In these volumes the second decade of the sixty-year diary of Charles Francis Adams, the third of the family's statesmen, is begun. As was true of the two earlier volumes of the *Diary*, the section appearing here has not before reached print.

Covering the period from Adams' marriage in September 1829 to the end of 1832, these volumes record the early years of his maturity during which he was seeking to find his vocation. Engaged in the day-to-day management of John Quincy Adams' business interests in Boston and Quincy, he nevertheless had no inclination toward commerce or the active practice of law. Son and grandson of Presidents, proud heir to a name already great and controversial in American politics, he also at this time considered himself "not fitted for the noise of public life." Dependent for support on his father and father-in-law but determined to maintain his independence, he devoted his available time to a program of studies and writing that would prepare him for a career he hesitated to name but in which he wished distinction. His own public career still years away, he was drawn at this period to the study of American history and his famous grandparents' papers, an effort that would continue and that would make him the family's archivist and editor.

These volumes offer manifold opportunities for an enlarged understanding of a complex and able man who was later to assume positions of high responsibility. In addition to furnishing innumerable personal and familial insights, this portion of the diary is of capital importance for the historian of society and culture. Probably no more detailed and faithful record exists of Boston life in the period.

The Adams Papers are edited at the Massachusetts Historical Society. Mr. Friedlaender is Associate Editor of the Papers, and Mr. Butterfield is Editor in Chief.

The Adams Papers

L. H. BUTTERFIELD, EDITOR IN CHIEF

SERIES I

DIARIES

Diary of Charles Francis Adams

Diary of
Charles Francis Adams

MARC FRIEDLAENDER and L. H. BUTTERFIELD

EDITORS

———— ☆ ————

Volume 3 · *September 1829–February 1831*

THE BELKNAP PRESS
OF HARVARD UNIVERSITY PRESS
CAMBRIDGE, MASSACHUSETTS

1968

Funds for editing *The Adams Papers* were originally furnished by Time, Inc., on behalf of *Life*, to the Massachusetts Historical Society, under whose supervision the editorial work is being done. Further funds have been provided by a grant from the Ford Foundation to the National Archives Trust Fund Board in support of this and four other major documentary publications. In common with these and many other enterprises like them, *The Adams Papers* benefits from the continuing and indispensable cooperation and aid of the National Historical Publications Commission, whose chairman is the Archivist of the United States.

Library of Congress Catalog Card Number 64–20588 · Printed in the United States of America

This edition of *The Adams Papers*

is sponsored by the MASSACHUSETTS HISTORICAL SOCIETY

to which the ADAMS MANUSCRIPT TRUST

by a deed of gift dated 4 April 1956

gave ultimate custody of the personal and public papers

written, accumulated, and preserved over a span of three centuries

by the Adams family of Massachusetts

The Adams Papers

The acorn and oakleaf device on the preceding page is redrawn from a seal cut for John Quincy Adams after 1830. The motto is from Cæcilius Statius as quoted by Cicero in the First Tusculan Disputation: *Serit arbores quæ alteri seculo prosint* ("He plants trees for the benefit of later generations").

Contents

Descriptive List of Illustrations

Folded in, facing p. 162 of Caleb H. Snow's *Geography of Boston*,
Boston, 1830, is "A Map of Boston, County of Suffolk, and the
Adjacent Towns, A. Bowen Sc." The original engraving is 12″ x 12″
and as reproduced here has been cropped at the sides. Excepting
only Weston, a few miles beyond the map's western edge, the map
encompasses the entire sphere of Charles Francis Adams' activities,
1829–1832. That the map was drawn or redrawn only a short time
before publication is clear from its inclusion of such recent construc-
tions as Western Avenue over the Mill Dam in the Back Bay to Brookline, 1821; the Granite Railway in Quincy, 1826; and the Warren
Bridge and Mill Pond triangle, 1828 (see below, p. 305–309). The
map records other features of special relevance to Charles Francis
Adams' activities and those of his family at this period: the route
of the Middlesex Canal through Charlestown and Medford (see
below, p. 153), "Prest. Adam's Seat" and "Payne's [i.e. Penn's]
Hill" in Quincy, &c.

Abel Bowen (1790–1850), born in New York State, came to Boston as an apprentice to his uncle Daniel Bowen, a printer. By 1812
he opened his own shop as an engraver on copper and wood, pioneer-
ing in introducing the craft of wood-engraving in Boston. Many of
the next generation of Boston artists and engravers were trained by
him. After lithography was brought to Boston by John Pendleton,
Bowen made use of that technique as well. Bowen was responsible
for the preparation of the illustrations in a number of books relating
to Boston, its history and appearance, and for the publication of some
of them himself. The most important of these were Caleb H. Snow's
History of Boston, issued in parts in 1825, in which were seventeen
full-page copperplates and woodcuts; Bowen's *Picture of Boston*,
1829; and Snow's *Geography of Boston*, 1830. He was the principal
figure in the "Boston Bewick Company," which began in 1834 to
bring out *The American Magazine of Useful and Entertaining
Knowledge*, publication of which continued through three volumes to
1837, all heavily illustrated, mostly with woodcuts. The illustrations of buildings in Boston and vicinity which follow are, with one
exception, selected from Bowen's work. See the article "Abel Bowen"
by William Henry Whitmore in Bostonian Society, *Publications*, 1
(1886–1888):29–56, with illustrations following.
Courtesy of the Massachusetts Historical Society.

ix

2. THE STATE HOUSE AND HANCOCK AVENUE FROM THE MALL, 1830   218

Bulfinch's State House, built along Beacon Street at the head of the graceful curve of Park Street and dominating the Common from its eminence, was for many years a favorite subject for the graphic artist. Numerous representations of the façade from the Common were done from a point that allowed the inclusion of the John Hancock residence on its Beacon Street site just to the west (left) of the State House. The draftsman, M. E. D. Brown, in shifting his angle of vision slightly to the east (right) and eliminating the Hancock house, provided us with a rare glimpse of the street, "under the shadow of Boston State House," and of the tops of its row-houses, which Henry Adams described in the opening passage of *The Education* as "the little passage called Hancock Avenue" which ran "from Beacon Street, skirting the State House grounds, to Mount Vernon Street, on the summit of Beacon Hill." There "in the third house below Mount Vernon Place" Charles Francis and Abigail Brooks Adams took up residence following their marriage on 3 Sept. 1829, to remain until 1842 (see below, p. 2).

Brown's admirable view was chosen as the front cover of the "Grand Centennial March," published in sheet-music form (Boston 1830), which Charles Zeuner had composed for the two-hundredth anniversary celebration in September 1830 of Boston's settlement. The lithograph as well as the drawing may well have been Brown's work. He is known primarily as a lithographer, and as an excellent one. This would have been a very early work, antedating by two years his appearance as an artist in Philadelphia and by five his reappearance in Boston (George C. Groce and David H. Wallace, *The New-York Historical Society's Dictionary of American Artists, 1564–1860*, New Haven and London, 1957). He may have been one of the two Browns listed by Bowen among the distinguished artists who had been in his employ and received training from him (William Henry Whitmore, "Abel Bowen," Bostonian Society, *Publications*, 1 [1886–1888]:35).

Courtesy of the Boston Athenæum.

3. NAHANT AND THE NAHANT HOUSE   218

Fourteen miles to the north and east of Boston at the tip of a peninsula extending three or four miles into the sea is Nahant, which in the first half of the 19th century was Boston's most fashionable resort during the summer season. The lively picture it presented is described in Margaret Morton Quincy's evocative account of "a project of pleasure" with her mother and sister at Nahant in 1824 (*The Articulate Sisters*, ed. M. A. DeWolfe Howe, Cambridge, 1946, p. 50–61).

Opinion was that Nahant's location "for picturesque beauty and sublimity of scenery . . . is not surpassed by any on the American coast." Its hotel was well known for the excellence of its table and for the variety of the entertainment. "Large and commodious stables are appended to the hotel, and a bathing house for warm and cold baths, and floating baths for those who may prefer the bracing action of sea water. . . . Nahant has many amusements—angling with the rod may be enjoyed as a pleasant recreation, standing on the rocks. . . . Game too is abundant in the vicinity; but there are few amusements or pleasures superior to that of riding, at suitable hours of the day, on the beach. A beautiful building in imitation of a Grecian temple, stands on an eminence near the hotel, in which are two elegant billiard rooms. There are also convenient covered bowling alleys." (*Bowen's Picture of Boston*, 2d edn., Boston, 1833, p. 300–303; see also, below, p. 305.)

The engraving, in which many of these attractions are shown, is the work of Ammin & Smith from the drawing by J. R. Penniman. It was among the plates Bowen used when publishing Caleb H. Snow, *History of Boston . . . with Some Account of the Environs* (2d edn., Boston, 1828, following p. 427).

Courtesy of the Massachusetts Historical Society.

4. THE FIRST CHURCH IN BOSTON, CHAUNCY PLACE   218

Chauncy Place, just off Summer Street, so-called because it had been the site of an orchard and garden cultivated by the Reverend Charles Chauncy when he was the minister of the First Church, had been the property of the Church since 1680. The decision to build a meetinghouse on the site was taken in 1807 at the same time that it was decided to sell the "Old Brick," located on Cornhill Square, which had served the First Church for almost a century. The new edifice, actually the fourth since the founding of the Church in 1632, was apparently constructed to the plans of Benjamin Joy by Asher Benjamin, who was appointed inspector and superintendent of the operation. The building, 70′ x 75′, was constructed of brick and was in use from 1808 to 1868, at which time it was sold, the congregation moving into its new building at Marlborough and Berkeley streets. Perhaps the decision to abandon the old structure, with which Adamses and Brookses had long been identified (see below, p. 14), contributed to Charles Francis Adams' decision on his return from England to Boston in 1868 to seek a different congregational affiliation. Actually the Chauncy Place building had never met with the congregation's approval, the principal complaint being the lack of light. During the years of its use it was several times remodeled, principally in 1842, but never satisfactorily. (Arthur B. Ellis, *History of the First Church in Boston, 1630–1880*, Boston, 1881, p. 235, 270–271, 306–312; Caleb H. Snow, *Geography of Boston*, Boston, 1830, p. 98.) Bowen's engraving was used first in his *Picture of Boston*, 2d edn., Boston, 1833, facing p. 128.

Courtesy of the Massachusetts Historical Society.

5. THE ADAMS TEMPLE (FIRST CHURCH), QUINCY   218

Charles Francis Adams and George Washington Adams represented their father at the dedicatory service of the Adams Temple on 12 November 1828 (see volume 2:307). Six years had passed since John Adams had conveyed to the town of Quincy, by deed dated 29 June 1822, tracts of land owned by him, on some of which were granite quarries, and had created the Adams Temple and School

Fund to administer the property and to carry out the purposes for which he had made the gift. The first of these purposes was "the completing and furnishing of a Temple to be built of Stone, to be taken from the premises, for the Public Worship of God, and the public instruction in religion and morality, for the use of the Congregational Society in said town." To that end the Supervisors of the Fund were charged to devote all the income derived from the property to the building of the Temple until it was completed. By 1826 the Society's funds and the accumulated income in the Adams Fund were held sufficient for work on the Temple to be begun.

Alexander Parris of Boston (1780–1852), on recommendation of Solomon Willard, was selected as the architect. Parris, whose work in Boston since 1816 had already established him as one of the leading exponents of the Greek Revival style, was the architect for St. Paul's Church on Tremont Street (1819) and for the Quincy Market (1824–1826), both of which he designed with the pedimented porticos and monolithic columns of granite that he was to use for the Adams Temple (Walter H. Kilham, *Boston after Bulfinch*, Cambridge, 1946, p. 21–24; *Dictionary of American Biography*, New York, 1928–1936, under Parris). John Adams' use of the word "temple" for the church he wished built, his specification of granite for its construction, and his coupling to the building of a temple the building of a classical academy all suggest that Parris' design was in full compliance with the donor's intent for the church.

The Temple was completed at a cost of $30,488.56, of which $2,402.63 was derived from the accumulation in the Adams Temple and School Fund. The granite from the quarries given by John Adams used for the entire building except the four columns and capitals, is presumably not included in these figures. John Quincy Adams' subsequent accomplishment in 1829 of his long-held plan to complete the granite chamber beneath the portico in which he had had the remains of his parents reburied and to install behind the pulpit in the meetinghouse a memorial tablet and bust was at his own charge. (William S. Pattee, *A History of Old Braintree and Quincy, with a Sketch of Randolph and Holbrook*, Quincy, 1878, p. 242–244; William Churchill Edwards, *Historic Quincy, Massachusetts*, Quincy, 1954, p. 136–141; and below, p. 55–56.)

Bowen's engraving of the Adams Temple reproduced here was apparently made by 1829 (see below, p. 24–25) and seems to have been intended for use in his *Picture of Boston*, first published in that year. However, the plate was not included in that work until its third edition was reached in 1837. In March 1835 the drawing was used to make a larger engraving for Bowen's *American Magazine of Useful and Entertaining Knowledge*, 1:289. There the drawing is signed J. Kidder. James Kidder of Boston was a painter of landscapes as well as a draftsman; he was working for Bowen as early as 1823 (George C. Groce and David H. Wallace, *The New-York Historical Society's Dictionary of Artists in America, 1564–1860*, New Haven and London, 1957).

Courtesy of the Massachusetts Historical Society.

6. TREMONT STREET IN 1830, SHOWING THE TREMONT THE-
ATRE AND THE TREMONT HOUSE   218

This drawing of Tremont Street, used by Abel Bowen as the frontis-
piece for both his *Picture of Boston* and Snow's *Geography of Boston*,
is of the prospect toward the Park Street Church at the corner of
Park and Tremont streets as observed from where Beacon Street enters
Tremont from the right. The large structure which faced both on
Tremont and Beacon streets, on the site of the present Tremont
Building, is the Tremont House, opened in 1829. Immediately be-
yond it is the Granary Burial Ground. Directly opposite the Tremont
House is the Tremont Theatre, built in 1827.

The competition between the new Tremont Theatre and the older
Boston Theatre on Federal Street proved so ruinous to both in 1828
that the lessees of the Tremont Theatre took over the Boston Theatre
for four years with the intent to keep the house dark. Hence it was
that until the end of 1832 there was but one theater in Boston in
which regular dramatic performances were given. The Tremont
Theatre, which had been established by "persons who believed the
time had arrived when something should be done to raise the character of the Boston stage," soon became sufficiently successful so that
it "receives patronage from the most wealthy and fashionable" (*Bow-
en's Picture of Boston*, 2d edn., Boston, 1833, p. 204–206). The
building was planned to be worthy of the patronage it sought. The
architect clearly derived the façade of Quincy granite, with its four
Ionic pilasters and Tuscan Doric antæ supporting an entablature and
pediment, from the west wall of the Erechtheum in Athens. He joined
to this an Italianate podium containing three identical segmental-
arched openings symmetrically placed within the rusticated central
section and gave to the whole wide and ample proportions. An
architectural rendering reflecting its quality appears on the jacket
of Walter H. Kilham, *Boston after Bulfinch*, Cambridge, 1946.
Within the arched doors was a wide hall from which a stairway
ascended to the boxes, "the lobbies for the promenade, and separate
drawing rooms, communicating with an elegant saloon in the cen-
tre" (*Bowen's Picture of Boston*, 2d edn., p. 207). The building
was sold to a Baptist Society in 1842, became known as the Tremont
Temple, and burned in 1852.

The Tremont House, architecturally "an epoch-making work,
original (almost revolutionary) in plan and with an exterior so
simple as to be almost austere," was at the same time perhaps the
first hotel in America of the modern type (Talbot Hamlin, *Greek Revival Architecture in America*, New York, 1944, p. 112). When the
New York Commercial Advertiser noted that "The Bostonians have
boasted much of their great hotel, the Tremont House. But they have
not boasted too much. It is indeed a noble edifice, and as a hotel . . .
above all praise," the *Boston Patriot* proudly reprinted the tribute (3
August 1831, p. 2, col. 3). Within a year of its construction its
importance was recognized by the publication of a handsome volume
on the hotel, consisting largely of architectural drawings: William
Havard Eliot, *A Description of the Tremont House*, Boston, 1830.
The building of Quincy granite fronted 160 feet on Tremont Street

and 104 feet on Beacon Street. Within were elegant public rooms, derived from Greek prototypes, and 170 rooms for guests. The portico at the principal entrance was 37 feet 6 inches long and its four Doric columns twenty feet high. The cost of the Tremont House when opened was $300,000; it remained in use until 1894 (same, p. 4–15; *Bowen's Picture of Boston*, 2d edn., p. 215–218; Kilham, *Boston after Bulfinch*, p. 32–34).

The architect of both the Tremont House and the Tremont Theatre was Isaiah Rogers (1800–1869), who, after four years with Solomon Willard, had opened his own office in 1826; he remained in Boston until 1834, when he left to continue a notable career in New York and Cincinnati. "He was undoubtedly the greatest architect of the Boston group . . . one of the most remarkable designers of the entire Greek Revival movement." (Hamlin, *Greek Revival Architecture in America*, p. 111, 114–117; *Dictionary of American Biography*, New York, 1928–1936.)
Courtesy of the Massachusetts Historical Society.

7. **THE GRANITE RAILWAY, QUINCY** 219

The horse- or ox-drawn cars devised by the inventor-engineer Gridley Bryant to convey the massive granite blocks from the "Railway Quarry" and the "Bunker Hill Quarry" in Quincy to the navigable waters of the Neponset River for transshipment to the Bunker Hill monument site in Charlestown have their place in the history of American railroads (see below, p. 307). The cars or carriages had wheels six feet in diameter, the wheels shod with iron half an inch thick and flanged on the inner side of the rim. Suspended by chains from the axles was the load-carrying platform which could be raised or lowered by machinery on the top of the car. Two or three cars could be coupled for conveying blocks twenty feet or more in length. A sixteen-ton load could be carried on a three-car train which moved at a speed of three miles an hour on tracks that descended eighty-three feet in the nearly four miles from quarry to wharf. The tracks were of wood faced with iron and were laid on a bed of broken stone with a gravel surface. See *Bowen's Picture of Boston*, 2d edn., p. 286–288; William Churchill Edwards, *Historic Quincy, Massachusetts*, Quincy, 1954, p. 105–108. Bowen's representation of a train on the Granite Railway is from Caleb H. Snow, *Geography of Boston*, Boston, 1830, p. 159.
Courtesy of the Massachusetts Historical Society.

8. **THE BOSTON ATHENAEUM AND GALLERY, PEARL STREET** 219

The Boston Athenæum, founded in 1807, had moved its location twice when James Perkins give to it his house at 13 Pearl Street, on the west side near High Street. After the house and that next to it had been converted and remodeled into a single structure under the direction of Solomon Willard, the third of Boston's triumvirs of the Greek Revival, the Athenæum occupied the building in 1822 (Mabel M. Swan, *The Athenæum Gallery, 1827–1873*, Boston, 1940, p. 3). Here the Athenæum remained until 1849, when it built its present quarters on Beacon Street. The interior of the Pearl Street building was described in 1829: "On entering, the visitor finds himself surrounded with the busts and statues of heroes and learned men of antiquity. At his left ... is the Reading Room, in which are found the newspapers and journals of the present day, with complete files of periodical publications for many years back. In this room it is contrary to etiquette, to hold any conversation whatever. On the right is a large and convenient room where the proprietors hold their meetings, and the trustees transact their business. This room is tastefully decorated with statuary and paintings. The Librarian's room and a conversation room, complete the apartments on the lower story. The second and third story contain the library" (*Bowen's Picture of Boston*, Boston, 1829, p. 38–39).

In 1826 it became possible to proceed with plans to construct a separate building on the Pearl Street property in the rear of the library to house a gallery of paintings and a lecture hall (see below, p. 124–125, 235). Plans for the building were made by Willard, and the Athenæum Gallery held its first public exhibition of paintings in May 1827.

Visible to the right in Bowen's engraving is the windowless third story "lighted only from the top, in a manner peculiarly adapted for the exhibition of Paintings" (*Bowen's Picture of Boston*, p. 39–40, facing p. 204; Caleb H. Snow, *Geography of Boston*, Boston, 1830, p. 105–106).
Courtesy of the Massachusetts Historical Society.

9. "RODE INTO TOWN WITH ABBY, AND LEFT HER AT THE BATHING HOUSE"   219
"In large cities, it is necessary to have bathing-houses; in places of a scattered population, they may be dispensed with; and yet warm baths will require a house anywhere. Several have been erected in Boston within the last twenty years—of which we believe Mr. Braman's, below Charles Street and not far from Beacon street ... on the margin of Charles river or bay, is the largest and most convenient. The building is two stories, eighty feet in length, and fifty in breadth—and it has fifty bathing rooms. The water is salt, both the warm and cold. Connected with the building ... is a large apparatus for a swimming school. ... This, we understand, is the only school for teaching the art of swimming in the United States." *American Magazine of Useful and Entertaining Knowledge*, 1:512 (August 1835). Charles Francis Adams' quotation above is from page 304, below.
Courtesy of the Massachusetts Historical Society.

10, 11. THE BROTHERS OF CHARLES FRANCIS ADAMS: GEORGE WASHINGTON ADAMS AND JOHN ADAMS 2d   314
That these two portraits, never alienated from the family, are of Charles Francis Adams' older brothers seems certain. The earliest unmistakable reference to these likenesses occurs in an article, "The Household of John Quincy Adams," by Harriet Taylor Upton in *Wide Awake*, 27 (1888):363–377. The paintings are there reproduced, the subject of each identified, and the ownership of both fixed in

William Clarkson Johnson, then of Newburyport. Johnson (1823–1893) had been the husband of Mary Louisa Adams Johnson (1828–1859), who was the only child of John Adams 2d to live to maturity (see Adams Genealogy). The present owner, Mrs. Waldo C. M. Johnston, is the great-granddaughter of that marriage. Neither on the paintings themselves nor in Mrs. Upton's article is there indication of artist or date.

However, in that article the reproductions of these paintings appear on the same page with the portrait of Charles Francis Adams painted by Charles Bird King in 1827 (see volume 2:vii, and facing p. 144). With the age of one of the sitters known, then the portraits of the three brothers, each of a sitter of nearly the same age, support a view that each was painted within a year or two of the sitter's reaching the age of twenty-one. A date of 1820–1825 can thus be assigned to the portraits of George Washington Adams (1801–1829) and John Adams 2d (1803–1834) with some confidence.

Other affinities among the paintings suggest that all were the work of a single artist. Charles Bird King (1785–1862), an American artist who was one of the best known portraitists resident in Washington during the years that John Quincy Adams was Secretary of State and President (1817–1828), had his studio (see volume 1:48) quite close to the Adams residence, 1820–1825, at 1333 F Street, exchanged visits frequently with the Adamses (John Quincy Adams, Diary, *passim*), and is known to have painted in the years 1819–1827, likenesses of John Quincy Adams, Louisa Catherine Adams, her sister Mrs. Nathaniel Frye Jr., and Charles Francis Adams all from life, as well as two portraits of John Adams after earlier Stuarts (Andrew Oliver, *Portraits of John and Abigail Adams*, Cambridge, 1967, p. 192–195, 221–222). King would have been the likely artist of portraits of others of John Quincy Adams' family commissioned within those years. This presumption is not weakened by a comparison of the George Washington Adams and John Adams 2d portraits with two Adams portraits known to have been done by King, that of Charles Francis Adams and the one of John Quincy Adams now in the Redwood Library and Athenaeum, Newport, Rhode Island. The sitter's pose; the placement of the figure and the space it occupies on the canvas; the disposition and treatment of hands; the representation and style of collar, stock, and waistcoat; and the rendering of eyes and mouth—all are strikingly similar in the four paintings.

If the likenesses of George Washington Adams and John Adams 2d are by King, then questions may be raised about the usual identification of George Washington Adams as the subject of the painting reproduced on the left-hand side of the page, and John Adams 2d, book in hands, as the subject of the other. The sole authority for the identification of the separate likenesses is the article in *Wide Awake* and current family tradition, apparently based on that ascription. Even assuming that the identifications in *Wide Awake* do in fact accord with the opinion of William Clarkson Johnson, the then owner, the acceptance of Johnson's verdict, unless he had written records available to him, would be subject to limitations: at John Adams 2d's death fifty-four years before, his daughter Mary Louisa Adams, subsequently Johnson's wife, was six years of age and Johnson was eleven; John Adams 2d's widow, Mary Catherine, had died in 1870; Mary Louisa Adams Johnson in 1859. The only other portraits known that may be likenesses of George Washington Adams and John Adams 2d, two which hang in the Old House at Quincy, provide no help in identification since their association with either brother rests entirely on perceived resemblances to the portraits reproduced here. If the likenesses of the brothers are examined with the assumption that they are by King but without prior identification of the individual subjects, the possibility that the painting said to be of George Washington Adams may be of John Adams 2d and vice versa, becomes more distinct. The four portraits by King of Adams men rather easily fall into two pairs, each pair distinguished by the coats in which the artist has clothed his sitters. The sitters in the John Quincy Adams portrait in the Redwood Library and in the portrait hitherto called John Adams 2d both wear coats of the same type with three brass buttons identically placed. Charles Francis Adams and the sitter for that hitherto called George Washington Adams wear robes or gowns with velvet collars and flowing sleeves. That the two paintings in each pair were done within a fairly short span of time seems evident. The dates 1819–1822 for the John Quincy Adams and 1827 for the Charles Francis Adams portrait are known. The other "brass button" painting would then have been done several years earlier than that of the other gowned figure. Such a conclusion would, in accordance with their ages, point to the identification of the person in the coat with brass buttons as George Washington Adams, the gowned figure as John Adams 2d. Again, the known dates of residence in Washington of each brother would be consistent with the view taken that George Washington Adams' portrait was painted before that of John Adams 2d. George Washington Adams was in Washington after his graduation from Harvard from 1 October 1821 to 14 August 1823; thereafter only for a month or less in 1825 and in 1828 (Adams Papers files). John Adams 2d, however, was at Harvard until 1823, after which he was in Washington for most of each year until 1827 (volumes 1–2, *passim*). A reversal of the identifications is supported further to some degree by the "prop" which the artist has placed in the hands of one of the brothers. A book would have been highly appropriate for George Washington Adams, not so for John Adams 2d. See the references to each below, *passim*.

Addendum: Further information that sustains the conclusions conjectured above came to light only after the text for this volume had been set in pages. What has been said has therefore been allowed to stand without change. Confirmation comes from the discovery in the MS Diary of John Quincy Adams that he continued to sit to Charles Bird King for his portrait until 10 November 1823 and, what is of more significance here, that on 31 May 1823 George was also sitting to King. That King was indeed the painter of George's likeness, and that the portrait was done in 1823 at the same time that his father's was completed, makes virtually certain (a) that King also did the portrait of John, (b) that the sitter for the portrait reproduced on the right-hand side of the page, which is in a number of ways a companion to the John Quincy Adams portrait, was George. We may now reverse the traditionally given identification of the portraits of the two brothers. Fortunately it has been possible to incorporate this correction and new information in the caption under the portraits, facing p. 314 below.

Courtesy of Mrs. Waldo C. M. Johnston, Old Lyme, Connecticut.

12. PLAN OF THE TOWN OF MEDFORD IN 1830, BY JOHN SPARRELL 314

Sparrell's map (Massachusetts State Archives, Maps of 1830, volume 3, p. 10) shows the town of Medford contiguous to Charlestown on the south and east, its town square just over five miles northwest of the State House in Boston. Within the town, the most prominent of the topographical features was the Mystic or Medford River, a tidal stream, whose northward and westward course from the Charlestown line to the point on the western boundary of Medford where the river widened to become Mystic Pond was marked by numerous loops and bends. A second was the Middlesex Canal which entered the southern bounds of Medford close to the river and followed a course just to the west and south of it until a crossing was effected by means of a lock and aqueduct (see the following item in this Descriptive List of Illustrations), beyond which the canal continued just to the east of the river and Mystic Pond. This generally northward course has become the present Summer Street to Winthrop Street, West Street to Boston Avenue, Boston Avenue to High Street, and then Sagamore Avenue, which continues along the Mystic Lakes as Mystic Valley Parkway. See below, p. 236, 249; Lewis M. Lawrence, The Middlesex Canal, Boston, 1942 [processed], p. 110; "Plans of the Middlesex Canal with the Neighbouring Roads, Buildings, &c. Surveyed for Loammi Baldwin by George R. Baldwin. Sept. & Oct. 1829," Office of the County Engineer, Middlesex County Court House, East Cambridge; and "Survey of Middlesex Canal" [1829], Baldwin Papers, volume 6, Field Book No. 5, Baker Library, Harvard University.

On the Sparrell map, just to the south of Mystic Pond is the Weir Bridge. The road from West Cambridge crosses this bridge and in Medford as High Street is a main artery into Medford Square. Shortly after High Street crosses the canal it is joined from the north by a road running parallel to the canal. This is Grove Street. The next road parallel and to the east of Grove is Woburn Street.

The estate of Peter Chardon Brooks in Medford by 1830 had been enlarged to more than three hundred acres and included the lands to the north of High Street, to the west of Woburn Street, and to the east of the river and the Mystic Pond northward to a point beyond "the Partings," the Pond's narrow waist as shown on the map (see also, below, p. 300). He also owned the tongue of land to the south of High Street, east and north of the river. The canal ran through the Brooks property for more than a mile. Brooks' residence, Mystic Grove, stood on the west side of Grove Street not far north of

High Street. See below, p. 10; volume 2:xi; *The Medford Historical Register*, 30:1–23 (March 1927).

Also in Medford was the farm of eighty acres which had been owned by John Adams, and afterward by Thomas Boylston Adams (see below, p. 236). Its location on the map is in the area south of the river and west from Medford Square, roughly halfway between the aqueduct and the first bridge to the eastward. It too lay on both sides of the canal. "A Plan of President Adams' Land taken for the Middlesex Canal ... 1806," Baldwin Papers, volume 6, Drawings 1803–1805, Baker Library, Harvard University.

Courtesy of the Secretary of the Commonwealth of Massachusetts, Archives Division.

13. RUINS OF THE STONE AQUEDUCT WHICH BORE THE MIDDLESEX CANAL OVER THE MYSTIC RIVER IN MEDFORD   314

The stone aqueduct, constructed by the Middlesex Canal Company in 1829 to replace an earlier wooden one, together with the lock at its western end were the means by which the canal crossed the Mystic River at the site of the present Boston Avenue bridge. The rebuilt aqueduct was 135 feet long with the stone abutments on each bank about a hundred feet apart. Supporting the aqueduct as it spanned the river were three massive stone piers. The aqueduct had an inside width of fourteen feet, with the surface of the water in it about ten feet above the water-level in the river at high tide; the trough was of timber and plank. The aqueduct remained in use until the canal was abandoned in 1852 after which it fell into decay until 1873 when the stonework served as the foundations for a highway bridge at Boston Avenue which was later superseded by the present bridge. (Christopher Roberts, *The Middlesex Canal, 1793–1860*, Cambridge, 1938, p. 195; Lewis M. Lawrence, The Middlesex Canal, Boston, 1942 [processed], p. 110.) The view illustrated is from a reproduction in *The Medford Historical Register* (volume 20, frontispiece [January 1917]) of an oil, unlocated, said to have been painted in 1865.

Courtesy of the Medford Historical Society.

14. "I GOT HOLD OF THE TRIAL FOR THE MURDER OF MR. WHITE AT SALEM . . . AND COULD NOT LEAVE IT QUICKLY"   315

No other event of the year so held the public interest in Boston in 1830 as the murder of Captain Joseph White of Salem, the consequent apprehension of the suspected perpetrators, and their trials (see below, p. 207–208, 248–249, 303–304; quotation from p. 303). In satisfying the curiosity aroused first by the shocking manner and circumstances in which the deed was done and then by the prominence of the accused, the newspapers returned to the case again and again during the six months from the act to the convictions. The limitations imposed by the court upon the press in reporting the trials during their progress invited pamphlet publication of the testimony, &c., immediately upon the conclusion of the trial. Four

such pamphlets are known, and others doubtless would be turned up in a bibliographical search. *The Trial in the Case of the Commonwealth, versus John Francis Knapp, for the Murder of Joseph White, Esq. of Salem, Mass.*, is a report of the proceedings in Salem from the convening of a grand jury by the Supreme Judicial Court on 20 July to the conclusion of the first trial of Frank Knapp on 13 August. Its titlepage representation of the murder distinguished it from competing pamphlets. One of the pamphlets was in Charles Francis Adams' hands on 18 August.
Courtesy of the Massachusetts Historical Society.

15. RECORD OF CHARLES FRANCIS ADAMS' EARLIEST BORROWINGS FROM THE BOSTON ATHENAEUM   315

A ledger of 537 pages sturdily bound in sheep, reinforced with calf hinges and corners, and labeled on its spine "Entry of Books Borrowed: 1: 1827–1834" is one of the numerous items of considerable bibliographical interest in the archives of the Boston Athenæum. The arrangement was intended to be alphabetical by shareholders with each proprietor assigned a page for the recording of his borrowings. However, changes in the membership during the years covered by the volume necessitated that an index of members' pages be inserted at the beginning of the volume. Pages 20–21 are used to record the borrowings of Charles Francis Adams from the date of payment of his first annual subscription on 4 January 1830 to a borrowing on 11 July 1834, which utilized the last bit of space on the pages and required a transfer of his entry to a second volume. Each page has two columns of entries, each entry consisting of the date of the borrowing; the shelf number of the work borrowed; the author and/or title of the work in greatly abbreviated form; the volumes borrowed of a multivolume work, the format of a single-volume work; the date on which the work was returned. The entries are in several hands, being made apparently by whoever of the staff was in attendance. The illustration is of the topmost section of the left-hand column of page 20 and includes those borrowings made from 18 January to 4 August 1830.

This new method of entering borrowings was made possible by the compilation and publication early in 1827 of the first complete catalogue of the Athenæum book holdings, recording for each title its shelf number in the Athenæum and full bibliographical information. This catalogue was supplemented in 1830 by a second catalogue constructed on the same plan and listing those volumes which had been added since 1827 (see below, volume 3:120, 133–134).

From the cryptic entries of the titles borrowed by Charles Francis Adams, 1830–1832, and their identification by means of the two catalogues, an essentially complete record of the books borrowed by him in these years has been constructed. It is included in the present volumes as an appendix (volume 4:436–444; see the introductory note there).
Courtesy of the Boston Athenæum.

Foreword

With the publication of the third and fourth volumes of the *Diary of Charles Francis Adams*, the Adams editorial enterprise moves a step further toward one of its several objectives: the presentation of complete, accurate, and annotated texts of all three of the statesmen's diaries, which comprise collectively an almost unbroken, and during long periods overlapping, record of American life as observed and experienced by Adamses over more than a century and a quarter.

Volumes 1 and 2, published in September 1964, were edited by Mrs. Aïda DiPace Donald and her husband, Professor David Donald of The Johns Hopkins University. The Donalds had been drawn to this task by a conviction that probably no hitherto unpublished diary kept by an American in the 19th century contained greater riches for the inquiring student of that period; and in carrying out their task they placed the stamp of their scholarly skill and authority not only on the volumes they edited but, in a more general way, on the edition as a whole. For this the editor in chief and all others concerned in the Adams enterprise at the Massachusetts Historical Society and Harvard University Press are and must remain deeply grateful. But upon the appearance of the first two volumes Mr. Donald was obliged by the pressure of his other scholarly commitments to withdraw from his role as co-editor, and in view of this circumstance Mrs. Donald likewise resigned. Editorial operations on the *Diary of Charles Francis Adams* were thereafter resumed at the headquarters of the enterprise in the Massachusetts Historical Society.

These operations have been concentrated in the hands of Mr. Marc Friedlaender, for many years a professor of English literature at the University of North Carolina, Greensboro, who, after five years as a publisher, joined the Adams staff at the beginning of 1965. His interest in *The Adams Papers* predated by a considerable time his affiliation with the enterprise, for it was he who, as an editor at Atheneum Publishers in New York City, had provided the stimulus for a paperbound reprint edition of *The Adams Papers* and had the oversight of the volumes as issued by Atheneum. It is only proper to say that he has performed the lion's share, or more, of the editing of the two volumes of Charles Francis Adams' *Diary* now published, has seen them through the press, and has written the Introduction which follows.

It is proper to say further that the Introduction deals with only a few themes in the diary record now spread before the reader, and dismisses a number of others on which it would be easy and agreeable to comment — for example the remarkably full and faithful, though dispersed, account furnished by this document of Boston's social, economic, and cultural life in the 1830's, and the accompanying physical growth of the city. These and other matters have been deliberately omitted in order to deal with the most basic themes running throughout this segment of Adams' massive and intensely personal record: his continuous effort to find his true nature between those poles of passion and restraint that had always marked, and would continue in the future to mark, the Adams character; his developing sense of responsibility as a dynastic heir, which, since the diarist's conception of it clashed—or *seemed* to clash—with his father's conception, led to one of the frankest series of exchanges between a son and a father on record; and, finally, his yearning search for a vocation, which he accidentally discovered in the course of these years but did not have the satisfaction of knowing he had done before these volumes close.

If none of these questions is resolved in the text of the diary, neither is any one of them categorically answered—by anticipation of future evidence—in Mr. Friedlaender's probing commentary. To judge by the amount of study being given to the subject in the 20th century, the problem of growing up as an Adams was one of the most unusual and difficult feats a human being could be called on to perform in the 18th or 19th century. It seems to be agreed that the difficulties were compounded as the generations of the family succeeded each other. In the present volumes is assembled a voluminous mass of new data on the most conspicuous figure in the third generation of the dynasty. That among them are many trivia and frequent *longueurs*, the editors must be the first to admit because they have been the first to cope with them. The volumes of C. F. Adams' *Diary* so far published, and some that will follow, document a slow starter's painfully slow start toward mastery of himself and thereby toward his important place in the political, diplomatic, and cultural history of his country and his central place in the Adams story for half a century. In the ever-enlarging view we now take of both history and psychology, no evidence in the personal record of such an evolution is wholly irrelevant to an understanding of it.

Adams himself presciently felt the force of this truth and furnished his editors with convincing arguments for proceeding as they have. Among the many books he read during the years spanned by these volumes was Boswell's *Life of Samuel Johnson.* In his diary entry for 30 March 1831 he remarked that Boswell's book contains "much the best Picture of [Johnson's] mind. None has ever been so fully laid bare to the public, and none could exemplify more strongly in itself the singular medley of weaknesses and power of which the human mind generally is composed." At that moment Adams was doubtful whether "such books are a blessing, for they tend to destroy all the Romance about perfection of character." But when, a few years later, he began his lifelong, if often interrupted, task of editing large portions of his family papers for publication, he started with the letters of his celebrated grandparents, in order, he said repeatedly and in a variety of ways, to expose the hidden springs of action that lay behind the momentous events in which John and Abigail Adams participated. And in the preface to his last filio-editorial undertaking, the monumental *Memoirs of John Quincy Adams...from 1795 to 1848,* carried out at the close of his active life, Adams echoed this early commitment to recording directly the personal testimony on which our understanding of the past must ultimately rest, as distinct from and better than reconstructing the past at second-hand, from partial evidence, and according to what we *wish* to think those who acted and were acted upon in "history" were like.

L. H. BUTTERFIELD
Editor in Chief

Introduction

1. CHARLES FRANCIS ADAMS, DIARIST, 1829–1832

Near the end of the period covered by the present volumes, Charles Francis Adams characterized his diary as "a pretty monotonous record of the very even tenour of my life."[1] In a sense the appraisal is a just one. Certainly, Adams' daily life from his twenty-second to his twenty-fifth year was marked by no spectacular incident and was passed without essential variation. Married on the day before these journal entries begin and already installed in the house he would occupy for the next thirteen years, the diarist was able to maintain his pattern of activities without interruption. Visits to his parents in the Old House at Quincy and to his wife's parents at Medford were the only occasions during these years on which he left Boston, other than for a day's outing or errand to a neighboring town: Cohasset, Weston, Cambridge, Woburn, Nahant. That the rhythm of his existence was maintained without break is suggested by the *events* which loom large in the journal: the birth of a daughter, the death of his mother-in-law and of his uncle, the emergence of his father from retirement to reenter public life as a member of Congress. And if his days passed with little interruption, it is also true that his time was given largely to occupations of no public moment: to the management of his father's not very extensive property in Boston and Quincy and to the keeping of his accounts, to a law practice that was never more than nominal and that he made no effort to extend, to the pursuit of a program of studies which he set for himself and which during the period of these volumes produced comparatively slight results. His Sundays differed from other days only in the regular substitution of the meetinghouse, morning and afternoon, for the office, and of the reading of sermons for secular literature. The journal entries do reflect faithfully the limited range of his activities, and make understandable, if mistaken, his verdict on himself: "I am nothing, and shall be nothing, but a daudle[r] over trifles."[2]

Charles Francis Adams was no less hard a judge of the literary interest his journal might have. In comparing his literary attributes

[1] Diary, 6 Feb. 1832 (vol. 4:235).   [2] 25 May 1831 (vol. 4:55).

xxv

with those of his brother George, he found his own work not the equal of his brother's in "aptitude of language and power of style."[3] His estimate of his own qualities, "Nature gave me no flights. It endowed me with a tolerably strait forward sense and middling Judgment,"[4] while consistent with the evidence offered by the style in which he wrote his journal, neglects to say what he says elsewhere and what is abundantly evident, that the unadorned and commonsensical style is an achieved rather than a natural style, the product of continued study and of self-discipline. On rereading a volume in which he had several years earlier allowed himself to record his transient feelings, he was gratified to find the entries "so prettily written,"[5] and again, before destroying some of his old letters to his brother George, he was struck by his earlier style: "I have lost ground since then, at least in genius if not in morals. I could not write so sprightly a letter now if I was to try ever so hard."[6] But that the sacrifice was deliberate becomes explicit when, on hearing one of his former classmates preach in figurative language, Adams writes, "I could not help reflecting what a severe hand had corrected my style, giving no Quarter to my Flowers, which were mere daisies along side of this man's lilies and Tulips."[7] The new and disciplined character which he resolutely assumed upon marrying could make him at times regret the cost. "I am getting sobered down. The serious part of life has already set it's hand upon me.... [I]t is a melancholy reflection to see the shores pass as I sail by and to think that I am never to see them again."[8] But he also had the satisfaction of recognizing, at least at moments and particularly toward the end of the period surveyed in these volumes, that adherence to the program of reading and writing he had imposed upon himself had brought gains: "I feel as if my style was not without power and that it ought to take better."[9]

However, though permanently submerged, there is a strain that sounds now and again, here and later, to unsettle us: "[T]here is a charm to me in ... allusion that I never can get over. In many respects, I am not fit for the matter of fact world of this Century."[1] Such a remark from the diarist of these years, who appeared to move so easily within the tasks he set for himself, can only evoke surprise, if not disbelief. Nor is this reaction lessened after a further appraisal. One must sense that, despite his occasional complaints, there were in him qualities that made the chores with which he was occupied—the col-

[3] 8 Sept. 1829 (vol. 3:6).
[4] 20 July 1831 (vol. 4:93).
[5] 15 Oct. 1829 (vol. 3:46).
[6] 1 Aug. 1831 (vol. 4:103).

[7] 2 Jan. 1831 (vol. 3:394).
[8] 30 April 1830 (vol. 3:225).
[9] 24 Nov. 1832 (vol. 4:404).
[1] 19 Oct. 1832 (vol. 4:381–382).

lecting of rents, the balancing of accounts, the cataloguing of books, the secretaryships, the copying of letters—all congenial to him. Whether he records, "I ... draughted an Alphabetical list of Stockholders, which was perhaps needless, but I like to arrange things regularly," or "I was busy during the morning in pasting labels into my father's books—Not a very appropriate occupation but one which I feel never will be done unless I do it," the recognition of the response in himself is evident.[2] The conscientiousness and humility with which he carried out the responsibilities he felt devolved upon him from the quarterly payments he received from his father and his father-in-law are perhaps only the obverse of self-distrust. "I have only steadiness of character, without the boldness of enterprise essential to success—and without any confidence in myself"; "the safest way for a man distrusting his abilities [is] to begin small and attempt things gradually."[3] These are characteristics he never wholly lost; it would seem that there was always the desire to reach "my journey's end without risk of my neck."[4] Such tendencies, deeply ingrained, do rather confirm the accepted image of the man than justify the romantic image of one out of harmony with the matter-of-fact world.

Further, when we proceed to examine the countenance the world saw in these years and afterward, we seem to find nothing to suggest that the gravity of demeanor, the imperturbable calm, was not the outward mark of a tranquility of mind, of acceptance of the world and assurance of his place in it. This is the picture of the man we are given, seen in later years, by his sons Henry and Charles Francis Jr., each with a different bias, in Henry's *Education* and in Charles' life of his father. And when the diarist was only twenty-two his father already spoke of him as "grave and steady,"[5] and remarked on his "sober enquiries after truth."[6]

We have been prepared, however, by the earlier volumes of his diary to know that it had not always been so with Charles Francis Adams, that in his youth he had had another character in which his passions were not so rigidly controlled.[7] Although at the time of his marriage he could say, "I care little about dissipation for time has made me sick of it. I have had more than my dose,"[8] three years later his

---

[2] 17 Feb. 1831 (vol. 3:424), and 23 Sept. 1832 (vol. 4:367).
[3] 8 Sept. 1829 (vol. 3:6), and 9 May 1830 (vol. 3:232).
[4] To the Editor of the *Boston Patriot,* 29 June 1830, quoted at vol. 3:271.
[5] To Charles Francis Adams, 18 Dec.

1829, Adams Papers.
[6] To the same, 13 May 1830, quoted at vol. 3:226.
[7] See vol. 1:xxviii–xxxix and the passages there cited.
[8] Diary, 12 Sept. 1829 (vol. 3:13).

view of himself at that earlier time seems closer to the fact: "Much has been said upon the danger of marrying early, but for a man constituted like me I believe it to be something of a safeguard."[9] It was well observed by a reviewer of the first two volumes of the *Diary* that Adams even after he achieved respectability "found continence extremely difficult."[1] Nor, despite appearances, did he ever completely subdue the other passions that marked the inner man. Among those who had long known Adams and appraised him after his death was James Russell Lowell. He penetrated the exterior to exclaim, "How often must his calm have been that of suppressed passion! . . . [I]t was harder for him than for most men to be circumspect and prudent."[2] In the years of the present volumes Adams sometimes seemed to himself deficient in masking his warmth among a cold people: "[T]here are moments when the impetuosity of my natural character will burst forth and then it rushes with tenfold violence. . . . I ought daily to set before myself some monitory sentence to guard me from the natural and powerful tendency of my own passions. In other climates, it would matter little, but here where the natural character and manners are cold, mine appear unpleasantly. I must learn to press down, to restrain the intense force of my feelings."[3]

Yet we judge that his reputation for reserve and coldness must already have been won when, after listening to a sermon by Ralph Waldo Emerson which Adams understood to mean that "the general reputation of a man is the correct one," the diarist, looking to himself, took issue: "A Man's whole character is rarely known, and in many cases the substitution in public opinion of certain leading traits occasions an entirely mistaken estimate. A man may be warmhearted in nature yet cold in his general manners. He is called haughty. . . . It is undoubtedly true that the world can sometimes, though it may not always, be deceived."[4]

Rejecting his father's and grandfather's passionate openness, Charles Francis Adams' characteristic behavior was to restrain any display. The course he set for himself in this regard was so rigorous a one that he seldom allowed himself even the indulgence of recording his feelings in his diary. The routine and meager references to his wife that are to be found in it are the mark of this rigor, rather than an indication of any failure in his marriage or any want of affection

[9] 3 Sept. 1832 (vol. 4:356–357).
[1] *Times Literary Supplement*, 28 Oct. 1965.
[2] Massachusetts Historical Society, *Proceedings*, 2d series, 3 (1886–1887): 150.
[3] Diary, 20 Dec. 1832 (vol. 4:424).
[4] 29 April 1832 (vol. 4:288).

for Abby—an affection that we deduce from other evidence was deep and abiding.

Beginning in 1826 and continuing for eight or nine years, he did allow himself some expression of his "views and feelings of the hour" in a separate book, which he would ultimately destroy though not before recording that he found the entries "not discreditable to me." When he read the volume over at the point that he was "busy in the work of destruction," we hear again of the "speculative and solitary tendencies I had," along with the renewed declaration of satisfaction that he had overcome them and in so doing "realized [i.e. accomplished] much more than I then even vaguely anticipated."[5] During the years he was writing in it, on at least one occasion when he opened the book he "could not avoid pouring out the current of my feelings at length."[6] More explicit statements of their character are rare in the diary, and when they occur they are in the context of what has been put away, but never quite:

> The beauty of the day, the rich colouring which the Autumn had given to the leaves of the Woods, and the picturesque effect of the wild scenery . . . gave a kind of romance to the Expedition. . . . I have from early associations in life felt a singular fondness for that scenery which by others is always considered wild and desolate. It seems in some measure to harmonize with a particular tone of mind in me formerly cherished but now repressed which seeks melancholy for pleasure. I can see more beauty in the roughness of nature than the softness of artificial cultivation, more attraction in a spot where man seems never to have been than where his labour has made all things smooth. Indeed my feelings today reminded me of early dreams long since vanished and not till now revived in any degree. They were the offspring of idle hours of musing then and are worth no more than the pleasure which remembrance gives to early feelings of all kinds. I have indulged them only here. . . . For after all I am no loser by the changes which have come over me. Why should I be savage, and lonely[?][7]

The solitary and melancholic, sensitive and passionate man, "unfit for the matter of fact world of this century" does then exist within the years of these volumes, but he is to be found out usually in ways more indirect than his own words. His preference among the poets for Collins, Gray, and Byron is confirmatory;[8] so perhaps is the large place occupied by accounts of Arctic exploration in the list of books borrowed by Adams from the Boston Athenæum during these years.[9] The

[5] MS Diary, 8 Aug. 1868.
[6] 15 Oct. 1829 (vol. 3:46).
[7] 9 Oct. 1829 (vol. 3:39–40).
[8] See vols. 1 and 2, *passim*, and the diarist's Literary Commonplace Book, Adams Papers, Microfilms, Reel No. 312.
[9] See vol. 4, Appendix.

powerful effect exerted upon Adams at each return to Mount Wollaston, "pretty and wild," adds another dimension.[1] Still another may be his preference for the Greeks, who "shone through the powers of the mind," maintained strongly against his father's preference for the more worldly and practical Romans.[2]

More problematic in its relevance to this aspect of the diarist's personality, because attributable to other traits and influences as well, was Adams' aversion to commerce, to the vulgarity of "money," to "State Street," to which Henry Adams gave emphasis in his extraordinarily deft portrait of his father as a kind of 18th-century man in *The Education.* Nevertheless, in the responses he records in the diary to men of current wealth and station when he encounters them at meetings of the directors of the Middlesex Canal or of the Boston Athenæum, at public meetings in Faneuil Hall, at the dinner tables of Benjamin Bussey and Peter Chardon Brooks, or in his reflections, one hears in the tone of his disapproval something of the same strain: "The passion for wealth is perhaps the most universal on the Globe. Its operation is to narrow the liberal feelings, to check nobility of soul. If there is any reproach to be made to people in this Quarter it is this."[3] Or again when his wife's cousin gives up his post in an Insurance Office to study theology: "Poor fellow, I pity him. He forgets the fact that Wealth gives Power, learning only indigence and contempt."[4]

Only after a probing search in these directions do Adams' consuming fears that he would be childless, morbid fears because they were groundless, become explicable and a consistent element in the man's temperament. Clearly, he had entertained those fears for some years before his marriage. Within a month of that event he had adverted to his fear, and in less than two he wrote, "I fear now ... that my dread will be realized."[5] In 1831, after the birth of the Adamses' first child, when giving thanks for the year's blessing, Adams wrote that it "had dispelled doubts and fears which for many preceding years had slightly shaded my path, and had justified me to myself for my conduct in some important particulars."[6] And in the immediate joy of that event he was led to "look back upon past time, ... the fears and hopes which possessed me, and which were spread throughout my writing whether in this Journal or in my letters."[7]

[1] 26 June 1830 (vol. 3:268); see also the entries for 27 Aug. 1830 (vol. 3:309–310) and 14 Sept. 1832 (vol. 4:362).
[2] See, for example, the entry for 26 Dec. 1831 (vol. 4:205 and *passim*).
[3] 25 Sept. 1831 (vol. 4:145).
[4] 17 April 1831 (vol. 4:30).
[5] 2 and 27 Oct. 1829 (vol. 3:33 and 58).
[6] 31 Dec. 1831 (vol. 4:208).
[7] 13 Aug. 1831 (vol. 4:110), and,

The fear of childlessness in the years before that fear was exorcised, was the dark underside of the strongest of Charles Francis Adams' passions, his utter devotion to the family name and character. Nor was that dread entirely debilitating, for the fear itself was a goad to achievement and right action: "I am the only Stock of an old House, and is not the object glorious to continue it in character even if I do not it's name[?]"[8] And beyond the fear that the family would become extinct was the fear that its reputation might suffer in its descendants: "[W]hat becomes of the family which we love to cherish[?] Perhaps this is a part of fate. I know not but with a very good end, for it would be better that it should cease than degenerate to become a proverb."[9]

It is clear that pride in the role of sole and final custodian of the Adams heritage was an operative passion, but there was in it too a romanticization of fact. Charles Francis Adams was not the last of the line. There was his brother John, who at the time the present volumes commence already had a child and would have another before the end of the period covered by them. But John lived in Washington, and for the diarist the true sphere of the family was Massachusetts. So that to say, "I am now the last scion of the race in this State,"[1] was but a more precise way of saying, "I am the only Stock of an old House." Moreover, John's first child was a daughter, as was his second; and John was in commerce, and not successfully either. The business (the financial responsibility of John Quincy Adams) and the presence of John and his family in Washington to manage it, were, to Charles Francis Adams, hindrances to the day when his father would return to the home of his fathers in Massachusetts, there to carry out his familial responsibilities in writing the life of John Adams. Washington too, and for many reasons, was a part of his own life that Charles Francis Adams preferred to ignore.[2]

In another sense, Charles Francis Adams' failure during these years to take effective note of John as a sharer in the family heritage is attributable to the diarist's fascination in exploring what were to him antithetical and complementary aspects in the characters of himself and his dead brother, the brilliant, amiable, and dissolute George Washington Adams; in exploring how between them was divided the whole Adams inheritance of mind and morals. It was a construction in which there was no place for a third. In that construction, by being

for example, see the entries for 8 Nov., 11 Dec. 1829; 16 May, 3 and 10 Oct. 1830 (vol. 3:70, 101, 237, 332, and 336).

[8] 10 Dec. 1829 (vol. 3:100); see also the entry for 7 Nov. 1831 (vol. 4:171).

[9] 10 Sept. 1830 (vol. 3:317).

[1] 16 Sept. 1829 (vol. 3:17).

[2] See vol. 1:xxvi–xxxiii.

saved by George's example from the weaknesses to which they were both subject, by acquiring through persistent study and imitation George's strengths in which he, Charles, was deficient, and by supplying the moral strength which George lacked, Charles could qualify himself to stand in the line of his father and grandfather. The image of George is never absent for long in the diary of these years and always appears in a monitory guise for the diarist.[3] The hoped-for end was all but mystical: "I have often thought that had we been able to form one character out of the advantageous portions of our two, Success would have been certain."[4] The continued use by Charles of the common-place books, the account books, the blank books that George had prepared, may reflect a kind of symbolic effort to achieve this union as much as it does a Yankee thrift. Something of this is evident in the note that Charles wrote at the commencement of his continuation of the commonplace book, "The Elements of Knowledge," that George had planned and begun: "Had perseverance only been his to fill the sketch he was so fully able to lay out, perhaps he would still have been among us, our pride and support. But since it was not the will of Providence that it should be thus, all that remains to me is to benefit as much by his good purposes as I can, and supply the deficiencies which in him prevented their execution. I therefore adopt here all that has been inserted and shall continue the extracts."[5]

Basic to the realization of Charles Francis Adams' purposes for himself and for the family was the assumption by him of a moral character that was unassailable. The devotion to duty, the humility, the regularity, the gravity that mark the Diary in these years are aspects of it. In the absence of evidence of strong religious convictions, the fixed habit of church attendance morning and afternoon and of sermon-reading afterward was the visible sign of the preeminence of the moral commitment. The want of confidence in his own abilities and powers made essential the acquisition of certainty of conscience: "The world can get along exactly as well if I do nothing. Perhaps better as there would be one less to crowd it. But this tone is incorrect. So long as I am placed in it, I must not reject my duty, because others do so. It is essential to me that my conscience should be clear."[6] It was the means by which he was able to put his trust in "a higher power," a phrase that runs like a refrain through these volumes. "I make my humble supplica-

[3] See, for example, the entries for 8 and 9 Sept., 16 Oct., 12 and 24 Nov. 1829; 14 April, 26 Oct. 1830 (vol. 3:6–8, 47, 73, 84, 213, 347, and *passim*).

[4] 30 July 1831 (vol. 4:101).
[5] Adams Papers, Microfilms, Reel No. 295; quoted at vol. 3:388–389.
[6] Diary, 19 Dec. 1832 (vol. 4:424).

tion to God, though I cannot feel now as if I could complain if he tried me a little. Yet I feel as if I had a pure heart and a willing mind to obey Counsels wherever they might end."[7] Thus armed, he was able to advance without hesitation upon those matters he thought vital to himself and to the Adams family "with a sense of independence and justness of feeling, without which I should be as a broken reed."[8]

The assurance was so complete that in his passages with John Quincy Adams, no mean antagonist, over pursuits that should most properly occupy the father, the son spoke in tones more conventionally heard from a parent:

> Three years have now elapsed and they have been witnesses to the most extraordinary irresolution I ever knew you seized by. . . . I have not been gratified by your election to Congress. I have felt little satisfaction in your occasional productions, for the reason that they employ the time in momentary objects, which should be devoted to a durable monument to your reputation. . . . I know that you can never be charged with any thing like Indolence in fact, but the moral effect is the same as if you could.[9]

To this exhortation, John Quincy Adams entered a defense, an Adams defense, that there were obligations owed to the Nation and to the Plymouth congressional district: "I am acting under a sense of duty. . . . My election to Congress was a *Call*. . . . [F]rom the dwellers of my native land. From the scenes of my childhood—Almost from the Sepulchres of my fathers."[1] But the son was not to be put off with the plea of a duty that transcended the *familial* duty: "[I]f the call on the part of your Constituents was of such a Nature as to make this acceptance of it a *duty*; was it so imperious as to put in the back ground other Calls which perhaps are not less urgent[?] . . . You say, it is 'Almost from the sepulchres of your fathers.' There is another, from which 'Almost' may be suppressed."[2] What he had set himself to persuade his father to was the prosecution of a life, perhaps more properly a vindication, of John Adams.[3]

In truth, Charles Francis Adams recognized in his father, and with satisfaction, the same inflexibility, the same response to what he conceived to be his duty, the same want of tact in his relations with those whose motives he questioned, that were characteristic of the diarist

[7] 10 Dec. 1829 (vol. 3:100).
[8] To Louisa Catherine Adams, 21 Dec. 1831, quoted at vol. 4:201–202.
[9] To John Quincy Adams, 12 Nov. 1831, quoted at vol. 4:175.
[1] To Charles Francis Adams, 22 Nov. 1831, quoted at vol. 4:187.
[2] To John Quincy Adams, 30 Nov.–

1 Dec. 1831, quoted at vol. 4:189.
[3] See the letter of Charles Francis Adams to John Quincy Adams, 12 Nov. 1831, quoted at vol. 4:175–176; also the journal entry of 24 June 1830 (vol. 3:267); and the editorial note on Jared Sparks, vol. 4:xii–xiii.

himself.[4] Father and son understood one another's character and manner, respected each other, and maintained their separate beliefs: "We keep up a kind of warfare that gives the letters a little spirit, and though apparently differing very much, agree well enough in the main. I tie my faith to no man's sleeve."[5]

As befitted one of this temper who was not "an unqualified admirer ... of any man living or dead,"[6] Charles Francis Adams, despite being overwhelmed by the breadth of John Quincy Adams' learning,[7] recognized limitations in his father: "He wants the profound wisdom which gives knowledge it's highest lustre, he is not proof against the temporary seductions of popular distinction to resist which is the most solid evidence of greatness. Yet if he is not in character like Washington, he is a very extraordinary man for the times we live in."[8]

But if he had limitations, he was still, for Charles Francis Adams, the only instructor to whom he could profitably apprentice himself for training of the mind. Although there were times when instruction was sought and imparted directly, the son's spirit was not of a sort to admit much profit from a master-student relationship: an effort was required to come to terms with his father's influence. More effectively and frequently, the educational method took one of two forms, the first, disputation, the second, emulation. The first was consciously entered upon, the second not with full realization or admission that it was taking place. At times there was an easy passage from the one to the other.

The pages of the diary for these years and the correspondence record many instances of debate being pursued between father and son on varied subjects, the son often taking his position opposite to that of his father with deliberation and purpose. They disputed among other topics the superiority of the Greeks to the Romans, Demosthenes to Cicero, the ancients to the moderns; the planning of gardens; the right of Parliament to legislate for the American colonies; Indian removal; political Antimasonry.

Instances of the son's emulation of his father are discoverable only accidentally. The reader of the diary and the person who examines Charles Francis Adams' later career will find many more and perhaps

[4] See the entries for 19 April and 20 Sept. 1831; 30 Nov. 1832 (vol. 4:31, 141, and 409).

[5] Charles Francis Adams to Louisa Catherine Adams, 21 Dec. 1831, quoted at vol. 4:201–202.

[6] Charles Francis Adams to John Quincy Adams, 30 Nov.–1 Dec. 1831, quoted at vol. 4:189–190.

[7] See, for example, the entries for 27 Sept. and 25 Oct. 1829 (vol. 3:29 and 56).

[8] Diary, 28 Sept. 1830 (vol. 3:328–329); see also the entry for 3 Oct. 1830 (vol. 3:331).

reject some of those alleged here. They may be of little moment, as when Charles Francis one evening read aloud from the American poets as his father had done less than two weeks before.[9] They may reflect more sharply an underlying competitiveness, as when Charles Francis undertook to translate from the works of Marmontel the identical tale that John Quincy had translated years before and published in the *Port Folio*, a copy of which Charles Francis had been reading a month before.[1] They may be of a larger and less well-defined sort, as in the son's adoption for himself of a program of improving his style by translating from the classic orators and of making himself a master of the literature and principles of oratory, a subject to which his father had devoted himself over many years and in which he was an acknowledged master.[2] They may relate to an extended interest on the part of Charles Francis in studying and writing about a current issue with which his father had become publicly identified. Here more than elsewhere the pattern of emulation begins in disputation to end in an arrival at almost identical conclusions. An example may be seen in the attitudes of father and son toward Freemasonry and their identification with Antimasonry.[3]

During the years covered by these volumes and for some years thereafter, in one area only is there no evidence that the son would follow the course set by his father: in the choice of politics and public life as a profession. Charles Francis undertook the disputation on this subject for no educational purpose and in no speculative vein. He rejected outright the thought of such a career for himself on a number of counts: his own temperamental unsuitability, the lack of opportunity so long as his father remained in the arena, and the unhappy experiences of each of the Adams statesmen at the hands of an ungrateful citizenry. He recognized his bent as in the direction of studies and writing. What ardor he could summon was "the ardor for literary distinction."[4] He described his ambition as of an "extensive but not of an extravagant kind. It is rather a desire of distinction from reputation than from place."[5] Thus committed, he gave all the hours that he could save from those office and family chores to which he felt bound, to reading and writing. The breadth and extent of his reading during

---

[9] John Quincy Adams, Diary, 10 Oct. 1831, quoted at vol. 4:154; Charles Francis Adams, Diary, 22 Oct. 1831 (vol. 4:161).

[1] Diary, 15 Oct. and 20 Nov. 1832 (vol. 4:379 and 403).

[2] See vol. 4:xvi–xvii.

[3] See vol. 4:x–xii and the entries for 22 May 1831, 20 Aug., 26 Nov. 1832 (vol. 4:53, 349–350, 407).

[4] 10 Oct. 1830 (vol. 3:336).

[5] 18 Aug. 1830 (vol. 3:303). The word "place" is here used in the sense of "official position."

these three years will be evident. The articles that he wrote and published in newspapers and journals make a more impressive list than one would guess from reading the diary entries themselves;[6] and they are of good quality as well. Although he was not then or later satisfied with the reception his writing received, he was justified in his reaction to the articles when he came upon them again nearly forty years afterward: "In reading them over I am not displeased with them, and am amazed at the industry they display, and the independence they maintain. They did not make for me the reputation that they deserved."[7]

The major subjects of his reading and his writing during the years covered by the present volumes, in addition to the subjects that have already been alluded to in the course of this Introduction, were American history and contemporary public issues. On the last, at the time these volumes end, he had concluded, "I . . . never shall succeed as a political writer. Let me turn then as soon as possible to Literature."[8] By literature he clearly meant historical literature, particularly that which related to the New England past, to the Puritan and, ultimately, to the Adams contribution. These were themes which continued to stir him:

My own impression is that the New England character has not been justly appreciated, that men have taken the start in giving false and unfavourable views of the early settlers which it will take long years to shake off. But whether by previous study or occupations I am the fit person to shake it off remains to be seen. At any rate it would be an honourable quest, and peculiarly appropriate in me, the descendant of one of the clearest of its lines, not undistinguished in its history. My thoughts flow in upon me far too fast to speak them even if I would. But they are only fit for secret meditations.[9]

When, in May 1831, he began in earnest to sort and arrange his grandfather's papers, he was reaching toward his ultimate vocation in the nonpublic sphere, though he could not yet sense it—the editing and publishing of the family's papers.[1] At the time he was aware only of an interest absorbing enough to cause him to break his established routine: "The day was fine, but I concluded that I would not go to

[6] See the Chronology, vol. 4:447–449.

[7] MS Diary, 4 Oct. 1869. See also the entries for 24 Nov., and 5 Dec. 1832 (vol. 4:404 and 413).

[8] 15 Dec. 1832 (vol. 4:421).

[9] 15 April 1830 (vol. 3:214).

[1] On this entire aspect of Charles Francis Adams' career, see the summary account and appraisal in *Diary and Autobiography of John Adams*, ed. L. H. Butterfield and others, Cambridge, 1961, 1:xxvi–xxx, xlvii–lii; *Adams Family Correspondence*, ed. L. H. Butterfield and others, Cambridge, 1963, 1: xxxii–xxxviii.

Boston.... I sat down accordingly and worked from eight o'clock until two very steadily at the Papers.... [A]s I am occasionally very much inclined to read over several interesting ones my course is stopped. An acquaintance with the incidents of his life embraces a knowledge of the history of the whole period. And I feel as if I ought to seize every opportunity of knowing facts relating to the times. The hours flew rapidly."[2]

What prevented his coming *then* to an understanding of his true vocation was the conviction he held that *this* was the proper and essential work to occupy John Quincy Adams for the rest of his life. On this ground primarily, but also because of what seemed to one of his decorous turn of mind an impropriety in one who had been President, Charles Francis Adams lamented his father's decision to accept the "call" to Congress. "His course ... has not been calculated to raise him in the judgment of the public. The examples of Washington, Jefferson and Madison have produced so strong an effect that a departure from their line of policy is considered as a departure from true dignity. I think his only course is to set seriously about writing a biography of my Grandfather and a thorough examination of his papers."[3] He therefore stubbornly persisted in his effort to lure his father from Washington to the family archives and the writing chamber at Quincy:

Does my grandfather's reputation stand so high that it will need no mending or restoring? ... Even at this moment, a deliberate attempt is made to rob him of all credit for knowledge of political affairs in a trying Crisis and moreover to prove him wrong where he has always been thought right. Is this nothing? Here is a gross perversion of history ... obtaining the authority of time and prescription, while the destruction of it is still left to chance ... [F]rom the clearest lights of my understanding I do feel impressed with a conviction that his story is not fairly told. ... You know it all better than I do. ... If this is an important duty, which you and you only can perform, is it wonderful that I feel provoked that the performance of it should be hazarded by ... the doubtful (to say no more) advantages of the ... all exhausting political warfare of a Seat in the House of Representatives?[4]

Until events forced him to realize that John Quincy Adams would never leave the public sphere while he lived, Charles Francis Adams still searched for his vocation.

[2] Diary, 28 May 1831 (vol. 4:57).
[3] 12 Nov. 1831 (vol. 4:174–175); see also the letter to JQA of the same date quoted in the note to that entry, and the entry for 3 Oct. 1830 (vol. 3:331).
[4] To John Quincy Adams, 30 Nov.– 1 Dec. 1831, quoted at vol. 4:189–190.

2. THE MANUSCRIPTS AND THE EDITORIAL METHOD

Before the period covered by the present volumes Charles Francis Adams had settled upon an appropriate form for the entries in his journal (see volume 1:xxxix–xl). Later, despite an inclination at times "to attempt some new method," he concluded that "the old way after all suits my taste and my habits. There is now no good reason to change it" (below, p. 238). From 1827 onward he was to follow a single form that was to remain essentially unchanged and to continue without any significant break until 1880.

The journal entries from 4 September 1829 to 31 December 1832, the time spanned in the present volumes, are consecutively written in three manuscript-diary volumes. In the Adams Papers serial numbering they are designated D/CFA/5, 8, and 9 (Microfilms, Reel Nos. 59–61). Adams' own numbering of the volumes differs from the numbers assigned in the Adams Papers as they now stand; an explanation of the discrepancy is given in volume 1:xxxvii–xxxviii.

From 4 September 1829 to 16 May 1830, the journal entries occupy the pages in D/CFA/5 that the diarist had left blank when he packed the volume away in July 1827 preparatory to leaving Washington for Boston. Thereafter, from 31 July 1827 through 3 September 1829, he had used two other volumes, D/CFA/6 and 7. On the day following his marriage, to mark the change in his life made by that event, Adams began anew in the earlier-used manuscript volume with the sentence with which the present volumes open: "An accidental circumstance which deprived me of this Book at the proper Season for continuing my Journal in course, has carried me through two other Books with as many years and it is only now as a Married man that I resume my record of events here" (below, p. 1–2). The volume, bound in tooled green leather, measures 8½″ x 6½″ and contains, in its two parts, 354 pages; in its second part alone, 260 pages.

Beginning on 17 May 1830 (below, p. 238) and continuing through 31 December 1831 (volume 4:208), the journal entries are continued through the 321 pages of D/CFA/8, a vellum-bound volume, 10″ x 8″, with a red leather label on its spine. On the front cover is written in George Washington Adams' hand, his name and "Boston 10th October 1827." One might conclude from the blank pages left at the end of the volume that when Charles Francis Adams had made his entry for the end of the year he wished thereafter to have the beginning and end of his diary volumes coincide with the beginning and end of calendar years. In this he was only intermittently successful, although he did accomplish it in the volume immediately following.

The ninth volume of Charles Francis Adams' diary (D/CFA/9) contains two full years of journal entries, 1 January 1832–31 December 1833, of which the first year's entries are included within the present volumes (volume 4:209–433). The manuscript volume, measuring 10″ x 8″, is bound in half calf with green boards; its spine is now missing; and it contains 368 pages.

The editorial method followed in volumes 3 and 4 of the *Diary of Charles Francis Adams* has, with slight modifications to be noted, been that followed in the two earlier volumes of the *Diary*. That method, including textual and annotational policy, has been explained fully in the Introduction to those volumes, 1:xl–xlvi.

Adams did not customarily paragraph his journal entries during the years covered by these volumes. Paragraphing has been introduced where shifts of time or place or subject seem to demand it.

With respect to punctuation, the editors of the present volumes have concluded that it is possible to rationalize Adams' use of the dash mark. His dash has been retained rather than converted to a period where he has capitalized the word following the dash but where the matter preceding the dash does not constitute a grammatical sentence. The editors believe that in such instances Adams did not use the dash as a proper concluding mark for a sentence but to separate introductory participial or absolute elements from the rest of the sentence. The decision to retain the author's dash mark in those situations, but to use the period as the concluding mark for full sentences, has all but eliminated what seemed to be Adams' addiction to the fragmentary sentence, and also the need to introduce any semicolons, a mark he very seldom used.

What was said in the Introduction to the earlier volumes (1:xlii) about the rendering of Adams' notation of the hour and minute of arising and retiring, and of the telegraphic style of his "Index" diary (D/CFA/1) is not relevant here since neither the notation nor the "Index" is used during the period covered by these volumes. Similarly, the policy adopted earlier on canceled matter and editorial insertions has not had to be employed in these volumes. However, during these years Adams did introduce a new element in his diary: the notation of place. Beginning with the first page of D/CFA/8 (below, p. 238) and continuing regularly thereafter, each page of the manuscript diary has at its head a notation of place. These place notations have a fixed position irrespective of whether the top of the page marks the opening of a new journal entry or the continuation of an entry from the preceding page. By means of the notation Adams indicates his abode or changes in it during the period covered by the entry or entries on that page. His practice in the manuscript has been normalized in these volumes to include the place notation, italicized, just above and to the left of the date at the beginning of any entry where a *change* of abode is recorded, but to omit the place notation elsewhere. In those instances where Adams has written in the manuscript the names of both the place from which and the place to which he went, both names have been retained. In those instances where a change of abode for a day is evident in the text of a journal entry but not recorded in a place notation in the manuscript, the editors have supplied and bracketed the place notation.

The statement made in the Introduction to the earlier volumes of the *Diary of Charles Francis Adams* (1:xlv) about the annotation of books and other publications mentioned in the Diary must now be expanded in one particular. In addition to recording, for the books Adams mentions, the edition and present whereabouts of those he owned or used in his father's or grandfather's library, the editors of the present volumes have been able to include bibliographical information about the substantial number of books Adams borrowed from the Boston Athenæum beginning in January 1830. All such borrowings have also been listed in the Appendix (volume 4:436–444; see also above, p. xix–xx).

Acknowledgments

The viability of the Adams Papers as an ongoing enterprise and the completion of each unit the editors project depend upon a number of collaborating agencies and upon the individuals who in their continuing commitment to the Papers have come, in our view, to personify those institutions. The gratitude of all who are a part of the Adams Papers to these institutions and persons has been expressed many times. Because the present volumes are the last that will be brought to editorial completion while he remains the director of one of the most important of all these institutions and because it was he who, from the outset, perhaps more than any other person understood the scope and import of the enterprise and has labored always and in a multitude of roles to forward it, we here single out as in certain vital respects "the onlie begetter," Thomas J. Wilson, Director of Harvard University Press, 1947–1967.

Had we not many times observed them with all professional skill and eagerness serving the needs of other scholars who come to use its superb collections, we would believe that the members of the staff of the Massachusetts Historical Society reserved the major part of their time and energy to satisfying our wants. Each person at the Society has been many times a friend of the Adams Papers. Sensible of each of them, from their number we must here name Mr. Stephen T. Riley, Mr. Malcolm Freiberg, Mr. John D. Cushing, and Miss Winifred V. Collins.

An institution second only to the Massachusetts Historical Society in providing help in the many fields that are of concern to us and to which this great library has relevance is the Boston Athenæum. The director, Mr. Walter Muir Whitehill, and the staff have not only responded willingly to our every request but also been mindful of what would be of interest to us whenever they encountered it. For these continuing boons we express our gratitude to Mr. James E. Belliveau and to two former staff members, Miss Margaret Hackett, now retired after many years of service, and Miss Susan Parsons, whose untimely death saddens us. Our thanks also go to Mrs. Jane N. Garrett, Mr. David M. K. McKibbin, Mr. Jack Jackson, and Mr. Donald C. Kelley.

In the far reaches of Harvard University's libraries and special collections we have had the ready assistance of many in making the materials under their care available to our use and in imparting needed information in their special competences: in the Archives, Mr. Kimball C. Elkins; in the Baker Library, Mr. Robert W. Lovett; in the Law School Library, Miss Edith G. Henderson; in the Theatre Collection, Miss Helen D. Willard and Mr. Arnold Wengrow.

Mrs. Wilhelmina S. Harris, Superintendent of the Adams National Historic Site in Quincy, has been unstinting in her support of the Adams Papers. She and her staff have always given that help and forbearance we have needed to ask for on numerous occasions.

We record with gratitude too the essential aid we have received from Mr. Leo Flaherty at the Massachusetts Archives; Mr. Sinclair H. Hitchings at the Boston Public Library; Mrs. Harriet Ropes Cabot at the Bostonian Society; Mr. John Snelling at the Middlesex County Engineer's Office, Cambridge; Mr. William C. Edwards at Quincy; Mr. Marcus A. McCorison at the American Antiquarian Society, Worcester; and from the Library of the Grand Lodge of Masons in Massachusetts.

The editing of the present volumes has been facilitated by the willingness of specialists to resolve questions or difficulties that have arisen in particular matters: on portraiture, Mr. Andrew Oliver, New York City, and Mr. Charles D. Childs, the Childs Gallery, Boston; on political cartoons, Mr. Roger Butterfield, New York City; on architecture, Mr. Stephen Friedlaender, Cambridge.

The enterprise has been fortunate too in having drawn in these volumes on the professional competences of Mr. E. Harold Hugo and his assistant, Mr. William J. Glick, The Meriden Gravure Company, Meriden, Connecticut, on matters relating to illustrations; of Mr. George M. Cushing Jr., Boston, photographer; of Mr. Burton L. Stratton, Printing and Publishing Associates, Plymouth, in the styling of the appendix; of Mr. James Menzies and the Harvard University Printing Office; and of the production staff of Harvard University Press. The editors offer their special thanks to Mrs. Ann Louise C. McLaughlin, Harvard University Press, through whose hands and under whose eyes all the copy for these volumes passed and is the better for having done so.

The editors have reason to be grateful to Messrs. Stephen T. Riley and Malcolm Freiberg, Massachusetts Historical Society; to Professor Robert E. Moody, Boston University; and to their own former colleague Mr. Wendell D. Garrett, *Antiques* magazine, New York City, for the care with which they read the galley proofs for these volumes and for the improvements they have effected thereby.

Each member of the staff of the Adams Papers, past and present, who has participated in the process by which the present volumes have been brought to completion has earned our salute. The transcription of the manuscripts of the diary for these years was accomplished by Mrs. Elizabeth E. Butterfield, Mrs. Rita V. Cherington, and Miss Jean Willcutt. Miss Lynne G. Crane, while she was on the staff, and, after her departure, Miss D. Maureen Clegg have borne the heaviest burden in forwarding this editorial effort in all its aspects. Other members of the staff who have participated in the work are Miss Amber B. Cox, Mrs. Glynn Marini, and Mrs. Elinor Johnston Smith, at earlier stages; and, currently, Mrs. Susan F. Riggs, Mrs. Sarah I. Morrison, and Miss Gene Bishop. Also a participant in the months since he came to the Adams Papers as Fellow in Advanced Historical Editing, under a Ford Foundation grant administered by the National Historical Publications Commission, is Mr. Gaspare J. Saladino.

Guide to Editorial Apparatus

In the first three sections (1–3) of the six sections of this Guide are listed, respectively, the arbitrary devices used for clarifying the text, the code names for designating prominent members of the Adams family, and the symbols describing the various kinds of MS originals used or referred to, that are employed throughout *The Adams Papers* in all its series and parts. In the final three sections (4–6) are listed, respectively, only those symbols designating institutions holding original materials, the various abbreviations and conventional terms, and the short titles of books and other works, that occur in volumes 3 and 4 of the *Diary of Charles Francis Adams*. The editors propose to maintain this pattern for the Guide to Editorial Apparatus in each of the smaller units, published at intervals, of all the series and parts of the edition that are so extensive as to continue through many volumes. On the other hand, in short and specialized series and/or parts of the edition, the Guide to Editorial Apparatus will be given more summary form tailored to its immediate purpose.

1. TEXTUAL DEVICES

The following devices will be used throughout *The Adams Papers* to clarify the presentation of the text.

[. . .], [. . . .]	One or two words missing and not conjecturable.
[. . .] [1], [. . . .] [1]	More than two words missing and not conjecturable; subjoined footnote estimates amount of missing matter.
[ ]	Number or part of a number missing or illegible. Amount of blank space inside brackets approximates the number of missing or illegible digits.
[roman]	Conjectural reading for missing or illegible matter. A question mark is inserted before the closing bracket if the conjectural reading is seriously doubtful.
⟨*italic*⟩	Matter canceled in the manuscript but restored in our text.
[*italic*]	Editorial insertion in the text.

2. ADAMS FAMILY CODE NAMES

First Generation

JA	John Adams (1735–1826)
AA	Abigail Smith (1744–1818), *m.* JA 1764

Second Generation

JQA	John Quincy Adams (1767–1848), son of JA and AA
LCA	Louisa Catherine Johnson (1775–1852), *m.* JQA 1797
CA	Charles Adams (1770–1800), son of JA and AA

Mrs. CA	Sarah Smith (1769–1828), sister of WSS, *m.* CA 1795
TBA	Thomas Boylston Adams (1772–1832), son of JA and AA
Mrs. TBA	Ann Harrod (1774?–1845), *m.* TBA 1805
AA2	Abigail Adams (1765–1813), daughter of JA and AA, *m.* WSS 1786
WSS	William Stephens Smith (1755–1816), brother of Mrs. CA

Third Generation

GWA	George Washington Adams (1801–1829), son of JQA and LCA
JA2	John Adams (1803–1834), son of JQA and LCA
Mrs. JA2	Mary Catherine Hellen (1806?–1870), *m.* JA2 1828
CFA	Charles Francis Adams (1807–1886), son of JQA and LCA
ABA	Abigail Brown Brooks (1808–1889), *m.* CFA 1829
ECA	Elizabeth Coombs Adams (1808–1903), daughter of TBA and Mrs. TBA

Fourth Generation

JQA2	John Quincy Adams (1833–1894), son of CFA and ABA
CFA2	Charles Francis Adams (1835–1915), son of CFA and ABA
HA	Henry Adams (1838–1918), son of CFA and ABA
MHA	Marian Hooper (1842–1885), *m.* HA 1872
BA	Brooks Adams (1848–1927), son of CFA and ABA
LCA2	Louisa Catherine Adams (1831–1870), daughter of CFA and ABA, *m.* Charles Kuhn 1854
MA	Mary Adams (1845–1928), daughter of CFA and ABA, *m.* Henry Parker Quincy 1877

Fifth Generation

CFA3	Charles Francis Adams (1866–1954), son of JQA2
HA2	Henry Adams (1875–1951), son of CFA2

3. DESCRIPTIVE SYMBOLS

The following symbols will be employed throughout *The Adams Papers* to describe or identify in brief form the various kinds of manuscript originals.

D	Diary (Used only to designate a diary written by a member of the Adams family and always in combination with the short form of the writer's name and a serial number, as follows: D/JA/23, i.e. the twenty-third fascicle or volume of John Adams' manuscript Diary.)
Dft	draft
Dupl	duplicate
FC	file copy (Ordinarily a copy of a letter retained by a correspondent *other than an Adams*, for example Jefferson's press copies and polygraph copies, since all three of the Adams statesmen systematically entered copies of their outgoing letters in letterbooks.)
Lb	Letterbook (Used only to designate Adams letterbooks and always in combination with the short form of the writer's name and a

	serial number, as follows: Lb/JQA/29, i.e. the twenty-ninth volume of John Quincy Adams' Letterbooks.)
LbC	letterbook copy (Letterbook copies are normally unsigned, but any such copy is assumed to be in the hand of the person responsible for the text unless it is otherwise described.)
M	Miscellany (Used only to designate materials in the section of the Adams Papers known as the "Miscellany" and always in combination with the short form of the writer's name and a serial number, as follows: M/CFA/32, i.e. the thirty-second volume of the Charles Francis Adams Miscellany—a ledger volume mainly containing transcripts made by CFA in 1833 of selections from the family papers.)
MS, MSS	manuscript, manuscripts
RC	recipient's copy (A recipient's copy is assumed to be in the hand of the signer unless it is otherwise described.)
Tr	transcript (A copy, handwritten or typewritten, made substantially later than the original or than other copies—such as duplicates, file copies, letterbook copies—that were made contemporaneously.)
Tripl	triplicate

4. LOCATION SYMBOLS

MB	Boston Public Library
MBAt	Boston Athenæum
MH	Harvard College Library
MH-Ar	Harvard University Archives
MHi	Massachusetts Historical Society
MQA	Adams National Historic Site ("Old House"), Quincy, Massachusetts

5. OTHER ABBREVIATIONS AND CONVENTIONAL TERMS

Adams Genealogy

A set of genealogical charts and a concise biographical register of the Adams family in the Presidential line and of closely related families from the 17th through the 19th century. The Adams Genealogy is now being compiled and will be published as a part of *The Adams Papers*.

Adams Papers

Manuscripts and other materials, 1639–1889, in the Adams Manuscript Trust collection given to the Massachusetts Historical Society in 1956 and enlarged by a few additions of family papers since then. Citations in the present edition are simply by date of the original document if the original is in the main chronological series of the Papers and therefore readily found in the microfilm edition of the Adams Papers (see below). The location of materials in the Letterbooks and in the volumes of Miscellany is given more fully and, if the original would be hard to locate, by the microfilm reel number.

Adams Papers, Microfilms

> The corpus of the Adams Papers, 1639–1889, as published on microfilm by the Massachusetts Historical Society, 1954–1959, in 608 reels. Cited in the present work, when necessary, by reel number. Available in research libraries throughout the United States and in a few libraries in Europe.

The Adams Papers

> The present edition in letterpress, published by The Belknap Press of Harvard University Press. References to earlier volumes of any given unit will take this form: vol. 2:146. Since there will be no over-all volume numbering for the edition, references from one series, or unit of a series, to another will be by title, volume, and page; for example, JA, *Diary and Autobiography*, 4:205.

Brooks, Book of Possessions
——— Farm Journal
——— Waste Book

> The MSS of Peter Chardon Brooks Sr. in the Massachusetts Historical Society consisting of:
> "Book of Possessions," 1 vol., and containing documents gathered by Peter Chardon Brooks relating to the history of his family and his estates;
> "Farm Journal," 13 vols., 1808–1848, a diary primarily devoted to matters relevant to his Medford estate but containing some entries of family concern;
> "Waste Book," 8 vols., 1789–1848, more properly styled "Private a/c Ledgers," a record of his personal holdings, income, and expenditures.

Everett MSS

> The papers of Edward Everett in the Massachusetts Historical Society. Included are a diary, 62 vols., 1814–1864; letterbooks, 67 vols., 1825–1864; and a chronological file of letters received, 18 boxes, 1819–1865.

M/CFA/3

> The account book of CFA as manager of JQA's business affairs in Boston, 1828–1846; Adams Papers, Microfilms, Reel No. 297. The payment of routine agency bills, the receipt of rents from tenants, fully recorded here and sometimes alluded to in CFA's journal entries, have not ordinarily been specifically annotated in the text.

M/CFA/9

> The record of CFA's personal receipts and expenditures, 1829–1844; Adams Papers, Microfilms, Reel No. 303.

6. SHORT TITLES OF WORKS
FREQUENTLY CITED

Adams Family Correspondence
> *Adams Family Correspondence*, ed. L. H. Butterfield and others, Cambridge, 1963– .

A. N. Adams, *Geneal. Hist. of Henry Adams of Braintree*
Andrew N. Adams, *A Genealogical History of Henry Adams, of Braintree, Mass., and His Descendants*, Rutland, Vt., 1898.

AHR
American Historical Review.

Alden, *Medical Profession in Norfolk County*
Ebenezer Alden, *The Early History of the Medical Profession in the County of Norfolk, Mass.*, Boston, 1853.

Allibone, *Dict. of Authors*
Samuel Austin Allibone, *A Critical Dictionary of English Literature, and British and American Authors, Living and Deceased, from the Earliest Accounts to the Middle of the Nineteenth Century...*, Philadelphia, 1858–1871; 3 vols.

Annals of Congress
The Debates and Proceedings in the Congress of the United States [1789–1824], Washington, 1834–1856; 42 vols.

Bemis, *JQA*
Samuel Flagg Bemis, *John Quincy Adams*, New York, 1949–1956; 2 vols. [Vol. I:] *John Quincy Adams and the Foundations of American Foreign Policy*; [vol. 2:] *John Quincy Adams and the Union.*

Biog. Dir. Cong.
Biographical Directory of the American Congress, 1774–1949, Washington, 1950.

Boston Directory, [year]
Boston Directory, issued annually with varying imprints.

Boston Streets, &c., 1910
City of Boston, Street Commissioners, *A Record of the Streets, Alleys, Places, Etc., in the City of Boston*, Boston, 1910.

Brooks, *Medford*
Charles Brooks, *History of the Town of Medford, Middlesex County, Massachusetts, From its First Settlement in 1630 to 1855*, rev.... by James M. Usher, Boston, 1886.

Calhoun, *Works*, ed. Crallé
John C. Calhoun, *Works*, ed. Richard K. Crallé, New York, 1853–1855; 6 vols.

Catalogue of JA's Library
Catalogue of the John Adams Library in the Public Library of the City of Boston, Boston, 1917.

Catalogue of JQA's Books
Worthington C. Ford, ed., *A Catalogue of the Books of John Quincy Adams Deposited in the Boston Athenæum. With Notes on Books, Adams Seals and Book-Plates*, by Henry Adams, Boston, 1938.

CFA, *Diary*
Diary of Charles Francis Adams, Cambridge, 1964– . Vols. 1–2, ed. Aïda DiPace Donald and David Donald.

CFA2, *R. H. Dana*
Charles Francis Adams Jr., *Richard Henry Dana: A Biography*, Boston and New York, 1890.

Chamberlain, *Beacon Hill*
>Allen Chamberlain, *Beacon Hill: Its Ancient Pastures and Early Mansions*, Boston and New York, 1925.

Col. Soc. Mass., *Pubns.*
>Colonial Society of Massachusetts, *Publications*.

Commonwealth *Hist. of Mass.*
>Albert Bushnell Hart, ed., *Commonwealth History of Massachusetts: Colony, Province, and State*, New York, 1927–1930; 5 vols.

DAB
>Allen Johnson and Dumas Malone, eds., *Dictionary of American Biography*, New York, 1928–1936; 20 vols. plus index and supplements.

Dict. of Americanisms
>Mitford M. Mathews, ed., *A Dictionary of Americanisms on Historical Principles*, Chicago, 1951.

DNB
>Leslie Stephen and Sidney Lee, eds., *The Dictionary of National Biography*, New York and London, 1885–1900; 63 vols. plus supplements.

Duberman, *CFA*
>Martin B. Duberman, *Charles Francis Adams, 1807–1886*, Boston, 1961.

Edwards, *Historic Quincy*, 1954
>William Churchill Edwards, *Historic Quincy, Massachusetts*, Quincy, 1954.

Farmer-Storer Trial
>*Report of a Trial: Miles Farmer, versus Dr. David Humphreys Storer, Commenced in the Court of Common Pleas, April Term, 1830, from which it was Appealed to the Supreme Judicial Court, and by Consent of Parties, Referred to Referees, Relative to the Transactions between Miss Eliza Dolph and George Washington Adams, Esq. Son of the Late President of the United States*, Boston, 1831.

Ford, ed., *Statesman and Friend*
>Worthington C. Ford, ed., *Statesman and Friend: Correspondence of John Adams with Benjamin Waterhouse, 1784–1822*, Boston, 1927.

Frothingham, *Everett*
>Paul Revere Frothingham, *Edward Everett: Orator and Statesman*, Boston, 1925.

Fuess, *Webster*
>Claude M. Fuess, *Daniel Webster*, Boston, 1930; 2 vols.

Gallatin, *Writings*
>Henry Adams, ed., *The Writings of Albert Gallatin*, Philadelphia, 1879; 3 vols.

Greenleaf, *Greenleaf Family*
>James E. Greenleaf, *Genealogy of the Greenleaf Family*, Boston, 1896.

Groce and Wallace, *Dict. Amer. Artists*
>George C. Groce and David H. Wallace, *The New-York Historical Society's Dictionary of Artists in America, 1564–1860*, New Haven and London, 1957.

HA, *Education*
> Henry Adams, *The Education of Henry Adams: An Autobiography*, Boston, The Massachusetts Historical Society, 1918.

HA, *Gallatin*
> Henry Adams, *The Life of Albert Gallatin*, Philadelphia, 1879.

HA, *Letters*, ed. Ford
> Henry Adams, *Letters of Henry Adams (1858–1891)*, ed. Worthington C. Ford, Boston and New York, 1930; 2 vols.

HA, *New-England Federalism*
> *Documents Relating to New-England Federalism, 1800–1815*, ed. Henry Adams, Boston, 1877.

Hamilton, *Papers*, ed. Syrett
> *The Papers of Alexander Hamilton*, ed. Harold C. Syrett and others, New York, 1961– .

Harvard Quinquennial Cat.
> Harvard University, *Quinquennial Catalogue of the Officers and Graduates, 1636–1930*, Cambridge, 1930.

JA, *Diary and Autobiography*
> *Diary and Autobiography of John Adams*, ed. L. H. Butterfield and others, Cambridge, 1961; 4 vols.

JA, *Earliest Diary*
> *The Earliest Diary of John Adams*, ed. L. H. Butterfield and others, Cambridge, 1966.

JA, *Works*
> *The Works of John Adams, Second President of the United States; with a Life of the Author*, ed. Charles Francis Adams, Boston, 1850–1856; 10 vols.

Jay, *Correspondence and Public Papers*
> *The Correspondence and Public Papers of John Jay*, ed. Henry P. Johnston, New York and London, 1890–1893; 4 vols.

JQA, *Letters on Silesia*
> John Quincy Adams, *Letters on Silesia, Written during a Tour through That Country in the Years 1800, 1801*, London, 1804.

JQA, *Memoirs*
> *Memoirs of John Quincy Adams, Comprising Portions of His Diary from 1795 to 1848*, ed. Charles Francis Adams, Philadelphia, 1874–1877; 12 vols.

Mass. Register, [year]
> *The Massachusetts Register and United States Calendar*, Boston, 1801–1847; 47 vols.

MHS, *Colls., Procs.*
> Massachusetts Historical Society, *Collections* and *Proceedings*.

Morison, *H. G. Otis*
> Samuel Eliot Morison, *The Life and Letters of Harrison Gray Otis, Federalist, 1765–1848*, Boston and New York, 1913; 2 vols.

NEHGR
> *New England Historical and Genealogical Register.*

NEHGS, *Memorial Biographies*
  Memorial Biographies of the New England Historic Genealogical Society, Boston, 1880–1908; 9 vols.

NEQ
  New England Quarterly.

Niles' Register
  Niles' Weekly Register, Baltimore, 1811–1849.

North Amer. Rev.
  North American Review, Boston, etc., 1815–1940.

Odell, *Annals N.Y. Stage*
  George C. D. Odell, *Annals of the New York Stage*, New York, 1927–1949; 15 vols.

OED
  The Oxford English Dictionary, Oxford, 1933; 12 vols. and supplement.

Pattee, *Old Braintree and Quincy*
  William S. Pattee, *A History of Old Braintree and Quincy, with a Sketch of Randolph and Holbrook*, Quincy, 1878.

Portraits of John and Abigail Adams
  Andrew Oliver, *Portraits of John and Abigail Adams*, Cambridge, 1967.

Quincy, *Figures of the Past*
  Josiah Quincy [1802–1882], *Figures of the Past, from the Leaves of Old Journals*, ed. M. A. DeWolfe Howe, Boston, 1926.

Register of Debates in Congress
  Register of Debates in Congress, 1824–1837, Washington, 1825–1837; 14 vols. in 29 pts.

Richardson, ed., *Messages and Papers*
  James Daniel Richardson, ed., *A Compilation of the Messages and Papers of the Presidents, 1789–1897*, Washington, 1896–1899; 10 vols.

Webster, 2d edn.
  Webster's New International Dictionary of the English Language, Second Edition, Unabridged, Springfield, Mass., 1957.

Whitehill, *Boston: A Topographical History*
  Walter Muir Whitehill, *Boston: A Topographical History*, Cambridge, 1959.

Winsor, *Memorial History of Boston*
  Justin Winsor, ed., *The Memorial History of Boston, Including Suffolk County, 1630–1880*, Boston, 1880–1881; 4 vols.

WMQ
  William and Mary Quarterly.

VOLUME 3

Diary 1829–1831

Diary of Charles Francis Adams

SEPTEMBER 1829.

FRIDAY 4TH.[1]

An accidental circumstance which deprived me of this Book at the proper Season for continuing my Journal in course, has carried me through two other Books with as many Years and it is only now as a Married man that I resume my record of events here. The occurrence gradually brings to mind the passage of the intervening time, in which I have enjoyed much and suffered much, in which my life has passed away rather in pleasure than in profit. The waste of time has been considerable but I am still gratified with the idea that it has not been without good purposes and pure thoughts, and that I can now lay claim with reason to being both a wiser and better man than formerly.

This morning found me established as a married man in Boston—Hopes, fears, dread and every thing else merged in the actual event. I arose rather early and after breakfast went to the Office where I occupied myself the larger part of the morning.[2] My father came in from Medford with Thomas B. Adams,[3] and called at my Office. I took the opportunity to speak to him of Mr. Degrand's proposition in relation to a Mortgage, but he did not seem disposed to listen to it. He is a singular man with regard to the management of his property. Investments with him are Chance things.

Edward Blake called to see me with some disposition to quiz but I did not allow it much.[4] I went to the House and found Abby alone.[5] She had seen a number of persons today, principally of the family however. My father had been there and had been kind. He certainly has made amends now for the unfortunate difference of last year.[6] Now is not a time to recollect. I passed the afternoon at home with Abby, as I was indolent, and also fearful she would be dull.[7] But Mrs. P. C. Brooks came in with Miss Carter and Miss Gorham and passed the Afternoon.[8] The evening at home alone with Abby. I wrote a Letter to my Mother,[9] just notifying her of our condition—Happy indeed. My course of existence has been today an unclouded one, it has been what I suppose I may fairly say the summit of human enjoyment. I have been favoured wonderfully, and on my knees I thank the

I

divine being for having so bountifully filled out my measure, even to so unworthy a servant.

¹ The following entries through 16 May 1830 derive from the second (and last) part of the volume of his diaries which CFA designated as No. 2, but which in the Adams Papers serial listing is No. 5 (D/CFA/5; Adams Papers, Microfilms, Reel No. 59). CFA had earlier used the volume for entries beginning 18 June 1826 and ending 27 [i.e. 17?] July 1827, then put it aside. On 31 July 1827 he began a new volume numbered 3, but which in Adams Papers serial listing is No. 6 (D/CFA/6), and on 17 Oct. 1828 still another volume numbered 4, Adams Papers No. 7 (D/CFA/7). Having completed both volumes, he returned to the remaining blank pages of D/CFA/5, preceding the entry for 4 Sept. with a note: "27 July 1826 [i.e. 31 July 1827]–4 September 1829. The Diary for the Intervale between these dates is contained in No. 3 and 4." The first sentence of the present entry provides an explanation. For a description of the MSS see Introduction and vol. 1:xxxiv–xl, esp. p. xxxviii, note 5, and p. xxxix, note 9.

² CFA, since the death of his brother George in May 1829, had occupied George's former office at 23 Court Street; see vol. 2:373, 382, 383. The building stood on land which had been bought by JA in 1772, by JQA from him in 1793, and was the site of JA's law office and of JQA's for a time. See JA, *Diary and Autobiography*, 2:63–64. It had a frontage of 22½ feet on the north side of Court Street and a depth of 160 feet (Nathaniel I. Bowditch, "Records of Land Titles," 26 [1834–1835]:153, 160, Bowditch MSS, MHi). In 1829, Prentiss Whitney occupied the first-floor store and the house at the rear (M/CFA/3 and *Boston Directory*, 1829–1830). Above, were at least two floors of offices. CFA's office and a smaller room opening from it, unrented at this time, were on the first of these (vol. 2:385, and below, entry for 17 Oct.). The other offices were occupied by attorneys also, currently George Gay, D. A. Simmons, and Thomas Welsh Jr. (M/CFA/3 and *Boston Directory*, 1829–1830).

³ Thomas Boylston Adams Jr. (1809–1837), JQA's nephew and a lieutenant in the U.S. Army, was currently on furlough from military duties and aiding his uncle at Quincy as amanuensis; see vol. 1:5; 2:406; Bemis, *JQA*, 2:186; Adams Genealogy.

⁴ Edward Blake, Harvard 1824, a college friend and an attorney, had been CFA's "first groomsman" at his wedding the day before (vol. 1:206, 2:425).

⁵ After their wedding in Medford on 3 Sept., CFA and his bride Abigail Brooks ("Abby") had returned to Boston to occupy the house at 3 Hancock Avenue which her father, Peter Chardon Brooks, had purchased in May for their use (vol. 2:376, 378–379, 432). They would remain in it until 1842.

Hancock Avenue, "under the shadow of Boston State House, turning its back on the house of John Hancock," was a short street or "little passage" running "from Beacon Street, skirting the State House grounds, to Mount Vernon Street, on the summit of Beacon Hill" (HA, *Education*, p. 3). Its situation is suggested in the view of the State House reproduced in the present volume. Opened in 1825, Hancock Avenue was obliterated in 1915 in preparation for the construction of the West Wing of the State House (*Boston Streets &c.*, 1910, p. 227; Chamberlain, *Beacon Hill*, p. 151). No. 3, "one of that pretty row of houses by the side of the State House" (Charlotte Everett to Edward Everett, 1 July 1829, Everett MSS, MHi), was the third house from the corner of Mount Vernon Place on a lot with 25 feet frontage, 69 feet in depth. Cornelius Coolidge, who owned the land and recently built the row, sold No. 3 to Brooks for $11,000 (Brooks, Waste Book, 1 June 1829).

⁶ See vol. 2:271, 313, 336–337.

⁷ CFA customarily uses "dull" in the sense of "depressed" or "melancholy"; e.g. see vol 2:422, and below, entries for 9, 15 September.

⁸ Mrs. P. C. Brooks Jr., ABA's sister-in-law, was the former Susan Oliver Heard (vol. 2:153–154 and Adams Genealogy). Anne Carter and Julia Gor-

ham were ABA's closest friends; Anne was one of her bridesmaids; Julia had not been at the wedding, perhaps because of the recent death of her father, Dr. John Gorham. See vol. 2:158, 167, 186, 360, 432.

[9] Letter missing. Because of ill health, Mrs. Adams (LCA) had been forced to remain in Washington at the time of CFA's wedding (vol. 2:388–389).

SATURDAY 5TH.

Morning to the Office as soon as I found Abby had somebody with her to amuse her. Obtained for my father the Dividend upon his Stock of the Fire and Marine Insurance Company and upon my own and wrote my Journal,[1] made up my Accounts. This occupied much of my time—So that I found it was time for me to return as I had promised before I was aware of it. I found Abby with a number of visitors, her sisters Eliza and Susan with Edward and Blake and Quincy.[2] The morning therefore passed away rapidly. After dinner I remained at home and idled the time away very pleasantly. Mr. Frothingham dropped in for a minute but seemed a little dull.[3] The evening passed quietly. I was a little apprehensive of the tone of her spirits as this was an evening when she expected to be at home,[4] or at least felt a little tempted to regret her absence. But though I perceived a cloud she had too much kindness to show it much and that made it lighter to herself. Indeed I have the utmost reason to be satisfied with her today and ever since our marriage—she has been kind and affectionate, patient and good tempered so that I have been as happy as circumstances well could make me.

[1] In June JQA had purchased eighty shares of Fire and Marine Insurance Co. stock at $50 per share. This dividend, the first thereafter, amounted to $150 (M/CFA/3). CFA owned three shares (vol. 2:306).

[2] That is, Elizabeth (Boott) Brooks (1799–1865) and her husband Edward Brooks (1793–1878), ABA's oldest brother and an attorney (vol. 2:168 and Adams Genealogy); Susan Brooks; Edward Blake; Edmund Quincy (1808–1877), CFA's kinsman and a groomsman (vol. 1:153; 2:433, and Adams Genealogy).

[3] The Rev. Nathaniel Langdon Frothingham (1793–1870), minister of Boston's First Church, was the husband of ABA's sister Ann (1797–1863); see vol. 1:103, 2:149; Adams Genealogy; *DAB*.

[4] That is, in Medford.

SUNDAY 6TH.

I was at home during the whole of the day. Abby would not go out to Meeting and I did not feel as if I could leave her alone. How we passed our day it is impossible for me to tell but I can truly say it was to me unmingled happiness or the intoxication of pleasure. I had formed moderate expectations only and they have been entirely exceeded—And Abby's conduct is perfectly delightful. The gentleness, and moderation she has displayed, with the attention to me have made

3

her far more dear than ever to me and have given me moments of felicity which could not be improved. Sidney and his Wife,[1] and Chardon came in and Julia Gorham in the course of the day and they laughed and made amusement in plenty,[2] and in the evening Mr. William Emerson called to see his old pupil.[3] I do not much like any of the Emerson family without knowing any reason for positively disliking them, excepting perhaps hearing from Abby's own lips that one of them had been once a favoured friend though at a time when she was so young as to be unable to judge. This might have been a reason, had I not been able to trace the dislike earlier than my acquaintance with her. Poor Edward has suffered so much subsequently however that I feel pity for him.[4] And I have been a successfull rival with too many advantages not to cause in him some regrets at the inequalities of life. I am sorry for I do not feel disposed to boast of advantages which are not my own but resulting from accident. I am full of gratitude for every thing.

[1] ABA's brother, Sidney Brooks (1799–1878) and his wife, the former Frances Dehon, had come for the wedding from New York where he was a partner in the firm of Davis & Brooks, importers. See vol. 2:103, 165, 197–199; Adams Genealogy; Brooks, Waste Book, 17 Jan. 1824, 19 Aug. 1826, 8 March 1828.

[2] P. C. Brooks Jr. ("Chardon") (1798–1880), another brother of ABA, was a partner in the firm of Sargent & Brooks, merchants, of 49 Central Wharf (*Boston Directory*, 1829–1830); see vol. 2:149 and Adams Genealogy.

[3] William Emerson (b. 1801), Harvard 1818, was the oldest of the three sons of Rev. William Emerson, minister of the First Church until his death in 1814. He was apparently the "Mr. Emerson" to whom Peter C. Brooks made payments in 1820 for "Abby's schooling" (Waste Book, 3 May, 25 Sept., 16 Nov. 1820). However, his younger brother, Ralph Waldo Emerson (b. 1803), Harvard 1821, was also one of her teachers, for on 29 Dec. 1824 Brooks recorded payment of $8 for a set of Cowper "presented by 'Miss Abby' to her instructor Mr. Ralph W. Emerson" (same).

[4] On Edward Bliss Emerson (1805–1834), Harvard 1824, formerly a fellow law student of CFA's in Daniel Webster's office, see vol. 1:206, 2:242, 254.

MONDAY 7TH.

Morning at home until ten o'clock with Abby. Then finding she had some of her friends coming, I went to the Office. Wrote my Journal but wasted my time considerably otherwise. Mr. Curtis called in to see me for a minute or two and we had much conversation respecting Mr. Boylston's Will and the arrangement and disposal of his Estates. I have not yet been able to finish the Deed.[1] After this I went to see Mrs. Longhurst and my father's other Tenants. But I obtained from them nothing but promises. Money seems now to be a difficult thing to obtain. And there is so much due to my father that it is high time to collect it. I have done my best.

Thence to the House to dinner. Found numbers of her relations with Abby and therefore she had become over excited. It is wonderful to see on what high pressure her spirits go, and sometimes I am really frightened for her lest they should prove too much, Afternoon passed restlessly, giving orders and directions for the evening. My father came in early and I asked him up in my Library. The rest of the family came too.

This was the Evening upon which Abby was to receive her Company and when she was to be fairly launched into Society. She was dressed magnificently and really looked quite a new thing. Her marriage has had a wonderfully beneficial effect upon her appearance so far and we are perhaps more struck with the contrast as she now comes out of black.[2] The Company both in character and number was highly flattering. All the most distinguished people in Boston favoured us and if I did not feel resolved not to be elated, I think I might with some reason. But all this is mere show. I hope I have too much sense not to see that it is all but as the passing shadow,[3] and that I have other and deeper duties to perform, to support and sustain my character, in the event of which there is much doubt. But I hope I shall be aware of my situation, and that adulation to my Wife is not respect for myself. The Company went early.

[1] Ward Nicholas Boylston (1747–1828) of Jamaica Plain, kinsman and friend of JQA (vol. 1:442 and Adams Genealogy), had by his will appointed as coexecutors of his estate, his wife, JQA, and Nathaniel Curtis (1774–1857) of Roxbury, a merchant of integrity and judgment (vol. 2:178; Francis S. Drake, *The Town of Roxbury*, Roxbury, 1878, p. 427).

The executors, faced with the prospect of conveying numerous parcels, wished a deed form prepared that would serve them generally. CFA had been chosen to prepare the somewhat complex instrument and was named conveyancer for the estate. See vol. 2:418; JQA, Diary, 1 Aug., 19, 25 Nov. 1829; and below, entries for 11, 16–18 November.

[2] ABA's brother, Ward Chipman Brooks, had died in March 1828; see vol. 2:223 and Adams Genealogy. It would appear that the Brooks sisters had continued to wear black since that time. Charlotte (Brooks) Everett had written to her husband on the subject, 1 July

1829, saying "there is little chance I think of my being able to have it off" (Everett MSS, MHi).

[3] Father and son shared similar views of such occasions, but JQA, less accustomed to the prevailing mode, is more explicit:

"It was near nine, when the company began to come, and by half past ten, all excepting the family had retired .... There is a fashionable formality in these wedding visits, and subsequent parties, different from the practice heretofore, and objectionable in many cases for its expensiveness. The Lady sends her Cards with her maiden name, and on the back of it At Home, such an Evening. The bridesmen introduce all the Visitors, to the bride with as much ceremony as at an European Court presentation. The dresses of the Ladies are too costly: and this wedding visit is succeeded by evening parties or dinners given by friends" (Diary, 7 Sept.).

Those other than family whose presence JQA marked were the Chevalier Huygens, the Minister from the Netherlands, with his wife and two daughters; Lt. Gov. Thomas L. Winthrop; Daniel Webster; Rev. Henry Ware, the Hollis Professor of Divinity at Harvard, and wife; Mr. and Mrs. Richard Derby; F. C. Gray; Jared Sparks.

TUESDAY. 8TH.

Arose this morning and breakfasted a little late, my wife being quite unwell. I sat with her until Susan Brooks came in, and I then went to the Office. Morning passed in writing my Journal and in arranging my papers. Chardon Brooks dropped in for a minute to speak about some Coal which he had engaged for me and to talk a little over the party. My Office has fallen into terrible confusion ever since the departure of my boy and I do not know when it will be restored. Returned to the House and found Mrs. Everett there, who was soon followed by her husband, Blake, Quincy and Mr. Lowell.[1] Abby however was not over well to receive them. After dinner I sat with Abby and commenced reading to her Devereux a new Novel by the Author of Pelham.[2]

Julia Gorham interrupting us, I walked to the Office and became unconsciously engaged in reading portions of my brother's Journal scraps which affected me exceedingly.[3] There is much moral to be learned from his Life and the candor and warmth with which it was set down made me reflect upon his character and mine. He possessed all the cultivation of mind essential to his success, he held what is infinitely more to the purpose than any thing in my possession, an aptitude of language and power of style which made a fascinating writer. I have only steadiness of character, without the boldness of enterprise essential to success—and without any confidence in myself. Much of his record affected me much, particularly his ample details of his love affairs with Mary which materially affected his life—ever afterwards.[4] Not that a marriage with her would have made him happy for I never believed any such thing, but his object of living was broken, and a chance was given to his weaknesses and evil inclinations to gain ground which never afterwards could be recovered. His Journal is interesting as a moral lesson to warn all young men and especially myself.

I returned home and found Abby alone. The Evening was quietly passed at home and I read a portion of Devereux to her. Quite happy.

[1] Charlotte (Brooks) Everett (1800–1859), the second eldest of ABA's sisters, and her distinguished husband, Edward Everett (1794–1865), currently a member of Congress, had been hosts to ABA in Washington in early 1827 at the beginning of CFA's courtship of her; see vol. 1:8; 2:x, 92, 97–113 *passim*; *DAB*; Adams Genealogy.

Probably John Lowell (1769–1840). Massachusetts Federalist and a leading member of the bar, on whom see vol. 2:311 and *DAB*.

[2] Edward George Earle Lytton Bul-

wer (afterwards Bulwer-Lytton), *Devereux*, 3 vols., London, 1829.

[3] GWA's efforts to keep a diary had been sporadic. However, what survives must represent but a fraction of the successive false starts. CFA, although an admirer of his brother's literary talents, eliminated from GWA's papers those that CFA judged would be damaging to his brother's name or painful to the family. The only section preserved is that for 1–23 Aug. 1825 (M/GWA/1, Adams Papers, Microfilms, Reel No. 287). However, there are other pieces preserved of a related character: a series of weekly letters to Claudius Bradford from 4 Sept. to 30 Oct. 1817, each of which is composed of journal entries for the intervening period; an account in five "essays" of a journey from London to Paris in 1817, written in early 1818, each of which he signed "Sterne" and entitled "A Sentimental Journey"; an "Introduction" to a contemplated "Review of the year 1825," which is in fact a memoir of his life up to that year. The remainder consists of a collection of poetical and prose compositions done at college, 1817–1821; poems copied by his mother in her commonplace book; "The Influence of Natural Scenery on Poetry," his commencement part at Harvard (MH-Ar); and an essay "Elements of Knowledge," dated 21 Dec. 1826, which was intended as an introduction to an anthology and to which CFA on 25 Dec. 1830 appended an appreciative note calling it "one of the best specimens of his mind" (Adams Papers, Microfilms, Reel Nos. 271, 287, 288, 291, 295).

[4] GWA had become engaged in 1823 to his first cousin, Mary Catherine Hellen (1806?–1870), with whom CFA had earlier been in love, and who subsequently chose the third brother, JA2, becoming engaged to him in 1827 and marrying him in 1828. See vol. 1:xxvi, xxix, and Adams Genealogy.

WEDNESDAY 9TH.

Morning passed very happily. To the Office but there had for the first time a little fit of dullness occasioned by old reflections which I dreaded, and which I had heretofore escaped. Engaged at the Office in writing out the Deed for Mr. Curtis which I completed, also in my Journal and in performing sundry Commissions. Paid Mr. Forbes part of my debt to him it being so large that at this time I was unable to settle the whole.[1] Indeed my father having given me no assistance at all on my Wedding, I am a little pressed for the amount to pay my furniture with.[2] I then went home and found much Company had been with Abby and that Edmund Quincy and Henrietta Gray were still there.[3] They were making so much noise and disturbance that it did not please me. I detest boisterous people—and boisterous fun. Abby is now and then impelled into it by others, for she has herself little fondness for it and is displeased when she sees it elsewhere. I love her most dearly in her quiet moments when affection is her principal feeling. Then she is invaluable.

She has lost some rings and several other things since her being here which renders it doubtful whether we have not a thief in the House. A circumstance as unpleasant as it was unexpected. I do not know what to think and to do about it. Afternoon at the Office—read more of George's Journal and was led to reflect upon the waste of my own time which must not be much longer. He always had some method in his head of a useful kind even to the last when his power to execute them was totally extinct. I am allowing all my days to run to waste unless I start to make a barrier early. I must soon reflect upon a division of time and a concentration of purpose. For if God gives me life to act, I feel as if I was not made to suffer my powers "to rust in me unus'd." This will do to think of. On my way to inquire for Miss Carter who has been sick since Monday, I met Miss Gorham who had come from there and walked home from there with her.

Evening, a party and Supper to my wife at Mrs. P. C. Brooks. Not a great many, principally Strangers—Mrs. Otis, Mrs. Ritchie, Mrs. Gilman and others.[4] I felt a little dull, and not very talkative but I got through the evening, more rapidly than I had anticipated. Returned home, tired and sleepy at twelve. I did propose declining as much as possible every civility as I feel a little anxious about my means and am desirous that they should rather be over my wants than that I should have to beg for more of either of my Fathers.

[1] These payments to William Forbes of $60.45 for "horse hire on account" and of $67.50 on 1 Dec. 1829 for "horse hire in full" are recorded in CFA's account book (M/CFA/9). CFA continued to manifest concern about the cost of horse hire: "as we are very economical we make our respective parents send in their carriages for us when they wish to be favoured with our agreeable company" (CFA to JA2, 21 Sept. 1829, Adams Papers).

[2] JQA's wedding gifts were "a Cameo ring with two hands joined" to ABA (JQA, Diary, 4 Sept.), three Stuart portraits of JA, JQA, and LCA (vol. 2:426–429) along with "the lion's share" of three dozen small bottles and a dozen and a half magnum bottles of wine to CFA (CFA to JA2, 21 Sept., Adams Papers).

Although CFA had had James Sharp make him some furniture for the new house, the bill for which did remain unpaid for several months (vol. 2:428 and below, entry for 21 Jan. 1830), ABA's father made her a wedding gift of most of the furniture and house furnishings, as he had done for his other daughters. These purchases for her included linens, &c. from John Fox—$142.96; china, glass, &c., from Joseph S. Hastings—$219.82; silver, furniture, &c., from J. B. Jones—$711.41; mahogany furniture from George Archibald—$1,071.13; carpeting, mirrors, &c., from John Doggett—$700; bedding, &c., from James H. Foster—$196; and miscellaneous items to a total expenditure of $3,798.91. In addition he made the couple a gift of $300 (Brooks, Waste Book, 6 July, 7, 14 Aug., 4, 11, 22 Sept., 17 Nov., 1 Dec. 1829).

[3] Henrietta Gray (1811–1891) was a first cousin of ABA; see vol. 2:155, 433.

[4] Mrs. Ritchie was accompanied by her husband. Perhaps he was William Ritchie, Boston merchant, who lived at 3 Cambridge Street (vol. 2:272), where CFA had had lodgings for a time (vol. 2:150). Mr. and Mrs. James Otis were of New York. Mr. and Mrs. Edward Everett were among the other guests (Everett, Diary, 9 Sept. 1829).

THURSDAY. 10TH.

Morning to the Office as usual but I was able to do little or nothing as I had hardly seated myself before my old friend Richardson dropped in.[1] I was very glad to see him and we talked pleasantly for a considerable time. He has not seen me since my marriage and at first he seemed to feel a little awkward, but he soon got over it and we then chatted very pleasantly an hour or two. He is one of the only men with whom I can say I have been exceedingly intimate, and although our present circumstances are such as to separate us considerably from each other, yet I like to see him to remind me of old times. We were interrupted by Thomas B. Adams who brought me a Note from my father with some Commissions to execute.[2] I performed some and postponed others—for consideration and conversation with him. Mr. Curtis also called, and asked as to the Deed which I had prepared and which he requested me to send to my father to be executed, which I accordingly did.

I then returned home and having agreed to dine with Mr. Brooks at Medford,[3] I drove out there with Abby. Found there Mr. and Mrs. Everett, Mr. and Mrs. Frothingham, Mr. and Mrs. Brooks, Miss Gorham her sister,[4] and ourselves. The dinner was pleasant enough and the time passed rapidly. Abby was not so much affected as I had expected, and luckily a visitor happened to come in who was not pleasant and broke up any feeling the parting might have otherwise created. We started early, in order to take tea at Mrs. Everett's. He is a singular man and puzzles me exceedingly. But sincerity is not his forte.[5] I like her although she has many decided faults.

We left early and returned to town with a fine Moon and a cold night. But the ride was pleasant. After stopping to inquire how Miss Carter was, we returned home, and from thence went to spend the Evening at P. C. Brooks's.[6] They are pleasant, agreeable and kind hearted people and I ought to like them very much, but now and then a little vulgarity escapes them which annoys me exceedingly. I am always anxious to do my best, but I cannot copy the same style and this makes me appear a little like a silent censor, and as if I was making myself a little high about it. But this must be for I will not do what I think degrades me, and though they may dislike my notions, yet I trust to the rest of my manner to show that I wish to make no offence. P. Chardon is a clever fellow, exceeding good natured, but very brusque, with whom I have always endeavoured to keep on the best terms, and whose attentions are exceedingly obliging.

[1] John Hancock Richardson, CFA's Harvard classmate, long-time friend, and correspondent, was an attorney with an office in Newton, Mass. (vol. 1:12 and *passim*).

[2] 9 Sept. (Adams Papers). The commissions included the acquisition of three pair of blankets, the purchase and installation of a Rumford stove for his kitchen and of sundry Franklin fire-

places, the exchange of a $50 bill for smaller ones, requests for several books, and conveying his "paternal love" to ABA with an invitation to visit at Quincy to "come and stay and go" as at "a second father's house."

[3] Peter Chardon Brooks (1767–1849) and his wife Ann Gorham (1771–1830), ABA's parents, had their home in Medford (vol. 2:ix–x, 105; *DAB*; Adams Genealogy), living in a mansion built by Brooks in 1805 on ancestral land (vol. 2:xi, illustration facing 305). The house, situated on splendidly landscaped grounds and with farm lands adjacent, though generally known as "Elms Farm," within the family was called "Mystic Grove" (letters of Charlotte Everett to Edward Everett, Everett MSS, MHi). Entertainment in the household in 1829 was restricted partly because of the death of Ward C. Brooks the year before, but more especially because of the poor health of Mrs. Brooks during the whole year (vol. 2:359–429 *passim*; Brooks, Waste Book, 31 Dec. 1829; Charlotte Everett to Edward Everett, 12 April 1829, Everett MSS, MHi).

Brooks took great pride in the estate, reacquiring all the lands held by his grandfather before division between heirs and purchasing additional parcels. On the location and bounds of the lands, see p. xviii and the map of Medford in this volume. In his "Book of Possessions" (Brooks MSS, MHi) are the deeds and papers relating to the property beginning in 1709 and a record of his own improvements. He several times gave a history of the holdings in his Waste Book, and in his Farm Journal he recorded from 1808 to 1848 production figures, daily activities, the weather, &c.

[4] Elizabeth Gorham (1769–1845), Mrs. Peter C. Brooks' only unmarried sister, continued to live in Charlestown, the Gorham family home, until sometime after 1823, when she moved to Cambridge (T. B. Wyman, *The Genealogies and Estates of Charlestown*, Boston, 1879, 1:424; *History of the Harvard Church in Charlestown*, Boston, 1879, p. 105). She had been visiting her sister since 5 Sept. (Brooks, Farm Journal).

[5] CFA's reservations on this aspect of the character of Edward Everett, which find some corroboration from the judgment of others and from events (see vol. 2:418; Frothingham, *Everett*, p. 272–273, 354, 428–429; CFA2, *R. H. Dana*, 2:279), persisted almost to the end of Everett's career. Only in the last four years of Everett's life (1861–1865) did CFA find a change in him:

"In his last days he reappeared in another and better character. The progress of events had brought him to a point where his fears no longer checked him, for his interests, such as might at his age be supposed to survive, ran on all fours with his convictions. As a consequence he spoke forth at last with all his power what he really felt. The change was wonderful. From that time I felt myself drawn to him as never before. . . . To me his four last years appear worth more than all the rest of his life, including the whole series of his rhetorical triumphs" (CFA to Richard Henry Dana, 8 June 1865, Dana Papers, MHi, printed in CFA2, *R. H. Dana*, 2:280).

[6] Mr. and Mrs. P. C. Brooks Jr. lived at 3 Chesnut Street (*Boston Directory*, 1829–1830).

FRIDAY. 11TH.

Morning after a deal of trouble at home, to the Office. One of the troubles of Housekeeping—My Wife not being accustomed to keeping her things locked, most unluckily left her Jewels exposed and the consequence has been that she has lost several things. Suspicion rested upon the Servants, and I thought it necessary in consequence to examine them all. I went through the form of searching all their things without any idea of finding any thing, for it would be absurd to suppose that Servants would not make away with things immediately that suspicion rested in the least upon them. This was as disagreeable a thing for a little affair of life as any I ever went through. I can fix suspicion upon nobody, but it is very certain that the things are missing.[1]

At the Office, I wrote my Journal, and a letter to Mrs. Longhurst.[2] We keep up a brisk correspondence by which I am in hopes of receiving her rent in time. But she is slow, though not quite so impudent as formerly. This and a few Commissions took me all the morning and I returned to dine. My spirits were rather depressed, as I was actually suffering from my old trouble.[3] I am a singularly fated man. The Afternoon was passed at home with the exception of a walk to the Office of the Daily Advertiser in order to put in an Advertisement for the lost rings. This done I returned and found my Furniture returned home. I am much pleased with it, and hope now soon to enter into a new system of life. The past week has been a kind of delirium which must soon pass off and leave us sober and quiet. I hope shortly to be able to start well in what I have undertaken, although I confess that at this moment of time, I am a little in a maze, which ought not to last very long.

The Evening came and with it, the recollection that we had been invited to a party at Mrs. Quincy's at Cambridge. As it was made for us, I could not decline the civility although we felt it to be irksome. We accordingly dressed and rode to Cambridge with Blake and Henrietta Gray. It was the first time that I had put my foot into that house for years. My old prejudices were so powerful that while my situation in life was doubtful I could not bring my pride to submit to the disagreeable style of the family.[4] But now at least, I feel free from any scruples and do not therefore make such resistance to patronage. We reached there at nine and found quite a collection of Cambridge people. I saw several of them and made my bow in the old way. How changed since I stood in the same room four years since. Incidents have rolled over me wonderful to think of and singular to relate. Let me pour out my soul to God in gratitude for his mercies and in the earnest and humble prayer that he will support me in prosperity as he has in adversity for they are equally hard to bear. Returned to town by eleven.

[1] Since the theft took place on 7 Sept. the likelihood is that it was during or just preceding the time ABA "received her company." On the 9th three rings, along with other things apparently of less value, were missed. One was a pearl ring, the second had three garnets set with pearl, and the third was the "Cameo ring with two hands joined" which JQA had given his daughter-in-

law on the preceding Friday. See above,
entry for 9 Sept.; *Boston Daily Advertiser*, 12–19 Sept. 1829, p. 2, col. 5.

[2] To Mrs. M. B. Longhurst (LbC,
Adams Papers); see also vol. 2:415, 430.

[3] CFA had long been subject to head-
aches and digestive disorders, minor ill-
nesses usually accompanied by melancholy; these are frequently mentioned in
his early diaries.

[4] Josiah Quincy (1772–1864), president of Harvard since Jan. 1829, and
Mrs. Quincy, the former Eliza Susan

Morton (1773–1850) (vol. 1:150, 2:
339; Adams Genealogy), were living in
Wadsworth House, which still stands in
Harvard Yard. It would appear that CFA
by "that house" is referring not to the
home of Harvard's presidents, but rather
to the Quincy household. The last time
that CFA had noted in his diary that he
had been to the Quincy's was on 4
Sept. 1824 in Boston. He then recorded
that the evening had been a pleasant
one despite the airs of Mrs. Quincy and
her daughter Susan (vol. 1:311–312).

SATURDAY 12TH.

The morning brought with it better spirits and more contented
feelings. I went to the Office after having advised Abby in some of her
household misfortunes consequent upon the loss of her rings. One of
her servants leaves her and deprives her of the expected gratification
of going to Medford. I went to the Office and occupied myself in my
various methods. I arranged my Money Accounts, and paid for my
Father, J. H. Foster's bill—it was large and I felt a little qualmish
about having given so much for the repairs upon Hancock Street, but
it was passed and unavoidable and so I paid the Money.[1] Mr. Curtis
called upon me to see about applying for Administration upon the
Estate of Thomas Boylston in order to recover some Money which has
been obtained on the other side of the Atlantic. He intends applying on
Monday. I passed the rest of the morning in looking up the case and
in trying to find a proper form but I could not succeed. Our law in
this branch is very deficient to young beginners.[2]

Returned home and dressed to ride to Charlestown to dine with
Mr. Everett as by agreement.[3] They having invited my wife to a
dinner as a bride. The company consisted of Mr. and Mrs. Hale,
Sidney Brooks his wife and her sister, Edward J. Lowell and ourselves.[4]
It was tolerably pleasant although a little too boisterous. Abby suffered
her spirits to run away with her, which I regretted although I have
seen but little of it, to annoy me, since my marriage. How much
women gain by tenderness and affection and softness, and how much
they lose when they depart from the character although an artificial
soft woman is least of all to my taste. It should be pure nature.

Owing to our arrangements, we returned to town and Abby being
fatigued and retiring early, I seized the occasion of going for the first
time into my study and arranging my books and writing papers a
little. I then took up the first volume of Laharpe's Course of Literature

and read some pages of the Introduction,[5] feeling more decidedly comfortable in a literary way than I have before since I left Washington. The gaiety of today puts a stop to our share as I hope and in future we shall attempt to resume a little of the old course of things in families. I care little about dissipation for time has made me sick of it. I have had more than my dose, and now I am anxious to look to ulterior and more honourable objects in life.

[1] James Hiller Foster (1773–1862) had a large upholstery and wallpaper store or warehouse at 224 Washington Street (*Boston Directory*, 1829–1830). The bill paid was for $123.53, of which $41.64 was for "repairs–papering" in August at 55 Hancock Street (M/CFA/3). Foster was married to AA's niece, Elizabeth Smith (1771–1854); see vol. 1:155 and Adams Genealogy.

[2] The executors of W. N. Boylston's will (see above, 7 Sept., note) found it necessary to assume the administration of the estate of his uncle Thomas Boylston (1721–1798), on whom see Adams Genealogy. W. N. Boylston had administered the estate skillfully but much was unsettled when he died, most importantly—and as it turned out, most unfortunately—the matter of recovering upwards of £10,000 sterling which had been collected by an English agent, Petty Vaughan, under a claim against the French government (JQA, Diary, 25 June; 8, 9 July; 1, 4, 11 Aug. 1829). The immediate problem was to draw new letters of administration in such a way as to satisfy the English courts that the executors of W. N. Boylston could deliver to Vaughan a full discharge on receipt of the funds and to satisfy the Massachusetts courts that the powers being conferred were properly limited and that jurisdictional issues were resolved. CFA was engaged in drawing papers during Sept.–Nov. 1829. When presented to the Suffolk County Probate Court in Boston they provided, by agreement of the executors, that letters of administration were to be issued in the name of JQA alone, with the other two executors named as bondsmen in the amount of $80,000. (JQA, Diary, 17, 28–30 Sept.; 31 Oct.; 9 Nov. 1829). On the later history of the claim, see below, entry for 13 Jan. 1830.

[3] At this time the Edward Everetts had their home at Winter Hill in Charlestown (Everett, Diary, 12 Sept. 1829).

[4] Nathan Hale (1784–1863) was the publisher of the *Boston Daily Advertiser* at 6 Congress Street. His wife was the former Sarah Preston Everett, sister of Edward Everett. Their home was on Tremont Place; see vol. 2:169 and *Boston Directory*, 1829–1830.

Mary M. Dehon was the sister of Mrs. Sidney Brooks (vol. 2:185).

[5] Jean François de La Harpe, *Lycée ou cours de littérature ancienne et moderne*. CFA continued his reading in La Harpe on the ancients until 14 November. JQA owned an edition published at Paris in 16 vols., 1820, now in MQA.

SUNDAY. 13TH.

Morning quietly at home writing my Journal, a thing I have not had an opportunity of doing before on this day for a long time. I enjoyed it exceedingly for it gave me an idea of home which is in itself exceedingly pleasing. I attended divine service this morning with my wife at Mr. Frothingham's Meeting House. It was the first time I had ever been to it but as I am not one of those who think that religion is to be found in particular places alone, I am perfectly willing that it should always be my place of worship for the future.[1] My wife was dressed as a bride and people stared as they usually do.

The remainder of my day was passed at home. I was almost entirely devoted to my Wife who was lonely and a little unwell. Marriage comes to her as a great change and some of it's features do not please her altogether; to be sure it is a great change for her to go from ease and entire freedom from care to a condition involving them both. But I cannot feel altogether as if she should repine at the change for if she has lost some advantages, she has gained others which should compensate in the end although it is natural enough that at first they should not be sufficiently appreciated. I read aloud during the afternoon and evening a considerable portion of Devereux to her, a new Novel which I do not think much of.

My own situation is somewhat changed. I am called upon for attentions which are altogether new to my system of life and to make sacrifices which in the selfish method of philosophy which I formerly cherished are entirely unknown. It gives me however a pleasure to perform them now which in my old notions I could never have experienced, and which arises entirely from a desire to do what I believe to be my duty.

[1] That the minister of the First Church, Nathaniel Frothingham, was married to Ann Brooks was but one of the ties the Brooks family had to the First Church. Peter C. Brooks noted repeatedly that his mother's great-great-grandfather was the celebrated John Cotton, the church's second minister (Waste Book, 4 March 1818; "Book of Possessions," Brooks MSS, MHi). Mr. and Mrs. Brooks seem to have attended the First Church from the time of their marriage. Their first child, Edward, and four other children, including ABA, were baptized there. Mr. Brooks served the Church in numerous ways through the years; he held pew No. 77.

The Adams family was not without First Church connections. JQA and his wife had their marriage at Allhallows, Barking, London, 1797, entered in the First Church records; they had CFA. GWA, and JA2 baptized there; and JQA was a pewholder from 1802 when the church was located on Washington Street. CFA's affiliation, sometimes active, extended to 1868 at least.

See Richard D. Pierce, ed., *The Records of the First Church in Boston 1630–1868*, Col. Soc. Mass., *Pubns.*, vols. 39–41 (1961). An engraving of the First Church meetinghouse, 1808–1868, on Chauncy Place just off Summer Street is reproduced in the present volume. See above, p. xi.

MONDAY 14TH.

Morning at the Office after reading for a little while in Devereux to Abby who was suffering from a violent head ach and whose spirits were consequently somewhat affected. It is impossible for me to reach the Office quite so early as I formerly did, at least at present. Perhaps I may do better in time. I reached it however just in time to meet Mr.

Curtis who came to me requesting to know what was necessary to be done. I told him to apply to the Judge, and at his request drew up an Application for Administration of Thomas Boylston's Estate on the part of the Executors. This took a considerable portion of the morning. I then called upon Mr. Brooks for a few moments and had conversation with him upon the loss of those rings,[1] then went to see Mr. Head as to the character of my Servant William, and then returned home having been unsuccessfull in my attempt to find him.

Wrote my Journal at home before dinner. Conversation with Abby upon some unfortunate history which has happened within our observation. Miss Julia Gorham came in and I went down according to appointment to see Mrs. Longhurst as to the condition of the House she lives in. She appears to have come to her senses and I feel therefore considerably more disposed to assist her. I looked at the House and asked Hollis the Carpenter who lives next door to call and see me about it. I will do what I can without incurring too much expense. I then went to the Office and after spending an hour there, returned home to find my Wife and Miss Julia in my study. The latter young lady took tea here and I escorted her home.[2] In the evening I read aloud to Abby in Devereux as long as she felt able to sit up, after which I was so much interested as to finish the volume. It is a tale written by a strong mind but more laboriously put together than his preceding productions and written so very artificially as to injure it's effect. We are always seeing a labour for point and never are allowed a moment when something is not absolutely required.

[1] Peter C. Brooks' counting room and office was at 10 Court Street (*Boston Directory*, 1829–1830).

[2] Julia Gorham lived with her mother, Mrs. John Gorham, whose home was at 1 Park Street (same).

TUESDAY. 15TH.

Morning to the Office after some Conversation with Abby upon the circumstances of my previous history. I talked with her in kindness and in confidence and she seemed fully to meet it although much which I said could not have been welcome. Mine is not a first though a young love and I am not fully subject to the impulse of the freshness of feeling which makes the first moments of marriage sometimes so intoxicating. But in recompense, my engagement has been a constantly increasing matter of happiness and my marriage has crowned and hitherto more than crowned my hopes. If I loved Abby before, it has been with reserve, which the peculiar sensitiveness of her character forced upon me, as I never felt as if I could speak frankly to her of every thing. The thing is now altogether different. We are now intimately and closely tied and our thoughts and feelings are entirely united. May they continue to be so is my constant prayer.

Mr. Hollis called at my Office. He is a Carpenter whom it has been the practice to employ upon the Houses belonging to the Agency and take it from his rent.[1] I directed him to look at Mrs. Longhurst's roof and Pump, to form some estimate of the cost to repair it and report to me. Mr. Conant is one of my father's Tenants at Weston, he brought with him a Letter from his Brother Amory Conant, the Lessee of the Farm, giving notice that he intends quitting the place in April, having lost money by his experiment this year. I conversed with him upon the subject and tried to encourage him, but it seemed to me that he was resolved to go unless I granted him some allowances out of his rent. I was disposed to think of it if he would consent to destroy the clause in the Lease allowing either party six months notice. He said he might agree to it on consideration and so we parted, I first agreeing to go to see him on Friday.[2] Mr. Curtis called to leave the Petition with me to go to Quincy for my Father's signature. I obtained powers also from the State Bank and wrote one for the Boylston Market in order to obtain his signature also for them in order to draw the October Dividends.

This being accomplished I returned to dinner. Abby received from my brother John's wife a congratulatory Letter,[3] in which she mentioned my Mother's being sick, which was not agreeable news. After dinner and accompanying Abby to make a few purchases, she and I started for Quincy in my father's little Carriage which came in for us. We found my father and Abby Adams, General Dearborn and his daughter, Thomas B. Adams Jr. and Louisa C. Smith.[4] The evening was a little stupid, the weather being cold and raw. I felt dull and melancholy upon many accounts too numerous for me to mention, as my associations with the house and it's present condition seemed to bring my thoughts in unison with the autumnal character of the season. General Dearborn left some handsome Manuscripts for my father's perusal. He is an author, but how good cannot be judged from the very elegant binding and manuscript which make the visible shape.[5] Conversation in the evening about them, and subsequently with my father upon subjects more interesting. He is a little dull, at being alone, and at the news from Washington, and I do not wonder at it, but he persists in his intention of remaining here until the season is far advanced.[6]

16

[1] Daniel Hollis, a Quincy man, had occupied tenement No. 2 at 101 Tremont (earlier Nassau, then Common) Street for nearly sixteen years under an arrangement by which the yearly rental (from 1824, $125) would be offset against work performed, chiefly carpentering, on the houses and stores in the Agency. GWA, during the period of his management, had also accepted notes from Hollis. CFA came to look upon the whole arrangement with less and less favor. He attributed the wretched condition in which he found much of the property, in some measure at least, to Hollis' inadequacies as a craftsman and to slovenliness induced by age and indulgence. Repeated annoyances led CFA, reluctantly and after numerous reprieves, to end the arrangement in Aug. 1830. See vol. 2:406; CFA to JQA, 31 Dec. 1829 (LbC, Adams Papers); M/CFA/3.

[2] CFA was successful in his efforts to keep Silas and Amory Conant as lessees of the somewhat run-down Weston farm bequeathed to JQA by W. N. Boylston (vol. 2:228, 244, 409). JQA agreed to CFA's plan by which half the rent would be expended on improvements. They remained at least through 1832, paying $125 annually (JQA, Diary, 17 Sept. 1829; M/CFA/3).

[3] Missing.

[4] Abigail Smith Adams ("Abby") (1806–1845), later Mrs. John Angier, was a daughter of TBA; see vol. 1:20 and Adams Genealogy. On Gen. Henry Alexander Scammell Dearborn of Rox-bury, see vol. 1:327 and *DAB*. Accompanying him was Miss Julia Dearborn (JQA, Diary, 15 Sept. 1829). Louisa Catherine Smith (1773–1857) was a niece of AA, a sister of Mrs. J. H. Foster; see vol. 1:99 and Adams Genealogy.

[5] The works in manuscript by Gen. H. A. S. Dearborn which he left with JQA consisted of two volumes upon the Grecian orders of architecture and two volumes of a Life of Christ (JQA, Diary, 15 Sept.). Neither is among the subsequently published works of Dearborn. The "splendid manuscript work" on Greek architecture was on the President's table, 28 Oct. 1829 (Everett, Diary).

[6] JQA had written that he would return at once to Washington to attend his wife in her illness if he could in that way contribute anything to her return to health. However, LCA was in agreement with him that he should remain at Quincy until late November when the plan to bring GWA's remains there for reburial could be carried out. As the season progressed, he wrote that it "has never been out of my thoughts" and that he was determined to see the remains "under my own care deposited by the side of my beloved Sister, in the Tomb." (JQA to LCA, 8 Nov.; also JQA to JA2, 16 Sept.; JQA to LCA, 17, 26 Sept.; LCA to JQA, 17 Sept., Adams Papers.) The rites were performed on 24 Nov.; see entries for 23, 24 Nov., below.

WEDNESDAY 16TH.

Morning exceedingly chilly and disagreeable, so that the house and Country seemed raw and uncomfortable. We took Breakfast and I felt very anxious to get away. It would be difficult for me to describe exactly my feelings today. In reflecting now upon the singular condition of our family, it seems as if my father was left to himself and as if, after him, I was the only person who could be expected to take the old property. Now in this there is much difficulty. For my tastes are not very warmly engaged in it and there is little or no temptation excepting that which springs from my decided attachment to the family name and character. I am now the last scion of the race in this State and upon me it must fall or upon some collateral branch of the name.

The place is itself falling into decay from the want of practical qualities in my father to keep it up, and I have other avocations to call me to different scenes. The future is always uncertain and it is possible my father may settle these questions by a very definitive step, and relieve me from all doubt about the matter.[1] Such a step would however afford me no pleasure. It has nothing but mortification to attend it. And though I am preparing my mind for it, it is only as an anticipation of evil.

We left Quincy in the little Carriage and arrived in town just in time to avoid the rain and see Mrs. Brooks who had come in to see Abby.[2] She appeared sick and out of spirits and seemed to mourn the loss of Abby. This affected the latter who was dull in consequence all the afternoon. It rained heavily and I remained at home. Abby's spirits have been generally good, even better than I had expected, under this separation and upon the change in her condition. I have not had occasion to feel as if I had done wrong, nor can I now repent of it. The engagement was long and was becoming unnecessarily extended, and I was playing the part of a fool with little or no satisfaction. It is impossible for me to confess the difference of my sensations now. I amused Abby with conversation and in the evening read aloud in Devereux. The comfort of home was strongly contrasted in my mind with the cheerlessness of my father's at Quincy.

[1] During 1828–1829, JQA had entertained several designs as alternatives to the unsatisfactory living conditions at the Old House. These included the purchase of a home in Boston (vol. 2:287–288), building a new house in Quincy (CFA to JA2, 21 Sept. 1829, Adams Papers), and apparently giving up Massachusetts residence altogether. Ultimately he went no further than the repair of the Old House, on which he was then engaged.

[2] This was the first day on which Mrs. Brooks had been well enough to come into Boston since 27 Aug. (Brooks, Farm Journal, 16 Sept.).

THURSDAY. 17TH.

Morning at the Office as usual. My occupations are not now decided enough and I must take early opportunity of fixing them. This was the day fixed for the sale of my brother's books and I accordingly went down to Mr. Cunningham's[1] and attended. They were generally sold at a very great sacrifice, so that I stopped the sale of the most valuable of them. The remainder being worthless to me and more desirable to my brother's affairs in the shape of a little money, I suffered them to go, although there was not a single volume that did not go below it's value. This passed much of my morning, but on returning to my Office, I again felt the necessity of doing something. My brother's Journal again fell in my way and I was struck with the superiority of his general pursuits, to those which I have fallen into during the last three months. This must be amended.

After dinner as Abby went out, I passed the Afternoon in my Study and made an attempt to arrange the remainder of my Books. Finding that they are so numerous, I have come to the conclusion to put them in double rows, which will thus accommodate them all until I feel able to make some arrangement at a future time, which may suit them more conveniently for reference. This took up most of the Afternoon. The remainder and the evening were passed in reading Devereux and Conversation with Abby. The book was dull and so we preferred talking.

[1] Probably Joseph L. Cunningham, auctioneer at Federal and Milk streets (*Boston Directory*, 1829–1830).

FRIDAY 18TH.

Arose early having felt slightly unwell this morning from an attack of pain in the stomach rather common to me at this season of the year though I have not felt it before this year. After breakfast, I started to go to Weston to arrange the affairs of my father in that place for the season. I was imprudent in not being thicker dressed for it was colder than I had expected. I suffered more in my ride than I should have done, and than considering my attack of the morning, was altogether safe. I called for Richardson on the route and he accompanied me there. Upon our arrival, we immediately took to the Kitchen fire, and with the assistance of this externally and the revivifying influence of something internal properly administered, we began to feel able to do something. Having met Col. Jones, the Auctioneer and in appearance the teetotum of the town,[1] his brother and our two tenants, we sallied forth in quest of the Woods. We walked round them and through them and felt pretty thoroughly fatigued before we returned. Indeed as I felt far from well, I was compelled to hurry home as fast as possible. But I saw and heard enough of the Wood to feel satisfied that if properly sold it will bring a considerable sum to replenish my father's Treasury. Not a disagreeable prospect. But we must stand the chances of sale and these are capricious enough. I made arrangements with the Auctioneer to get the sale advertised, and the measurements made, and allotted about one half to the Hammer and the Axe. The remainder shall go next Autumn.[2] This job being finished we returned to the House and dined. The Tenants had made preparation for us and it was essentially necessary that I should so far assent to their arrangements as not to appear too proud to sit down with them. We made quite a dinner party and had a very tolerable meal upon Chickens. But feeling so unwell, I was not enabled to support that character which I had wished and desired. I was therefore glad to get away and return to town, which I did at a rate sufficiently rapid, so that I was at home before three o'clock. Miss Julia Gorham spent the day with Abby which was a relief to me as I was fatigued and out of spirits. I seized an hour while she was out and commenced La Harpe's Course of Literature with his Analysis of Aristotle but I could not progress very far from the want of the habit of reading which I have lost, but must now endeavour to resume. Evening with Abby reading Devereux which I finished.

[1] On Col. John Jones of Weston, see vol. 2:251. CFA's meaning here is unclear. He may have meant that Jones was a *little* man, or one who spins about busily like a top; see *OED*: "teetotum." Or perhaps there was a confusion or blending with "factotum."

[2] The auction of the cut wood was held on 13 Nov. (see below under that date), and netted $407. The second sale, in 1830, brought in $428.25. An annual sale thereafter through 1835 brought revenue each year in excess of $500 (M/CFA/3).

SATURDAY 19TH.

Morning to the Office. Finding myself in want of occupation I commenced Marshall's Book on Insurance in order to make myself more familiarly acquainted with that subject.[1] I read a little but was interrupted by visitors. D. Orcutt, one of my father's tenants came to tell me he could pay me no rent and he quits the house in consequence.[2] He is an everlasting talker and detained me discussing all his prospects until I became so tired as to manœuvre him away. He offers security however so that the rent is not absolutely lost. My father also came in and sat some time talking of his necessities, which at this time are many. I therefore walked down to the New England Soap Stone Factory in order to send for one thing most needed, a close fireplace for his large room. The remainder of the things required I must defer attending to until next week.

My father dined with us and as I had in the morning attended to the receiving some wine which he has been so kind as to give me, which had just arrived from Washington, I thought I would open a bottle for him—but it disappointed us, for it felt the effects of transportation very much.[3] Our dinner was however an exceedingly pleasant one, as my father was in a mood for Conversation and we talked of Shakespear with great vivacity. He disclosed then his singular views of the plays of Othello, and Macbeth, which rather amuse than convince me though they are undoubtedly worthy of consideration. We sat some time and afterwards I had only time to write a little during the absence of both my father and my wife upon separate errands. He returned only for a moment previous to departing for Quincy and it was not long afterwards that we found Mr. Brooks had sent his little Carriage for us, to go to Medford. I had expected this would be the case though I confess I did not wish it. My own happiness hitherto has been un-alloyed, but there is danger that the feelings which Medford engenders divide and separate us and bring on difficulty. I had hoped that we should have gone tomorrow in order to return on the day succeeding without difficulty but now I feared that the result would not be so promising. This brought an unwelcome cloud upon my spirits, which every thing that followed in the course of the evening was calculated to increase. For it made me uncomfortable in spite of myself to think that Abby should prefer her home to me—and I am peculiarly sensitive to the very looks of Mr. and Mrs. Brooks because I feel that they are a little displeased with me for doing what I could not in justice to myself avoid. Sidney Brooks and his Wife, and Mrs. Frothingham were there making a pretty large party, and for the whole of the evening I felt as restless, and uncomfortable as I did at any time during my engagement.

¹ Samuel Marshall, *Treatise on the Law of Insurance* . . . , 2 vols., London, 1802.

² David Orcutt, a cabinetmaker, rented tenement No. 3 of 101 Tremont Street at $150 per year. When he left the premises on 23 Oct., he was $112 in arrears (vol. 2:417; M/CFA/3; and *Boston Directory*, 1829–1830).

³ See entry for 9 Sept., above.

SUNDAY. 20TH.

I did not arise in better humour than when I retired the evening past. And I continued feeling quite low spirited throughout the day. I attended Divine Service with Abby in the morning and heard Dr. Follen preach a Sermon without a Text. This is strange and I do not know how to like it; old prejudices are strong against the innovation and even without them, I think the evident object of the institution is to illustrate and explain passages of the Scriptures, and that it is therefore much more clearly effected by setting before one the end to which all conclusions must be directed. In modern times, texts have been falling into unpopularity but as I think very unreasonably, and I believe it would be found that much less will be found to remain in the memory of the common classes of people who are most benefitted by these Addresses, through the medium of a process of Orationizing, than by the old practise of familiar texts. Dr. Follen is a German who is attached to Harvard College and since his residence in this Country has taken to Divinity.[1] He reads English well for a foreigner. He dined with us. After dinner I went to walk and not to Church for he was rather too dry.

On my return, found Mr. Shepherd who was soon after followed by Edward Brooks and his Wife.[2] These are the most agreeable part of the family to me, though I have seen much least of them.[3] They are tolerably merry people, and so they enlivened us much at tea. Mrs. Brooks looked and appeared fatigued and sick. The evening passed in conversation with Mr. Brooks upon fruits and then old Boston history—rather dry—but I try to interest myself in these things. Afterwards, a Conversation with Abby, which it will do well to remember, though I should be foolish to detail it here.

[1] Charles Theodore Christian Follen (1796–1840), Unitarian clergyman and first professor of German literature at Harvard, had come to the United States in 1824 (*DAB*).

[2] Resin D. Shepherd, father of Ellen Shepherd who had married ABA's brother Gorham Brooks earlier in the year, was a Boston merchant living in Watertown; see vol. 2:165 and Brooks, Farm Journal, 20 April 1829.

[3] Although the Edward Brookses maintained a house in Boston at 4 Bulfinch Place (*Boston Directory*, 1829–1830), apparently they preferred to remain aloof from society and family at their well-situated place in Watertown; see vol. 2:249. CFA's expressed liking for Edward continued. A Harvard graduate (1812) and a lawyer, increasingly he assumed the management of his father's extensive business interests, having "the whole care" from 1833 onward and earning his father's entire approbation (Brooks, Waste Book, 26 April 1848). His concerns extended to public matters as well. In 1828, he had written a series of articles, appearing in the *Courier* signed "Brougham," proposing the establishment of a university in Boston (Edward Everett to Alexander H. Everett, 19 Nov. 1829, Everett MSS, MHi). See also Brooks, *Medford*, p. 530–531.

MONDAY 21ST.

Returned to town this morning in Mr. Brooks' Carriage with him, Miss Lydia Phillips,[1] and Mr. Frothingham, thus leaving Abby at Medford not to return until tomorrow. This was one of the hardest struggles with myself that I ever made. I wanted her dreadfully to return with me, although I could not be angry with her desire to remain, and so after reflection I determined to give my consent to her staying, intimating at the same time that I should not return in the evening as she wished me to. There was to be a Medford party at Mrs. Frothingham's, and as these to me are shocking bores and I see no reason on earth for me to subject myself to them, I preferred even a separation for a day. Medford itself under present circumstances is a disagreeable place as it divides with me more than I wish it did the affections of my Wife. I feel therefore more pain than pleasure in being there at all, and I regret that it should come in such a hurry to put a check, to the heretofore delicious current of our honeymoon. Had Abby returned with me, I should have perhaps adored her for the sacrifice, but I did not expect it and I was not disappointed.

My morning was partly taken up by a long walk into Front Street and an order for my Wood for the Winter. I took ten Cords of a Mr. Stephen Child at five dollars a Cord. I then called upon Mr. Cunningham the Auctioneer to see about the late Sale, but I found the Books had not yet all been called for, so that no settlement could be made. The remainder of the morning was passed at the Office reading Marshall on Insurance, a book of some value and not without interest, particularly in the history of Marine Law in general, a subject with which I ought to be better acquainted. After my lonely dinner at home, I went to the Office and superintended it's cleaning up—a thing which it needed exceedingly. A woman called upon me about Mr. Farmer and that affair.[2] I dread to see her as much as I do him, but it seemed only a friendly visit to congratulate me on my marriage. My evening was passed in my study alone. I seized the occasion to write a long letter to John,[3] and then read further in La Harpe in which I finished his Analysis of Aristotle on Poetry and commenced Longinus. I retired to my lonely apartment and tried in immediate sleep to forget that it was the first time since my late marriage that I already was alone.

[1] Lydia Phillips (b. 1804), of Andover, was ABA's first cousin; see vol. 2:364.

[2] Miles Farmer, indebted to GWA, had given him the use of a room for Eliza Dolph and their illegitimate child. Farmer was continuing his efforts, begun after GWA's death, to obtain money by threat of disclosure. See vol. 2:376, 382, 403–404.

[3] CFA's brother in Washington. On JA2 (1803–1834), see vol. 1:xxvi–xxvii, 6, and Adams Genealogy. A portrait of him appears as an illustration in the present volume. CFA's letter (in Adams Papers) expressed at once satisfaction in his married state and concern over their mother's health and spirits. He reported also JQA's plans to alter the kitchen and fireplaces at the Old House and to convert his bedroom to a library.

TUESDAY. 22ND.

Arose rather late and after breakfast which I took in my solitary way, I waited for Abby's return. She came, but in exceeding low spirits and much affected by having been left alone during the night. I remained with her for some time but finding her still depressed I went out to the Office. My morning was spent in reading Marshall which interested me considerably. Richardson called in and spent an hour with me discussing matters and things in general. He did not seem to be so lively as usual. Indeed time with him has produced much change.

In reading Marshall I occasionally read the cases referred to which delays me considerably in my regular progress.

Returned home to dine and conversed further with Abby upon the affairs of yesterday. Our happiness returned more gushingly than ever, and I remained at home the whole of the afternoon and evening. I read one or two Articles in the first Volume of the New Monthly Magazine, while Abby was writing a letter to my Mother,[1] and afterward finished La Harpe's Analysis of Longinus, which was interesting so that I retired feeling much more happy and contented than ever.

[1] Letter missing. LCA in replying writes of it as a "very affectionate letter" (LCA to ABA, 1 Nov., Adams Papers).

WEDNESDAY. 23RD.

Morning after leaving Abby, I went down to the Office and sat reading Marshall a large portion of the time. As I become more regular I find myself better able to allot my time to my duties without obstructing or interfering with any. Mr. Hollis called upon me to tell me he had examined some of the repairs as required and made a report wishing me to go and see for myself with the Carpenter's assistant whom I had required. I pointed out some time during tomorrow. Another person whose name I did not know called with a plate of the Meeting House at Quincy and to ask my opinion as to its Title. I was a little puzzled, for I felt modest about giving to it the proper name.[1] Captain Willis Howes was the Master of a trading vessel between this and Alexandria and called to be paid the freight for certain boxes, which I paid. Mr. Carey sent a Man with Copies of my Father's inscriptions to his Father and Mother, which I corrected and sent to Quincy.[2]

Dined with my Wife at P. Chardon Brooks' where I was amused as I always am, for I calculate when there to do nothing but laugh. The strange originality of his character makes up for some defects in delicacy, and one is induced to smile at what could not strictly be approved. My dinner was a very pleasant one and as Abby staid until evening, I returned there to tea and remained there until near ten o'clock, listening and laughing for I seldom say much. They have been exceedingly kind to us and I feel much obliged to them, as I do not know that I please them—but I have heretofore said so much that I shall only go into needless repetition to continue. So we returned home.

[1] The "plate" was perhaps that made by Abel Bowen from the drawing James Kidder did of the new First Church building at Quincy, built according to

JA's directions and from his gift of a fund for its erection and the establishment of a classical school in Quincy. The building, dedicated 12 Nov. 1828, became known both as the "Stone Temple" and, perhaps more properly, as the "Adams Temple." Bowen's engraving is reproduced in this volume. See above,

p. xi–xii; vol. 2:307; and Bemis, *JQA*, 2:111.

[2] Alpheus Carey to JQA, 23 Sept. (Adams Papers). On Carey and on JQA's inscriptions for the marble monument to his parents, see vol. 2:399 and entry for 25 Oct., below.

THURSDAY 24TH.

Morning to the Office and then according to appointment to the Houses in Tremont Street to look at the roof of Mrs. Longhurst's. I found there Mr. Trask who deals in Composition [roofing] work and examined it with him. From what he said I concluded to have both of them slightly done for the present. The Houses are hardly worth very thorough work.[1] Returned to the Office and read Marshall during the remainder of the morning. Mr. Whitney the tenant in Court Street has notified me that he intends leaving that House,[2] but I insist upon notice legally given. It is very wrong for a person to quit in such manner. But it seems now altogether probable that I shall have a number of these tenancies on my hands, as Orcutt also quits on the first of the month. I also passed half an hour in forming some kind of estimate of my late brother's affairs. They turn out rather favourably for him.

After dinner I remained at home with Abby until five o'clock when by her request I went down and paid a visit to Miss Anne Carter. She is just recovering from a cold caught in the evening of my marriage in riding to town with us. She seems frail as a bruised reed, and does not give promise of a long continuance of life. But I said so two years since and she is not yet worse. I am partial to her as a friend of Abby's, for she was a creditable selection. On my return I found Abby alone, and spent the remainder of the day and evening with her in conversation interesting to ourselves. My happiness still continues, increased rather than diminished by our temporary separation. May it long continue and may we feel ever grateful for the blessings we enjoy. I read to her in the evening Mackenzie's short tale of Louisa Venoni,[3] but it did not strike me as so pretty this time as upon a former perusal.

[1] Mrs. Mary B. Longhurst, dressmaker and milliner, occupied No. 103 Tremont Street at the corner of Boylston Street (*Boston Directory*, 1829–1830, and below, entry for 3 March 1830). The accounts of neither 103 nor of 101 and 105, also owned by JQA, show any repair charges at this time. However, S.

and W. Trask were paid $43.60 on 19 Oct. for undescribed goods or services (M/CFA/3).

[2] Prentiss Whitney's annual rent for the store and the house in the rear of 23 Court Street was $300 for each. He was heavily in arrears in his payments on both. CFA's difficulties with him extend

through the fall and spring and are resolved only after suit is instituted. See
below, entry for 27 April 1830; CFA to
JQA, 2 Feb. 1830 (LbC, Adams Papers);
M/CFA/3.

[3] "Louisa Venoni" by Henry Mackenzie is included (3:291–304) in the
edition of his *Miscellaneous Works* (3
vols., Glasgow, 1820) owned by CFA,
now in MQA.

FRIDAY 25TH.

Morning rainy and unpleasant. After lounging at home as usual considerably longer than I should have done properly, I went to the
Office and passed some time quite uninterrupted in reading Marshall.
I found little or nothing today however which struck me as new.
Called upon Mr. Brooks for the sake of the visit, conversed upon his
intentions for the Winter and regretted to find that he intends remaining there.[1] This makes me feel thankful however that I had not
another Winter to go through in my character of suitor. Mrs. Brooks
is wrong in remaining there and it will much surprise me if she
survives the season. Her spirits will not stand the still-dullness of her
own condition.[2] But I saw that the plan was approved and so I uttered
not a syllable of opposition. Indeed from delicacy I would not wish to
intrude my opinion.

Mr. Curtis called upon me for a few minutes in relation to Mr.
Boylston's affairs and to know when my Father would be in town. In
regard to this, I had expected that he would come tomorrow, but the
letter which I especially directed to be sent to Quincy, has been
regularly found in my Box each Morning since Wednesday, so that
in despair I called upon Abby Adams at Mr. P. Foster's and gave it
to her to take this afternoon.[3] There was a thunder shower in the
afternoon so that I remained at home and read a portion of a History
of the United States by a certain Mr. Graham, which passes through
my hands from Mr. Sparks to my Father.[4] It is said to be the best
extant. Abby went after the rain to see her friend Miss Carter. In the
evening I read to her Mackenzie's Man of Feeling or rather the first
portion of it.[5] But she did not appear so much interested as I expected.
Afterwards a little of La Harpe.

[1] Until 1827, the Brooks family each
year moved into Boston from Medford
in November, remaining until May.
However, in that year Mr. Brooks sold
the house on Atkinson Street in which
they had lived for 24 years, the neigh-
borhood being no longer suitable (Waste
Book, 16 July 1827). Thereafter they
planned to remain at Mystic Grove the
year round (same, 1 Jan. 1828). In
1829 Mr. and Mrs. Brooks were alone
in the house for the first time, their
children married or living in Europe.
However, Ann Frothingham and her
children spent the summer months with
her parents, and Charlotte Everett and
her children, the winter months.

[2] During her long illness Mrs. Brooks
suffered periods of aberration and melan-
cholia (Charlotte Everett to Edward
Everett, Jan.–April, Nov.–Dec. 1829
passim, Everett MSS, MHi).

[3] Phineas Foster, a merchant, was married to Frances Harrod, a sister of Mrs. TBA. They lived at 5 Bulfinch Place (vol. 2:260; *Boston Directory*, 1829–1830).

[4] The 1827 edition of James Grahame's *The History of the Rise and Progress of the United States* ..., 2 vols., London, in MQA has CFA's autograph. It was a book which continued to in-

terest CFA; see below, entries for 3 April–1 May 1830 *passim*; 13 April, note.

On Jared Sparks (1789–1866), currently the owner and editor of the *North American Review*, see vol. 1:79, 312; *DAB*; and numerous entries below.

[5] *The Man of Feeling* is also included in Mackenzie's *Miscellaneous Works* (3:1–147); see preceding entry.

SATURDAY 26TH.

Morning to the Office. Occupied in reading a little of Marshall but I did not progress much. I cannot very fully explain how the time was passed but it went and apparently not without its uses. My father came in as I had expected and sat with me an hour. He seemed in very good spirits and talked upon a multitude of things, more especially the inscription which he is making to my Grandfather's memory, and also of my Mother from whom he receives good accounts this morning.[1] I am very glad to hear of this as I had feared much for her. He talked also of business and gave me commissions as usual. Little or nothing occurred otherwise. I returned to dine.

My father and Mr. Brooks dined with me.[2] I did not feel easy as is my custom. When is it that I do feel easy in presence of Mr. Brooks—and why do I not? These questions are to me inexplicable. Perhaps the sense of my being a little dependent upon him for a good opinion is the thing which works upon me as a check. I have always felt as if there was a doubt about me upon his mind and as long as this lasts it does not seem to me probable that I shall ever alter. The dinner was therefore not nearly so pleasant to me as that which we had on last Saturday, and I was very glad that it was done.

In the afternoon Mr. Curtis called to see my father and I went up with Mr. Brooks to have him examine the Bookcases as he proposes having some made at his own house. Thus the time passed until the Carriage called for us by agreement to go to Quincy. And we started at five. Upon leaving, I met my Classmate Cunningham who has just returned from Europe.[3] He does not look so well as he did and I had no opportunity to do more than barely recognize him. Our ride was through Milton and we did not reach Quincy until quite late and I was very cold. Indeed I found today that I had in some manner caught a cold which was not a pleasant idea to me. For it always gives me an impression that I have contracted a habit of body a little unfavourable. After a good Supper and a little Fire which was not by any means uncomfortable, we spent the evening very quietly in amusing Conversation until an early retirement.

[1] Mainly a report on her health: weak, but mending. Affectionate messages for CFA and ABA (to JQA, 21 Sept., Adams Papers).

[2] Relations between the Adams and Brooks families appear to have been generally cordial, particularly after the engagement of Charles and Abby in Feb. 1827. There were numerous visits of Mr. and Mrs. Brooks at Quincy and of JQA and LCA at Medford sometimes of several days' duration (Brooks, Farm Journal, July-Oct. 1827, Aug. 1828, July-Aug. 1829 *passim*). On a number of occasions, the two men were invited to dine at the same table in Boston houses; they went together on a day's excursion to Lowell, on an ocean fishing trip by steamboat (same, 5, 18 Sept. 1827), and, much later, on a trip to Niagara and Canada with ABA, 6 July-1 Aug.

1843 (Brooks, Farm Journal, and JQA, Diary, for that interval). From 1819 to 1827 Mr. Brooks owned a cast of the Binon bust of JA and in the latter year acquired a framed engraving of JQA (Waste Book, 1 May 1819, 6 July, 27 Aug. 1827). No serious political differences between the two men had developed. Earlier a Federalist, Brooks in those years was a contributor to Whig causes, deeply concerned in the career of his son-in-law Edward Everett whose entrance into politics JQA had fostered and who remained an Adams supporter through the Presidential term (Frothingham, *Everett*, p. 75–116 *passim*, 134, 295; Bemis, *JQA*, 2:74).

[3] On Francis Cunningham, with whom CFA had been on terms of some intimacy at Harvard but not since, see vol. 1:130, 232–302 *passim*.

SUNDAY 27TH.

Morning fine but of the clear cold weather rather showing the season of November than our present month. My cold was quite bad during the whole day. We all attended Meeting during the day and heard Mr. Lamson of Dedham preach two quite sensible discourses. He is a fluent and ready writer, but not strong enough to give his pieces effect. The congregation looked to me smaller than I expected, but those who were presented were quite struck with the novelty of a bride, and so they looked at us well. Thomas and Isaac Hull dined with us and so we made quite a family party.[1] In the afternoon as my Uncle came to see us and to invite us down there,[2] we concluded to walk down and drink tea with them so as to return in the evening to be with my father. We found all the family comfortably situated and had quite a tolerable time. In the evening much company came in consisting of old acquaintances from the upper end of the town. My Uncle seems to be a Slave to this Company. It overruns his House and I do not wonder that it disables him from paying his way with his limited income. But I do not see by what code of morality my father is bound to impoverish himself and his children to keep them in idleness and a condition they cannot probably remain in. I am sorry for the Children because this is the punishment occasioned by the fault of the father.

We did not remain long, nor probably until the whole of the number who visit had arrived, and returned to find Josiah Quincy sitting with my father.[3] The conversation was literary and turned upon the belief of literary men. It astonishes me more and more to perceive the extent and reach of the acquisitions of my father. There is no subject upon which he does not know a great deal and explain it with the greatest beauty of language. He has in the course of this day opened his information upon the subject of painting, of music and of historical characters—All of which have been handled with perfect ease and familiarity. He is a wonderful though a singular man, and now displays more of his real character than I have ever before seen.

[1] Isaac Hull Adams (1813–1900) was the younger brother of Thomas Boylston Adams Jr.; see vol. 2:159; above, entry for 4 Sept.; Adams Genealogy.

[2] On Thomas Boylston Adams (1772–1832) (TBA), JQA's brother, see vol. 1:xxiii–xxiv, 163–169 *passim*. His household in 1829 consisted of his wife, the former Ann Harrod (1774?–1845), on whom see vol. 1:13, and six children, all unmarried; see Adams Genealogy. For several months the family had been living in "the old Ruggles House," located at what is now Elm and South streets in Quincy; see vol. 2:370, note.

[3] Josiah Quincy (1802–1882), fourth of the name, son of President Quincy of Harvard, was an attorney, but is best remembered today as the author of a valuable book of reminiscences of Quincy and Boston entitled *Figures of the Past*, originally published Boston, 1883, new edn. by M. A. DeW. Howe, Boston, 1926. On Governor Lincoln's staff, he is sometimes referred to as Colonel. See vol. 1:154; *Mass. Register*, 1830, p. 90; Adams Genealogy.

MONDAY. 28TH.

The weather this morning was clear and cold and we enjoyed our ride to town notwithstanding my own peculiar inconvenience from the violent cold which I had contracted. My father came in with us, to finish the papers respecting Mr. Boylston. After an hour at home and seeing Mr. Frothingham, who was from Medford, I went to the Office and read a little of Marshall but was much interrupted by the arrival and departure of different individuals between my room and the Probate Office—Mr. Curtis and my father and several others. They found a difficulty about bonds and as I believe did not settle it after all. So that my father left town having accomplished little or nothing. Mr. Champney is one of my father's Tenants and called to pay some arrears which were due on his tenements.[1] He is in appearance a very clever young man and though in arrear, it seems to have been only for the reason that he was allowed to go behind.

Returned home to dinner and passed the afternoon in my study, writing and arranging my Accounts. My cold has had a very unfavourable effect upon my spirits and temper—and Abby and I had a conversation at dinner which gave me regret. For I perceive so very strongly the seeds of difference between herself and a member of our family now absent but who may still hereafter be thrown into some intimacy with us, that I fear the result will scarcely be agreeable, and endeavour earnestly to correct it.[2] Evening with Abby at home, but not pleasant as I suffered much and she was a little out of sorts. This evening R. Sturgis was married again to Miss Hubbard and we had a portion of the Serenade.[3] It was flat and poor.

[1] John Y. Champney, an ensign in the City Guards, occupied tenement No. 1 of 101 Tremont Street until Oct. 1830 at an annual rent of $150 (M/CFA/3; *Mass. Register*, 1830, p. 244).

[2] Probably Mrs. JA2; see entry for 8 Sept., above.

[3] Russell Sturgis, an attorney whose office was at 16 Court Street, was married to Mary Greene Hubbard, daughter of John Hubbard, merchant, of 7 Somerset Street (*Columbian Centinel*, 30 Sept.; *Boston Directory*, 1830–1831).

TUESDAY. 29TH.

Morning rainy and unpleasant. I arose suffering very heavily from my cold. I do not know how or when I could have contracted it but it seems as severe as any I have had. At the Office engaged in reading Marshall, and in making out the accounts of my father's Agency for the quarter. Mr. Child sent me a letter requesting the use of my late brother's Uniform. I told him in reply, first in a letter and then verbally when he called to see me that I did not feel at liberty to let him have it in that manner,[1] that I wished to part with it but felt it impossible to allow the value of it to be diminished constantly by these occasional uses. He allowed the reasoning and seemed puzzled to know what to do and so left me. Mr. Curtis called and left a letter from my father in which he complains of not hearing from his man to put up a fire place for him.[2] This compelled me to go and find him after dinner which was not at all agreeable as I felt much more in a humour for remaining at home. My comfort was entirely destroyed during the day and evening although I felt all the luxury of a comfortable home. Mr. Child made me go to the Office at seven o'clock in order to come to a decisive arrangement about the Uniform. He concluded to take it and give me the appraised price which I thought very low. He paid me only a small part in hand and promised the remainder in ten days. I know what his promises are but I was foolish enough to give them up and do much more than was altogether suitable to my conscience.[3]

[1] Correspondence missing. On David Lee Child (1794–1874), who succeeded GWA as brigade-major of the City Guards (*Mass. Register*, 1829, p. 107; 1830,

p. 92), see vol. 2:152, 351, and *DAB*.

[2] JQA to CFA, 29 Sept. (Adams Papers). The reference is to the brother of Ward Litchfield, agent of the New

England Soapstone Co., probably Allen Litchfield, mason, of 28 Myrtle Court (*Boston Directory*, 1829–1830).

³ Child purchased at this time only

parts of the uniform (hence "them"). The price was $85. CFA to JQA, 26 Feb. 1830 (LbC, Adams Papers).

WEDNESDAY. 30TH.

My morning after going to the Office was very much taken up by the calls of different individuals, and though my cold made me suffer exceedingly I did not feel able to abandon myself to it. My father came in to make some arrangment in respect to the Affairs of Mr. Boylston which he succeeded this time in completing. My Uncle called for his quarterly payment due tomorrow, which I paid in advance, as I did also both the girls.¹ Col. Davis called to see my father and to request a conversation.² Mr. Curtis came in about Mr. Boylston's Affairs, Mr. P. Whitney to notify me of his abandoning the House in Court Street formally, as he was a little out of temper about my binding him for another quarter. I was engaged also in making up the Accounts of the Agency for the quarter and the Bills for the next quarter. Thus my time passed until dinner.

The afternoon was passed in a walk with Abby, making some purchases for Miss Smith at Quincy, and calling to see Mr. Cruft about my father's library which I was to see about transporting. He was not at home but I saw his wife, her Mother Mrs. Smith and brother.³ She could not however inform me of any thing. I then returned home and passed some time in my study—The noise which the military were making on the Common interrupting me considerably. It was a horrible day of Review. Evening at home, reading aloud a little of the Man of Feeling, to Abby, my cold having improved.

¹ The two daughters of TBA, namely Abigail Smith Adams (mentioned earlier in this volume) and Elizabeth Coombs Adams (1808–1903) (ECA), being both of age, received their proportionate share of interest on mortgages under the terms of JA's will. The payments to each were $45 quarterly. For himself and his four minor sons, TBA received $225 quarterly. See vol. 1:99, 2:387; M/CFA/3; JA, Will, inventory, and estate papers, Adams Papers, Microfilms, Reel No. 181; Adams Genealogy.

² On John Brazer Davis, see entry for 31 Oct., below.

³ Edward Cruft, merchant, lived at 6 Pearl Street (*Boston Directory*, 1829–1830). His wife, the former Elizabeth Storer Smith (1789–1859), was a daughter of Hannah (Carter) Smith (b. 1764) and William Smith (1755–1816) who was a first cousin of AA. The brother spoken of is probably Thomas Carter Smith (1796–1880). See vol. 1:224, 334; 2:19; and Adams Genealogy.

OCTOBER 1829.

THURSDAY. OCTOBER 1ST.

Morning at the Office, arranging the Affairs of the Quarter. Received my father's tax bill for the year and my own for the first time.[1] This makes me in all respects a Citizen of Boston, as well in it's disadvantages as it's benefits. I then took a walk to Union Wharf which is at the North end of Boston leading out of Ann Street and is a considerable distance. I found no advantage from going as I did not come when the Ware house was open which contained my father's books. But Mr. May set me in a way to obtain them.[2] He was the owner of the Wharf and pointed out to me the Liverpool Packet which was just ready to go out of the Harbour, this being her regular day of sailing—and further commenced discussing political subjects upon which I went away, to call upon Mr. Lyman's agent, by name Bigelow who informed me he would meet me down there at three.[3] Bicknell, the Captain of the Sloop which was to take them called at my Office and I fixed the same time for him. Orcutt, my father's tenant, called to tell me he was unable to pay me and asked me to take security. I want the money, so referred him to others to raise it and pay me, which he refused to do as he probably has found that he cannot. I postponed the subject, although I presume it is my only chance of getting any thing. Thus went the morning and I found I had read little or nothing.

The afternoon was taken up partially in another visit to Union Wharf where I saw the Trunks and Cases but could not get them out. I made such arrangements however with Mr. May that it will render needless any further effort on my side.[4] I then called at Mrs. Frothingham's but she was not at home. The remainder of the afternoon was passed at home. The evening was taken up in two visits—One to Mrs. Gorham and her daughter and one to Mr. and Mrs. Frothingham who have just returned from Medford, for the Winter.[5] Their house looked cold but we had some good Wine and returned home after nine o'clock.

[1] The tax bill of $115.19 on JQA's Boston property was paid on 18 Nov. (M/CFA/3). CFA's own account books show no payment of taxes in 1829 nor that he owned any real property at this time. Taxes on the house at 3 Hancock Avenue were paid each year by Mr. Brooks, who retained title to it (Brooks, Waste Book, 27 Dec. 1834).

[2] Probably Henry K. May of 6 Union Wharf (*Boston Directory*, 1829–1830).

[3] Perhaps Theodore Lyman, merchant, of 4 Bowdoin Square, and Benjamin Bigelow of Bigelow & Bangs, merchants, 15 Long Wharf (same).

[4] On 3 Oct., the lighter sloop *Flash*, Captain Bicknell, arrived at Quincy with 38 boxes and 5 trunks of books. Some, accumulated during JQA's years in Europe, had been packed in England in 1817 and subsequently stored in Boston. Some, the books that constituted his library in Boston when he left for Russia in 1809, had been on deposit at the Boston Athenæum until 1822, then boxed and stored. Some had been lately sent from Washington. The cargo was delivered from wharf to house in four wagonloads, then placed in the woodshed for shelter until unpacking could be completed. See above, entry for 23 Sept.; JQA, Diary, 3 Oct. 1829; Walter

Muir Whitehill, "Three Letters of John Quincy Adams," *Athenæum Items*, No. 62 (July 1955).

[5] The Rev. and Mrs. Frothingham lived at 24 Summer Street (*Boston Directory*, 1829–1830).

FRIDAY. 2ND.

Morning at the Office. Spirits rather low. I hold it silly to mention the cause for as my father once said, there are many things which must not be mentioned even there. But disappointment is the most painful thing in life, and I feel fearful that I am about to suffer it. I passed a considerable part of the morning in reading Marshall. Mr. Gay called to pay me his rent.[1] Another person to ask about the House which Mr. Whitney quits, and with these interruptions I got quite clear. But my attention is so distracted by them even when so few, that I can understand my brother George's objection about it. I am beginning to feel as if I dare not indulge the aspirations which I formerly made, and as if for one kind of happiness, I had voluntarily cast off prospects of another. I hope not however. I shall find it difficult to reconcile my mind to the truth even when it comes to convince me of my negligence.

Returned home and passed the afternoon reading to her passages of the Man of Feeling. It does not take. Perhaps there is too much of the abstruse in the sentiment and feeling which it contains for her. I was not myself aware of the extent of it until this reading, and certainly should not have commenced my attempts with it had I been. We were interrupted by a succession of persons—Mrs. Frothingham for a few minutes, Sidney Brooks who drank tea with us and passed a part of the evening and Mr. Degrand, the rest. The latter has found me out and is resolved to visit me.[2] On some accounts I regret it, on others it ought to be a matter of gratification to me as he might be a valuable friend. But I do not feel as if I had the means to make friends for myself. My own external manners are so repulsive. I have at times treated this very person with the most decided symptoms of coldness, but he has got over it and is here. Perhaps this does not speak well for his pride. But he is generous to forgive it. Perhaps he may imagine my assistance likely to be worth something—in which he will be mistaken. Be that as it will. He remained here until time to go to bed.

[1] George Gay's annual rent for his 23 Court Street office was $80 (M/CFA/3).

[2] Peter Paul Francis Degrand, stock-broker of 65 Broad Street (*Boston Directory*, 1829–1830), was a long-time political supporter, often unwelcome, of JQA; See Bemis, JQA, 2:22, 74, 137–138. His earlier approaches on both business and political matters, CFA had repulsed; see vol. 1:155–156; 2:310. Although CFA did use him as a broker from time to time, other association was out of the question; see entry for 29 Nov., below.

SATURDAY 3RD.

Morning at the Office, after seeing at the House, Mr. Conant, one of the Tenants of the Farm at Weston. He came to make inquiry respecting my determination in regard to the place. I told him that I supposed I must accede to his Terms in the end but proposed an experiment in order to try and find whether the place would not be so improved as not to need all. He said he thought they could agree to it.[1] I was occupied during the morning in reading Marshall, and in drawing up the Accounts of my brother George's affairs which I am desirous to commence closing. I accordingly again wrote to Genl. Winthrop for a settlement of his debt.[2] As I went into Hilliard's I obtained some further Numbers of the Library of Useful Knowledge and obtained a Life of Sir Isaac Newton which I read—And wondered at.[3] A mathematical genius is a singular gift and a precious one, but which I never could envy perhaps appreciate. Indeed there is no character on record which I would not sooner desire to equal and my taste must therefore be considered as decidedly poor.

Home to dine and as Abby went out in the afternoon I passed it in reading La Harpe. His remarks upon the Epic and the different specimens in ancient times which approach it are very interesting and I only broke off in the evening to go down for Abby to Mrs. Frothingham's. Calling in to see how the Private Debating Society flourished, a meeting of which was called for tonight, I found only Quincy, and Park, the President and Secretary and myself.[4] This looked poorly so I went in to Mrs. Frothingham's and took a little Supper and chatted with them for an hour before returning home. I feel infinitely more at my ease with them now than formerly.

[1] See entry for 15 Sept., above.

[2] Brig. Gen. John Temple Winthrop was commander of the 3d Brigade, 1st Division of the Massachusetts Militia ("City Guards"), in which GWA had been a major and to which he had made a loan in 1827; see below, entry for 13 Oct.; *Mass. Register*, 1829, p. 93.

[3] Hilliard, Gray & Co., booksellers, were at 134 Washington Street (*Boston Directory*, 1829–1830). The volumes of the *Library of Useful Knowledge* (1827–1842), published by The Society for the Diffusion of Useful Knowledge, London, were issued first in parts. Among the works included in the *Library* was *Lives of Eminent Persons* (1833), which had appeared in 13 parts, one of which

was a life of Newton, adapted by Sir H. Elphinstone from the French of J. B. Biot.

[4] The Private Debating Society, to which CFA had been elected a year earlier and which met on Saturday evenings from October to the beginning of April, though earlier said to have been the Boston Debating Society (vol. 2:309), was distinct from it and the other "public" debating society whose officers and meeting days were different from those mentioned in the present entry and in later ones. See *Mass. Register*, 1829, p. 142. Edmund Quincy and Edward Blake were among those who were both active in the Society and friends of CFA. On John Cochran Park,

the secretary, an attorney with office at 16 Court Street (*Boston Directory*, 1829– 1830), see entries for 21 and 28 Nov., below.

SUNDAY. 4TH.

Morning opened with heavy rain which ceased however at the time commonly fixed to go to Meeting. I went to Mr. Frothingham's and heard him deliver a Sermon upon the Communion, which had to me not much interest. It is a subject upon which I have not as yet felt disposed to pay much attention, nor have I felt that my religious opinions or method of life need any such support or confirmation. Returned home and passed the remainder of the day with Abby. She was suffering from the cold which I have just ceased to have. It seems to extend every where probably occasioned by a chill in the air which has a tendency to check the perspiration of the system too suddenly. Mr. Blake called in for a few minutes only to talk of Miss Hubbard's marriage &ca.

I amused myself in reading La Harpe, who is the most amusing critic without exception that I have read. He discusses the Ancient Tragedy, and the plays of Æschylus and Sophocles with great spirit. I have been so interested in him as to wish that I only had more time to devote. But this at present is impossible. My wife is lonely and at times depressed, and she requires more attention than usual from the sensitiveness of her nature which has ever been too much indulged. Our evening passed quietly as they usually do and with much comfort. I certainly am too much favoured to think of complaining.

MONDAY. 5TH.

Morning at the Office, weather cold and blustering. On my way I called upon Mrs. Sidney Brooks to give some of my Wife's Commissions to her as she is starting for New York soon. Abby herself was too unwell to think of going out. I sat a few minutes with her only and merely asked a few common place questions as usual. And this was the end, for I take no interest in her. She is a woman of a kind I have seldom met with and to tell the truth with all her good qualities I do not desire to.[1] But it is impossible for me to define the precise reason, and so I will not attempt it. At the Office I was engaged most of the morning in making up the account of the sales made on my brother's Account and mine producing for his share about sixty dollars and for mine thirteen. I am so disappointed by the result of the Dividends of the Banks today that I need every thing I can scrape. I do not receive a dollar upon twelve hundred invested in three several

Banks which I call very bad luck. This is owing to the misfortunes which have befallen the Manufacturing Interest in this section of [the] Country and the prevailing depression of trade.[2] A man called to see the House in Court Street vacated by Mr. Whitney, and I went over it with him. It was disgusting in the extreme for it has been neglected most abominably. This will cost something to put in repair, and money is tolerably scarce now. Indeed I have seldom known a time when there was so much difficulty in raising it. My father's income is considerably curtailed, and the vacancy of several houses makes it probable to be more so.

On my return to dinner I went in to see the Furniture of Dr. E. H. Robbins advertised to be sold and was much disappointed in it. He is a Bankrupt and his assignees in consequence sell his elegant superfluities. They are not very numerous. Afternoon at home with my Wife who was suffering very much with a cold. I did nothing. My father came in for half an hour after some purchases in order to begin living in his study with a fire, a necessary thing on such a day as this. He remained however but little while. In the evening Mr. and Mrs. Frothingham came in and passed an hour very agreeably.

[1] During her visit to Boston, Mrs. Sidney Brooks presumably was at the home of her parents at 7 Bulfinch Place (*Boston Directory*, 1829–1830). Frances Dehon's background had led Mr. and Mrs. Peter C. Brooks to regard Sidney's marriage as "a sore thing." Her father, William Dehon (d. 1833), though currently successful as an auctioneer, was held in some contempt in the Brooks household for his lack of cultivation, while Mrs. Dehon was mocked for her pretensions (Charlotte Everett to Edward Everett, 23 Dec. 1827, Everett MSS, MHi).

[2] On the depressed state of trade and manufactures, see below, entries for 27 Oct., 31 Dec., and notes there.

TUESDAY. 6TH.

Morning cold but the weather was clear and the day fine. I went to the Office, but not early as my wife was quite sick with a bad cold caught some days ago. I began to be alarmed about her and was exceedingly doubtful of the expediency of her going to Medford as she proposed. For this purpose I called to see her father to know whether her Mother would go in the Carriage to carry her home, but I was unable to ascertain as he could not be found. I then went to the South end of the town to obtain the Dividend upon the Shares of the Boylston Market for October, and one unclaimed for April last, which the Treasurer, Mr. Knapp gave me an order to obtain.[1] I was occupied in this manner all the morning.

Sidney Brooks called to see me for half an hour and I took the opportunity to ask him concerning the most expedient way of conveying here the remains of my brother. He appeared to hesitate considerably about it but said he would attend to it.[2] He delayed again so now he goes tomorrow. All this being over as I was returning home, I met Abby in her Mother's Carriage and so found her positively gone. The consequence was a lonely dinner at home, and a return to the Office in the afternoon to remain until John[3] came with the Chaise as my Father had promised to take me to Quincy. I remained reading a file of Newspapers of an ancient date 1809 at my Office until the time when he came and I immediately started on the return. The ride was cold but not unpleasant though I was glad to reach a warm room. I found the family at tea and with them Mr. and Mrs. J. H. Foster and Mr. Degrand. Miss Foster is now staying with her Aunt.[4] They returned home before nine and soon after the family retired.

[1] JQA owned 12 shares in the Boylston Market purchased at $100 a share. The April dividend was at the rate of $2, the October at $3.50. John Knapp, the treasurer, was a counselor with office at 14 State Street; the Market was at Washington and Boylston streets. See M/CFA/3; *Boston Directory*, 1829–1830.

[2] See above, entry for 15 Sept., note. CFA seems to have been led to ask his brother-in-law's help because of Sidney's New York residence. See further, JQA to Sidney Brooks, 7 Nov. 1829 (LbC, Adams Papers).

[3] JQA's servant John Thomas.

[4] Elizabeth Anne Foster (1802–1875), visiting her aunt, Louisa Catherine Smith, at the Old House, was the eldest of the thirteen children of the J. H. Fosters. She was AA's grandniece. See vol. 1:99, 155, 157, and Adams Genealogy.

WEDNESDAY. 7TH.

Morning clear and weather warm, so that the weather was fine when we started for the purpose for which I came out—Surveying or overlooking a survey to be made of the old farm on Penn's Hill. My father presuming that I am the only son likely to remain in the State is desirous of giving me information which he never possessed in the same circumstances and of which he felt very much, the want.[1] I am therefore induced to consent to the arrangement which breaks up my home considerably.

We started after breakfast, our party consisting of my father, Thomas B. Adams, Mr. Humphreys a Surveyor from Weymouth, two men to carry the Chain, and myself.[2] We started from the upper Corner on the old Plymouth Road above the old House, the Birth place of my father and his Father before him. Our Survey was of a lot of land including the two Houses and about one hundred and eight Acres of land.[3] The boundaries being rather irregular and a portion of it fresh Meadow, it was quite a slow affair so that it was nearly four before we were thinking of a return home. I obtained some acquaintance with this property which I never had before and perhaps attached a little more idea of value to it than heretofore although in truth it is most unmanageable property as to any change to be made of it. But after all property is but a pure business in this life giving more care than pleasure. And if I could only feel sure of being beyond any want, I should care but little what my father's pursuits might be. I returned considerably fatigued from the exercise. We of course dined late and though I attempted some kind of conversation with my father it resulted in nothing as we both of us inclined to sleep. I therefore retired early.

[1] After three days in the woods and swamps, JQA wrote that the survey was of "lands which I have owned twenty-six years, without knowing how they were bounded, nor even where some of them were" (JQA to LCA, 11 Oct., Adams Papers).

[2] Lemuel Humphreys was the surveyor, William Spear and one Baxter, the chain bearers (JQA, Diary, 7 Oct. 1829).

[3] The Adams farm, at the foot of Penn's Hill in Quincy, was established by Deacon John Adams, CFA's great-grandfather. The house on the northern side was the home of JA's parents (and is now called the John Adams Birthplace), that adjacent to it on the southern side was the home of JA and AA after their marriage in 1764 (now the John Quincy Adams Birthplace). See JA, *Diary and Autobiography*, 1:15, note, for a fuller account and same, p. 256 for a drawing of the homestead made by Eliza Susan Quincy in 1822; also Waldo C. Sprague, *The President John Adams and the President John Quincy Adams Birthplaces*, Quincy, 1959. The houses, given to the city of Quincy in 1940 by the Adams family, are in the care of the Quincy Historical Society and are open to the public.

THURSDAY. 8TH.

Contrary to my expectation this morning, I found the weather very clear but with a cold Easterly Wind which promised to give us a little want of comfort in the continuation of our purpose today. But as it was dry this was of less importance. Having suffered yesterday from my father's promising to return to dine without due consideration, I took precautions today which proved useful as we did not return until five o'clock. Our party today had lost Thomas B. Adams who had other engagements and was besides quite satisfied with yesterday's experience, and it had gained Deacon Josiah Adams, one of the elders of the town who from his proximity to the spot and familiarity with the land was of great service to us in ascertaining the limits.[1]

We this day surveyed a quantity of land amounting to about forty three acres described in the Deeds as Pasture land but which time and neglect had covered with a thick growth of wood. This made our travelling slow and rather heavy, so that it was half past three o'clock before we completed the survey. I think I shall remember the land. After a slight meal upon what we brought with us, we closed the day with the examination of a small lot called the Quincy Meadow on the east side of the Plymouth old road containing six or seven acres—At the present price of land in the vicinity quite valuable and much better situated than I had supposed my father's land to be. This occupied us until sunset. The day had been unpleasantly cold and my father had suffered very severely from one of these Colds which are now prevalent and from which I am myself but just recovering. I was glad to be able to get home, where we found dinner waiting for us, no disagreeable event. I was so fatigued and heated that I could not keep myself awake and so went to sleep early in the evening.

[1] Deacon Josiah Adams (1763–1844) and Deacon Ebenezer Adams (1762–1841) were brothers residing in Quincy (A. N. Adams, *Geneal. Hist. of Henry Adams of Braintree*, 1:410). Their grandparents, Ebenezer Adams (1704–1769) and Anne (Boylston) Adams, were brother and sister of Deacon John and Susanna (Boylston) Adams, JQA's grandparents (same; see also Adams Genealogy).

In JQA's account of the survey, he refers on the two first days to the presence of Deacon Ebenezer, whose lands abutted those of JQA for a distance and who wished to swap lands and open ditches; not until the third day was Deacon Josiah's aid sought as the party moved over a quite different territory (Diary, 7–9 Oct. 1829).

FRIDAY 9TH.

The morning arose in great beauty. The East Wind which so much troubled us yesterday had spent itself in the course of the night in a frost which covered the hills and valleys with a white mantle, the sure harbinger of a clear day. The day was in effect lovely and admirably calculated for our purpose. We again started this morning on the next survey. Leaving Mr. Josiah Adams' house to which we rode as yesterday, we took him for our guide, and with the same party we proceeded to those spots strictly called Wood lots to be surveyed today. Our day's work was much the most laborious of any we had undergone, as we were obliged to pass through swamps and the luxuriant undergrowth of the woods which at once impeded our progress and increased our exertions. Now and then an ascent of rocks presented itself after surmounting which we only saw below us a grove of oaks almost impenetrable to relieve our sight. Add to this, the knowledge of our guide gave out when we had passed one half our course and the rest was a mere attempt to get out of the wilderness before sundown. So that on the whole we had rather a useless day's work.

I do not know how it happened but instead of suffering from the labour, I enjoyed it. The beauty of the day, the rich colouring which the Autumn had given to the leaves of the Woods, and the picturesque effect of the wild scenery, a glimpse of which we caught occasionally on the high grounds as we climbed over them, gave a kind of romance to the Expedition which prevented my feeling the labour and the fatigue. I have from early associations in life felt a singular fondness for that scenery which by others is always considered wild and desolate. It seems in some measure to harmonize with a particular tone of mind in me formerly cherished but now repressed which seeks melancholy for pleasure. I can see more beauty in the roughness of nature than the softness of artificial cultivation, more attraction in a spot where man seems never to have been than where his labour has made all things smooth. Indeed my feelings today reminded me of early dreams long since vanished and not till now revived in any degree. They were the offspring of idle hours of musing then and are worth no more than the pleasure which remembrance gives to early feelings of all kinds. I have indulged them only here, and even here perhaps too much. For after all I am no loser by the changes which have come over me. Why should I be savage, and lonely. Why should not I delight in the society and converse of others as other people do. Enough of this.[1]

We took our rustic dinner at sunset in a singularly rough spot and I have seldom relished food so much. This closes my surveys for the present, perhaps entirely. I have on the whole enjoyed them, and yet I do not regret much the end. We have not accomplished more than one half the farm but I can spare no more time. I have gained now a sufficient knowledge of the location of it to assist me materially in whatever I may at some time or other hereafter have to do. It will be long hereafter I hope and believe before any such call will be made upon me. Perhaps I may be the first to leave the World and things cease to be of interest to me at the idea. Perhaps I may have no interest to obtain the information. But these things are only troublesome to think of and lead to no good. We must trust to the Divinity for much—for all.

After our return I felt so little fatigued that I took the opportunity to look over a Volume of Block's History of Fish, a most splendid work which is among the books my father is now opening.[2] This is a beautiful Library and if I live I promise myself much pleasure from it. I obtained a good deal of information in relation to many fish which in appearance are familiar to me, though I was able to give but a very superficial attention to them as the time was short before I retired.

[1] JQA's diary entries for these three days are richer in detail and more comprehensive than CFA's. CFA's, as here, are more reflective and sensitive to land and weather. A rooted responsiveness to the more romantic aspects of nature and of literature, the association of melancholy and loneliness with the sub-

lime, is evident in CFA's poetic taste which ran strongly to Byron and the works of such 18th-century figures as Collins and Gray. See vol. 1:110, 114, 129, 159, and CFA's literary commonplace book, p. 1, 61–62, 262–263 (Adams Papers, Microfilms, Reel No. 312). The feeling that in indulging this sensitivity toward which he was drawn there was a moral danger, he had expressed too in his college years in his estimate of Byron (vol. 1:220–221, 418); now it was more than ever in his mind as he reflected upon GWA and himself. See entries for 15, 16 Oct., 24 Nov., below.

[2] Marc Eliéser Bloch, *Ichtyologie, ou histoire naturelle ... des poissons*, 6 vols. in 3, Berlin, 1785–1788. JQA's copy with his bookplate is in MQA.

SATURDAY 10TH.

The morning was clear but a little cold, and brought with it the close of my stay at Quincy. It has been in some respects agreeable, but in others it has been otherwise. My absence from home and my wife has made me anxious and uneasy, particularly as she left me unwell. I accordingly was glad when the time came for John to take me into town in my father's Chaise. Abby shortly after my arrival came in and was much pleased to return. I was glad to come home and find myself again fixed comfortably in my usual avocations.

I went to the Office soon after and there attended to my father's affairs; Drew the Dividend for October upon his Shares in the Neponset and West Boston Bridges.[1] This together with the arrangement of my Accounts consumed a considerable portion of the morning and the rest I devoted to Abby at home. As the weather was fine I walked out with her in the afternoon to make one or two purchases for the House after accomplishing which and leaving her at the turning to Mrs. Frothingham's I walked down again to the Office. It was a lucky walk as I found Mr. D. L. Child there just ready to pay me for the Uniform which he purchased some time since. I confess I was agreeably surprised and received the money with great satisfaction as it enables me to arrange all the smaller accounts of my brother's Estate directly. He is not famous for punctual payment and this made it the more gratifying that he should relieve me from difficulty so soon. Returned home, and employed myself in writing my Journal which my absence had thrown in the Back ground. The Evening was passed at home and I read aloud to Abby the Life of Richardson taken from Scotts Biography of the Novelists, which seemed to please and interest her considerably.[2]

[1] The dividends were $54 on six shares of the Neponset Bridge and $25 on five shares of the West Boston Bridge (M/CFA/3).

[2] In choosing to read aloud here and during the succeeding ten days from Sir Walter Scott's *Biographical and Critical Notices of Eminent Novelists*, CFA was selecting material he thought likely to interest ABA from his earlier reading (see

vol. 2:389–391). The lives are in the third volume of the Boston edition of Scott's *Miscellaneous Prose Works*, 6 vols., 1829, CFA's copy of which is in MQA.

SUNDAY. 11TH.

Morning cloudy and damp. Arose and passed an hour in my study in writing. After which I went to Meeting at Mr. Frothingham's and heard him deliver a Sermon not a single word of which remains in my memory. He is not a good Preacher for he has not the quality of taking hold of the Hearer's attention. This is a tact only possessed by some men and it is the great secret of seizing one's mind whether voluntarily or not. Some men do it almost instinctively, and without forcing nature, others by artificial means such as startling paradoxes or new doctrines but whether in one or the other, they all need it to keep up reputation. Mr. Frothingham is an exceedingly amiable man and he is also a man of talents but he has misconceived his line. He has not the art of fascinating public attention like some of his Brethren.[1]

After dinner as Abby still had too much Cold I went alone and heard another Sermon which interested me as little. I am sorry for this as I esteem Mr. F. and feel the exertion he makes to please, but it is impossible to correct the facts. The remainder of the afternoon and evening was passed at home, part of it passed in finishing the Life of Richardson by Scott. It is very light stuff. Scott is rather a pleasing but an exceeding shallow writer. His reflections all lie on the surface and have only their simplicity and their showy qualities to recommend them. After Abby had retired, I read La harpe's remarks upon the Ancient Comedy in which I thought him much too severe upon Aristophanes, to whom he allows a very small share of merit. I am not a very competent Judge but from what I have read of the translation by Mitchell of his Plays I think they have merit to redeem the unquestionable objection which exists in their coarseness.[2]

[1] Frothingham's qualities as a writer of sermons and as a pulpit orator are the subject of CFA's comments on many later occasions. See also JQA to CFA, 13, 21 Feb. 1830 (Adams Papers).

[2] Thomas Mitchell, translator, *The Comedies of Aristophanes*. CFA's copy of the Philadelphia edition in 2 vols., 1822, is in MQA; but see below, entry for 25 Jan. 1830.

MONDAY. 12TH.

Miss Oliver, the Tenant of the House in Hancock Street called to pay me her rent for one quarter before I had left the House this morning. This with the various other sums of money I had received on Saturday made a considerable amount which I did not know what to do with as I could not deposit it in the Bank—A portion of it being money which the Bank will not take.[1] I was on that Account compelled to go round and pay Bills of my Fathers, my brother's Estate and my own in order to get rid of it. This and the arrangement of my Accounts consequent upon it occupied a very considerable part of my morning. But I accomplished much, for I made great progress toward a final settlement of the affairs of George which have been so long delaying upon my hands. My Money Accounts are now a little complicated for I have three different tracks to keep of money received and expended, and in paying small bills I draw from what I have in my pocket which makes the transfer from the several deposits difficult, to preserve precisely correct. I made a settlement with Hilliard and Co. which is final and not unfavourable. This is the last of a series of dreadfully heavy bills which my poor brother inflicted upon himself at that Store and to them may be traced partially his state of mind in his later days.[2]

The afternoon was passed partly at the Office and partly at the House but I can recollect little of any consequence which happened. The evening went with more use and pleasure. The first part of it was passed in reading to Abby Scott's Life of Fielding which was tolerably interesting, the second was more jovial but not quite so agreeable to my own taste. Mr. and Mrs. Frothingham came in with Mr. and Mrs. Everett and passed the evening pleasantly enough. Now and then a sip of some warm Whiskey Punch served to enliven us and to chase away care. They left us shortly after ten o'clock to our meditations, and I then read a Chapter of La Harpe upon the Ancient Comedy of the Romans, Plautus and Terence.

[1] JQA's account was in the United States Branch Bank Boston (M/CFA/3). It was the policy of the Bank of the United States during the presidency of Nicholas Biddle, 1823–1833, to refuse to accept state bank notes not redeemable in specie.

[2] The booksellers, Hilliard, Gray & Co., were paid $65 (M/CFA/3). It was,

perhaps, with thoughts similar to those of CFA, that JQA, in contemplating his father's and his own lifelong passion for books and their acquisition, reflected that collecting "must be associated with vigorous economy, with punctual accountability, and with judicious and untiring industry" (Diary, 17 Oct. 1829).

TUESDAY. 13TH.

Morning at the Office a portion of the time engaged in my usual business of looking over accounts, and arranging further those of my brother's Estate so far as to settle all existing demands against it excepting that from his Tailor which must wait. I feel myself however quite fortunate in having progressed so far. I then went to make purchases for my father after which I went down to the Estate belonging to my father in Common Street to look at the state of the Property and inquire after Orcutt who had not been near me since the memorable time when he announced to me that he should be unable to pay me. I found he had not yet quitted the Tenement and his Wife who in appearance was quite an honest creature seemed hurt even at the intimation that they should leave without a settlement—A thing I had a little apprehended. I saw Hollis the Carpenter and gave him directions for attending to Mrs. Longhurst's Pump and some few other things which appeared requisite and necessary to be done, and then left them to return home and see Abby who was going to Cambridge, to pay visits. I had thought of going with her but upon reflection thought it would be best to return to my Office and read a little of Marshall. But as my ideas could not easily be fixed I went into Mr. Kinsman's Office to see about the Note which the City Guards owe to my brother, and from thence I dropped in and chatted with Davis and Winthrop for an hour or so.[1] A man, name unknown called to see me about the Rumford which my father had asked me to order him and I then gave him as good directions upon the subject as I was able.

On returning home I found Abby returned and Miss Julia Gorham in company with her who dined here. My afternoon was passed in my study, reading La Harpe and arranging my Library after a different mode. I want to make some thing like a systematic arrangement. Evening at home, Abby was not disposed to listen to reading so I did nothing until nine after which I read another Chapter of La Harpe and commenced reading the New Testament regularly with the five first Chapters of Matthew.

[1] GWA had lent the City Guards $102 on 7 July 1827 to be repaid with interest (CFA to Commanding Officer, City Guards, 29 June 1829, LbC, Adams Papers). The original sum and interest were still unpaid when CFA closed his administration of GWA's estate in Feb. 1830, despite numerous efforts to collect. However, CFA's confidence that the debt would be paid was justified; see below, entry for 10 April 1830.

Henry W. Kinsman was a lieutenant in the Guards and an attorney (*Mass. Register*, 1830, p. 244). On him and on Thomas Kemper Davis, see entry for 18 Nov., below. George E. Winthrop, CFA's Harvard classmate (vol. 1:80), was still reading law and was later admitted to the bar (*Mass. Register*, 1832).

WEDNESDAY. 14TH.

Arose a little earlier and by this means succeeded in getting to the Office a little earlier than heretofore. The morning was quietly passed partly in reading Marshall, partly in the settlement of my Accounts. My interruptions were not many. Dr. Storer called and I settled with him.[1] This closes the affairs contracted with the Estate of my Brother by a business not over creditable to any of the parties concerned. I paid this considerable demand with less difficult[y] because I did not wish to hear what probably might have been disclosed to me. The whole affair ought to be forgotten. My mornings are not now spent satisfactorily. I feel as if I should be doing something more creditable than settling accounts and talking nothings. But at present I am not in the way of commencing with spirit. John has promised to send me the Trial of Dr. Watkins and I have expected it in order to try my hand and expend my time upon it, but he does not keep his resolutions.[2] I must talk with my father upon it.

Afternoon at home, reading La Harpe's view of the Ancient Fable and Satire, with his parallel between Horace and Juvenal. The reading of this Author has inspired me with a Taste for Ancient Literature and I propose directly to turn my attention again to the Latin Classics, and to become more completely the master of their Style than I have yet been. This will require study but I am equal to it. In the evening I read to Abby, Scott's Life of Smollett which is not so interesting as either of the preceding. It is too long, and mixed up too much. He borrows to save himself the trouble of writing, and makes the whole book appear like a Catch penny thing which in fact it was. After Abby retired, I again read La Harpe and five Chapters in Matthew, and reflected more upon the beauty of the precepts of Jesus Christ as given in the Sermon on the Mount than I had hitherto done. It merits deep consideration.

[1] Dr. David Humphreys Storer had been attempting since GWA's death to collect from the administrator of his estate for medical services allegedly rendered by Storer to Eliza Dolph in childbirth. See vol. 2:382, 392, 403–404. Settlement was made for $37 (M/CFA/3).

[2] CFA had asked JA2 in a letter on 21 Sept. (Adams Papers) to send him a newly published pamphlet complete with all the papers on the case of Dr. Tobias Watkins, a JQA supporter and appointee at the Treasury who had been removed by Pres. Andrew Jackson and then convicted of embezzlement (see vol. 1:51; 2:399). CFA was resolved to write an article on the case for a Boston legal publication to which he had been invited to contribute. JA2 had apparently responded to the request, but the letter is missing. Soon afterward he did send the pamphlet to Quincy (CFA to LCA, 30 Oct., Adams Papers). Although it is clear from letters of JQA to JA2 and to LCA complaining of unanswered letters to John and from letters of LCA to JQA explaining John's failure to write that JA2 was not so faithful a correspondent as were others of the family, nevertheless the lack of any recorded surviving letters to any of the Adamses from JA2 after childhood points to a later systematic removal from the family papers. Numerous references in the family papers to the receipt of letters from JA2 confirm this.

THURSDAY. 15TH.

The morning afforded us one of the finest specimens of Autumnal weather, we have had this season. I was at the Office but am ashamed to say that I wasted my time very much. The want of a systematic plan of study forces itself upon my attention more and more every minute and today in opening a book in which for the three last years I have usually written a little at this season of the year, I could not avoid pouring out the current of my feelings at length.[1] It is strange and not without pleasure to me to read these successive memorials of fleeting years, and it is rather gratifying to my vanity to find them so prettily written.

My friend Richardson called to see me this morning and I asked him to dine with me. The rest of the time was passed in turning over the leaves of old Newspaper files and skimming over the disgusting records of old political Battles. How much there is of passion, how much littleness of soul in these miserable contests. Richardson dined with me and sat a little while afterwards, the rest of the afternoon was passed in reading La Harpe's view of the merits of the Minor Latin Poets which is not such as to tempt one much to the perusal. I have read but little of them, and therefore can express no opinion of my own.

The afternoons are however so exceedingly short as to afford me but small means to progress in my studies, and while the evenings are wasted as this one was in conversation of no use and productive of nothing agreeable I do not feel able to reconcile myself to my course of life. Abby is so fatigued as to feel often unable to keep awake, and I therefore this evening to please her did nothing; but our conversation was worse than profitless in it'[s] consequences to us both, and it decided me to take a different course in future, and be mindful of the precept pursued both by her father and mine, that there is no time which cannot be usefully employed. Evening after she retired, I sat up an hour, reading La Harpe upon the sacred Scriptures, an eloquent answer to Voltaire, and five Chapters of Matthew which led me to design examining the Life of Christ by Jeremy Taylor,[2] in order to form some decided and original opinion of the character of our Saviour.

[1] This "book" cannot be identified and is evidently missing from CFA's papers.

[2] CFA owned an edition of *The Life and Death of . . . Jesus Christ* published at London, 2 vols., 1811, now in MQA. As indicated by his autograph, it had earlier belonged to GWA; there are numerous marginal notations in his hand.

FRIDAY 16TH.

Morning to the Office, occupied in re-examining for a final disposition the old papers and accounts of my brother. I found two or three which might be of some use and one or two more which I ought to have had before. How much money has been lost by my father through his negligence and how badly the Houses look which have been under his care. Poor George. Much merit as he had for his spirit of literature and his generosity of heart, he was eminently unfitted for the duties and common occurrences of life. His mind was thoroughly speculative, at times philosophical, but always unequal to what the world terms common sense. With a keen sense of right, he was unable to resist wrong in an alluring shape, and with a bitter recollection of the past, he could not turn to improvement for the future. Thus his life was a continued scene of virtuous resolutions, and vicious transgressions, of violent repentance and passionate repetition.

Thomas B. Adams called in and I asked him to dine with me. He came to make a settlement with respect to the purchase of some of my brother George's Clothes, upon which we agreed very shortly. He goes on Monday for Charleston.[1] Miss Mary B. Hall from Medford also dined with us making in this manner quite an enlargement of our family circle.[2] The afternoon was elegantly spent in the household occupation of bottling my Whiskey and in continuation of La Harpe's criticism of the sacred writings which is very interesting although from my losing the habit of reading I am obliged to make more effort to condense my attention. Evening at home reading Scott's Life of Cumberland which my Wife did not relish. I am afraid I must give up the point of creating any thing like a decided interest in literature and this grieves me for I cannot waste my time in worthless and trifling conversation. I read afterwards more of La Harpe and five Chapters of Mathew before retiring.

[1] Lt. Adams was stationed at Fort Pickens, S.C.
[2] Mary Brooks Hall was a first cousin of ABA; see vol. 2:155.

SATURDAY 17TH.

My morning at the Office was considerably interrupted by visitors who came for different purposes of business so that although I attempted something in the way of reading, my success was not greater than a Chapter or two of Marshall. Dr. Storer called upon me further upon the business relative to the affairs of my brother, with a claim which I could not at least at present admit. I conversed with him and found that he had involved himself by his hasty character in a scrape which he was anxious to have me help him out in, but I told him I could not, and he left me to arrange as well as he could upon my promise that I would attend to it not as a legal but an equitable claim upon any balance which might exist after the settlement of the Estate.

I fear it will be but small. But on the whole I have done better than I had expected.

Mr. Conant, my father's Tenant at Weston called merely to tell me that he thought he should remain on the Farm for the five Years under the new conditions which we made at our last meeting, which makes another disagreeable business off my hands. This Farm is a plague and no profit. Mr. Orcutt came to tell me that he should not move until next Week and that he should try to raise some Money upon Mortgage to settle with me before going to Connecticut. He like many others is driven out of Boston by the pressure of the times. This is the first time that he has been to my Office perfectly sober, and I thought much better of him. His rectitude of principle however still remains. Mr. Payson is the Tenant of the Store below my Office and came to tell me he was ready to move whenever I found another Tenant.[1] I must therefore advertise directly. This makes the fourth of my Father's places of occupation becoming vacant on or before the first of January and I foresee trouble enough with them, and some diminution of revenue. Thus my morning passed and I returned home in order to go with Abby and dine with Chardon. Mr. Heard and his daughter Mary were there.[2] Our dinner was good and nothing remarkable passed. I have always the same series of feelings when there, and have already described them so repetition is absurd.

Returned home to read La Harpe upon eloquence and became somewhat interested in his Analysis of Quinctilian. This put me in mind of the Meeting of the Debating Society which I attended. The number was but slender and gave but poor encouragement for the support of the Club, but we notwithstanding had a debate and I made an effort. It was not [as] happy as those last Winter, and reminded me of the defects of my conversation. But I feel as if practice and a little attention previously, which I could not give tonight, would cure it. Finished the evening at Chardon's, returning with my Wife at ten, and omitting my reading by forgetfulness.

[1] The firm of (Henry) Payson & (Jacob) Gutterson, dry goods, which had a store in Court Street, was apparently dissolved (*Boston Directory*, 1829–1830, 1830–1831). Payson does not appear in CFA's account books.

[2] John Heard Jr., attorney, and the father of Mrs. Chardon Brooks, lived at 6 Walnut Street (*Boston Directory*, 1829–1830).

SUNDAY. 18TH.

Morning cloudy with an air chilly and uncomfortable. I attended divine service all day at Mr. Frothingham's Meeting House whither I suppose I shall go in future regularly having thus started in married life. We heard this morning Mr. Greenwood upon the observances of the world, Courage and fortitude.[1] His style is peculiar but interesting and I was interested considerably more by him than by the more musical style of Mr. Frothingham. He is practical and direct, instructing the minds of the plainest of his hearers and not below those of the most cultivated. Mr. Young in the afternoon.[2] Text, "Thy Kingdom come." He writes well and reads well, but his delivery is bad, and he has a defect in his pronunciation which materially operates upon any thing he might be able to say. But I was on the whole agreeably disappointed by him. The Boston Clergy have certainly a very high standard of style in writing introduced by the models of Mr. Everett and Mr. Buckminster.[3] It now remains only to create an equal ambition to excel in Oratory. And this led me to entertain the idea of writing something upon the subject and reading for the purpose. I do not know whether I can find time for the purpose but I certainly have the disposition, and something I must soon do I think is certain.

I passed the remainder of the day and evening in reading the Preface to Jeremy Taylor's Life of Christ which I read twice over with great care. It deserves the perusal, being an argument in support of Christianity as being derived from the principles of Natural Law originally fixed by the Creator and being therefore the revival among men of those feelings which time and corruption had obscured. He argues that the world was established only with two Laws—The love of God, which leads man to be holy and pious, the love of our Neighbour which leads us to act with justice and creates our other social duties, and the love of ourselves which teaches prudence and sobriety. This last however is only subsequent. Thus my evening was useful and I felt better for it. Conversation with Abby and some Chapters in the New Testament before retiring.

[1] Francis W. P. Greenwood was minister at King's Chapel (Unitarian), Tremont and School streets (*Mass. Register*, 1830).

[2] Rev. Alexander Young Jr. held the pulpit of the New South Church (Unitarian) on Summer Street; see *DAB*.

[3] Edward Everett, before his academic and political careers opened, was, from 1813 to 1815, the successor to Joseph S. Buckminster as minister at the Brattle Street Church (Unitarian). On both, see *DAB*. For a brief account of the leading figures in the contemporary Unitarian clergy in Boston, including Greenwood and Young as well as Buckminster and Everett, see Winsor, *Memorial History of Boston*, 3:475–476.

MONDAY. 19TH.

Morning at the Office. Weather exceedingly warm and for the season a little unusual. I went down this morning and attended a meeting of the Stockholders of the State Bank in order to satisfy myself in regard to the condition of the Company.[1] Much excitement has been produced in the Community by the omission of this Bank to make any Dividend this Season. The losses of the Bank have been very heavy and a Committee was raised in order to inquire into them and produce the result which they did. The losses have been considerable and owing to the state of the times, not unattended however with some negligence on the part of the Directors. To punish this negligence an attempt was made to remove the present Board of Directors and elect an entirely new Set. I did not very well see the expediency of such a measure, as it seemed to me hazardous to bring an entirely new set into the management of a Capital so large as this, at a time when all property of this kind is in very depressed circumstances, but I thought it would be expedient to make a partial change in order to serve as a warning to the old Directors, and to bring in some new who had a deeper interest in the Capital Stock of the Company—It being a singular fact that six of the Directors have but forty two shares in the aggregate. That is to say that one half the board own about 2500 dollars in a Capital of 1800,000. I voted therefore eight of the old Board with four others of the New List whom I supposed to possess the most Capital in the Company.

This took much of the morning, the rest was spent in a Call upon Mr. Brooks, where I talked about things in general, and in Conversation with Thomas B. Adams Jr. who called and sat with me for an hour or so. He returns to Charleston, leaving this tomorrow, his furlough being about to expire. I was unable to do any thing this afternoon as he again called at my house shortly after I had commenced my afternoon's occupation and remained until after tea. He came to take leave of Abby before going away. I know too well what it is, not to feel somewhat sympathizing for him. Passed the evening with Abby at Mr. Frothingham's, and enjoyed much a little Supper which we had.

[1] JQA owned at this time sixty shares and CFA seven shares of stock in the State Bank. They had been purchased at par: $60 a share. See vol. 2:286 and M/CFA/3.

TUESDAY. 20TH.

Morning at the Office. A man named Brown called upon me about this eternal business of George's, and I was obliged to go over the same business with him that I did with Dr. Storer and satisfied him as little. I then went down to the State Bank and found that all the Directors had been elected yesterday with the exception of Mr. Henshaw,[1] who upon hearing it had withdrawn. I do not know but this may be on the whole the most desirable result. There is no fault attaching to the

Directors and they have had warning enough to prevent their negligence, hereafter. The trial today was between Mr. David Ellis and Mr. John Henshaw brother of the late Director.[2] I knew nothing of either, but as the Bank had lost by the Jackson partiality of the former [director] I thought the best course was to prevent any political bias influencing a man's mercantile transactions, Mr. Ellis as I presume, not being partial on any side. As the meeting was small and nothing likely to be done on the subject of the application for a renewal of the Charter, I returned to the Office and busied myself arranging my papers which have fallen into great confusion. My Office is now cleared of the rubbish which was to go to Quincy and I shall now feel as if I could sit down and pursue my regular occupations more methodically. I called in and paid a short visit to Mr. Brooks. These calls are a little irksome for they are always interrupting the busy time of a person always busy. I do not think myself ever at liberty to say more than a brief inquiry after Mrs. Brooks, and often feel as if I was intruding to do that.

Afternoon at home. Tried to divide my time so as to read a little, write a little, and arrange a little. Commenced making a Catalogue of my Books, which will be a considerable labour. Read some of the Commencement of the Book on Animals published by the Society for Useful and Entertaining Knowledge in England and was interested by it.[3] The account is simple and pleasing. The evening was however passed in visiting Mrs. E. Brooks and Mrs. F. Parkman, the latter is a Cousin of Abby's, sister to Miss Hall.[4] Her husband is a singular man, quite in character with the rest of the family in eccentricity, but withal a man of good and charitable feelings. Returned home to read my Chapters in the new Testament before retiring.

[1] David Henshaw, collector of customs at Boston (*Boston Directory*, 1829–1830).

[2] David Ellis, merchant, and John Henshaw of Henshaw & Co., druggists, of 21 and 33 India Wharf, respectively (*Boston Directory*, 1829–1830).

[3] In 1829 the Society for the Diffusion of Useful Knowledge, London, began publication of *The Library of Entertaining Knowledge* with a volume on quadrupeds entitled *The Menageries.*

CFA's set, 51 vols., London, 1829–1838, is in MQA.

[4] Mrs. Francis Parkman, formerly Caroline Hall (b. 1794), was the daughter of Nathaniel Hall and Joanna Cotton (Brooks) Hall, and a sister of Mary Brooks Hall. Her husband was minister of the New North Church, Hanover Street (Congregational); their son, Francis Parkman, was the future historian (*DAB*). They lived on Somerset Place (*Boston Directory*, 1829–1830).

WEDNESDAY. 21ST.

Morning clear but cold. The weather being of that fine Autumnal kind of which we have now so much. To a man in the vigour of health, no climate is more agreeable than this at the present season, though when any thing like debility exists the keen air becomes too searching. A great change has taken place in my frame in this regard, for I now relish with much satisfaction the air which two years since cut through me. At the Office, where I wrote a Letter to my Father upon the subjects on which I required information, the rumford and the Boston property,[1] at the same time intimating an intention of going to Quincy this week which I upon seeing Mr. Brooks afterwards, regretted as I decided upon going to Medford.

I then walked to the South End of Boston in order to inquire about Mrs. Bittner whom I had long since sued and had execution against her.[2] She pleads poverty and I have too much heart to make a lawyer. I must give her time. From thence I went to the Store of Messrs. John D. and M[oses] Williams[3] to make an inquiry about some Wine for ordinary use. I tasted some which I thought quite good, but deferred a decision until I should be able to see one of the gentlemen themselves. My walk did me a great deal of good, and I returned home to dine with a good appetite.

The afternoon was occupied in reading La Harpe and forming Castles in the Air about a review on the subject of eloquence, which I am resolved to attempt even if I never show it. To this effect I have laid down a course of some length for myself. Continued my Catalogue. In the evening I read to Abby the lives of Goldsmith and Johnson in Scott's Biography of the Novelists. She took much interest in them and I was paid for my labour. She is capable of being made an exceedingly fine and sensible girl, but her powers have been suffered to run to waste in the endeavour to support her natural disposition. My affection for her increases. Finished the Gospel of St. Mark and began that of Luke this evening.

[1] Letter missing. JQA, in acknowledging its receipt, indicates that CFA asked JQA's wishes on further expenditure for the installation of the Rumford stove in his kitchen and on the policy to be followed in dealing with tenants in view of the likelihood of numerous vacancies (22 Oct., Adams Papers).
[2] Probably Elizabeth Bittner, dyer, of 560 Washington Street (*Boston Directory*, 1829–1830). CFA had sued Mrs. Bittner on behalf of his tenant, Daniel Hollis. Efforts to collect the judgment were protracted; see numerous entries, below.
[3] Wine merchants, they were at 757 Washington Street (*Boston Directory*, 1829–1830).

THURSDAY. 22D.

I accomplished more this morning than usual before going to the Office, and my library in which my servant had made a Fire was so comfortable I regretted exceedingly to leave it. At the Office my time was better spent than usual as I completed a considerable portion of Marshall on the nature of Warranty in Insurance notwithstanding a number of interruptions from various people, some calling for Money, others about the Tenement which Orcutt is about to vacate. This seems to be in much demand as no less than three people have been this morning for it in addition to others heretofore. The only danger in these cases is as to the admission of persons of doubtful character or credit, no security being required. I saw a person today whom I should be willing to admit, as she looked tolerably respectable. The morning passed in this manner rapidly until I found it had reached the time when I promised to go to Medford with Abby. I was obliged therefore to hurry home and found myself just in time. We had a pleasant though a cold ride, as I had not clothed myself as a man should in these times. But in walking in the sun in town, the weather is deceptive. We found Mr. and Mrs. Brooks as usual, Chardon and his Wife, and Mr. Burnap, the Clergyman in Baltimore, a very disagreeable man.[1] My appetite was somewhat improved by the Country Air, and on the whole we did justice to the fare. Judge and Mrs. Lyman of North-ampton came in after dinner and passed the afternoon.[2] They are friends of Mr. and Mrs. Brooks and he is an agreeable and gentle-manly man. At this season the sun sets early and as Abby was desirous of returning home before night, we started at about sunset, and stopping only a moment at Mr. Everett's to find them not at home, we reached our own house to take Tea and for me afterwards to read a little of La Harpe with the usual five Chapters of St. Luke.

[1] Rev. George Washington Burnap, a distant kinsman of Peter C. Brooks, was a nephew of Massachusetts governor John Brooks (d. 1825); see vol. 1:238, 2:155; JQA, Diary, 26 Aug. 1827; Brooks, Farm Journal, 26 Aug. 1827, 22 Oct. 1829.

[2] Probably Levi Lyman, chairman of commissioners and register of deeds, Hampshire co. (*Mass. Register*, 1829).

FRIDAY. 23D.

Morning fine, with the ground covered with a brilliant white frost, which in it's appearance resembled snow. At the Office, Mr. Orcutt called to ask me about the applications for his house and to remon-strate against the admission of a certain Mrs. Wells one of the appli-cants.[1] I cut him short being obliged to go according to appointment to see Mrs. Lewis. She commenced as all Tenants do by abusing the House and finished by requiring repairs and a diminution of rent. The lease of this House by Dr. Lewis expires on the 13th of December, and the rent has hitherto been punctually and fully paid. Rents have fallen and I think it myself very doubtful whether this House could longer be let at it's present rate.[2] I promised however to refer the matter to my father. On returning to my Office, I found two applicants for the Tenement, both anxious to take it, and having heard a very good character of Mrs. Wells from Dr. Lewis who offered to be bound for her rent, I thought this better evidence than Orcutt's and so admitted her, so that this Tenement has not been a moment on my hands. Should I make arrangements with Mrs. Lewis, the House and Store in Court Street will be the only things [left?][3] of my anticipated trouble. I had time also to read a portion of Marshall, but not with steady or fixed attention. Afternoon at home, reading La Harpe on the Writings of Demosthenes and Cicero, subject of eloquence. I attempted a commencement of my project but was dissatisfied with the result. Continued my Catalogue. Miss Julia Gorham took tea here after which I read the account of the Cat tribe in the Library of Entertaining Knowledge.

[1] Mrs. M. Wells did become the occupant of Tenement No. 3 at 101 Tremont Street, remaining until 13 Aug. 1830. Her monthly rent of $12.50 was, in general, paid promptly (M/CFA/3).

[2] Dr. Winslow Lewis, the husband or son of Mrs. Harriet Lewis, was unsuccessful in securing a reduction in the annual rental of $450 for the house at 105 Tremont Street. When the house became vacant, CFA was able on 1 April 1830 to obtain a rental of only $375 (M/CFA/3).

[3] Word omitted in MS.

SATURDAY 24TH.

Morning at the Office as usual. Occupied myself in reading Marshall as much as I could, but owing to frequent interruptions was impeded somewhat in my progress as well as understanding of it. My father came in to talk of a variety of things and to ask me to go to Quincy with him which was arranged. I then seized the opportunity to consult him about his property here and the disposition of it and he gave me Carte blanche with it as he always does with his Agents. No wonder that they have cheated him. But as it is my intention to do by him as faithfully as I should were the case my own, I feel rather heavily the weight of the responsibility. Mr. Orcutt again called to intimate to me that I had admitted a bad tenant and to tell me he had not yet succeeded in raising any Money, a much more important and less agreeable piece of information. I told him to make another effort and if that did not succeed I would then myself take the Mortgage he offered as his Security. This with the payment of one or two small demands against my Father which were presented and one Post Office Account rather larger than I could quite comprehend, passed the morning.

My father dined with me as did John Gorham, brother of Miss

Julia.[1] Dinner much as usual excepting that I thought Abby made a little too much display, for the occasion and for my economical feelings. The weather was mild so that we rode to Quincy with my father after sunset without being uncomfortable, and that too by the way of Milton as we did before when I confess I suffered a little. We reached my father's to take tea, found Miss Smith as usual, and Mr. William Greenleaf who is now occupied as secretary to my father, in copying the papers which Thomas left.[2] He is not uninteresting. We snatched a moment to look at my father's library which is gradually developing itself.[3]

[1] John Warren Gorham was a student at Harvard, class of 1832. In addition to the intimacy of ABA and Julia Gorham, the families were close. Mrs. Brooks (Ann Gorham) was a cousin of Dr. John Gorham, Julia's father. The Brookses' son, Ward Chipman, between 1822 and 1826 studied medicine in Dr. Gorham's office. Following the death of Dr. Gorham in March 1829, Peter C. Brooks contributed toward John's schooling for several years. See Brooks, Waste Book, 8 Aug. 1822, 26 May 1826, 27 March 1829.

[2] William Cranch Greenleaf (1801–1868), grandnephew of AA, succeeded his cousin, Thomas Boylston Adams Jr., as amanuensis. See vol. 1:434 and Adams Genealogy.

[3] JQA's diary entries reveal that since the arrival of his books he had been engaged assiduously in unpacking the trunks and boxes and shelving the volumes. According to Bemis, there were 5,000 to 6,000 books in the collection (*JQA*, 2:188). The want of space to house it properly caused JQA to call it "l'embarras des Richesses; I have been half a century, as greedy of books as Helluo was of the Salmon's belly. No such Library exists in the hands of any other individual in the United States; but I have never had the enjoyment of it; nor can I expect to have it now or hereafter for the remnant of my days. ... The want of a place in which a Library can be stowed is an inconvenience which nothing but wealth can escape. A large house; and a very large Apartment are indispensable. These I shall probably never possess, and must make up my mind to finish my days without them" (Diary, 17 Oct. 1829).

SUNDAY 25TH.

The morning was bright and fair and the air as mild as Summer, so that I enjoyed the day considerably. We all attended Divine Service both in the morning and the afternoon and heard Mr. Whitney preach two Sermons of very indifferent interest. He is a preacher who looks ill suited to his new Pulpit and does not raise the character of the mind in it's aspirations after good.[1]

But the most remarkable incident of the day was the first appearance of the Tablet which my Father has caused to be erected to the memory of his Father and Mother. It is very pretty and quite ornamental although in the utmost simplicity. The inscription was written by him, and is chaste and simple, merely recalling the dates and the incidents which made their lives so peculiarly memorable.[2] I felt perhaps an undue elation upon seeing it but what is the objection. They earned their reward and it is but a humble one after all, and why should not I feel proud that they merited the distinction among men.[3]

Much of the day was passed in conversation with my father upon subjects of more immediate importance, relating to his affairs, and afterwards in examining his numerous books of which he has a fine Collection. They are selected generally with judgment and to great advantage, being rare and not elsewhere to be obtained. My passion for literature was much increased by the sight of the many books which surrounded me, all of which I felt as if I was anxious to read, and most of which it is more than probable I never shall touch. For what is the life of man and especially of one who has duties of other kinds to perform. All this was a little dull to Abby, especially the refined tone of Conversation of my father which is perhaps a little too literary now for the taste of the present age. My own information is often puzzled by it. But as I am fond of instruction, I like this means of enlarging it. The evening was passed at home. One or two visitors came in, Mr. Beale and Mr. Daniel Greenleaf,[4] but they soon left us, and I passed an hour reading Mrs. Thrale's Correspondence with Dr. Johnson.[5]

[1] On Peter Whitney, minister of the First Church in Quincy since 1800, see vol. 1:157. The pulpit was that in the new stone edifice, in use for almost a year.

[2] JQA had asked for CFA's and ABA's presence on the occasion, also the anniversary of the marriage of JA and AA, "as a special favour and if I may presume so far, would put it in the form of a Mandamus, and command you to come 'Laying all other things aside' " (to CFA, 22 Oct., Adams Papers; JQA, Diary, 25 October). The bust of JA in white marble by Horatio Greenough (vol. 2:400; JQA, Diary, 20 June 1829) and the tablet beneath, on which Alpheus Cary had carved JQA's tribute to his father and to his mother (vol. 2:399 and entry for 23 Sept., above), had been put into place only on the preceding Thursday. On that day JQA had also had their names carved on the granite stones in the crypt to which their remains had been removed from the churchyard on 1 April 1828 during the construction of the Adams Temple (JQA, Diary, 22 Oct. 1829; Bemis, JQA, 2:187). The tablet and bust are illustrated in Daniel Munro Wilson, *The*

"Chappel of Ease" and Church of Statesmen [Quincy], 1890, facing p. 103; the inscription printed in Bemis, JQA, 2:125 (where the text is incorrect in one particular: the date of AA's birth given on the tablet is "November 11/22 1744"). See also *Portraits of John and Abigail Adams,* p. 231–232, 234.

[3] The self-reproach of pride in the erection of the memorial, evident in JQA's diary as well as here, is the more understandable from the fact that "There are few such monuments existing in this Country, and indeed very few Churches of durable structure, in which they could be placed. There are three in the Stone Chapel at Boston—All of ante or anti-revolutionary personages." It was after an inspection of these with Cary that JQA decided upon the form the memorial would take, deriving it principally from the monument to the wife and daughter of a colonial governor, William Shirley. (JQA, Diary, 9, 18 July, 22 Oct. 1829.)

[4] George W. Beale (1782–1851) in 1792 had built a house just to the west of the Old House on Adams Street, Quincy. At least two sketches by him, one of the Old House and one of Mount

Wollaston, survive; see further, vol. 2:151.

Daniel Greenleaf (1762–1853), an apothecary and doctor, had been a Quincy resident since 1797; see vol. 2:153 and NEHGS, *Memorial Biogra-*

phies, 2:34–37.

[5] Hester Lynch (Thrale) Piozzi, *Letters to and from Samuel Johnson ...*, London, 1786. There is a copy of the 1788 edn. in 2 vols. in MQA.

MONDAY. 26TH.

It was impossible to desire a more agreeable day than this. The air was soft and entirely different from that which is our usual climate at this season. I cannot help enjoying it's mildness, though I am far from complaining of that which is more severe. After breakfast Abby and I returned to town in the little Carriage. I went to the Office as usual and spent the morning in reading Marshall without much interruption, Mr. Clapp, the Mason being the only person who came, in order to inquire at what time he could go to Quincy which I told him.[1] I had expected to see Orcutt but was disappointed.

After dinner, Abby and I went to pay a visit to Mr. and Mrs. Alex. H. Everett who have just arrived from Spain.[2] He is one of those who have suffered proscription by the New powers and is now arrived to see what he can do with himself here. I confess for my own part that I do not easily perceive any cause for him which would be at all eligible. He has not what may be called an active character and here what can be done without one? He looks very well and has grown quite showy in his dress since I last saw him. She has become quite European and a little affected, I think, but always a pleasant woman. Our visit was short and I returned to my study to commence operations seriously as a student. I devoted a short time to continuing my Catalogue and then opened the subject which I am about to commence with the study of Auger's preliminary Dissertation to the Works of Demosthenes.[3] Singular as it may seem to myself I am resolved to attempt the Orations for the Crown in the Original.[4] And I started in the Work fairly today. This is the only way to begin the subject of Oratory with any view to understand. I studied uninterruptedly until nine, when I went to Mr. Frothingham's for Abby who passed the Evening there. Edward Brooks was there and we had a comfortable Supper enough.

[1] James Clapp of Chambers Street, near Poplar, Boston, contracted to do repairs at the Old House to the kitchen and chimney, for which he was paid $60 on 19 Nov. (*Boston Directory,* 1829–1830; M/CFA/3).

[2] Alexander Hill Everett (1790–1847), a brother of Edward Everett, had been a law student in JQA's office and subsequently JQA's private secretary in Russia. During JQA's administration he had been chargé d'affaires at The Hague and most recently minister to Spain. Within the year he would become, with his brother-in-law Nathan Hale, owner and editor of the *North American Review*. His wife was the former Lucretia Orne Peabody. See vol. 1:294–295;

DAB. Whether the Everetts were already living in their house at 38 Summer Street is doubtful (*Boston Directory,* 1830–1831).

[3] Demosthenes and Æschines, *Oeuvres complètes, trad. en françois ... par M. l'abbé Auger.* The edition published at Paris, 6 vols., 1793, owned by JQA, is in MQA. Auger's "discours préliminaire" is at 1:1–151.

[4] Æschines and Demosthenes, *The Orations on the Crown.* An edition in the original Greek with English notes by Alex Negris was published at Boston in 1829; the copy in MQA has CFA's bookplate and numerous marginal notes in his hand.

CFA's translation, here begun, was carried on until early January (CFA to JQA, 10 Jan. 1830, Adams Papers). A fragment of the translation of Æschines is preserved in CFA's literary commonplace book (Adams Papers, Microfilms, Reel No. 312); of Demosthenes, among some papers on eloquence in a folder of literary efforts (Adams Papers, Microfilms, Reel No. 317).

TUESDAY. 27TH.

Morning fine but colder as the warm Clouds had dissolved in rain during the night and left us a Clear sky. I went to the Office as usual and was less interrupted than common. P. P. F. Degrand came in to give me my Newspaper which he had taken from my box to take to Quincy but as he did not go, he returned it to me. He told me that Mr. John Hubbard had yesterday assigned his goods and chattels away to others in order to rid himself of his liabilities as a Member of the Canton Factory.[1] A fraudulent proceeding as I suspect though it will not be considered as censurable by the majority of men. That does not alter the stubborn nature of the fact. I then went to obtain the numbers of the Gazette containing the notice of the Estate of Thomas Boylston, for my Father, and tried to see Mr. Tarbell about the remnant of my Law business but I could not find him.[2] The rest of the morning occupied in reading Marshall on Insurance—The nature of loss, and general average. There is little satisfaction in reading over particular cases when the principles are the desirable things. And the principles of Insurance lay in a pretty narrow compass.

In the afternoon, having worked an hour upon my Catalogue, I sat down and finished Auger's preliminary discourse, after which I was induced to look into Mitford and became again infinitely provoked with his impudent perversion of History.[3] This consumed the two hours devoted to study in the Afternoon, and the Evening was passed with my Wife. She begins to feel the irksome loneliness of new married life considerably and this produces occasional depression of spirits. I regret it particularly as I fear now there will not be a termination to these sufferings and that my dread will be realized, but I still trust not.[4] Evening closed with five Chapters of Luke.

[1] The factory failure is probably that of the Neponset Woollen Co. in Canton, Mass., which under the presidency of Harrison Gray Otis had been formed in

1827 to take over the plant of the Boston Manufacturing Co. after its failure. See Daniel T. V. Huntoon, *History of the Town of Canton*, Cambridge, 1893, p. 545–546. The slump in textile manufactures, with resultant failures, was so severe in 1829 that various stratagems were resorted to, including giving away shares of stock, to avoid assessments. See Caroline F. Ware, *The Early New England Cotton Manufacture*, Boston, 1931, p. 91–92, 134–135. John Hubbard was probably the merchant of that name residing at 7 Somerset Street; see entry for 28 Sept., above.

[2] Thomas Tarbell was married to Lucy Tufts, daughter of Cotton Tufts Jr. (1757–1833) and Mercy Brooks (1763–1849) who were doubly related to AA. See Adams Genealogy. CFA had had a room at the Tarbell home, 11 Avon Place, from 10 Nov. 1828 to 23 June 1829, and friendly relations had been maintained. Tarbell, an importer and merchant, had interested himself in and sought to forward CFA's legal progress both by putting small claims for collection into his hands and by sending him other clients with claims to be prosecuted. Those claims, aside from his work on matters relating to JQA's affairs and as his agent, seem to have constituted the sum of CFA's practice during his first year or two at the bar. See numerous mentions in vol. 2; and below, entries for 30 Oct. 1829–1 Feb. 1830 *passim*.

[3] William Mitford, *The History of Greece*, which CFA read while at Harvard, is frequently mentioned in vols. 1 and 2.

[4] See below, entry for 8 Nov. and note.

WEDNESDAY 28TH.

Morning cool but fine. At the Office as usual and but little interrupted. A Copy of the Life of Arthur Lee being left here for my Father I was tempted to look over it to find the papers which were said to relate to some misunderstandings between the American Mission in France during the revolution. I had heard the disclosures were important but I found little that was new. This is a new publication from the pen of R. H. Lee.[1] Richardson called in for a few moments but had little or nothing new. Orcutt called to tell me he could not raise the money, but did not yet despair. I suppose I shall be compelled to take his property. He then talked upon other subjects so as to detain me until dinner, a practice not pleasant of his, but I think his honesty about this debt meritorious.

At home, Miss Julia Gorham dined and passed the afternoon with my Wife. I continued my Catalogue, finished Auger's Treatise upon the habits of the Greeks, read over La Harpe's Sketch of Demosthenes and nibbled at the beginning of Æschines, but as it was late, I postponed the attack until tomorrow when I am resolved to begin. In looking at the Greek today I felt a little more encouraged about it, and gave myself a little more credit than I did for my acquisition at College. Miss Julia Gorham remained here until after tea when Abby went to pass the Evening at her sister Susan's, and I accompanied her. We found Mrs. Frothingham there and Chardon and her husband soon after came in. We had as usual a little sociable Supper and a very pleasant time. These things are always agreeable because they are easy. And I feel now very differently about them than when I was engaged for I feel as if I had a kind of right to be considered a part of the family, and therefore much less sensitive as to the opinions which may be formed of my conduct.

[1] Richard Henry Lee, *Life of Arthur Lee, LL.D. . . . With His Political and Literary Correspondence*, 2 vols., Boston, 1829. The author was a great-nephew of Arthur Lee; his biography was based on the extensive papers of the Lees in his custody and was one of the earliest (and most unsatisfactory) compilations of sources for the Revolutionary history of the United States. Lee dedicated the work to John Quincy Adams, stating in his dedicatory letter that JQA would find in Arthur Lee's writings "a spirit of patriotism congenial with your own." The copy of the biography in MHi was presented by CFA in 1849. CFA had a natural interest in Arthur Lee's correspondence because Lee and JA had, together with Franklin, been fellow commissioners from the Continental Congress at Paris in 1778–1779, had corresponded extensively, and had made common cause in the bitter and protracted dispute over the conduct of Silas Deane, JA's predecessor as joint commissioner. For JA's contemporaneous and retrospective accounts and views of the "misunderstandings" to which CFA alludes, see JA, *Diary and Autobiography*, 2:304 ff., 345–350; 4:43, 68 ff.

THURSDAY 29TH.

Morning chilly and many Clouds reminding us of the rapid approach of Winter. I was at my Office all the morning and occupied in reading a part of the Memoir of Arthur Lee which is interesting. He certainly took a very considerable part in the early Stages of the revolution and that on a stage where he was in some measure alone. I found some letters from my Grandfather which struck me as favourably as any thing I had ever read of his.[1] The force and fire which was so characteristic of him are both to be found here in full strength. Arthur Lee was apparently a favourite of his. I read also a little of Marshall. My interruptions were numerous but not long. Richardson came in only for a few minutes to warm himself, Mr. Curtis with a letter for my Father which he wished to send directly and Mr. Clapp the Mason to consult about the Rumford at Quincy. My father wants every thing put into it, which will materially increase the expense and be of little use. I gave the Mason my own opinion and he went to follow it.

After dinner and continuing my Catalogue I commenced the Oration of Æschines upon the Crown and read twenty lines for my afternoon's work. It was not as difficult as I anticipated and I had time after translating them to read the Summary of Auger and his remarks upon the two Orations. My afternoon was thus well and usefully employed. Evening passed downstairs with Abby, and read the second part of the Menageries published by the Society for Useful

Knowledge containing the Account of the Camel and the Deer. But it seems to me the publication would be more useful if it took the Horse and the Cow, animals which we know by observation, but of which we may still desire information. Read five Chapters of John.

[1] Eleven letters from JA to Arthur Lee, 1778–1788, are printed in R. H. Lee's *Life of Arthur Lee*, 2:242–262; see note on preceding entry.

FRIDAY 30TH.

Morning at the Office, a Cold Storm threatening us all day. I was engaged in reading the Memoirs of Arthur Lee which I found quite interesting. The foreign transactions of the United States are fully developed in them, with some slight reflection upon the character of Franklin. This is not much of a favourite with me. There is too much selfishness in his philosophy, though I do not doubt that it has been serviceable in the world.[1] My interruptions this morning were numerous. Mr. Tarbell came up to see me having heard I had called once or twice. I inquired what was to be done with Titcomb who has been so long on my hands,[2] and with the other accounts which I have in my possession; he told me to begin again with the first and do as well as I could with the others. He sat with me talking half an hour pleasantly enough upon subjects in general, and then gave way to Col. Davis, who came to ask when my father would be in town for he wished to see him to which I gave as a reply that I could not tell. Mr. Danl. Hollis is the Carpenter superintending my father's houses and called to get instructions as heretofore directed. I went to look at the House behind the Office and found it in wretched condition. I told him that at present nothing could be done, that I must wait until the present tenancy expired, but that then I expected him to do a great deal. Luckily I have contrived to run up against him as I have indeed with all the Tenants, a pretty heavy bill of arrears for rent, and this will go a good way towards the expenses for repairs which will now be found necessary.

Dined at Mr. Frothingham's with Abby. Nobody else. Tolerably pleasant although nothing remarkable. But I felt more at home. We were amused with a letter from Sidney Brooks' wife to mine, full of her usual nothings.[3] After dinner, I walked again to the Store of Messrs. John D. and M. Williams and succeeded this time in making a selection of some Wine. I purchased some Sherry at two dollars the gallon, thinking that if it turned out well I should then like to keep some of it as choice Wine, which I could not do if I bought cheaper, however fine it might prove. There is much Charlatanerie about Wine especially in the name. And I have seen so much of it as to induce me to make an experiment thereupon.[4] Returned to my Study too late to do anything in the regular way, so I continued La Harpe's Analysis of Cicero's Orations, until late, when I again went to Mr. Frothingham's to call for my Wife. The night was very stormy but we reached home before the floods came.

[1] For a brilliant, though thoroughly partisan, elaboration of this judgment on Franklin's character, see CFA's account of JA's relations with Franklin written a quarter of a century later, in JA, *Works*, 1:317–320.

[2] The claim against Titcomb, after numerous delays, was succesfully concluded. See entry for 23 Dec., below.

[3] Letter missing. CFA's general practice when he became custodian of the family's papers seems to have been to destroy letters that had been addressed to Adams wives, except letters written by members of the family.

[4] The intent seems to be related to a request to JA2 contained in an affectionate letter to LCA, to obtain "Antoine's mixture" for wine cooling. However, the effort proved abortive because Antoine Giusta, still employed as valet in the White House, informed the family that "by order he can have no intercourse with ours" (CFA to LCA, 30 Oct.; LCA to CFA, 15 Nov., Adams Papers). On Antoine Giusta see vol. 1:84 and Bemis, *JQA*, 2:159.

SATURDAY 31ST.

The first incident which happened this morning was a fire, and not far from my House. We heard the alarm which proved to be from a house next to that occupied by Mr. Thomas Perkins, commonly called short Tom.[1] It was kept under, luckily for had it once burst out, the wind was so high that in all probability the whole block would have been consumed. I went to the Office in the midst of a violent Storm of rain, and enjoyed a very comfortable portion of time in examining the Life of Arthur Lee, especially the Documents, which are very interesting as they respect the History of our Revolution. Mr. T. Welsh came in to speak to me about the purchase of his former residence in Hancock Street, which is offered now for Sale at five thousand dollars.[2] I made several inquiries about the property, and satisfied myself that it would on the whole be a very safe purchase—And if possible intend to prevail upon my father to purchase it. It would prove better property than his Stock in the State Bank and might prevent his transferring the money to Washington on less safe speculations. I hope to see about it next Week.

My father himself made his appearance and upon my proposing it seemed to relish the plan without giving me definite instructions upon it. He came in through the Storm, in order to despatch a letter to Mr. Vaughan on the business of the Estate of Thomas Boylston,[3] and to do some other business in relation to that Estate. As he was here I sent for

Col. J. B. Davis who had some conversation with him upon the present state of political affairs highly interesting to me. Poor Davis feels himself in a very bad pickle, for he now does not know what course to take and whom to support and therefore feels restless until he can get some ground to stand upon. The prospect of the promotion of Otis to the government of the State seems to provoke him no little—And well it may.[4] My father dined with me and was disposed to remain all night but John, his Servant was obliged to return so that he decided to go through a very disagreeable storm. I lost the afternoon for study, and so was obliged to satisfy myself with a little of La Harpe, who gives the Orations against Verres and Catiline, a due share of attention. Evening, read to Abby the beginning of Clarissa Harlowe,[5] and closed as usual with five Chapters of John.

[1] Thomas Perkins lived on Sumner (afterwards Mount Vernon) Street which bounded Hancock Avenue at one end (*Boston Directory*, 1829–1830). CFA gives his familiar name, perhaps to distinguish him from Thomas Handasyd Perkins, father and son.

[2] Thomas Welsh Jr. (1779–1831) was a son of Dr. Thomas Welsh (1752–1831) and his second wife, Abigail Kent (1750–1824), who was a first cousin of AA (vol. 1:15, 99). Along with Harriet (d. 1857), a daughter of his first marriage, Dr. Welsh and Thomas had lived at 20 Hancock Street (*Boston Directory*, 1828–1829). GWA had rented a room there and lived at the house at the time of his death. Although Thomas, an attorney, continued to have his office at 23 Court Street, JQA's building, he had earlier in 1829 had severe reverses, been imprisoned for debt, and lost his property (vol. 2:375, 399). On those members of the Welsh family mentioned, see also Adams Genealogy.

[3] JQA to Petty Vaughan, 31 Oct. (LbC, Adams Papers).

[4] John Brazer Davis (d. 1832) was editor of the *Boston Patriot* (1824–1831) and a long-time political supporter of JQA. See Bemis, *JQA*, 2:22, 206; and MHS, *Procs.* 49 (1915–1916):

178–256. His purpose at this meeting was to persuade JQA to allow him to publish immediately the "Reply to the Appeal of the Massachusetts Federalists" (JQA, Diary, 31 Oct.), which JQA had written earlier in 1829 while his defeat was still sharply felt and which was particularly bitter in its charges against Harrison Gray Otis. Those of JQA's friends who had seen the document had advised against its publication; Davis however, in order to bolster his position, would seem to have been overstating the likelihood of another Otis campaign for the governorship. Otis, the mayor of Boston, had left the state scene after the decisive defeat of the Federalists in 1824.

JQA's reaction to the plea to publish was "to wait yet sometime" (JQA, Diary, 31 Oct.). The "Reply" remained unpublished until 1877, when HA included it with the other documents in the controversy in *New England Federalism, q.v.* p. v–vii. See also Bemis, *JQA*, 2:167–176; Morison, *H. G. Otis*, 2:243–246, 249–251.

Davis was to be further identified with the Adamses in antimasonic politics of 1830–1831 and as an early encourager of CFA to write for publication.

[5] JQA's bookplate is in the London edition, 2 vols., 1795, in MQA.

SUNDAY. NOVEMBER 1ST.

The morning was misty and wet, with the air cold and chilly. I attended Divine Service alone all day, at Mr. Frothingham's, and heard him deliver two Sermons, the one in the Morning upon the character and sufferings of Christ adapted to the service of the Communion, the other in the afternoon upon the inutility of the many controversies of the day upon abstractions. I agree with him in this, and approved the Sermon much. He stands almost alone in this doctrine however, as the Church here on all sides is rather of a Church militant. And this is probably one reason why as he makes no exciting stir, he makes no proselytes. I do not pretend to influence any man's opinion but I think it would be desirable on all sides that peace should be the offspring of religious belief, for otherwise it rather hardens than improves bad passions. I read on my return home, Jeremy Taylor's Exhortation to the Imitation of the Life of Jesus Christ.[1] He is a powerful writer of the old school, and his piety and earnestness make a warm style which is at once pleasing and affecting. He is clear withal and lays down rules of moral conduct applicable to human life, which is after all the great end of religion if preachers would but remember it. I read also Walpole's Castle of Otranto which I have long ago read, and I confess was better pleased with it from memory than from the re-perusal.[2] In the evening continued reading Clarissa Harlowe to Abby, and finished the Gospels.

[1] A part of the matter prefatory (1:3–17) to the *Life of Christ.*
[2] Horace Walpole's famous "Gothic" novel, first published 1764.

MONDAY 2D.

I had two hours of this morning tolerably uninterrupted in which time I read much of the rules of Pleading in Marshall's Law of Insurance. The weather was very chilly and disagreeable, a continuation of the storm of Saturday which in it's effects proves much worse than I had supposed it to be. Mr. Curtis came in, to learn what my father desired to see him about on Saturday which I told him and he seemed quite sorry. It does not amount to much after all.[1] Col. Jones the Auctioneer at Weston came to notify me that a sale of the Wood at Weston would take place on the 13th day of this month. I was glad to hear of this as I began to be apprehensive that I should not get the business done and it is desirable on account of my father's situation that it should bring him some Money. I can hardly dare to hope although it is worth a considerable sum. The sale I shall feel obliged to attend. He had not left me before Titcomb came, being brought up by my threat that I would prosecute him directly. I got nothing out of him but promises, which he supposed might go down smoother from the circumstance of his bringing a Client with him. A certain Captain

Lufkin who wanted to get his share of a Mackerel trip which he had earned some time in the year 1824. This is the first Client I have had since my Marriage. His case is a doubtful one, and after examination, I postponed a decision until he obtained stronger papers, which he promised to do and then left me.[2] My Uncle, T. B. Adams called and finding me so busy went away again. He was doubtless a little surprised. Thus my morning was fully taken up.

After dinner, I continued my Catalogue, and read another portion of the Oration of Æschines which was a little more difficult. I believe I mastered it at last. As Abby had gone out, I had two hours more which I spent in reading La Harpe on the remainder of Cicero. This Author writes well, but was too full of the French revolution not to crowd in much matter foreign from his subject, which however interesting to an auditory politically excited, agrees little with calm literary disquisition. I came across a violent tirade against the excesses of Robespierre, this evening, which find their true place not in discussions of Oratory but in History. At eight I went through the rain to Mrs. Frothingham's for Abby, and found there, Mr. and Mrs. Everett, Mr. and Mrs. Edward Brooks, Mr. and Mrs. Frothingham and Abby. We had a little Supper and on the whole a pleasant time, but I felt a little silent. I do not know how it is but there is something about the singular character of Mr. Everett that shuts me up completely. Returned at ten.

[1] The papers of administration of the estate of Thomas Boylston which JQA had sent to Petty Vaughan on 29 Sept. not having reached him, JQA had on the 31st, without Curtis' help, secured a duplicate set, had them authenticated at the offices of Probate and of the Secretary of the Commonwealth, and turned them over to CFA for dispatch by the *Amethyst* sailing the next day (JQA, Diary, 31 Oct.).

[2] Nothing further is heard of Captain Lufkin's claim unless the action taken by CFA against a member of the crew of the ship *Gold Hunter* is in pursuit of it. See entry for 16 Nov., below.

TUESDAY. 3RD.

Morning rainy and weather appearing much as it has done for some time back, Previous to my going to the Office I called upon Mrs. Lewis in the House at the Corner of Common Street to ascertain her determination with respect to it as her Lease expires shortly. She begged for time until the Spring to move, provided I would make a reduction of one third in her rent, which I did not feel myself authorized to do, so that after some talk, I found to my regret that this House was also to be upon my hands. I therefore quitted her, to go to my Office and write some advertisements for the Patriot and Daily Advertiser which I carried down myself to those Newspapers.[1] I have now two houses which become empty on the opening of the year and my Father will lose two hundred and sixty dollars a quarter until they are filled, which is something of a loss. And I am to have the trouble of directing the repairs which must infallibly be considerable. The rest of the morning was passed quietly at my Office, and I read Marshall pleasantly enough, and made some further arrangements in my Accounts by which I hope to be able to form a tolerable estimate of the profits of my Father's real Estate. After dinner I read Æschines as usual and accomplished more in my short allowance of time than I had previously done on any single day. My preparatory reading has been such as materially to assist me in my labour. But it is nonetheless not at all a slight undertaking for me, more particularly the part of translation. In the evening, I read a portion of Clarissa Harlowe to my Wife who was suffering from a head ache, and afterwards continued La Harpe whose account of the two Plinies is interesting, and with them I finish the second part of his book relating to Orators.

¹ The advertisement offering to rent the house lately occupied by Dr. Winslow Lewis and the store numbered 23 Court Street with the dwelling house in the rear, to be had separately or together, appeared in the *Boston Daily Advertiser* in the issue of 4 Nov., p. 2, col. 6.

WEDNESDAY. 4TH.

Weather cleared off during the Night so that upon this morning it had turned cool and promised an entrance upon Winter. I went to the Office as usual. Had some Conversation with Mr. Welsh about the House in Hancock Street and from that diverged until we got upon the last Election and the prospects of Mr. Webster. He was explaining his agency in the matter when I was obliged to leave him to see Mr. Degrand who came up to ask if I had any orders for the sale of the State Bank Shares, belonging to my Father. I told him, No, and we then proceeded to talk upon subjects in general relating to Stocks and Property of all descriptions which he seemed to have a pretty accurate knowledge of—But talked in an ambiguous manner as all brokers do. After him Richardson called and sat a few minutes talking as usual of nothings. I engaged him to accompany me to Weston next week which he assented to. Dr. Welsh came in apparently to give me some Message but did not owing to the presence of Richardson. The remainder of the morning passed in completing Marshall on Insurance, the Chapters on the Insurance of Life and of Fire which led me to examine the Policies of the Mutual Fire Company, and I then found myself having spent the morning. Afternoon, as usual occupied with Æschines, a considerable passage of whom I read, but did not complete the whole of my task in the short time I had to perform it in. Two hours each afternoon are not a very large allowance for a study resumed after a lapse of four years or more. My time is not yet entirely employed to my satisfaction. Evening, read a part of Clarissa Harlowe, to Abby, but we were interrupted in our pursuit by the entrance of Mr. Hall, the Clergyman of Northampton, and Cousin of Abby's.[1] His was a short visit, and after it I read a Chapter of La Harpe upon the early Historians of the first Class.

[1] On Rev. Edward Brooks Hall see vol. 2:419 and entry for 8 Nov., below.

THURSDAY 5TH.

Weather cold and affording us the experience of what here may be called the second Stage of Winter. I went to the Office earlier than usual and sat there with little interruption all day. But I did little as I had forgotten to bring with me from my House the book I proposed to read. I therefore amused myself with looking over the Journal des Scavans a little old volume containing four Numbers.[1] But the reviews seemed to be for the most part Theological and uninteresting, and I considered the time as passed unprofitably on the whole.

Mr. Degrand came to know what my opinion of the sale of Stock was, which took place yesterday. I am fearful that my father will not be able to sell out just now at par as that yesterday brought but 59 and a fraction. I have therefore made no propositions and am glad of it. But Bank Stock is now so reduced that I should think it a tolerably safe investment for any person not desiring a great interest. I am on the whole well satisfied that it should be so as I do not feel alarmed about my Stock. After this I had no visitors and so I returned home earlier than usual in order to see Abby who had been unwell this morning and felt quite low spirited. I found Miss Anne Carter with her, and shortly after Mr. and Mrs. Everett came in; they all dined with us, and we had a stiff and disagreeable dinner. Why and wherefore I cannot say, but this feeling has grown on me so, that it is now absolutely intolerable. Afternoon, Occupied in study. I completed my translation which should have been made on a preceding day, and continued Æschines but finished little. I find translation easier than I thought. Words arise very rapidly. In the evening, Clarissa to Abby, after which a Chapter or two of La Harpe on the later Historians. But this branch of his subject is very quickly closed.

[1] *Journal des Sçavans par de Hédouville* [Denis de Sallo], Paris and Amsterdam, 1665–1798. In its early years published with some irregularity as a weekly or bi-weekly, it became a monthly in 1724. Of JA's set, five volumes, for parts of 1780, 1781, are now in MB.

FRIDAY. 6TH.

Weather Cold. I should like this Winter as I am now in a condition which will promise something like permanency, to set a Thermometer and record in a general way in this Book the various changes of our Climate.[1] There is much that is curious to learn from this and much that remains in the memory to future times. I went to the Office and was hardly interrupted during the whole course of the morning. I began reading Pufendorf's Devoirs de l'homme et du Citoyen,[2] being his own abridgment of his larger work, and in order to exercise my skill in writing I began a translation of the Preface, which I found easy and pleasant. My idea now is to practice writing in all shapes until I get to a state satisfactory to myself, that is a state, when my pen will be a source of confidence. I accomplished five pages, in translation, and read the whole Preface. It put me much in mind of that of Jeremy Taylor, excepting that the one merely draws the lines between Natural Law and Theology, the other bases the latter upon the principles of the former and carries them out.

My morning was satisfactory. Mr. Brooks came in for a single moment to ask me to go to Medford tomorrow to which I acceded. The remainder of the time was usefully passed. After dinner I read for two hours to my Wife instead of the usual time in the evening, in the Story of Clarissa Harlowe. It is too long and minute. Trifles seldom deserve recording excepting in a Journal where they bore only the person interested.[3] I read the usual quantity of Æschines but found him rather harder than usual. I translated all I had done [due ?] yesterday and had time for a little of the Philosophy of the Ancients in La Harpe before going to Mrs. Frothingham's after Abby who had passed the Evening there. I found them much the same and hospitable as ever, for they entertained me with Oysters and other nice things, and then we returned home.

[1] CFA did not pursue his intent.

[2] Samuel Pufendorf, *Les devoirs de l'homme et du citoyen, trad. du Latin par Jean Barbeyrac.* A copy of the 1735 Amsterdam edition in 2 vols. (MQA) has TBA's signature and JQA's bookplate. Also there, are copies of the 1718 Amsterdam and of the 1756 Amsterdam and Leipzig editions.

[3] That is, the person involved or concerned, namely, the writer himself.

SATURDAY 7TH.

The morning set in dark and hazy, and it soon began raining, and continued hard and steady during the whole day. I went down to the Office and sat there all the morning without serious interruption. I began the work of Pufendorf but unaccountably I could gain very little ground indeed in the pursuit of it. The author appeared difficult and my mind was in one of those moods when it seemed impossible to fix it to any thing permanent so that I spent the time in reading over the first Chapter without the Notes, which I postponed to some other time. But was discontented with my morning. I tried to see Mr. Brooks but could not succeed. Dr. Welsh came in for a single moment to inquire whether in making an appraisement of the books of a deceased person, they should be valued singly or in the Mass. I told him that I had in my brother's case pursued the former plan and thought it much the most advisable, but was doubtful whether it was generally practised.

After dinner, I read a considerable portion of Æschines and translated what I had read yesterday. But it occupied me fully for the entire afternoon so that I had the evening only which I passed in reading Clarissa Harlowe to Abby. This book possesses considerable interest although it does trail into interminable longueurs. Richardson had great talent at description and that until it extended to objects of the smallest and minutest nature—and his mind was not so exalted as to be able to look beyond them, at higher and more distinguished marks. I am glad to have a chance to read loud as it exercises my lungs which have been for some time unused to public delivery. After Abby retired I read La Harpe's Chapter on the Philosophy of Plutarch.

SUNDAY. 8TH.

The rain ceased during the Night but gave way only to a high Wind and chilly weather. As we were disappointed in not being able to go to Medford yesterday we determined upon going this morning. I sent and borrowed the loan of Chardon's Gig and horse, and we went out accordingly, in time to attend Meeting, and warm ourselves a little previously. We found Miss Parks there on a visit to her Aunt, otherwise the family as usual.[1] We attended at Meeting and heard Mr. Edward B. Hall, the gentleman who came to see us on Wednesday. He is in bad health, and for the first time preached today. His Sermons were tolerably well calculated for effect among an audience of commonly informed people and were practical enough. But the ideas were ordinary and common place. His powers are not very great. But he seems to have cultivated what he had with zeal and success. His illness and the destitute circumstances in which his abandoning his profession would leave him, render him rather an object for sympathy and compassion.[2] Mr. and Mrs. Everett were at Meeting in the afternoon, and were at the House for a few Moments. He seems to be a little depressed and she very considerably so. And what reason have they for such feelings; not much. But so it is, the perversion of feelings of nature. She mourns for what others and I would consider a blessing.³ In the evening, as the night was fine, Mr. Brooks asked me to go down and see Mr. Jonathan Brooks and his family, which I accordingly did with him. Mr. Jonathan was not at home, but we saw his daughters and sat with them, some time. The elder is goodnatured, but they are both foolish from a sense of blue stockingism which makes them appear to pretend more than they are worth.⁴ Mrs. Stetson, the Minister's Wife was there also.⁵ We returned early and retired soon after.

¹ Mrs. Peter C. Brooks' sister, Mrs. Warham Parks of Charlestown, had two daughters unmarried in 1829, Rebecca (d. 1837) and Elizabeth (1800–1871); see vol. 2:266.

² Rev. Edward Brooks Hall (b. 1800), of Northampton, was a son of Nathaniel Hall of Medford and his wife Joanna (1772–1841), a sister of Peter C. Brooks (vol. 2:155). The two families were close, and the Halls were recipients of financial help from Mr. Brooks. Edward's illness being diagnosed as tuberculosis, with Brooks' support he left in early January for a winter in Cuba. (Charlotte Everett to Edward Everett, 6, 27 Dec. 1829, Everett MSS, MHi; Brooks, Waste Book, 9 Jan. 1830.)

³ The birth of the Edward Everetts' third daughter in 1827 occasioned great disappointment to both parents. Mrs. Everett, again pregnant, through 1829–1830 expressed repeatedly in letters to her husband her absorbing fear that they would be denied a son. These plaints ended only when she was delivered of a boy (below, entry for 6 May 1830). CFA's desire for a child, evident here, seems to become an overriding concern of husband and wife as the months pass, though he alludes to it in the Diary generally by indirection; see, for example, entries of 27 Oct., 10, 11 Dec.

1829; 16 May 1830. The state of mind of the two "poor disconsolate children" after five months of marriage is such that in reporting to her husband a bantering but bitter exchange with them Charlotte Everett is led to reflect "Better have all girls, than no children at all!" (10 Feb. 1830, Everett MSS, MHi). After two more months she and they had concluded that ABA "will never have any. It will never do to joke her or her husband about it—for it is a very sore subject to them" (13 April 1830, same). On 10 Sept. 1830, CFA admits the bleak outlook in his Diary. When on 13 Aug. 1831 he records there the birth of their first child, he gives full expression finally to the depth of his desire.

⁴ First cousin of Peter C. Brooks, Jonathan Brooks (1765–1847) was also an Adams relative. Brother of Mercy Brooks (Mrs. Cotton Tufts Jr.) (1763–1849), he was the son of Thomas Brooks (1732–1799) and Mercy Tufts (1742–1813), AA's first cousin. See Adams Genealogy. His wife Elizabeth (Albree) had died in 1826; his daughters were Elizabeth (b. 1797) and Lucy Ann (b. 1810) (Brooks, *Medford*, p. 529).

⁵ On Rev. Caleb Stetson of Medford see vol. 2:155, 427, 433.

MONDAY. 9TH.

Morning clear and pleasant for the season. As soon after breakfast as practicable we returned to town. I was better pleased with this visit to Medford than with any previous one. After a few moments at my house, I went to the Office and sat down to read as usual. I began the first Chapter of Pufendorf again, but was soon interrupted so as to be unable to resume it again this day.

My father came in and spoke to me about a Number of things which he had desired to have done and I accordingly undertook to do his Commissions whatever they might be. He wished to see Mr. Curtis and accordingly I sent for him and as they were in my Office and conversing upon the subject of Mr. Boylston's Affairs, I was unable to do much of any thing. Nor did they go until nearly time for me to return home. Mr. Lewis came to see me as I was going with the acceptable offering of some rent—Altogether an agreeable thing. I conversed with him a little upon Mrs. Lewis' removal, in which she seemed to intimate that I had been a little too precipitate. I told him that I should like to talk with him about it, as I had no doubt but that we might agree upon the subject finally. And so there is yet hope of letting the House. Returned after depositing the Money, and upon going home, found Mr. Everett and my Father sitting with Abby. Alexander, I mean, for the other one I generally call by his name. They made us wait for dinner some time and put me no little out of humour.

In the afternoon, Mr. Frothingham came and examined my library with which he seemed not a little pleased. But I was prevented from reading or studying the whole afternoon, and in the evening, I passed the time in reading to Abby from Clarissa Harlowe, after which I completed La Harpe's Chapter upon the Philosophy of Cicero.

TUESDAY. 10TH.

Morning Cloudy and warm. I went to the Office as usual and passed my time in translating a part of the Preface of Pufendorf, but was less interested in the work and did not do it so well. There is much sense in this Preface, rather clumsily given and it is my desire to make my translation express the ideas even more clearly than the original. Whether I shall succeed I do not know, nor care, but I hope the attempt will do something to facilitate my powers of writing. They say practice makes perfect. Why not so with me? And are there many men who use themselves to it equally. I again attempted the first Chapter of Pufendorf but did not succeed in mastering it even this morning which makes me almost despair. I should not have taken so long to have read the larger work. It is to be allowed that the arrangement of it is clumsy for it forms divisions and subdivisions according to the ancient mode, which only serve to perplex and entangle.

I returned home without having been much interrupted, Mr. Champney, my father's Tenant in Common Street being the only person, who came to tell me he could not yet pay me. I told him I was sorry, but could wait a little longer. Afternoon, passed in continuing my Catalogue which has nearly come to it's end, and a further portion of Æschines. I completed all my task and felt better satisfied than I did yesterday. My translation of this Oration goes on with perseverance and upon it's success will depend the continuation of it to that of Demosthenes, which is the most important, and would certainly be much the most beneficial one. My time however is so limited that much must be done in a very little while, and I must hurry even what I now do. In the evening I read to Abby some of Clarissa Harlowe, interesting but interminable. She is a little too apt to prose, as all *very* good people are.[1] I continued La Harpe in his Chapter upon Seneca. He is warped by his ideas of the French Revolution and tries one.

[1] CFA has unconsciously shifted from a comment on the novel to one on its title character. Both CFA and JQA frequently used *prose* as an intransitive verb in the pejorative sense of talking or running on tiresomely.

WEDNESDAY 11TH.

Morning fine but the Weather becoming more and more decisive. I have not yet succeeded in taking a result from my Thermometer which I placed some days since for observation, but only in my Study. At the Office reading a part of Pufendorf where I succeeded in accomplishing the first Chapter after so long a struggle. It is exceedingly difficult to comprehend the meaning and to embrace the general tendency of the author. I went on with the translation of the Preface which I hope to make tolerably clear. It is on the whole better than the Book. I finished the first draught so that tomorrow I propose to make a fair Copy.

Mr. Curtis came in for a Minute to tell me that he wished by my father's request, to consult older Counsel upon the forming of a Deed as my father thought I had inserted what was superfluous. I told him I was willing. The deed was the best result of my Judgment and aided by good advice; if they did not feel confident I should be glad that they would consult others and Mr. C. P. Curtis was fixed upon.[1] This was a little mortifying but I have some command of my temper to bear these things, thank Heaven, and I can rest satisfied with the conviction that I gave what I was asked for, my own opinion.

Returned home, and in the Afternoon, read a portion of Æschines as usual, and translated according to custom. The legal Argument is a little dry. My wife went out to tea and this afforded me an opportunity of continuing my studies, which I did with La Harpe, who writes with partisan fury against Seneca and disgusts me. With some justice, he mixes much of the contrary. At eight I went to Chardon Brooks' to meet an assembly of the family which is held as I am told weekly at each others houses. That tonight embraced all those in town excepting Mr. Frothingham. It was stiff and cold owing to the low spirits of Mrs. Edward Brooks who from some cause or other was cold enough to freeze the whole. I am not pleased with what I have seen of her conduct at either of the Meetings which I have attended this season, and this I regret for I think him deserving of a more fortunate fate. We returned before ten.

[1] Charles Pelham Curtis, Harvard 1811, had his law office at 16 Court Street (*Boston Directory*, 1829–1830).

THURSDAY. 12TH.

Morning fine and clear. At the Office as usual. Commenced the corrected translation of the Preface of Puffendorf and finished one page in one of the unfinished Blank books of my poor brother.[1] He had attempted a series of answers to Field's Interrogatory Analysis of Blackstone, and as usual had left off very early. I have resolution to finish what I begin if nothing else, and if possible shall exemplify it in this Preface. I began the second Chapter of the Treatise but was interrupted by my Father who came in and sat an hour or more. We had some Conversation upon the late publications of R. H. Lee and the works of Mr. Jefferson[2]—And upon the course Mr. Sparks is likely to take in his history which he[3] thought would not be agreeable to his notion of History.[4] I left him to attend an Auction where I had expected to find a Copy of a French Work, Arts et Metiers. But it had been previously sold. I returned to my Office to read a little further. Col. Quincy came in to give me the result of the application made by my father to the Athenæum to have his name reinstated among the Proprietors of that Institution—It was with a Certificate of a Share.[5]

I returned home and dressed myself to attend a Dinner at Govr. Winthrop's. The Company consisted of my father, uncle, Mr. Brooks, Mr. Everett, Frothingham, Ed. Everett, Brimmer, Welsh, Genl. Dearborn, Gorham, and myself.[6] The dinner was handsome as usual, and I felt more in the humour than I have for years. I sat between General Dearborn and Robert Winthrop and was on the whole very well entertained. I did not leave until the latest went and until I had drunk quite as much wine as was consistent with the bounds of propriety. I walked down to Mrs. Frothingham's after Abby and amused them a good deal with the liveliness of my Conversation. Returned before ten o'clock.

[1] Missing.

[2] Thomas Jefferson, *Memoir, Correspondence and Miscellanies,* edited by his grandson, Thomas Jefferson Randolph, in 4 vols., the first attempt at a collected edition of Jefferson's works, appeared in 1829, first at Charlottesville, then at Boston. JQA's judgment of Jefferson as revealed therein was bitterly critical; see JQA, *Memoirs,* 8:270 ff.

[3] JQA.

[4] Jared Sparks had in process an edition of *The Diplomatic Correspondence of the American Revolution,* which was published at Boston in 1829–1830 in 12 volumes.

[5] Josiah Quincy (1802–1882) was the secretary of the Boston Athenæum (*Mass. Register,* 1829, and see entry for 27 Sept., above). On the controversy between JQA and the Proprietors resulting in the restoration of his share, see below, entry for 26 Feb. 1830. Upon its restoration to him, JQA transferred the share to CFA (entry for 25 Nov., below).

[6] The home of Thomas Lindall Winthrop, lieutenant governor of Massachusetts, 1826–1832, was on Beacon Street at the corner of Walnut (*Boston Directory,* 1829–1830). His son, Robert Charles (1809–1894), also present, later a member of Congress and a senator, had graduated from Harvard the year before and was reading law in Daniel Webster's office (*DAB*); his political career was to be closely intertwined with those of both JQA and CFA. JQA in his account of the occasion (Diary, 12 Nov.) lists the guests somewhat more fully. Those not previously identified were Benjamin Gorham, member of Congress and ABA's uncle (vol. 2:152); George Watson Brimmer, merchant and Beacon Street resident (*Boston Directory,* 1829–1830); and Joseph Coolidge, Harvard 1817, who had married a granddaughter of Thomas Jefferson.

FRIDAY 13TH.

I was obliged to rise early this morning in order to get ready to go on my expedition to Weston to sell the wood off part of that Farm. I obtained my breakfast early and started with the air most nipping cold. The morning was a true November specimen of our Climate and though cutting not uninvigorating nor without a tendency to excite and enliven. I stopped for Richardson at his House, and he accompanied me from thence. We arrived there after the time appointed and found a very considerable number of persons collected for the sale. The wood proved rather unsatisfactory to the purchasers. It happened that the Auctioneer had with a view to my Interest so divided off the portion to be sold, as to include in this day's sale all the thinnest and poorest of the Wood, and owing to the quantity and the small size of the Lots, the rest could not be inserted today. Much murmuring resulted from this, but nonetheless what was offered brought by the general consent of all a very fine price. We remained out all day, having only some Crackers and Cheese and Rum for the whole of our Dinner. I confess I did not like much the nature and character of the Company, because they were very coarse, but I adapted myself as well as I could to my situation which in all places is wisest, and so I talked with all who would talk with me.

The day was on the whole fatiguing, and it was not until after sunset that we had completed our day's work. We were then obliged to return to the House and take Tea out of complaisance. The sum of what was sold today amounted to only four hundred dollars. This was hardly worth coming out for. But as I was told that almost every stick had brought its price I was compelled to be satisfied. I was unable to discover the quantity that remained, though my Tenants the Conants thought full two thirds of what I had designed to sell. If so, it is well though I distrust it and much fear the quantity will fall short. At any rate I think it probable that I shall stop for this Season, provided my Father is not of a contrary opinion. So far I feel confident that his Interest has been fully preserved.

We started at last and had a dark and a cold ride home. I left Richardson safe at his house and came through without any accident, to my great gratification, for it is now some time since I gave up my inclinations for Nocturnal excursions. I returned home at eight having been absent twelve hours, and feeling burnt and uncomfortably chilled, rather a singular combination but the most uncomfortable to which the human frame is subject. Mrs. Francis Parkman was with my Wife, so that I was obliged to amuse her though myself infinitely fatigued. Her husband came in at Nine and sat for half an Hour. I was so tired as to be glad when they left us. So after taking something warming I retired.

SATURDAY 14TH.

My eyes opened this morning to behold the snow lying thickly on the earth. This was to me exceedingly sudden and unexpected, and as I must confess not very welcome for it seemed to presage an early Winter. The warmth of the day however produced rain and made all of it disappear faster than it came. I was at the Office as usual, and attended to my portion of the translation of the Preface though it must be allowed that I did not feel quite so brisk as I wish I did. The fatigue of yesterday as well as the cold had produced very disagreeable effects upon my lips and face. I read a portion of Puffendorf as usual, though interrupted in the middle to go down and see if I could not obtain some Flower Roots for my Wife which I did—One bundle for Thirty Cents. I then returned and continued the second Chapter of Pufendorf which I finished.

My feelings were such in the Afternoon that I could not attend to Æschines and so devoted myself for the larger part of it to writing up my Journal which my busy avocations for two days past had prevented my doing. This took up so much of my time that I had only enough left to finish the Declamation of La Harpe against Seneca and the remaining Chapter which concludes his Course of Ancient Literature. I have been on the whole amused, entertained and generally instructed, though I have not implicit confidence in his judgment or his taste. And my opinion has gone on decreasing. I read in the Evening almost uninterruptedly in Clarissa Harlowe to my Wife, going only for a few minutes to the Meeting of the Debating Society where I did not see sufficient promised to pay me for the absence from home. There were but three or four persons present and those not very promising Debaters. I returned directly and finished reading only at nine o'clock.

SUNDAY. 15TH.

The morning was clear and cold. We determined to go to Medford, according to promise while this fair weather lasted. Accordingly we started after breakfast as we did on last Sunday, arriving there just before time to attend Divine Service. I went morning and afternoon and heard Mr. Stetson deliver what I did not doubt were sensible Sermons, if I had been sufficiently fortunate to have been able to have attended to them but I was not. My attention would not turn as I would have it so I was fain to give up the Contest and a judgment. Mr. Brooks was much pleased with the Sermon. The day passed otherwise without any thing worthy of notice. I wasted as much time as I always do.

In the evening as Abby was anxious to make some visits among her Medford acquaintance, her father and I accompanied her to Mr. Stetson's in the first place, where we saw the Parson in his prime condition and his small Wife. They were as usual, the former a wriggling nervous man of sense, the latter a very quiet unmeaning woman. We soon left there and went to Miss Osgoods, two Maiden ladies, daughters of the old Parson,[1] who take after him in manners and in drawl, but appear to be tolerably intelligent from the small opportunity I have of judging of them. We went from there to see Mr. and Mrs. Hall with whom we spent over an hour.[2] We thus accomplished an evening's work. This business is a little irksome to me, but it is proper and I consider it one of those fitting sacrifices of the married State which I have made perhaps as much for my own good as the general one. We returned home late in the evening and retired soon afterwards.

[1] Dr. David Osgood, Stetson's predecessor as minister at Medford, had two unmarried daughters, Lucy and Elizabeth. See *Medford Historical Register*, 2 (1899): 106–118; Brooks, *Farm Journal*, 12 March 1830.

[2] On Nathaniel Hall and his wife Joanna, see above, entry for 8 Nov., note.

MONDAY. 16TH.

The morning was cloudy and very cold. I have not experienced a day yet which felt so cheerless and wintry. We returned to town suffering very considerably from the cold. After warming my body which had become thoroughly chilled, I went to the office. My time was so much taken up with other occupations as to render me unable to continue my translation. Having seen by the Newspaper that the Gold Hunter, a vessel was arrived from Cronstadt, I was obliged to issue a Writ immediately to take one of the Men who was on board in satisfaction of a debt which I have had in my hands to collect for a very considerable time.[1] Mr. Titcomb called to see me to talk a little for he never seems ready to pay. Mr. Curtis came to show me the Deed Mr. C. P. Curtis had made in place of my own. It varies only by abridging my own. He gives an opinion accompanying it which I do not agree with—And against which I am disposed to write an opinion. My deed is perhaps too good for the purchaser but not on that account the less acceptable to me who am anxious to give that which I think will bind. Mr. C. also left with me Papers to make an assignment of all the Property belonging to Mr. Boylston in Maine. I had not time to do it today and to tell the truth scarcely felt in the mood.

I returned home and read in the Afternoon a page of Æschines, translating as much. This business progresses slowly and consumes much time but I flatter myself it is done thoroughly and will show me tolerably well the spirit of the Ancient Orators so that comparing it with Cicero and with our Modern eloquence we may form some accurate idea of their relative merit compared to each other. Evening passed in reading to Abby in Clarissa Harlowe which drags its slow length along. After which a little of the Life of Admiral Blake.[2] But from some reason or other I was not satisfied with the day's work.

[1] Perhaps relates to "Henderson's case"; see below, entry for 19 Nov., note. The *Gold Hunter*, Captain Gray, had docked on the 14th (*Columbian Centinel*, 18 Nov. 1829).

[2] By Samuel Johnson. CFA's copy of the London edition of Johnson's *Works* in 12 vols., 1823, is in MQA; the life of Blake is in 9:41–62. CFA copied two passages from it in his Literary Commonplace Book (Adams Papers, Microfilms, Reel No. 312).

TUESDAY 17TH.

Morning cloudy, which afterwards changed and became a warm and heavy rain throughout the day and evening. I went to the Office and was very busily engaged in making an assignment according to Mr. Curtis' paper and request to me. I was so doubtful as to the form that I went to consult with Mr. Kinsman and after some conversation I made out An Indenture of two parts assigning to General Salem Towne all the Interest which the Executors had to certain Notes and Papers relating to a particular Estate at Mount Desart in the State of Maine. The finishing the thing occupied me very nearly the whole morning as I had also to draw up a kind of quitclaim in case any land remained unsold. Mr. Curtis called to see me for a moment but he had changed his mind about the Papers and so left them again with me. I was glad of this as I shall still have an opportunity of Drawing up an explanation of my own deed as differing from that of Mr. Curtis, the lawyer consulted by him.

I returned home and in the afternoon read my usual quantity of Æschines which was easy and rather interesting. I comprehend this Oration infinitely more fully than I had expected. Perhaps had I continued Greek I should now have been perfectly master of the Language and just at the Age to begin to relish it. As it is I have hardly the time to pursue it. But I find the difficulty of not having a Greek and English Dictionary which must facilitate the study considerably. Having become a Member of the Society for the Diffusion of Useful Knowledge I was desirous to hear the Introductory Lecture for the Winter course this evening,[1] but it stormed so hard and my wife seemed so lonely I decided upon remaining at home and finishing the second Volume of Clarissa Harlowe in reading aloud to her. I also concluded the life of Admiral Blake, which is not much.

[1] Recently formed, the Boston Society for the Diffusion of Useful Knowledge currently had as its president, Daniel Webster. The lecturers for the year were Webster, Edward and Alexander Everett, Dr. Walter Channing, Professor Francis Lieber, Rev. Alonso Potter, Dr. John Park, Dr. Chandler Robbins, William Sullivan, and John Pickering (*Mass. Register*, 1830, p. 159). The lectures were regularly held at the Boston Athenæum on Pearl Street (see below, entry for 5 Feb. 1830).

WEDNESDAY. 18TH.

Morning cloudy but as mild as Summer. I went to the Office and was occupied much of the morning in giving an opinion upon the

Deed of Mr. Curtis as opposed to my Deed, in drawing a Quitclaim Deed which I could approve of, and in making a process of Foreign Attachment in Henderson's case. All which I did and moreover translated a portion of Pufendorf as usual but not quite so much to my satisfaction. I was not this morning quite so much in the spirit of it. Called to see Mr. Kinsman and Mr. Davis.[1] Conversation with them upon various subjects, particularly with one upon the Note of the City Guards, with the other upon the news of the engagement to be married between Mr. Webster and Miss Le Roy of New York. He has been so long talked about that it is desirable to have some end put to it.[2] Mr. Curtis called for a few moments and took all the papers which had been left with me. I was thus quite glad to have had an opportunity to have given an opinion in defence of my own deed, and devolving the responsibility of it upon another. I am satisfied as I get my perquisites also.

Returned home and after dinner, read as usual my portion of Æschines besides bottling a very considerable portion of Whiskey, a duty I am obliged to attend to now that I have a House of my own and things to keep, though not over agreeable. In the evening I continued reading to my Wife a portion of Clarissa Harlowe, commencing the letters of Lovelace, which are amusing enough though rather broad. Being desirous of becoming acquainted with the Older Authors rapidly, I began late this evening Potter's Translation of the Tragedies of Æschylus, with his Preface.[3] My only complaint is that I cannot find time enough for all my avocations.

[1] Henry W. Kinsman and Thomas Kemper Davis had read law along with CFA in Daniel Webster's office at 33 Court Street. Kinsman was farther along in his career than the others, having been admitted to practice by Oct. 1827, a full year before CFA, and remaining afterward with Webster (vol. 2:170; Fuess, *Webster*, 2:319). CFA took Kinsman legal questions on which he had had experience.

Davis, first in his Harvard class (1827), was still a year or more away from admission to the bar (*Mass. Register*, 1831). CFA's conversations with him were nonprofessional, often on literary matters; CFA valued them and regarded him highly. See, for example, the entry for 28 April 1830, below. Thomas Kemper Davis is frequently referred to in vol. 2 (1964 edn.), but he is erroneously identified at 2:199 and thus in the index as Timothy K. Davis.

[2] Since the death of Webster's first wife in Jan. 1828 there had been rumors linking him to several ladies; see vol. 2:360; Fuess, *Webster*, 2:383–384. His marriage to Miss Caroline LeRoy, 17 years younger than he, took place in New York on 12 Dec. (Fuess, *Webster*, 1:358–360).

[3] Of the two editions in MQA of the *Tragedies* translated by R. Potter and published at London, that of 1779 in 2 vols. has JQA's bookplate, that of 1809 contains a note in CFA's handwriting.

THURSDAY 19TH.

My days now pass in so regular a routine, that I feel as if it was hardly necessary in my Journal to do more than repeat. I went to the

Office as usual and translated and read a portion of Pufendorf as usual. I then read over what I had done and was satisfied with it. On the whole it appears to me clearer than the original from which I took it. This is not saying a great deal however in this particular instance. I paid my father's Tax and service for this year and settled with Mr. Clapp, the Mason who has done my Father's Kitchen at Quincy. This leaves me exceeding little of his Funds in my hands and a good many debts to pay. I wish his Tenants were better pay, and gave me less trouble. Mr. C. P. Curtis called upon me to inform me that Captn. Rogers whom I had sued on Henderson's Account had accepted a Draught for one hundred dollars from Henderson and was therefore desirous of being discharged.[1] I was very sorry for this as I had fully expected to obtain this Money. But in this present case the costs will be considerable and probably the satisfaction nothing. I returned home a little dull about it.

Afternoon occupied in reading and translating as usual in Æschines and found myself at the close of the dry Argument upon the time when and place where a Crown should have been conferred in Athens, which constitute the two first points of the Oration. The remainder being more to the Character of Demosthenes and History of Greece will be more amusing, though I confess I think already he has made a good attorney's case. As Abby was gone out to drink Tea, I took the time to read Potter's Translation of The Prometheus Chained of Æschylus. It appears literal and correct, and gives me a better idea of the piece than I could get from the original. I read La Harpe's Opinion and that of Cumberland in the Observer. The former considers it as an Epic fragment rather than a Play, to which he says it has no pretensions, the latter admires it's wildness and striking imagery. Such may be considered the distinct tastes of the two Nations which these Individuals represent, and a good comment may thus be afforded upon the Standard of Taste. I think myself the middle the best ground. The play is essentially poetical and not dramatic, but not more so than most of the ancient plays which have no possibility of assimilating themselves to our present notions of the drama. I called at Mrs. Dexter's for Abby where we sat for a little while.[2] It was rather dull and I was glad to get home.

[1] A reconstruction of the action in which Henderson was defendant must be conjectural and incomplete. Scattered entries in the Diary indicate that CFA, acting under instructions from Thomas Tarbell, who was himself acting for an unnamed principal, had entered suit against one Henderson apparently for debt. Henderson, in turn, seems to have been a creditor, being owed by Captain Rogers, among others. A trustee had been appointed to handle his affairs, but CFA had tried, apparently, to collect directly from his debtors some of the moneys due

Henderson. His efforts in this direction were thwarted by Captain Rogers' acceptance of Henderson's draught for $100, thus making Rogers free of indebtedness to Henderson or to Henderson's creditors. Having failed to obtain this money and not confident of his case in court, CFA finally offered a settlement of the claim for one-half the amount plus costs.

[2] Mrs. Catherine (Gordon) Dexter, whose late husband Samuel Dexter had been secretary of war in JA's administration, was particularly fond of ABA; see vol. 2:160, 342. Mrs. Dexter's residence at this time was at 1 Franklin Place or 28 Beacon Street (*Boston Directory*, 1829–1830, 1830–1831, and entry for 20 Dec., below).

FRIDAY 20TH.

Morning at the Office. Weather changed again and become cold. I found the glass in my room about 42. degrees of Fahrenheit. I have not as yet succeeded in placing it out. I continued my method of translating. This Preface seems to me on nearer inspection not so satisfactory as it did at first.[1] There is much irrelevant and much illdigested matter, but the substance differently arranged would comprehend all that we wish to have upon the limits of the Sciences of Natural and Civil Law. I have obtained clear ideas of them by reading it, which I cannot say I had before. Called to see Mr. Tarbell and talked with him upon this business of Henderson's which by it's ill success disgusts me. He said he would obtain instructions. Wrote a short letter to my Father in answer to his of the other evening which I put into the Post Office on my return home.[2] Authorized Degrand to purchase two shares of the Atlas Insurance Company if he could get them for ninety eight. I do not expect to get them.

After dinner I read my usual portion of Æschines and began his review of the Life of Demosthenes. This constitutes the essential of the Oration. I read also Potter's Translation of the Supplicants of Æschylus which I do not admire so much. The only remarkable thing in it being the principles of public liberty which were then held as exhibited in the mouth of the King of the Greeks. Nothing new has been discovered since. I then went down to hear Dr. Walter Channing deliver a Lecture upon the Education of the Ancients, before the Society for the Diffusion of Useful Knowledge.[3] It was pretty but not well adapted, and it was not long. From thence, to the house of Edward Brooks, to the regular weekly meeting of the family, where we had a tolerably pleasant hour and returned home before the Clock had struck ten.

[1] Pufendorf's preface.

[2] CFA's letter is missing. JQA's letter, enclosing one just received from Sidney Brooks stating that GWA's remains had been placed on board ship for Boston, asked CFA to send notice of the vessel's arrival and to help in the safe dispatch of the case to Quincy (19 Nov., Adams Papers).

[3] Walter Channing (1786–1876),

Boston physician, professor of obstetrics and medical jurisprudence and dean of the Harvard Medical School, co-editor of the *Boston Medical and Surgical Journal* (*DAB*).

SATURDAY 21ST.

Morning to the Office. Weather cloudy but not cold. Engaged in writing as usual some of my Preface. I find this business so easy that I have lost my taste for it. My design in future in reading authors in a foreign Tongue will be to translate in my Common Place only the Passages which strike me as particularly,[1] and these I will attempt to finish as much as possible. Several persons came to see me to ask for Money on account of my Father's Improvements in his Kitchen. I paid as far as I was able,[2] but could not come near the amount demanded. I do not know what it is advisable to do. Must see my father about it.

Read a Chapter or two of Pufendorf, and was considerably instructed upon the nature and duties of man in his condition apart from Christianity. He follows the three great divisions which seem to be always laid down, the duties to God, to fellow Men and to one's self. The morning seemed to pass rapidly. Mr. Curtis called and redelivered to me the Indentures of Assignment, with a request to insert a Clause releasing the Executors from any Bonds entered into by Mr. Boylston to give Deeds, a Clause he had forgotten to state to me before. I therefore occupied myself with this.

In the afternoon, read my usual portion of Æschines, where he begins his attack upon the policy of Demosthenes, which constitutes the essence of his Oration. I translated as usual but I am fearful that I shall not arrive at the whole force of the original from my inability to devote time enough to the force of the Greek. Attended this evening a Meeting of the Debating Society. It was quite full and on the whole a tolerable debate upon a trite subject, Duelling. I was appointed Secretary and acted in that capacity in the absence of Park, but was obliged to leave before it broke up as I had left my Wife at Mrs. Gorham's. She returned home before me as it was.

[1] Thus in MS. Word omitted after "particularly"?

[2] A payment of $28.75 was made to John G. Loring & Co., coppersmiths, of Portland and Ivers streets (M/CFA/3; *Boston Directory*, 1829–1830).

SUNDAY. 22ND.

Morning cloudy attended with a drizzling rain, making the day very unpleasant though quite warm. I attended divine service at Mr.

Frothingham's, both in the morning and the afternoon and heard him deliver Two Sermons, to neither of which I attended much. The one in the afternoon was upon Charity to the Poor, and in aid of the Contribution box served regularly on the Sunday before Thanksgiving, and it was good as I thought for it's intended purpose. I returned home and read for the Afternoon Jeremy Taylor's Account of the Conception and Nativity of Jesus Christ.[1] His style is extraordinary, sometimes brilliant, at all [times][2] nervous, and strong, but not infrequently obscure. It is the old vigour of that class of Writers who though subsequently excelled by the smoothness and polish of later ages has in itself never been surpassed. Indeed our times are not like those, we force much and produce little. In the evening I read to Abby part of Clarissa Harlowe. The letters of Lovelace have much power in them and a great deal of wit, not formerly appreciated by me when I read them here and there out of connection. Mr. Everett called in to tell us he was going tomorrow morning to Washington— His departure being accelerated by the account of the Boat. He sat only a single minute, so that we resumed Clarissa and continued it until bedtime.

[1] *Life of Christ,* 1:31–39.
[2] Word omitted in MS.

MONDAY 23D.

Morning very dark with rain. The weather unusually warm and the Storm attended with Thunder and Lightning. I went to the Office as usual, and very shortly after went down to look after the Susan and Phœbe, the vessel in which the remains of my poor Brother were returned here from New York. The rain was such as very thoroughly to drench me before I had completed my business. I found the vessel at the head of Long Wharf and saw the Captain who made an arrangement with me to deliver the case which contained his remains any time during tomorrow morning. I accordingly returned to my Office and wrote a Note which I sent out by the Driver of the Stage to let my Father know it, and direct accordingly.[1] But in the performance of all this I became so wet as to think it expedient to go home and dress myself over again, which I did with much haste. The Storm while it lasted was very great but it did not continue long after dinner. I returned to my Office, saw Mr. ⟨Charles P.⟩ Nath. Curtis who was at my Office and received Instructions in regard to Henderson. The former came to see my father and I told him the Storm was such he could not come.[2] In the afternoon I read as usual my portion of Æschines and was engaged a considerable time in making my usual translation of the same Author.

My former Man Servant left me today.[3] Although a good man, in knowledge of his business, yet his temper and character are very intolerable, and as his Wages are high I have thought it advisable to send him away and take another more manageable and cheaper one. These are the smaller troubles of life. I also sent today to Mr. Stetson ⟨fifteen⟩ twenty five dollars as a present to him for marrying me,[4] rather a late affair, but it was only yesterday that Abby informed me he had never received any thing. The truth was that I supposed it customary here for the lady's Parent to arrange that article in the Wedding affair, but as it is not, I took an opportunity immediately to repair my thoughtless omission. In the evening I read a part of Clarissa Harlowe to Abby—The series of letters recounting their skirmishes.

[1] Letter missing. JQA's response, as agreed, was to send by the sexton at Quincy authorization to CFA to receive the remains (JQA to CFA, 23 Nov., Adams Papers). The *Susan and Phoebe*, Captain Baker, had docked on Saturday (*Columbian Centinel*, 25 Nov. 1829).

[2] The meaning is not certain. A possible reading: At my return, Mr. Nathaniel Curtis was at my office to see my father, but I told him that the storm had prevented my father from coming in.

I also received instructions [from Mr. Tarbell(?) for response to Mr. C. P. Curtis] in regard to Henderson. See entries for 19, 20 Nov., above.

[3] "William" seems to have been replaced by "Benjamin." See entries for 14 Sept., above, and for 13 Feb. 1830, below.

[4] The payment of $25 to Caleb Stetson is recorded in CFA's account book, 1829–1844 (M/CFA/9); but see below, vol. 4, entry for 28 March 1831.

TUESDAY. 24TH.

Morning at the Office. Weather again turned off clear and cold. I went early this morning to be ready for any call which might be made upon me. Soon after I had reached there, Mr. Hubbard the Sexton of the Parish at Quincy came and I accompanied him to the Vessel where I saw the remains of my poor brother transferred to his Waggon and on their road to their final resting place.[1] It gave me at the moment a strong feeling of melancholy, for I knew him well and was witness to much of the latter part of his feverish dream. For such it was indeed. Here was the close of all his views, and if his steps were retrograde during the latter part of life even in spite of himself, here they met a termination almost too abrupt to afford our feelings any solace. Much in him there was that I admired, much that I wish I could imitate, but still there was unfortunately more that was equally unfit for him and for me.[2] And I rest comforted in the strong conclusion that I have come to that he would not have lived for his own good had God spared him longer. May Heaven deal mercifully with his Soul. His earthly remains lie with those of his Fathers.

I spent an hour in the Supreme Court hearing Mr. Webster and Judge Orne sparring upon an Insurance case.[3] The former has a magnificent way with him. It strikes me with wonder whenever I see it. It is power in truth over our fellow creatures. I would give much to possess it—And why not try? The field is open to the bold, the perservering and the brave. I am conscious of some power that way. Why not endeavour to turn it to some advantage.

I translated a little but not much of Pufendorf. This work lags in it's latter end. I also attended a sale of Flower roots in which I purchased a considerable number, they going very low. I carried them directly home. Afternoon as usual, reading Æschines but instead of doing all my common quantity of Translation, I took a part of the time to read Mr. Mitford's Account of the Two Orations on the Crown which made me as angry as it always does. Although I must agree with him in the force of evidence adduced on the two first points of the Oration of Æschines. But I do not as yet see the same weight in the third. As I was about to continue Clarissa to Abby, we were interrupted by Edmund Quincy who came and sat pleasantly all the Evening.

[1] Mr. Hubbard reached Quincy about half past one. There, in the presence of JQA and W. C. Greenleaf, after a short prayer by Rev. Peter Whitney in the graveyard opposite the Adams Temple, the remains were placed in the family tomb next to the grave of JQA's sister, Abigail (Adams) Smith (AA2), who had been reburied there in 1813. (JQA, Diary, 24 Nov.; JQA to LCA, 24 Nov., Adams Papers; CFA, Diary, 14 March 1832; Ford, ed., *Statesman and Friend,* p. 110.)

[2] The literary character of this passage, the Shakespearean echoes, may derive from CFA's identification of GWA with poetry, as well as with some aspects of the flawed or tragic hero.

[3] Peters, Pond & Co. *v.* Commonwealth Insurance Co. Daniel Webster and Lemuel Shaw were counsel for the plaintiffs; Henry Orne and William Prescott for the defendants (*Columbian Centinel,* 2 Dec. 1829, p. 2, col. 5).

WEDNESDAY. 25TH.

Morning at the Office. Weather bright and cold. I attempted a little translation but did not progress far before Mr. Curtis came in to see and meet my father who got there half an hour afterwards. I went into the Supreme Court for a little while but found them still occupied upon the details of the Insurance Cause. My father and Mr. Curtis called to finish the Conveyances which were to be made of Mr. Boylston's property before his going away. They sat all the morning, and signed the conveyance of Land to John Bullard, the

Assignment and the Deed to Towne, which were acknowledged before Mr. Gay as Magistrate. I then had some conversation with my father upon his Affairs, which are not now at this moment entirely easy. We made arrangements by which he will be relieved for the present, to be taken out of the next proceeds from his Estate here.[1] He has very much changed his nature as to expenses here, for now he has been so long accustomed to large funds that the restraint of his private means comes upon him. I hope he will not be driven to incroach upon his Capital at all for should that happen, my own expectations must soon be realized. I am anxious myself to make provision against such an event gradually, so as[2] that I may relieve him from the pressure of my Allowance—Although I think that it is not much more than my labour on his account deserves.[3]

My father dined with me and in the afternoon transferred his share of the Athenæum to me, for which I am very much obliged to him.[4] It will be of considerable service to me. He then started to go to Medford whither Mr. Brooks had invited him to go to spend Thanksgiving.[5] I went to my study and passed a short afternoon in finishing the Suppliants of Æschylus. It is a very simple specimen of the original drama. The fifty daughters of Danaus fly from Egypt to avoid marrying the Sons of Ægyptus, they call upon the King of the Greeks to protect them, who promises so to do, the Herald of the Bridegrooms comes to claim them and is refused. As La Harpe observes this is rather a Dramatic Poem, but we do not feel the less bound to admire it upon that account. It's simplicity is one of it's principal charms, but after all so far as we can judge at this day it seems affectation to think these Plays superior to our modern productions. The latter have the advantage of being compelled to reach a standard already assumed, an advantage not to the author but to the merit of the piece if successful.

In the evening, Abby had the usual meeting of her family with the addition of Mr. and Mrs. Alex. H. Everett. The Evening passed off not very pleasantly, to me, on some accounts. But these are my misfortunes not my fault. I am apprehensive of experiencing this bitterness more strongly perhaps as I go on. Mrs. Everett is a pleasant woman and I should be very glad to be on good terms with them while they live here.

[1] JQA and Josiah Quincy (1772–1864) were co-executors of the estate of JA, of which JQA was a principal legatee (JA, Will, inventory, and estate papers, Adams Papers, Microfilms, Reel No. 181). On 27 Nov. JQA executed a note to the Executors borrowing $600 from the estate to be repaid in 60 days with interest (JQA, Diary). On 28 Jan. 1830, CFA as agent deposited $606 to

the Executors' account in the U.S. Branch Bank (CFA to JQA, 2 Feb. 1830, LbC, Adams Papers).

[2] Thus in MS.

[3] CFA received from his father $250 quarterly as allowance and fee for managing JQA's Boston property and financial matters (M/CFA/3).

[4] On the proprietor's share in the Boston Athenæum transferred by JQA to CFA, see below, entry for 26 Feb. 1830

and note.

[5] JQA had wished CFA and ABA to spend Thanksgiving at Quincy. The invitation from Mr. Brooks had resolved the problem for all. However, Mrs. Brooks' illness impelled one of their daughters to the view that "there ought to be no one here while Mother is in her present state" (Charlotte Everett to Edward Everett, 25 Nov., Everett MSS, MHi).

THURSDAY. 26TH.

Morning opened cloudy and with rain. I sat in my Study after breakfast and wrote a letter to Mr. Sparks [1] besides doing some other little necessary things. As it was the day devoted to Thanksgiving, I was unable to have a command of my time, sufficient to sit down to any serious occupation. I only read two or three of the pieces in the Melanges Litteraires of Voltaire, which only tended to confirm me in my great admiration of the particular elegance of that Author.[2] Writing as he did upon all subjects it is wonderful to perceive how delightful he can be upon them all. We were called for and so I stopped.

We rode to Medford with Mrs. Frothingham, and Mrs. E. Brooks. The day was rainy throughout and what might be strictly called gloomy. But I did not feel it quite so much as heretofore, although far from being in very exalted spirits. We found on arriving, Mr. and Mrs. Brooks, Mrs. Everett and children, my father, Edward Brooks and Mr. Frothingham the two latter just arrived before us. The time passed pretty much as such time has often passed before, in the demolition of eatables which were given us in fair quantity and quality. I sat next to Mr. Frothingham and Eliza Brooks and did not derive much pleasure from their Company. The former is not a man to my taste, the latter is a pleasant woman but reserved and distant. The dinner passed off tolerably and in the Evening as Abby and I were to return with my father tomorrow morning, the Company left us to return before dark. We were therefore at home alone, and passed the evening very quietly in Conversation upon miscellaneous matters. It was a little sleepy but on the whole passed off well. I feel a species of constraint here which I cannot get over in any way and it troubles me exceedingly for I am aware that it hurts me with Mr. Brooks and with the rest. Strange to say, I feel it no where else excepting here and at home when they are present. For with strangers it seldom happens.

[1] (LbC, Adams Papers). Upon request of Jared Sparks that he be allowed to examine and copy JA's letters on public matters during the Revolution and JA's second mission to Europe with a view to their publication in *The Diplomatic Correspondence of the American Revolution,* JQA had brought to CFA's house 21 volumes of JA's letterbooks and written Sparks that he might have access to them *there* (13 Nov., LbC, Adams Papers). CFA repeats the terms and offers the use of his study for the work any mornings in the week.

[2] In the Deux-Ponts, 1791–1792, edition of the *Oeuvres complètes* of Voltaire in 100 vols., *Mélanges littéraires* is vol. 68. JQA's copy is in MQA.

FRIDAY. 27TH.

We returned to town this morning, my Wife in the little Carriage with my Father, myself with Mr. Brooks. The weather had cleared off and was rather pleasant although the roads were obstructed with the snow which fell in quantity of about three inches upon a surface during the Night. Such are the varieties of our weather. I found my father at the Office, and we then performed a considerable number of the remaining little pieces of business necessary to be transacted previous to his leaving this part of the Country. This took a considerable time and I had not much of the morning left. The remnant of it was taken up in reading a Number of the Edinburgh Review which I had brought with me from Medford which had an interesting article upon America and one upon the Drama.[1] I read them with much interest and although I cannot think that they are fair or correct Articles yet I must allow them to be interesting. My father who looked into one of them appeared much incensed. He is almost too quick however upon matters relative to this Country.

After dinner, I occupied myself in making a draught of what I had translated during the two last days of Æschines into my little pamphlet book,[2] and as Abby went down to take tea with Mrs. Frothingham, I read Potter's Translation of the Seven against Thebes of Æschylus and tried to steer clear of the excessive partiality of Potter on the one side, and the other extreme of La Harpe on the other. Æschylus must not be read as an Author of Dramas of the present day. But he contains much which has never been since exceeded. I had barely time to finish, before it became time to go down and hear Mr. Channing's second Lecture to the Society of Useful Knowledge. It was upon Climate acting physically, and upon Diseases the effect of Climate or Soil, particularly alluding to those which go under the names of Yellow or Malignant Fever. It was interesting, to some extent, although not in itself so much so as to pay me for my trouble in coming down. On my return, called for Abby at Mrs. Frothingham's, this lady being sick with a headach we hurried home, and I passed another hour in reading Voltaire's criticisms upon Moliere's Plays.

[1] The *Edinburgh Review* for June 1829 contained an article on the ancient and modern drama (p. 317–361) and an article on the United States, ostensibly a review of James Fenimore Cooper's *Notions of the Americans by a Travelling Bachelor*, 2 vols., London, 1828, and *Travels in North America* by Capt. Basil Hall, 3 vols., Edinburgh, 1829 (p. 473–525). Peter C. Brooks had subscribed to the *Edinburgh* for a number of years (see Brooks, Waste Book); his file of the magazine is in MHi.

[2] See above, entry for 26 Oct., note.

SATURDAY 28TH.

Morning damp and chilly, I went to the Office unusually late. After doing my usual business of little things which take up time though I hardly know how to describe them, I went into Court and heard Mr. Webster in the Insurance Cause taking to pieces the Depositions of the opposite side. He has great power in the prodigious clearness of his ideas which leads him to results at once. Admiration of Mr. Webster is not a voluntary thing, for when I have not been near him for some time I begin to think less of him, but the moment I again hear any exhibition of him, I am compelled to award him the merit which is his due. He is a good model to study in order to know what constitutes the particular power which he wields, so as to be able to place it before us for imitation. Clearness of the Mind is the great and essential requisite. I was obliged to leave the Court in order to go and see about one or two little Commissions before the time came for me to leave town and go to Quincy.[1]

I delivered to Josiah Quincy Jr. the Share in the Athenæum to be transferred to me, who upon the occasion informed me of his fortune in having a Son last Evening—A great fortune as it had been somewhat questioned heretofore. He has been married two years or more.[2] I was really very glad. On going to my Office, I found I had been sent for and I accordingly hurried to get ready to go out of town. My preparations were soon made and I hastened home, found Abby just returned from walking. The town is full of a scandalous affair arising from an elopement of John C. Park and a Miss Moore the daughter of Col. A. Moore, a brother of our profession. It is an affair which will very much injure him, who before stood tolerably well.[3]

At last we started in my father's Carriage and rode to Quincy having a very cold and dreary ride—The weather being severely influenced by a chilly North Easter. We reached Quincy before three and in time for the dinner for which we were invited. My father previous to his departure was for going to make a return to the civilities of the Gentlemen of Quincy and accordingly invited them to dine. The Company consisted of Messrs. Miller, Beale, Thos. Greenleaf, Danl. Greenleaf, Marston, T. B. Adams, Smith, W. C. Greenleaf, myself and my wife, the Revd. Mr. Whitney and Mr. Douglass, Miss M. Foster and the rest of the family.[4] My seat was cold and uncomfortable, near the door. But the dinner got through much better than I had expected considering the want of necessaries for large entertainments. They went early and we spent the evening at home in conversation.

[1] A verdict for the plaintiffs, whose case Webster argued, was returned on 30 Nov.; the sum at issue was $12,000 (*Columbian Centinel*, 2 Dec. 1829, p. 2, col. 5).

[2] Josiah Quincy (1802–1882) had married Mary Jane Miller two years earlier (*Columbian Centinel*, 8 Dec. 1827). The son was Josiah Phillips Quincy (1829–1910); see *DAB* and Adams Genealogy.

[3] The marriage of Park to Miss Mary F. Moore, oldest daughter of Col. Abram Moore, had taken place on 23 Nov. (*Columbian Centinel*, 28 Nov.). Miss Moore's mother, who was Miss Woodham, had been an actress in Boston. The bride "is said to be without character, and some have doubted whether he or Ned Prescott ought to have felt obliged to marry her. At any rate, Prescott was a Groomsman and accompanied them to Brattleboro, where I am told they are to live. This is a most mortifying affair to poor Dr. Park and his family; and it produces a great excitement in town" (Charlotte Everett to Edward Everett, 29 Nov., Everett MSS, MHi).

[4] Of the sixteen at table, Edward Miller, George W. Beale, Thomas Greenleaf, and TBA were newly constituted Supervisors of the Classical School at Quincy provided for by JA's Temple and School Fund. Others in the company, in addition to those clearly identified by CFA, were John M. Gourgas Jr. (affianced to ECA; vol. 2:387), John Marston, Mr. Douglass, William Smith, his sister Louisa Catherine Smith, and their niece Mary Smith Foster (b. 1807), daughter of the James H. Fosters (JQA, Diary, 27, 28 Nov. 1829).

SUNDAY. 29TH.

The rain poured in Torrents during the Night, and continued in a kind of drizzle throughout the day. I attended Meeting with my Father both in the morning and afternoon and heard Mr. Bowes Whitney preach two sermons in themselves tolerably sensible, but injured from the badness of his manner as well as from the unusual ugliness of himself.[1] Personal appearance certainly does produce an effect very sensibly felt in delivery by a speaker. And as to manner, if Men really were only sensible of the difference in the effect of the same piece of composition when properly and when not properly read, they would turn again to their School rooms to try their hands.

Mr. Whitney dined with us, and so did Mr. Degrand who came out here in a Carriage from Boston and who spent the whole day here. This was not over agreeable to me as I do not feel desirous of a great deal of acquaintance with him in a familiar way and yet I do not care about so entirely shutting him out as to make it unpleasant to me to meet him at my Father's, which I shall always be liable to in the future.[2] His boldness is disagreeable and his general unpopularity here so great as to attach even to those who are with him. Mr. Brooks has expressed to his daughter a dislike so strong of him as to affect me materially as well in the feeling of restraint which it puts upon my Independence of action, as in the disagreeable situation it puts me into, regarding the Man. He remained here until nearly ten in the evening, talking of all sorts of things very unreservedly although in addressing himself to my Wife he received some rude rebuffs. I felt as if I ought not to check her although I did not know how to approve of it. I had no time for reading of any kind and little for Conversation with my Father.

[1] Nicholas Bowes Whitney (d. 1835), Harvard 1793, was Congregational minister in Hingham (*Mass. Register*, 1830).

[2] See above, entry for 2 Oct., note.

MONDAY. 30TH.

The morning was delightfully clear and pleasant for us to return to town but we did not succeed in getting away very early. So many things were there which I was desirous of picking up before I finally left the House. The Carriage looked a little overloaded, but I could not avoid that. I was merely bringing in the Books which I thought I should need this Winter. Our ride was exceedingly pleasant and we reached home at about 12 o'clock. I went to my Office and there found Mr. Degrand's Intelligence of yesterday true that Mr. James H. Foster's Store in Washington Street had been burnt down to the ground.[1] This is a severe and disagreeable blow to a man like him though I doubt whether it will deprive him of an enjoyment the less. For I strongly suspect that accumulation is his fancy.[2]

I was occupied at my Office in arranging and settling my money affairs for the Month and in those of my Father which have got behind hand so much that I was to day obliged to advance a considerable sum to Mr. William Howe on account of his deficit.[3] This puts me to considerable inconvenience myself as I am now about settling my own affairs for the quarter, having now been married just three months. I called at the Store of Dorr and Allen, Auctioneers and made settlement with them upon the things I sent them of my brother and received from them a sum which again put me in funds for my brother's Estate.[4] I feel encouraged about this now.

After dinner, at home writing up the deficiencies which my last three days have cost me. This absence is a severe drawback upon me and puts a great stop to my plans for my own improvement. Mr. Sparks called upon me this evening and talked upon my Grandfather's papers which he is to see and compare at his pleasure—at my Study. We digressed upon Arthur Lee and the whole account of the revolution upon which we did not agree.[5] I had no time for any thing else and in the evening read to Abby from Clarissa Harlowe.

[1] Foster's store was in "the very large wooden building, corner of Summer and Washington streets" (No. 224). The fire, which broke out in the building next door, consumed both buildings, neither of which was owned by the occupant. Foster's stock, valued at $20,000 and on which there had been $8,000 insurance, was only partially destroyed (*Columbian Centinel*, 2 Dec. 1829, p. 2, col. 5). Shortly, Foster reopened his business at 156 Washington Street, remaining there for thirty years. See Richard D. Pierce, ed., *The Records of the First Church in Boston 1630–1868*, Col. Soc. Mass., *Pubns.*, 41 (1961):1000.

[2] Foster, married to a niece of AA's, had a reputation within the family for canniness in financial matters (see below, entry for 19 Jan. 1830). For many years he had in his charge the affairs of the First Church in Boston, serving as deacon from 1815 to 1862, most of that time as sole deacon, and also for varying times as clerk, treasurer, and moderator. He was also an overseer of the poor. Same, vols. 39–41 (1961).

[3] Probably William Howe, tinsmith, of 7 Marshall Street (*Boston Directory*, 1829–1830), for work done on the Old House.

[4] (Alfred) Dorr & (J. M.) Allen were at the corner of Milk and Congress streets (*Boston Directory*, 1829–1830).

[5] To Arthur Lee's position in his controversy with Silas Deane and Franklin, recently defended in the *Life of Arthur Lee* (see entries for 28–30 Oct., above), Sparks was strongly antipathetic. JQA disagreed with the Sparks view more strongly than did CFA; see Sparks to JQA, 18 Jan.; JQA to Sparks, 24 Jan., LbC; JQA to CFA, 5 Feb. 1830 (all in Adams Papers). Sparks gave full expression to his animadversions in his review of the book in *North Amer. Rev.*, 30: 454–511 (April 1830).

TUESDAY. DECEMBER 1ST.

Morning at the Office a little earlier than usual. I find that I waste so much time as to make it necessary for me to attempt a little reformation in this particular. I was occupied after getting there in continuing the translation which still hangs upon my hands. I accomplished enough today to leave only a little more behind. My time was also much taken up in the usual round of Accounts for my Father. Mr. Wells the son of my new Tenant called and paid me one Month's rent, thereby contradicting Orcutt's story,[1] and showing what may be often seen in the world, that those who talk much and against others are not perfectly clear themselves. I have not heard from Orcutt for a long time and suspect he has run away.

My time was consumed effectually so that I was obliged to return home and from thence to Abby's brother Edward's where I had agreed to dine. It was entirely a family party, consisting of us four and the dinner was as dinners usually are, good without any thing remarkable. Edward Brooks is a singular man with singular opinions and therefore does not pass for so much as he is worth. He carries his notions perhaps to an extreme and therefore affects his character, but on the whole I think him less known than he ought to be.

I returned home and it being too late for Greek had only time to read the article upon the Seven against Thebes, in La Harpe, to read all that Brumoy has to say upon the three plays already read,[2] and to begin the Agamemnon of Æschylus. This piece has many beauties, to my taste. The opening of it is so picturesque. The solitary watchman, the appearance of the flame after long and tedious vigils had made it doubtful if it ever would appear, and the description of the Communication of fire signals by Clytemnestra, with the beautiful Chorus upon the flight of Helen seem to me to have been seldom exceeded in grandeur in subsequent times. I was obliged to stop to go down to Mrs. Frothingham's to the regular weekly Meeting of the family where I did not enjoy myself over much.

[1] See entry for 23 Oct., above.
[2] Pierre Brumoy, *Le théâtre des Grecs*. JQA owned an edition published at Amsterdam in 6 vols., 1732, now in MQA.

WEDNESDAY 2D.

Morning at the Office. Engaged in making my Translation, which on this morning I completed, and read over the Whole with some gratification. It satisfies me better than any thing I have ever yet attempted, and shows that I have been imperceptibly improving. But there is still much to do. We may express tolerably well the ideas of others long before we shall be able so to dress our own as to make them attractive or powerful. I must strive to do this, for here and in speaking lie the great *powers* of man. All the rest is the mere trash of the mind.

I was occupied the rest of the time in reading rather an uninteresting article in the Edinburgh Review upon the Utilitarians and Mr. Bentham's School.[1] Just as I was about leaving my Office, Mr. Jones came in from Weston to pay a portion of the Money for the Wood sold the other day at that place. This was very agreeable as I had been exceedingly in want of Money on my Fathers account. I could not wait to talk over much of matters as it was my usual time for dinner. I went to the House and found that Mr. Brooks had been so kind as to make a present to us of some Fenders which was exceedingly obliging in him.[2] My father sent in his Trunks. I was obliged to attend to these things so much as again to lose my Greek studies which was very provoking. At this rate I shall never come to an end. I succeeded in reading the rest of Agamemnon and all the Commentaries upon it. I do not agree with La Harpe and do admire the piece, though I cannot altogether judge from the translation which makes sense sometimes of what I suspect is at this day thoroughly inexplicable. The latter half does not please me so well as the first, though the prophecy of Cassandra is noble Poetry. But the Chorus makes one laugh in the midst of terrors by the coolness of it's reasoning and the simplicity of the dialogue.

I had barely time to finish my avocations when my father arrived in town and I went down to see him. He had decided to go off tomorrow morning, and I made arrangements with him in regard to the future. He leaves me this Season with an unusual share of responsibility of which I hope not to prove unworthy. He transferred to me a share of the Quincy Canal, and treated me so kindly as to make me feel, how differently from what I had done.[3] Dr. Parkman called for a few moments to see him.[4] Otherwise quiet.

[1] The review of Mill's *Essays on Government*, 1828, in the *Edinburgh* for March 1829 (49:159–189), had provoked the *Westminster Review* to reply. The articles on utilitarianism in the June and October issues of the *Edinburgh* (49:273–299; 50:99–125) were rejoinders.

[2] Mr. Brooks, in recording the purchase of the fire screens for ABA, describes them as "2 elegant brass fenders for her parlors" (Waste Book, 29 Dec. 1829).

[3] Thus in MS. See above, entry for 4 Sept. and note.

[4] Probably Dr. George Parkman, Harvard 1809; see vol. 2:158.

THURSDAY. 3D.

My father left us this morning before daylight in the Providence Stage. I felt his departure more than I had expected. He has been so kind to me and I have been in the practice of such frequent communication with him this Summer as to make me feel as if one of my supports was leaving me. I hope his absence will not be for a long time. He promises to return in April, though I am afraid that circumstances will prevent him from coming quite so soon.

I went to the Office, obtained the Fenders which Mr. Brooks gave us, and made my regular deposits in the Bank, for the Quarter.[1] It is now just three Months since I was married and on the whole I have had happiness uninterrupted, as mortals ever enjoy. And let me here as ever take occasion to be grateful to a benevolent Deity for the benefits and advantages enjoyed, and pray that I may never abuse them.

I was obliged to hurry myself and make the arrangements about my Father's Horses. He left them upon my hands in such a manner as to compel me to act at once without hesitation. I therefore went down and employed Mr. Forbes my Stabler in all that was requisite to keep the Carriage in good order,[2] and to send the Horses for the Winter to Weston. I think sufficiently well of the Tenants there to be willing to trust them. Thus went the Morning. In the afternoon, after returning from dining at Mrs. Frothingham's where Abby and I had been invited, I sat down and studied some of Æschines being resolved not to lose this fourth day of the week. I succeeded in making a translation, and as Abby was out, read until late, thus finishing the fifth of the pieces of Æschylus, called the Choephoræ. One of the most interesting of them all. I read La Harpe's opinion of it which is favourable. But the French lean too much to Dramatic effect. Went for Abby at eight o'clock. The Night was severely cold.

[1] CFA deposited $300, the first of the regular quarterly payments from Peter C. Brooks they were to receive during his lifetime. This sum represented interest at 6 percent on $20,000 which Mr. Brooks kept on his books as an advance against ABA's "portion." While his sons received varying amounts of their inheritance as their business enterprises required, his three daughters, beyond the cost of their homes, received only the interest on sums which increased as Mr. Brooks' wealth increased and as the sons required larger amounts of capital. In 1829 the Frothinghams were receiving $450 quarterly, the Everetts $500. These sums remained constant until 1833, when the payments to the Adamses went to $400, those to the Everetts to $750. From 1837 Adamses and Frothinghams also received $750 quarterly, the interest on $50,000. From 1840, the Everetts' payments went to $1,250 (Brooks, Waste Book).

[2] William Forbes' stable was at Water and Devonshire streets (*Boston Directory*, 1829–1830).

FRIDAY 4TH.

Morning at the Office as usual. Time occupied partly in reading the Edinburgh Review. This number has much strong writing in it, but not a great deal of that which is better than show, real substantial foundation. My time passed rapidly and I did not seem to do much, but our days are now so short that they do not admit of the performance of a great deal. I paid the long unsettled bill of my Carpenter Mr. Ayer who made my Book Cases, and felt very glad at being able to free myself from that debt.[1] I had been in hope to make an Investment this Winter but instead of it find myself barely able to pay all my Debts. These were not large neither. But my disappointment at the failure of the Banks to pay Dividends, and my not yet obtaining any of my Fees for my professional Services have had some effect in producing this. I hope still not to let the Winter entirely pass without making some attempt to this effect.

In the afternoon, I read a part of Æschines but being interrupted by Mr. Sparks and his Clerk for a little while I was unable to read as much as I had wished or to do all my task of translation. I this afternoon read what is called his beautiful passage upon the parental affections. It is good but now it would be trite. After tea I went down to hear Dr. Walter Channing deliver a Lecture upon Aqueducts and the modes of conveying water. It gave me a little information but not as much as I had trouble so that I was not quite paid. On my return I found Edmund Quincy at my House who sat and chatted for a little while quite pleasantly. He is disposed to be quite sociable and I am very well satisfied that he should be. I afterwards read Brumoy's Analysis of the Choephoræ and Plutarch's Life of Demosthenes.[2]

[1] Thomas Ayers, housewright, of 23 Chambers Street, was paid $133 (vol. 2:420; M/CFA/9).

[2] JQA's bookplate is in the edition of Plutarch's *Lives* published at London in 6 vols., 1758, in MQA.

SATURDAY 5TH.

Morning at the Office. Finished the remainder of the Edinburgh Review. This publication is carried on with much talent and power, but not in the very best taste. The articles have a grandiloquence about them that is injurious to them when analyzed, though it makes an effect apparently. This occupied all my morning with the exception of only a short time that I was occupied in making inquiries upon the obtaining a Certificate for a poor Pensioner at Quincy, Rufus Davis by name, who by an accident lost his some time since—A business committed to me by my Father.[1] I only ascertained the steps it would be necessary to take. I then went to see to the purchase of some Liverpool Coal and purchased a Chaldron at twelve dollars, which is very cheap, considering that in the last Spring I was obliged to give at the rate of eighteen, one third more. Thus went the morning.

I occupied my afternoon in pursuing the study of Æschines which as far as I have gone, has been pretty well analyzed, though it takes so much of my valuable time that I think I shall be unable to continue in the same path. I must remain satisfied with translations. My field is wide, and only now do I begin to feel the incitements of a powerful ambition. It excites me at every moment with an indefinite preference which seems to remind me that I ought to fulfil the duties to which my station designs me. But it is wrong to be carried away too fast, there is time, and there must be opportunity.

In the evening I went down to the Meeting of the Debating Society but found that we were shut out, the consequence of which was that

the Members who came were obliged to return home and this unfortunately for the Society which is on it's last legs. I had gone prepared to oppose the resolution which I apprehended Quincy would
make to put an end to the Society, instead of which I returned home
and very quietly read Clarissa Harlowe to my Wife.

[1] JQA had undertaken to help Rufus Davis, a veteran of the Revolution, recover
his pension by filing a new certificate, but the process had not been completed when
JQA left for Washington (JQA, Diary, 17 Oct. 1829).

SUNDAY. 6TH.

The morning opened fine and mild but continued not in the same
mood. The heat of the weather soon formed Clouds, and the atmosphere became thick and hazy. I attended divine Service all day and
heard Mr. Frothingham preach, without giving the attention he seemed
unable to command. I cannot help thinking when in a Church that
I could read the man's own Sermon much better than he could himself and that perhaps had I the opportunity I might rapidly acquire
reputation. But this opportunity is probably not soon to be afforded
me and this may be all for the best, by the time which it may give to
mature what is yet only in weakness and unformed. But my visions are
now so strong that I must at least attempt to dispel them, and then
perhaps the result will show me my dreams like a Cloud in the distant
prospect, fast vanishing into thin Air.

I wasted the day. My wife seemed anxious for my Company and I
could not deprive her of it, although I omitted Jeremy Taylor, who
has not been altogether so well used heretofore as I could have wished.
Miss Julia Gorham dined with us but remained a very short time
afterwards. I read in the Evening a part of Clarissa Harlowe to my
Wife. The Story is becoming very deeply affecting. It has much more
power than I had imagined.

MONDAY 7TH.

Morning at the Office. Weather cloudy with mist. I began reading
over Mr. Williston's Book of the Eloquence of the United States.[1] It
is a large collection and it seems to me something of a labour to undertake to read it through. Indeed I do not know that I shall entirely
succeed, but I hope to do so at least sufficiently to be able to attempt
something in the shape of an Essay upon that subject even though I
should not endeavour to print it. My time is now coming when to be
successful I must at least dare. I suffered from no interruption during

the morning and was thus enabled to go on with great and unaccustomed rapidity.

In the afternoon I read Æschines and translated but the spirit has gone from this business as I feel that I am not sufficiently master of the Language to be able to go through with such a translation as I should desire to make. The Evening was spent in reading Clarissa Harlowe to my Wife excepting an hour in my Study when I attempted to embody some of my thoughts on the subject of Eloquence, but without any result in the least satisfactory to myself. They say perseverance will conquer all things, if I possess any talent so it shall with me. The evening was warm and misty, so that I sat in my study until past eleven o'clock.

[1] E. B. Williston, compiler, *Eloquence of the United States*, 5 vols., Middletown, Conn., 1827. JQA's copy, with marginal notes in CFA's hand, is in MQA.

TUESDAY. 8TH.

Morning at the Office. The weather was lovely, more like the softness of the latter part of Spring than our harsh and chilly weather of the Season. It was too warm to have need of Fire, a thing remarkable to say in these days. I was occupied during the morning in reading Williston, and feeling still the strong fury for writing I sat down and wrote a few pages upon the subject. They pleased me better than any thing I had written before and the arrangement of the ideas met my satisfaction more. My allowance of time however was so small that I could not finish as I was obliged to return home uncommonly early in order to go out to Medford with my wife and Mrs. Chardon Brooks who had agreed to go and dine there. My father sent Abby a letter from Philadelphia which place he had reached on Friday Evening.[1] We rode to Medford together in a Carriage with both Windows down more as if it was Summer than Winter.

We found Mrs. Brooks and the family much as usual. She is not well but on the whole seems considerably better than she was during the Summer. Our dinner was much as usual and I felt just as I usually do. I do not know why it is that I can say so little as I do at that house, but it does seem to me as if my tongue was tied when I get into it. Habitual caution, and the fear of committing myself upon many subjects in which I know I do not feel as they do, is perhaps the reason. For with my Father, how different is it. We remained there until nearly sunset, when we started with the additional company of Mrs. Everett and Chardon. Mrs. Frothingham's child has been very ill with Measles, so that Abby wished to go and see how it was. We went accordingly, found it better and from thence we passed over to Eliza's to the usual weekly Meeting. I went earlier and it was at first rather dull, but it ended pleasantly and we returned home in rain. Mrs. Everett going with us to stay the Night.[2]

[1] To ABA, 4 Dec.; ABA had made gloves for him. She replied on 13 Dec. (both letters in Adams Papers).

[2] Charlotte Everett, coming to Boston for a party at the Nathan Hales on the 9th, decided to spend two nights with ABA in an effort to relieve her own low spirits induced by her pregnancy and Mrs. Brooks' condition. The children remained at Medford (Charlotte Everett to Edward Everett, 10 Dec., Everett MSS, MHi).

WEDNESDAY. 9TH.

Morning at the Office. Continued my Writing which I carried on with spirit and rose from it with an impression that I had done famously. How very deceptive is self judgment. We incline most impartially to judge and yet the little whispering spirit within us distorts every thing till others know not what we would intend, and then scorn and derision follow the result of the deception. I thought I had clearly shown my talent, and perhaps I have erred in believing even in the existence of any thing extraordinary. At any rate my time passed very rapidly and I had no leisure for any thing else. My interruptions having become much less numerous than they were previous to my father's departure, I am now able to perform much more than at any previous time since the Spring, and I hope what I may do will result in some useful purpose.

After dinner I was occupied as usual in my portion of Æschines which I read with more pleasure than usual as it was uncommonly easy. Mrs. M. B. Longhurst sent me a part of her rent due on account of the House in Tremont Street and I was very glad to be able to receive it, as at last it brings my Father out of all his embarrassments for this Quarter at least. After my time for Æschines was done, as Mrs. Everett and Abby were to go to Mrs. Hale's, I sat and commenced a letter to my Father in which I stated to him fully my causes of trouble in study. He has written me very usefully heretofore and will I hope continue to do so. I could not conclude before it was time for me to go, as Mrs. Hale had a small party of friends and must not be neglected. These small parties of friends are great bores in general and this was assuredly no exception to the rule. It was apparently given to Alex. H. Everett and his Wife. I was tired to death and very glad to get away quite early, as I felt exceedingly fatigued.

THURSDAY IOTH.

Mrs. Everett left us this morning. I went to the Office as usual and passed the morning. My studies were much as usual, engaged in reading Mr. Williston's Book and reflecting upon what I had written. It is very certain that I do not feel quite satisfied with the result but I yet do not feel despair, perhaps what I have done may form a Nucleus for much better things. I arranged my father's Affairs and obtained the proper balances of my books at the Bank. My money Accounts take up a little time, but on the whole look pretty well at present. I passed some time in reading the Message of the President to Congress which arrived here in the unprecedented time of thirty one hours and some minutes from Washington. It is on the whole a better document than I had expected, certainly not written by him, but rather singular in the amount of propositions started in it. I have a little wondered at those respecting the Judiciary and the Bank of the United States.[1] I must reconsider this a little.

After dinner as usual I read a little of Æschines and translated what I had read for the two last days. This Author becomes rather easier after leaving the technical parts of his Argument and consequently a little more interesting. As Abby was going out, I sat after tea and wrote another Letter to my Father in which I very candidly detail to him the difficulties which surround me, and my hopes to overcome them.[2] I do earnestly hope to overcome them, for with me much should be done to establish that character I am ambitious to sustain in this Community. Are my visions dreams? Perhaps, but I never cherished them so much till now. I am the only Stock of an old House, and is not the object glorious to continue it in character even if I do not it's name. The fear in this last regard is the only fear I entertain,[3] but it would be strange even if I was to be fully happy in every thing. I make my humble supplication to God, though I cannot feel now as if I could complain if he tried me a little. Yet I feel as if I had a pure heart and a willing mind to obey his Counsels wherever they might end. Enough of this. I called for Abby at Mrs. Gorham's and copied part of my Letter.

[1] See entries for 14, 15 Dec., below.

[2] (Adams Papers) Reflecting the purposiveness and confidence evident in the diary entries of the preceding five days, CFA analyzes his problems, asks JQA's advice on a course of study and action that would seem designed to lead to a public career, and rationalizes the direction of his current employments as (1) a mastery of the principles of eloquence through the study of the models of ancient oratory; (2) the improvement of his literary style by translating, writing essays, letters, &c; (3) a full exploration

of American history before and after the Revolution.

[3] See above, entry for 8 Nov., note, and below, next entry.

FRIDAY. IITH.

Morning at the Office as usual. Passed a considerable part of the morning in reading Williston's Eloquence of the United States, and the different Speeches made in the Convention of Virginia upon the adoption of the Federal Constitution.[1] The reflection which most strongly occurs to me continually in reading it is how totally erroneous the spirit of their predictions of it's evils was and how differently it's actual parts of weakness are situated. The weakness of the Constitution seems to be in the great power of the House of Representatives, as opposed to the Judiciary and the Executive, and the method of election of the latter. But this may happen to be speculation equally vain with all the rest. On the whole the plan has worked admirably and disappointed all the croaking of the opponents to it's adoption. Perhaps it might not be a profitless study to look into the subject historically and critically.

I called to see Mr. Brooks and Josiah Quincy Jr. Talked a little, pleasantly enough with both of them.[2] My morning flew away, and it became time for me to go and dine by invitation with Chardon Brooks, the result of which was that I read no Greek this afternoon. My married life subjects me to a few interruptions which are not agreeable, but considering every thing I incline to the opinion that on the whole I gain. Lord Bacon said very truly long ago that "wife and children are impediments to great enterprises." Why should I so foolishly long for the latter. My spirit verily is restless. I copied my Letter to my father and then went to hear what Dr. Lieber had to say upon the Fall of the Turkish Empire,[3] previously slipping in to the Athenæum thus commencing upon my newly acquired right. I wasted my time for I saw nothing of interest. Dr. Lieber's Lecture was good in itself but being an attempt to pronounce a language necessarily acquired in an imperfect manner at least in pronunciation, it rendered the situation of an auditor unpleasant. I spent the rest of the evening at Chardon Brooks'. We returned in the rain.

[1] The speeches of Patrick Henry, Edmund Randolph, James Madison, and John Marshall delivered in the Virginia Convention in 1788 are in Williston's *Eloquence* at 1:73–251.

[2] Josiah Quincy's law office was at 27 State Street (*Boston Directory*, 1829–1830). He served as his father's agent in matters relating to the administration of JA's estate, as CFA did his.

[3] Francis Lieber (1800–1872), Ph.D. Jena 1820, was editor (1829–1833) of the *Encyclopedia Americana*, the first volume of which had appeared in October (*DAB*).

SATURDAY 12TH.

It was cloudy with wind and rain during the day, being one of those heavy storms of which we have had so many during this Season. But as the wind was from the South it was warm and by thus keeping off the severity of the Winter more than paid me for it's violence. I was at the Office engaged in reading Williston, and in a variety of occupations too minute to describe. Mr. Curtis called upon me for the settlement of the affairs of Mr. Boylston, and I agreed to finish with them if Mrs. Boylston would call upon me early next week. I also succeeded in passing an Account against the Estate which George had made my Father pay. It was very small to be sure but it will now pay Jones's new charge against my Father. Orcutt too came up to see me, just as I began to feel a little afraid I had suffered a total loss from him. He told me the usual Story and as I had got tired of it I finished off by offering to take his Interest in the Estate he speaks of as security for the payment of the debt. He promised next week to make a final settlement. I intend to press him. It is better to get beyond contingencies.

After dinner, I studied Æschines as usual but did not accomplish as much as I ought to have done, considering that I have added an hour to my time. My *writing* does not progress as I wish it did. I am almost in despair. The evening was taken up in reading to Abby from Clarissa. The storm was such that I could not go out to the Debating Society, being impressed with the notion that we could not have a meeting. Here is another branch in which I aim at success and feel as if circumstances were against me. Can I not pronounce the words, I will.

SUNDAY. 13TH.

The morning opened clear and cold—The weather of that bracing kind which promises health and not suffering. We went to Meeting all day and heard in the morning Mr. Walker of Charlestown,[1] in the afternoon, Mr. Emerson.[2] Their Sermons were neither of them first rate, not even so good as their's are generally, but nevertheless there is a fine tone of masculine feeling in them which denotes a considerable advancement in the tone of the pulpit. It is that which I most complain of in Mr. Frothingham that he is deficient in this very tone. Mr. Walker leads too much the Church Militant, he is rather over disposed to talk at the powers of others, and their doctrines, and their authority, as if he was jealous of it, but he is still a strong powerful preacher and among the best with us. Mr. Emerson has talent and manner which with us is more rare, but his health is indifferent and he has none of the greater powers of the Orator.

I passed part of the day in reading a Discourse of Jeremy Taylor upon the nativity of Jesus Christ. There is wonderful vigour in the style of this man, and though he has faults arising from obscurity of expression and perhaps pedantic language, yet these are trifles compared to his force and the wonderful beauty of his ideas. I also wrote a letter to my Mother[3] due long since, and on the whole did better than I expected. My ideas flow easily in letter[s], but they will not elsewhere. In the one, the careless writing is all natural, in the other it imposes restraint. The remainder of the evening was passed in reading the old Journal of my Grandfather when but a young man of twenty one or two years old.[4] It seems to have been nothing but an exercise, to express ideas which in his mind were worthy of it, and on the whole it is admirable. His account of his Writ is also very good.[5] How very similarly have I felt at times and particularly now when my trustee process plagues me. It took me all the evening.

[1] On Rev. James Walker (1794–1874), referred to at vol. 1:419, see below, entry for 23 Dec. and note.

[2] Ralph Waldo Emerson was minister of the Second Church, Middle Street, 1829–1832. His sermons are referred to at vol. 2:223, 338.

[3] Letter in Adams Papers. CFA had last written on 30 Oct., to which LCA had replied on 15 November.

[4] This passage marked the beginning of CFA's study of JA's papers—a task that was to occupy him at intervals for many years and that culminated in CFA's edition of his grandfather's *Life and Works*, 10 vols., 1850–1856. JA's "old Journal" was a volume of heterogeneous character into which *inter alia* JQA had earlier in 1829 had T. B. Adams Jr. and W. C. Greenleaf transcribe JA's journal entries of 1755–1759 (D/JA/47, Adams Papers, Microfilms, Reel No. 3). With these CFA had compared the two booklets in JA's own hand from which the transcription had been made (CFA to JQA, 20 Dec. 1829,

Adams Papers). Later, when he came to the arranging of JA's papers, CFA numbered these booklets "Paper Book No. 1" and "Paper Book No. 2" (designated D/JA/1 and D/JA/2 in the Adams Papers). The entries which CFA had found admirable in reading are those printed in JA, *Diary and Autobiography*, 1:1–85.

[5] JA, *Diary and Autobiography*, 1:48–50, 62–65. JA recounts the doubt and uneasiness he experienced in drawing a writ in his first case as a practicing lawyer (Field *v*. Lambert) and his anguish when the writ proved defective. His notes written preparatory to drawing the writ and a draft of the writ itself, JA put into another booklet that became separated from his papers during his lifetime and was newly discovered in 1965 in VtHi (JA, *Earliest Diary*, p. 89–90, 93–95). A full editorial review of Field *v*. Lambert and the problems it presented the young JA appears there also (same, p. 13–14, 82–89).

MONDAY. 14TH.

Morning at the Office. Time passed rapidly and yet I did but little. Went to the State Bank and got three Shares of the Stock belonging to George formerly, transferred to me for which I pay par, making in all ten Shares belonging to me in that Institution, where I propose to stop.[1] The Dividends are now so small there that I feel in some measure indisposed to set much of a stake in the Establishment, though for security I do not know that I could do better. At any rate I will do no more there, indeed I could not if I would. All my Stock is not invested in the best manner. A man in my situation finds it hard to come at correct information because I feel unwilling to ask for it lest I should excite attention. I design selling the six shares remaining of George's and transferring the whole to the Fire and Marine or some other Insurance Company, to my father. For otherwise I am afraid he will call for it to go to Washington. And I am fearful of the result of his speculations in that place. It may make him rich and it may produce an effect directly the reverse.[2]

I then called to see Edward Blake who notified me that we were put upon a Committee together last Saturday Evening to decide the affairs of the Bank of the United States in our Debating Society.[3] Here is a fine opportunity. We talked for an hour and then I went to vote for City Officers and to get a Mortgage recorded of my father's Property to pay the bequests of the Will. Thus went the morning. I forgot to say however that I received a letter from my Father,[4] containing the receipt from Philadelphia. But the seal had evidently been violated and this induced me to go round and attempt to discover if I could trace it to any body here. I satisfied myself that it was not done here, the next thing to know is if it was done at Washington. I wrote to my father this afternoon to know.[5] We shall soon hear if the Post Office is really not to be trusted.

The afternoon was passed in reading Æschines as usual and translating some part of what I had already done. The Oration is a powerful one. There is a great deal of reasoning talent in it. The Evening was spent in reading aloud in Clarissa Harlowe to Abby, the interest of which goes on increasing. It is written with an accuracy wonderfully minute.

[1] CFA's seven shares had been purchased for him in Sept. 1828 upon his coming of age by GWA with funds provided by a gift from JQA (vol. 2:286). The shares had a par value of $60 (M/CFA/9).

[2] Since JQA's acquisition in 1823 of the Columbian Mills (flour and meal) located in Rock Creek in the District of Columbia, they had proved a heavy drain on his resources and were requiring ever more capital. In 1829, with the assumption of responsibility by JA2 as manager, JQA's hopes for the mills had been again renewed; see Bemis, JQA, 2:197–200, and entry for 17 Dec., below.

[3] MS reads "Societies." Agitation against the Bank of the United States, a privately owned, profit-making institution which was the depository for public funds and had monopolistic control over the money supply, had been growing in

the East during 1829, a depression year. The issue, dormant for some time, had been brought to the fore also by the election of Jackson, who held well-known antibanking views. Now that the President in his first Message had raised doubts about the constitutionality of the Bank, the question would be debated until it reached full maturity as the main issue in the election of 1832.

⁴ 9 Dec. (Adams Papers).

⁵ (LbC, Adams Papers). See entry for 29 Dec., below.

TUESDAY 15TH.

Morning at the Office. My time much taken up without being well able to ascertain how. I sat down and wrote upon the subject of the Bank of the United States. My ideas flow too fast. The great point with me now is to methodize, to arrange and above all, to condense. I wanted information as to facts and went to see Mr. Davis and ask him whether he still had in his possession the Copy of the works of Alexander Hamilton in order to see his report on the Bank.[1] I did not find that but he gave me a Manuscript of Hamilton's Opinion given to General Washington, in opposition to those of Mr. Jefferson and Mr. Randolph,[2] which I read with great interest. It takes what seems to me a very strong view of the question. After all, it is one of those subjects furnished by the Constitution which will always admit of two sides and of consequent division in public opinion. I was obliged to pay attention to other things so that I could not devote my whole morning to it, but I became so interested as to pursue the subject in the afternoon, and to write several pages of matter which may become useful hereafter. My only difficulty is that I have too many Irons in the Fire. Patience and Coolness.

I went to see Mr. Tarbell understanding he had called. I found him and he gave me Instructions to pursue the two Writs on Mr. Gilman's Account which I propose to do.[3] I read none of my Greek today, and on the whole passed the time in a silly fit of enthusiasm.

The Evening came, and with it the regular time for the weekly Meeting of the Family which was this Evening at Chardon's. I went and passed the time much as usual. A little stupid or so, but that is always the case. I have not talent for indiscriminate Conversation and I know so little of Boston people that I cannot talk of them. This makes me feel terribly stiff. Will the feeling ever cease. I thought it would with my Marriage.

[1] An edition of the *Works* of Hamilton in 3 vols. had been published at New York in 1810. The "Report on a National Bank" [1790] is at 1:59–110.

[2] That is, Hamilton's communication to Washington, 23 Feb. 1791, submitting his "Opinion on the Constitutionality of an Act to Establish a Bank" along with "the reasons which have induced him to entertain a different opinion" from that of the Secretary of State and Attorney General (Hamilton, *Papers*, ed.

Syrett, 8:62–134). When CFA located a copy of Hamilton's *Works* two days later at the Boston Athenæum, he found that the document had also been printed (1:111–155), along with the "Report."
[3] See below, entry for 21 Jan. 1830.

WEDNESDAY 16TH.

Morning at the Office. The day looked fair and mild after the quantity of rain which fell during the Night. I was occupied as usual excepting that my Morning seemed if any thing shorter than ever. My accounts took a considerable part of my time. My father's dividend upon his Shares in the New England Insurance Office coming due, I went to receive it. It amounted to eight hundred and sixty four dollars, being eight per Cent upon the Capital.[1] This result is very gratifying as the Investment last July was urged by me and was entered into by my Father with a little hesitation. It now pays him the small advance he made for it besides giving him a half yearly Interest nearly as large as he would have got for the whole year had he continued his property in the Stocks. So that at any rate it has turned out well.

These arrangements being made, Edward Blake came up to see me about the Meeting on Saturday Night and to talk generally. He sat only for a little while and talked pleasantly enough. I do not know whether I shall be able to find time enough during this week to do all that I wish owing to the multiplicity of engagements which distract me from pursuing the study but if I do not, I lose an opportunity which I ought to be ashamed of omitting.

I was called off shortly after one o'clock to go to Medford with Mr. and Mrs. Frothingham and Mrs. Brooks to dine, Abby going out with her Aunt Gray. The dinner party consisted of Mrs. Gray and her daughter Mrs. Story,[2] Chardon, the persons already named and the family. It was tolerably pleasant, rather more so than usual. I sat next to Mrs. Gray and felt rather more at my ease than I commonly do. It became time to return at sundown. I came back with Mrs. Gray, after stopping a few moments at Mrs. Hall's. This family are very much distressed by the very unfortunate situation of their son Edward, who is gloomy in the extreme. His health having given way and his situation as Clergyman of a Parish at Northampton being quite too laborious for him, he is thrown upon his friends without money, with a wife and two Children. We reached town and received Mrs. Everett who again came in to pass some days. We dressed and went to a party at the Miss Inches.[3] It is the first time I have been in any considerable Society this Winter. The party was numerous and very select in it's character. I have been out of society so long as to feel but little acquainted with any body. The party was on the whole barely tolerable. Returned early.

[1] JQA held 108 shares of New England Marine Insurance Co. stock purchased for $10,929 as a replacement for his investment in United States 6-percent stocks which were paid off 1 July (vol. 2:395–396; M/CFA/3). The office of the company was at 34 State Street. Peter C. Brooks was one of the directors (*Boston Directory*, 1829–1830).

[2] ABA's aunt, Mrs. Mary Brooks Gray (1769–1842), was the widow of Samuel Gray of Salem (vol. 2:155). Mrs. Franklin Story (b. 1800, Elizabeth Gray) was her oldest daughter (Brooks, Waste Book, 5 March 1821, 7 Jan. 1823; CFA, Diary, 1 Feb. 1833); she is referred to, vol. 2:408 (1964 edn.), but there erroneously presumed to be Mrs. Joseph Story (Sarah Wetmore).

[3] The Misses Elizabeth and Susan Inches lived at 21 Fayette Place (*Boston Directory*, 1829–1830).

THURSDAY. 17TH.

Morning at the Office. Weather quite cold but nevertheless tolerably agreeable. I was engaged much of my morning in settling accounts for my Father and myself. I paid those of Doggett, the Picture Framer and Jackson the Painter.[1] So that now there are exceedingly few outstanding debts against him or myself. My time was interrupted so that I had little opportunity to do any thing in the way of reading or arrangement of matter for my Opening on Saturday. Mrs. Boylston, Mr. Curtis and Genl. Towne came to finish executing the Papers relating to Mr. Boylston's Estate—Which was all done. Mr. Orcutt came to tell me that he could get no Money but we came to no arrangement. I went to see Mr. Brooks to get Mrs. Everett's Letters, got into a conversation with Edward Brooks and Thos. W. Phillips which took up much time.[2] From thence went to see Degrand, authorized him to buy some Fire and Marine Insurance Stock for my Father and to sell the Shares in the State Bank formerly belonging to George. This is an Operation I am going to hazard in order to diminish the amount of Stock which my father will be likely to transport from here to Washington, to experiment upon in the Mill. It will also be likely to turn out better in it's Dividends than the Bank.

My time passed rapidly, and I found it time to go down to dine according to agreement with Mr. and Mrs. Frothingham. They asked us to dine with them and so I cannot escape. The dinner was pleasant as usual, perhaps a little more so, and after it I went to the Athenæum and spent the afternoon in reading Hamilton's report upon a National Bank. It is a good production but not exactly what I expected for it's application was to Banking in general rather than to the expediency of a Bank for the Nation. This however is fully treated in the paper he presented to the President which I read over again. My time passed rapidly. I think this Library will be of immense use to me. As I was to go to a party tonight, I went home to dress and then walked to the place, Mrs. Bradley's of Pearl Street—A relation of Mr. Frothingham's, but not in the best Society.[3] I found there few people whom I knew, but by stirring among the young men and speaking to all the ladies, I got through one hour which may fairly be reckoned among the wasted. Returned home without Mrs. Everett as she went to Mrs. Frothingham's.

[1] See M/CFA/3; M/CFA/9. John Doggett & Co. were at 12 Cornhill; Ebenezer Jackson, painter, lived at Milk and Bath streets (*Boston Directory*, 1829–1830).

[2] Thomas W. Phillips' law office was at 11 Court Street, close by Mr. Brooks'

(*Boston Directory*, 1829–1830). Charlotte Everett's letters from her husband were customarily addressed to Mr. Brooks' office.

[3] Rev. Nathaniel Frothingham's sister, Joanna, was Mrs. Josiah Bradlee (Col. Soc. Mass., *Pubns.*, 40:446; 41:1076).

FRIDAY 18TH.

Morning cloudy with a chill of snow in the Air. I went to the Office and passed my morning quietly though not very busily. Mr. Orcutt came to see me and to talk over matters more, but not to arrive at any distinct settlement of his debt so that I was desirous of getting rid of him. He seems to have no sort of disposition to leave the place without settling with me so that I do not feel anxious about him. It is probable that I shall be obliged to take security so that it matters very little to me when it is done. Mr. Titcomb also came to me being desirous to settle the matter for which he was sued. He brought me a watch as a pledge, but I declined taking it, as such a thing was totally useless to my purpose which is the Collection of Money, for my Employer. The rest of my time was taken up in attempting to digest my plan for my argument tomorrow night. It goes hard.

As Mrs. Everett is in town, the relations seem disposed to entertain her, and make much of her. We consequently dined at Chardon's today, and had a tolerably pleasant time. Nobody there but Mrs. E. and Abby. After dinner I went to the Athenæum to look at the Files of the Newspapers containing the Debates in Congress on the Bank, which I did. But I was totally unable to make any thing of an examination of the subject as my time was very limited. I merely ascertained a few facts respecting the decision on the subject, in 1811 and 1816.[1] This will aid me a little in the few observations I propose to make tomorrow night. I remained at the Athenæum reading until late in the Evening when I found it was time to go in and hear Dr. Lieber deliver his Lecture upon the State of the Turks. This was rather better than the former one, but still it made me feel angry. The information it contained was not so much as in the preceding Lecture, much being repeated.

I got away at eight o'clock and went to Chardon's to spend the evening where I found Mrs. Gray, Mrs. Story and Henrietta [Gray], Mr. and Mrs. Frothingham. I talked a great deal with Mrs. Everett, and took an opportunity gently to intimate that I thought she was not correct in the course she pursued to her husband. I did it very delicately and in such a manner as to prevent her feeling hurt with me, which succeeded. Whatever my opinion of Mr. Everett may be, generally, I think that so far as regards her, his course deserves much consideration. And though she may feel impatient at the progress of circumstances it is not proper for her to check the course of her husband's career.[2] We returned at ten. The snow still holds off.

[1] The charter of the first Bank was not renewed in 1811. The second Bank of the United States was not established until 1816.

[2] Mrs. Everett's dissatisfaction with the progress of Edward Everett's political career was probably a reflection of the disappointment he felt that the seat he sought in the Senate had gone to Webster and of his frustration in the House in the new administration (Frothingham, *Everett*, p. 111–112, 120–130 *passim*). His next preferment, to the governorship, did not come until 1835.

SATURDAY 19TH.

The snow was falling gently but fast when we arose this morning but it ceased soon after I reached the Office. My time here was little interrupted during the morning so that I had much opportunity to mature my reflections on the question of the Constitutionality of the Bank. I studied the subject as much as I could and found myself tolerably well able to perform the beginning. After my return home I devoted all the Afternoon to it and in order to [*word omitted*] a more thorough understanding of it, I wrote down my ideas. They appeared to come fluently enough. I then looked into the Speeches of Mr. Clay to find the two which he made upon the different sides of the Question.[1] They are curious in themselves. I had read them before but not with the same attention to a particular point. My day was in this manner totally given to the arrangement *mentally* of what I was to say, and this is by far the most difficult part of the duty of a Speaker. The exercise is one absolutely necessary, for otherwise how could it possibly be in the power of an individual to take any latitude, when he must always be careful to keep in recollection the track which he must follow, to carry through even an argument.

After tea I went down and found collected a considerable number. Our debate was animated and interesting. I did even better than I had expected, and in my reply was enabled to trust myself to some animation without any fear of stumbling. My success this evening will I hope only add a stimulus to my ambition to go on and perfect myself in this species of Oratory. I succeeded this evening tolerably for a first attempt but how very far short of my idea of an Orator. If I can only pursue that to the extent my Imagination carries me, there will be no limits to the effects which such a result might produce. Returned home at ten and retired.

[1] Clay spoke in the Senate against rechartering the Bank in 1811, for the Bank's reestablishment in 1816. An edition of *The Speeches of Henry Clay* had appeared in 1827, Philadelphia and New York.

SUNDAY. 20TH.

Attended Divine Service all day, at Mr. Frothingham's Church. The day fine for this month but a little windy. Mr. F. preached in the morning a Sermon which I did not see the end of. It was refined and drawling. My ideas of Eloquence are running away with me. They carry me into an enthusiasm which makes me feel unreasonably disgusted with the attempts of others. Mr. Motte preached in the afternoon.[1] I recollect him well, as the Classmate of my brother George and at one time his College Chum. He had a reputation there which like nearly all those formed at that place disappoints when brought to the trial of the World. I think he has some ability but not of a kind to produce the greatest effects. And who among us has, when we consider what the Pulpit is, and the great field for the most magnificent effects of intellectual power. But I will think no more about this. It is foolish to speculate when it is necessary to practise.

I wrote a short and very indifferent Letter to my Father today,[2] and read a Discourse of Jeremy Taylor upon the Nursing of Infants.[3] Taylor was a sensual man by nature, or his imagination could not have been so lively, upon subjects which cold men cannot make themselves eloquent upon. He is quaint and very obscure, and this discourse on the whole did not please me. I afterwards read the portion of the Furies of Æschylus not before read, reviewed the whole Play, and then went in with my Wife to see our Neighbour Mrs. Dexter.[4] Mr. W. Foster came in during our stay there.[5] And in conversation a singular mistake occurred. He made an allusion to the cold and reserved manners of my Father in a manner rather surprising to me. I presume he did not recollect who I was. But it was rather an awkward affair to the poor man as he made several attempts to recover it which only plunged him deeper. I pitied him and tried to help him out. But the thing was unpleasant. Returned early.

[1] Mellish Irving Motte (d. 1881), Harvard 1821, was the minister of the South Congregational Society, Washington Street (*Boston Directory*, 1829–1830).

[2] Letter in Adams Papers.

[3] That is, Discourse 1: "Of Nursing Children, in imitation of the blessed Virgin-Mother" (1:52–65), a part of the section on the Nativity in Taylor's *Life*

of Christ.

[4] Mrs. Dexter had lately moved to 28 Beacon Street (*Boston Directory*, 1830–1831).

[5] Perhaps the William Foster who had been a neighbor of Mrs. Dexter on Franklin Place and now lived at 55 Beacon Street (*Boston Directory*, 1829–1830, 1830–1831).

MONDAY. 21ST.

Morning clear and mild as the middle of Spring. I went to the Office and busied myself as much as possible with my few Law affairs and my Accounts. My Journal being transferred to my Office takes off a considerable part of my available time. I wrote and tried to read a little of Williston but Richardson came in and sat for half an hour, and I went down to see Degrand about my Stocks for another half. He does not succeed in making a disposition of them. I regret this for I had hoped to have done well in that business.

My afternoon was taken up in copying my Letter to my Father and again attempting an Article upon Eloquence. The result does not satisfy me. I wish it would. My feelings impel me strongly to write, but nothing that comes from my pen comes near the idea I have formed of excellence. It is all tame, languid and dull. Under these circumstances I begin to doubt whether I shall ever succeed in this line of pursuits. The patience is not in me to study that excellence which is necessary to distinction. I grasp too high at once, my hold is not firm, and I find I have caught at a slender twig which will not support my weight. The evening was spent in continuing Clarissa Harlowe to Abby, and afterwards, continuing my writing.

TUESDAY. 22D.

Morning clear but rather colder than it has been. I went to the Office as usual and was occupied in my common avocations. I read a considerable portion of Williston with interest, though the Speeches did not strike me forcibly. They are of too temporary a character to please me. A part of my time was taken up in early preparation for sending in my Account Current, to my Father. I design it to be very thorough and satisfactory. The account was prepared as far as possible on one side, but nothing done in respect to the Letter to accompany it. My time was a little interrupted by the visit from Mr. Jones of Weston to bring me a little more of the proceeds of the sale of Wood at that place. This money comes in tolerably well. I do not know that now I shall want to receive any more, as the sum in my hands of my father's is now quite large enough, and nearly all demands are satisfied. He gave me some unpleasant News about the Horses, saying that one of them was unwell. I am glad I did not take him and have the trouble of him. But I feel sorry that they should be getting sick. This is the worst of Horses.

I returned home at dinner time and in the afternoon studied Æschines again after a lapse of some time. It grieves me exceedingly that I am unable to go on as I wish, but obstacles seem to be throwing themselves in the way constantly which only fret me to death. Patience is an essential requisite to a man, and although I had supposed that my experience in life had given me no trifling share of it, I do yet find myself frequently mortified by my want of it. I could not quite accomplish my regular purposes, as I went down to see the family, the regular meeting of whom happens once a week, and for this week with my Wife. These meetings are not pleasant from the circumstance that there is no community of feeling in the family. Edward and his Wife are entirely different from Chardon and his, and they all have no points of resemblance with mine. This consideration is deeply painful to me, for I see little in future so far as they are concerned to encourage my natural and good feelings which burn to disclose themselves.[1] My own family are now removed from me and they have in some measure lost that interest in me the want of which I feel though my age deprives me of it. But enough of this. It answers only for a Journal, perhaps not for that. The time was passed tolerably.

[1] His dissatisfaction with his aloof posture at these gatherings of the Brooks family in Boston and Medford led CFA to believe that he was considered by them "a great nothingarian who has no better amusement than to sit silent, communing with the stars" (CFA to LCA, 13 Dec., Adams Papers).

WEDNESDAY. 23RD.

Morning at the Office. The Officer came and settled with me for Titcomb's business which clears that Law business from my Docket which has been standing there for a very considerable time. I am very glad it is settled for it had worried me a good deal throughout the Summer.[1] I went down to Deposit the sum on hand and to see Mr. Tarbell about the other little affairs which he had intrusted me. He directed me to wind up, so that as soon as possible I propose to make a close in the affair. I then met Degrand and found that he had not been yet successful in his transactions for me, which is a matter of trouble to me. The shares of the State Bank have fallen below par so that I gave more for mine than I could have got them at in the Market. But as mine is a permanent Investment, I think the advantage it afforded me in the smallness of the Number more than overbalances the difference in price. I then went to the South End of the Town to see Sharpe the Cabinet Maker and pay him the amount due to him, and to see Mrs. Bittner for the settlement of that demand. She is poor and makes a very long face. I was obliged to make a very short one. This with a visit from Titcomb to talk over matters was quite enough to consume all the time till dinner.

Miss Carter and Miss Gorham, Abby's friends dined with us. I was out of humour. Afternoon, reading Æschines and reflecting upon an excellent letter I have received from my Father.[2] It is in the spirit of kindness. As a cousin of Abby's, Miss Bartlett married to Mr. Walker the Clergyman of Charlestown,[3] received her Company this evening, we went over with Mr. and Mrs. Frothingham and Chardon Brooks, a terrible bore but it was done to please Mr. Brooks. We returned shortly, and after a short Supper at Chardon's, went home.

[1] On the suit against Titcomb, entered at Thomas Tarbell's instance, see entry for 30 Oct., above.

[2] 18 Dec. (Adams Papers). A reply to CFA's letter of 10 Dec., on which see above, entry for that date, and note. He counsels perseverance in CFA's tripartite endeavors and suggests: (1) that each part be made auxiliary to the other parts; (2) that CFA reconsider his aversion to theoretic writers; and (3) that in his writing CFA attempt more complex forms, differing styles, and then begin to publish without revealing authorship.

[3] Catherine Bartlett (b. 1797), niece of Mrs. Brooks, was a daughter of Dr. George Bartlett (b. 1760, apothecary of Charlestown) and Mary (Gorham) Bartlett (1767–1832); see vol. 2:168, 270. James Walker was to remain as minister of Harvard Church, Charlestown, until 1839, when he would become successively Alford Professor of Natural Religion and President of Harvard, 1853–1860 (*DAB*).

THURSDAY. 24TH.

The morning was cloudy and damp, and I did not reach my Office until it was quite late. Indeed this practice of mine is bad, and ought to be corrected. I passed my morning much as usual—Not doing so much as I wished but having no moment unemployed. My spirits were rather depressed, owing to the constant struggle I am obliged to keep up to be at all Master of my own time. I confess I am disappointed in this. For one of the great reasons which had impelled me to urge so strongly the accomplishing my marriage, was the entire dissipation of time in which my engagement kept me. And now the same action in another form operates. Mrs. Brooks is anxious to see her daughter and to have her spend not hours but days and nights with her, and I am therefore under a pressure to avoid doing it. For they see only what I appear to be compelled to do, and judge from that, my time to be at my own disposal. I feel all this, and yet I feel more strongly what I believe to be a more urgent duty—That of fitting myself for all situations in life to which I may be called.

I read Williston this morning, the Speeches on the British Treaty.[1] They all want power, they need that force which is essential to Eloquence, that clearness which gives it power. I also prepared my Quarterly Account for my Father's inspection. It is long though tolerably clear. After dinner, I was engaged in reading Æschines which I enjoyed very considerably. The Greek is far from difficult, and I find some reason to flatter myself for the knowledge which I picked up at College, much more firmly than I had myself supposed. How delightful are these occupations. I read to my Wife, Clarissa Harlowe, my progress in this is slow, and I feel desirous now to get through it, to attempt something pleasanter and better. After she retired, I seized an hour to continue an Article upon Eloquence which upon reflection does not please me a bit better than any of the rest.

[1] The speeches of James Madison, William Branch Giles, Albert Gallatin, and Fisher Ames delivered in the House in 1796 on the appropriation bill to effectuate the terms of the British Treaty of 1794 are included in Williston's *Eloquence* at 1:332–463.

FRIDAY. 25TH.

The day was warm but damp. I went to the Office as usual and was occupied in reading Williston, and the Speech of Mr. Ames upon the resolutions of Mr. Clay on the British Treaty. It is certainly a more powerful piece of eloquence than any I have yet read. Mr. Ames was a very able man, and left behind him a very strong feeling of admiration of his character among a circle of admirers here.[1] But he became rather incorrect in his views during the latter part of his Life, being in ill health, and depressed circumstances. His mind was totally sound.

I also tried to form a Letter on the affairs of the Agency, a considerable portion of which was accomplished to my satisfaction. This was Christmas day and I reflected upon the probable condition of our family on that day. How will they spend the day this year, when those in place must feel in fear of seeing too much those who are out.[2] At any rate, the day brings no particular feeling with it to me now as I am here settled without any associations of family to remind me of it's return.

I read Æschines all the afternoon excepting a short space of time devoted to Mitford, who provokes me beyond tolerance. I think his Book ought to be thrown into the Fire. How much mischief History philosophically written, to use a fashionable word of the present day, by a prejudiced man, will occasion. I was pleased with my pursuits and my mind felt that kind of self satisfaction which is eminently soothing. I read to Abby, in continuation of Clarissa Harlowe, which becomes more and more interesting at every step. It is a very pathetic Novel indeed. And very moral for it contains much which would do well to be thoroughly understood by every young Lady. I sat an hour afterwards writing more and more on my Essay but getting more and more dissatisfied.

[1] Fisher Ames (1758–1808), member of Congress from Massachusetts and a leading Federalist (*DAB*).

[2] The meaning is uncertain, but would seem to allude to GWA's death during the year. In this context the sentence might be read: How will they spend the day this year, when those in place [i.e. living] must feel in fear of seeing too much [in their mind's eye] those who are out [i.e. dead]?

SATURDAY. 26TH.

Morning Cloudy but not disagreeable. I went to the Office, and occupied myself in looking up the facts relative to the Affairs with the Indians as given to us by the Message of the President of the United States. And I could not help being struck with the flimsy network of it's argument when I came to look into the thing—The Indian Treaties and the Controversy with Georgia.[1] But I could not devote my whole morning to it, and therefore sat down to draw up my Letter of Accounts to my Father which I did so effectually as to conclude to make another. This is always my way. But my morning passed and as I had advised Abby to go out of town to day to see her Mother I went down myself to Mrs. Frothingham's to dine. Found them at home as common and dined without any ceremony. From thence I went down to the Athenæum and in a great measure wasted the Afternoon. This may often prove the case unless I guard against it by some means or other. I did however read a considerable portion of Captain Hall's book upon America and was amused with it. I do not however agree with the notions taken by Mr. Everett of it.[2] No American need be afraid of such a work. We have got beyond that stage of existence when the hasty opinions of any single Individual can produce any permanent effect. Our Institutions are taking a solidity which will make us look to ourselves more and abroad less. Captain Hall is on the whole entertaining. His prejudices and his candor, his English feeling with his parental one all combine to make one diverted with him on the whole. But the book is not intrinsically worth much. I left off to go to the Debating Society where there was a very considerable meeting. The discussion on the Bank was renewed and continued during the whole evening. I spoke unpremeditatedly and was not so well satisfied with myself. But we closed the subject very thoroughly.

[1] As part of the Yazoo lands settlement in 1802, Georgia ceded to the United States the territory west of the Chattahoochee river for a cash payment and a promise that the Indians remaining within the State would be removed. Partly deterred by treaties entered into with the Indian tribes, government policy on removal from Georgia and other states in the years since had been discontinuous. In his Message of 8 Dec., President Jackson gave a new emphasis to the question. By inference holding the Indian treaties invalid on the premise that by them the tribes had set up independent governments within the boundaries of sovereign states, he affirmed that this could not be countenanced, that the Indians should emigrate westward or, remaining, submit to the laws of the states without special privileges. He proposed the creation of territory beyond the Mississippi to be guaranteed to the tribes occupying it. In 1830 Congress would make Indian removal national policy, and within the decade the process would be carried to completion.

[2] Capt. Basil Hall, R.N., *Travels in North America, in the Years 1827 and 1828*, 3 vols., Edinburgh, 1829. The book had been reviewed adversely in *North Amer. Rev.*, 29:522–574 (Oct. 1829), by Edward Everett, though not severely enough to satisfy JQA (Diary, 17 Dec.). On CFA's encounter with Captain Hall, see vol. 2:169.

SUNDAY. 27TH.

Did not rise very early this morning. But I hope to be able to do so for my time now slips away exceedingly fast. For the two past mornings I had succeeded in starting early but again fell back on this. As I did not feel desirous of reaching Medford very early, I read a little of Brumoy's Preliminary Discourses and two of Blair's Lectures upon Oratory which interested me very much.[1] They are full of interest to a young man who like myself is endeavouring to fix some school for himself to pursue. And they contain much advice which had occurred to my mind spontaneously. The whole study is exceedingly fascinating, and if I could only give my whole time to it, I should be pursuing the most anxious wish of my heart. I feel favoured in many respects, by the independence which I enjoy, by the circumstances of birth and character which I need not be ashamed of. Now if I can fill up the rest of the outline, I can enjoy a respect and consideration in society to be excelled by few individuals in the Country. I can support the the name at least respectably among us.

But I was obliged to think of going to Medford and so at eleven, I started and going through Milk row and Cambridge arrived just before dinner. Found the family as usual, excepting that Mrs. Brooks appeared to me suffering, though with a better appetite than she has had. We dined, and went in the afternoon to hear Mr. Stetson who preached a tolerably sensible Sermon upon the close of the year; This gentleman has some power, but his great corpulency is a drawback. We returned and spent the evening at home quietly. I had little or nothing to do, so occupied myself in looking over the Pages of the New Almanac gotten up under literary patronage. But, I should have preferred to have been at home pursuing a more useful purpose.

[1] CFA undertook to read Hugh Blair, *Lectures on Rhetoric and Belles Lettres,* in pursuance of JQA's advice to study some of the theoretical writers on oratory (above, entry for 23 Dec., note, and CFA to JQA, 3 [i.e. 4] Jan. 1830, Adams Papers). Editions published at London in 3 vols., 1793 and 1796, are in MQA, the earlier having JQA's bookplate.

MONDAY. 28TH.

The morning was cloudy when we arose, but it afterwards cleared up and became a beautiful day. One of those mild Winter days which make perhaps the pleasantest weather we have. We breakfasted and returned to town very pleasantly. It was very late however before I reached my Office. My time seemed scarcely a minute, for I found upon my Table two Letters from my Father which I read with much interest[1]—Though one of them in reply to my inquiries about the violated letter satisfied me it had been done at the Post Office. I had not done examining these when Richardson came in and sat some time with me. The time passed so rapidly that I did not profit at all of the morning. My only work was the accomplishment of a proper portion of Journal.

Richardson dined with me, and was very pleasant, and I felt more easily at my Table than I have commonly done. He did not remain long afterwards so that I had time to complete a portion of Æschines. The invective is the feeblest part of this Oration. By men who were conversant with the facts it is not wonderful that he was condemned. Mr. Mitford however follows him as if a heated partizan was as good an authority as the most unbiassed Judge, because he was not contradicted in his assertions, though he well knew, that frequently the best mode of refuting assertions of an extravagant nature is by leaving them alone. It is not probable, had Æschines possessed the power of answering Demosthenes, that he would have noticed many of the violent charges of the latter against him, though Mr. Mitford thinks

117

differently. I read also one of the Prefatory Discourses of Brumoy upon the Greek Theatre.

As Abby was out this evening, I went to call for her at Mrs. Carter's.[2] Her friend Anne being [*word omitted*] to entertain her and Miss Gorham. I spent an hour there much in my usual way, without any benefit to myself or any body near me. I like Conversation but it must not be trivial. We returned early. The night was beautiful for the Season.

[1] 21, 22 Dec. (Adams Papers). The first of these relates to the broken seal on JQA's letter of 9 December.
[2] On Mrs. James Carter, mother of ABA's friend Anne, see vol. 2:158. The Carters lived on Summer Street (*Boston Directory*, 1829–1830).

TUESDAY. 29TH.

Morning fine. I reached the Office quite early and had a fine opportunity for work. I was first interrupted by the entrance of Henderson and his Trustee, who are desirous of making a settlement. I told him I would compound on very favourable terms, and mentioned one half the demand with costs. He said he did not know, that he would go and see, which he did. I am now a little encouraged about this demand and hope very earnestly that I may be able to settle it, for I have little confidence in the result of a trial.

My next object was the framing a short letter to Mr. Barry which I did, complaining mildly of the violation of my Letter at the Post Office at Washington.[1] I do not know that it will produce any very particular effect, but it is curious to see the operation of it. I then passed all the remainder of the morning in drawing up a Letter to my Father upon the Affairs of the Agency which I completed, and now needs nothing but copying. I flatter myself that it is clear and distinct. My morning was thus usefully employed though with hardly any reference to literary pursuits. The practical affairs of Life demand Attention as much as any, for the science of living with respectability depends much upon the clear superiority of the receipts over the expenditures. I hope to keep this in view clearly myself.

It was time to go down by Invitation to see Mr. Frothingham where we were to dine. I found there Mr. Storrow, a gentleman residing in Paris, now here on a visit, a certain Dr. Fisher who is a friend of Mr. F.'s,[2] Edward Brooks, Abby and myself. The dinner was to me exceedingly dull. But somehow or other this seems universally the case, probably from the fact that I feel out of my element at them. I was glad to return to my room, but it being too late for Greek, I finished

Brumoy's Parallell between the Ancient and Modern Theatres and Franklin's Dissertation prefixed to his Translation of Sophocles.[3] This happened between my leaving Mr. F.'s and my return, for it was the evening of the Collection of the Family. The meeting was much as usual and ended in a spirit not a bit pleasant. This is not much to my taste. Nor does it make me feel in very good humour. Returned home early.

[1] To William T. Barry, Postmaster General of the U.S. (LbC, Adams Papers). To this letter Barry responded to JQA (8 Jan. 1830, Adams Papers) asking for particulars and promising fullest investigation. JQA answered Barry on the 9th (LbC, Adams Papers), but when he received a letter on the 14th from William Jones, postmaster at Washington, asking numerous questions and proposing an interrogation of JQA's servant (letter missing), JQA on the same day wrote indignantly to Barry (LbC, Adams Papers) that the investigation, if it was to be carried forward at all, should be carried forward by Barry. Barry's civil and apologetic reply (missing) disarmed JQA temporarily (JQA to CFA, 17 Jan. 1830, Adams Papers), but on the 28th he had to write Barry once more (LbC, Adams Papers) enclosing cover of a letter received that day open at one end. Coincidentally, in the same mail was a letter on political matters from his old supporter, John Brazer Davis, in which Davis expressed fears of the Post Office. On the 29th, JQA with some acerbity recounted the two "accidents" in a letter to Davis (LbC, Adams Papers), in consequence expressing caution about committing political comments to the mails. In the meantime, CFA, in better humor now than his father, tells the story with relish, admitting to making "a noise at the Post Office here, where poor Greene feels all the time like a condemned criminal and after flying round the town to convince every body of the enormity of the injury, I sat down quite satisfied that I had so much cause for complaint—and so little for regret. . . . [I]t is a very comfortable thing to feel ourselves sometimes wronged by people against whom we have no disposition to charge merit" (CFA to LCA, 17 Jan. 1830, Adams Papers).

[2] Probably John D. Fisher, physician, of 11 Hayward Place (*Boston Directory*, 1830–1831); Mr. Storrow has not been further identified.

[3] *The Tragedies of Sophocles, from the Greek by Thomas Francklin*, London, 1793. JQA's copy is in MQA. At p. 5–61 is "A dissertation on ancient Greek tragedy."

WEDNESDAY. 30TH.

Morning at the Office as usual—The weather a continuation of the fine season of warmth we so unexpectedly enjoy. I was engaged nearly the whole of my time in copying my Letter to my Father and finishing the Accounts previous to their transmission. I completed every thing so as to feel rather awkwardly when Dr. Lewis came to pay his rent and wind up his Lease. I begged him to postpone it which is a prayer I seldom make in cases of payment. I am going to have some trouble with that House. From some cause or other, George had very little while he was in the Agency. And now it comes all at once upon me, with the repairs which it will be necessary to make to put[1] upon the Houses so as again to rent them. I wrote fully upon the subjects and intend as far as possible to relieve myself from responsibility in the matter. Many persons called upon small affairs of different sorts too numerous to mention.

I had only leisure to look over a small portion of the Catalogue of the Athenæum which is just now published.[2] There are many good books, but too many which seem to have very little value attached to them. I suppose this a fact necessarily resulting from the Constitution of the Corporation, by which popular works are demanded, to please the taste of Proprietors who read only those. Returned home, and having wasted an hour of the afternoon in paying attention to the affairs of my Wine Cellar I read a considerable part of Æschines. Having left off the slow process of translation, I go on faster, but my schemes and my projects are so numerous that they puzzle me a little. In the evening, I read to my Wife a portion of Clarissa Harlowe where it is becoming most interesting. We were interrupted by Edmund Quincy who spent an hour in conversation in a very tolerable manner.

[1] Thus in MS.
[2] *Catalogue of Books Added to the Boston Athenæum since . . . January 1827,* Boston, [1830]. The extensive additions suggested to CFA that the institution had "incurred very heavy expenses in large Collections of Books" (to JQA, 3 [i.e. 4] Jan. 1830, Adams Papers).

THURSDAY. 31ST.

Morning Cloudy with a little rain, but yet quite warm. I went to the Office and was busy nearly all the morning in making up my Bills against my Tenants for the ensuing Quarter. My accounts on the whole present a pretty fair prospect. I have increased my Property a little during the past year, as well by my own efforts as by my father's kindness. But it still remains a little problematical to me whether the proceeds of my Income will entirely defray the expenses of my family establishment. We have as yet sailed before the Wind, having had no heavy expenses to weigh upon us. But when they come I shall then feel as if there was a trial to be made, and what may prove a severe one. It is my endeavour now so to increase my resources as to be able more firmly to meet any such events as may happen, and to be able to ease off the load of my dependence should it happen to press too hard, at any future moment. My Father's Affairs here look tolerably well.

My time was so nearly taken up with all this that I only read a few pages of Mr. Bayard's Speech on resisting the aggressions of France, and that not with the attention which the subject deserved.[1] Returned home and spent the Afternoon in reading Æschines as usual with whom I made great progress. Received a very pleasant letter from my Father, and sent him my own business Letter for the close of the year.[2] Thus the day passed agreeably enough. In the evening I had but a short leisure to read any of Sophocles in the Translations of Potter and Francklin,[3] for we were invited to a Ball of the Bachelors of the City. We accordingly went at the Hour of Nine and passed three Hours in dancing as usual upon occasions of a similar nature. I did not enjoy myself as much as I had expected. I do not know why because there were many young Ladies who seemed to be pleasing. But my wife was not well and for the first time I found that my situation was essentially altered. I was no longer the unmarried man. And there was a tedium and ennui attending what I did which had not formerly been the case. I was glad to get away and so was my Wife.

[1] Probably CFA is referring to the speech "On the necessity of resisting the agressions and encroachments of France" delivered in the House in May 1797 by Robert G. Harper, the only one on this subject included in Williston's *Eloquence.*

[2] 26 Dec.; CFA to JQA, 31 Dec., LbC (both in Adams Papers). CFA's review of the year, while noting some favorable developments in the Agency, dwells upon the depressed state of Boston real estate in 1829. He reports that rents have fallen by 25 percent within six months, that four or five hundred houses and stores are vacant, this of his own knowledge and on the authority of Mr. Brooks.

[3] In MQA, along with the translation by Francklin, is R. Potter's translation of *The Tragedies of Sophocles,* Oxford, 1819.

JANUARY. 1830.

FRIDAY 1ST.

The morning of the New Year broke bright and clear, though much colder than it had been heretofore. It is usually with me the season of reflection upon the past and the future. I have little to say in regard to the former for Circumstances have already occurred in the Interval since last year, in which I fully explained my feelings in regard to it. I commence this year in a new and responsible relation, and I look now to the future with more anxiety. My own feelings have nothing in them which I can condemn. I endeavour to keep up to the line of duty which my rigid sense of propriety marks out, and though not conscious yet of failure, the dread of it hangs still heavy on my mind. It is not probable that at any future time, I shall enjoy so fully the satisfaction of a contented mind as I now do. For the future is bright, beyond the possibility of realization.

I was busy all the morning in making up my Accounts against the different Tenants and sending them out. Mr. Lewis called upon me to settle the rent and I asked him what he thought the House would in future be worth. He gave me very little encouragement to expect it would be even what I had fixed it. He paid me his balance due in full, and took his final leave. Degrand called to know if I wished to make an Investment in some Stock tomorrow to which I assented, and gave him the necessary instructions to that effect. I arranged my own Accounts during the Month and paid myself the Quarterly Allowance due on this day to me by my Father.

Returning home, found my Wife quite unwell and comfortless. This was not at all pleasant. After dinner I went upstairs and read Æschines as usual—Nothing of interest occurring. Evening passed in reading to my Wife a part of Clarissa Harlowe in which we go along quite slowly. She was so unwell that she retired early and I sat two hours writing upon the subject of Eloquence. I was satisfied with what I did when I left off, but there is no possibility of telling how I shall like it when I look over it again. The day passed more quietly to me than any New Year's day I have passed for many years.

SATURDAY. 2D.

The weather still continued delightfully mild during the whole day. I was at the office engaged in my usual occupations—Arranging my Accounts which from some cause or other take up much of my time and talking much with Mr. Degrand who did not succeed in making any Investment for me as I had desired. I am not entirely sorry for this as what I saw did not present to me a vision entirely attractive. I was able to devote a short time to reading and became much interested in the Speech of Mr. Harper upon the ⟨British Treaty⟩ power of appointing Ministers lodged in the Executive.[1] It is a tolerable Speech, but disappoints me when compared to what I had heard my Brother say of it. It does not nearly equal that of Mr. Ames which I have lately read, on the British Treaty. I had not much time to think of these things and so was obliged to return home after seeing Mr. Brooks for a moment to tell him we should go out of town tomorrow.

After dinner I continued reading Æschines and endeavouring to make a more rapid advance than hitherto in which I succeeded and as I had a little time over and above, which remained besides, I devoted it to commencing a Letter to my Father, which I could not finish before it became time to go to the regular meeting of the Debating Society. I regret that I am always feeling so pressed for time, as to be unable to write to him as fully and regularly as I ought—

Because my Correspondence with him has the double merit of being interesting and useful to me. I was obliged to leave off, to go and hear the question of the Georgia Indians discussed. It was done in a lame and dull manner. The Committee were not a good one to do the subject justice, and those were absent who could give most interest to it. I was much pleased with my own extemporaneous success to revive the drooping spirit which had been distressed by the long harangue of Dr. Davis, neither studied nor connected in its parts.[2] Returned home late and retired after reading an article in the North American Review called a Year in Spain.[3]

[1] "On the constitutional powers of the President and Senate relative to the appointment of foreign ministers," delivered in the House, 2 March 1798, by Robert Goodloe Harper (Williston's *Eloquence*, 2:19–75).

[2] Probably Edward G. Davis, physician, of 17 Pearl Street (*Boston Directory*, 1830–1831). For CFA's views on the subject under debate, see below, entry for 21 Jan. and note.

[3] A review of *A Year in Spain* by Alexander Slidell Mackenzie, *North Amer. Rev.*, 30:237–259 (Jan. 1830). The (anonymous) reviewer was Willard Phillips.

SUNDAY. 3D.

The morning was bright and clear though somewhat colder than I had been accustomed to for the few days past. I had no time to do any thing at home, as we went to Medford according to agreement immediately after breakfast. I suffered a good deal from cold during my ride. But having reached there before Service began, we went down in the Carriage, and heard Mr. Stetson preach a Communion Sermon in which I did not take much interest. Then at home, time passed as usual pretty much. The afternoon, we again went to Meeting, and heard Mr. Hedge of West Cambridge, an old Classmate of mine.[1] I listened to his Sermon with attention. It was prettily written, but in a style rather singular for a Country Clergyman, whose parishioners do not much understand the nature of the sublime and beautiful. Their philosophical heads turn much more upon the practical and the simple.

We returned home and found Edward Brooks and his Wife just come to pass the afternoon. They were lively and pleasant, talked about the Ball, and made the time pass so rapidly that I hardly was sensible of it. These are on the whole the most to my taste of all the family. After tea, Mrs. Everett and I went to Mrs. Hall's to pay a short visit. They were all very dull and I was amazingly tired of my visit. Mary, the daughter is a Woman of strong mind and pleasing conversation but they are a doleful set at present owing to certain misfortunes which are upon them strongly.[2] We left them and spent an hour with the Miss Osgoods, a pair of old maids, daughters of the famous Parson Osgood of well known memory. They are tinged with old and disagreeable prejudices which make them to me very unpleasant, but as they are kind to my Wife, I cannot object to them. Returned early and retired as usual.

¹ On Frederic Henry Hedge, see vol. 1:425 and *DAB*.
² See above, entries for 8 Nov. and 16 Dec. 1829.

MONDAY 4TH.

We returned to town as early as we could make it out, which was not however before 11 o'clock. The heavy rain which had fallen in the Night gave us a beautiful day, and the ride was pleasant, but I had not reached my Office before I found that my business called for me. A Number of persons had called to receive their dues upon the arrival of the first of the year. I was very busy in making up my Accounts, but a little disappointed in my receipts which were not very considerable. My Uncle, T. B. Adams called in and made the usual settlement at the Commencement of the Quarter. Mr. Gilson came in and settled with me as to the little Law business I had done for him.¹ My Cash Accounts do not please me over much. There seems a deficiency in promptitude of payment, which I do not at all admire.

In the afternoon I called at Mrs. Foster's to see Miss Abby S. Adams and pay her the Quarterly Interest. Stopped in at Miss Oliver's but found her unprepared to settle with me. This business being done, I had barely time to go home and read a few pages of Sophocles, before it became time to go to the annual meeting of the Proprietors of the Athenæum. This was the first which I had attended. There was little or nothing remarkable which happened. Col. T. H. Perkins was chosen President instead of Mr. Quincy who withdrew.² I returned home and passed the Evening in reading Clarissa Harlowe to Abby, after which I saved time enough to finish my Letter to my Father.

¹ Perhaps Asa Gilson of Gilson & Foster, stablemen, of Hawley Place or Joshua Gilson of Gilson & Livermore, grocers, of West and Mason streets (*Boston Directory*, 1830–1831).
² President Josiah Quincy of Harvard had resigned the presidency of the Athenæum because of his "transfer to Cambridge." On Col. Thomas Handasyd Perkins, see vol. 2:151. CFA took his elevation to the presidency as a mark of the shift taking place in the direction of civic enterprises to those who had acquired wealth in commerce, remarking that since the institution "is now supported by the wealth of the Merchants, it is but fair the most liberal among them should have the credit" (CFA to JQA, 3 [*i.e.* 4] Jan., Adams Papers). By the application of such a measure, Col. Perkins was uniquely qualified. The building at No. 13 Pearl Street in which the Athenæum was housed from 1822 had been the mansion of and was the gift of Col. Perkins' late brother and partner, James Perkins. The construction in 1826 of the lecture hall and gallery in the rear of the library had been made possible by gifts of $8,000

each from Col. Perkins and James Perkins, the younger, and by matching funds raised by subscription (Josiah Quincy, *The History of the Boston* *Athenæum* . . ., Cambridge, 1851, p. 70, 96–97). Abel Bowen's engraving of the buildings is reproduced in the present volume; see above, p. xiv–xv.

TUESDAY. 5TH.

Morning at the Office. Occupied as usual in arranging my Accounts which take up considerable time and in writing my Journal which takes more. This ought to be changed for they neither of them merit quite so much attention as I give to them. I found time however to read several very interesting Speeches in Williston's Book, many of which on the Judiciary in 1802, I had read before.[1] They do not much vary the views I have taken upon the general question. My time passed rapidly and after dinner, having paid a visit at Mrs. Foster's, and settled with Elizabeth[2] for the Quarter, I returned and read a considerable portion of Æschines with relish. Finished my despatch to my Father which was somewhat long, and as Abby was out I wrote something more upon my Dissertation. It is a little too bold to publish I fear, and not good enough. I have not yet made up my mind whether to offer it for publication. But if I do, I must make it up to have it rejected.

I was soon reminded of the necessity of going to Edward Brooks' to the usual meeting of the family. Chardon and his Wife were not there and our Meeting was much the pleasantest we have had this Winter. I see clearly that the misunderstanding with them is the cause of all our disagreements and I regret it. We remained until ten, and I then came home quite pleased with my evening.

[1] The speeches of Stephens T. Mason and Gouverneur Morris in the Senate and of William Branch Giles and James A. Bayard in the House in 1802 on the repeal of the Judiciary Bill of 1801 appear in Williston's *Eloquence* at 2:82–235.

[2] His cousin ECA.

WEDNESDAY. 6TH.

Morning at the Office. As Miss Oliver this morning sent me a portion of her rent I was again occupied in arranging my Accounts, though they did not take up quite so much time as usual. I was engaged in reading Williston and the sharp Speeches of Mr. Giles and Mr. Bayard upon the Judiciary Bill of 1802. Mr. Beale of Quincy called in to see me having heard I had made inquiry respecting the meeting of the Quincy Canal Company. He told me that the meeting would be held at six o'clock on Tuesday next which is a very inconvenient hour to me. But I agreed to attend as my Father is desirous that I should. He gave me also the unwelcome news that the Neponset

Bridge Company made no Dividend this Quarter. I am somewhat disappointed at the State of my father's funds, this month, and am thus taught the necessity of never anticipating too much. This Company is a rarely failing source of revenue. But so it is, it fails when most calculated upon.

After dinner I was as usual occupied reading Æschines in his close where he attempts to anticipate the objections of his Adversary and so evidently exhibits the great dread he entertains of him, but I did not finish the Oration. As Abby was again out I continued my Essay upon Eloquence. Although I get dissatisfied as I go on, yet I am resolved to persevere, and after my whole plan is finished I will then look it over to criticize. This evening I was not in the spirit, being oppressed with a bad cold upon my Lungs. I left off to call for Abby at her sister Anne's, after which, I read over the Lives of Demosthenes and Cicero by Plutarch.

THURSDAY. 7TH.

The morning was cloudy and threatened snow, but it finally cleared away and became very fine, as if it seemed difficult to break up the continued series of fine weather which we have enjoyed. I was at the Office all the morning engaged in my usual duties and in reading Williston. I made a call and sat with Mr. Davis for a few minutes. Mr. Cruft also came and informed me of a Fire which had occurred during the Night in the House owned by my Father and occupied by Mrs. Oliver.[1] This is not agreeable News for it is probably too small to be covered by my Father's Insurance. I deferred going to see it however until I should be sent for. After dinner I went to see the spot where the Fire took. The Kitchen came very near being destroyed. It was luckily saved from the violence of the Enginemen, so that the Expense of repair will probably be trifling. From thence I went down to meet Chapman and Pickering upon a Committee upon the affairs of the Debating Society which kept us an hour.[2] We looked over their Affairs and made out a case, not of the most flattering kind. I left them to go to the Office and meet Mr. Hollis my father's Carpenter, and direct him to estimate the amount of damage done so as to ascertain if the Insurance Office will pay it. Thence home where I read only a little of Sophocles before Tea. The evening was passed in reading Clarissa Harlowe. We progressed beyond the catastrophe and I was exceedingly affected by it. Seldom have I read a book which excited my sympathies more. After Abby retired, I read some articles in the North American Review but went myself to bed early.

[1] The house owned by JQA at 55 Hancock Street was occupied by Miss A. B. (or A. R.) Oliver and N. K. G. Oliver, schoolteacher. See M/CFA/3; CFA to JQA, 2 Feb., to Miss Oliver, 10 April 1830 (both LbCs and in Adams Papers); *Boston Directory*, 1830–1831.

[2] Jonathan Chapman Jr., CFA's Harvard classmate and friend (vol. 1:101 and numerous references thereafter), was an attorney, 16 Court Street; Edward Pickering, also an attorney, was at 21 State Street (*Boston Directory*, 1830–1831).

FRIDAY 8TH.

Morning fine. I went to the Office as usual but was so much interrupted that I could do little of my reading. The first visit that was paid me was by Rufus Davis the revolutionary veteran whose business had been entrusted to me by my father. He is an odd looking character and full of the wildness peculiar to the poorest of that Class. I cannot say that I admired my Client but as I was obliged to pay him some attention on my father's Account I thought I would do it out of Charity. I carried him to the Pension Office but Mr. Lilly, the person who had seen me and directed me how to act, was absent and nothing could be done so that poor Davis must go to the trouble of coming again and I must also again be bored.

A man came to apply for my father's House in the rear of Court Street and in consequence I was obliged to go and look over it with him and look at it's very miserable condition. I engaged to repair if he would take it, and he agreed to let it go till tomorrow before giving an answer. I was obliged to send for the workmen in order to go and see how soon it might be put in order for occupation. My talking with them consumed much time, and Mr. Jones coming in from Weston kept me afterwards for a considerable time after my regular season for dinner. I settled with him. Mr. Curtis called to give me a Deed to make out for the Boylston Estate. Thus was I full of occupation.

The afternoon was passed in reading Æschines and after my usual portion of this, the Œdipus of Sophocles in the translations of Potter and Francklin. The time in this manner went rapidly until evening when I went down to hear the Lecture of Mr. A. H. Everett before the Society of Useful Knowledge. It was a historical view of the State of Society in the World, in which he examined the different doctrines of perfectibility, improvement, the reverse, and a stationary condition. His manner is tolerably good, but not equal to his brother's. I was on the whole tolerably well satisfied. On my return I tried to read Clarissa but was prevented by Mr. Degrand, and Nathl. Hall who paid short visits here, the latter to take leave,[1] so that we read but little of Clarissa.

[1] Rev. Nathaniel Hall (b. 1805), younger brother of Rev. Edward Brooks Hall and nephew of Peter C. Brooks, was on the point of his departure for Cuba, having in his care his brother, who was ill (Brooks, Waste Book, 9 Jan. 1830).

SATURDAY 9TH.

Morning at the Office. Weather fine as usual. I was very busy all the time. Chapman sent over to me his report for the Debating Society which I signed as a Member of the Committee and returned. Then came the applicant for the House, who after some conversation upon the subject agreed to take it from the first of February at the old rent paid by Mr. Whitney, abating the Taxes.[1] And I thought it wise to close with him at once and undertook to have the House prepared for his reception by that time. I then took up my Journal, after which the Deed which Mr. Curtis had left for me to do. This took me some time. Then I filled up an Indenture of Lease for my new Tenant to sign. Thus my whole time was pretty much occupied.

After dinner, I continued Æschines as usual and came to the close of the argument, the Peroration being now the only part which I have to read. I do not like so well this close for it displays a degree of timidity not held before, and not becoming in a man who is Accuser, and has therefore brought his risk upon himself. I then sat down and attempted a continuation of my Essay upon Eloquence which I brought down tolerably well to a close, a few remarks only remaining to be added as generalizing. I read it all over and was better satisfied than I had expected. From thence I went to attend the meeting of the Debating Society. The subject this evening was not an interesting one, it was upon the question now agitating the Community of legalizing Medical Dissections by furnishing bodies to Physicians, from the Alms Houses and other Establishments where those die who have few friends to feel for them. The discussion was much more interesting however than I had expected and we were detained a considerable time by the Speakers upon it so that I returned not until ten.

[1] William Tenney became the tenant of the house at the rear of 23 Court Street on 1 Feb., remaining there until May 1833 and paying his $75 quarterly rent with punctuality (M/CFA/3).

SUNDAY. 10TH.

The Weather we have so much enjoyed has at last come to an end. We arose this morning in darkness, with a storm raging without. I did not myself feel over well, and this is so rare an occurrence with me now that I feel restless under it. I did not go to Meeting this morning, but took the opportunity to write a Letter to my Father,[1] containing a kind of Analysis of the Oration of Æschines which I have just finished. I put some labour into this in order to show to my Father that in my reading I am not trifling. And though it is a little amusing that I should address such a thing to him yet I hope he will feel gratified by my exertion if not entertained by my subject.

My Wife was quite sick all day with a violent cold which weighs upon her. I went out in the afternoon to hear Mr. Pierpont preach.[2] His sermon was tolerable. It's difficulty was that it was not sufficiently clear. But he has much merit in his correctness of reading. I cannot say that I quite like his *tones*, or his *breadth* of pronunciation of particular words, but on the whole I was pleased. I returned home, finished four pages to my Father, and passed the Evening in reading Clarissa aloud. I was much fascinated with this part of the Book and began to think that Richardson merited his fame, an impression which I had not fully given to me, I admit, hitherto.[3] But the conduct of Clarissa after her dishonour is a noble effort of the mind. I afterwards sat an hour continuing my Essay on Eloquence.

[1] Letter in Adams Papers.
[2] John Pierpont was the minister of the Hollis Street Church (Congregational), Boston (*Mass. Register*, 1830).
[3] Thus in MS.

MONDAY. 11TH.

The morning was clear but colder than any we had endured this Winter. I went to the Office as usual and was engaged in occupations which prevented me from paying any attention to Williston. I was called down to oversee the work which the Painter was putting upon the House in the rear of this, at a season most unfit for the purpose. I looked over it and gave the necessary directions, being glad to get back to my room. But I was soon called away to go and inquire of Mr. Tarbell whether he knew any good man of whom to obtain Butter, a domestic errand but a very necessary one. I stopped to converse a little while with him about his little affairs in my hands and then returned, but my day was gone, I could not put any thing more into it.

The Afternoon was passed in reading Æschines which was the conclusion of the Oration on the Crown. I admire it on the whole. How far it is superior to the long and laboured efforts of our day, when power is overlooked in the search for it. I then continued my Essay in a way I did not like. The evening was spent in reading aloud in Clarissa, wherein we progress slowly. I afterwards read the Article on the North American Indians.[1]

[1] Probably the review bearing the running-head title "Removal of the Indians," *North Amer. Rev.*, 30:62–121 (Jan. 1830). The (anonymous) author was Gov. Lewis Cass.

TUESDAY. 12TH.

Morning cold. At the Office as usual, and engaged in doing my work upon the usual affairs, but on this day I was exceedingly hurried. Rufus Davis again came to me, and again I went with him to the Pension Office where I saw all the steps necessary to procure for the man his new Pension, and I went through them all and forwarded to Mr. Eaton secretary of War, the Papers. This took much time. I then went into Court and heard Judge Putnam deliver his Opinion in the case of the Warren Bridge.[1] The Court delivered their various Judgments seriatim, no two being agreed altogether, but on the essential point being equally divided. I could not wait to hear Judge Parker. Returned to the Office, and continued doing what I could but that was little. Josiah Quincy came in and sat a little while, then Mr. Curtis came on business, and he detained me until dinner time so that the whole morning went and I returned home. I forgot to state that I had received a Letter from Mr. Barry this morning quite respectful.[2]

The day was cold, but as it was the time fixed for the Meeting of the Canal Company at Quincy, I started at half past three. My ride was a cold and very disagreeable one but I reached my friend Mr. Beale's before five. With him I had a little conversation, but finding that I should not be able to see my Uncle's family after the Meeting I decided to go before, so I went up and found only the Girls as the remainder of the family had gone to Exeter to place their son John at school. Whether this is done by them or by my Father, I do not know.[3] I sat with them a little while talking pleasantly enough, until it became time to go to the regular Meeting. I found the Members of the Company present.[4] They elected their Officers and among others I was chosen a Director which I accepted and hope soon to know a little more about the affairs of the Company. Little else was done, the great point of paying the Interest on the Notes was not settled, and I returned to town feeling that here was another source of disappointment to me in the expectation of Funds. So that now I am compelled to abandon my cherished idea of investment. My ride was not quite so bad as I had expected. It was lighter, and I arrived in town before ten. Abby had been attending the usual Meeting at Chardon's.

[1] The Supreme Judicial Court sitting in chancery had heard the application of the proprietors of the Charles River Bridge for an injunction against the proprietors of the Warren Bridge on the ground that construction of a second bridge connecting Boston and Charlestown, located only a short distance from

the first, constituted an impairment of its rights. Chief Justice Isaac Parker and Justice Samuel Putnam delivered opinions supporting the application, Justices Morton and Wilde opposing. There being no majority, the application failed (*Columbian Centinel*, 13 Jan., p. 2, col. 5). The case is more fully discussed in vol. 2:264.

² The letter from the Postmaster General, W. T. Barry, is missing; on the occasion for it, see above, entry for 29

Dec. 1829, note.

³ CFA learned shortly that JQA in November had proposed that if TBA's son, John Quincy (1815–1854), be sent to Phillips Exeter Academy JQA would pay the board and tuition of $200 a year (JQA, Diary, 8, 30 Nov. 1829; JQA to CFA, 5 Feb. 1830, Adams Papers).

⁴ Although CFA owned a share in the Quincy Canal Company given to him by JQA, CFA attended so that he could represent JQA's interest.

WEDNESDAY. 13TH.

The Weather was cold and the sky cloudy this morning when I went to the Office. It began to snow but it did not moderate sufficiently to allow of the fall of any quantity. I was engaged in the supervision of the repairs necessary for the House in the rear of my Office. It gives me much trouble, as I find myself standing in danger of being taken in constantly by workmen or others who think me young and easy to be imposed upon. One man cautions me, and another man cautions me until I feel as if I had rather more to do than I was able. But this is my first trial on this Agency. So long as Houses are occupied, it is an easy business, but when empty, and they need considerable repair, the trial begins.

I called in a few moments to see Mr. Brooks, and wrote a part of a letter to my Father on business, from which I desisted to see Mr. Curtis who came in to talk over the unfortunate affair of Mr. Vaughan. My father wrote me a letter upon the subject,[1] but we decided upon nothing. He advises Mr. Curtis to go to England in person, but he seems rather doubtful upon it. Returned home. After dinner read the remarks by various Authors upon the Œdipus of Sophocles, La Harpe and Brumoy, who agree in their praises. It is a good tragedy but not so much to my taste as the wilder ones of Æschylus. I also finished my Dissertation which upon reading over I did not admire. It did not appear to me as well as I expected. Evening at home reading Clarissa, until Mr. William Brooks came in who sat with us for a very considerable time.[2] He is a cousin of Abby's, and was tolerably agreeable.

¹ 8 Jan. (Adams Papers). Following the dispatch to Petty Vaughan, the English agent of Thomas Boylston, of papers designed to effect the transfer of funds collected by Vaughan from the French Government and due the Boylston estate (see above, entries for 12 Sept., 2 Nov. 1829, notes), Vaughan acknowledged

their receipt but delayed proceeding because he was "sick in bed." A second letter from him to JQA, enclosed by CFA in his letter of 31 Dec., brought information that Vaughan had, at some point after collecting the funds, placed them in the hands of his uncle, William Vaughan, whose failure Petty Vaughan had now to report. Though JQA had known and respected William Vaughan for nearly fifty years, he suspected that Petty Vaughan, knowing of his uncle's financial straits, had placed the money with him, hoping thereby to provide him temporary relief. JQA's proposal that Nathaniel Curtis, his coexecutor, go to England, like other efforts initiated to recover the funds, came to nothing. CFA seems to have been involved in this phase only as a conveyor of messages and correspondence. See JQA, Diary, 8, 13, 23, 28 Jan.; JQA to Nathaniel Curtis, 8 Jan.,

to Nathaniel Curtis and Mrs. W. N. Boylston, 13, 23 Jan., 4 Feb. (all LbCs and in Adams Papers).

[2] William Gray Brooks, a son of Peter C. Brooks' brother Cotton Brown Brooks of Portland (1765–1834), in 1833 married another cousin of ABA's, Mary Ann Phillips (b. 1808), daughter of Lydia (Gorham) and John Phillips of Andover. Their sons included Phillips Brooks (*DAB*). William Gray Brooks' Diary in 9 vols. (1838–1877, with breaks) is among the Brooks MSS, MHi.

THURSDAY. 14TH.

Morning misty but cold. The fog seemed to attach itself to every thing and freeze as it came, so that every thing presented a white and glossy appearance in the Streets. The grass had the white frost on it which we so often see in the Autumn and the Trees were clothed with uncommon beauty. I went to the Office and was engaged in overlooking my Workmen in the business they were about. They go on pretty briskly. But I heard something so much against the character of my Tenant that I felt very much depressed about it, and to counteract any danger of the kind drew up a Lease which will bind him. My satisfaction is that my repairs must sooner or later have been done, and so I shall not have been hasty. But my prospect of letting it will not be very good if I cannot get the present applicant to take it.

My morning was pretty much taken up in bustling without coming to any precise result. I went upon change, resolved to finish the affair of my father's Investment and purchased five shares of the State Bank of Mr. Degrand at 59½. This is reinvesting the money I paid for my Shares with one hundred and twenty dollars beside—All I can do.[1] I then calculated my power of meeting the Note on the 29th and concluded to send to Mrs. Longhurst and try her as a resource.[2] Returned home and passed the afternoon in reading, and correcting my Essay which I like less and less. When shall I ever be satisfied? But I corrected freely, and thought it was improved. I then read the first part of the Œdipe of Corneille which I thought tolerably poor.[3] It is a Frenchified Drama, in the strictly ludicrous sense. The evening was passed at home quietly reading Clarissa without interruption, after which I had time to finish an article in the North American Review upon the American System.[4]

[1] In GWA's estate were nine shares of State Bank stock which upon settlement of the estate would become the property of JQA. CFA had purchased

three of these shares from the estate at par in December mainly to provide cash needed in the Agency account at that time. Adhering to his policy of keeping Agency funds fully invested and taking advantage of the decline in the market, CFA used the cash which had accumulated in the interim to restore the three shares to JQA's holdings and to add two more. The transaction was completed in the following week with the transfer of the remaining six shares in GWA's name to JQA. (M/CFA/3)

[2] Despite his failure to collect any part of the $405.49 by which Mrs. Long-

hurst was in arrears (CFA to JQA, 2 Feb., LbC, Adams Papers; M/CFA/3), CFA was able, on 28 Jan., to meet the due date of JQA's sixty-day note to the executors of JA's will.

[3] CFA owned an edition of *Oeuvres de P. Corneille* published at Paris in 12 vols., 1824, now in MQA; "OEdipe" is in vol. 7 of this edition.

[4] The (unsigned) article relating to British opinions on the American tariff system was by Alexander H. Everett, *North Amer. Rev.*, 30:161–216 (Jan. 1830).

FRIDAY. 15TH.

Weather misty, and in going to the Office, I found the sidewalks so slippery as to be in a degree dangerous. I stopped at Mr. J. H. Foster's to decide about a paper for the Entry and rooms in Court Street, talked with him a little and made a selection which might by some be thought tolerably pretty. Overlooked the workmen as they were going on, and felt satisfied on the whole with the Work. I have hurried them pretty rapidly and feel tolerably content so far. I then finished the draught of the Lease and delivered it to the proposed Tenant for reflection and consideration. He seemed so willing to take them that I could hardly entertain a suspicion. But in this world caution is an essential thing. I recommenced my Letter to my Father, but had only time to write one half of it before dinner—The time having passed thus rapidly without my being able entirely to account for it's passage.

I was reminded that I had engaged to dine at Mrs. Frothingham's. So I went at the appointed hour, and found assembled Mr. and Mrs. P. C. Brooks, Abby, a certain Miss Emily Lee and myself as the company. Being between the two latter I felt a little awkward and so did not enjoy myself over much. I felt much anxiety also weighing upon my mind in regard to this Agency business. After dinner I went down to the Athenæum without much purpose and so I did very little. I looked over books and wondered how little I had read. My principal end however was to obtain a Catalogue[1] which I did. I then read a large part of the third Volume of Captain Hall's Travels and consumed my time until seven when I went in to hear Mr. Alexander H. Everett deliver his second Lecture. My opinion is very well settled that this is not his line. As a Writer he has few equals but his defect is that which is universal, in manner. I returned to Mr. Frothingham's and after a little Supper we went home.

[1] See entry of 30 Dec. 1829, above. An earlier catalogue of the Athenæum's books added before 1827 had been published in that year.

SATURDAY 16TH.

I find I have omitted a day. These two records must therefore be transposed in future readings.[1] The weather was misty but no rain. I went to the Office, when it soon after began, and continued all day. My time was much taken up in paying off Accounts and settling my Affairs which I did pretty satisfactorily. I was also overlooking the Workmen in the House in the rear, this together with the finishing my Letter to my Father and copying it[2] engrossed every part of my disposable time before dinner, so rapidly does it go. I do not know that I ought to blame myself but it does seem to me as if I could not employ all the time I ought to and yet bring about so little. I felt pretty well satisfied too, with this day, for little of the time had dropped through my hands.

Returned home and in the afternoon occupied myself in copying out my Essay with great alterations, though I feel now as if I should not print it but merely write for my own satisfaction, as an attempt to handle a subject in a continued manner. I had the afternoon and evening all to myself and continued busy in my Study, Abby having gone out, to pass the evening with Julia Gorham. I finished the Œdipe of Corneille and began reading Lord Kaimes.[3] The Œdipe of Corneille is remarkable as displaying the contrast of the French character with that of the Greeks. The subject is handled by the latter in the stern spirit of ancient liberty, the former on the contrary, introduce the gallantries of love, and the courtly maxims which are the results of a spirit of haughty despotism. Voltaire did much to set this matter in it's proper light subsequently, and by doing so damned this play, but after all the French are not proper subjects to understand the spirit with which the ancient Greeks wrote. Few of them are not something tainted with the radical foibles of the Nation. In commencing Lord Kaimes I am adding to my burdens, but I feel convinced that it is essential to me to read him.

[1] The editors have placed this entry in its proper chronological sequence.
[2] 15 Jan. (LbC, Adams Papers).
[3] Henry Home, Lord Kames, *Elements of Criticism*, 3 vols., Edinburgh, 1762.

SUNDAY. 17TH.

Morning cloudy with rain in the afternoon and evening. It was warm and not exactly seasonable weather. I attended Meeting and heard Dr. Lowell preach a Sermon.[1] It was not very interesting. My own thoughts were much occupied with the letter which my father wrote me received yesterday; and the advice which it contains.[2] I have set about reading Lord Kaimes Elements of Criticism though with so many other things begun upon, I feel a little puzzled by this great diversity of things but hope in time to be able to accomplish all that I propose.

Much of my time was taken up in writing a Letter to my Mother.[3] She was so low spirited in what she wrote that I think it only a duty to do what I can to assist her. I begin to suspect that all is not precisely agreeable at Washington to her, that the scene presents much she cannot admire and much she is not fond of thinking about. I aimed therefore at being light and airy in my style and at expelling blue devils from her mind. Perhaps I shall succeed as badly as heretofore for every letter I have yet written has brought me a very *maussade* answer.[4] If so I must give up writing.

I heard Mr. Frothingham in the afternoon but was overpowered by drowsiness. The remainder of the evening was passed in reading the Continuation of the Life of Christ in Jeremy Taylor, Clarissa Harlowe to my Wife, and Lord Kaimes after she had retired.

[1] Charles Lowell was the minister of the West Church, corner of Cambridge and Lynde streets (vol. 2:395).

[2] 11 Jan. (Adams Papers). Pursuing his suggestion that CFA read more of the theoretical writers on rhetoric, JQA had recommended Lord Kames along with *The Philosophy of Rhetoric* by George Campbell (2 vols., London,

1776), and the works of the Abbé le Batteux.

[3] A reply to her letter of 27 Dec. 1829 (both in Adams Papers).

[4] That is, sulky or cross. CFA is referring to the correspondence between them since his marriage. His efforts on this occasion seem to have been more successful; see entry for 29 Jan., below.

MONDAY. 18TH.

Morning at the Office. Weather tolerably cold. I dropped in to see how the Workmen came on and found Mr. Hollis tolerably busy at his Work. I begin to feel better satisfied with him than I have been. He seems to work with tolerable diligence which is the great thing. Mr. J. Y. Champney called upon me to pay me some rent though not as much as he owes me. I was glad to get any thing. I spent much of the morning for once in reading the Speeches in Williston only going out to try to find the residence of Mr. Trueman for the purpose of returning him a visit.[1] I was not successful.

On my return I wrote my Journal and Mr. John Knapp came in to talk to me and give me some idea of the condition of the Boylston Market. His present proposition is to purchase an adjoining Estate which is offered to the Corporation, by which they in their limits will not be so confined. He came to know whether I would assent in the name of my Father if such an arrangement were to be made. I told him I could not tell but that I would write for information in time for the annual Meeting which will take place on the first day of February. Thus the morning passed and I returned home to dine.

I found Miss Julia Gorham with Abby who dined and passed the day with her. I wrote a Letter to my Father about this Market Stock,[2] and spent the afternoon in reading Mitchell's Preliminary Discourse to his Translation of Aristophanes. This is another digression but it cannot be helped and I hope to be through it soon. The work is very interesting though the political effect designed to be produced by the work rather weakens the deductions and Statements made of the Athenian character—Taken too in connection with Mitford who is evidently the basis of the writer's views. There is yet much spirit in the style and a classical taste which is very refreshing. I accomplished the Discourse and a part of the translation of the first play of the Acharnæ. The spirit is very well supported in it.

[1] Perhaps Robert Trueman, who lived at 3 West Cedar Street (*Boston Directory*, 1830–1831).

[2] LbC in Adams Papers. The land adjoining the Market had been occupied by a rival market and was needed for expansion. The land had recently been bought at auction by two or three stockholders of the Boylston Market who now offered it to the company at the price they had paid. The proposal was to issue additional stock to the amount of the cost.

TUESDAY. 19TH.

Morning cold and clear. At the Office where I had many persons to see me. Mr. Whitney the Tenant of the House came to talk about the rent which is due to him. He was very anxious to have me take off the Quarter's rent upon the House which I charged him, but I declined very positively so as to make him assured that I should not.[1] After much conversation he withdrew, making me suspect that he designed making an appeal from my decision. I care very little if he does. My own duty in managing the affairs of the Agency is performed.

Mr. Leighton called upon me at last upon the Affairs of the Housewright Association and promised an early settlement.[2] I then went to receive the Dividend upon the Massachusetts Hospital Life Insurance Office Stock.[3] Met there Mr. Foster who talked to me upon the subject of the Boylston Market and tried to get me to go into the plan. Indeed I should not feel at all unwilling to follow him, notorious as he is for his clearness of[4] Money affairs.[5] I hope my Father will return a favourable answer. I then made the Deposit and returned to my Office to consider over the matter of a Letter from Mr. Vaughan to my Father. I tried to find Mr. Curtis but not succeeding opened the letter at a hazard. Returned home and in the afternoon had a copy taken, after which I sent on the original with a letter of my own.[6]

I then passed some time in reading Mitchell's Aristophanes, finished the Acharnæ and was induced by it to open Brumoy's Account of the same author in which I did not go far before evening, when I went down to see the family at their usual Meeting on this Evening. The Meeting was much as usual, without material interest and only better than others because the individuals were not at open war. I did not relish it much. The Society is not that to which my own taste inclines.

[1] Prentiss Whitney had vacated 23 Court Street on 1 Jan., owing a large arrearage. In addition, it was CFA's contention that the terms of his lease required payment to 1 April. Whitney asked for withdrawal of this claim as a part of a settlement. CFA instituted suit against him for the total amount. CFA to JQA, 2 Feb. (LbC, Adams Papers).

[2] The Boston Housewright Association, represented apparently by Charles Leighton, housewright, of the firm of Lee & Leighton, Portland Street (*Boston Directory*, 1830–1831), had made arrangements to rent the room opposite CFA's office at $35 a year, but the matter had not yet been concluded nor payment made.

[3] JQA owned thirty shares of Massa-

chusetts Hospital Life Insurance Co. stock for which he had paid $100 a share. Dividends, paid annually, were currently at $7 a share (M/CFA/3). The company offices were at 50 State Street (*Boston Directory*, 1830–1831).

[4] Thus apparently in MS, but CFA very likely meant to write "cleverness in."

[5] James H. Foster's reputation has been mentioned earlier (entry for 30 Nov. 1829 and note).

[6] The letter from Petty Vaughan is missing; it contained further information relating to the funds due the Thomas Boylston estate. CFA, in his covering letter, also relayed to his father Foster's advice on the Boylston Market matter (19 Jan., LbC, Adams Papers).

WEDNESDAY. 20TH.

The morning was dark and lowering and soon after turned into rain. I went to the Office as usual and was busy in making my usual progress in my affairs. My calls were numerous, among others Miles Farmer came up and attempted to take me in. I could not easily keep my temper because he most evidently came to gull me. I was more angry perhaps than I should have been, but it satisfied him that I was not to be imposed upon. He left me, I trust for the last time. My Tenant has not been near me since he received his Lease. I am a little afraid of the circumstance, but I went to see how Hollis came on and was pretty well satisfied with the progress made.

Abby had agreed to go to Medford today notwithstanding the weather. So I returned home at one o'clock and after waiting a little while, went out in a Carriage with Mrs. P. C. Brooks and Mrs. Frothingham. Upon our arrival we found that Mrs. Brooks was not so well.

Indeed I never saw her when she seemed more suffering. It seems to me pretty clearly evident that her term of life is rapidly drawing to a close. But this is too unpleasant a subject to be whispered, and indeed it seems to me it is a severe thing for the consideration of that family. Her influence in cementing them is strong though scarcely felt. When it is gone, I cannot precisely tell what will be the end of it. And it is as well not to attempt to look forward. We dined there and remained while the rest returned to town.

I had much conversation with Mr. Brooks who treated me very kindly. It is somewhat remarkable how different impressions influence me with regard to him. I suppose this depends much upon his feelings to me which vary as much. My coldness he cannot admire and yet at times I cannot help it. It is my bane every where. I retired early as usual.

THURSDAY 21ST.

The morning was bright and clear but tolerably cold. After breakfasting we came into Boston with Mrs. Everett and Mr. Brooks in his Carriage. I went to the Office and during the whole morning was busy with my affairs. Many persons came in to talk and more to bring bills all which I paid off as fast as I was able and relieved myself from a very considerable load. Mr. Sharpe came and received his Money at last, which makes the last debt contracted before I was married. My different suits were settled and I paid Mr. Tarbell the balance due upon Mr. Gilman's Collecting efforts after paying myself for my Costs.[1] This is the best business I have done in the Law, excepting Mr. Boylston's and my Administration, which indeed embraces every thing.

My Tenant came to tell me he could not swallow so strong a Lease. But he seemed anxious to take it and I felt rather doubtful of the representations of Hollis. Indeed from all the information I could gather, I was inclined to think that he was a good man. He said he would call again. I am still in hopes I shall be able to settle with him, and get the load off my Shoulders. Mr. Leighton came to tell me he was about to settle for the hire of the room opposite for which I rejoiced. But no signs were there of Money. He promised tomorrow. The key was given up, and I went in to look at the rooms. They are in better condition than I anticipated. And I feel pretty nearly confirmed in my resolution to attempt to let mine, and occupy these. Thus passed the morning.

I went to dine with Chardon Brooks by agreement. Abby is out all her time.[2] My head did not feel very well owing to a slight indigestion.

138

I got through Dinner and went home to my study, but owing to my head did not enjoy my reading as much as I might have done. I merely finished Brumoy's Dissertation without having read it very carefully. This over, I went to a Meeting which was called in favour of the Cherokee and Creek Indians in the question with Georgia. It was very full. I never had seen a thing of the kind before. But it was not very famous for its soundness or its deliberation. The Speakers were men of no character and the resolutions were foolishly violent.[3] I could not get out until they adjourned when I went again to Chardon's and after a Supper and Glass of Whiskey Punch returned home feeling a severe headach.

[1] CFA's accounts provide no information on what his fee was for legal work done for Thomas Tarbell nor on the identity of Gilman.

[2] That is, at Medford with her mother.

[3] The Jackson administration's policy on Indian removal is detailed above, entry for 26 Dec. 1829, note. The statewide meeting in the Representatives Hall of the State House was called in protest against that policy and against the actions taken by the state of Georgia to remove the Indians. At the meeting's conclusion, resolutions were adopted unanimously holding that removal would be a violation of solemn pledges and treaties by the Government of the United States which "would probably bring upon us the reproaches of mankind, and would certainly expose us to the judgments of Heaven" (*Columbian Centinel*, 23 Jan., p. 3, col. 1). In reporting the tenor of the meeting to his father, CFA wrote: "There was a man there talked of sending a thousand regulars into Georgia with as much coolness as if he was going to take a breakfast and was thought sensible too" (24 Jan., Adams Papers). JQA, interested, suggested that CFA should have taken the opportunity presented to gain experience in speaking to a large audience (to CFA, 5 Feb., Adams Papers). To this, CFA replied that he had expressed his opinions on the subject earlier (see above, entry for 2 Jan.) but had not spoken on this occasion because he would have begun "in opposition to the whole current of the Community. And had I failed the effect upon me would have been permanent." He stated for his father his own conviction, arrived at after endeavoring "to examine that subject in its *practical* bearings without out reference to the abstract and impracticable views of moralists," that "the Indians must submit or remove," adding his hope that all could be managed peaceably and voluntarily (CFA to JQA, 14 Feb., Adams Papers). In measured response, JQA wrote:

"You took a very judicious course, in refraining from the debate at the meeting about the Indians. It would not have been prudent to make your first Essay at public speaking on the unpopular side of a great question of national policy—and perhaps you was not so well prepared upon that subject as you may be hereafter. You have not investigated it as a question of Justice—of Morals—of Politics—of Natural—Conventional—Constitutional, and federal Law—of Natural History and of Political Economy. It is all this and more" (21 Feb., Adams Papers).

For an account of the policies on the Indian question followed by JQA during his administration, see Bemis, *JQA*, 2:79–87.

FRIDAY. 22D.

Morning mild and pleasant. Went to the Office as usual—My time as much occupied in affairs of business. My tenant called upon me to talk over the matter and from what he said I feel disposed to close the agreement with him. It is not worthwhile to listen to the conversation of such a man as Hollis whom I do not entirely think well of, when after inquiring of the Officers in town who would be very likely to know, I find they have no acquaintance whatever with the man. This would prevent the supposition that he is notorious which was Hollis' assertion. On the whole I begin to think Hollis is a poor fellow—This being the second time he has put me in fear of Tenants without good apparent reason. I had an applicant also for the House in Tremont Street, and took it upon me to offer the House upon my own responsibility for three hundred and seventy five dollars. This is a great diminution but it cannot be helped. I lose more by letting the House stay empty. Mr. Leighton called and paid me the rent for the room opposite which winds up that business. I now think of fitting up and advertising them both and moving myself upstairs—Which would put the Building again upon its proper footing. But all these things involve expense which ought to be considered. But if the benefits anticipated were sure they would overbalance them in a very few months. If I get my Houses off, perhaps I may try it. Thus went the morning. I passed the afternoon reading Mitchell's Aristophanes, The Comedy of the Knights, after which I tried to think over something to say upon the Militia Question tomorrow night, but could hit upon nothing.

Mr. Brooks intimated to me that his Wife was very ill today. I am very fearful her disorder is rapidly approaching to it's termination, and poor Abby is in tears about it. But I apprehend she has much more to suffer yet. We went out this evening to a little party at Mrs. Dehon's which was pleasanter than usual and I thought it was ten when the hour of eleven frightened us home.

SATURDAY 23RD.

Morning cold but pleasant. I went to the Office as usual. Found myself occupied without knowing how, first in the receipt of a Letter from my Father which I read with pleasure, as it had nothing in it of a disagreeable or depressing nature.[1] This and the writing my Journal took up an hour. I then went to ask after Mrs. Brooks, and was told that she was much the same, though it was hoped that the applications made would relieve her. My proposed Tenant, Mr. Gilbert then called upon me, who had been to see Mrs. Lewis, and had been much shaken in his inclinations for the House by the series of representations, or rather misrepresentations she had made. This was not a little provoking and I felt out of temper, it being enough that I should reduce the rent. He left me promising an answer on Monday. I then went to Mr.

Edward Blake's Office to meet with the Committee on the Militia for the Debating Society.[2] We sat nearly two hours and talked of every thing without coming to any conclusion. I was obliged to leave off because I was fearful that I had lost my Tenants at the Office. I shall not feel easy until the Houses are let. On returning to it, I found Mr. Degrand had called to let me know that he had transferred the shares of the State Bank which had been purchased for my Father, so that I went down and concluded the business by adding these with the remainder of George's making eleven to the sixty already owned by my Father. This took the rest of the morning.

The Afternoon was spent in reading Mitchell's Translation of the Knights of Aristophanes, and comparing the Letters copied by the copyist of Mr. Sparks with the originals in the Letter books. They are very interesting and it will be a good way for me to read them. But in objecting to any for publication I feel a little doubtful of my Judgment and dislike the responsibility. After tea, I went down leaving my Wife at Mrs. Frothingham's to the Meeting of the Debating Society. It was respectable and the discussion upon the subject of Dissection was continued with great interest. I felt much more engaged in it than I had expected, but the cold was so great that we adjourned early without coming to any decision or without hearing all the information upon the subject. The evening was severe. I returned home with my Wife at nine.

[1] JQA to CFA, 17 Jan. (Adams Papers).
[2] Blake's office was at 5 Court Street (*Boston Directory*, 1830–1831).

SUNDAY. 24TH.

Arose very late this morning, the weather more cold than at any preceding time this Winter, and I feeling unwell from a severe cold caught upon my preceding one which had not altogether left me. Went to Meeting at Mr. Frothingham's this morning and heard him deliver a much better Sermon than usual. I was quite pleased with it though I felt severely the cold during the Service. I was glad to get home, from which I resolved that I would not again stir, during the day.

Miss Julia Gorham and Mr. [Edmund] Quincy dropped in, the former by chance, the latter by invitation and they dined with us very pleasantly. Quincy remained all the afternoon, conversing about things in general. He is tolerably agreeable, and has a kind of superiority about him to the generality of [ou]r young men which I do not dislike. He has tastes which are in themselves rare and which do ennoble a man, let people say what they will. He left us at dark when I felt much

worse with the oppression from my cold, than heretofore. Being somewhat upon my breast it alarmed me a little.

After tea, I read to my Wife a little of Clarissa Harlowe but we were
soon interrupted by the entrance of my friend Edward Blake who came
in and talked with us agreeably for a couple of hours. It would give me
a good deal of pleasure if I could select a number of young men to frequent my house such as these and a few like them. I reject many of
the coarse and disagreeable persons I meet in Society and even the
rough in manners, for with these I cannot coalesce. But my notions are
perhaps a little too fastidious upon these subjects—And I shall only succeed in quite excluding myself out of young men's society. Be it so.
I am independent. After he had gone and Abby had retired, I sat down
and wrote a long Letter to my Father in reply to his two last, which
took up until near twelve o'clock.[1] The weather was cold and I was
glad to retire.

[1] For this letter, see above, entry for 21 Jan., note.

MONDAY 25TH.

The morning opened cold and dark, the weather moderating produced snow, and the day was dull throughout. I went to the Office but
was not occupied so pleasantly or properly as I might have been. Mr.
Gilbert called to let me know that he declined taking the House owing
to the high rent, a thing I very much regret though I do not see how I
can diminish it more in conscience. I then went to inquire how Mrs.
Brooks was. Mr. B. seemed much discouraged and told me to go and
ask Mrs. Frothingham to go out to Medford with him which I did and
then returned to give her consent. I do not know what to think of the
case, but I cannot help feeling as if it was not yet so bad.

Mr. Curtis called to see me to let me know part of the scandalous
transaction of Petty Vaughan and the course thought advisable to be
taken in the case by Mr. Lowell.[1] Josiah Quincy also dropped in, for
a minute only and did not seem able to say what he wanted. Returned
home and passed the afternoon reading Mitchell's Translation of the
Knights with Brumoy's remarks upon the same Play. There is great
spirit in the Translation though the Comments upon republican usages
are altogether unjust. He gives a dash, I notice at the Americans in
one of his Notes, though manifestly ignorant to a great degree of our
Institutions.[2] This rather affects the correctness of his inferences in
the others. Yet he is amusing. As to the merit of Aristophanes I have
not yet made up my mind, but La Harpe's opinion is deserving of consideration. My Cold was very severely upon my Chest all day, but I

felt on the whole better. I read aloud to my Wife in Clarissa in the Evening. Edward Brooks and his Wife called to tell us his report from Dr. Stevenson, which was rather encouraging.[3] I then read part of the Clouds of Aristophanes.

[1] John Lowell, although retired from active legal practice, had in 1817 successfully represented Ward Nicholas Boylston in England in an earlier phase of the protracted effort to recover the funds owed to Thomas Boylston's estate (MHS, *Procs.*, 1st ser., 2 [1835–1855]: 161). Following the failure of William Vaughan, Lowell was called into consultation on further steps. See JQA, Diary, 28 Jan.; JQA to Nathaniel Curtis and Mrs. W. N. Boylston, 4 Feb. (LbC, Adams Papers).

[2] In an explication of Agoracritus, the type of vulgar and unprincipled leader of the people ("The Knights," Act 4,

scene ii), Mitchell remarks: "The picture itself is such as a republic only could furnish, and something like a parallel to it might, I believe, be still found in the free states of America" (*The Comedies of Aristophanes*, London, 1820, 1:274). The note does not appear in the American edn. (Phila., 1822), which CFA owned and which is in MQA.

[3] Dr. J. Greely Stevenson, whose office was at School and Tremont streets (*Boston Directory*, 1830–1831), had been called to Medford for consultation upon Mrs. Brooks' condition (Brooks, Farm Journal, 25 Jan.).

TUESDAY. 26TH.

Morning bright but cold. The severity of our Winter is coming upon us quite rapidly. But it is now so far in the Season that luckily it cannot last very long. I went to the Office as usual, and was occupied in making up my Accounts and those of the agency. I called upon Mr. Brooks to inquire how Mrs. B. was and was told she was much the same. But they had hopes that she would now improve. I then went to pay Hilliard and Co. their Account against myself and my father. This being done, I went back to my Office and was called upon by Richardson who sat for half an hour talking but apparently in rather low spirits—His father being about to go away and leave him in charge of the family.

Mr. Tenney came up to tell me he had not got his security but would shortly have it and spoke so well and so confidently that I thought myself foolish for having got into difficulty about him. I think I have got rid of that concern. Now still remains the one in Tremont Street, and these Offices, which are matters for future meditation. Mr. Curtis also came in to show me Mr. Lowell's Opinion about Mr. Boylston's affairs. It is clear but a little discouraging. Returned home and after dinner occupied in writing a revised copy of my Essay in a book,[1] and continuing the Clouds of Aristophanes. A most singular work—Especially the passage inserted in the middle of it, which would lead one to suppose that it belonged to some other Play, and requires many more perusals to become master of. Mr. Sparks then called upon me to ask about the papers copied, and left some which I looked over directly. They contain nothing but what is creditable to him in an extreme degree,[2] in my mind. His patriotism was not exceeded by that of any man during the whole of our revolution. I read in the Evening a part of Clarissa Harlowe to my Wife though my Cold was so severe that I was unable to do more than grunt aloud. After she retired, I went on with the Wasps of Aristophanes.

[1] For his exercises in composition, CFA often used the blank pages in volumes in which GWA's literary projects had been left unfinished. It was in one of these, GWA's literary commonplace book, that CFA copied a version of his Essay on Eloquence (Adams Papers, Microfilms, Reel No. 294).

[2] That is, to JA.

WEDNESDAY 27TH.

Morning cloudy with a chilly air. At the Office as usual and for once without interruption and without particular business. Received a letter from my Father containing the Deed of the Boylston Estate to Gleason, and a Power of Attorney to me to appear and vote about the affairs of the Boylston Market.[1] He expresses satisfaction at my manner of proceeding, which is all that I can possibly desire. I then went to see Mr. Brooks, first however going to return two visits—One to Mr. Trueman and one to Genl. Lyman which were due long ago.[2] This being off my mind, I felt much better. Mr. Brooks said, his wife was a little better, but the physicians discouraged him by giving no hopes of a recovery. I have long foreseen this, though it is a most melancholy thing to think of. For his family are scattered to the winds immediately upon it. There is no more of that kind of union which has heretofore so strongly prevailed.

I passed the remainder of the morning in reading Williston, and was much pleased with the Speeches this morning, on the Embargo.[3] There is much animation in them. They read better. The afternoon was passed in finishing the Wasps of Aristophanes of which Mitchell has made two pieces. They might well be so for all the connection they have with each other. I then read Brumoy's version of the same pieces and after reading the Edinburgh and Quarterly Review I believe I shall have established a tolerable knowledge of the Old Comedy of the Greeks.[4] I regret however that Mitchell did not himself translate the Clouds, for Cumberland whom he has followed though correct is a little tame. He gives one no definite idea of the peculiar character of the Poet. Brumoy is good in his criticism though Mitchell has transferred much of the valuable matter to his Notes. Read to Abby in Clarissa which on this evening was very interesting. It snowed violently during the after-noon.

[1] JQA to CFA, 22 Jan. (Adams Papers).

[2] Theodore Lyman Jr. (1792–1849), political enemy of JQA, preceded John T. Winthrop as commanding general of the 3d Brigade, 1st Division, Massachusetts Militia ("City Guards") in which GWA had been a major. (*Mass. Register*, 1827, p. 105; 1829, p. 107; on Lyman, see also *DAB*.)

[3] The speeches in the Senate, Nov. 1808–Feb. 1809, of William B. Giles and James A. Bayard are in Williston's *Eloquence* at 2:391–410, 486–516.

[4] The articles would seem to be the essay on the ancient and modern drama in the *Edinburgh Review*, 49:317–361 (June 1829); the reviews of Frederick Schlegel, *Lectures on the History of Literature, Ancient and Modern* (principally on "The Clouds"), and of Thomas Mitchell, *The Comedies of Aristophanes*, in the *Quarterly Review*, 21:271–320 (April 1819); 23:474–505 (July 1820).

THURSDAY. 28TH.

Morning cold but clear. At the Office as usual occupied though not so usefully as I had hoped all my time might be passed. I first regulated my accounts and called to see Josiah Quincy with whom I had some small matters to settle respecting affairs under the will of my Grandfather. We exchanged Mortgage deeds, the new one in my hands for the old and cancelled one in his. I then went to the Branch Bank and paid to the credit of the Executors the sum of six hundred dollars with six more for interest upon that sum for sixty days the date of my father's Note given for the sum. The Note however not being in town could not be delivered up. I have thus far done pretty well with the business of my Father's Agency—And now he is in my debt a little.

Mr. Isaac P. Davis called upon me to talk about a Frame for the Picture at Philadelphia, of my father which Sully is finishing. I promised to send to him. Mr. George Brimmer called to see the estimate of the same apparently for curiosity.[1] My own time was passed in correcting the Quarterly Accounts made up for the two Quarters preceding George's decease which make a heavier balance than ever against him. It serves little purpose to look back upon them. He paid for his privilege in heavy suffering.

Returning home, I found Miss Elizabeth Phillips come to stay a week with Abby.[2] She is a Cousin from Andover. After dinner I sat down to study, and read the review of Aristophanes in the Edinburgh and North American with the remarks of Schlegel on the same Author and Cumberland's Numbers in the Observer upon the Greek Comedy.[3] They are very interesting. After tea for the first time I sat upstairs, and again tried the old subject[4] on another tack, in the shape of a Newspaper Essay. Mr. C. C. Paine called however and interrupted me,[5] though I resumed afterwards and did not retire until it was very near midnight. The night was cold.

[1] Isaac P. Davis, wealthy Boston merchant, was a friend and patron of the painters Gilbert Stuart and Thomas Sully (William T. Whitley, *Gilbert Stuart*, Cambridge, 1932, p. 157 ff.; James Thomas Flexner, *Gilbert Stuart*, N.Y., 1955, p. 155 ff., 167; John Hill Morgan, *Gilbert Stuart and His Pupils*, N.Y., 1939, p. 36, 40, 69). Stuart in 1825 had undertaken a full-length portrait of JQA, but had completed only the head when the artist died in 1828. Sully was employed to finish the work, and JQA conferred with him in Philadelphia a month before about its early completion (JQA, Diary, 5 Dec. 1829).

The verifiable facts are not entirely separable from the lore that early grew around the painting. Ward Nicholas Boylston did commission the portrait and apparently from the beginning intended to present it to Harvard. The commission, said to have provided for the payment to Stuart of $1,000, was for a full-length portrait "as much as possible like" that of JA which Copley had painted in 1783, which had come into Boylston's keeping about 1811 and which Boylston, with the tacit approval of the Adams family, bequeathed to Harvard. Perhaps because he desired that the two works be alike in all respects, to match the court dress in which Copley had painted JA, Boylston wished that JQA be painted attired in the formal costume that JQA had worn as Minister to the Court of St. James's. However, JQA is said to have been resolute in his preference for "the plain American dress." It may be that the failure of Stuart to complete more than the head before his death is to be attributed rather to the failure of Boylston and JQA to compose their differences than to Stuart's habitual dilatoriness in bringing his portraits to completion. In any event, after the deaths of both Stuart and Boylston, Sully, engaged with money provided in Boylston's will, painted the figure "in the plain costume that best becomes a true republican." (CFA to JQA, 29 Jan. 1830, LbC, Adams Papers; same to an unidentified recipient, March 1872, original not located, printed in Martha Babcock Amory, *The Domestic and Artistic Life of John Singleton Copley*, Boston, 1882, p. 87 ff.; *Boston Patriot*, 4 Aug. 1830, p. 2, col. 1.)

Having completed the canvas, Sully sent to Davis, for JQA's approval, proposed patterns for the painting's frame. Before referring the question to his father, CFA consulted Nathaniel Curtis, who as coexecutor with JQA of Boylston's will would have to approve the expenditure. Curtis, while assenting to any arrangement, wondered whether the frame too should not be made to match that of the JA portrait. In order that comparison might be more readily made by the frame maker, he or Mr. Brimmer suggested that John Doggett of Boston, whom Brimmer recommended as "much the best framer in the country" and who was for many years Stuart's close friend and framer, be employed. Doggett agreed to meet Sully's price (CFA to JQA, 29 Jan. as cited above; Mabel M. Swan, *The Athenæum Gallery, 1827–1873*, Boston, 1940, p. 5). JQA concurred with Curtis' point but expressed a further preference for the cheapest (to CFA, 5 Feb., Adams Papers). When these decisions were made known to Davis, he, perhaps because of his connections with Sully, was "exceedingly fretted" and begged that the least expensive of the Sully designs be chosen as the most expeditious way of having the work finished in time for the portrait to be hung in the Spring Exhibition (CFA to JQA, 26 Feb., LbC, Adams Papers). To Davis' further importunities, CFA responded by referring him to Curtis for final decision. The work was done by Doggett, apparently, and was not ready for delivery until late in July. (Entries for 25 March, 24 July, below; *Boston Patriot*, as cited above.)

[2] Elizabeth Phillips (b. 1805), a daughter of John and Lydia (Gorham) Phillips, later the wife of William Stevens of Andover (Henry Bond, *Genealogies of Watertown*, Boston, 1855, p. 886).

[3] *Edinburgh Review*, 34:271–319 (Nov. 1820); *North Amer. Rev.*, 14: 273–296 (April 1822); Frederick Schlegel, *Lectures on the History of Literature, Ancient and Modern*; Richard

Cumberland, *The Observer*, Nos. 135–140. Copies of the two-vol. Philadelphia, 1818 edn. of Schlegel with GWA's marginal notes (vol. 2 only) and of the three-vol. London, 1822 edn. of *The Ob-* *server* with CFA's bookplate are in MQA.

[4] That is, "Eloquence."

[5] Charles Cushing Paine, Harvard 1827; see vol. 2:224.

FRIDAY 29TH.

This was the coldest morning we have had this Winter—The Glass being at about zero. It is not often in this latitude that we have it much more severe, though we do have it as much so once or twice every season. I went to the Office and then called at Mr. J. H. Foster's to select some Papers for the Offices in order to prepare them to let well. The Weather is not favourable for the repairs. Received a letter from my Mother in much better spirits, which rejoiced me very much.[1] For I have so long been in the habit of receiving dull letters from her that this moderate one is quite agreeable.

My morning was passed uninterrupted by visitors of any sort. I read much of Williston, especially the speeches upon the admission of Louisiana, and had my opinion somewhat raised of the oratorical powers of Mr. Quincy.[2] Called in to see Mr. Blake on the subject of the Militia, but as Chapman was indisposed, the Committee did not succeed in gaining a Meeting. Stopped to ask Mr. Brooks who reported things at Medford much as they were. Mr. Curtis called to speak of Mr. Petty Vaughan's matters, and I then submitted the case to him concerning the Frame of the Picture, and agreed to write to my Father upon the subject. I did accordingly write the Letter in the Afternoon,[3] and passed the remainder in reading a most interesting review of the Works of Demosthenes in the Edinburgh.[4] The writing is masterly. It is wonderful to look at this and not be struck with the prodigious inferiority of our periodicals. And the reading only interested me the more deeply in the study of Oratory, fascinating in the greatest degree. I could now lay down my mind to the application with the utmost ease. My zeal is revived and much increased. The whole evening was thus taken up and I finished all my work except Lord Kaimes to whom I returned, but I shall be compelled to give more than one perusal to him.

[1] 24 Jan. (Adams Papers).

[2] The speeches of Josiah Quincy (1772–1864) and of George Poindexter delivered in the House, Jan. 1811 (Williston's *Eloquence*, 2:415–454).

[3] LbC in Adams Papers; see entry immediately preceding.

[4] The Auger translation was reviewed in three issues of the *Edinburgh Review*, 33:226–246; 36:82–110 and 483–516 (Jan. 1820, Oct. 1821, Feb. 1822). CFA elaborates his opinion on the series in a letter to JQA, 14 Feb. (Adams Papers).

SATURDAY 30TH.

Morning clear and cold. Went to the Office as usual. Occupied in my usual avocations though my time as usual seemed to slip away much faster than I could clearly account for. I had leisure to finish Mr. Bayard's speech upon the Embargo and in that manner to finish this volume of Williston. Received a letter from my Father upon business affairs though of no great consequence. It merely recommended to me certain occupations in business affairs which I am willing to adopt.[1]

Went to Blake's room where I found the Committee and we sat as usual discussing things in general without arriving at any definite conclusion. I was called away to attend to Mr. Tenny who had got his security to offer which I accepted and I drew up the Lease according to the last agreement, and we agreed to sign and seal on this afternoon at four o'clock. Accordingly after dinner I was obliged to return to the Office and meet him, when we in effect finished the job, and I am glad to be able to say that this House is actually out of my hands. Now there still remains the other one.

The afternoon was in a degree wasted. I sat with Mr. Welsh, discussing affairs in general with him until it became quite late. He is a singular man, but on the whole much more tolerable than one might be apt to suspect. From his Office, I went to the Athenæum where I passed half an hour in looking over the Edinburgh Review, an Article on Education probably written by Mr. Brougham.[2] I then found it was time to go to the Meeting of the Debating Society. The Weather was severely cold, but the Meeting was large and the discussion upon the subject of Medical Dissection was continued, so that we were saved the exposition of Militia affairs. We have gone on increasing gradually in our Members until we have become quite respectable. Returned home calling for Abby and Miss Phillips at Mrs. Frothingham's in a bitter cold night.

[1] JQA to CFA, 25 Jan. (Adams Papers). The recommendations were that CFA number each of his business letters consecutively, that he write all letters on paper of the same size, and that he use covers on his letters so that the letter itself would not suffer mutilation on the breaking of the seal.

[2] Perhaps the article on military education in the June 1829 issue (49:388–420), read for its bearing upon the debate on militia affairs shortly to be begun and participated in by CFA (entries for 6, 13 Feb., below).

SUNDAY. 31ST.

Arose this morning to find the weather changed to intense cold. Every thing even in the parlour was frozen. The change was as sudden as it was disagreeable. I had no glass properly exposed to ascertain the degree but mine even in its sheltered situation sunk as low as eight, sixteen degrees lower than at any preceding time.

After breakfast, we went to Meeting and heard a certain Mr. Sewall preach, Mr. Frothingham having gone to Washington.[1] My feet were so cold during the service that I could not feel comfortable and the preacher was not over lively. We returned home, our two ladies quite regretting they had come out at all. As my father was strong in his recommendation of going to Church in his yesterday's letter, I thought I would go again when I found that the weather had moderated. Mr. Ripley preached.[2] I know this young man from reputation at College. He has not kept up to it, and this afternoon he was quite long and tedious. Attendance at Church is no doubt a good practice, but to hear much of what is said in the Pulpit is a little fatiguing. Some things we think we can say better. Others we would not say at all. This may be vanity and self exaltation but we still can hardly avoid the reflections when we come to know what constitute the body of our Preachers.

Returned home to look over some more letters of my Grandfather copied by Mr. Sparks. One only I withdrew. The rest were admitted without objection. But I do not precisely know how far Mr. Sparks ought in justice to carry his selections. In the [parlor?][3] as my study was so cold, I sat with the ladies and read to them a part of Sir Charles Grandison, an amusing book, for it's peculiarities though not for it's merits.[4] We were stopped by the entrance of Mr. Edmund Quincy, who passed the rest of the evening with us.

[1] Rev. Charles C. Sewall of Danvers or Rev. Samuel Sewall of Burlington (*Mass. Register*, 1830). Mr. Frothingham preached in Washington on 31 Jan., 7 and 14 Feb.; on each occasion JQA was in the congregation (Diary entries for these dates; JQA to CFA, 13 Feb., Adams Papers).

[2] George Ripley, Harvard 1823, was minister of the Purchase Street Church, Boston, until 1840 and was afterward a principal figure on the *Dial*, in the Brook Farm experiment, and among the Transcendentalist philosophers (*DAB*).

[3] Editorially supplied for word omitted in text.

[4] Samuel Richardson, *The History of Sir Charles Grandison*, first published in 1754. CFA owned an edition published at London in 7 vols., 1817, now in MQA.

FEBRUARY. 1830.

MONDAY. FEBRUARY. 1ST.

The morning presented the appearance of the depth of winter. The Snow was falling heavily and the sky was dark. I arose and went to the Office. My morning was much taken up, very much in affairs connected with my father's Agency. As my former tenant, Whitney was still very dilatory in his payment I wrote him a Note on Saturday designed to be final.[1] I went down in the mean time to see Mr. Tarbell about some little Commissions of mine, and to the meeting of the Stockholders of the American Bank. There were so few and my interest was so small, I was ashamed to appear so I returned, and went to the meeting of the Proprietors of the Middlesex Canal.[2] The Exposé was not a very favourable one in my mind. The receipts exhibited a great falling off from last year and the expenses as usual have been very heavy. There was much reasoning attempted to prove that the Stock was not in a low condition but I did not feel convinced by it. The pro-jected railroad has hurt it much and the expenses which are so heavily laid on will injure it more. The Dividend is eight dollars upon the Share—Worse than either of the years preceding. I was chosen a Di-rector at the Meeting for the next year and I hope to be able to become master of the subject in time.[3] But I confess my idea is that the property is bad enough.

Returning to my Office I found a Note from Mr. Whitney[4] of such a character that I thought it advisable to act at once, so I left the Ac-count to be prosecuted by Mr. Kinsman. This will produce a crisis though I am now much afraid I shall lose the Money. This business of collecting rents is a wretched affair. I have not now a single Tenant who pleases me. But it is advisable to take a short course with such Men and see what the end of it will be.

Returned home to dine and in the afternoon began the Oration of Demosthenes for the Crown, in which I proceeded a little way well. This will be no mean labour. But I now was called to attend the Meet-ing of Proprietors of Boylston Market which I went to accordingly. The faces were all new and strange to me excepting Mr. Foster's and Mr. Knapp's. Yet as soon as I was known Mr. J. D. Williams[5] treated me with so much attention as to make me feel very much ashamed. He is one of our rich men yet exceedingly illiterate at first sight, and as I suppose somewhat sensible of the superiority of some who have greater advantages of Education. He accordingly singled me the best educated man in the room out in a very disagreeable manner. The question was upon the purchase of a certain property adjoining, and having given my father's assent to that arrangement I thought it was sufficient.[6] But I had some duty to do. Mr. Greene and I were tellers to pronounce who were elected as Directors, which we did in announcing the old set, and after deciding that the sale of the new shares should happen on Satur-day next we adjourned. This time is too early for me or my Father, but as Whitney may disappoint me I could not in any event use the chance of investing for him.[7]

[1] Letter missing.

[2] The office of the company was on Pond Street near the Charlestown Bridge (*Boston Directory*, 1830–1831). The Adamses' interest in the Middlesex Canal was substantial. JQA had been one of the original subscribers at the company's organization in 1794, taking five shares. He had increased his holdings by two shares before 1802 and purchased twenty-five more in 1817–1818. JA had become an owner of thirteen shares before 1806, and these had passed to JQA at JA's death. In turn, JQA had given two shares to GWA and two to CFA in 1828 (vol. 2:303). The family holdings of forty-five shares had cost, principally by the one hundred assessments levied from 1794–1817, in excess of $15,700, or an average of more than $350 a share. When CFA set up the Agency's books in 1829, the shares had an assigned value of $250 each. The total amount realized on the investment, in dividends paid from 1819 to the company's liquidation in 1853, was $559.50 a share. (M/JQA/12, Adams Papers, Microfilms, Reel No. 209; M/CFA/3; Christopher Roberts, *The Middlesex Canal*, 1793–1860, Cambridge, 1938, p. 41–44, 179–184, 227.)

[3] CFA's election as a director, his first to an important semi-public or public post, was to be followed by annual re-election until he withdrew in 1852. He was a member of the Standing Committee of the directors from 1840 to 1843. See Roberts, *The Middlesex Canal*, 1793–1860, p. 222–224.

[4] Letter missing.

[5] Probably John D. W. Williams of the firm of Hall & Williams, merchants, 38 Central Wharf (*Boston Directory*, 1830–1831).

[6] JQA to CFA, 22 Jan. (Adams Papers).

[7] CFA had recommended the purchase of some of the newly issued shares, but JQA thought the indicated price too high and had some apprehension about over-expansion in the company. (CFA to JQA, 19, 29 Jan., LbCs; JQA to CFA, 22 Jan., 5 February. All in Adams Papers.)

TUESDAY. 2D.

The morning was cloudy and cold though not to be compared with what has preceded. I went to the Office and employed myself as usual. I have directed Whitney to be sued, but am fearful the project was not a wise one. We must wait and see. I occupied myself in drawing up a Letter upon business to my Father in which I stated to him very exactly the condition of the Property, to relieve myself from much of the weight which I feel hangs upon me.[1] This now hangs considerably upon my spirits. I called to see Mr. Brooks about the News from Medford which was good, and to see Josiah Quincy about the Note of my Father but could not see him. Thus as usual vanished my morning without my being able fully to account for it. And thus it is always, and thus I am afraid it ever will be in future, but we must have Courage, and go on with the task assigned us.

After dinner I read a portion of my Demosthenes as usual and gained time enough after it to draw off a copy of my first Number of Essays upon Oratory. I am now resolved upon offering it, and on the whole am tolerably well satisfied with the neatness of the style. It is a good study to me and whatever may be it's failure to attract attention, I shall feel a little more confidence in my own powers for appearing before the public. I design offering this to the Editor of the Massachusetts Journal,[2] if he accepts it, Well, if not, try again. That is my father's motto, and I will follow it.

I left off to go to Mrs. Frothingham's to the weekly Meeting which had been omitted last week on account of the sickness of Mrs. Brooks. The number commonly present was increased by the addition of Miss Parks, Miss Phillips and Miss Wells, a niece of Mrs. Edward Brooks.[3] The Meeting professed to be lively but was not a whit more agreeable to me than they usually are. After my return, I sat up some time to read a part of Lord Kaimes.

[1] LbC in Adams Papers. Although he writes at length on the generally depressed state of business, CFA's principal concern is about the $1,134.24 in accumulated past-due rentals.

[2] That is, David Lee Child.

[3] Frances Boott Wells was the daughter of Frances (Boott) and William Wells Jr., see vol. 2:258, 268.

WEDNESDAY. 3D.

Morning cloudy with snow but it soon stopped and produced a pleasant day. I went to the Office as usual and was engaged in the transaction of business for some time. I claimed the Dividend upon the Middlesex Canal Stock for my father, my brother's Estate and myself, and deposited the amount in the Bank. This sum relieves me from all embarrassment but I had hoped for better results. My anticipations of having a sum sufficiently large to make a handsome investment is entirely vanished, and if I can now from the proceeds of the Quarter pay expenses of repairs and have a fund sufficient to pay off the charges accruing on the first of April without trenching upon next Quarter I shall think I have done very well—Which is one of the vicissitudes to which property is liable. I do not much relish this management of property, it has too many cares, troubles and vexations attending it to make the business agreeable, particularly in depressed times.

At my Office I was occupied in copying my Letter to my Father, and preparing it to send away. I also sent to Mr. Child my first Number thus taking the final leap. It will come out on Saturday, and I must begin to prepare another Number.[1] I had a number of visitors, Chardon Brooks about some Tickets to the Theatre, and Workmen to get Orders about the Houses. Returning home I found that Miss Elizabeth Phillips was going to Charlestown instead of to the Theatre which put me in some quandary for I had a Ticket for her. I sent it back however to be disposed of. Abby was disturbed by the cross occurrence. It was not very well.

At four I went to a Meeting of the Directors of the Middlesex Canal at the Office of Mr. William Sullivan.[2] We proceeded to elect the Officers for the year and do all the necessary business. The Company has been of late years managed by a standing Committee in connection with Mr. Eddy the Agent.[3] I do not know how far this plan is entirely correct, but I do not feel as yet at all qualified to make any motion to alter it. It took the afternoon and I came away with a report made to the Board of Directors by Mr. Sullivan which I design copying for information.[4] On returning home, I prepared myself directly to go to the Theatre with Abby and Miss Parks who came from Mrs. Frothingham's. The play was King John, the two leading parts taken by Mr. Booth and Mr. E. Forrest.[5] I was on the whole agreeably disappointed in the piece and the acting. Booth ranted less than I had expected but he hardly went through a buffoon afterpiece without evincing symptoms of his infirmity. Returned in a shower of snow, Miss Parks coming to our House.

[1] The first number of CFA's essay on Eloquence appeared in the *Massachusetts Journal* on 20 Feb.; see the entry for that date and note 3 there. No further numbers were published.

[2] A member of the directors' Standing Committee, Sullivan had his office on Court Square (*Boston Directory*, 1830–1831). His father, James Sullivan (1744–1808), attorney general and governor of Massachusetts, had been an originator of the plan for the Canal and the principal figure in its early history. See Roberts, *The Middlesex Canal, 1793–1860*, p. 28, 30, 31, 34, 222.

[3] Caleb Eddy, who served as superintendent, treasurer, and clerk of the corporation, had assumed the agency in 1825 and would continue until 1845 (same, p. 222).

[4] The history, problems, and prospects of the Middlesex Canal were matters of continuing interest to CFA. In Feb. 1829 he undertook a thorough study of the Canal; see vol. 2:339–344. His paper and his copy of the Sullivan report are preserved in one of his composition books (Adams Papers, Microfilms, Reel No. 315). CFA's early position on railroad building was clearly affected by his interest in canal enterprises (CFA to

JQA, 2 Feb., LbC, Adams Papers; below, entry for 26 Feb.). The Middlesex Canal, joining the Charles River basin and the Merrimac and planned as a first link in a water route from Boston to the St. Lawrence, was particularly vulnerable since the most insistent proposal being advanced was for a railroad paralleling the Canal from Boston to Lowell. The Canal's obsolescence was rapid after trains loaded with cargo began to ply the route in 1835. See Roberts, *The Middlesex Canal, 1793–1860*, p. 26–27, 154–158, 170–175, 191–196. A part of the canal's route is shown on the "map of Boston and the adjacent towns" reproduced in the present volume.

[5] The performance, the play's first in Boston, was at the Tremont Theatre before a "crowded and fashionable audience." John was played by Junius Brutus Booth (1796–1852), Falconbridge by Edwin Forrest (1806–1872), Lady Constance by Mrs. Duff. In the farce, *Amateurs and Actors*, which followed, Booth was Geoffrey Muffincap (*Columbian Centinel*, 3 Feb., p. 3, col. 4; 6 Feb., p. 2, col. 6). An engraving of Tremont Street and Theatre is reproduced in this volume.

THURSDAY. 4TH.

Morning clear and pleasant. Went to the Office and was busy nearly the whole of my Common period of time in copying the report of Mr. Sullivan upon the state of the Middlesex Canal. It is in many respects a valuable paper containing much information upon points where I could not gather any at the period of my last winter's examination. The theoretical portion I dissent from, and the inclination to further works seems a little singular after the misfortunes of those already perfected. But all which relates to the facts which the Writer by experience well knew is valuable. I devoted the larger part of my disposable time to it, afterwards only calling upon Mr. Brooks to inquire how Mrs. B. was.

Mr. Blake sent me a notification to attend the Meeting of the Private Debating Society at four o'clock in the afternoon but when the time came I found myself so comfortably seated reading Demosthenes in my warm room that I could not reconcile myself to going in the cold to do nothing. I accordingly pursued the study of my Greek with much pleasure. I have the assistance of so many Authors and Commentators that I hit the sense with a good deal of ease. Miss Julia Gorham spent the day here with my Wife and we had an agreeable time. I tried to write my second Number but could not please myself. On the whole, the day passed quietly but with little interest. I did not retire until late.

FRIDAY 5TH.

Morning clear. The weather is now steady Winter, and not in itself very disagreeable. The snow now lies hard on the surface and makes a pleasant chance for sleighing. At the Office, engaged in finishing Mr. Sullivan's report which I did. This has taken me a good deal of work. But I find upon comparing it, that it is in fact no longer than the abstract I made last year. After it was finished I went to Mr. Foster's to give directions about the putting on of the Papers as I am now rapidly going on with the repairs of the two Offices—My first attempt at speculation, I am a little afraid it may fail.[1] But at any rate it relieves me from the responsibility of paying so much rent, myself, or at least of costing so much to my Father. I feel a little delicate about that at the present time when his income comes very close with his expenditure.

I asked Mr. Foster to buy one Share of the Boylston Market Property for me, in case he purchased himself and not without. I also paid two remaining Accounts against my brother's Estate. There is now a single one left, and as Mr. Stone this day gave me hope that the Note of the City Guards would be soon paid in part, I believe I shall proceed at once to close the Administration.[2] This and calling to see Mr. Brooks was all I did, and Richardson coming in to spend half an hour interrupted me in my closing my Journal, so I returned home, and spent the afternoon in reading Demosthenes.

My afternoon studies are the pleasantest portion of my life. They are so far removed from the bustle and noise and risks of my morning occupations, and they are so much more profitable to the mind. I tried to write another Essay but failed. The attempt to handle the subject properly is difficult. At seven, I walked to the Athenæum to hear a Lecture delivered by Dr. Park upon the knowledge acquired by Sensation.[3] An easily written, agreeable Lecture, containing a good deal that is practical and pleasant. Stopped at Mrs. Frothingham's for Abby who passed the evening there, and we sat down to a little Supper very agreeably. After which we returned home by a brilliant but rather cold Moon.

[1] See entry for 22 Jan., above. In an effort to create more rentable space in the 23 Court Street building, CFA was moving his office to a previously unused area on the floor above.

[2] Ebenezer W. Stone was Adjutant of the 1st Regiment, 1st Brigade, 1st Division of the Mass. Militia ("City Guards"), *Mass. Register*, 1830, p. 93.

[3] Although Dr. John Park had his degree in medicine, he was not in practice. His office was in the Boston Lyceum. (*Boston Directory*, 1830–1831; *Mass. Register*, 1830, p. 159.)

SATURDAY 6TH.

Morning to the Office. Weather again severely cold, although I did not feel it nearly so much as before. My Wife received an amusing Letter from my Father,[1] which I read. It is full of the Washington scandal, but sarcastic enough. I was very much prevented from attending to any thing in particular, by several visits I made. One to Mr. Brooks to inquire how Mrs. B. did, one to Edward Blake to know what the result of the meeting of the Committee was. I was very little interrupted however while at the Office, so that I had opportunity to finish the record of my Diary, which had been lagging behind.

In the afternoon, instead of reading Demosthenes, I was engaged in making preparation for some few remarks I had to submit at the Meeting in the Evening.[2] My arrangements this day were short, for my only duty was that of attack of a proposition without submitting any thing for a substitute. But I pursued the course I always propose, that of methodizing my ideas in such a manner as to present a clear and definite statement of my grounds of argument, and not going at all out of the way. I accordingly attended and succeeded in submitting my propositions very distinctly. They brought on an animated discussion which lasted till quite late, and though myself considerably attacked, I had no opportunity to reply, a thing perhaps a little lucky for me, for I was perhaps a little too warm. We adjourned, and I returned home tolerably well content—My powers of speaking being undoubtedly improving.

¹ 31 Jan.; an answer to ABA's letter of 13 Jan. (both in Adams Papers).
² In its first three meetings in February, the Debating Society devoted itself to the subject of the militia. What the views were that CFA presented at these meetings is not known.

SUNDAY. 7TH.

Morning again severely cold. Miss Phillips who returned to us on yesterday, Abby and I attended divine Service this morning and heard Mr. Emerson preach a Sermon upon Charity. It was good as most of his are. There is a degree of practical sense running in them enough to interest, and to improve, a quality not always strong in the efforts of our Clergy. My feet were so cold that I could not enjoy it as much as I otherwise should have done. This weather is thorough Winter. After dinner, the ladies inclined to remain at home, so that I went out alone and heard Mr. Sewall again preach a Sermon upon temper, it was sensible but long and poorly delivered. It might have been made a very good thing. Returning we had a little flurry of snow which soon brought on Clouds to promise to us still more.

I passed the afternoon in examining Copies of the Letters of my Grandfather for Mr. Sparks, and finished for him a considerable number, though it occupied us until late in the evening. Many of these are interesting, some of them powerful, showing a mind and a pen not of a trifling character. It is something agreeable to me that I can look to my Parents with so much pleasure. It may be improper pride, if so may God forgive me. But I think it is a humbling reflection to add to it, that I am a son, a very lazy and indolent son, doing very little for my own support.

In the evening, I read a part of Sir Charles Grandison to the young ladies who soon found a more agreeable subject in a little Supper of devilled Turkey legs. I read Lord Kaimes afterwards. This Author is full of instruction and must be read again and again.

MONDAY 8TH.

The Snow had fallen heavily and had already given to us a very considerable addition to our mass of snow and extended the probable period of our sleighing indefinitely. I went to the Office as usual and was busy all morning in making out my Account as Administrator of the Estate of my poor brother. It was not long and I finished and copied it in time to submit to the Judge of Probate today. He hesitated about receiving it and finally advised me to send it to my Father, ask him to settle the Fee and give me a release, which would then close the Administration. I accordingly was obliged to return and write a letter to my Father upon the subject,[1] and as I was writing I thought I would add a little upon other subjects, particularly the astonishing sale of the Shares of the Boylston Market at 25¼ to 29¼ advance, which is beyond expectation.

Mr. Curtis called to ask if I had any News from my Father. He had nothing to say. This business took up all my time so that I had none left to write even my Journal. Returned home. After dinner, Abby went to see her Mother with Dr. Stevenson, and Miss Phillips was left to compare letters for Mr. Sparks with me. I also copied the letter to my father, and thus went the afternoon without touching my Demosthenes. Abby did not return until late, and then a little dejected by the condition in which she found her Mother. I am fearful the closing scene is rapidly coming. Miss Julia Gorham came to pass the Evening and I therefore went upstairs but my room was so cold, I could pursue no regular study, so I looked over King John.[2] After the ladies retired as usual I read Kaimes.

[1] LbC in Adams Papers; the enclosed inventory, prepared for the Court, is missing.

[2] There are seven editions of Shakespeare now in MQA; of these, four have JQA's bookplate and one (8 vols., Edinburgh, 1769) bears an inscription dated 1815 from JQA to GWA. CFA noted in his copy of the Isaac Reed edition (12 vols., London, 1820) the date on which he first read or witnessed each play. A one-volume, London, 1827, edition is inscribed in CFA's hand: "Abby B. Brooks from Charles Francis Adams, January 1st 1829."

TUESDAY. 9TH.

Morning at the Office. Time occupied in making my record for the three preceding days which was somewhat laborious. Called in to see Mr. Brooks who seemed to speak as if his Wife was better. Richardson called for a few minutes and Mr. Curtis. The latter read a letter for my Father which arrived here from the House of Baring, being another act of Mr. Petty Vaughan's Play. I enclosed this with a bill for Thomas J. Hellen and sent them both to my Father.[1] But on reflection I find my morning wasted very much in the manner they all are. This is bad but I hardly know how to correct it.

I returned home and after dinner devoted myself to the Oration on the Crown in which I made some progress. The text is not so difficult to understand as that of Æschines, and the style is more polished. I feel pleased as I go on. I took part of the time, as the ladies were out, to attempt a little of my second Essay. Mr. Child not having published my first in his Saturday's paper gives me a little respite. Perhaps he may not publish it at all—How do I know. If not he ought to return it agreeably to my request. I succeeded in forming a skeleton of an Essay, this evening which I shall fill up at leisure. It embraced the prominent points of defective deliberative Oratory. I then recollected it was time to go to Edward Brooks' to the weekly Meeting. The usual persons were there, and the guests enumerated at the last Meeting, with the addition of Mr. Shepherd who came in upon a visit without any intention of interfering. Our time was merry but I did not enjoy it; We returned and I read some of Lord Kaimes.

[1] The letter from Baring's is missing. On Thomas Johnson Hellen (1809–1833), nephew of LCA, see vol. 1:6, and Adams Genealogy.

WEDNESDAY. 10TH.

Morning at the Office. The Weather which for three weeks past has been cold this day moderated so much that the snow began to disappear with amazing rapidity. I have now become so much accustomed to it that I rather regret this, for it makes only an interruption in our winter Weather and not a final change from it. My last Evening's Supper gave me a slight uneasy head ach which made me feel unable to do much, and the condition in which I found my Office distracted my attention. The People were in it making repairs. I think it is about to be fully worth what I think I ought to ask for it. But there are now so many Offices empty that I am fearful I shall not get rid of it, just at present.

I passed the morning in reading the Speech of Mr. Quincy upon the New army Bill so noted for its violence and the reply given to it by Mr. Clay.[1] There is some eloquence in it, but the want of judgment, Mr. Q.'s prominent weakness throughout life is manifest. I then called to see Mr. Brooks who was again low spirited and I went to inquire of Quincy what the result of my Note for *the Note* was, but it was not to be found so my pursuit was fruitless.[2] My morning passed and the Afternoon was taken up in looking over and correcting Letters for Mr. Sparks. This is a disagreeable business at all times, and particularly when suffering a little from indisposition. I read aloud in the Evening, a little of Sir Charles Grandison to the Ladies and afterwards read Lord Kaimes.

[1] The speeches of Josiah Quincy (1772–1864) and Henry Clay, delivered in the House, Jan. 1813, are in Williston's *Eloquence* at 3:5–76.

[2] Josiah Quincy (1802–1882) had not been able to locate JQA's note to the executors of JA's will so that it could be returned, payment having been made; see entry for 28 Jan., above.

THURSDAY. 11TH.

The morning was warm and pleasant. Quite a change from what it has been, and the snow went off in quantities until about twelve o'clock when it began to freeze and grow cold again. At the Office as usual. Received a long and gratifying letter from my father,[1] which I read with pleasure, excepting in the business part where he charges the funds in my hands with a still further burden in the education of John Quincy Adams, his nephew, which fact explains to me what before was dark in the matter of the visit of my Uncle to me yesterday morning—He being seldom inclined to favour me excepting when demands are to be made.

I proceeded in my usual occupations. Wrote several Notes to my Tenants and read a part of Mr. Poindexter's Speech on the Seminole War.[2] Mrss. G. A. Otis and S. Brown called to request my subscription to a fund for establishing a Post Office. I subscribed as it is probable it will benefit my father's property in Court Street. Mr. E. Clough called to speak about the Share in the Republican Institution belonging to my brother. He notified me that the Government declined taking it and asked me if I would not take it for myself. This establishment is now of so little use that I think it exceedingly questionable whether it is worthwhile to keep it up. But seeing Mr. Rayner the President of it afterwards he told me that he thought it likely a motion would be made to wind it up this next annual Meeting, and accordingly I should get what I wanted.[3] I asked Mr. Brooks how they were at Medford, and his answer was, much as usual. I tried to find Mr. I. P. Davis, but could not succeed.

The paperer was this day busy with the other Office I was about to move into. He finished and beautified it in such a manner as to make it look entirely another thing. How badly this building has been treated. And now I am afraid I shall do it no good. Had it been so managed at the time of the Fire, it would have yielded richly.[4] After dinner I read Demosthenes with pleasure. A fine author and one constantly to be studied. I am an admirer of his pithy, meaning[5] style. There is no trifling. And I propose to make him my study. Made a draft of my Essay No. 2. and in the evening read Sir Charles Grandison to the Ladies, and finished Kaimes to myself but I must read him again.

[1] 5 Feb. (Adams Papers).

[2] George Poindexter's speech delivered in the House, Feb. 1819, is in Williston's *Eloquence* at 3:128–183.

[3] On Ebenezer Clough, John Rayner, and CFA's effort to have the Republican Institution buy back GWA's share in it, see vol. 2:411–412 and note.

[4] Ten brick buildings and some wooden structures on Court Street had been destroyed by fire on 10 Nov. 1825, forc-

ing 35 attorneys to find other quarters. The spread of the fire was checked at the building adjoining 23 Court Street (*Columbian Centinel*, 12 Nov. 1825, p. 2, col. 3). Since rebuilding had not been completed until the end of 1826, office space had been in great demand (Brooks, Waste Book, 10 Nov., 27 Dec. 1825; 14 Nov., 30 Dec. 1826).

[5] Thus in MS, for "meaningful"?

FRIDAY 12TH.

The cold was again extremely severe with us. But I have now become so much accustomed to the temperature which now is common that I mind it very little. Such a thing is habit, and such a change does the agreeable difference of a comfortable home of one's own produce. At the Office as usual, where I was occupied as usual in reading Williston. My morning however was considerably wasted as is commonly the case. I must labour to introduce a change. Tried to find Mr. Isaac P. Davis but could not succeed. Went to the City Bank to get an old Book balanced which belonged to my Brother. Called upon Mr. Brooks for a moment and paid a short visit to Kinsman. Mr. Whitney appears to make no start in any way, and the City Guards affairs progress slowly.

After dinner I continued reading my Demosthenes, which became a little more difficult—But on the whole still very fascinating. Mr. Sparks called to see me about my letter to him, and seemed a little startled by my father's words.[1] He was for returning the whole, but I thought this would not do, so that I talked over the matter and advised to the withdrawal of several Letters not excepted to heretofore by me, and going on a little more cautiously in the future.[2] I was glad to get over this business so well, for I feared it would lead me into a scrape.

I began in the evening to read Sir Charles Grandison to the ladies, but we were soon interrupted by the entrance of Mr. and Mrs. Walker from Charlestown, who passed the evening with us. He is an able and an agreeable man and I was glad to see him. She as I have said before is my Wife's Cousin. We passed a very pleasant evening. They were quite agreeable, and we all finished with a little Supper and some Whiskey Punch which had a very sensible influence in enlivening the group. They left us at ten.

[1] On 11 Feb. CFA had written to Jared Sparks (LbC, Adams Papers) communicating JQA's decision stated in a letter to CFA, 5 Feb. (Adams Papers), to withhold consent for Sparks to use a letter about which CFA had asked on 24

Jan. (Adams Papers). The letter in question was upon public matters and was therefore eligible under the terms JQA had originally fixed, but in it JA had expressed views about Franklin intended as private observations.

Acting on JQA's instructions, CFA had also had to go beyond this and reverse decisions previously made allowing the use of a number of other letters written to individuals on public matters. Permission thereafter would be restricted only to "such public dispatches from JA to Congress as were not in the Department of State but which ought to be included in a publication ordered by Congress."

² Sparks was so "nettled" by the new decision that he seemed inclined to use nothing on these terms. CFA, wishing to avoid a public charge of "illiberality" against his father, modified JQA's strict rule so as to allow the use of letters written to public characters on public subjects as long as private observations upon individuals were not included (CFA to JQA, 14 Feb., Adams Papers).

CFA's new rules, in point of fact, conformed to Sparks' earlier statement of intent (Sparks to JQA, 18 Jan., Adams Papers). However, in the period since

JQA granted access to the letterbooks (above, entry for 26 Nov. 1829, note), he had come to regret that he had done so (JQA to CFA, 5 Feb., Adams Papers). This change had been brought about (1) by the appearance in the *North Amer. Rev.* for Jan. 1830 (p. 1–25) of Sparks' review of Timothy Pitkin's *A Political and Civil History of the United States, 1763–1797*, a review which JQA viewed as a "gross and wanton outrage upon the memory of John Jay" (to CFA, 5 Feb.), and which had provoked a bitter public controversy between Sparks and John Lowell (*Boston Advertiser*, 7, 8, 9, 11, 15, 16, 19 Jan.); (2) by JQA's becoming aware of opinions held by Sparks about Arthur Lee that JQA felt constituted "an outrage equally unjust" (see above, entry for 30 Nov. 1829, note); and (3) by sharp differences between Sparks and JQA over James Grahame's, *The History of the Rise and Progress of the United States* (JQA to Sparks, 24 Jan., LbC, Adams Papers).

Contributing also to CFA's difficulties were the crustiness and arrogance of Sparks (CFA to JQA, 24 Jan., Adams Papers).

SATURDAY. 13TH.

Morning clear and cold. Our weather as yet does not moderate. I have very seldom known a more severe month. I went to the Office, after having marketed in the absence of Benjamin, my Man Servant who went home sick. I found this rather a new business, but still attempted to do as well as I could. It is an essential article of knowledge.

My time at the Office was passed very much in preparing some methodical train of reasoning for any argument which might take place tonight, upon the much talked of subject of the Militia laws. I inquired of Mr. Brooks as usual, and found that Mrs. B. was not much altered. I found Mr. I. P. Davis and delivered to him the patterns of Frames which had been returned to me by my Father. Nothing happened otherwise. Mr. Sparks had a conversation of a few minutes about the Papers and made a request that I would again look over those I had last examined, and reject what might not come within my father's rule. I did so in the Afternoon but found none to make objection to.

The remainder of the Afternoon was passed in methodizing and modifying the remarks I thought of submitting to the Society. This labour costs me much time and trouble. But it is very beneficial for it habituates me to the practice of bringing ideas in a train and of managing them to an effective purpose. We met as usual in the evening though the meeting was small. I had expected that the discussion would fall through, instead of which it became animated and it was my luck to bear the whole brunt of the battle, for nearly all the Speakers were on the other side. I made a very few remarks but with very considerable warmth. I had been a little nettled at the tone of the remarks of A. W. Fuller,[1] and I replied in a manner perhaps not altogether agreeable to him. One effect however I found my warmth produce upon my Speaking, it checked the flow of my ideas so as once or twice to put me in the hazard of losing my train. But on the whole I was very well content. Adjourned without a settlement, and called for Abby and Miss Phillips at Mrs. Frothingham's to return home.

[1] Abraham W. Fuller, counselor, whose office was at 31 Court Street (*Boston Directory*, 1830–1831).

SUNDAY. 14TH.

The morning was severely cold. I attended divine service at Mr. Frothingham's Church in the morning, and heard Mr. Sewall preach rather a dull Sermon. He is not an agreeable man to my fancy. My wife went to Medford with her brother so that Miss Phillips and I kept house. Our dinner was quite comfortable, and in the afternoon as it was cold, I remained at home, and wrote a long letter which was due to my Father.[1] Our Correspondence is now a tolerably agreeable one, being upon common subjects of interest and having no reference to objects of an unpleasant nature. I write, generally speaking of my literary occupations, and he replies in his most pleasant vein. After I had finished, I read aloud to Miss Phillips, a Sermon of Jeremy Taylor's on Meditation. It was in his peculiar style, flowery and pedantic but containing much sterling sense. He advises in it practical Christianity, and is very severe upon the spiritual effervescencies which so frequently distinguish those who aim at extraordinary piety. The Sermon was good and served the purpose better than Mr. Sewall's. Abby did not return until late in the Evening. I read a little of Sir Charles Grandison, but Edward Brooks came in to enquire about his Mother. Abby gives, I think a very unfavourable account.[2] But I feel unwilling to alarm or distress her.

[1] Letter in Adams Papers.
[2] Perceptible loss of strength and an increase both in the frequency and in the duration of periods of aberration characterized Mrs. Brooks' condition (Charlotte Everett to Edward Everett, 14 Feb., Everett MSS, MHi).

MONDAY. 15TH.

The weather still cold, but cloudy. Went to the Office as usual and that part of my time which was not occupied in writing my Journal, was passed in reading Williston. I this morning examined Mr. Pinkney's Speech upon the Treaty making power—A very able thing and bearing much more highly the marks of careful polish than any thing I have yet read.[1] This was a very able man. His power was clouded with a little affectation, but on the whole I incline to the belief that he is more respectable as a Speaker in the eye of the future than any man we have had.

I called to see Mr. Brooks who was this morning exceedingly discouraged. He had conversed with Dr. Swan and had derived little or no consolation from his opinion.[2] I am afraid that the case is desperate. Thus the morning passed and I went home. The afternoon was passed in inspecting the Copies of some more letters of my Grandfather, in reading a portion of Demosthenes, and in finishing the copy of my letter to my Father which my wife could not complete. I receive many more interruptions than I wish I did, in the prosecution of my most profitable studies. In the evening after calling at Mrs. Frothingham's to know how she was, and being informed that she was relieved from her sudden attack I returned home and was just beginning to read Sir Charles Grandison to the Ladies, when Edmund Quincy came in and sat all the evening until quite late. He is quite fond of coming here, and somehow or other, we seldom have a single entirely uninterrupted evening at home.

[1] William Pinkney's speech in the House, Jan. 1816, Williston's *Eloquence,* 3:231–254.
[2] On Dr. Daniel Swan of Medford, the Brookses' family physician, see vol. 2:206 and *Medford Historical Register,* 1 (1898):116–118, portrait facing p. 116.

TUESDAY. 16TH.

The morning cloudy with a kind of drizzle which freezing when it reached the pavements made the walking slippery and dangerous. I got down as well as I could and upon arriving safe at the Office went about my usual avocations. This morning was not much interrupted so that upon finishing my usual day's record, I sat down and read with attention two or three Speeches in Williston—Those of Messrs. McLane and Sergeant on the Missouri Question, and Mr. Hayne's on the Tariff with Mr. Webster's on the Greek Question.[1] The latter I recollect to have heard. It was an able though perhaps not in itself a proper effort. The question was not in itself one which would pay a man for the trouble and risk in raising it. On the whole I was better satisfied with this morning than with any for a long time preceding.

Mr. Farmer called upon me again and being a little impertinent, I ordered him out of the Office, which as I hope will put a stop to his visits. That affair is not yet over. But time enough has passed to make me indifferent about it. Moses Thompson came to present a bill.[2] He is a plaisterer whom I have dismissed on account of intemperate habits. He made a charge which I could not settle unless I previously arranged with Mrs. Longhurst. So I told him to postpone it. Returned home and passed the afternoon reading Demosthenes. Mr. Kingman called about the House in Common Street but declined the rent. My Greek was easy. I regretted to hear the despairing account of Mr. Brooks. The case is hopeless.[3] The evening came and I went to the usual family Meeting at Chardon's. Mrs. Frothingham was so sick, she could not go, so that the party contained all it had last time excepting her. It was very agreeable, and we came away early enough for me to read a Chapter of Lord Kaimes.

[1] Louis McLane and John Sergeant in the House, Feb. 1820; Robert Y. Hayne in the Senate, April 1824; Daniel Webster in the House, Jan. 1823 (Williston's *Eloquence*, 3:277–363, 378–416, 470–524).

[2] His address was 37 Warren Street (*Boston Directory*, 1830–1831).

[3] Mr. Brooks had continued to maintain hope of Mrs. Brooks' recovery, but on the day following he wrote with resignation to her brother, Benjamin Gorham, in Washington; to their son, Sidney; and to their son-in-law, Edward Everett (Brooks, Farm Journal, 17 Feb.).

WEDNESDAY. 17TH.

The morning was cloudy and weather disagreeable. I went to the Office as usual first going to inquire of Mr. Brooks what the proposed arrangement might be, as to Abby's going to Medford. He told me she would go out with her Aunt, Mrs. Gray, probably to remain until tomorrow. I then returned to the Office. Mr. Russell Freeman called upon me, he is the ejected Collector of Newburyport and has lately returned from an exploring visit to Washington, he came to me only to make acquaintance and to say he had seen my father and family well.[1] Mr. Jones called upon me from Weston to inform me he had a little more money, proceeds of the sale of Wood at Weston. I was quite glad of this for I fear the funds of this Quarter will turn out but poorly. The remainder of the morning was passed in finishing Mr. Hayne's Speech upon the Tariff of 1824. It is good but it is a little surprising that this should have been the course taken by the Southern Gentlemen. For in raising up a new Market for their Cotton here what is it to them if they lose a little elsewhere, and but little for Great Britain must take what they want, because they can get none so good and so cheap any where else.[2]

Miss Phillips and I dined together, Abby sending me a Note saying that her Mother was worse even than she expected, and wishing to stay. Miss Phillips left me after dinner so that I passed the whole afternoon and evening in my study. I read a portion of Demosthenes as usual with all the critical remarks in themselves a material assistance. In the evening not having written for a long time to my Mother I sat down and made one out,[3] though now it is hard to write as she has very much ceased to interest herself in the smaller affairs of my situation. I am sorry, but I think she does not think so nearly of me as she used to do. Retired to a solitary room.

[1] Although Russell Freeman was a friend of JQA (Bemis, *JQA*, 2:183n.), CFA had only a minimal respect for him, holding him to be "a gambler in politics" (CFA to LCA, 17 Feb., Adams Papers).

[2] Thus in MS. The meaning seems to be that because of the lack of competition the purchasers (Great Britain) must pay what the growers demand.

[3] The letter to LCA is that cited above.

THURSDAY. 18TH.

Morning mild and pleasant. Went to the Office as usual and to see Mr. Brooks who told me he had brought my Wife in with him so that I need not go out. His report of the condition of Mrs. B. is such that I think it likely she will not live many days longer. Returned to the Office and after finishing my usual Diary I sat down to read Plutarch's Lives of Demosthenes and Cicero which I wish to set before me as constant studies. They are deeply interesting in themselves as exhibiting the greatest specimens on record of perfection in the highest powers of man.[1] My morning was gone before I thought. Only one interruption. That not welcome. A man by the name of Haskell came to me to present a bill for lumber used in the House behind my Office.[2] Mr. Hollis being the responsible man, I sent him off, but as this was one of poor George's loose practices, I was obliged to pay it only calling Hollis pretty severely to account. I think I should benefit the Agency much if I could dismiss him.

Found Abby at home, but exceedingly dull and dispirited. I am sorry but cannot help it. She must now go through a hard trial, one of the first she has been subjected to. I called upon Dr. Stevenson to know his opinion—it is decided.[3] I then for the rest of the afternoon read Demosthenes with usual interest. In the evening, resumed Clarissa Harlowe with my Wife, so long interrupted.[4] After which I read part of Lord Kaimes.

[1] JQA, animated by CFA's letters reporting his studies in the ancient orators, had recently returned to the reading of Cicero and found his old enthusiasm unabated. He sought to communicate his passion in a series of letters to CFA in the course of which he calls Cicero "the noblest spirit that ever lived in the Tide of Times" (22 Dec. 1829; 11, 17 Jan., 5 Feb. 1830, Adams Papers). CFA, deep in his studies of the Greeks and relying heavily on three articles in the *Edinburgh Review* (see above, entry for 29 Jan., note), entered a strong defense of Demosthenes as the greater (CFA to JQA, 14 Feb., Adams Papers).

[2] Perhaps Levi Haskell, who had a wood wharf at the foot of Poplar Street (*Boston Directory*, 1830–1831).

[3] Dr. J. Greely Stevenson had, along with Dr. Daniel Swan, been in regular attendance upon Mrs. Brooks since 25 January. Dr. John C. Warren had also been called in consultation on three occasions. Dr. Stevenson's call on the 18th was the last. (Brooks, Farm Journal, 25 Jan.–18 Feb. *passim.*)

[4] On 27 Jan., *Clarissa Harlowe*, which CFA had been reading aloud to ABA for three months, was put aside to be replaced on 31 Jan. by *Sir Charles Grandison*. The interruption can be explained if the copy of *Clarissa* they had been reading was the same copy which ABA sent to her mother at her mother's request. After Mrs. Brooks' condition worsened, Mr. Brooks and Charlotte Everett took the copy up and planned to read it through (Charlotte Everett to Edward Everett, 31 Jan., Everett MSS, MHi).

FRIDAY. 19TH.

The morning was extremely mild and agreeable. I went to the Office and occupied myself as usual in my reading going out only to see Mr. Brooks for a moment. He said Mrs. B. had been a little better yesterday and recommended my going out with Abby to see her this afternoon which we accordingly decided to do. I met Isaac P. Davis who asked me to get that business of the Picture done. But the principal part of my time was passed in reading Williston—The Speeches on the Panama Question made by Mr. Berrien in the Senate and Mr. Webster in the House. The surprising thing to me is to perceive how the ingenuity of man was occupied in perverting the objects of that measure. And how blindly men rushed into opposition on selfish ends of a measure intended for a great good. But so it is in human nature. And great national views must in a free government occasionally meet with great checks and discouragement. The surprising thing is that they prevail so much on the whole. Mr. Berrien is a narrow minded Sophist quibbling in a small way.[1]

I received this morning a letter from my Father in answer to mine upon business and allowing me my Fee for Administration. But where to get the Money a little puzzles me.[2] We dined hurriedly, and I then with my Wife started for Medford. The riding was good and we went fast. But Mrs. Brooks was so sick that it was not thought advisable that I should see her. She had been quite revived yesterday, only to sink back further today. So I sat in the parlour and conversed with Mr. Brooks whose spirits are very much depressed. But getting upon indifferent subjects we managed tolerably well. Mrs. Everett looks sick and is dull.[3] But my Wife bears all this very badly. It totally discomposes her system and makes her fit for nothing. I grieve for her, yet find it myself hard to bear.[4] My maxim adopted many years ago is true. We in marrying and thus doubling our means of enjoyment and happiness also double the sources of pain. We returned just at dark which is now much later than it has been. And on arriving at home I sat down to get a little more comfortable and to read a little of Clarissa Harlowe, after which, Kaimes.

[1] The speeches delivered in March 1826 by John Macpherson Berrien and in April by Daniel Webster are in Williston's *Eloquence* at 4:14–96. CFA had been present in the House during several days of the debates on "the Panama Question," one of the crucial issues arising during JQA's Presidency; see vol. 2:39–41, 85. The Congressional debate was on the proposal, strongly urged by the President and by Secretary of State Henry Clay, to authorize sending United States representatives to the Inter-American Congress to be held at Panama and on restrictive amendments to that authorization that would limit the freedom of the United States representatives to negotiate. For an account of the episode in the vigorously pursued but ultimately unsuccessful effort of JQA and Clay to achieve a larger Latin-American policy and to foster the creation of a Congress of American Nations, see Bemis, *JQA,* 1:550–561 and, for an even more extensive treatment, Arthur P. Whitaker, "Tempest over Panama" in his *The United States and the Independence of Latin America, 1800–1830,* Baltimore, 1941, p. 564–602.

[2] In ordering that the matter of a fee for administering GWA's estate be referred to JQA (above, entry for 8 Feb.), the Judge of Probate had said that he had decreed $100 in similar cases, but CFA had pointed out to him that in this case he (CFA) enjoyed the use of much of the inventoried property (CFA to JQA, 8 Feb., LbC, Adams Papers). JQA fixed the fee at $100 (JQA to CFA, 12–13 Feb., Adams Papers).

[3] Although sisters of Mrs. Brooks and Mr. Brooks were in attendance, Charlotte Everett, pregnant, felt that, with her sister Ann Frothingham too ill to come to Medford, the family burdens upon her were overwhelming (Charlotte Everett to Edward Everett, letters of Jan.–Feb., Everett MSS, MHi).

[4] CFA's regard for Mrs. Brooks was beyond the ordinary (below, entry for 23 Feb., note). To this had been added his awareness for more than a year that her illness was a mortal one. Combined, they had made "a strong reason for my urging my marriage so soon . . . for she was exceedingly distressed at the idea that she should not live to see it" (CFA to LCA, 17 Feb. 1830, Adams Papers).

SATURDAY 20TH.

Morning hazy but soon changed to a clear sun and a lovely day. I went to the Office as usual and passed my time much as usual, first reading Mr. Hayne's Speech upon the Western Lands, a bitter Phillipic upon the course of the Eastern States. The truth is that the course of these States during the War was and is totally indefensible and it is a weak point to touch, but still it is not generous to touch so often the subject. The people here have came to their senses and punished the Authors of those measures by removing them from public life. And the other States ought to accept of this as sufficient without pushing farther.[1]

I went to see Mr. Brooks but found his Office closed which led me to conclude that the closing scene was rapidly approaching. I then passed the remainder of the morning in reading Mr. McDuffie's Speech upon the Amending the Constitution as to the election of President.[2] It is a better Speech than I thought, though too long and not sufficiently laboured. Returning home I found Abby had received a letter from Medford intimating that her Mother might not live through the day. She was of course very much affected. After dinner I read Demosthenes as usual. My first Article upon Eloquence was published this morning but so obscurely placed that I do not think it has justice done to it.[3] Miss Julia Gorham came in to pass the Evening so that I went out and attended an unusually full meeting of the Debating Society. The discussion upon the Militia was renewed but not carried on with vigor, as none of the warmest Members joined in it. But the question approaching to a decision, I waited till the close and found that my side of it prevailed, after which I went rapidly home.

[1] CFA was reading the newspaper reports on the great debate on public-land policy in the United States Senate during Jan.–Feb. 1830. The protagonists were Daniel Webster, who had shifted with New England from a narrow to a broad construction of the Constitution, and Robert Y. Hayne of South Carolina, who made the most of the threat of federal "consolidation" and the near-treasonable course of New England leaders in opposing the War of 1812. Hayne's speech opening the debate had been printed in the *Columbian Centinel*, 6 Feb., p. 1, cols. 2–5; his rejoinder to Webster appeared in the issue for 20 Feb., p. 2, cols. 2–5. Publication of Webster's speech followed; see below, entries for 27 Feb., 3 March.

[2] George McDuffie's speech delivered in the House, Feb. 1826, is in Williston's *Eloquence* at 4:97–152. See below, entry for 2 March and note.

[3] *Massachusetts Journal*, 20 Feb., p. 1, cols. 3–4. The communication appears under the rubric "Literary," bears the heading "No. 1," and is signed "Orator."

SUNDAY. 21ST.

The day was again exceeding lovely and beautiful. I attended divine service this morning and heard Mr. Sewall preach a long and tedious Discourse which did not please me at all. Abby went to Medford, her Mother being still alive, with her brother Chardon. And I had a solitary dinner at home. My amusement consisted in reading Kaimes until I received a Note from Edward Brooks with the request of Abby that I should go out to Medford to bring her in. This seemed so strange a part of the plan that I did not know what to do, but after going to Mrs. Chardon Brooks' and conversing with her, I found her husband was to stay all night, so I went down, got a Chaise and started off. Upon arriving I found that Mrs. Brooks was still living though very low and all the family present very much affected. It was a melancholy spectacle and in itself exciting as well as affecting. I remained downstairs talking with the family until after tea, when just before my starting to return I received a Message from her expressive of a desire to see me. This I had not expected today but I went immediately. The scene was a melancholy one for she was unable to speak yet anxious to express to me her feelings. She was altered totally, and looked as if Death already claimed her in all but one little spot. I had never seen before, any one so situated and I felt the sadness of the spectacle, but I was not so horror struck as I expected. There was nothing of that shocking nature which my feelings had anticipated. She apparently had sent for me to express her kind feelings and was unable, and I felt the signal she made of it more than expression. God rest her kind soul. She has done her duty on earth, and sees no terrors in a better place. The loss of her family is greater than her own. We returned to town and after calling at the houses of the different relations to let them know the facts so far as we knew, we passed the remainder of the evening at home.[1]

[1] Mrs. Brooks' last day seemed equally extraordinary to all those who recorded its details. After a night during which she had been unconscious and at the point of death, at about eight in the morning she had revived and was "sensible and collected" (Brooks, Farm Journal, 21 Feb.). For some days there had been "much alienation of mind, but on the last there was none. The voice only was gone" (CFA to LCA, 13 March, Adams Papers). She saw successively each member of the family. When Abby kissed her "she sent for me by a sign to Abby and a strong exertion to arti ulate my name.... [F]or the few moments I was there she seemed to be attempting to express to me words of affection" (same). "After these interviews she drew her cap over her Eyes and tried to compose herself" (Charlotte Everett to Edward Everett, 23 Feb., Everett MSS, MHi), "taking her leave of us all with the utmost resignation and tenderness and then requesting us to leave the room" (Brooks, Farm Journal).

MONDAY. 22D.

Morning pleasant, but it turned out a damp and disagreeable day. I went to the Office and wrote my Journal as usual, but my head did not feel in good order. Saw Mr. Brooks' man Foster who came to town with Chardon, and announced to me that Mrs. B. expired last night at twelve o'clock. Thus is the melancholy scene closed. I have been for some time expecting it but yet I feel a regret at having lost an indulgent Mother and a kind friend.

I presented my Account of my brother's Estate this day to the Judge of Probate who accepted it and thus closed that affair. This was all the business I did, and as I was going home to see my Wife, I met Chardon who gave me a little thing to do which puzzled me a little.

It was to get a plate for the Coffin. I never had been called to perform a similar Office but after going around to ascertain some distance, I found the proper person and gave the necessary directions.[1] Knowledge of this kind is useful in practical life for it may often help a friend. I know but little of it. I then ordered Mourning and afterwards went home. The constant friends of Abby, Miss Julia Gorham and Miss Carter were with her during the morning. I found her something better than I expected. We dined alone, and I passed the afternoon in trying to finish the Inventory of George's Affairs to deliver to my father. But I could not quite succeed. This last part is a tedious business.

After tea, I read aloud to my Wife a part of Clarissa Harlowe and finished the 7th of 8 volumes. It is a little long but still quite interesting. My Nerves and stomach were however so much out of order that I did not enjoy it. The excitement has been considerable and painful. After Abby retired, I tried to write a little Notice of her Mother, as my small tribute for the affection which she expressed for me on her dying day, but my head was in such pain that I am fearful I did not do justice to my subject. I retired in much suffering.

[1] Thus in MS. The intended meaning might be paraphrased: "after going about at some length to ascertain who the proper person was, I found him and gave him the necessary directions."

TUESDAY. 23D.

Morning again delightful. I went to the Office, and was occupied in continuing the abstract of my brother's Inventory. This took me nearly the whole morning—A very tedious and not an agreeable job. The result I am also a little in anxiety about. I finished however my little tribute to the memory of Mrs. Brooks and sent it to the Newspaper.[1] It is not so good as I wish it was, but I do not now feel capable of doing any thing better. My head is not great at writing. I am unable to produce any thing very extraordinary or striking. But Mr. Brooks should pardon the effort in the good intention.

As Abby was occupied at Mrs. Frothingham's in working, I went down to dine there. She looks better than she did, though still apparently an invalid. Mr. F. her husband has not yet returned which to her was matter of great regret.[2]

After dinner I went home and passed the afternoon in my study reading Demosthenes in which I progressed exceedingly. There are some difficulties occasionally but I have so many good Notes and commentaries that I get along easily. I attempted another number upon Oratory but without spirit. How much writing in it's effect dwindles from the inspiration in which it is written. My ideas are not strong enough. The truth is that today I fell into a kind of melancholy train of ideas. My ambition seems to have lost it's tone, my mind it's hopes. I look to the future with some dread, for what will be likely to turn out as the result. My father must be my adviser and advocate in cases where I may feel too weak to stand for myself. The evening was passed in my Study reading Walker's Rhetorical Grammar,[3] a book I do not incline to think very favourably of. It makes too much of small matters. My Wife returned at nine, and I tried to sit up and read Lord Kaimes but found myself quite unable from weariness.

[1] CFA's unsigned tribute appeared in the *Columbian Centinel* for 24 Feb., p. 3, col. 2. It concluded: "The writer has known the subject of this, for a period in time perhaps comparatively short; but long, if that time is measured by the opportunities he has had of *watching* the rich abundance of her charity, of *witnessing* the strength of her parental attachments, and of *experiencing* the living warmth of her love." His tribute privately expressed was no less warm: "Goodness of heart was her eminent attribute . . . , her benevolence flowed as

from a continual spring" (CFA to LCA, 17 Feb., Adams Papers).

[2] Mr. Frothingham arrived on 24 Feb. in time for the funeral. Though he had left Washington the week before, his sister-in-law wrote that "his immoderate love of New York has kept him there, notwithstanding Ann wrote him of Mother's illness, and of her being sick herself" (Charlotte Everett to Edward Everett, 23 Feb., Everett MSS, MHi).

[3] John Walker, *A Rhetorical Grammar or Course of Lessons in Elocution*, London, 1785.

WEDNESDAY. 24TH.

The morning was again clear and lovely. I went to the office however feeling heavily and not yet free from head ach. My time was taken up in writing my usual record and in removing my books and book cases thus commencing my start to a new room. Whether my project succeed or not of letting this one, I am at any rate under a much less heavy charge to my father—As I shall take good care of a room liable to be abused, and render it respectable while I am in it. I only completed the thing partially as I was obliged to return hence early for the purpose of preparing myself to go to Medford, to pay the last tribute to the remains of Mrs. Brooks. My notice appeared this morning and caused some sensation—The members of the family ascribing it to Dr. Stevenson or to Mr. Palfrey.[1] Mr. Frothingham paid it a very pretty compliment. He arrived this morning, and upon Abby, Chardon and his wife and my reaching Medford we found him and the rest of the family assembled. Mr. Brooks behaved with tolerable composure, and the children acted naturally and without affectation. There was no superfluous and overstrained grief, it was silent, noiseless and gave room for the sympathy of others. Mr. Stetson made a tolerably appropriate Prayer, though not so possessed of the kind of feeling which in my mind a Clergyman should have. The idea would force itself into my mind that the being acting for us was worldly, and not possessed of that high sense of the *end* of his vocation which exalts the spirit to speak in the tones of power to men. But still the prayer was by no means bad.

Those who came from Boston were a considerable number, besides the connexions of the family. We followed the body to it's final resting place, and I felt my eyes tingle as the last duties were performed. I looked at the face, contrary to my common practice and I was struck with the placid state of the Features expressing the uncommon quiet of the mind when it departed. On returning home, to Mr. Brooks, we did not wait, but came back to Boston where we passed the Evening quietly.

[1] Three days later, CFA's authorship was known. "It gratified my Father very much" (Charlotte Everett to Edward Everett, 27 Feb., Everett MSS, MHi).

On Rev. John Gorham Palfrey, kinsman of Mrs. Brooks, see vol. 2:266 and *DAB*.

THURSDAY. 25TH.

Morning hazy but gave way to the Sun. This weather is delightful and pays for all the severity of the preceding period. I went to the Office and was busy all day in making my Inventory and returns to my Father of Affairs of my brother's Estate. The loss on the sales is considerable, rather more than I had expected, but as those affairs are arranged it matters little. I was also busy in removing, to my new Office. This makes the third I have occupied since my being in Boston.[1] I hope it will be the last. I should be willing to charge myself forty dollars a year for it if my father should feel himself at all embarrassed. It satisfies me much more than the extravagant appearance of the other one. My Law Books were all removed today, and tomorrow I propose to commence occupation.

Returned home and found Mr. Sparks had left business enough for me to do for the whole afternoon, but I hope that it will be the close. It took me not only the afternoon but the evening to do it. Miss Julia Gorham dined here, and in the evening Edward came in and sat a little while talking very pleasantly.[2] I like some points in his character much—Others not quite so well. But as to conversation, he is generally agreeable. We had a very quiet day and nothing at all remarkable about it. I retired as usual.

[1] From Nov. 1828 to April 1829, CFA had rented an office at 10 Court Street; see vol. 2:306, 371.

[2] Probably Edward Brooks.

FRIDAY 26TH.

Morning fine. The Weather for the past week or ten days gives new life to a man, though I must confess that during nearly the whole of it, I have been a little annoyed by a headache which is not agreeable. My time was taken up very much at the Office in settling my Account with my Father of George's Affairs. I drew up the Account, Inventory and my own Letter upon business which explains the whole. But the work took up all my morning so that I had not time to copy the Letter and finish off the whole to send to him today.[1] It is all of it a laborious business. But I have progressed thus far and now hope to go through clear this week. Returned home, and after dinner was engaged in comparing letters for Mr. Sparks until four when I went to attend a Meeting of the Middlesex Canal Company Directors. We were called to see about the propriety of taking further measures in regard to a Rail Road projected to go from here to Lowell. Our remonstrance produces no effect, and the Committee of the Legislature have reported a bill to carry into effect the purposes of individuals by an Act of Incorporation. I am afraid the Canal will be a poor concern. We remained rather longer in time than was necessary, but I went down from there to the Athenæum and obtained my Certificate in the Athenæum as a Proprietor which settles that business. This is a great privilege, and one which was obtained in rather a singular manner.[2] I returned home to tea and was just in time, after which I was occupied until late in examining the copies Mr. Sparks has taken of papers. He has drawn rather largely but on the whole if it was not so much trouble to me, I should be glad to have the letters appear in that collection.

[1] CFA to JQA, 26 Feb. (LbC, Adams Papers). The administrator's account showed assets of $3,245.07 after deducting all charges. Against this sum were JQA's claims against the estate, consisting of GWA's note for $2,065 and unexplained deficiencies in GWA's Agency account of $1,093.24. The Court had signed an order for distribution of all the assets to JQA. For this letter, see also below, entry for 20 March, note.

[2] At some time before 7 Sept. 1829, JQA, as was proper for one who had been a member and proprietor since 1807 and a benefactor through the deposit there of a large part of his library from 1809 to 1822, had sought to avail himself of the privileges of the Boston Athenæum but had been informed that

he was no longer numbered among the proprietors. He thereupon wrote a letter of inquiry. There followed an exchange of letters culminating in his reinstatement and in the issuance to him on 11 Nov. of a proprietor's share, No. 255. See Walter Muir Whitehill, "Three Letters of John Quincy Adams," *Athenæum Items*, No. 62, July 1955, where the letters are printed and the circumstances recounted. Two weeks later JQA transferred the share to CFA and after further reflection wrote him:

"The share as a proprietor of the Athenæum which I gave you, I consider as the portion which I took out of the hand of the Amorite with my bow. It had been taken from me in a manner which for the thousandth time taught me how tenacious a man must be of his own interests and rights in this world, and how unceremoniously they are disposed of when entrusted to the memory, justice or generosity of others. I acknowledge with pleasure the liberality of the present Directors of the Athenæum when the facts were made known to them, and I should rather have abandoned my right than attempted to recover it for any other purpose than that of transferring it to you. . . . May you drink deep of the fountain there open'd" (26 Dec. 1829, Adams Papers).

SATURDAY 27TH.

Morning at the Office. Weather mild and pleasant. I was at the Office and spent a large part of the time reading Webster's Speech which should have been occupied in my duties. But it had just arrived and was so fascinating that I could not resist it. It is a fine effort upon a subject in itself rather hard. For a mere resolution of inquiry is not and has seldom been considered a matter to talk much about. The Speech itself is one upon a small subject, defence from attacks upon sectional differences. It has nothing to recommend it of the great views and enlarged purposes of a real Statesman. It is a quarrel about small things.[1] I had no great time however to think of it for I was obliged to copy my Letter to my father and I had a long interruption from Mr. Whitney, whom I had sent for to converse upon the debt he owes me. Our conversation was earnest and I made him liberal propositions until I thought I could go no farther, but he was stubborn and would not give me more than three hundred dollars, which was altogether too little, so we parted. Mr. Ayer came to tell me, he should leave his Store, but he said he had a Tenant who was ready to take his place at a higher rent.[2] I told him that under those conditions I was willing to let it go.

I was excessively hurried to finish my Letter, because my Wife had engaged to go out of town in her father's carriage rather earlier than was convenient to me. But I got through at last, and returned home, where I found my Wife and we rode to Medford with Mrs. Hall. Nothing remarkable took place. I found Mr. Brooks rather dull and heavy, and unable to keep up his spirits, but we tried to talk to him. Chardon came out in the afternoon, and we did as well as we could in conversation until night. But the loss to Mr. Brooks is sensible every hour of his time. His home is not now what it was, but far otherwise.

[1] The first half of Daniel Webster's reply to Hayne, delivered in the Senate on 26 Jan. and later studied by generations of American schoolboys, was published as extra sheets to accompany the *Columbian Centinel* and *Boston Daily Advertiser*, 27 February. See above, entry for 20 Feb. and note 1 there; below, entry for 3 March.

[2] C. C. Ayer dealt in dry goods; he was insolvent, but CFA accepted him as a tenant of at least part of the store at 23 Court Street vacated by Prentiss Whitney. His account was not settled until 5 May. (Brooks, Waste Book, 17 Dec. 1830; M/CFA/3.)

SUNDAY. 28TH.

The morning was bright and fine but far colder than it has been for a long time. The weather becoming more in the character of the Climate. After breakfast we had all the members of the family out here excepting Mr. Frothingham and Mrs. P. C. Brooks. This is in compliance with an invariable custom in this Country of offering Prayers upon the Sunday succeeding the death of a person.[1] We accordingly all went to Meeting and heard Mr. Stetson deliver a Prayer and a Sermon on the subject which might have been in better taste if they had been shorter and less laboriously drawn. On the whole the effect was unsatisfactory. It did not seem to put the thing in the right light.

We returned home and dined after which we again went and heard an account of the Clergyman's experiences during three years in which he had been settled. This was perhaps well calculated for his people, but to strangers it was nothing. At the same time, I could not help being fully convinced that the labour of a Clergyman was rather unsatisfactory, and difficult, to please is difficult in every situation, particularly where dependance creates a necessity to do so. After tea the expedition from Boston returned home. And we had the Company first of Mr. Stetson, and then of Mr. Hall and Dr. Swan. They talked something of Medford affairs not over interesting to me. But I got along as well as I could. I pity Mr. Brooks considerably, but cannot help thinking it a sacrifice for me to do what I am doing.

[1] Mr. Brooks expressed it as "having a note up for the death of Mrs. Brooks" (Farm Journal, 28 Feb.).

MARCH. 1830.

MONDAY. MARCH 1ST.

The morning was much colder than any of the preceding for a very considerable number of days, and the ground was frozen hard and stiff. We started to return to town in Mr. Brooks' Carriage with him. The riding was hard and rough. Having arrived we went directly to my Office, where I found a letter from my Father.[1] It was long and quite pleasant, and revived me considerably. At the same time, I had a letter from Miss Longhurst my Tenant,[2] declaring her inability to pay and throwing herself upon my mercy. Here is a deficiency of five hundred dollars at once, making over a thousand dollars loss of rent during this Winter, a circumstance exceedingly hard for my father's funds here. But I must struggle along. This fact leaves another House empty for she must move, and I must do as well as I can with the House. But it is a little hard that all these things should fall at once upon me in the first taking of my Agency. I found the Store empty also. But I believe this is tolerably provided for. I was then occupied in writing my Journal and drawing my Accounts out for this month. Every thing in the way of rent is falling backward, and I am excessively disturbed about it. My demands upon the first of April it is now tolerably ascertained cannot be met by the balance upon this Quarter. And I had like a fool expected the surplus would be nearly two thousand dollars. So much for anticipation. My morning was pretty much taken up in this manner, and I returned to dine.

The Afternoon was passed in a useless though necessary labour— That which my father wished of having his name pasted into his books. My Wife and I were engaged all the afternoon and yet we accomplished only a small portion. The Evening was passed in reading Romeo and Juliet to my Wife—She never having read the Play, a singular circumstance being one of Shakspeare's most beautiful efforts. I finished the three first Acts. This is a difficult Author to read aloud. He has so many breaks and bursts and difficult obsolete expressions. I did not feel fully satisfied with myself but hope to find in this exercise means of improvement. Afterwards Lord Kaimes. There was a considerable Fire seen in an easterly direction.

[1] 21 Feb. (Adams Papers); on literary matters, particularly on oratory, ancient and modern.
[2] Letter missing.

TUESDAY. 2D.

Morning cold and Cloudy, making quite a dull day. I went to the Office as usual and was quite uninterrupted all the morning. My father's Affairs trouble me considerably for now I have all my Tenants in arrears, and they do not come to me to make settlement but leave me to go to them, which is mighty disagreeable. Mr. Gay came to tell me that Whitney had put his case in their hands, and to beg that I would compound for three hundred dollars. I told him I thought it hard, but he said that I had better take it. Upon reflecting and consulting Mr. Kinsman I thought I would take 350 and will make the proposition tomorrow, as a final one, if rejected I then will refer it to my father and finally to arbitration, which will prevent going to Law. This is a monstrous disagreeable business but so it is.

I passed most of the morning in reading Williston and finished most of the Speeches of modern time in Congress, many of which hardly merit insertion in a Collection of Eloquence. The Speech of Mr. McDuffie however is an able effort, it stands well compared with the rest.[1] Mr. Webster's second part reached us this morning.[2] It is better than the first and really powerful, but I cannot help feeling regret at the occasion being so small. As my Wife passed the day at Mrs. Frothingham's, I went to dine there and had a time pretty much as usual. Returning to my room, I resumed Demosthenes but after such an interval that my relish for it today was injured. I completed my usual quantity however. The abuse of Æschines is a little in bad taste, according to our present notions. He speaks of his Mother in a manner which would in these days provoke a duel. In the evening, I finished reading to Abby, Romeo and Juliet, and commenced King Lear, but my voice was so husky that I hardly did it justice. Afterwards I continued Lord Kaimes. Beauty of language.

[1] The fourth volume of Williston's *Eloquence* contains speeches delivered in the House in Feb. 1826 by George Mc-Duffie and Henry R. Storrs on an amendment to the Constitution to provide for the election of President and Vice President by a uniform system of voting by districts and to prevent their election from devolving upon the respective Houses of Congress (p. 97-192), and speeches delivered in Congress between 1824 and 1827 on a variety of topics by Peleg Sprague, Edward Livingston, James Barbour, Henry Clay (p. 193-260).

[2] *Boston Daily Advertiser*, 2 March, p. 2-3.

WEDNESDAY. 3RD.

Morning cold but clear, latterly as a violent March Wind arose and dispersed the fog. I went to the Office as usual and was occupied the larger part of the time in reading Williston. The conclusion of Mr. Webster's Speech came on however and I sat down to read it carefully. It appears to be an exposition of his principles in opposition to the doctrines at present advanced by South Carolina. It is in the latter part argumentative in a high degree, but after all the subject does not form a true foundation for so large and unwieldy a superstructure. I think it may be ranked high as a defensive operation, and in opposition to the host of things laid upon the other side, but in itself it has not the merit which many other of his speeches on *measures* are entitled to claim.[1] I also made some progress in Williston, finishing the Speeches in the deliberative style and beginning the Judicial, with Alexander Hamilton's defence of Croswell,[2] of which I did not think much. I had one or two interruptions, one from a person who came to tell me that my tenant Miss Longhurst had closed her career as a Milliner in Jail, and I am a loser of five hundred dollars without remedy. So much for that besides having another House upon my hands. Hollis the Carpenter came and I settled with him for the Quarter ending February 1st. My store is about being on my hands too. All this is trouble, and expense, vanity and vexation of spirit. After dinner I went down to the property and gave directions for repairs in order to get them ready to rent again, as soon as possible. This is now a poor property. Pity it was not sold during the time when land was so high. I returned and read Demosthenes but not comfortably. Evening was passed in reading Lord Kaimes. His strictures are generally clear, but I feel unwilling to give up some passages which are favourites with me, though criticized by him.

[1] Printed as a supplement to the *Boston Daily Advertiser* for 3 March. See above, entries for 20, 27 Feb. and notes there.

[2] On an indictment for a libel on President Jefferson, delivered in 1804 before the N.Y. Supreme Court (Williston's *Eloquence* at 4:261–290).

THURSDAY. 4TH.

Morning clear, and tolerably mild. At the Office as usual, where I was occupied in reading Williston. Drew my quarterly Check from Mr. Brooks and deposited it. My funds appear now in a condition tolerably healthy and so I hope to invest a little more. The affairs of my father are in a condition so doubtful, that I feel in duty bound to do every thing by which I may assist myself.

Mr. Jackson the Painter called to take my directions about the Houses, in Tremont Street, which must be put in order as soon as possible.[1] Richardson came in for a little while to talk, though he appeared suffering with a cold, and Mr. Whitney passed an hour, upon whom I exerted all my powers of persuasion to induce him to pay me three hundred and fifty dollars in full settlement, but without effect. This is the toughest affair I have ever yet had to go through, because it seems to me that this man is relying upon my accepting three hundred dollars, and thus is going to run into twice the expense to get me out of the trifling balance. He left me promising to give me an answer tomorrow. I called in a moment to see Mr. Brooks. All the rest of the morning was passed in reading Mr. Hopkinson's very good Speech upon the trial of Judge Chase and Mr. Emmet's upon Col. Smith and Mr. Dexter upon T. Selfridge.[2] The first I think much the best. It is clear, comprehensive and forcible and though not worked up quite so much as it could have been, yet shows no little skill and talent. On the whole I did a tolerable morning's work.

Afternoon passed as usual in reading Demosthenes, but I have lost the general train of reasoning and feel less interested. I tried to get it up again by looking over La Harpe's Analysis but it is not clear. I shall have to take Auger's. My Study was cold as I am circumscribed in fuel owing to the great use made of it by the copyists.[3] Evening, engaged in reading Lear to my Wife. After which Lord Kaimes.

[1] Ebenezer Jackson completed the painting of the Tremont Street houses during the next month and was paid $152.74 on 26 April (M/CFA/3).

[2] Joseph Hopkinson upon the impeachment of Justice Samuel Chase, Thomas Addis Emmet in the trial of William S. Smith, Samuel Dexter in the trial of Thomas O. Selfridge, all 1805–1806 (Williston's *Eloquence*, 4:291–383).

[3] That is, by Jared Sparks and his assistants.

FRIDAY 5TH.

Morning fine. The weather like Spring. I went to the Office as usual and was occupied in reading Williston very pleasantly. Commenced Mr. Pinkney's Speech in the case of the Nereide but did not progress very far in it before I was compelled to stop by a number of interruptions.[1] Mrs. Wells came today to pay rent for two months of her Tenement and to notify me that she should be unable at this rate to remain in the House longer than the end of this month. Thus another of the tenancies will be vacated which almost discourages me —Nearly one half of my sources of profit from real Estate thus becoming stopped and the amount of funds called for to supply repairs being enormous. I feel excessively worried at this responsibility upon me. Mr. Champney also called to talk about his rent. He seemed also to be half tempted to move but did not know what to do. I told him that I would be as liberal as I could but that I was very much pressed. He is a man I like and if Hollis had not been so engrafted on the property I should incline to transfer the work to him. At it is I must keep the rod over the latter and make him do his duty. Thus much for the morning.

Abigail S. Adams, my cousin dined and spent the day with Abby. I have not seen [her] for a long time. She was pleasant. After dinner I went to the Estate in Tremont Street and looked over it, with a view of giving the proper directions to begin the work of putting in order. The furniture of Miss Longhurst was sold today, and I went in to see what could be done to put it in good order. It needs touching considerably. I gave Dr. Wendell notice to quit and on the whole imagine I did not consult my interest in having him remain.[2] Thus ended the matter. I hope I shall rent these two Houses at least. The afternoon was so spent, that I did nothing more but sat with the Ladies until evening talking. I. Hull Adams her brother came to take her away, and after that I read Lord Kaimes.

[1] William Pinkney before the U.S. Supreme Court, 1815 (Williston's *Eloquence* at 4:442–486).
[2] Dr. Wendell had taken a room temporarily at $1 a week in the house at No. 105 Tremont Street after it was vacated by Mrs. Lewis (M/CFA/3).

SATURDAY. 6TH.

Morning cloudy and dark. I went to the Office as usual and was occupied in my usual affairs all the morning. Mr. Jackson the Painter called to tell me that he wanted an order against Dr. Wendell, which I accordingly gave. This man begins to be an annoyance. My feeling about these Houses distresses me. But my only business is firmness, and perseverance. Deacon Spear came to tell me that my father had forgotten to send on his orders about the letting the Farm at Quincy, and requested me to give notice of it to him, which I promised to do.[1] Mr. Whitney presented to me a Note giving his final refusal to my proposition. I then sat down, and wrote the whole matter to my Father and requested him to decide how to proceed.[2] For my own part I think I should resist, but what he will think proper to do, I am unable to say. The matter is a troublesome one. My time was thus entirely taken up. A tax gatherer from Randolph came to see me and to ask the payment of a large bill of twelve cents, tax upon the Estate of my Grandfather in Randolph. I paid it.[3] A gentleman came in to inquire the rent of the two Houses in Tremont Street, and detained me a little while. He did not continue long however the rent being too high. Returned home and after dinner copied my letter and read some of Demosthenes. But my occupations in study are now much interrupted, and I do not so entirely relish him as I did. My own feelings too are not quite so agreeable. I have a head ach much of the time which is very disagreeable, and something new.

After tea, I went to the Meeting of the Debating Society, and heard argued the question of Imprisonment for Debt, taking but little part in it myself. The Meeting was moderately attended, and the subject pretty well debated. Adjourned, and read afterwards at home, The Arabian Nights.[4]

[1] Spear, who was acting in JQA's behalf in Quincy, had urged JQA to rent out the Penn's Hill farm, had had people interested in taking it, but had not received authorization from JQA. Moreover, the most favorable time for leasing was passing rapidly (CFA to JQA, 6 March, LbC, Adams Papers).
[2] Same.

[3] Perhaps reflecting a putative interest in the farm in South Braintree, later Randolph, left to JA's younger brother Elihu by their father and subsequently possessed by Elihu's oldest son; see JA, *Diary and Autobiography*, 3:277.
[4] GWA owned an edition published at London in 4 vols., 1819, now in MQA (vols. 1 and 4 only).

March 1830

The Morning was misty with Clouds, but mild. Immediately after breakfast, I started with my Wife to go to Medford. We had a very tolerable ride for the air was mild. Arrived, we found the family as usual, with the addition of Miss Mary B. Hall.[1] We went directly to Meeting and heard Mr. Stetson preach a Communion Sermon, after which I walked home, enjoying my walk very much. It was one of those early Spring days which make one agreeably sensible of even the slight change of atmosphere that has taken place, when things begin to thaw in the shade. After dinner, I again attended Church and heard Mr. Hedge of West Cambridge preach a tolerably good Sermon, upon the vicious search after excitement which so generally prevails. Mr. Hedge is a young man of tolerable talents and more acquirement. He talks a little too learnedly about things in general, for the comprehension of his Parish, but time and reason soon cure that. He wants judgment, and that is seldom mended.

We returned home in the rain, and passed the remainder of the day and evening in reading the English Papers, which are amusing. But the occupation is not a very creditable one. It seems however to be destined that I shall waste my time.

[1] Mary Brooks Hall remained with her uncle after the death of Mrs. Brooks until 20 March, taking on many of the household duties that Charlotte Everett, pregnant and not well, was unable to assume (Charlotte Everett to Edward Everett, various dates, Feb.–March, Everett MSS, MHi).

Morning mild and clear. We returned to town from Medford and I went directly to the Office. My time was taken up insensibly without having any particular way of accounting for it. Two or three persons called upon me about the Houses, among others, Mrs. Harriet Lewis, the former Tenant. I talked with her, and was very glad of the opportunity to explain to her some facts which I had formerly heard about her. She was warm and earnest in denying them. There is no knowing how to go on with these women. I would rather never have to do with them. Mr. Jackson came to me to talk about the Dr. and I gave him special orders to remove his things. I also wrote to Dr. Lewis respecting some injury that was done to the House, and to Mr. Child about the Uniforms.[1] Thus went most of the morning.

The afternoon was passed in an examination of the Houses, and giving directions how to mend them. My own opinion is that the rent of these at the price I set them is low, but I have no means of ascertaining, and no applicants who close with me. My idea of the trouble of property increases daily. There is little affording a steady settled income, beyond the influence of chance. And with a little money now upon my hands, I find myself seriously puzzled to know what to do with it. The chances are great and on the whole the profits small. Returned home and it being too late to attend to Demosthenes I passed the remainder of the afternoon in pasting Papers to my father's books, a dry but necessary duty. The Evening was spent at home in reading to my Wife the rest of Lear. She was so unwell from a cold however that she could not enjoy it, and I felt nervous and lowspirited. The responsibility of this property now hangs very heavily upon me. Read a part of Walker's Rhetorical Grammar.

[1] Both letters missing.

TUESDAY. 9TH.

Morning at the Office. Weather very much changed from being mild to a tolerably severe degree of cold. I passed the time much as usual. Finished the fourth volume of Williston and not having the next to continue with, I was obliged to take up Hall's Law Journal.[1] I am more and more worried about my Father's affairs. The Fire and Marine pay no Dividend as I am told, and thus I am cut off from almost every source of supply. I went to see Mr. Brooks and talked a little with Mr. Welsh, which made the whole of my morning. Regret follows waste, but little amendment is the result.

A Tenant came and applied to me for the House, or rather Tenement next to what was Miss Longhurst's. This was the only person today. The afternoon was passed in reading Demosthenes, and taking refuge in the beauties of the style from the anxieties relating to personal matters. I made good progress today, and relished it more.

In the evening, the usual meetings of the Brooks family which had been interrupted by the melancholy event, were resumed at my House. This was on the whole also the most pleasant we have had. I felt rather more at my ease, and was able to carry through the evening more feeling of my own situation. But there is still something wanting. The meeting was tolerably gay, considering the circumstances. How soon grief wears off from the young and active. We can none of us expect to be lamented beyond a short day or two after we cease to live.

[1] The fourth volume is concluded with Daniel Webster's speech in the impeachment of Judge James Prescott, 1821 (p. 487–508). James E. Hall edited the *American Law Journal and Miscellaneous Repertory*, 6 vols., Phila., 1808–1817.

WEDNESDAY. 10TH.

Morning dark and cloudy. Went to the Office as usual. But felt exceedingly dull and depressed all day. My father's business weighs upon my mind and in addition to this more troubles come upon me every day. Dr. Storer called upon me today about that old affair of Farmer's. It seems this man has sued him for defamation of character, as some time in the Spring he wrote a letter, imprudent and silly enough to be sure.[1] He came to me to inquire of me whether I would see his Counsel, Mr. Fletcher. I am glad this gentleman has been selected for the purpose,[2] though I am deeply grieved that the whole affair has happened. What the development may be is impossible to say, and all of it through the folly of this young man. His imprudence always precipitates him into scrapes.

My Uncle Judge Adams called in to see me and interrupted us. He came to inquire about money and I was obliged to tell him I was as poor as a rat. This is true now and likely to be true hereafter. I do not admire present appearances. After seeing Mr. Brooks as usual, and going to make a purchase of some Coal, I had time to sit down and read one or two of Williston's Selections in his fifth volume. They were Orations on the famous Boston Massacre by Warren and Hancock,[3] and I cannot say that they were great models for imitation, being extremely turgid and in false taste. There certainly has been an improvement in our productions in this Country. More solid matter and less wind, though even now there is enough.

Dined at Chardon Brooks' with my wife. Time pleasant. Afternoon at home, reading Demosthenes in which I made good progress. But how superficial is merely a single examination of such an author. In the evening I read to my Wife the first half of Sheridan's Comedy of the School for Scandal and was amused as usual with it's wit. If any thing the replies have too much point to be natural. Walker's Rhetorical Grammar.

[1] The letter of Dr. D. H. Storer to Miles Farmer on which Farmer was to base his suit for libel was written on 31 July 1829 (*Farmer-Storer Trial*, p. 6, 16–17).

[2] Richard Fletcher's law office was at 10 State Street (*Boston Directory*, 1830–1831). CFA's acquaintance with him began when they both boarded at Thomas Tarbell's, 11 Avon Place; a mutual respect soon developed; see vol. 2:264, 348, 371, 400.

[3] The orations of Joseph Warren (1772 and 1775) and John Hancock (1774) are at p. 5–42.

THURSDAY. 11TH.

Morning cloudy, but mild. Went to the Office as usual, and passed my time in writing my Journal. Mr. Hurlbert is a man who was burnt out of his premises last Fall and now applies for this Store beneath. After a little conversation and some provisions on both sides, I let him have the Store and two rooms overhead for the sum of three hundred dollars, an arrangement which suits me very well, for the rooms above I cannot let for any other purpose, and now are better disposed of than lying waste.[1] I immediately went to give directions to Hollis and the others for the purpose of beginning. This relieves my mind a little. If I could now only get rid of the other two houses. This arrangement compelled me to be very active and brisk in trying to get rid of the dust and rubbish which has accumulated in the garret above. I have been anxious ever since I was in the Agency to do it. I read consequently but very little of Mr. Williston.

Returning home, I found Miss Elizabeth Phillips passing the day with Abby. I forgot to mention the fact of the decease of Winthrop Gray this morning. He has lived a worthless life and leaves little regret behind him. The great misfortune of his life was the possessing too much property too early.[2] I passed the afternoon in reading Demosthenes quietly and pleasantly at my Study. The progress I am now making is considerable. My spirits were a little improved today though still not excessively bright. I passed the remainder of the evening in finishing for my Wife the School for Scandal. The latter scenes of the Play delighted me as much as ever. The brilliant wit of them is astonishing. But after all there is more point than nature, though nature not exaggerated would probably on a representation prove very flat. After Abby retired, I sat up and read further Walker's Rhetorical Grammar though I found nothing in it extremely remarkable.

[1] Jesse P. Hurlbert dealt in paper hangings (*Boston Directory*, 1830–1831). His long tenancy in the Court Street building here begun, ultimately included the house in the rear and office space as well (M/CFA/3). For the two rooms, seemingly on the fourth floor, which he was allowed to use, for storage perhaps, he paid the increased cost of the insurance on the building.

[2] Winthrop Gray (1804–1830), a first cousin of ABA, was the oldest son of Mary (Brooks) and Samuel Gray. Having squandered "a considerable fortune" by "every species of dissoluteness" and contracting diseases brought on by dissipation, he died at "Tremont House" after surgery following convulsions. (CFA to LCA, 13 March, Adams Papers; Charlotte Everett to Edward Everett, 10, 12 March; Peter C. Brooks to same, 22 March; both in Everett MSS, MHi.)

FRIDAY. 12TH.

Morning bright though rather cool. I went to the Office as usual and was as usual very much disturbed in the disposal of my time, and interrupted more than usual. My first was an application for the refusal of the House in Tremont Street, No. 2, which I accordingly gave until tomorrow. The Store being let and this House, I shall feel less the weight of the remainder, but it is too much to have the whole property upon my hands at once. Since my coming into the Agency I have changed every Tenant but three and the Offices. And very necessary it was, for the old ones had become very poor and very irregular. I hope now that things will go on better. I have still however much to do, and many places to let. May luck befriend me.

Mr. Eddy called to notify me [of] a Meeting of the Directors of the Middlesex Canal, this afternoon, and I had some conversation with him. I think under his direction for a few years more things will be apt to improve, provided we may ward off the rail road. He has much more energy and capacity than have ever before been displayed upon this Canal. Mr. Welsh offered me an administratorship upon an Estate in town, the only objection to which was in the bonds. I felt doubtful about it and took time to consider. This was nearly all I did. I saw Mr. Brooks for an instant and then read over for study Washington's Farewell Address several times.[1] In the afternoon, I bottled a considerable portion of my Sherry which should have been done long ago, and attended the Meeting of Directors of the Canal. The business was quickly done. I spent part of the time in looking over the records of the Corporation, and could not help smiling at the account of it's early proceedings. How changed we are as a people. Returned home, and in the evening read to my Wife Beppo and Parisina by Lord Byron, beautiful poems.[2] After which finished Walker's Grammar.

[1] Williston's *Eloquence*, 5:110–128.

[2] CFA had been in his college years an enthusiastic reader of Byron; see numerous references in vol. 1. GWA owned an edition of Byron's *Works* published in Paris, 2 vols. in one, 1826, now in MQA. Also there, is the New York edition in 8 vols., 1825, owned by JQA.

SATURDAY. 13TH.

Morning at the Office. The weather was hazy and became warm in the course of the day. I passed the time in reading the Newspapers, and in the many kinds of interruptions to which I have for a few days past been subjected. An applicant came for the House No. 2 and requested the refusal of it, which I gave. Deacon Spear came in from Quincy and showed me a letter from my father giving directions about the Farms there.[1] In this letter he seems to express it as doubtful whether he shall be here before the month of May. This rather surprises me but I presume it to be owing to my Mother, whose health will not permit her to come on sooner. I talked with the Deacon about affairs in Quincy, and drew from him facts respecting the Farms which I was to set down to write to my Father immediately. As soon as he went, I sat down to do so and wrote him very particularly the condition of the property.[2] How far I had gone, and proposed to go. The weight upon my mind is very great. Returned home.

In the afternoon, I went to the performance of the last Office to the body of poor Winthrop Gray, not from any feeling for him, but from respect to his Mother who is a very estimable woman. Returned I was then engaged in copying the letter and thought I would take the broken remnant of the afternoon for the purpose of writing a letter long due to my Mother. It was principally upon the subject of the death of Mrs. Brooks, giving some particulars respecting it. It did not perfectly satisfy me in the writing as things rarely do, but in such cases I do not stop to correct.[3] I barely finished it in time for tea and my usual visit in the evening to the Private Debating Society where the former question was again debated, and finally settled. The argument of Mr. A. W. Fuller settled it the contrary way to what I had formerly thought my vote would be. I detest opinionated self conceited men stiff in their prejudices. Did not get home until late.

[1] In the letter (missing) JQA authorized Deacon Spear to undertake to lease the houses and farm at the foot of Penn's Hill (JQA to CFA, 11 March, Adams Papers).

[2] CFA to JQA (LbC, Adams Papers). Spear's recommendations were that the offer of Harvey Field to take the farm and that of Curtis and Hardwick to renew their lease on the house be accepted. According to prior understanding, Spear had purchased from rental income three acres of salt marsh for addition to the Mount Wollaston estate.

[3] Letter in Adams Papers; its contents are discussed above in entries for 21 Feb., 11 March, notes.

SUNDAY. 14TH.

The morning was cloudy and soon after breakfast it began to rain in torrents. The first approaches of Spring. We were prevented from going to Medford so early as we intended but by eleven o'clock it cleared up so that we could go out to dine. Found the family as usual, but rather more alone. I felt a little inconvenience from head ach which increased as the day advanced, and by evening became quite serious. Attended divine service in the afternoon and heard Mr. Stetson preach, though without attending to him much. Somehow or other I felt drowsy and dull.

The remainder of the day was passed in reading superficially the Memoirs of the Court of Napoleon by Bausset, a book owned by Mr. A. H. Everett.[1] I was somewhat surprised by his ideas as they were new to me, though I did not feel thoroughly convinced by them. He intimates that the escape from Elba was connived at by the Allied Powers, in order to give them the excuse for removing Napoleon to St. Helena and to divide France, but this last plan was defeated by the unanimity of the people. I am inclined to the opinion that the risk was too great for had they been defeated at Waterloo, a thing not impossible, the result might have put much at stake to them.

A short time was passed in conversation with Mr. Brooks. I wonder at and admire his remarkable shrewdness of character. It has brought him to his present prosperity and seems to be an infallible guide to success in worldly affairs. Retired feeling quite unwell.

[1] Louis François Joseph de Bausset, *Mémoires anecdotiques sur l'intérieur du palais et sur quelques évènemens de l'Empire, 1805–1814*, Paris, 1827. Although the work was translated as the *Private Memoirs of the Court of Na-* poleon and published in Philadelphia, 1828, the copy which A. H. Everett lent to Charlotte Everett at Mystic Grove was in French (Charlotte Everett to Edward Everett, 13 Jan. 1830, Everett MSS, MHi).

MONDAY. 15TH.

The morning was cold and clear. We returned to town, though rather late. I went directly to the Office where I received a notice that the President of the Mutual Office had declined responsibility for the building while the repairs were going on. I accordingly went down to see him, and conversed with him upon the subject. The result is that I must hurry the changes as much as possible, for while they are in this condition, the responsibility upon me will be prodigious. I had several applications for the Houses on Tremont Street and went down to see what opinion to form of them. After some thinking and ordering the Papers at Deacon Foster's with whom I had a good deal of conversation, I decided upon my pieces. Upon returning to my House, I found Mr. Spear the former applicant had decided to take it, and gave me his references, so that I think I shall get this out of my hands.[1] On the whole I am exceedingly encouraged, about this property. My workmen are all executing with great rapidity and I hope by the first of April, the whole of this property will be working on finely. I was thus taken up all the morning. In the afternoon, I went down to inquire Mr. Spear's references and thence to the Office to give orders, feeling so anxious about the Property I did not like to leave it. On the whole, I feel better satisfied with it than at any time. It seems to be renovating briskly. The Evening was spent reading Byron to Abby.

[1] John I. Spear, auctioneer (*Boston Directory*, 1830–1831), occupied No. 103 Tremont Street, the house formerly rented to Miss Longhurst, until Feb. 1831 at an annual rental of $300 (M/CFA/3).

TUESDAY. 16TH.

Morning clear. At the Office, after inquiring and ascertaining the character of Mr. Spear. Found the reference so good that I decided upon accepting him. Gave my directions to regulate the Store and overlooked the Workmen in their progress which was tolerably satisfactory.

Mr. Brackett called and found himself anticipated about the House, but took the refusal of the other.[1] I hope in this way to get rid of both, and with an application this morning for a Tenement I hope this will close all my distresses about letting the real Estate. Now the trouble comes on respecting funds. Having received a letter from my Father respecting the Arrears I immediately addressed a Note to Whitney offering him what I considered as my final proposition.[2] If this is not accepted I am afraid I shall be reduced to the gratification of sending him to prison which will hardly suffice to pay the demands coming upon the Property here on the 1st of April.

I had an hour's work in drawing Leases of the Store and House which I have let, and the morning wasted away to a very small remnant, which I spent in reading some Eulogies of Washington in very bad taste.[3] Returned home. Afternoon passed in reading Demosthenes, in which I made considerable progress. Then came down again to the Store, to see that all was safely arranged for night. For my workmen do not yet get through. I repent a little letting it so low, but next year I hope to redeem the deficiency. And I think the permanency of the Tenant will remedy the defect. Returned and read Campbell's Rhetoric, a work I am going over again. Found it was time to go over to the usual meeting of my Wife's family which tonight occurred at Mrs. Frothingham's. It was tolerably pleasant. I was occupied merely in laughing for it is always impossible for me to talk, when so many louder voices are collected to make more noise. Returned at ten extremely drowsy.

[1] Rufus Brackett, owner of a leather store (*Boston Directory*, 1830–1831), became the tenant of No. 105 Tremont Street at the corner of Boylston, occupied earlier by Winslow Lewis, at an annual rental of $375. He remained in the house until Nov. 1832 (M/CFA/3).

[2] JQA had refused to give advice as to the proper course to take with Whitney, leaving the decision to CFA (JQA to CFA, 11 March, Adams Papers). The letter to Whitney is missing.

[3] The eulogies by Henry Lee, Fisher Ames, and John M. Mason, 1799–1800, are in Williston's *Eloquence* at 5:129–172.

WEDNESDAY. 17TH.

Morning cloudy. Went to the Office as usual, but being about to try to make a settlement with all the little outstanding debts to this concern, I accordingly went out to see about it. First I went to see if I could not save by a threat a little remnant of Miss Longhurst's debt to me. Wales was the person, a dealer in dry goods in Washington Street.[1] I talked with him but the result was not encouraging, and for fear of getting into a useless passion about it, I retreated. The effort will not cost much, and it may save a trifle.

From thence after dropping in, to see the condition of the Houses I returned home, to my Office, where for the balance of the morning, Mr. Miles Farmer annoyed me exceedingly with his account of the affair still pending between himself and Storer. The former has been imprudent and the latter rash, and thus every body is to suffer from their folly. I talked with Farmer very rationally and tried to convince him that the best course was to wind it up. He appeared half inclined to listen to reason, and half to passion. I still hope it will be arranged. Received a Note from Miss H. Welsh requesting the payment of the debt due to her from my brother, which I answered forthwith.[2] My troubles now are considerable. I am involved in three suits at law, and am without funds to meet my father's debts. A most unpleasant situation. But I hope for the best and anxiously look for the clouds to scatter. After dinner I read Demosthenes, my study for this afternoon is easy. Received a letter from Miss Longhurst,[3] trying to get me this money, but I am afraid it is too late.

Went down to see that all was safe at the Store and Office. A violent Storm came on with very high wind and rain, which beat fearfully all night. I was in great dread for my responsibility, but the evening was passed quietly and pleasantly in reading Lalla Rookh to my Wife,[4] whom I am teaching to like Poetry. Afterwards, Campbell's Rhetoric.

[1] The store of Samuel Wales Jr. was at 397 Washington Street (*Boston Directory*, 1830–1831). Presumably he had fared better than the other creditors.

[2] The letters from and to Harriet Welsh are missing. On the debt see be- low, entry for 20 March, note.

[3] Missing.

[4] CFA owned an edition of Thomas Moore's *Works* published at New York in 5 vols., 1821, now in MQA.

THURSDAY. 18TH.

Morning at the Office as usual. The weather was still rainy but cleared up bright at noon. My time was very much broken by interruptions. Farmer came up and went on with his long story and tired me to death. I told him to be gone, as he was prosing away more than ever. But the thing does not appear to be nearer settlement than ever. The lawyers for the parties have acted very handsomely and it is quite a relief to be treated by persons of such a character. Farmer is such a poor Tool that I do not imagine that I can be easily rid of him. Mr. Cruft came up to make inquiry about the way to forward a letter to John, and he sat here with me for an hour or two in which time I consulted him in respect to the character of the Atlas Insurance Company, in which I contemplate investing a trifle.[1] His account of it is very favourable and may probably decide me. Mr. Spear the Tenant of the House in Tremont Street No. 2. came to finish off, and so we completed the Leases and that business. He takes possession Monday. Some others called making application for houses which were soon settled, but on the whole I had very little time to myself.

The afternoon was passed in reading Demosthenes, which I did with much satisfaction—Though I have been so much interrupted as to make the impression of the Oration as a whole very feeble upon my mind. How many interruptions I have had, and how many disagreeable things are now on my mind.

The repairs on the Store being finished I went down and notified the President of the Mutual Office of the fact, and requested him to call and see it, which he agreed to do.[2] He is a very disagreeable man to me. I went to see the store, and found Cruft, for whom I did his little business. Evening, reading Lalla Rookh, not so interesting as yesterday evening, but still rather pretty. Afterwards Campbell's Rhetoric. But all my studies are now somewhat interrupted by my anxieties about temporal affairs.

[1] Edward Cruft was a director of the company (*Boston Directory*, 1830–1831, p. 21).

[2] Turner Phillips was the president of the Mass. Mutual Fire Insurance Co. at 60 State Street (same, p. 23).

FRIDAY 19TH.

The day was beautiful and I went out very early in order to have an opportunity to see Mr. Fletcher upon this disagreeable business of Storer's. I talked with him for a very considerable time and though we came to no conclusion about it, yet I sincerely hope he will exert himself to settle it. I foresee however that it will be a source of uneasiness as to money. I shall have it as a tax upon me I fear. The Directors of the Insurance Company came to see about the House and in consequence charged me a small addition of premium. I went to see them and paid, then to the Houses in Common Street, then to Town Meeting to see the new Law for the election of Mayor, knocked in the head,[1] then to see Mr. Brooks and finally to my own Office where Mr. Brackett called and positively took the Corner House in Tremont or Common Street, so that now all the Houses of size are off my hands for one year at least. I called in to see Mr. Wales and talked with him, coming down finally to the proposition to accept the costs.[2] The rest of the morning was passed in drawing up the Leases, so that on the whole I can scarcely be said to have had one moment of time to myself.

Abby had engaged me to go and dine at Mrs. Frothingham's today which I did and found there Mr. and Mrs. P. C. Brooks. Our time was much as usual, tolerably agreeable, thence to the Athenæum where I did not stay long. At home however I did but little and found my mind so distracted as to profit very little even from that. My situation is disagreeable enough, involved in law suits, with demands hanging upon me of my father's and funds coming in with excessive slowness, I feel troubled beyond measure. Nothing now goes right. I find pitfalls at every step. Evening at Mr. Frothingham's but dull.

[1] The legislature at its last session had passed an act proposing an amendment to the city charter as to the election of mayor. At the town meeting held in Fanueil Hall and moderated by Mayor Otis, a motion that consideration of the act be indefinitely postponed passed overwhelmingly (*Columbian Centinel*, 20 March, p. 2, col. 3).

[2] Part of CFA's endeavor, apparently, to establish JQA's claim among Miss Longhurst's creditors.

SATURDAY 20TH.

Morning at the Office. The day was fine, and I walked out without my coat. The first thing I did was to go and see Miss Welsh and make a final settlement of our affairs—George's last just debt.[1] His expenditure for the last fifteen months of his life must have been enormous, as he had spent his own allowance of a thousand five hundred dollars, eleven hundred dollars of my father's, and was in debt five hundred more. I am very unwilling to think it, but cannot blind my eyes to the facts, and the deduction from them, that he did not cease to live too soon. The moment was the crisis for his reputation and there is now nothing known of a positive nature against him. Poor fellow. His own evil passions dealt hardly with his better nature. The weeds grew very rank and choked the useful productions which grew too luxuriantly to allow depth of root.

From seeing Miss Welsh, I crossed over to the Houses in Tremont Street and was much pleased with their neat appearance inside. Thence to the Office—Where I was interrupted by the appearance of the creditor of Miss Longhurst who trusteed the Misses Haskins—Mr. Wales. He is a stubborn, dogmatical young puppy, but he had the advantage so I was obliged to play prudently to save remnants, so I was glad to compound the matter for four dollars—better than nothing. I then went back to see the ladies and got my order accepted to put it out of doubt.[2] Dr. Storer called to see me, being somewhat frightened and to consult about the terms of a reconciliation. He has got himself into a scrape and me too, and I suppose he thinks I should help him out, so I foresee a tax of Money for the folly of a rash young man. He left me in much agitation. I do not yet see clearly through the business. Thus, this morning was as much broken up as all the rest, and gave me no time for any mental business. I am resolved not to think so much of my father's affairs and wait patiently the result of all.

After dinner I read Demosthenes as usual and accomplished a considerable portion, but the interest is gone. I read La Harpe's examination over. It would not do. The spirit has for the present departed from me. In the evening went to the Meeting of the Debating Society and took my part in the discussion of the subject of the expediency of Theatricals, which was warmly contested.

[1] At the time CFA settled GWA's estate, Harriet Welsh had requested that the payment due her and her father, Dr. Thomas Welsh, for GWA's rent during the last weeks of his life be further delayed, suggesting the possibility that the sum due might be offset against Thomas Welsh Jr.'s arrearage on his office at 23 Court Street (CFA to JQA, 26 Feb., LbC, Adams Papers; and see above, entry for 31 Oct. 1829, note). The matter was settled by the payment to Harriet Welsh of $31.66 and by a credit to Thomas Welsh Jr's account of $15 (M/CFA/3).

[2] The situation is unclear. On 25 Feb., while Miss Longhurst still had her dressmaking establishment at 103 Tremont Street, CFA charged rent for two rooms in the house to the Misses Haskins at $25 a quarter. Perhaps earlier they had occupied the rooms as tenants of Miss Longhurst; at least they seem to have been indebted to her. Apparently it was their indebtedness that the creditors were contending for and on which CFA reached a somewhat disadvantageous agreement with Wales. On 3 April CFA collected $6.60 from them, representing rent from 25 Feb. to 22 March, when the new tenant, Mr. Spear, took possession (M/CFA/3).

SUNDAY. 21ST.

The morning was lowering and an easterly wind made it chilly and disagreeable. In order to avoid the rain we started from Boston early after breakfast and reached Medford just as the shower was beginning. We found the family much as usual, having only the addition of Miss Elizabeth Phillips.[1] We attended divine service and heard Dr. Ware deliver a Sermon which I recollect very well as an old one at Cambridge in my time.[2] Dr. Ware is a sensible man and a clear writer, but so dry that it is next to impossible to keep the attention fixed. I tried it but did not succeed. He dined at Mr. Brooks, but I do not enjoy his Company much as I respect him. Our dinner was dull and Afternoon Sermon drowsy. The remainder of the day was passed as usual without much to remark. I finished the volume of Bausset's Napoleon which I began last Sunday in which he carries out his proposition. A very questionable one in fact, but ingeniously drawn up. Medford has lost much of it's attraction however, in the mistress of the house.

[1] Elizabeth Phillips, on the day before, had taken Mary B. Hall's place in the Brooks household (Charlotte Everett to Edward Everett, 21 March, Everett MSS, MHi).
[2] Henry Ware was Hollis Professor of Divinity at Harvard (*DAB*).

MONDAY. 22D.

The morning came in the most lovely shape of Spring, bright and warm. We returned to town and I found myself at the Office writing with my windows open, a thing in itself unusual at this season, perhaps imprudent. But the day was most uncommon. I was engaged during the time in reading, which I did with much less interruption than usual. Mr. Farmer came in very much humbled in his tone and talked of a settlement and reconciliation very strongly. I urged him to make it and he went away with the feeling so strongly upon him, that I feel as if I may escape this unlucky business without much injury. I hope the very lowering state of things is gradually cooling off and growing bright. But still there is much to trouble me. The very considerable amount due to me from Whitney, the small sum actually in hand are troubles which at present annoy me. Miss Longhurst's failure also is a troublesome thing. Mr. Haskell came to have his bill of repairs paid upon the Store, which after having canvassed it considerably I settled.[1] To me who am in a great measure ignorant and inexperienced in matters of this kind, it is no small source of uneasiness that I am subject to so many chances of imposition.

I read several Eulogies in Williston and was scarcely pleased with any. They are not sufficiently in the natural style. Too turgid.[2] Afternoon reading Demosthenes, in which I go on so rapidly now that I soon shall finish this Oration. A noble effort and strongly illustrative of the power of words. Every one should remember that words are things. Evening at home. Abby was unwell, and it was not at all agreeable.

[1] J. Haskell, housewright (M/CFA/3; *Boston Directory*, 1830–1831).
[2] Eulogies of Alexander Hamilton by Harrison G. Otis and Eliphalet Nott, of Thomas Jefferson and John Adams by William Wirt (Williston's *Eloquence*, 5:191–229, 454–503).

TUESDAY 23RD.

Morning as it opened surprised us with the sight of snow. After such a day as yesterday, it might have been expected, but it certainly was not welcome. I went to the Office, and passed the day pretty quietly. Mrs. D. L. Child called upon me to tell me that her husband had been arrested and was in prison, and she herself paid the amount of the sword.[1] This was an agreeable settlement of a disagreeable affair. I am sorry for Child's misfortunes although circumstances had led me to expect them. Mr. Brackett, my new Tenant at the corner of Common Street, and Mr. Hurlbert of the Store, called in and I finished the business of the Leases—So that now, every bit of my father's heavy real Estate is under Lease. I hope, to give me less trouble than heretofore.

I had a comfortable time reading Williston and progressed considerably. Mr. Everett's Address to the Phi Beta Kappa is an admirable thing of it's kind.[2] I see nothing after all, that equals it in this particular line of exertion. It is fine, and presents much for reflection and example. Mr. Webster does not succeed so well in this kind of effort, but his best specimen is strangely omitted in this Collection—The Address at Plymouth.[3] After dinner, read my portion of Demosthenes, and wondered at the artful method he uses of acting upon the feelings, of the people of Athens. How is it that the art has been lost. How is it, that by not recurring to the models of Antiquity as Students in Sculpture do to the works of it's masters, men do not attempt to catch some of the spirit of brilliant eloquence.

Afterwards, I read Silas Deane's Address to the American People, in order to explain if possible the difficulty resting in my mind about him, but it did not do it. He was however either a knave or a coward, no matter which so far as his character for patriotism is involved.[4] Then went to Edward's, where we had a very pleasant time. Chardon not being there allowed us an opportunity to talk and that very pleasantly. He is too noisy for comfort. Returned home at ten in the snow.

[1] This payment of $15 (M/CFA/3), together with the earlier payment of $85 by Child, brought to settlement the sale of GWA's accouterments to Child, who succeeded GWA as brigade major. Child had begun to serve sentence following his conviction in a libel action against him as editor of the *Massachusetts Journal* (vol. 2:351). Lydia Maria Child, in addition to being an unusually attentive wife, was conducting the *Massachusetts Journal* alone during Child's imprisonment and engaging in numerous other projects as means of support. Her books for children, her *Frugal Housewife*, and her other unconventionalities made her the subject of sometimes violent comment. See Charlotte Everett to Edward Everett, 10, 28 Jan., 13, 20 April, Everett MSS, MHi; *DAB*.

[2] Delivered at Cambridge, 26 Aug. 1824; in Williston's *Eloquence* at 5: 262–298. CFA had attended the Phi Beta Kappa exercises that year as an undergraduate and had then pronounced good that part of Everett's oration that he heard; see vol. 1:301–302.

[3] *Discourse, Delivered at Plymouth, December 22, 1820, in Commemoration of the First Settlement of New-England*, Boston, 1821. There were four editions before 1827.

⁴ *An Address to the United States of North America* . . . , London, 1784. On the long-argued controversy relating to Deane's conduct as an American com-missioner at Paris during the early years of the American Revolution, see above, entry for 28 Oct. 1829, note.

WEDNESDAY. 24TH.

Morning clear, and mild enough rapidly to dispel the snow which had only fallen to vanish. I went to the Office and occupied myself as usual, in reading Williston, and in arranging the accounts of my Father and bringing them down to the present time. The result of the Quarter is yet doubtful, but things look better than they did. I may scrape through. If I do, I shall be entitled to more credit than from the ignorance of the circumstances I shall probably get, and should the affair of Whitney be once settled, I shall feel easy in my mind.

I read today Mr. Webster's Eulogy of the two Presidents.[1] It is good, but rather overlong. In all addresses, the great art is to be short. And though here it required time to do justice to the subject yet it inevitably makes it tedious. Deacon Spear called to know my father's decision, which I could not give him. I talked a little with him and agreed to let him know what should be done. My other interruptions were few and of little or no consequence. I called to see Mr. Brooks and went down to look at a Dictionary of Natural History which I had a great mind to buy,[2] but on reflection what good can books do to me, the Money is worth more to all intents and purposes. Returned home and passed the afternoon reading Demosthenes, as usual, though the Oration for the Crown is rapidly coming to an End. I am glad of it for on the whole, it has consumed quite time enough.

The evening was passed with Abby, in reading Lalla Rookh aloud, the story of the Fire Worshippers. It is on the whole the best in the work. Though I cannot say I am partial to the broken metre which is used throughout. It is hard to read, and harder to understand. Occupied afterwards upon Campbell's Rhetoric. Strictures upon style, which are for the most part good, but time has operated a change in many respects even since he wrote.

[1] On Adams and Jefferson, in Williston's *Eloquence* at 5:374–414.
[2] Probably *Dictionnaire d'histoire naturelle*, 36 vols., Paris, among the works advertised to be sold at auction at Cunningham's (*Columbian Centinel*, 24 March, p. 3, col. 5).

THURSDAY. 25TH.

Morning clear and tolerably mild. Went to the Office as usual and passed my morning in reading Williston and in business affairs. This Agency is far from being an agreeable business, so many little trifling demands and applications, and so much trouble about the rent. But as I have undertaken it, I will carry it through without any winking. Mr. Brigham called upon me to make arrangements respecting the payment of Money due on the Canal Notes.[1] I agreed to go to Quincy on the first of the month. A letter from my Father received this morning is in very low spirits and advises me to sell stock to make up my payments.[2] I am sorry to see this kind of thing operating upon him for it portends more ominously to the ruin of his property than any thing I have yet seen. Mr. Isaac P. Davis called about the Picture of my Father.[3] I recommended to him an arrangement with Mr. Curtis. Thus passed the morning.

Returning home to dinner, I found P. Chardon Brooks and his wife there according to invitation, and they dined with us. He is a clever fellow, but evidently feeling under heavy restraint with me. My own character is so grave, that he can make nothing of it. I wish to be on good terms with him as with all the other members of the family, but I fear it is more difficult work to be cordial than one might suppose. After dinner the time was so much consumed, that I had only time to finish two pages of Demosthenes, and a short time to read a debate carried on at the close of the Administration of Washington upon the Answer of Congress to his Speech.[4] It is curious, as it develops the principles of the day and the very unfinished speaking of the men. I am somewhat amused by the sense of novelty which every Speaker appeared to experience.

In the evening, I finished Lalla Rookh to my Wife. It is a Poem of much glitter and some sweetness, of too much to cloy, and sicken entirely yet not enough to keep alive. The constant description is agreeable at first but gradually becomes fatiguing. Edmund Quincy also spent an hour or two pleasantly.

[1] Probably Josiah Brigham of Quincy, to whom JQA wrote on canal matters, 13 Jan. 1835 (LbC, Adams Papers).

[2] 19 March (Adams Papers). The tone of the letter reflects the discomfort he was experiencing from a "hoarse Catarrh." He wrote that the sale of State Bank stock was to be resorted to only if other sources of funds to meet the quarterly obligations on 1 April proved unreliable.

[3] That is, about a framer for the portrait.

[4] The debate in the House took place on 13–15 Dec. 1796. It was reported in Thomas Carpenter, *The American Senator, or a Copious and Impartial Report of the Debates in the Congress of the United States ... during the Present Session, Being the Second of the Fourth Congress*, 3 vols., Phila., 1796–1797; a copy, with JQA's bookplate, is in MQA.

FRIDAY. 26TH.

The opening of the day brought with it winter and storm. The snow was several inches deep already, and rapidly increasing with a violent wind from the Eastward. I hesitated long before deciding to go to the Office, a business not of the pleasantest. When there however, I was paid by receiving a letter from my Mother in tolerable spirits speaking of arrangements to come on.[1] I am a little doubtful whether this is not all Smoke as usual. We shall see. She speaks very doubtfully of Mr. Everett.[2] I do not exactly know why, but so much like a snake are his windings, that it is impossible at a distance to guess at them. Dr. Storer called in about this business of Farmer's. The latter insists upon the sum of two hundred dollars which I think an enormous piece of extortion, and accordingly I am of opinion that the suit must go on. We talked it over and I could not help feeling galled at the idea that the scoundrel had of his hold over me. If it must be war, it shall be, and damned be he, who first cries, hold. Mr. Welsh spent an hour in conversation, the rest of the time was passed in reading Clinton's Address to the Society at Columbia—A very uncommonly good production, with which Williston's book closes.[3] I have derived some benefit from this work, though not disappointed[4] by the general impression it leaves of dissatisfaction. There are few specimens of true Eloquence, much rant, great bad taste and a good deal of brilliancy. At home after dinner reading Demosthenes on the Crown, which I am rapidly closing. Tomorrow finishes.

My wife has today been quite unwell and suffering. In the evening, I tried to resume Clarissa Harlowe in the last volume, but she was unable to hear. So I advised her to go to bed, and sat myself reading Campbell on Rhetoric, until I came to a metaphysical Chapter which posed me though I read it twice, and it is on a question which is curious. Why do sensible men sometimes write nonsense?

[1] LCA to CFA, 20 March (Adams Papers). A departure for Quincy during the course of the following month was contemplated.

[2] LCA reported that Edward Everett had not called since he had dined with the family during Mr. Frothingham's stay in Washington. Relations with Everett had become "cold and formal."

[3] DeWitt Clinton's address to the New York Alpha of Phi Beta Kappa at Union College, Schenectady, July 1823 (Williston's *Eloquence*, 5:504–528).

[4] Thus in MS, but "not" seems clearly intrusive.

SATURDAY. 27TH.

Morning clear and the snow began to melt with great rapidity. I went to the Office as usual and passed most of the morning in writing to my Father.[1] Dr. Wendell called upon me and paid his little balance, which thus clears off another of the very disagreeable trifles that have been pressing me. I hope in time to get through them all. My letter was upon business and a brief and clear statement of his affairs. Not over flattering to be sure, but still worthy of attention. Half an hour was passed attending a Stock Sale,[2] which turned out however in nothing material. I have funds to invest but fear I shall not be able to make them fully available, just yet, this I regret, as the Atlas Stock which I propose to purchase went low.

Returned home and after dinner was employed in reading Demosthenes, and finishing the celebrated oration on the Crown.[3] It is a great effort and deserving perpetual study. The remarkable point is that he manages so well to throw over the whole the strong colouring of truth. Who can help feeling as if he had truth on his side when he recapitulates his services and his motives? Who does not feel as if Æschines his accuser is playing a low game? On the whole, I think I have been fully paid in this study, by the insight given me into the power of words. Who does not feel the truth of Mirabeau's explanation of his power when he said that he always considered Words as *things*.

The Evening was passed at the usual meeting of the Debating Society. The question of Theatrical Exhibitions was again brought up and discussed. I took no part in it however this evening as I had on the last exhausted all I had to say. It was a little singular that Chapman followed my ground precisely. We carried our point. This was the closing evening in this season. In looking back to the beginning, I find I have not lost my time, for in ease and self possession, in the knowledge of division and exposition, I have made considerable progress. This is all however, but little compared to what I wish.

[1] LbC in Adams Papers.

[2] At noon in Merchants' Hall with Stephen Brown as auctioneer (*Boston Daily Advertiser*, 27 March, p. 3, col. 5).

[3] CFA marked the completion of his study of the oration in the original, begun on 29 Oct. 1829, by writing a lengthy critique in the form of a letter to JQA, 2 April (Adams Papers).

SUNDAY. 28TH.

The morning was bright but chilly with a harsh March wind blowing. Immediately after breakfast, Abby and I went to Medford. The ride was the least pleasant I have had this year—My provisions against the cold not being such as they would have been in Winter. We found the family as usual, Miss Phillips still there. I went to Meeting all day, and heard Mr. Stetson preach two rather dull Sermons. He is a man of considerable sense, but it is obscured by his being so corpulent and consequently indolent. His mind is rather above the common order, of Country Clergymen. The remainder of the day was passed at the House as usual. Little or nothing remarkable happening. I read more of Monsieur Bausset, but not with much interest. The close is put in to fill up four volumes. The French are full of bookmaking, which is a business tolerably easy in these times, and particularly where Napoleon is concerned, who in every little incident of his life, is now a subject of interest to the Nation.

Medford is a different place since the death of Mrs. Brooks. I do not feel even the degree of interest I then had. What a loss is the head of a family to all the younger members, for the binding force being gone, division comes. What I have said heretofore in this Journal, is likely very soon to prove true. I pity Mr. Brooks very much.

MONDAY. 29TH.

Morning mild, and had there been no snow on the ground, would have been as lovely as last Monday. Went to town with Abby. At the Office where I found a letter from my father inclosing a draught upon the Branch Bank here for three hundred dollars.[1] This is at once a relief to me in his pecuniary affairs. It is rather matter of surprise that he can remit to me from there, but since I cannot inquire, my only satisfaction is that I am now out of immediate difficulty. I went to the Bank and deposited the money, then hearing that Mr. Brooks' famous law case of last Summer was receiving it's quietus in Court, I went in and heard the latter part of Judge Parker's Opinion. It was decidedly favourable to Mr. Brooks, confirming the settlement of 1808, but allowing the Plaintiff to correct the account so far as it might be wrong by the admission of Mr. Brooks. This will probably cost him four or five thousand dollars, which is a cheap way of getting rid of a demand of more than one hundred.[2] I went up to see and to congratulate him upon it. He seemed affected by the expression of sentiment of his friends. I am glad of it on his account as I hope that he will now rest quiet.[3] The decision was an able one.

The rest of my morning was passed at the Office in reading Mr. Holmes' Speech in the Intelligencer.[4] It is a severe dressing of Mr. Benton and must have made him feel unpleasantly in many particulars. This debate in the Senate may have a very good effect in showing that New England is both able and willing to defend herself from all attacks ungenerously made against her.

The afternoon was spent in reading Auger's translation of the Oration on the Crown by way of review. But I was not in good mood for study and did not manage it well. Auger takes liberties and cannot give the force of his author. Evening reading Clarissa to my Wife, and afterwards, reading more of Campbell's Rhetoric, a very sensible book.

[1] 24 March (Adams Papers). Uneasy over the impending quarterly obligations and desiring to avoid the sale of stock earlier considered, JQA sent the order on his personal funds.

[2] On the case of Henry Farnam, administrator for the estate of Tuthill Hubbart, *v.* Peter C. Brooks, see vol. 2:390.

[3] "Poor Father! I scarce ever saw him so much Excited! He said more than 20 gentlemen came to offer him their congratulations." In speaking of the court's decision "he wept like a child!" About Mr. Webster, his attorney, and Mr. Wirt, attorney for the plaintiff, "he could not restrain his tears. 'Mr. Wirt I shall always *love* for his peculiar kindness to me while he was here and for his having told me that he would never again plead a cause against me.' " (Charlotte Everett to Edward Everett, 30 March, Everett MSS, MHi). For further expression of Mr. Brooks' intense satisfaction in the outcome, see Brooks, Waste Book, 31 Dec. 1830; "Autobiography" in Book of Possessions, Brooks MSS, MHi; Brooks to Edward Everett, 21 April 1830, Everett MSS, MHi.

[4] The speech of John Holmes, U.S. Senator from Maine, delivered on 18 Feb., was printed in the *National Intelligencer*, 25 March, p. 2, col. 1 through p. 3, col. 2.

TUESDAY. 30TH.

Morning mild though with an East Wind. At the Office as usual. Time passed in a rather useless manner. As I have finished Williston and not yet assumed any other reading, I found myself soon at a loss what to do, after I had got through the measures proper for bringing my Accounts into order for settlement. I got hold of a copy of Bacon's Essays however, which could not but be good reading, and studied two or three of them with the usual pleasure. Wonderful the power of that man's mind. Strong and sound thought.[1]

I tried to find Mr. Degrand to talk to him about Atlas Stock, but could not, so that I must go into Market and appear a buyer tomorrow if I wish to invest at all. Called to see Mr. Brooks, and afterwards gave the proper directions for the little repairs I wish in this building. I am now getting my Carpenter to attend to little minutiæ very well. And I am gradually bringing all this property into better condition than it has been for a long time back. The Store looks now exceedingly well, and on the whole I feel tolerably satisfied with the present appearance of affairs.

Whitney came up to see me and seemed disposed to settlement. He agreed to pay me a part Cash, and a part by Note, but as he appeared unwilling to close, I acted in rather a Cavalier Style, satisfied that my appearing a little careless would have a better effect than my former anxiety. We parted standing as we were.

I dined with Abby at Chardon's, as usual. Afternoon at home passed in reading the reviews of Demosthenes in the Edinburgh over again. They are excellent and if not a little too sneering and dogmatical would deserve the first rank for papers of criticism. As I had felt a little inclination to head ach during the day I thought it would be advisable to walk a little. The Evening was fine, and I had a pleasant though lonely stroll on the Common. After which I went to Chardon's to the usual weekly Meeting, which was pleasant as they commonly are.

[1] Bacon was one of the authors to whom CFA returned many times. He had read the *Essays* with some regularity early in 1824 (see vol. 1:23–68 *passim*). Of CFA's two copies of the *Essays, Moral, Economical and Political* in MQA, that published at Chiswick, 1822, has his signature and the date 1824. The other (London, 1822), originally GWA's, has CFA's bookplate, marginal comments, and a note dated 1831 in CFA's hand, together with an inscription to JQA2 dated 6 Oct. 1853.

WEDNESDAY. 31ST.

Morning thick and cloudy, with a slight rain and a cold Easterly wind. Went to the Office as usual and was engaged in making up my Quarterly Accounts. Miss Wells a daughter of my tenant in Tremont Street called to pay me a month's rent and to say that they would stay another month. Mr. Whitney called to make a settlement but just as we were closing I started off upon the Shed he left, and we separated wider than before. Thus a moment's rashness has I fear lost all prospect of a peaceable recovery of this large sum, and though I repented very soon, it was too late. He was gone. I had not time to think much upon it, for I went down to attend the sale of stocks at Merchants' Hall in order to buy some Atlas Insurance Shares, but I did not succeed in getting them. I made a bargain however with Mr. Degrand for five at a quarter of one per cent advance, which settles the amount of my investment,[1] then to my Office where I finished all that was requisite for the Quarterly Account. The amount of it exceeds two thousand dollars,[2] and it is wonderful to me how it should have been spent, but so it is, that there is not enough to meet the payments tomorrow. My mind is a good deal troubled about it. I hope never hereafter to have so many crooked[3] things to work.

The afternoon was passed at the Office in the hope of coming to a settlement with Whitney, but Mr. Gay his attorney intimated to me, that the time was gone by. I am afraid it has, and my father suffers dearly for my experience.[4] Returned home dull. Read a little of Carpenter's Senator without much relish. In the evening I read to Abby from Clarissa, excepting an hour which was passed pleasantly in a visit from Edward Brooks. He is quite an agreeable man and not valued near enough.

[1] The recorded price in CFA's personal account book is $500 (M/CFA/9).

[2] This total for expenditures by the Agency during the quarter includes the

routine payments of \$315 to JA's heirs, CFA's fee of \$250 as agent, the repayment of \$843.56 borrowed in the preceding quarter, and the purchase of securities in the amount of \$297.50 (M/

CFA/3).

[3] In the sense of being *tortuous, out of order, awry* (*OED*).

[4] Thus in MS. A mistake for "inexperience"?

THURSDAY. APRIL IST.

The day was lovely, full of the softest feeling of Spring. I went to the Office early and passed my morning in making up the accounts falling due at the commencement of the Quarter. I was in some degree of trouble about having funds sufficient to meet the demands accruing today besides what I wanted to invest. Degrand called upon me however quite early and there was no retreating so I drew the Check and the transfer was made at the Atlas office to my name of five Shares putting this business beyond a doubt. I was then busy in financiering until I was relieved by the voluntary settlements of Messrs. Gay and Welsh, by means of which money I was enabled to prepare the necessary payments if required. I then sat down and read the new Number of the North American Review which contains some quite interesting Articles—One by Mr. Sparks upon the Life of Arthur Lee which will give many and among others my father, a pretty exciting sensation.[1] I confess I do not altogether admire the tone and style of it. But it seems to be a defence of Franklin by means of attack, which pleases Mr. Sparks much, but which is a fault of his temper. My mind however is so disorganized that it is impossible for me to make much headway in any purely literary subject just at present.

I went out to Quincy in the Afternoon, thinking that I should scarcely soon have an opportunity of a more lovely day. The roads were not over good, and as I thought I should not have any conveniences for my horse, I took my Servant Benjamin with me to take care of him at the Stable. Looked into the House and found every thing much as it was. The rain seemed to have injured it much less than I had anticipated.[2] Every thing looked natural and pleasant. From thence I went to Mr. Brighams where I received two years Interest upon the Quincy Canal Notes,[3] from thence to find Deacon Spear to discuss the matter but I could see him only a minute. He told me however that the House was let. This proves to me how wary a man should be in his prices and how ready people are to impose upon him.[4] Thence to my Uncle's where I found all the family but Abby who was still in town. I settled with Elizabeth, but as my Uncle was coming into Boston tomorrow postponed the rest until then.[5] Returned home to tea and passed the evening reading to my Wife from Clarissa, after which Campbell, a sensible author.

¹ *North Amer. Rev.*, 30:454–511 (April 1830). JQA had hoped to the point of publication that the review would not appear (to CFA, 24 March; CFA to JQA, 2 April; both in Adams Papers).

² CFA was urging JQA to authorize repairs to the Old House that would seal the leaks, long in need of attention (27 March, LbC, Adams Papers).

³ The accumulated interest on the notes amounted to $105 (M/CFA/3).

⁴ Spear had maintained that some reduction in rent would be necessary before the two houses could be let; JQA had refused; the houses were then taken at the former rental (JQA to CFA, 19 March; CFA to JQA, 2 April; JQA to CFA, 8 April; all in Adams Papers).

⁵ That is, the quarterly payments to TBA's minor children.

FRIDAY. 2D.

Morning not so pleasant, the wind being easterly. At the Office as usual. Occupied in my Accounts as usual. Received a small portion of rent from my Tenant Hurlbert, and paid the customary due to my Uncle who called for it. I then went down to see Miss Abby Adams and made a settlement with her thus clearing out this business. Returned to the Office and began attempting a careful review of Marshall's fifth volume.[1] I fear much I have lost the power of close application but as now I shall be able to be more released from affairs of business, I am resolved to begin upon a new tack, and try to see whether I cannot profit more by studies which ought to be most important to me, for the mere temporal affairs are after all, a matter of exceeding small consideration. I did however accomplish a considerable portion of Marshall and succeeded in getting the general impression as to the condition of affairs at the commencement of the peace of 1783. Marshall is considered a prejudiced historian of this period, which is probable, but yet he is the only one.

The morning slipped away with great rapidity, and not disagreeably although it must be confessed this affair of Whitney's hangs upon my mind. After dinner I sat down and wrote a letter to my Father upon the subject of my studies,[2] which exhausted the whole morning and finally did not satisfy me at all. But I have no time to write over. It is a difficult thing to write well, at least so exactly as I have a desire to know how. Whether I shall ever succeed in reaching the standard of my wishes, is at any rate doubtful. But practice, they say makes perfect, and there is no want of that. In the evening, I continued Clarissa Harlowe aloud to my Wife and read the Will and subsequent events to her death. They are tame. The action seems to be over, it is a superfluous fifth Act in a play and injures the unity of the Novel. Afterwards, Campbell, on the arrangement of words.

¹ On the editions of John Marshall's *Life of George Washington* in MQA, see vol. 1:13.

² Letter in Adams Papers.

SATURDAY 3RD.

Morning fine. Went to the Office expecting to have considerable time to read Marshall, but as it turned out entirely interrupted. My first visitors were not unwelcome, being my two Mr. Conants from Weston, with a part of the money due upon the Notes for the sale of Wood upon the property there. This was not quite expected so soon, but it does not come out of season, and certainly not inopportunely. I then went to the Miss Haskins and received the amount of their debt in settlement, which finishes another of the small things in my way. Thence home, where I had Mr. Ayer to consult me upon a point of Law of some interest to him—My only Client for a considerable portion of time. He does not incline to Law, and so he left me hesitating, which as I know commonly amounts to nothing. Deacon Spear came in to ask if any thing was to be done upon the Quincy Property and to ask about repairs, to which I made a very negative reply. In this manner however, I found that the whole of my morning was gone and I could not even find a moment to open Marshall. Then came my time for depositing by which I was a good deal puzzled, for much of the money given to me was in a currency not received at the Bank.[1] This is always annoying me—An inconvenience sufficient to balance almost the advantage of exchange, with Washington. As it was I was obliged to carry home a balance.

In the afternoon, commenced Graham's History of the United States—a chapter or two well read, which I had read before was all I accomplished, but it was done tolerably well. The evening, as the Debating Society has ceased to hold its sessions, was spent at home reading the closing part of Clarissa Harlowe, one of the last letters is good as a recommendation of what a young lady should be, and as conveying very good moral instruction, but as part of the Novel, it is not a little dull. Closed the Evening with reading Campbell, which this evening, I finished.

[1] That is, in state bank notes not redeemable in specie; see above, entry for 12 Oct. 1829, note.

SUNDAY. 4TH.

The morning was cool but clear. After some deliberation, we decided upon going to Medford, and as usual went in Mr. P. C. Brooks' gig which we borrowed. Having arrived there, we went to Meeting with Mr. Brooks all day, and heard Mr. Parkman of Boston preach two Sermons. One upon the dangers of adversity, and another which though I liked parts of it, is entirely out of my recollection. Mr. Parkman has certainly improved very much within a few years. He has parted considerably with an ugly whine he used to have, which made a sensible thing appear in his mouth silly. I am inclined to believe that this gentleman by reason of some eccentricities of appearance and manner has been very considerably underrated. After all, sterling merit lies in the mind and heart.

The remainder of the day was passed much as usual. I was occupied in reading several articles in the American Quarterly, Mr. Walsh's production,[1] which in this last Number has considerable talent, and smartness, though I cannot say that I admire much the sentiment in one or two instances. The Evening was passed in conversation with Mr. Brooks who was very pleasant. His kindness of manner produces an effect to bind me here to attend him at least once a week, when much happens in regard to Charlotte which I would much prefer to have had omitted.

[1] On Robert Walsh (1784–1859), of Philadelphia, editor of the *American Quarterly Review*, 1827–1837, see *DAB*.

MONDAY. 5TH.

The day was bright and clear. We returned to town after breakfast, and I went to the Office directly. My time was taken up first in writing my Journal and next in settling my accounts. I went down to claim my Dividend upon the Stock of the State Bank which paid this morning at the rate of 2 and a quarter per Cent,[1] a small matter but better than nothing. I received and deposited the sum. The rest of the morning was passed in reading though not without such interruptions as to render Marshall very difficult to understand. I cleared out the room opposite in order to have it ready to let. I had my Carpet shaken and set in my inner room so as to have it ready to occupy myself for the summer, and arranged my Accounts with regularity and method. Returned home and passed the Afternoon in reading Mr. Graham's book, in that portion which relates to the State of Virginia. It is very well but it does not come quite up to my expectation, being for a shorter period than I had supposed and embracing much less of the Colonial History. The Account is however a fair one, as coming from an inhabitant of the old Country, and treats the whole principle with more of a philosophical and less of an angry turn than any preceding Writer. Why may I not attempt an Essay upon the subject.

I had time also to look over some Copies of papers taken by Mr. Sparks order relating to minutiæ of the Treaty of 1783, but not in themselves over interesting. The evening was spent in reading Clarissa

Harlowe, to which I gave a final close. It has taken more time than it deserved,[2] still the book has merit, much thought and moral influence. I afterwards began my father's Lectures upon rhetoric, and was surprised agreeably by them, for they contain almost every thing which in my new Articles, I had thought to have said, and express it much better. I never read them before.[3]

[1] That is, at $1.35 a share (M/CFA/3).

[2] Reading aloud in the evenings from Richardson's *Clarissa* had begun on 31 Oct. 1829 and been pursued with fair regularity save for one hiatus (above, entry for 18 Feb., note).

[3] Delivered by JQA as the first Boylston Professor of Rhetoric at Harvard, 1806–1809, they were published as *Lectures on Rhetoric and Oratory*, 2 vols.,

Cambridge, 1810. For a lengthier tribute, see CFA to JQA, 17 April (LbC, Adams Papers). See, further, Donald M. Goodfellow, "The First Boylston Professor of Rhetoric and Oratory," *NEQ*, 19:372–389 (Sept. 1946). Of the three copies in MQA, one bears GWA's signature and JQA's bookplate; one was presented by JQA to TBA in 1810; and one is without indication of ownership.

TUESDAY. 6TH.

Morning at the Office. The Easterly winds have now set in and give the usual disagreeable chill to the Air. I walked down to State Street, and received at the Boston Bank the Dividend of Stock, being one third of their Capital—My share being one hundred and fifty dollars and reducing thus much my Capital in Bank Stock. This amount is already invested in the Atlas Insurance. Whether for better or for worse remains to be seen. I then obtained the Dividend of one per cent in the American Bank—A very large distribution for one year. This Company has lost part of it's Capital. My little property has on the whole been far from prosperous,[1] having done very little for it's increase in the way of profit. Returned to my Office and spent the morning in reading Marshall, where I made considerable progress, yet I feel dissatisfied with that book. It does not contain that extent of philosophical view which I should have expected from such a pen. My morning time is not available as I would wish. So many interruptions occur, and so much trouble in regard to the pecuniary affairs of the moment that the mind is distracted and unsteady. I hoped to day, that Whitney would come to settle. He did not. I had expected the rent from the House occupied by the Olivers. They fail to pay this Quarter, making another trouble upon my hands.[2]

After dinner, I read Beverley's History of Virginia, Part the first. A curious book published in 1705 a copy of which happened to belong to George.[3] It relates the History of the Settlement plainly and apparently in a very concise and impartial way. I then began Grahams,

Account of New England. He is a warm Advocate of the Puritans, and justly so for in England they have been much misrepresented. I was then called down to spend the Evening at home at the usual meeting of the Brooks family, which was this week at my house. It was as usual tolerably pleasant, but not so much so as some of the later ones have been.

[1] CFA's holdings were six shares of stock in the Boston Bank purchased at $75 a share (vol. 2:286), three shares in the American Bank (vol. 2:288, 339).

[2] No rent on 55 Hancock Street having been received from the Olivers since early January, CFA wrote to Miss Oliver on 10 April (LbC, Adams Papers) suggesting removal unless regular and sub- stantial payments could be assured.

[3] Robert Beverley, *The History and Present State of Virginia*, published at London in four parts, 1705. The copy in MQA is without indication of GWA's ownership, having the signature of David Evans, 1753, JQA's bookplate, and a brief note in CFA's hand on the title-page referring to a position taken by Beverley antithetical to that of Grahame.

WEDNESDAY. 7TH.

Morning cold and blustering. I went to the Office as usual. Heard of the murder of Mr. Jos. White at Salem, a shocking affair enough. Found in his bed this morning stabbed and bruised in the head. The City was a good deal excited about it.[1] Read this morning Genl. Harrison's Pamphlet and was satisfied by it, that his vanity and ignorance of the whole had made a fool of him.[2] The worst danger of all to public men comes from themselves. Many are fully equal to prevent surprises from others, who are totally overset by some strange and insidious enemy in their own persons. Although this gentleman was most certainly ill treated, yet he proves himself fully unfit for the place he was occupying. I also read something of Marshall, relating to the early debates in Congress which formed the parties in the Coun- try. These are interesting but they are not managed by Marshall as I should have supposed a man of his powers would have done. He wrote it in too much haste, and did not leave his mind to form conclusions, instead of merely hurrying over premises. But there is notwithstanding much information to be derived from the work. It contains a definite and not altogether a dry statement of facts, and explains the motions of parties, though by one side asserted to be partial.

I received today the Dividends upon the Stock in Neponset and West Boston Bridge.[3] The latter is again becoming tolerable stock. My father's personal Property here is generally good. And all, both real and personal, tolerably productive. If his other property was equally so, he would have been a wealthy man.

The afternoon was passed in reading Graham's History of the United

States, the portion relating to New England is very interesting as it conveys a clearer and more impartial account than any preceding Historian. I also compared Robertson.[4] In the evening, I began reading aloud to my Wife a part of Eustace's Tour in Italy,[5] in order to render myself a little more familiar with places in that country. It was pleasing. After it, I read part of my father's Lectures, and found in them much food for reflection.

[1] The 81-year-old Captain White was murdered with hatchet and dirk (*Boston Daily Advertiser*, 8 April, p. 2, col. 1; *Columbian Centinel*, 10 April, p. 2, col. 3). The crime became "an all-engrossing topic" for nearly two months until announcement was made that the perpetrators had been discovered, again during their trials, and afterwards, because of the prominence of some of the accused. See below, entries for 29 May, 18 Aug. and notes there. The murder, developments subsequent thereto, and the trials of the accused are reconstructed in Charles Pelham Curtis' "The Young Devils and Dan'l Webster," *American Heritage*, 11:52–54, 101–103 (June 1960); also in Howard A. Bradley and James A. Winans, *Daniel Webster and the Salem Murder*, Columbia, Mo., 1956.

[2] With his letter of 31 March (Adams Papers), JQA had sent CFA *Remarks of General Harrison Late Envoy . . . to the Republic of Colombia, on Certain Charges Made against Him by That Government*, Washington, 1830, which tended to justify the Bolívar government's contention that Harrison had involved himself in their domestic conflicts (*DAB*, article on William Henry Harrison). CFA amplified his views on Harrison in a letter to JQA, 17 April (LbC, Adams Papers).

[3] These amounted to $79 on JQA's six shares of Neponset Bridge and five shares of West Boston Bridge stock (M/CFA/3).

[4] William Robertson, *The History of America*. GWA's autograph is in an edition published at London in 4 vols., 1803, now in MQA. Also there, is an edition published at Basel, 3 vols., 1790, with JQA's bookplate.

[5] John Chetwode Eustace, *A Classical Tour through Italy*, an. 1802. CFA owned an edition published at London in 4 vols., 1815, now in MQA.

THURSDAY. 8TH.

This was the day appointed according to immemorial custom for the annual fast—One of the practices of the puritans of whom I am reading.[1] I did not therefore go to the Office, but passed my time in reading the ninth and tenth books of Robertson. They are written with a great appearance of fairness but he did not feel the great points of character he was describing, and his inclination is rather to slur than to praise.

I attended Divine service at Mr. Frothingham's and heard a good Sermon, to which however I could not listen, perhaps from my unfortunate habit of inattention. This practice of fasting is now in a great measure done away. Few people think it proper to pursue it and perhaps as the circumstances of the Country are changed it is now without what was once its most rational purpose.

The remainder of my day was passed usefully in reading Graham in which I made considerable progress and in writing a little upon the subject. It is useless to read much without writing, for the impressions soon wear away from the mind unless stayed by some attempt to fix them more permanently than reading will do. The subject of our ancient history makes itself on the whole much more interesting to me than heretofore, and I think I shall follow it with much more earnestness. No person in this Country who professes to be well informed should be ignorant of it, and I who call myself a young man of distinction should be least of all so. Looked into Marshall's first volume and found myself following implicitly Robertson and Chalmers.[2] The more I see of this work, the less I think of it. Judge Marshall has however revised his first work. Evening, Eustace to my Wife, and afterwards my father's Lectures. This is a day delightfully spent. How far preferable to the disgusting troubles of the world, yet it cannot always be enjoyed and perhaps the mixture gives it a keener relish.

[1] The spring fast-day, announced by governor's proclamation, was observed in Mass. on the first or second Thursday in each April (W. DeLoss Love, *The Fast and Thanksgiving Days of New England,* Boston, 1895, p. 510–514).

[2] George Chalmers, *Political Annals of the Present United Colonies, from Their Settlement to the Peace of 1763,* Book 1, London, 1780. See entry for 15 April, below.

FRIDAY 9TH.

Morning at the Office. The day promised fair but became gloomy and cold. I passed the larger part of my time in reading Marshall. The prolixity of his volume makes it tedious. I feel wearied by its minuteness, though the importance of the period to our History makes it necessary. The subsequent time makes very evident the influence which the division of parties at the early period of the Administration of Washington, has exerted. It is to be felt now, as the principles of contest between the parties are effectively the same—The same division between the friends of the national and the friends of the State power. I was occupied in this manner the whole time, excepting a small portion in which I called upon Mr. Brooks, and went to the Estate at the South end, to see about a partition wall which was thrown down in the gale the other evening.[1] After arranging it's repair I walked in and made an arrangement with Miss Longhurst to settle her rent by taking her Note, which finishes that business.[2] I then walked to the Washington Bank to receive the Dividend upon the Boylston Market Stock which was four dollars upon the Share, being quite a comfortable thing at this time.[3] This is excellent Stock.

Thence back to the Office. As this was the last day to which entry could be delayed, I was compelled to make up my mind what to do in Whitney's case. After much doubt and hesitation and misgiving, I at last concluded to go on. I hope I did right, but right or wrong, I mean to pursue the best interest of the employer. The issue is not with us. I trust to a higher power. My own judgment will often be found wanting. John Gorham dined with us, and after dinner I finished Graham's first volume and the Account of New England. I then read the Account of it in the "European Settlements,"[4] and part of Mr. Webster's Plymouth Oration, which does not seem to me to treat the subject exactly. The Evening which was to have been taken up in reading Eustace, was passed in conversation with [Edmund] Quincy who came to visit us.

[1] On 5 May 1829, shortly before the crisis in his financial affairs was reached, Thomas Welsh Jr. had deeded to JQA an "estate in High Street" with an assigned value of $250 as partial settlement of the arrears on his 23 Court Street office (vol. 2:375; M/CFA/3).

[2] The amount was $489.01 (M/CFA/3).

[3] The Washington Bank was at 471 Washington Street (*Boston Directory*, 1830–1831). The dividend amounted to $48 (M/CFA/3).

[4] Probably the Abbé G. T. F. Raynal's *Philosophical and Political History of the Settlements and Trade of the Europeans in the E. and W. Indies*, 8 vols., London, 1783. An edition belonging to JQA, in the original French, published at La Haye in 11 vols., 1774–1781, is in MQA.

SATURDAY 10TH.

Morning cold and gloomy. I went to the Office and passed my time as usual in reading Marshall, excepting a small portion of it devoted as usual to the regulation of my Accounts. Mr. Kinsman called upon me to pay a portion of the Note of the City Guards to the Estate of my brother, and to discuss the matter of Mr. Whitney's Affair. I left the settlement of this altogether to him, if he can make terms with him, it is well and much more than I can. I hope this disagreeable business will terminate without a reference to law, but if it is not my mind is made up. I have only the course of decision to take. My character always was one which verged to obstinacy in points where it was based upon belief of right and now when the conviction of justice is most prevalent, it is rather hard to yield to the sense of expediency.

Marshall was not over interesting but I got along tolerably in progress. At home found Mr. Brooks who dined with us. I was very glad to have the opportunity to receive him in this way, without ceremony or parade. And he was very mild and pleasant as usual. He left us immediately, and I occupied myself during the afternoon in reading and writing upon Mr. Graham's History. I feel as if I might be able to write upon this subject but I do not know whether it does not require more perseverance than I am equal to. And yet it is a shame to say so. But the subject is interesting and I propose at any rate to pursue it for my own instruction.

The Evening was passed in reading Eustace to my Wife. This author is full of prejudice, and John Bullism but yet has a cultivated mind, and much that is entertaining and instructive. After this was finished, for the Evening I read some Articles in the North American Review upon Jefferson's works and others.[1]

[1] A review (unsigned) by Andrew Ritchie of T. J. Randolph's edition, *North Amer. Rev.*, 30:511–551 (April 1830).

SUNDAY 11TH.

The morning was cheerless and gloomy, the East Wind prevailing in all its severity at this period of the year. Abby and I went together to Medford to pass the day as usual. We found Mr. Brooks and Mrs. Everett much as usual. We attended divine service during the day and heard Mr. Briggs, a clergyman from Lexington deliver two serious discourses one upon the immortality of the soul, the other I have forgotten.[1] They were very well calculated for the Country being simple, and solid, but full of common places which very much diverted my attention. He dined with us at Mr. Brooks', and we found him very pleasant and agreeable. I was much pleased with him, as he was lively without stiffness, conversible without the starch piety of some. On the whole he is a favourable specimen of the Country clergy, around Boston.

The remainder of the day was spent in reading some Articles in a late number of the Quarterly, which present the state of England in a view totally new. Indeed though no one could help being astonished that Britain has kept to such a height so long, yet the inevitable course of things is not to be stopped to indulge men with wonder. The debt of England is a load no nation can march under without staggering. It remains yet to be seen whether this will not finally fall with a ruinous crash. Conversation general.

[1] Charles Briggs, Harvard 1815 (*Mass. Register*, 1830).

MONDAY. 12TH.

The dark, cold, and gloomy weather continues. We returned to town this morning, and I passed the morning at the Office. Received a letter from my father in reply to my Quarterly Account and otherwise containing nothing material.[1] Mr. Farrar the brother of my Father's Quincy Tenant called and requested some Garden seeds to begin with the place at Quincy, which I provided him with.[2] I obtained a large collection and hope now to be able fully to furnish the family with vegetables for the whole Summer. My time was so short and so cut up that I was unable to make any progress in Marshall, and on the whole felt dissatisfied. Mr. Forbes called and I paid him his very moderate bill, for the past quarter.[3] Returning home I was occupied in framing and beginning to execute the plan of an Essay which I have in my head upon the early History of the Country. I do not know whether it is not beyond my grasp, but at any rate I will try. I thought over the matter and only lament my want of preparation. The whole afternoon was passed in this manner. The Evening was occupied in reading Eustace to my Wife who was much pleased with the account of Rome. After which I passed some time in reading Hutchinson over to compare with Robertson.[4]

[1] 6 April (Adams Papers).
[2] In a letter of 31 March (Adams Papers), JQA had asked CFA to hire Farrar to prepare the soil and plant the vegetable garden at the Old House.
[3] Horse hire from William Forbes for the quarter was substantially reduced from what it had been before CFA re-

solved to make increased use of family carriages for trips to and from Medford and Quincy.
[4] An edition of Thomas Hutchinson, *The History of the Colony of Massachusetts Bay* ..., published at London in 3 vols., 1765–1828, is in MQA and has JQA's bookplate.

TUESDAY. 13TH.

Morning again gloomy and cold, with rain and snow. I went to the Office as usual and received a letter from my father upon miscellaneous subjects which was quite interesting.[1] The rest of the time was passed in reading Marshall, the fifth volume of which I finished. It has refreshed my memory upon the principal matters relating to the Administration of Genl. Washington, a period of history which is becoming every day more interesting and important. But it has dissatisfied me more with a work which is miserably poor in reflection, and withal carries with it no slight evidence of the feelings of party, and the hurry of agitated writing. But my pursuit of the earlier portion of our History engrosses me now infinitely more, and I intend to carry it on more fully in future.[2]

My time was entirely at my own disposal and I did little or nothing, my books not being here. I looked over my brother George's papers to see what was to be done with Mr. Whitney's claim, but could make nothing of it. Afternoon passed in thinking and writing. But to me it is exceedingly hard to do the latter and I try over and over again. I did begin in earnest today and am resolved now, to intermit as little as possible. Evening, Eustace to my Wife and the enthusiastic description of Rome—After which, the second volume of my father's Lectures.

[1] 8 April (Adams Papers).

[2] The idea of writing an essay in American history had been evolving since 3 April following completion of the reading of Robertson, Hutchinson, Chalmers, Marshall, and Grahame comparatively, and took final shape as a study of the Puritan inheritance in New England. CFA was engaged steadily during the next several weeks in preparing successive drafts. Submission to the *North American Review* in the form of a review of Grahame was followed, after considerable delay, by publication. See below, entries for 14 April–1 May; Adams Papers, Microfilms, Reel Nos. 294, 316; *North Amer. Rev.*, 32:174–195 (Jan. 1831).

WEDNESDAY. 14TH.

Morning at the Office. Occupied in Graham's second volume which is exceedingly interesting. It contains the History of the rise of the settlement of Maryland, the Carolinas, New York and Pennsylvania. The account of these so far as I have gone each presents distinct and strongly marked features. My views vary as I read, and I am fearful my attempt at writing will again terminate abortively. Yet my impressions are rather strengthened of the correctness of my own views. Perseverance is all I need, and confidence in myself which is very grievously deficient. I then took a short time to look further over the papers of my brother which still remain and I destroyed several of them. Then I went down to see some new books which are advertised to be sold tomorrow.[1] The temptation was considerable, but I was resolved to withstand it, as I have a plan to pursue which these things should not shake. Unity of purpose in life seems to be the great secret of success. My poor brother's records show much and bright talent, but constantly diverted by the seductions of pleasure, and even the trifles of life.

After dinner I sat down to my studies but being unable to procure Chalmers from the Athenæum I was in some measure deprived of the afternoon for having finished what I had to say of Robertson, I could not proceed, and therefore wasted much in reading trifles. The day was clear and pleasant, and my spirits which had been wavering now took a more steady balance. The Evening was short. I read only a little of Eustace, and afterwards my father's Lectures on Oratory.

[1] At the Julien Auction Rooms, corner of Milk and Congress streets (*Boston Daily Advertiser*, 14 April, p. 3, col. 5).

THURSDAY 15TH.

Morning at the Office. The day was mild and bright though the Easterly wind prevents any softness in the air. Occupied all the morning in reading Graham and was much interested in it. His account seems to be fair and tolerably impartial—Giving to every author in turn his due merit and correcting them properly when wrong. My mind is not firmly made up, I think or it would waver less about my purposes. This subject is I am afraid as yet beyond me. But I will persevere and finish something at any rate for myself, and then we shall see what can be done with it.

My time was very little interrupted. After dinner I went myself to the Athenæum, where I found Chalmers book, and took the opportunity to look over all the works upon America which I could find there. My general impressions become strengthened but as yet the mass is not woven so as to bear examination. My own impression is that the New England character has not been justly appreciated, that men have taken the start in giving false and unfavourable views of the early settlers which it will take long years to shake off. But whether by previous study or occupations I am the fit person to shake it off remains to be seen. At any rate it would be an honourable quest, and peculiarly appropriate in me, the descendant of one of the clearest of its lines, not undistinguished in its history. My thoughts flow in upon me far too fast to speak them even if I would. But they are only fit for secret meditations.

The evening was passed as usual, reading to my Wife out of Eustace the splendid description of the Church of St. Peter's at Rome. A magnificent subject. After it, I read Mr. Clayton's Speech in the Senate,[1] and a Lecture of my Father's. My spirits today exceedingly agreeable.

[1] JQA, in a letter to CFA (6 April, Adams Papers), had enclosed *Speech of Mr. [John Middleton] Clayton, of Delaware . . . on the Fourth Day of March, . . . the Resolution of Mr. Foot of Connecticut, being under Consideration* (Washington, 1830), with the statement that it "disputes the palm with that of Mr. Webster." CFA was more restrained in his judgment of it (CFA to JQA, 17 April, LbC, Adams Papers).

FRIDAY 16TH.

Morning clear, but still having much in it of the East Wind. I went to the Office as usual and read Graham without interruption during the morning so that I progressed very rapidly indeed. One reading however will hardly be sufficient. And much reflection and reconsideration will be necessary to form any thing like an agreeable production, or even a sensible one. The task I have undertaken too is a hard one and perhaps at this stage almost sure to fail. But then it has much ingenuity to recommend it.

My mornings now pass very quietly and without disturbance. The afternoon was spent in writing and that very steadily though as usual very much dissatisfied with my first draft. To write is easy, to write well is the hardest of all things. I have nearly finished my first sketch which is rough enough. This evening, being invited to Mr. Frothingham's I walked down and passed the Evening. Nobody but Chardon besides my wife and myself. Tolerably pleasant, but I took too much supper.

SATURDAY. 17TH.

Morning clear but with the usual chill in the Air from the East wind which is generally prevalent at this season. I went to the Office a little under the influence of a head ach from eating imprudently last evening. On this account, having finished Graham and finding that I was not equal to much attention to business, I thought I would take a walk. I accordingly went to the beginning of the Neck, and though not directly benefitted, found the advantage in the course of the day.

Called to see Mr. Foster and obtain my bill of him which he would not send in, I suppose fearful of my intending to make a change which I do contemplate, it is very certain. He told me also that I might have Mr. Knapp's share in the Boylston Market which we had been talking about. I have invested every thing I can for this Quarter already it must be allowed, but I believe notwithstanding I shall accept this offer.

I called also to see Mrs. Bittner and try to arrange with her about her debt to Hollis. She has gathered courage and is now very stubborn. I must see Hollis and settle the matter. Returned to my Office, found Deacon Spear who came to inquire for his Note, and to inform me that he designed paying it, upon the first of May. I accordingly sat down and wrote to him [*i.e.* JQA] about it which took the rest of the time.[1] Miss Julia Gorham and her brother John dined with us. My afternoon was not passed as profitably as might be because my head ach did not go off until the latter part of it. But I succeeded in reading over carefully the History of Virginia in Chalmers, Robertson and Graham.

The Sun set in all his glory tonight and shone in full upon the curtains of my room, throwing thus a blaze of living light upon my study. This is delicious, and never before, have I felt so fully the great value of this privilege. It cheers the spirits exceedingly. Evening at home reading Eustace to my Wife. Afterwards my father's Lectures.

[1] CFA inquired in the letter (LbC, Adams Papers) both as to the amount and the whereabouts of the notes. JQA replied on 23 April (Adams Papers), sending on the notes.

SUNDAY 18TH.

Morning clear, but with a cold and cheerless wind. I had anticipated a pleasant ride to Medford, but was somewhat disappointed. The east predominated too much. Arrived, we attended divine service all day and heard Mr. Stetson. I was so cold in the morning having imprudently left my great coat behind me that I could hear little. The subject however was prayer. In the afternoon, his sermon was upon Sunday Schools and somewhat severe upon the practices of his neighbours of the orthodox creed. I am not over fond of militant Theology, and therefore pay little attention to denunciations from the pulpit of any kind. It is a little unfortunate for Communities that they have in them commonly smart spirits who in the desire for self distinction which animates man as a race, seek those ways calculated to breed evil passions and disagreeable feelings in the hearts of fellow men.

But I am not going to moralize on hackneyed topics. The world must always be taken by every generation as it is, and if it is the work of half a life to come to an understanding of this nature, it only shows, what shadows we are, and what shadows we pursue. My time was lost. Dr. Swan paid a short visit in the evening.

MONDAY. 19TH.

This was the first morning that the Spring Season had manifested itself in an unequivocal manner, and therefore quite delicious. The air was soft and made our ride returning from Medford quite agreeable. I went to the Office and enjoyed a morning totally uninterrupted from any visit of any kind but not on that account entirely well spent. My books are at home and having finished Graham, I had nothing else to begin upon, so that I did little except to look over the series of letters written to my brother George by my father.[1] They are deeply interesting to me as evincing his constant unabated affection and anxiety for him and the trouble that his procrastinating conduct occasioned. If ever there was a son who had advantages from his father, it was he, and his mind and taste merited a better fate. But the past is not to be recalled, and we submit under the affliction more readily when we suppose that it is probably for the best.

The afternoon was passed in my study writing a rough draft of my Essay upon our early History. I was tolerably well satisfied with what I had accomplished, and if I can do it all in the same manner I hope it will do as my first effort in a long composition. But it will need revision and reflection, and my time is very short. I have so many inducements to continue it that I anxiously hope they will carry me through the necessary labour. The days have now grown so long that I have but a short time to read Eustace to my Wife and we progress slowly. After it, I accomplish something, and this evening finished my father's Lectures which have done me good.

¹ For the period from Oct. 1823, when GWA began to assume the management of JQA's affairs in Boston, to GWA's death in 1829, almost all of JQA's frequent letters to him, both the retained copies in letterbooks and recipient's copies, remain *in situ*. It is safe to conclude, therefore, that the file is practically complete. In contrast, however, only five letters from GWA to JQA during the some period have been located, all recipient's copies in the Adams Papers. CFA, on the basis of his own repeated statements in the diary that he had destroyed papers of his brother, must bear the major responsibility for the loss. However, we do not know whether GWA was systematic in keeping letterbooks, and we do know that JQA did not keep complete files of personal letters received. On the related problem of JA2's letters, see above, entry for 14 Oct. 1829, note.

TUESDAY. 20TH.

Morning mild and like Summer. I went to the Office as usual. This weather does not produce a very pleasing effect upon me as it used to, my mind is now rendered languid by it. I called upon Mr. Kinsman to see if there was any probability of a termination of the dispute with Whitney. But I find none. He is not altogether so active an Attorney as I took him for. Returned to my Office and passed my time in reading Graham over again. I accomplished the History of Virginia today and on the whole have no occasion to alter the impressions which the previous reading had made. I do not know whether I shall fully succeed in working it in. But is not the trial worth making. Shall I not obtain some degree of notice even for the attempt.

My time was very little interrupted. For a few days past I have not seen a soul, which is rather an unusual circumstance. The afternoon was entirely occupied in writing my Essay in which I made considerable progress and got through the violent charge of intolerance that has been made against them.¹ I do not know whether I have done to my side the justice it deserved, but I think it bears a strong face. My time was taken up until quite late, as this was the evening for the meeting of the family at Chardon's. I went as usual and we had a Supper much in the ordinary way. Returned quite early.

¹ That is, the Puritans in New England.

WEDNESDAY. 21ST.

The weather continues warm even to the sultry feeling of Summer. I went to the Office as usual and passed my time in reading

Graham's History of the settlement of New England. My interruptions were not numerous. A man called with a bill of Messrs. Russell and Randall, Pump makers, against the late Agency, which after much demur, I consented to pay. It was of three years standing, and done by the direction of Mr. Hollis who seems to have had Carte blanche during the preceding six years to waste, to spend and to destroy.

Mr. Champney is one of my Tenants and called to pay me a portion of his rent which was due and promised to me some time ago. I had begun to fear that it would not come at all, and was therefore glad to give him credit for it. The remainder of my time was much at my own disposal, and I took advantage of it to examine the early History of our forefathers with some attention but the subject multiplies upon me so rapidly that I hardly know what to do. I see so many branches and so many lights in which it may be taken that my mind is almost puzzled, and I begin to yield to despair. My time is so short and so much seems [*i.e.* needs?] to be done. My task is rather more than at present I feel equal to. Courage, there is a spirit to support the labour and a prize to reward it.

Afternoon, employed in writing, but my views were not bright nor clear. I did not accomplish much. The days now grow long. Evening, stopped in reading Eustace by Edmund Quincy who came to pay a visit and spend two hours. The rest of the time, reading anecdotes of distinguished characters.

THURSDAY. 22D.

Morning at the Office. The weather grows warmer rather than more cold and begins to make us feel as if Summer had really come. It is delightful to sensation but creates rather a languid feeling as to work. My time was not interrupted. I went to see Mr. Kinsman to inquire respecting Whitney whom I saw this Morning. He was not aware that he had returned from New York. Then read Graham but not regularly, and finding my head full of composing, I sat down and wrote off the concluding portion of my Essay. I think it is tolerably good but will require much careful correcting and laborious recomposing. I think the ideas are generally sound, though I am afraid a little of the reasoning, is open to question. It may not be good but it is so ingenious as to have convinced me, which I never thought it would.

The rough draft is now completed. And I must now commence the work of putting into a favourable shape. The afternoon was accordingly passed in this business, and I worked steadily and accomplished a large portion of the earlier, but not most laborious portion for

I. ABEL BOWEN'S MAP OF BOSTON . . . AND THE ADJACENT
TOWNS, 1830

See page ix

2. THE STATE HOUSE AND HANCOCK AVENUE FROM THE MALL, 1830

3. NAHANT AND THE NAHANT HOUSE

See page x

4. THE FIRST CHURCH IN BOSTON,
CHAUNCY PLACE

5. THE ADAMS TEMPLE
(FIRST CHURCH), QUINCY

6. TREMONT STREET IN 1830, SHOWING THE TREMONT THEATRE
AND THE TREMONT HOUSE

See pages xi–xiii

7. THE GRANITE RAILWAY, QUINCY

8. THE BOSTON ATHENAEUM AND
GALLERY, PEARL STREET

9. "RODE INTO TOWN WITH ABBY, AND LEFT HER AT THE BATHING HOUSE"

See pages xiv–xv

it includes little of the reasoning, and was better finished at first than the latter part of it. The evening was sultry. I finished the second volume of Eustace to my Wife, and continued my labour afterwards until eleven.

FRIDAY 23D.

The morning was sultry but before noon the wind changed and brought with it the chill to the air which always comes from the East. At the Office, occupied in reading Graham very attentively over—And reflecting upon the subject. Mr. Knapp called to let me know that he was ready to transfer the share of the Boylston Market Association which I had agreed to take. Accordingly [I] paid him one hundred and twenty five dollars for one hundred, a considerable advance, but as I suspect not more than it will always be worth. This rather cramps my means during this Quarter as it is unexpected, but I think I shall be able to clear it with a little attention. Nothing peculiar happened. The afternoon was passed in writing out the more difficult portion of my Essay, which troubled me a good deal but I progressed notwithstanding, and think it probable that now I shall finish it and have it ready to offer. It may want finish from hurry, but still it will be clear, and not without considerable ability—If I may be allowed to think so.

My wife was not very well today, and the change in the weather was not favourable to the spirits. I had no volume of Eustace from the Athenæum so was obliged to look over some things in the New Monthly which strikes me upon reviewing it as uncommonly feeble.[1] A matter of nothing. Afterwards I went to my study and spent some time in continuation of my labours in writing.

[1] *New Monthly Magazine and Literary Journal*, London, new ser., vol. 28.

SATURDAY 24TH.

Morning cold and rainy. I went to the Office as usual and passed the morning in a manner not quite so profitable as I might have done because I had not with me my books, the consequence was that I was driven to employ myself as I could. My time was principally taken up in looking over and destroying all the papers of a useless nature among the remaining things belonging to my brother. They are very numerous and though I have a great indisposition to doing any thing of the kind yet it seems useless to keep them.

Mr. Child, the Secretary of the Boylston Market Association called and I walked with him to the Market for the purpose of receiving the

Certificate of the Share purchased yesterday.[1] This business occupied but a few moments. On my return I sent a Note to one of my negligent Tenants and continued my business of destruction. After dinner I laboured hard, and finished the examination of the Essay I have written. It is now in a state of forwardness, and I hope now to get it ready before the next month. My Wife was quite unwell all day. In the evening I read to her a little from the Insect Architecture of the Library of Entertaining Knowledge.[2] It was interesting as it informed me of the fact that there were solitary bees, which I did not know before. The day was bad and I was not over lively.

[1] Perhaps Joshua Child, an employee of the Washington Bank with which the Boylston Market seems to have had a close relationship. The Market was at the corner of Washington and Boylston streets (*Boston Directory*, 1830–1831).

[2] The volume entitled *Insect Architecture* was published in 1830; on the *Library of Entertaining Knowledge*, see above, entry for 20 Oct. 1829.

SUNDAY. 25TH.

Morning cold and gloomy. We doubted a considerable time as to the expediency of going to Medford and finally hit upon that side of the alternative which was certainly the least prudent. But as our departure was deferred until eleven o'clock I passed two hours in examining and re-arranging my observations upon the American History. Having done this, I began reading Chalmers regularly in order to see what was to be said in addition of him. This book is the most violent misinterpretation of American facts that I have seen and that probably exists. The time came to go and we had a very uncomfortable ride indeed.

Arrived, and found at dinner with us, Mr. Walker, the Clergyman of Charlestown. He was quite pleasant, and in the afternoon I went to hear him. The Sermons he preaches are peculiar for the closeness of the reasoning and the simple texture of the style. He assumes a point and brings it forward in all it's shapes. His subject this day was happiness as an object. He touched very well upon the general weakness of man in not looking for happiness, but he did not very distinctly illustrate what he meant by the term. His *moral* was too short. But on the whole, there are few preachers whom I prefer to hear before Mr. Walker. The remainder of the day was passed in looking into Mather's Magnalia a copy of which Mr. Brooks has,[1] in order to look for the authorities for certain statements in Graham which I found generally correct. The book is a curiosity inasmuch as it is a strange specimen of a mind regulated with little judgment, and blunted by entertaining a too great multiplicity of objects, so that the leading ones are huddled with the indifferent and worthless without much discrimination.

[1] Cotton Mather, *Magnalia Christi Americana: or the Ecclesiastical History of New England.* An edition published at Hartford in 2 vols., 1820, is in MQA, but there is no indication that it is the copy that had belonged to Peter C. Brooks.

MONDAY. 26TH.

The day was mild but exceedingly windy, so much so that upon riding back to town I felt exceedingly apprehensive that we should be blown over. My head also felt a little out of order and when I reached home, my entire feelings were far from enviable. Found a note from Miss Oliver inclosing the amount of her taxes for the past year. I did not know what to do about replying to her and so prefer to let the matter go on as it does now, until next Quarter when I shall feel obliged to make a final decision according as she is able to pay. To the Office where Mr. Conant came in to pay me the balance of the sales of wood at Weston. It fell a little short of what I had expected, but it was not a final settlement. Mr. Kinsman came to tell me that Whitney had consented to compromise by giving his Note with satisfactory endorsers to which I assented. I put into his hands the demand against Ayer for Collection, being tired out by his want of punctuality. The remainder of my morning was taken up at the Probate Office where I assumed the responsibility of Administrator of New's Estate, signed the Bond and inclosed it to my Father for his signature and John's.[1] The latter I objected to in my own mind, but as two were necessary and I could ask no one else I sent it intimating an understanding that no risk was to be incurred by any one but my Father.

In this manner the morning vanished with great rapidity and I returned home. The afternoon was passed in reading over the Essay I had written and as on the whole I approved of it and thought if I once sent one it would help me to write constantly, I set about copying it, so that now I think I shall send it to Mr. A. H. Everett before the close of the month.[2] Once acquire confidence and I shall do better. My wife thinks the tone too positive and I believe she is right but I am not able to write milk and water. Evening, reading Eustace's Account of Naples to my Wife. It is interesting, though his positive tones ought to give me a lesson how disgusting they are. I afterwards continued copying.

[1] CFA to JQA, 26 April (LbC, Adams Papers). When Thomas Welsh Jr., himself disabled by circumstances from finding a bondsman, had offered CFA the administration of Robert New's estate, which consisted of real property that would have to be sold to satisfy debts that might prove as large as the amount

realized from the sales, CFA had asked his father for guidance. JQA had advised acceptance and had agreed to execute the bond required. (CFA to JQA, 13 March, LbC; JQA to CFA, 19 March; both in Adams Papers.) New had been a hairdresser on Cambridge Street (*Boston Directory*, 1829–1830); his life

story was a melancholy one (below, entries for 14 May; vol. 4, 27 June 1831).

[2] Everett had become the editor of the *North American Review* after he and his associates had purchased it from Jared Sparks (JQA to CFA, 24 March; CFA to JQA, 2 April; JQA to CFA, 8 April; all in Adams Papers).

TUESDAY. 27TH.

Morning bright and somewhat cold. Went to the Office as usual, and occupied myself in my father's Accounts and business affairs. Called to see Kinsman and found that Mr. Ayer was disposed to resist the claim of rent against him, which is very disagreeable indeed but I cannot see how to help it. A writ must be issued. The amount is trifling but the giving up would be making a sanction of injustice, which I never can do. But I dislike exceedingly going into one case when I am barely out of another. I received this day Prentiss Whitney's Note indorsed by Baker and Alexander payable in thirty days, for 308.75 clear of expenses, which is a miserable way of getting off, but it is not my fault.[1] This is the consequence among many others of the [eminently?] negligent system followed during the last Agency. We can only regret what is past. I had this morning another disagreeable business relating to George settled. Mr. Miles Farmer came up for the last time and after various attempts at extortion, which were strenuously resisted he consented to give me a total release of all demands whatsoever if I would give him up his Note which I consented to do.[2] So we exchanged receipts and he went away as I hope not to return to us very soon. I am tired of the sight of his face. Mr. Ayer my Carpenter came in wanting to be paid but I had not the money so was obliged to state the case. My purchase of the Boylston Market Share has embarrassed me. The rest of the time was not well spent.

After dinner I continued writing but felt less satisfied as I went along. Much occurred which puzzled me, and my Wife's conversation distracted me. But I progressed notwithstanding, and the more as this was the evening of the family meeting which takes place late. I went at eight. It was not over agreeable and I was glad to get home. The severity of remark upon writing a little discouraged me.

[1] CFA's total claim against Prentiss Whitney for unpaid rent on the store and house at 23 Court Street amounted to $433. The endorsers, T. M. Baker & E. Alexander Jr., had auction rooms at 81 Washington Street (*Boston Direc-* tory, 1830–1831).

[2] On Farmer's indebtedness to and counterclaims against GWA, see above, entry for 21 Sept. 1829, note, and references there cited.

WEDNESDAY. 28TH.

The morning was cool but agreeable. I went to the Office and occupied myself as usual, in doing little or nothing, yet I seemed employed. Called upon Mr. Kinsman to know whether any thing further had dropped from Ayer, found nothing. Sat down and got involved in a conversation with Mr. Davis about literature which kept me there sitting until after twelve o'clock. He is one of the few young men here of uncommon mind who has known how uncommonly to apply it. And it is a pleasure to have to do with him.[1] It is not a little singular that in a Community abounding so richly in all the means, there should actually exist so little of the end of education, literary excellence. Our system is perhaps slightly superficial in this respect, giving to all some thing and to none a great deal, but if it is so, the general advantage more than counterbalances the particular disadvantage.

I passed the rest of my morning in settling my money operations with my father's books, and in paying Hilliard and Gray, my Mother's subscription to the Juvenile Miscellany which I have stopped.[2] I took up a number of the Quarterly review which contained an Article upon the Speech of Mr. Brougham upon Law reform,[3] but I did not finish it before dinner time. In the afternoon, I wrote with great steadiness upon this Article which I am resolved to complete out of hand and make an experiment. It is well to get a foot hold first and much good may be done afterwards. I have been better satisfied myself than I ever was before, and have found no great occasion to alter or correct. The Evening was passed as usual in reading aloud from Eustace whose enthusiasm in Italy never ceases nor does his hatred of the French, but his style though too pompous is attractive. The glare[4] is tedious and description too much the same, but he pays for it in energy and vividness of colouring. Two hours are thus spent every night when we are at home, and two hours more are devoted to my Work.

[1] Thomas Kemper Davis (1808–1853), son of Isaac P. Davis, and CFA had literary interests so similar that CFA repeatedly records his delight in Davis' company; see, for example, above, entry for 18 Nov. 1829. It was only in later years that Davis applied himself more closely to the law. Early and late his enthusiasm for classical studies was such that upon his death it could be said that "he had read with studious attention every classical author, in the entirety of his works." Also, though he gave little attention to the modern foreign languages and the literature in them, "his acquaintance with English literature was perfect and exhaustive." To his learning and a "prodigious memory" was added a fluency that allowed him "to pour forth at will a perfect cataract of talk." Flavoring all was "a dash of eccentricity of thought and manner, controlled by thorough kindliness of heart and good temper." (A List of the Classical Books of Thomas Kemper Davis, given to Harvard College Library,

1855, by his mother Mrs. Susan Jackson Davis, together with a letter of transmittal from Josiah Quincy to Pres. James Walker and an obituary notice by Edmund Quincy, MS, MH-Ar.)

[2] A bi-monthly magazine, it had been founded in 1826 by Lydia Maria Child, who continued as its editor.

[3] *Quarterly Review*, 38:241–297 (July 1828). Henry Brougham's speech on the "Present State of the Law" was delivered in the House of Commons on 7 Feb. 1828.

[4] That is, *ostentation, showiness*.

THURSDAY 29TH.

Morning delightful. Went to the Office as usual and passed my time in reading with little interruption. Miss Wells only came to pay a month's rent for her Mother and to tell me that it was probable she should not leave the House. I am glad of this as she is the most punctual Tenant I have, and it makes all the arrangements of my real Estate fully and clearly settled. I now have a clear control and hope to go on swimmingly. My difficulties have been considerable owing to the loose mode of carrying on business heretofore pursued, and though I still fear there are black spots yet I hope to be able to prevent the preceding losses from happening at least so heavily again. The road once got smooth it is my fault if it becomes rough again. One of the Conants came from Weston with one of the Horses sick. I immediately had him carried to Mr. Forbes' Stable to be taken care of, but he did not seem to me to be in a very bad condition.

I went to dine according to appointment at Mr. Frothingham's and spent the afternoon in the Athenæum verifying my authorities. I found them all correct, and had some time at my disposal beside, which was passed in rather desultory reading. At the Post office where I obtained a letter from my father inclosing Deacon Spear's Notes which should be paid on Saturday.[1] I did not read it directly, but went for my Wife, and passed an hour eating Oysters. After returning home, occupied some time in reading and writing over my Essay. I begin to think it very superficial.

[1] JQA to CFA, 23 April (Adams Papers).

FRIDAY 30TH.

Morning lovely. One of those warm days in which the body feels languid but not unpleasant. They are rare in this Climate, but we have had several of them this Season. I went to the Office as usual and passed the larger part of the time in bringing up my Account Current with my Father for the month. Called upon Mr. J. H. Foster and paid him his bill for six months past which was no trifle,[1] exceeding one third my estimate of it. These repairs have been enormously expensive. But what was to be done. The Houses could not stand empty. And I do not feel as if I had done more than was absolutely necessary. My father's Agency Affairs require much time and attention, and the responsibility they impose is no trifle.

Called in to see Mr. Brooks for a moment and received a visit from Richardson at my Office. He was dull and I was dull. The fact is that I am getting sobered down. The serious part of life has already set it's hand upon me, for I do not find that elasticity of mind which formerly supported me. Perhaps my present happiness is of a nature more durable and less unequal. But it is a melancholy reflection to see the shores pass as I sail by and to think that I am never to see them again. The bright spots in life and the dark ones, happiness and misery all sink soon into one confused and undistinguishable mass in the distance, and every step closes a part of the view.

I read an Article upon Paley in a number of the Quarterly.[2] It was not very interesting. Another upon De Roos which I had no time to finish.[3] At home. Upon reviewing my Essay, I found a passage that did not please me and so I concluded to write it over again. This consumed one sheet and my Afternoon and Evening. Disgust with me always follows writing, and I liked my words little, but the change momentarily gratified me. Read Eustace to my Wife. Weather very warm.

[1] $115.15 for wallpapers (M/CFA/3).

[2] *Quarterly Review*, 38:305–355 (Oct. 1828), an essay-review of *The Works of William Paley*, 7 vols., London, 1825.

[3] Same, 37:260–297 (Jan. 1828), an essay-review of Lt. Fred. Fitzgerald de Roos, R.N., *Personal Narrative of Travels in the United States and Canada in 1826*, London, 1827.

SATURDAY MAY 1ST.

Morning very warm. Finished my last reading of my Article and all my doubts by writing a note to Mr. Everett and submitting the whole to him.[1] Good, bad or indifferent it is now of very little consequence for the die is cast. Thence to the Office. Deacon Spear called to take up his Notes. He paid me the sum of $408.80 being the amount without interest of the two. I thought this too little but it was so expressed and I could gain no more. This sum was deposited immediately in the Bank to my father's credit.[2] Mr. Tenney my new Tenant in the House behind this Office called to pay me his rent which became due this day; a proceeding which satisfied me very much, for I began to think that the constant failure to pay must proceed from some defect in my management rather than the fault of the Tenants. Called to see

Mr. Kinsman about the suit against Ayer, and on the whole had a very busy day of it, so that I was unable to devote any portion of the time to reading.

Passed the afternoon in writing a letter to my father upon the subjects touched in his of Thursday.[3] And my mind having previously run a good deal upon them gave considerable fluency to my pen. It is the first *differing* letter if I may so express it which I have written this season, and may if the season is not too late bring on something of a controversy.[4] Evening reading Eustace to my Wife as usual after which I passed an hour or two in copying.

[1] Despite some later reservations, A. H. Everett noted its receipt to JQA "with applause" (JQA to CFA, 13 May, Adams Papers), judging that "the literary execution is highly creditable to his taste and talent, as the substance is to his character and principles" (A. H. Everett to JQA, 4 May, Adams Papers).

[2] That is, in JQA's personal as distinct from the Agency account.

[3] JQA to CFA, 23 April; CFA to JQA, 1 May (both in Adams Papers).

[4] The "differences" were on two fronts. In his letter JQA had renewed an earlier dispute over ancient and modern eloquence; CFA, firmly holding to the ancients, in his entered a vigorous rejoinder. The second was of a more personal sort.

Both agreed on the superiority of Grahame to other historians of the American colonial period, and JQA moreover in giving his own interpretation of that history, especially as it related to the Puritans, and in surveying much of the territory that CFA had in his newly completed article, arrived, both in the appraisal of Grahame and of the spirit of liberty among the Puritans, at "exactly similar" conclusions. However, on the matter of the proper limits of the power of the British Parliament to legislate over the colonies and of whether Massachusetts had ever acknowledged that power, CFA registered his disagreement with JQA's views in terms that he was sure would cause JQA to think that his son had come under the heavy influence of Tory and "Scotch Jacobin" writers.

In his dissenting but excellently humored response (13 May, Adams Papers) to CFA's views, JQA affirmed that "the deductions which will naturally flow from that doctrine upon affairs arising in your own times, may be neither congenial to our institutions nor likely to prove acceptable to your Countrymen. Their tendency is to an overestimate of the rights of authority, and an under-estimate of the rights of the People." But, he concluded, "the course of your life, as well as the habitual meditation which you bestow upon all the topics which are likely to influence your practice has so far reconciled me to your political heresy that I willingly leave to time and experience the further modifications of opinions to which your continued sober enquiries after truth may hereafter lead you."

SUNDAY. 2D.

Morning cloudy with a mild wind blowing from the South. I decided upon remaining in town until eleven o'clock, during which time I finished copying my letter to my Father and arranged my Study which bore the marks of considerable reading without method. It ought to be a person's business to restore books to their places at least once a month or so. Without it a Library soon becomes a mass of confusion.

We had two or three Spring showers which served to render the air agreeable. At eleven we went out to Medford as usual, and found the face of things changed since our last visit from Winter to Spring. I took a short walk and mused in a tone half pleasing, half melancholy, the family had not returned from Meeting. They finally came accompanied by Mary Hall who dined here. The afternoon was passed at Meeting—A Sermon from Mr. Stetson extremely uninteresting to me. Afterwards time wasted listlessly. Evening, Mr. Jonathan Brooks —An amusing original.

MONDAY. 3RD.

The morning commenced very mild and pleasant but did not continue so. Clouds began to collect and we had hardly started from Medford on our return before the wind became east and put a stop to all the enjoyment of Spring. Having arrived I went directly to my Office. Made an inquiry about the Horse and found he had been taken ill and as Mr. Forbes inclined to believe, would not live. This is disagreeable news. But it cannot be avoided. Morning little interrupted. Mr. Hollis called to make his Quarterly Settlement. The balance against him is still large. I was as usual obliged to take his Note. Made a settlement also of his Writ against Mrs. Bittner, and gave up his Execution for him to deal with her as he thought best. Called to see Mr. Kinsman and inquire of him about the issue of the suit against Ayer. He had not yet made the Writ; I was sorry but think on the whole that it was as well. He began directly and the Writ was made before I left the room which will decide whether this does or not go to trial.

The remainder of my time was passed in reading Marshall, with whom I feel less and [less] [1] pleased as I proceed. He has little independence and all reliance upon a set of authors whom he condescends to praise, without being aware of the tendency of their books against the best principles of his Countrymen. Afternoon, having compared a portion of my grandfather's Correspondence for Mr. Sparks, I passed the remainder reading Mr. Chalmers. Mr. A. H. Everett sent me a Note to say that my Article could not appear until October which is a matter of regret to me as it will thus interfere with Mr. Quincy, but it cannot be helped. [2] Evening reading Eustace to my Wife, after which Chalmers who makes me exceedingly angry.

[1] Word omitted in MS.
[2] Everett's letter is missing. CFA is perhaps referring to the likelihood that President Josiah Quincy's scheduled oration at the celebration in September of Boston's founding would cover much of the same ground, and that in the normal course its pamphlet publication would come at about the time of the appearance of the October issue of the *Review*.

TUESDAY. 4TH.

Morning cold with an Easterly wind and a heavy rain. Went to the Office and passed my morning in reading Marshall attentively—My time having little interruption. A little shocked at the blindness with which such a man as Judge M[arshall] has followed the English Writers, without appearing to think that he is committing gross injustice to the character of his Countrymen, and still more disgusted that he should have been willing to praise them as he does, in his Preface. But it takes much time to become perfectly disenthralled from the mental after the civil power of others has been defied. We have long ceased to obey their Officers of War, or Peace, but we still remain subjected to the decided dogmas of their High Priests of Literature. How long this may endure it is impossible to say.

The rain passed away by dinner time. Afternoon occupied in reading Chalmers, whose misrepresentations provoke me exceedingly. He makes a most unfair representation of the early History of New England and puts in his wise saws and modern instances with the feeling of a man berating his enemy with reproachful words, rather than talking calmly of the history of the past.

I finished an Article in the Quarterly review upon Dr. Dwights Travels rather more good natured to the United States than such usually are.[1] And was prevented reading Eustace by the appearance of Edmund Quincy who spent the evening here.

[1] *Quarterly Review*, 30:1–40 (Oct. 1823); an essay-review of *Travels in New England and New York* by Timothy Dwight, the president of Yale. CFA's comment would seem to be directed toward the tone of the review rather than that of the book.

WEDNESDAY. 5TH.

Morning clear and mild. Another of the delicious days we have had this Spring. I have never known a pleasanter season in this Climate, and though the rapidity of the advance may check the fruits by a return of frost, I yet cannot help feeling as if we were fully paid for the risk perhaps for some loss. Called to pay a bill for China made a present to Mrs. Walker by my Wife at the marriage of the former. An old account. Then to see about the Horse of whom I received a most discouraging Account. I fear his case is decided. Then to the Post Office where I received from my father two letters—One returning the Bond executed,[1] the other inclosing two Pamphlets and a most bitter Satire upon the powers of the Nation.[2] I have rarely known him to deal in such excessive gall, but as it is only to me, the thing matters little. I should hardly feel desirous to have it disclosed to the world for they would attribute it to a motive which is far from the operating one.

Mr. Kinsman came in to pay me a debt of Mr. Ayer which I had ordered to be sued.[3] The writ settled the thing, and I believe it is all I now have to trouble me. Patience and perseverance have thus carried me through all the embarrassments of this season. My Agency affairs are on infinitely better footing, and I have cause to thank God for guiding me in the straight path which has brought me nearly out of my difficulties.

My time passed away rapidly in this way and I did not have a moment for Marshall. Afternoon taken up in writing a reply to my father which was tolerably good though infinitely qualified from his severity.[4] I say tolerably good but I hardly dare to think so. Evening very short, read a little of Eustace to my Wife and afterwards Chalmers.

[1] 30 April (Adams Papers).
[2] 28 April (Adams Papers). Of the pamphlets enclosed (both missing), one was on the U.S. Bank, the other, signed "Algernon Sidney," on the Presidential succession. The satire by JQA was contained in the letter itself.
[3] The net amount received in settlement was $41.67 (M/CFA/3).
[4] CFA to JQA, LbC, Adams Papers.

THURSDAY. 6TH.

Morning rainy but warm. The weather cleared up however very shortly afterwards and produced another lovely day. I went to the Office and passed most of my morning in reading Marshall, the interesting portion of whose history I have now finished. In reflecting upon what I should do next, I felt a marvellous inclination to take up Æschines and Demosthenes, though not a little awed by the amount of the labour which will be necessary to do any thing with it. I went to Hilliard's Store to see what was to be done and upon examining the work of Mr. Negris I thought I would purchase and go directly to work to see whether something could not be done out of it.[1] I propose to begin upon it coolly, to devote six months to the materials and the composition and if necessary to give two months more to the perfection. If I can make nothing more out of it, my labour will still not be lost. Called in to see Mr. Brooks who notified me of the birth of a son to Mrs. Everett, a matter which will delight them all—As Mr. Everett has been long regretting his want of one. Afternoon passed in my beginning of the Book of Mr. Negris, and found myself quite surprised that I had made myself so fully master of the text in my previous reading, but the Notes are very good. I read ten or fifteen pages easily. Evening Eustace to my Wife, after which I tried with little success to throw together some preliminary thoughts.

[1] On Alexander Negris' edition of *The Orations of Æschines and Demosthenes on The Crown* in the original Greek with English notes, and on CFA's efforts at a translation, see above entry for 26 Oct. 1829, note 4.

FRIDAY 7TH.

Morning clear with a cool West Wind blowing pretty strong. I went to the Office as usual and sat myself down to study Demosthenes with attention and to try my hand at translation. I expected to have proceeded much more rapidly than I did and found accurate translation to be difficult. Something must be given to the genius of the tongue. But my purpose will be at first to be sure to get the precise sense after which I shall be better able to render it into elegant English. Translation is more difficult than composition inasmuch as it requires that two languages should be made to convey the same ideas in the same spirit. But my occupation was so interesting as to engross me very much so that I did not go to see Mr. Brooks as I should have done. Afternoon passed in reading more of Æschines. It is now I find the benefit of having read this work, for I am no more puzzled and distracted by ignorance of words and thus since yesterday have read thirty pages in Negris which before cost me a month. I now also see the beauty of the style. I was able to pursue the subject until late in the evening as my Wife was out, and I only went down for an hour to Mrs. Frothingham's where we had a pleasant little Oyster Supper, and returned early.

SATURDAY 8TH.

Morning fine although the weather was very considerably cold. I went to the Office after receiving a visit from Miss Oliver my Tenant who paid me forty dollars of her rent on account and thus relieved me from much of my anxiety respecting that House. She has now materially diminished the weight of her debt, and having received a polite warning from me proves one of the most anxious to pay. My father's real Estate is now in the best condition, all the Tenants being now about to manifest the result of my care, in their increased sensibility to the duty of punctuality which had become somewhat dulled. After balancing my books at the Bank, and inquiring for the condition of the Horse which this morning was a little encouraging, I spent the rest of the time at the Office in translating more of Mr. Negris, and felt as if I had succeeded better today.

After dinner I went to see the furniture of Madame de Walewsky formerly Mrs. Humphreys who made a silly match, and now leaves

Boston to follow her husband, probably an impostor wherever he chooses to say. I know of no instance of greater folly in a woman, likely to be attended with more unfortunate circumstances to herself. Her large fortune will probably vanish under his hands, and then she is an old woman tied to a young and unprincipled spendthrift.[1] I could not help thinking of this when looking at her house, which was all comfortably and some of it splendidly fitted up. Returned home and read Æschines for two hours, after which I had agreed to go to Medford. Owing to the confinement of Mrs. Everett Mr. Brooks is left quite alone down there, and I therefore thought it would answer to go and spend two evenings instead of one. The evening was fine but cold and I thought I would vary our ride by going through Milk Row and the Old road near West Cambridge. We were paid for it in the beauty of the scenery which now shows the luxuriant freshness of the Season. I know nothing finer than the appearance of the Apple Orchards here in the month of May. Our ride was agreeable and we reached Medford directly after Sunset. The evening passed in conversation with Mr. Brooks.

[1] Mrs. Ann F. Humphreys was the wealthy widow of Gen. [properly, Col.] David Humphreys. Her property had been further enhanced by a bequest of $150,000 from her sister. On 31 Dec. 1829 she had married Col. de Walewsky, a Polish gentleman who was said to have served in Napoleon's army. She was 51, he 41. At his insistence that any other arrangement would be an offense to his honor, she allowed all her property to pass to his control. In the months after marriage the house became "a resort for the young rakes of the town who have been treated by the Col. with fine dinners and choice wines." The marriage, the ménage, and the reasons animating their removal from Boston evoked interest and gossip. The furniture, wines, &c. were on display at the residence, corner of Sumner and Mt. Vernon streets, and were to be sold there at auction on 10 May at 9 o'clock. (CFA to LCA, 17 Jan., Adams Papers; Charlotte Everett to Edward Everett, 4, 10, 24 Jan., 2 May, Everett MSS, MHi; *Columbian Centinel,* 5 May, p. 3, col. 6.)

SUNDAY 9TH.

The morning was fine but cold, and there had been a slight frost which tinged the leaves of the Clover, but Mr. Brooks thought not enough yet to injure the buds. The air continued so cold however throughout the day as to make me think that it would not pass off without nipping the fine promise of fruit. We attended divine service and heard Mr. Newell the Clergyman of Cambridge who graduated there the year before me.[1] He has been much praised for his ability and at College he stood high, but I confess that he very much disappointed me. It was artificial, laboured, and not striking. His thoughts were old and common place dressed very gaudily. Thus it is with many who are highly praised at Cambridge. They enter the world on too high a scale, and therefore run the chance of falling much more than rising. It is true that this is not always the case for great talent will force it's way through every obstacle, but I cannot help thinking now as I did when at College that the safest way for a man distrusting his abilities was to begin small and attempt things gradually.

I passed my loose time in reading a review of Mr. Cambreleng's report written at Baltimore, a pretty good thing and very thoroughly destroying all his sophistry. But Mr. Cambreleng is a thorough paced Englishman, turned New Yorker.[2] Evening, Messrs. J. Brooks and Furness, neighbours of Mr. Brooks came in, and the former entertained me with his conversation as usual. I think he is one of the few men you can properly style original.

[1] Rev. William Newell, Harvard 1824.

[2] On C. C. Cambreleng, a spokesman for the Jackson administration in the House, see vol. 2:35, 74, 151. His anti-protectionist *Report on the Commercial Intercourse with Foreign Nations* delivered 8 Feb. as chairman of the House Committee on Commerce and Navigation was ordered printed at government expense (*Niles' Register*, 37:422 [13 Feb. 1830]). In early April in Baltimore had appeared a pamphlet, *A Review of Mr. Cambreleng's Late Report from the Committee on Commerce*, by "Mephistopheles," i.e. Hezekiah Niles or someone closely associated with him in the cause of "the American system" (same, 38: 121, 137–138 [10, 17 April]). The charge that Cambreleng's position was to the benefit of Great Britain rather than of the United States was included (same, 38:156 [24 April]).

MONDAY 10TH.

Morning bright but very cold, for the season. There was a frost more severe than that yesterday morning, but whether it affected the fruit remains to be seen. This is certainly something of a drawback upon this Climate. We returned to town, but I felt cold and out of order all day. Went to the sale of Mrs. Humphreys things, but could not stay owing to the crowd and my disgust at being in such a place. Went from thence to the Office, after having given in my Probate bonds and obtained my Papers of Administration upon New's Estate. I have now assumed this trust and hope I shall be able to carry it through, without making any mistake. The balance of my time was occupied in copying the Papers.

My afternoon was not spent profitably as I felt heavy and my Greek progressed slowly. I made up much of my deficiency however in the evening. It is a true test of the thorough character of study to review it soon after when the parts which were skimmed over will again present difficulty. But on the whole my former reading was pretty solid.

My wife was unwell all day. Her health is failing totally much to my regret. This is the first trouble of married life and the greatest, as it creates anxiety of the deepest character. The Physician has been attending her for months without apparently bringing about any favourable change.[1] P. Chardon Brooks and his Wife came in and spent an hour or so in conversation. They are persons with very good feelings but I am sorry to say that the latter is a little dangerous. I must beware, for I sometimes as I did tonight say a wrong thing. It was again quite cold.

[1] Dr. J. Greely Stevenson (M/CFA/9).

TUESDAY 11TH.

The weather was cold and cheerless, and Abby was quite sick with a head ach so that I felt rather dull. Made inquiries about the Horse and received discouraging Accounts again. Indeed after reading what I saw in the Encyclopedia about the glanders, I have little expectation of his recovery. Mr. J. Y. Champney called and paid me the balance of his rent due on the 1st of April. This was unexpected, but it makes me quite easy, on that score. My Tenants now pay very well. I have no arrears excepting Hollis and Oliver. The former will require pretty strong management, for I shall never get any money out of him. The rest of my day was taken up in copying the Papers of Administration and studying the law upon them, which I find to be tolerably complicated. My course is not a perfectly clear one. I read the leading case making Administrators liable in their private capacity for a warranty of the title of their intestate, in the capacity of Administrator. Had no other time.

After dinner I read Æschines assiduously so that before I went to bed, I had finished the Oration against Ctesiphon. Thus have I done in six days what occupied me before two months. I also passed the evening in reading to my Wife from my Father's tour in Silesia.[1]

[1] CFA owned a copy of the edition of JQA's *Letters on Silesia, Written during a Tour through that Country*, published without the author's knowledge at London in 1804, now in MQA. It had borne the title "Journal of a Tour through Silesia" on its original appearance serially in *The Port Folio*, vol. 1, 3 Jan.–7 Nov. 1801.

WEDNESDAY. 12TH.

Morning clear and a little pleasanter, but still somewhat cheerless. This weather coming after that which was so pleasant makes the feeling of it just so much worse. I was tempted to diverge a little from my path and drop into Cunningham's Auction room where I found the books of Mrs. Humphreys going for little or nothing. There were many French and Spanish works which I should have been much pleased to have possessed and for a moment or two the temptation was exceedingly strong to remain. I mastered it however by going away. For me of all persons it is the highest degree of absurdity to purchase books—Having at my own house a very respectable collection of works, and at my Father's a very large one.

At the Office my time was passed in reading over the laws respecting Administration upon intestate insolvent Estates. And I then devoted an hour to Æschines, making some progress. But at my Office I have no facilities, and though my business which should properly take up my time here is not sufficient without hazarding much waste, yet in attempting to make any other use of the moments, I find myself as if working out of the line. Afternoon, began Demosthenes, whose Oration I find much harder on this second reading. Probably because I took only the sense when I went before. Evening reading the Tour in Silesia for an hour to my wife, and Demosthenes for two by myself.

THURSDAY. 13TH.

Morning cloudy, and threatening rain, which however did not come on heavily during the day. We had a few slight showers rather pleasant than otherwise. I saw nothing remarkable and found at my Office no occupation excepting writing out my Translation of Æschines which lags somewhat. It is a heavy work and the more I think of my own powers, the less I feel myself able to draw any conclusions favourable to my prosecuting my design. Should the article I wrote for the North American ever appear, I shall then be better able to form some clear idea of the probability of my success.

A man named Morse called to purchase the equities of redemption of New's estates. He wanted to make a speculation out of them and offered what I thought was very little. I told him that I could do nothing about them now. Mr. Degrand called to offer par for my father's Stock in the State Bank, about which I wrote to him immediately.[1] I do not know whether it would be advisable to sell or no.

Dined at Mr. Frothingham's very pleasantly with my Wife and Mr. Brooks. He gave us specimens of his new purchases of wines. None very excellent, many quite good, and all cheap. After dinner I went to the Gallery at the Athenæum and mused over the Pictures,[2] the afternoon was not favourable, and on the whole I was not so much pleased as I expected. But I must go again. Read a little of the Works of Mr. Jefferson and returned for Abby at nine, but too sleepy to work.

[1] CFA to JQA, LbC, Adams Papers.

[2] Designed to house the Athenæum's collection of paintings and thus the forerunner of Boston's Museum of Fine Arts, the Gallery occupied the top floor of the three-story addition, sixty feet long and fifty wide, built in the rear of and detached from the library of the Athenæum on Pearl Street. The building is visible in an engraving of the Athenæum reproduced in the present volume. The great room, twenty feet high, was lighted

"only from the top." A loan exhibition had been held each spring since 1827 to which the public was admitted on the payment of an admission charge (Mabel M. Swan, *The Athenæum Gallery, 1827-1873* ..., Boston, 1940, p. 10). The current exhibition had opened on 10 May and was to remain on view each day from 9 A.M to dusk until 17 July (*Boston Patriot*, 10 May, p. 2, col. 5; p. 4, col. 2). It was reviewed in six articles signed A.B. (same, 14–26 May).

FRIDAY. 14TH.

Morning dark with heavy rain. Went to the Office as usual. No letters from my father which I cannot help thinking a little strange. Something must be the matter to keep him so very silent about his coming in this direction. I am afraid it is again my Mother. My own spirits are much affected by this idea. But it cannot be helped. The great misfortune for a man is to marry and live at a distance from his natural home, for his Wife never gets a taste for her husband's proper residence, and this keeps him away from it.

The greater part of my morning was passed in my translation of Æschines which in this manner progressed exceedingly. I am engaged at present in ascertaining the meaning merely and design to beautify afterwards. Only one person came in, with an Account against New's Estate, and he gave me some account of the man, his life and the causes of his death. Intemperance, a natural leaning to which increased by the misconduct of all his children, brought him to his grave just as he saw the close of his property. He probably dies insolvent.

Afternoon continued Demosthenes but somewhat superficially as I had forgotten Negris and was therefore aware that I must go over it again. The style is very different and much more close than that of Æschines. I progressed rapidly during the afternoon and evening. And succeeded in reading a good deal to my Wife from the Tour in Silesia.

SATURDAY. 15TH.

Morning cloudy, but it cleared up in the course of the day into very fine weather. At the Office as usual. Little or nothing of interest occurred. I was busy in translating in which I made great progress. But it is dry and disagreeable work. I do not relish it much. No interruption at all. Went to the Bank and put in Prentiss Whitneys Note for Collection. This will settle that business in one way or the other, and get me out of another scrape in which I had thought myself deeply engaged. It remains to wind up with him his other small demands, about which I feel exceedingly unwilling—He having behaved in so very shabby a manner. But those demands must be settled.

Called for a moment to see Mr. Brooks after which I returned to the Office and continued Æschines. As my Wife wanted to go to Medford to pay some visits, I agreed to ride out early after dinner. We accordingly started at four and stopped at Mrs. Gray's, and afterwards at Mrs. Hall's, Abby's two Aunts. The former we did not find, the latter was upstairs and I did not see. After staying a short time, we went to Mr. Brooks. Found Edward Brooks and his Wife just leaving there for Boston. The evening was short, for Mr. B. and I took a ramble on the banks of the Canal and enjoyed the pleasantness of the west Wind. We went as far as the Farm which belonged to my Uncle and is mortgaged to my Father.[1] It is a fine situation and by a Tenant who could improve it would make a great Estate for the Country—But as it is, brings little or nothing. My Uncle obtains whatever benefit there is in it. We saw also the Aqueduct over Medford River which has just been made. A substantial work and likely to be durable.[2] But this Canal may after all be only finishing itself as a sacrifice to the rage of rail road improvement. Evening reading and Conversation.

[1] Originally JA's, the milk farm of eighty acres was owned in common by TBA and Rev. Joseph Barlow Felt of Hamilton. It lay to the south of the river on both sides of the canal about a mile southeast of the Brooks residence and a quarter of a mile west of Medford's center. See above p. xviii; *Boston Patriot*, 24 Nov. 1827, p. 3, col. 4; JQA to GWA, 4 Dec. 1827, Adams Papers.

[2] The walk along the canal from the Brooks Stone Bridge southward to the river was just over half a mile. The canal's course was through Brooks' lands along what is now Sagamore Avenue, under a bridge on the road to West Cambridge, now High Street, then along the present Boston Avenue to Medford Lock. Beyond it, the canal spanned the river by aqueduct. Both lock and aqueduct had been built in 1804. In 1829 the earlier supporting structure of wood was replaced with stone. The aqueduct and the course of the canal through Medford are illustrated in this volume. See above, p. xviii and xix; Roberts, *The Middlesex Canal, 1793–1860*, p. 195; and Lewis M. Lawrence, The Middlesex Canal, Boston, 1942 [processed], p. 110.

SUNDAY. 16TH.

The morning was fine but the air cold. The Wind having again become somewhat easterly. We attended divine service morning and afternoon and heard Mr. Stetson. He is quite a tedious preacher to me. I saw little in him to day to like. He may be a man of sense, but his way of shewing it is not attractive. We were very much alone at Mr. Brooks', and I felt today more than ever the vacuum occasioned by the death of Mrs. B. There is a kind of loneliness about it, particularly now when Mrs. Everett is upstairs which is very affecting. So different was it last year though her fate was then impending and how much more so the year before when I went up about this time and saw there Dr. and Mrs. Thayer of Lancaster.[1]

This is the last page of the first volume of my Married life.[2] Nine months have passed away very pleasantly, and my only regret is that my Wife is not with Child. I had hoped on her account much more than my own that she would have had an infant to soothe her loneliness. But it has not so turned out, and upon reflection I have had so many blessings showered upon me that I ought not to complain. I do not complain. This period of my life has had few things to make it bitter. And I feel too full of gratitude for what has been allowed me by a beneficent Creator, not to submit without a murmur to a privation his supreme wisdom has subjugated me to. My wife has lost a kind and indulgent Mother, but the blow had been so long coming that its force was broken. Its approach was gradual, and her sufferings were too melancholy to allow of much deep regret. Yet after all, she was a woman with as many fine domestic qualities, as in my life I ever saw, and to her family, her loss is not reparable. In general however my comforts have been many and my enjoyments great. May the future be as agreeable as the past, though this may be a presumptuous wish, I yet must hope it with humility.

The evening was chilly. Mr. and Mrs. Story, Miss Gray and her brother came and passed an hour in the evening,[3] and William G. Brooks another, so that the time rapidly glided away.

[1] See vol. 2:240.

[2] That is, of the volume (D/CFA/5) which CFA had used earlier for diary entries but put aside, then returned to as to a new volume on the day following his marriage; see above, entry for 4 Sept. 1829 and note 1.

[3] Francis A. Gray (1813–1888), ABA's first cousin, was Elizabeth (Gray) Story's and Henrietta Gray's youngest brother; see Brooks, Waste Book, 1 Oct. 1827; *Medford Historical Register*, 21 (1918):30.

No. 6   Diary

17 May 1830

31 December 1831 [1]

He, that hath passed the day without attention to the task assigned him, may be certain, that the lapse of life has brought him no nearer to his object; for whatever idleness may expect from time, it's produce will be only in proportion to the diligence with which it has been used.

Adventurer. No. 69.

[1] Titlepage of D/CFA/8 (Adams Papers, Microfilms, Reel No. 60), which begins where D/CFA/5, 2d *part*, ends and in which are contained all the journal entries CFA made between the terminal dates named on the titlepage. An explanation of the discrepancy between CFA's numbering of his Diary volumes and the Adams Papers serial numbering appears at vol. 1:xxxvii–xxxviii; see also, above, entry for 4 Sept. 1829, note. For a description of this Diary MS and of the other MSS from which the printed text of vols. 3 and 4 is derived, see the Introduction.

DIARY. MAY 1830

Medford–Boston [1]

MONDAY. 17TH.

Upon commencing another Volume, I always feel disposed to attempt some new method of keeping my Journal, which will have some improvements upon the ancient mode. But not having much to record it is not necessary to condense, and the old way after all suits my taste and my habits. There is now no good reason to change it. The practice of keeping a Diary is a part of my father's instruction to his Children. I believe I now am the only one of them who has persevered in it. Not that I have been without my qualms and hesitations. Most men's lives are not worth a daily laboured record. Why should I consider myself superior to the mass of beings? As a mere matter of value, a man's private Journal ranks low, and if I confined myself purely to such considerations I should never write a page in one again, but to me it has produced indirect results of considerable consequence in being the sole cause of a tolerable ease in style, which no part of a common education would have given me. It is an every day exercise in composition, and he who does not improve by it almost without any effort of his own, must be either a fool, or totally and wilfully negligent. My only surprise with me,[2] is far from flattering to my vanity, that I have not improved more. But he who writes indolently and is afraid to correct for fear of blotting his page will make but slow progress. Few men's first thoughts merit immediate transcription, and I may safely say that I have advanced more rapidly within a few months by studying corrections of style and finish of thought, than in all my preceding years. Yet had I not by my Journal habituated myself to labour in writing, I might have been deterred at the threshold. Enough, however about this.

I awoke at Medford, in the midst of a strong Easterly Storm, which was not so agreeable to my eyes as I could have wished. But after considering whether I would hazard my Wife in it or leave her at Medford, I could not decide upon the latter and so wrapped her up and we started after breakfast. The rain fell very straight and so did not materially affect us.

We reached home, and I went to the Office. My time was passed in translating Æschines, a work in which I progress but slowly. But it will if persevered in assist me more than any thing in the knowledge of labouring composition. Little or no interruption took place. I felt a little depressed at not receiving letters from home, for there has been no similar interval since my father left us.[3] Afternoon engaged in reading Demosthenes. New beauties strike me in this perusal, particularly his fine use of figures. I am as yet however barely skin deep in this Author, yet after finishing the Silesian letters to my Wife, I had the presumption to begin a critical notice of the Oration upon the Crown.

[1] By the name of a city (or cities), CFA begins here to indicate regularly his abode, or changes in it, during the period covered by each journal entry. At times he includes also the city in which a large part of the day was spent. See the Introduction for a description of his practice in entering the information in the MS and for a statement of the course which has been followed in adapt-ing the MS usage to the printed text.

[2] Thus in MS.

[3] The last letter from JQA had been received on 5 May. JQA, suffering from a prolonged and severe catarrhal cough and lumbago as well as an inflammation of the kidneys, was spending his days in reading, principally Cicero (Diary, 8–12 May).

TUESDAY. 18TH.

Morning cloudy and dull but subsequently cleared up. At the Office rather earlier than usual expecting to see a man on Mr. New's business. He came but I got little satisfaction from him. My head is now somewhat puzzled as to the proper course to take. Nearly all the morning went in translating Æschines which is a solemn piece of labour. Called for a moment on Mr. Brooks and having become sick of the monotony of my occupation, I sat down and tried at a draught of a political paper upon the present state of affairs. Wrote half a page three times over and did not like the result much. Afternoon at home. Considerable progress in the Oration for Ctesiphon. Came to the noble passage, called the Adjuration—A style of eloquence truly heroic.

At last, I received this evening a letter from my Father with a Note from my Mother giving some intimation of my probable residence this Summer.[1] The two do not agree in their Account of the arrangements for their Journey. And I am in a puzzle between them. But experience has taught me there is no knowing what will happen, from any discussion of it in our family a week beforehand, and I shall on that account pay but little serious attention to Quincy until another letter comes. Evening, as my wife reads Moore's Life of Byron,[2] I take out the good parts of Don Juan, both for the beauty of the poetry and as an illustration of the work.

[1] JQA to CFA, 13 May (Adams Papers); the letter from LCA is missing. JQA announced his intent to leave Washington on 25 May and to arrive at Quincy by the 29th; LCA would follow, traveling more at leisure.

[2] Thomas Moore, *Letters and Journals of Lord Byron, with Notices of his Life*, 2 vols., London, 1830.

WEDNESDAY. 19TH.

Morning bright. Went to the Office as usual, and sat down to my translation in which I made some progress. My interruptions were of a trifling character until twelve. Mr. Brigham from Quincy called to ask me whether I would purchase any Canal Shares at Quincy. I declined as well from inclination as necessity. My father has too many there for his interest, as I think. And I have need of immediate income. Mr. Brooks stopped in for a minute about some things he had for us, which sent me home, from whence, I thought I would seize the opportunity to go to the Gallery and waste an hour in lounging. Met there Dr. Davis and had a pleasant chat with him. He is a young man of a good deal of sense, and somewhat above the ordinary run of our youth. The Gallery pleased me better today.

Returned home and passed the afternoon in reading Demosthenes in which my progress was rapid. But I find that I a little slighted the latter part in my former reading. It is now necessary to finish in order to get ready for our removal. My review of it will scarcely succeed. I wrote a short answer to my Father which I barely got ready in time.[1] Then amused myself by reading to my Wife from Moore's Life of

Byron, a miserably compiled work though very interesting in itself, from the richness of the materials.

¹ LbC in Adams Papers. CFA proposed that, since his house in Boston would be closed for the summer, their three servants be employed at Quincy.

THURSDAY. 20TH.

Morning delightfully pleasant. Went to the Office and occupied myself a short time in writing an Article which I talk of contributing to a Newspaper by way of amusement. But I did not nearly finish it, from being interrupted first by my Uncle who came at last to claim the amount for the schooling of his Son which has been appropriated by my father to that purpose. He sat with me for some time, and while he was there Mr. Savage came in to inquire about a paper of my Grandfather's which he had often seen published but could not find. His object was to know whether I could lead him to it. I told him I would see about it.¹ I then went to an Auction to see whether I could make some convenient purchases for Quincy.² But without any success. At home found Miss Julia Gorham who was spending the day with my Wife. She is a pleasant as well as a sensible girl. Went out to the Auction again in the Afternoon but my walk in the shower which fell heavily about that time was all the benefit I received for my pains. The bad things were sacrificed but the good ones they were too wise to put up. Returned home and read the Oration for the Crown nearly to it's close, which took me until nearly the proper hour to go to Edward Brooks as we had been invited. Found there only Mr. and Mrs. Frothingham as Company. We had a very pleasant time and returned home at a seasonable hour.

¹ James Savage (1784–1873), one of the founders of the Boston Athenæum and long active in the Massachusetts Historical Society (president, 1841–1855), devoted himself largely to antiquarian pursuits (*DAB*). The paper he wished was the letter of JA to John Jay, 2 June 1785 (LbC, Adams Papers; printed in JA, *Works*, 8:255–259). CFA sent Savage a copy with the proviso that the docu-

ment not be published without the consent of JQA (CFA to Savage, 22 May, LbC, Adams Papers). Savage's work as editor is referred to below, entry for 26 June, note; entries for 27 June, 29 July.

² The stock of the Furniture Commission Co. was sold on the premises, Milk Street, beginning at 9 o'clock (*Boston Patriot*, 20 May, p. 3, col. 4).

FRIDAY. 21ST.

Morning clear but cool. Went to the Office after calling at several places to see about the different sorts of things necessary to be sent to Quincy. I almost made up my Mind upon several articles of Furniture which were offered at what appeared to me very fair prices, and I came very near an agreement with Forbes about a horse and Chaise for the Season. At the Office my time was spent for the most part in looking over the Papers of New upon which I have undertaken to Administer, but I only found enough to make it a little subject of regret that I took it at all. I see nothing but debts and bad paper which has accummulated on his hands.

As Abby let me know she was going to Medford with Mrs. Frothingham, I thought I would accept her husband's invitation that I should dine with him. After dinner returned to my Study and copied for Mr. Savage the letter he requested of me. This occupied me all the time that I did not spend in looking over the Copies for Sparks. Received Letters from the Post Office this Evening from John and my father.[1] The former informing me his Wife was coming, the latter authorizing me to sell the Stock of the State Bank. My plans are changed, and I wrote in reply that I should *not* go to Quincy.[2] But my time passed so that I hardly saw my Wife.

[1] The letter from JA2 is missing; that from JQA was written on 17 May (Adams Papers).

[2] To JQA (LbC, Adams Papers). CFA, to explain the reversal, wrote that the earlier decision to spend the summer in Quincy had been made despite considerable inconvenience to himself and ABA and some opposition from Mr. Brooks, but now that Mrs. JA2 and child were to be in the house "the only idea which overbalanced all these considerations, your and my Mother's probable solitude at Quincy, is not to have any foundation, my most advisable course is to stay where I am."

SATURDAY. 22ND.

My letters received last evening discomposed me very considerably. They changed my plans essentially as I do not feel willing to go to Quincy to take the chance of a divided empire, and yet I regret the loss of the Society of my Father. But after all I have so much comfort and pleasure in my own house with the knowledge that it is mine, and that my Wife is properly Mistress of it, that it is not worth the risk, to remove from it.

My first proceeding was to go upon Change and inquire what it was worth while to do about the Stock in the State Bank. I satisfied myself that it was worth more than par and went to my Office where I wrote out for the Press a political Article. Mr. Degrand called to know what the answer was to his offer and I told him, not that my Father accepted his former proposal, but that I wanted sixty and a half for sixty dollars, to which he assented, and the sale was agreed upon. I then negociated with him and he agreed to keep the Money until August, paying four and a half per Cent with these shares as

Collateral Security, to be referred to my father.[1] So much for business. I did little or nothing more. My friend Richardson came in and passed half an hour. And I agreed to go to the Athenæum at one. Accordingly we went and lounged for the hour before dinner. At home found my Wife quite sick—So that Richardson and I dined alone.

After dinner, I rode to Quincy on John's Affairs, to see William Greenleaf and to give directions about the House. Found things in much better order than I anticipated. William Greenleaf has an offer from John of a situation in his Flour business. But he would give no answer today so that I might have spared my pains.[2] Called to see my Uncle and his family. Found them well. Miss Elizabeth as usual on an expedition with her Lover. Having given all the orders possible, I returned. My Wife sick, lonely and out of spirits. I was obliged to close and dispatch two letters by this Mail before I could sit with her.[3] She suffers a good deal.

[1] The sale of 71 shares in the State Bank brought $4,295.50 (M/CFA/3). A large part of the amount realized was needed to pay to Thomas B. Adams Jr., upon his 21st birthday in August, his share as one of JA's heirs.

[2] Later, Greenleaf did decide to accept JA2's offer and set off at once for Washington (JQA to JA2, 28 May, Adams Papers).

[3] To JA2 (Adams Papers) and to JQA (LbC, Adams Papers). In the first, CFA wrote "I need not say that both my Wife and I shall feel exceedingly happy in seeing Mary as often as possible here as well as at Quincy." This proved sufficient to persuade JA2 and his wife that she should go to Quincy as had been intended before CFA's letter to JQA of the 21st arrived to provoke a "flurry" and consequent change in plan (JQA, Diary, 25–26 May).

SUNDAY. 23RD.

My wife was so unwell this Morning that we did not make any attempt to leave town. I went to Meeting at Mr. Frothingham's for the first time for several months. Heard him preach morning and Afternoon. His Sermons are highly laboured, and in themselves finished pieces of Composition, though the thoughts run hard. There is no natural and easy flow which is attractive even in its redundancy. I have noticed that his best Sermons are preached in the Afternoon. Probably because they are selected from the best of his efforts for a considerable period of time. My principal occupation was the correcting Copies for Mr. Sparks, which with all the time today I did not entirely finish. Mr. and Mrs. Frothingham, Miss Carter and Dr. Stevenson called to see my Wife. Evening, a Sermon of Dr. Barrow's,[1] and an attempt to write which failed.

[1] CFA continued to read the sermons of Isaac Barrow until very late in life. In the edition (5 vols., London, 1823) in MQA which has GWA's signature and JQA's bookplate, CFA has written the date at which he read each of the ser-

mons; many were read more than once and at intervals of as much as forty years. CFA's bookplate is in vols. 3, 4, and 6 of another edition (6 vols., Edinburgh, 1751), of which vols. 2, 3, 4, and 6 are in MQA.

MONDAY. 24TH.

Morning quite cold and the wind became Easterly and comfortless. We pay for our fine days in April. Went to the Office as usual, and passed the larger part of the morning in my translation of Æschines. This has grown tedious. Yet I feel as if once undertaken, it should not be abandoned, and as yet I have not even reached the place I arrived before at. Nothing particularly worth mentioning occurred. Called to see Mr. Brooks and to explain to him the reasons which had induced me to take my course in regard to my residence at Quincy. He appeared to acquiesce in the correctness of it though there is a something about it I relish very little. Undoubtedly his view can have little reference to mine and he perhaps feels little disposed to interest himself in a more distant when he has so many nearer connexions. So that I must act independently, trusting as I have nearly always done to my own judgment.

After dinner, I again went to Quincy, to open the House and give all the necessary directions in order to make one of my Servants comfortable, who has gone out there to clean and arrange previous to the arrival of the family. This is a troublesome matter, for which I shall get no great thanks, but still it is too bad to allow my Mother to come to a place in the condition in which that now is. I found all the Stores and all the Linen and Silver, and gave it to the Woman's charge. This kept me until quite late. I then returned and after tea, Edmund Quincy dropped in and amused us the rest of the Evening.

TUESDAY. 25TH.

Morning cloudy and cold. The Weather for some time past has been of the most disagreeable kind we have. The Easterly Wind quite sharp and piercing. After sending to be sold some of the books belonging to my brother, which are duplicates of those I myself possess, I went to the Office, where my time was passed in translating as usual. J. B. Davis called upon me about a Communication I had sent to the Patriot. His proposition was that he should put it under the editorial head of his paper, to which I very willingly consented although he proposes so much to adopt[1] it, as not to allow me the authorship. This may be flattering but I can scarcely fancy it fair. However this is a mere premier pas.

I got something beyond my former mark in translating Æschines before. Afternoon, began the final perusal of the same Orations in Reiske's edition to read the Notes.[2] But I begin to feel exceedingly wearied by an occupation of which even as yet I see little or no termination, and am moreover doubtful of my success. Yet as nothing new offers itself, and I am ashamed to turn back, it is as well to go on. Perhaps if I can find a light subject in the mean time, I will try it. Evening, read to my Wife a part of the Arabian Night[s]—Stories as amusing to me now as ever. After which I read more of Æschines.

[1] Thus in MS.
[2] The orations of Æschines with commentary are in vols. 3 and 4 of *Oratorum Græcorum*, edited by John Jacob Reiske, 8 vols., Leipzig, 1770–1773. The copy in MQA has JQA's bookplate.

WEDNESDAY. 26TH.

This being the day regularly assigned for the organization of the new Government of the State for the year, commonly called Election Day,[1] and no season for business, I remained at home and occupied myself very busily for three hours in my work upon Demosthenes, which progressed very considerably. I should have done more, had it not been for Edmund Quincy who called to pay a visit. Mrs. Frothingham and her children with those of Mrs. Everett from Medford came to complete the set. Our windows are very well adapted to the notice of all that is to be seen, and small children like these always admire such prospects very much.[2] It was wearisome to me. I went out with Quincy and finding my morning nearly gone, concluded to go to the Athenæum, where I passed my time between the gallery and the reading room. The Everett girls dined with us.[3] Afternoon passed in reading Greek and Latin Notes in Reiske's Edition, but it is now stupid. My nerves had got disordered so that I made unusually slow progress. Evening, read Arabian Nights to my Wife and after it, some of Plutarch's Lives, and Saverien's Philosophes Anciens.[4] My editorial Article appeared today in the Patriot, corrected.[5] I thought it good.

[1] Established usage dictated that on Election Day the legislature assembled, completed its organization, and elected its officers; then, with military escort, its members accompanied the Executive to the Old South Meeting House for the election sermon. In 1830 the sermon was preached by William Ellery Channing.

Beyond the events of the day, the whole week was largely given over to public functions, it being the traditional time for the religious and benevolent societies of the Commonwealth to hold their "anniversaries," i.e. annual meetings, in Boston. The investiture of the governor and lieutenant governor were the concluding ceremonies at the week's end. For this year's events, see *Boston Patriot*, 22 May, p. 2, col. 1; 26 May, p. 2, col. 4; 29 May, p. 2, col. 1.

[2] Not including infants in both families, there were four Frothingham boys

and two Everett girls. All were between the ages of five and ten (*First Church Records*, Col. Soc. Mass., *Pubns.*, 40 [1961]:449–452).

³ ABA's plans for the day for Ann and Charlotte Everett included taking them "to see the Rhinoceros and other Lions of the day" (Charlotte Everett to Edward Everett, 26 May, Everett MSS, MHi).

⁴ Alexandre Savérien, *Histoire des philosophes anciens jusqu'à la renaissance des lettres*, 5 vols., Paris, 1771– 1772.

⁵ CFA's communication which had been changed somewhat and adapted by John Brazer Davis as an editorial, and as such was unsigned, bore the title "The Next Presidency" (*Boston Patriot*, 26 May, p. 2, cols. 2–3). It called upon patriotic citizens, "unseduced by the glitter of corruption, and unawed by the intimidation of power," to begin the fight against the reelection of Andrew Jackson. Praise is given to the minority in the Senate for resisting encroachments upon liberty, and the members of the Congress are urged to lose no time in choosing a leader to make the fight. "The fundamental principle of the opposition, should be resistance against the PROGRESS OF CORRUPTION.... Let it not be said, by any true man, that he has not done every thing in his power ... to purify and restore the Republic."

Although it does speak of the President's "imbecility," the editorial is directed not so much against Jackson as against Vice-President Calhoun and Secretary of State Van Buren: "more dangerous public men ... never existed here."

THURSDAY. 27TH.

The morning was very pleasant, but the usual change took place at noon, and we were chilled by an Easterly wind. At the Office, but felt indisposed to translating; so that I read the laws upon the course of Administration upon insolvent Estates, and made a reexamination of New's Papers. Found nothing of any value. Mr. Kinsman called about a demand made in favour of New, and with some propositions to a settlement. I told him that I would attend to it. Mr. Greenough called to be paid his demand for the expenses of the Bust, a stale thing for which he ought to have been ashamed.¹ I called on Mr. Bowditch for a memorandum of New's debt to the Life Office but could get none.² Called also upon Mr. Welsh for it. He had mislaid it. Thus the morning passed.

The Afternoon found me engaged in an occupation very different from my usual ones. I had sent for Prior's Life of Burke to the Athenæum, and could not help sitting down at once to it's perusal.³ The character of the man, his eloquence, and the society in which he lived, all make him to me one of the most interesting individual biographies in the world. I could not leave excepting for an hour in the Evening to read to my Wife from Eustace. How valuable the privilege of the Athenæum is to me. I obtain books to amuse my Wife whose state of health depresses her spirits, and to instruct me—Though my own resources are very considerable. Continued Prior until I had nearly devoured the volume.

[1] Horatio Greenough had been commissioned by JQA to do the bust of his father to be placed above the memorial tablet in the Adams Temple at Quincy, and had also done a bust of JQA, both in 1828; see above, entry for 25 Oct. 1829; JQA, Diary, 20–25 Feb. 1828; and *Portraits of John and Abigail Adams*, p. 231–232, 234.

[2] Nathaniel Bowditch was a director and the actuary of the Massachusetts Hospital Life Insurance Co. on State Street (*Boston Directory*, 1830–1831).

[3] The copy of James Prior's *Memoir of the Life and Character of . . . Edmund Burke* at the Boston Athenæum is of the 2d edn., 2 vols., London, 1826.

FRIDAY 28TH.

Morning bright and pleasant. I went to the Office as usual and passed a great part of my time in translating Æschines. Mr. Chadwick came in and asked me to accompany the Directors of the Middlesex Canal tomorrow [1]—An arrangement to which I consented, providing I found no difficulty in my present situation at home, my Servant being gone to Quincy. Called to see Mr. Brooks and afterwards at the Bank to know if Whitney's Note had been collected, found it was not yet due.

Returned home for an early dinner, in order to be able to go out and see how things went on at Quincy. My Wife accompanied me today. We found things in considerable confusion, and our woman very much discouraged at the magnitude of the Work. Things had been left so very dirty as to multiply the work exceedingly. It made me feel badly, as it showed the mode of life pursued by my father during the last Summer. It will be different this year I hope, but I care much less about it. We remained looking round until evening when we returned through Milton. I received a letter this evening from my Mother in answer to my first, counting very much upon my being there.[2] Now I wait for the reply to my last, which will change the face of things. Evening, two hours of Prior's Life of Burke.

[1] Ebenezer Chadwick was one of the directors (Roberts, *The Middlesex Canal, 1793–1860*, p. 223).

[2] LCA to CFA, 23 May (Adams Papers).

Woburn—Medford

SATURDAY. 29TH.

Morning cloudy and threatening rain. After reading as much of Prior as possible, I went to the Office to stop only a few moments, before the proper time to go to meet the other gentlemen on the expedition. I went into State Street and after conversing with Degrand about the Salem Murder, the perpetrator of which has just been discovered,[1] and also about the nomination of Mr. Randolph as Minister to Russia, a late wise measure of the President,[2] I met the gentlemen and we got into Carriages to start for Charlestown where we stopped to see the new Mills, the superintendant's House and every thing which might be considered curious.[3] The set in our Carriage consisted of Mr. Coolidge, Mr. Baldwin, Mr. Joy and myself.[4] From this spot, we rode to the Aqueduct over Medford river which we examined. I had seen it but a few days before so it was no curiosity.[5] We then took the Canal Boat and went directly to Woburn. I saw nothing new excepting the breach made a few days since, and a stone lock which is certainly a very beautiful specimen of work. But the rage for railroads is increasing, and the determination seems to be to obtain one to go to Lowell at all hazards. The very one which will be ruinous to us. We arrived at Woburn in a shower, which changed to a settled rain for the afternoon. This is a beautiful place. I doubt whether any where a sweeter position for a residence could be found.[6]

Our body here assembled, and we found it consisted of ten of the Board and three visitors. Messrs. Guild, Sullivan, Coolidge, Thacher, Hallet, Chadwick, Joy, Baldwin, Eddy and myself,[7] with Mr. Coles of New York, Mr. Whitwell and S. Torrey of Boston. Our dinner was good, and the conversation pleasant, but the party was so mixed it made Conversation a little hazardous, particularly when upon the ticklish points of Politics. Unfortunately, Whitwell touched upon the Hartford Convention, and gave us his idea of that body immediately after his explaining to us how the nonintercourse laws were evaded. The connection seemed to be good, as the one who justified what he himself had practised, would not be there to justify what would bear him out among others in doctrine. I felt awkwardly enough, and did not like to join him in the Conversation, particularly before so many Federalists among whom Mr. Sullivan was, who had taken pains to treat me politely. But it was lucky the conversation was changed for I might have become worked up to speak. There was much other talk about the present state of affairs which might as well have been omitted.

We rose from dinner and returned home, I being unable to accomplish what I had intended, the stopping at Mr. Brooks', because the party went through West Cambridge, a different route. So that I was compelled to return to Boston before I could go to Medford. My wife was at the latter place, so that I took Chardon Brooks' horse and went out getting there late, a Short Conversation and went to bed.

[1] Rumor had followed rumor after the murder of Capt. Joseph White, and suspicion had been raised against a number of persons. However, on 27 May announcement was made that the case had been solved and arrests made. Confessions followed. Most of those involved were of good families. Accused as planners and instigators were two Salem brothers, Capt. Joseph J. Knapp Jr.,

married to the daughter of Capt. White's housekeeper and niece, and Frank Knapp. It was alleged that Richard Crowninshield Jr. of Danvers had committed the act, having been hired by the Knapps because he had a gang organized for robbery and deeds of violence. Crowninshield committed suicide in his cell before trial. The trials of the two Knapps resulted in the conviction and execution of both. (Charles Pelham Curtis, "The Young Devils and Dan'l Webster," *American Heritage*, 11:52–54, 101–103 [June 1960].)

[2] The damage done through the years both to JA and JQA by the rancorous enmity of John Randolph of Roanoke (Bemis, *JQA*, 2:132–133), and the outraged cries of the anti-Jackson press at the announcement of the appointment of the highly eccentric, if gifted, Randolph as minister, are grounds for a conclusion that CFA's words are to be understood as bitterly ironic and that he regarded the appointment as an additional proof of that "imbecility" in the President of which CFA had but lately written.

[3] The canal's point of beginning was at a landing on the Mill Pond at the foot of Mill Street in the area known as Charlestown Neck. Close by were the mills given over to the grinding of corn and sawing of timber. The mills, the milldam, and the pond were owned by the Canal Co., having been purchased in 1803 to provide a terminus with storage facilities for lumber and merchandise. Improvements had been made at various times thereafter. (Roberts, *The Middlesex Canal, 1793–1860*, p. 113; Timothy T. Sawyer, *Old Charlestown*, Boston, 1902, p. 464.)

[4] Joseph Coolidge, James F. Baldwin, Joseph B. Joy, along with CFA, were directors of the Canal (Roberts, *The Middlesex Canal, 1793–1860*, p. 223).

[5] See above, entry for 15 May.

[6] In its passage from Medford to Woburn, the canal, just beyond the Brooks estate and north of Mystic Pond, reached the Symmes or Aberjona River at about the seven-mile line. Here the river was crossed by another aqueduct; a short distance beyond were Gardner's Locks. Through Winchester to Woburn the canal's course was to the west of Wedge Pond and Mill Pond. Beyond the eight-mile line, after crossing Horn Pond Brook, the canal entered Hollis' Lock and soon thereafter, Woburn. The canal then followed close to the eastern shore of Horn Pond, and at the north end of the pond, beyond the nine-mile line, reached Horn Pond Locks and the Woburn landing. Close by stood the popular tavern, built and several times enlarged by the Canal Company. The attractions of the spot caused it to become a resort area, well known for many years. The locks at Woburn, which together with the recently rebuilt aqueduct at Medford were evidently the objectives of the directors' inspection trip, consisted of three sets of double locks with a total lift of about fifty feet. The lowest set of locks had been rebuilt in hammered granite in 1828. (Lewis M. Lawrence, The Middlesex Canal, Boston, 1942 [processed], p. 111–114; Roberts, *The Middlesex Canal, 1793–1860*, p. 195.)

[7] Directors not earlier identified: Benjamin Guild, George Hallet, Peter O. Thatcher (same, p. 223).

SUNDAY. 30TH.

Morning mild, damp but warm. We attended Divine Service all day and heard a certain Mr. Gannet of Cambridge preach, a man whom I had heard once before and who is certainly infinitely dull.[1] He dined with us, and gave us a good specimen of a pious, sincere, perhaps really good Clergyman with little or no head, and a face which was not very favourable. Mrs. Everett came down and I saw her today for the first time, since her confinement and the additional honor of her son. She looked quite well. But from some cause or other,

I have lost my desire to cultivate her acquaintance, and indeed, the general apathy and stupidity of my present manner, begin to strike me. I am much altered since my marriage. The gravity and seriousness of my pursuits, and the cares of life now weigh sensibly, so that my friend Richardson's remark the other day, is true.

Short walk and conversation with Mr. Brooks about his place, which now looks exceedingly well. It has much beauty and infinite capability. I should envy it if I allowed myself to do so. Mr. Swan, a gentleman living in New York called in the evening and it was passed in common conversation.

¹ On Rev. Thomas B. Gannett, see vol. 2:380.

Medford—Boston   MONDAY. 31ST.

The morning was clear and cool. On the whole the month of May this year has been far from pleasant. The East Winds have prevailed very much and checked the warmth which we enjoyed in April. Left Medford immediately after breakfast alone, as my Wife was to go with Mrs. Everett to her house in Charlestown to spend the morning. Found at home a short letter from my Father announcing his probable arrival for tomorrow, and a short Note from my Mother, as I expected full of disappointment.¹ I felt a degree of pain, but knowing that it would be folly in me to run any risk, my resolution was not changed. Never was there a measure of this kind upon which my mind was more clear.

Went to the Office, and after ascertaining that Whitney's Note was paid, and returning my Affidavit of Notice of Administration to the Probate Office, I sat down and read Mitford with my usual indignation. An abominable book. Afternoon, finished the first Volume of Prior's Life of Burke, and looked into Milton. My reading of the Poets has slacked so much that I find I must refresh. Evening reading Eustace to my Wife, and afterwards, examining the Oxford Elements of Logic.²

¹ The letter from LCA is missing; that from JQA (25 May, Adams Papers) on the matter of CFA's decision not to stay in Quincy has only a laconic "be it as you judge best."
² The book is not readily identifiable.

TUESDAY. JUNE 1ST.

Morning cloudy, damp and cold. Went to the Office as usual, and busied myself about my father's Accounts, preparing them for him in case he asked for them. On the whole they are in as good a condition as I could expect, leaving a balance of seven hundred dollars for him after paying the demands for repairs and the usual very heavy charges upon the income. Whitney's affair is settled, though not without a great sacrifice. I can only content myself with the idea, that nothing has been lost through my Agency. I immediately transferred to my father's Credit, a Sum sufficient to make up one thousand dollars on his book to begin with. He has arrears at Quincy sufficient to make up half as much more, besides the income of the shortly expiring Quarter.[1]

Read Mitford and felt as usual. It is a sin for a man to sit down to write a history if he feels in his bosom one iota of inclination to a prejudice against particular systems, for if he does, his work will surely taste of it. Heard in the Streets of my father's having started, and being in Baltimore and Philadelphia.[2] But decided not to go out to Quincy today. In the afternoon I began the second volume of Prior's Life of Burke and followed it up as fast as I had done the other. With many egregious faults of carelessness, it has some good points. But the subject of the work is the fascination to me. I have read all his works that I could find and wish I could get more. Evening, Eustace to my Wife, which we have nearly finished and I am not sorry—After which I continued Prior with unabated interest. Every study has given way to it.

[1] That is, overdue rents owing to JQA on his property in Quincy and the regular interest and dividend payments accruing on 1 July.

[2] JQA left Washington by stage on 27 May accompanied by his servant William. He stayed in Baltimore that night. Setting out again on the 28th, he arrived in Philadelphia ten hours later (JQA, Diary). Dispatches covering the journey of these two days reached Boston in time to be included in the morning newspaper of 2 June (*Boston Patriot*, p. 2, col. 2).

WEDNESDAY. 2D.

The morning was lovely, giving us the first specimen we have had of Summer Weather for some time past. I thought I should go to Quincy and went to order a vehicle when I found a letter at the Post Office from Philadelphia informing me of their probable stay at that place for some time, which of course disarranged me for the day.[1] I had anticipated the pleasure of meeting them so strongly that it certainly was a disappointment.

At the Office where I passed my time in translating Æschines and reading Mitford. News came this morning of the loss of the Ship Boston by fire, upon which a considerable sum was insured at the New

England Office, so that the expected Dividend will not be so large, and my Accounts are somewhat varied.[2] My friend Richardson called, but staid only a few moments. Returned home to dine and passed the afternoon in reading Prior. Finished the work with which I have been on the whole much pleased. It is a better estimate of Burke's character than any I ever read, and gives me many new ideas about him. I also read an Article upon him in the Edinburgh Review and another in the Quarterly.[3] The first by a political enemy, the last by a friend. Both not quite the truth, but the latter much nearer to it than the former. Evening, Eustace to my Wife. A strange and incomprehensible mixture this man. A Catholic Priest, a John Bull, and a warm republican. Three most incongruous characters.

[1] JQA to CFA, 29 May (Adams Papers). LCA, Mrs. JA2, daughter, and nurse (Mrs. Nowland), who had left Washington in the family carriage on the 27th, joined JQA in Philadelphia according to plan. However, since the journey could not be resumed before the 31st, the arrival of all in Quincy was necessarily delayed.

[2] The *Boston*, Capt. Mackay, bound for Liverpool from Charleston with a cargo principally of cotton, was struck by lightning and set afire on 25 May. Of her $20,000 insurance, half was carried by the Columbian office, half by the New England office (*Boston Patriot*, 2 June, p. 2, col. 1).

[3] A review of *The Epistolary Correspondence of ... Edmund Burke and Dr. French Lawrence*, London, 1827, in the *Edinburgh Review*, 46:269–303 (Oct. 1827); a review of Prior's, *Memoir of ... Burke*, in the *Quarterly Review*, 34:457–487 (Sept. 1826).

THURSDAY. 3RD.

Morning clear and warm. I went down to my Office early in order to find out something in relation to my father's arrival, but could not succeed. Concluded upon taking my chance of finding them.[1] So after making several arrangements, I went off in a horse and gig with my Wife at ten o'clock, and we soon reached Quincy. We found there my father only, he having left the rest of the party at Providence to come on more gradually. We did expect them before dinner but the time wore away and nobody came so that we dined without them. My father looks in very good health and seemed in tolerable spirits. We had a great deal of conversation upon general subject of politics and family matters. He did not seem quite so comfortably situated as he was last year.

At six o'clock my Mother came, with Mrs. J. Adams and Child.[2] They looked fatigued and worried. And bore the appearance which always so unaccountably attends all their proceedings.[3] I conversed with them briefly and argued the point with my Mother mildly, as to my determination not to go to Quincy to reside, but my Uncle and his family came in which shook our decision, and we left them late to return. Found the other Servants at our House who had come by Water.[4]

[1] JQA had written a note to CFA at 7 P.M. on the evening before, announcing his arrival at Quincy at 5 (Adams Papers), but apparently it had not been delivered before CFA left for Quincy.

[2] Mary Louisa Adams (b. 1828), daughter of JA2; see vol. 2:320 and Adams Genealogy.

[3] The family left New York on the afternoon of 1 June by steamboat *President*, Capt. Bunker, and landed at Providence the next day after a rough passage. JQA took the stage at once,

leaving LCA and her charges to follow by carriage. Because the child was seized with a "fainting or convulsion fit," LCA decided that they would remain overnight in Providence (JQA, Diary, 3 June).

[4] Mrs. Mary Ann Pitts, Mrs. Elizabeth Kirke, and daughter journeyed by sea. Leaving Washington on 21 May, they reached Quincy on the 4th (LCA to CFA, 23 May, Adams Papers; JQA, Diary, 4 June).

FRIDAY. 4TH.

Morning warm and pleasant. I did not feel very well myself as my Nerves had been disarranged by seeing the family yesterday and being obliged to attend to the disposition of the Servants. Received from Mr. Brooks his Check for the Quarter as usual, and deposited the Money at the Bank, with some also to the credit of my father. I then went and completed the transaction with regard to the Stock in the State Bank, and conversed wih Mr. Degrand upon it. The project seems to be to put that Institution upon a new footing, by reducing the Capital, and changing the head of it who has become unpopular.[1] Judge Hall came up and paid me a short visit this morning, inquiring about my father's arrival,[2] and the remainder of my time excepting a few minutes to see Mr. Brooks, reading Mitford. My head ached a little. Afternoon not spent to the best advantage as the time was cut up in getting the women off for Quincy, and in a sleepy turn that came over me.

Felt a little puzzled about the most advisable course to be pursued. My Mother is provoked, my Father grieved and my brother's Wife hurt by my decision. Yet it is undoubtedly a wise one. I see that it is at every step. Yet I feel sorry to cause so much uneasiness. The family is large and expensive, and I have no desire whatever to make it more so. I think my Father does not feel quite so well as he did. The care seems a little too much for him. Poor man, he is destined to have a load upon his shoulders full as heavy as he can carry.[3] Read Burke's Speeches upon America.[4] In the evening, Eustace, and afterwards, Logic.

[1] The president of the State Bank was E. A. Bourne (*Boston Directory*, 1830–1831).

[2] On Judge Joseph Hall, see vol. 2:154.

[3] CFA was not wrong in sensing a deep concern in JQA. In his diary entry on the same day JQA wrote, "I find it [the move] of oppressive magnitude and distressing charge." The number in the household at the Old House was swollen to two children and eleven adults: three members of the family and eight servants. With each of the family

unwell, JQA was provoked to write, "With a family so infirm, that every step I take is with fear and trembling, I cannot express what I feel. If I had concern only for my own life, my condition would be comparatively happy. I have no reliance upon Earth. May that from above be sure and stedfast." (JQA, Diary, 31 May; 4, 30 June.)

[4] The speeches on America are in vol. 2 of the edition of *The Works of . . . Burke* in 3 vols., published at London in 1792, which has JQA's bookplate and is now in MQA.

SATURDAY 5TH.

My Cook came in from Quincy with my father's man Kirke, and I had to obtain several things for the family directly. Called at Mr. Forbes' and found the Horse come from Weston this morning looking very well, and heard that the other one is growing better. I then went to see Bond the Watchmaker and inquired about the Clock Mr. Brooks has purchased for my Wife,[1] and about my brother George's Watch, which has returned well finished. The first was not quite ready, the other I directed if possible to be sold.

Conant from Weston came to my Office to settle for a year's rent and for the balance due from the Wood. After a long calculation, not very accurate, owing to the loose manner in which it was made in the first instance by the Tenants, I came to a conclusion to take Forty dollars in full for the balance remaining. This pays for the Winter's Care of the Horses and their board. Paid Ayer my Carpenter, and read Mitford. Afternoon spent in reading the Memoirs of Dr. Parr, a book from which I expected much amusement and instruction, but was very far from realizing my hope, for in the first part at least is a great deal of twaddle from one Field, the Author, who writes also very tamely.[2] Eustace for a very short time.

[1] Mr. Brooks recorded the payment of $26 for an "imported parlor clock donated to Mrs. Adams." Charles Bond, watchmaker, was at 37 Washington Street (*Boston Directory*, 1830–1831).

[2] William Field, *Memoirs of the Life, Writings, and Opinions of the Rev. Samuel Parr . . .* , 2 vols., London, 1828.

[*Medford*]   SUNDAY. 6TH.

Morning cloudy and cold. After breakfast we concluded upon going to Medford today as the family at Quincy are probably in a state of disorder and not ready to receive us. Our ride was not a very agreeable one, but we reached Medford in time to accompany Mr. Brooks to meeting. It was a matter of gratification to us to find that Mrs. Everett had left the House and given place to Mrs. Frothingham. This is a kind woman and not actuated by the same feelings in the least. I once felt much esteem for the other lady, but greater intimacy has not improved it. Though I do think she has many estimable points, I also consider she has as many quite the reverse. Mrs. Frothingham with half the pretention has twice the substance. It rained so that Mr. Brooks did not think proper to attend Meeting in the afternoon, so we remained at home. I tried to read the Edinburgh Review, but my attention was distracted and on the whole I feel as if I ought to put down the day as wasted.

Boston

MONDAY. 7TH.

Morning damp, and warm. We left Medford after breakfast, to return to town. I did not go to the Office however as it was not a business day.[1] The present is the holiday season in this part of the Country. Election week being the time in which most of the people from the Country choose to indulge themselves with the wonders and pleasures of a City.

My Wife feeling desirous of going to the Gallery of Pictures at the Athenæum, I took advantage of the day to go down with her. The exhibition strikes me less and less every time I go to see it. Though the good pictures are still worth attentive examination. There is a strong temptation held out there to buy. But I feel as if I could not properly purchase and must attend more strictly to those views which I have laid down for myself at present.

We returned late, and stopped at Mrs. Hale's to see Mr. Everett who has returned. He looks pale and thin, somewhat exhausted from his labours in the Session. After dinner, I continued Dr. Parr for a portion of time, and spent a part in seeing the show of the Governor's chairing with my Wife.[2] They say it always rains on this occasion. This day was no exception certainly, for we had a number of showers during the day. Evening, reading Eustace and afterwards Parr.

[1] The day of the Artillery Election, so-called, being the day celebrated as the anniversary of the founding of the Ancient and Honorable Artillery Company.

[2] The Governor was escorted from the State House to the reviewing area on the Common and there, as commander in chief, presided over the ceremonies in which resignations were received and new commissions were awarded to the officers chosen earlier in the day (*Columbian Centinel*, 9 June, p. 2, col. 5).

TUESDAY. 8TH.

Arose and found that instead of a bright day we were having a very heavy rain, with a warm south wind. This did not last, though we had occasional showers with thunder through the day. At the Office where most of my time was taken up in reading Mitford, the volume I wish to finish. It has been a matter of some satisfaction to me to find, that the impressions received from the book now are exactly the same with those I had in my first reading at College.

The literature of England for the early period of the nineteenth Century bears the characteristic strongly, of the times. The terror of the French revolution, and jealousy of the success of a rival nation threw nearly all the scholars in England into an attitude hostile to all institutions excepting such as supported the great weight of their own system. And as democracy was the most fearful enemy, it partook most largely of their enmity. The Tory party, Mr. Mitford, Mitchell the translator of Aristophanes, the Writers in the Quarterly Review, Walter Scott in his way, and many others which I cannot now recollect, have laboured with much assiduity and some success at this Oar. But they have perverted history, and unsettled political principle.

The Afternoon was devoted to Dr. Parr's Life. He to be sure went to another extreme, but perhaps the most correct one. Time should never hallow abuses, though change ought not to be *rashly* attempted. I took up the works of Sir Joshua Reynolds to inform myself a little more upon the merits of Painters, and the science.[1] This is a proper time to apply the information. Finished Eustace to my Wife in the evening, after which I attacked Logic. How multifarious is knowledge. How extended the ways of learning. Who can compass them all and yet who feels not the desire of trying more than he can accomplish.

[1] Sir Joshua Reynolds, *The Complete Works*. The edition published at London in 3 vols., 1824, in MQA, has GWA's autograph and CFA's bookplate.

WEDNESDAY. 9TH.

The morning was cloudy but turned off quite fine. I began another undertaking this morning in addition to my former ones, to which I have been led by reading Dr. Parr's Life, that is, the making a Catalogue of my Collection of Books. I propose to turn it to some account by learning the editions and their separate value and object. I began it this morning.

At the Office where I finished the volume of Mitford which I had been reading. The most prejudiced and unfair statements I ever read in History, compounded to produce an effect upon the occasional feelings of a people. I returned home quite early in order to go out with my Wife to Quincy. Accordingly we went and much to our surprise we found that my Mother was sick and confined to her room ever since Saturday, with a violent attack of erysipelas.[1] My father's spirits seemed much affected. Indeed I rarely recollect seeing him more dull. The time did not pass pleasantly to me, as the family seemed so disarranged. My father was regulating what he never did before, and Mrs. J. Adams doing nothing but sitting with her hands before her. The Child a nuisance, and altogether not over pleasant. The afternoon passed at my Mother's bedside, I afterwards conversed a little with my father about his plans and prospects and tried to excite his weakened purpose of writing my grandfather's life.[2] After which we returned to town, and I finished Dr. Parr.

[1] JQA pronounced it the "most terrific attack of St. Anthony's fire that I ever witnessed" (Diary, 8 June).

[2] "Charles urged me to resume the Memoir of my father's life, which I have already too long neglected. I have in truth here less time at my disposal than at Washington" (JQA, Diary, 9 June). An 85-page fragment in JQA's hand of a "Memorial of the Life of John Adams," dated 5 Aug. 1829 is in the Adams Papers (M/JQA/46, Microfilms, Reel No. 241) and was printed by CFA in JA, *Works*, 1:13–89.

THURSDAY. 10TH.

The weather was rainy and unsettled during the morning and cleared off in the afternoon. My morning was not spent profitably. I wasted part at home, and at the Office found it much cut up. Deposited more money to the credit of my father, and gave orders for the binding of some of his books, after which I called at Hilliards in consequence of my father's telling me he was the Author of the Chapters upon Greece in the Annual Register.[1] Tried to read the first part of it upon the domestic History but progressed very little.

Gave orders today for the purchase of a quantity of Shingles in order to begin upon the repair of my Father's Tenements which I have been meditating. I know of no time more favourable than the present, when I have funds which it is not likely I shall have again. I ordered the Nails and the lead and in this way expect I shall get through with this business very quickly.

After dinner I again began Æschines for a final reading, and passed an hour in pasting my father's Crest into his books, a necessary though not profitable work. Evening wasted doing nothing until nine when I read Logic, a little of Sir Joshua Reynolds and my continuation of Catalogue. A bright Aurora Borealis such as I never saw before.

[1] JQA was the author of the chapters on Russia and Turkey, as well as that on Greece, in the *American Annual Register* (New York, 1830). A draft of the chapters (10–15) in his hand is in the Adams Papers (Microfilms, Reel No. 492).

FRIDAY. 11TH.

A very fine day at last. At the Office after having gone down to see Hollis and the Houses which I propose to have shingled. Gave my directions about it but felt dissatisfied with Hollis. It is the very worst plan in the World to have a man pay his rent in work, for he charges just what he pleases and you can make no deduction. I propose by the close of this year to make a change unless this Hollis gets disposed to work differently, and to be more punctual in his payments. My present fear is that this one repair will bring on a great deal more.

Read a considerable portion of the Annual Register, particularly that which relates to Russia and Turkey. The style is that of my father, warm and brilliant. The views are his views, such as few other people think of holding. I am not sure that they are right, because with me every new question must be submitted to a process of reasoning before decision, but they certainly develope a state of things totally different from any previous idea of mine.

Returned home early because Mr. Brooks, and Mr. and Mrs. Frothingham were to dine here so as to go to Quincy.[1] Miss Julia Gorham was here likewise. The dinner was pleasant because I begin to feel more at ease at the foot of my own table. They left me early and I passed the remainder of the day in reading Æschines, continuing my Catalogue and concluding the trip to Flanders of Sir Joshua Reynolds.[2] Evening, Logic, both the Oxford Elements and Hedge's,[3] after which the Article "Painting" in Elmes Dictionary of the Fine Arts.[4]

[1] Members of the party, joined by ABA, made the journey to Quincy to pay their respects at the Old House; they were not able to see Mrs. Adams (JQA, Diary, 11 June).

[2] The "Journey to Flanders and Holland" is in vol. 2 of his *Works*.

[3] Levi Hedge, *Elements of Logick*, Cambridge, 1816.

[4] JQA's bookplate is in the edition of *A General and a Bibliographical Dictionary of the Fine Arts* by James Elmes published at London in 1826, now in MQA.

Boston—Medford
SATURDAY 12TH.

Morning fine and beginning to be quite warm. Went to the Office where I did very little owing to many interruptions. John Kirke, my father's man came to me, for directions having brought in with him the horse I sent for and being about to take out the other, who has much recovered from his illness, and now promises to get well. He brought in a letter from my father with some commissions to perform,[1] which I set about instantly. In the first place to get bottles for his Madeira, which I succeeded in doing though at what I thought a great price. I then went to buy some Porter and Ale which I thought I obtained low. Having finished this and bargained with Mr. Forbes about the hire of a Gig for the Summer which I obtained at a reasonable rate, I returned to the Office where I had a visit from my friend Briggs.[2] He has not been to see me for a long time. Indeed he was not ever a particular intimate of mine. George loved him much. At College I knew him and when he was studying here. I was glad to see him, and to hear that he was succeeding well at his place of residence, Augusta in Maine. But I could not help a shade of moral speculation upon thinking of the change which had come over both of us since we last met, and poor George has ceased to live. Richardson came in afterwards for a short time and after him Mr. Curtis upon nothing in particular.

After dinner I started off with my Wife to Watertown to pay a visit to Edward Brooks and his Wife, and Gorham and his Wife who have returned and are established at the place of Mr. Shepherd.[3] We had quite a pleasant time. Gorham Brooks was more civil to me than I had ever known him, but I shall never get over the first impression. He was guilty of no civility when I *first* came here and when I needed and felt grateful for attention.[4] His wife is pleasing. After tea we rode to Medford where we found Mr. Frothingham and Mr. Stetson. Evening quiet.

[1] JQA to CFA, 12 June (Adams Papers).

[2] Cyrus Briggs, Harvard 1821, is referred to in vol. 1:458; his undergraduate career was marked by numerous infractions of the rules and consequent admonishments, fines, and punishments; see entries in Records of the College Faculty (MH-Ar). Subsequently he studied medicine and received the degree of M.D. in 1826 (*Harvard Quinquennial Cat.*).

[3] On Gorham Brooks (1795–1855), Harvard 1814, another of ABA's brothers, see vol. 2:149 and Adams Genealogy. His wife, Ellen (1809–1884), was the daughter of Resin D. Shepherd of Watertown; see vol. 2:165 and above, entry for 20 Sept. 1829. Shortly after their marriage in April 1829 Gorham and his wife left for Europe, from which they returned on 4 June (Brooks, Farm Journal).

[4] For the earlier unpleasantness, see vol. 2:320, 367. The incivility to which CFA objected was perhaps not so much directed at him as it was characteristic of Gorham's social manner (Charlotte Everett to Edward Everett, 12, 26 April 1829, Everett MSS, MHi).

SUNDAY. 13TH.

Mild rain until twelve when it cleared off and by evening became cold. Attended divine service all day and heard Mr. Frothingham preach two very good Sermons. He has a finished and elegant style, and though it is a little too studied and laboured for general comprehension, yet I think it has much merit. I am more pleased as I know more of the man, for his social qualities are very creditable to him. Mr. Brooks goes on much as usual, his spirits a little revived perhaps. I find myself able to do little or nothing on Sundays, and must bend my mind down to be satisfied with the waste of time. Tried to read two or three Essays of Vicesimus Knox but with very little success.[1] Evening a short walk with Mr. Brooks and Mr. Frothingham along the Canal and returned to talk away the evening.

[1] The essays of Vicesimus Knox (1752–1821) were collected as *Essays, Moral and Literary*, 3 vols., and under the title *Winter Evenings*, 3 vols. Both collections went through numerous editions.

Medford—Boston—Quincy

MONDAY. 14TH.

Morning at Medford with the weather mild and pleasant. As soon after breakfast as possible we started to return to Boston and I was very busy after that in making my preparations to go to Quincy. This is an experiment, how to turn out remains yet to be seen. At the Office where I had little time to do any thing as I felt obliged to go out of town early. Received the Dividend of the New England Insurance Company for my father. This makes fifteen per cent they have paid within a year, and is very beneficial to my accounts. A man by name J. Q. Adams called to see me, said he was a Printer and came to beg the favour of being employed by my father in his contemplated life of my Grandfather. I told him that it not being written yet, there was quite plenty of time to think of printing it.

At a little before one I went for my Wife and we rode to Quincy to reach their dinner hour. Found my Mother better but still quite sick. My father full of care and much depressed. The family altogether in such a condition that I felt more like an outcast than at home. I do not think I shall manage a very long period.[1] My mother is sick, Mary discontented and my father depressed, and my wife ennuyè while I waste all my time. After copying a letter for my father,[2] I walked to the Judge's where I passed an hour. There was, as there always is, Company there.

[1] CFA and ABA came out for a "visit to us for some days" (JQA, Diary, 14 June).

[2] JQA to Messrs. Thomas & John Baring and Joshua Bates, 14 June (LbC, Adams Papers). The letter placed in the hands of the recipients the collection of the claims of the Thomas and Ward N. Boylston estates against Petty Vaughan and William Vaughan.

TUESDAY 15TH.

Morning at Quincy, instead of rain as we expected, we found a warm sun and a summer's day. My mother seemed a little better, but so many strange ways seem to have crept into the House that I feel no longer at home. We waited as usual when my father is in the case, pretty long before we could start for Boston. He had agreed to go and dine with us, so that my Wife accompanied us, and Abby Adams. We did not reach Boston until eleven, when I was hurried all the rest of the time. Went with my father to my Office, where we executed certain papers for the Estate of W. N. Boylston, Mr. Curtis and Mrs. Boylston being there for the purpose.[1] This over, a few Commissions, a visit to Mr. Brooks and my Journal took up the rest of my time, until dinner. My father, Miss Abby Adams and Miss Julia Gorham dined with us. The first was made heavy and sleepy by the weather so that we had little Conversation. At five we returned to Quincy, and I rarely recollect suffering more than we did during our ride—The heat being intense and the Carriage shut close. I was glad to be freed from this restraint, and to breathe a fresher air. The Evening was passed in the Portico,[2] in the first thing like a Conversation which we have been able to carry on, and this was mostly upon Political matters which do not materially interest me.

[1] The documents in support of the letter written the day before to the Barings and Joshua Bates had been prepared by John Lowell (JQA, Diary, 12, 15 June).

[2] CFA must be referring to the small covered entry or porch to be found in the representations of the Old House in the 1820's.

WEDNESDAY. 16TH.

Morning warm, but the wind changed to the eastward in a little while and a thunder shower in the evening cooled the air completely. I went to Boston, and spent an hour or more at the House in bottling the remainder of my Sherry Wine which turns out better than I had anticipated. I have now five dozen and a half to keep as choice wine, which will be worth nearly what I paid for the whole, besides the quantity used for the last six months. This done I went to the Office and was occupied there in my usual way of writing my Journal. I find my time now much more limited than it used to be last Summer as I go out of town to dine.

Called in to see Mr. Brooks and found him engaged so much that I did not stay long, and from there went to Quincy. Found my Mother so much better as to sit up and she seemed moreover in tolerable spirits. After dinner I sat down with my father to the work of a Catalogue of his Library.[1] How far we shall succeed I do not know. But the value of a library like that is essentially diminished by not knowing what is in it. We were interrupted by a visit from the two Mr. Everetts, Alex. and Edward. The former of whom spoke to me of my Article for his Review very openly and made me feel a little awkward. After a short visit they were driven away by the rain. Evening, a short and uninteresting conversation with my father.

[1] The catalogue was brought to completion on 12 October (see below, entry for that date). Among the sundry catalogues of Adams books in the Adams Papers this one has not been located.

Quincy–Medford
THURSDAY. 17TH.

Morning warm but the weather soon gave way to an East Wind which chilled the Air for the rest of the day. I breakfasted early and rode to town with my Wife, and after leaving her at the house I went to the Office to write my Journal and read a little of the Annual Register. But my time was much taken up first by a visit to my father's Tenements to see how the workmen got on with their work. I found that they had finished one side of the Houses and had begun upon the other. This is doing better than I had expected. The rest of the job may be longer but still it will be closed by the end of next week.

At twelve I went home to ask of my Wife to accompany me in one or two visits I was desirous of making, to Mr. and Mrs. Gorham and Mr. and Mrs. Webster. I feel as if I ought to keep up the current of those kind of acquaintance or I may be dropped myself. They were out and we left Cards. Returning we started for Medford and reached there early before dinner. The afternoon was nearly wasted. I did manage to read Dr. Channing's Sermon delivered upon the day of Election.[1] It did not please me. There is too much mysticism about it. Instruction is good for nothing if not plainly expressed, without metaphysics. Evening a walk with Mr. Frothingham and much conversation upon the family of Mr. Brooks, and his character. We agreed very much in our views. Mr. B. and his two daughters visited their Aunts until nine, after which a short conversation.

[1] William Ellery Channing's *Sermon*, preached 26 May at Old South Meeting House, had been published more than a week earlier (*Boston Patriot*, 7 June, p. 3, col. 3). On Channing, see vol. 2:182.

Medford–Quincy
FRIDAY. 18TH.

The morning was cloudy with cold wind and damp air. We left

Medford with an uncomfortable ride before us, and it was made still more uncomfortable by the running of my horse which frightened my wife not a little. After arriving, I went to the Office and passed my time as usual, in writing my Journal and doing little or nothing else. I wrote a Note to Mrs. Woods and one to Col. Tyler,[1] the two things I had set down for myself to do. Examined and corrected my Accounts with my father, and by that time it became necessary to start for Quincy.

We arrived without any accident to dine. The afternoon passed in making out more of the Catalogue of my father's books, though it progresses but slowly. Saw my Mother who seemed pretty well, growing better of her attack fast. She seems perhaps more lively than I had expected, but my father shows a manifest change. A kind of want of purpose which alarms me, as I think I see in it the source of much restlessness and of some danger. But I hardly dare to think much about it. Evening, a short visit from Josiah Quincy and his Wife, who have just come out here.[2] Conversation with my father.

[1] Mrs. Woods was indebted to the estate of Robert New; the letter to her is missing. CFA's letter to Col. J. S. Tyler (LbC, Adams Papers) requested him to make a further check to ascertain if a bill on the estate of GWA for a subscrip-tion had not in fact been paid by GWA before his death.

[2] Col. Quincy, his wife, and child were spending the summer at his father's house in Quincy (JQA, Diary, 18 June).

SATURDAY. 19TH.

Morning warm. Went to Boston, and passed my time as usual in a variety of occupations, first going to the House where I wanted a volume to be returned to the Athenæum. Then busied with writing Notes, to Mrs. Woods, about New's Estate, Col. Tyler about George's subscription, and to a certain Mrs. Bailey to try to recover something from that large demand.[1] All of this disagreeable business necessary to be done, without hope of good to come from it. I then went to the Athenæum and to execute one or two little Commissions with which I was charged by my Mother. Returning to the Office I found Mr. Curtis, who gave me some papers to carry to Quincy, relating to a Mortgage of real Estate in the hands of the Boylstons, which he had succeeded in selling.[2] Returned to dinner and was occupied all the afternoon in the Catalogue which my father and I are taking together.

My mother I am glad to find considerably better and more cheerful than I have known her for years. I am in slight hopes that she will find some things to recommend this part of the Country to her, and that finding herself now more independent than she ever was before, she will relish having a house of her own. My father seems to me however to be exceeding heavy, and not to take as well as he did the leisure with which he is perhaps overburdened. He thinks more of politics than I wish he did, but this is a necessary consequence of his situation in the Winter, in such a hot bed as Washington is. Evening my Mother went to ride, after which I had a little conversation with her. My father walked out to pay a visit or two, and I read Hume's Essay upon Eloquence.[3]

[1] The notes to Mrs. Woods and Col. Tyler are probably the same as those mentioned in the preceding entry; the letter to Mrs. Bailey is missing.
[2] Nathaniel Curtis negotiated the sale to the Treasurer of Harvard College of a mortgage for $10,000 on the Tremont Theatre (JQA, Diary, 19 June).
[3] CFA owned an edition of David Hume's *Essays and Treatises* published at London in 2 vols., 1788, now in MQA. The "Essay upon Eloquence" is in vol. 1.

SUNDAY. 20TH.

The morning began with a violent rain. So it has been for several successive Sundays. We (My father and I) went to Meeting in the morning in the Carriage, but in the afternoon it held up so that we walked. A certain Mr. Crafts preached but very flatly.[1] His style was ambitious without any foundation to sustain a flight. If a clergyman would form for his beginning plain sense strongly worded how much more it would take, particularly if he assisted the delivery of it with a little knowledge of manner. It is one thing to write well, another to read well. Many a man might easily afford to lose a little of the former character if he could gain in the latter, for bad speaking takes off half the effect of a good style, and good will grace even a defective one.

The weather was very disagreeable, being an Easterly Storm and I felt it more from being under the influence of a violent cold. I sat with my Wife nearly all day as she was quite unwell. In the evening, some conversation, for the first time with my father—This being the only occasion upon which he has not slept from weariness. Our talk was literary and not political, turning upon the character of the French drama, and upon versification in general, then upon Moliere whose plays we reviewed. Altogether, the pleasantest time I have had.

[1] Probably Rev. Eliphalet P. Crafts of East Bridgewater (*Mass. Register*, 1830).

MONDAY. 21ST.

The morning was cloudy, and the day attended with rain and a cold Easterly wind. After some deliberation, I concluded not to go to

Boston, a decision, I had no subsequent reason to regret, for I had a cold upon me which would have been made much worse by my visit without any outside coat to Boston. My father and I instead of it, went on vigorously with the Catalogue of his books, spending five or six hours in their arrangement, and in this way completed a great deal. He talks now of selling his Books, and so on. Every day astonishes me more at the change in his mind and feelings. The dejection is surprising, and the total indisposition to all the kinds of occupation which amused and interested him last year. He was so fatigued by his morning's work, that we did not resume it in the afternoon, and instead of it, I read a large part of Sheridan's Art of Speaking or Reading.[1] A good work, explaining very clearly the force of emphasis in the use of language. His illustrations taken from the book of common Prayer are clear and forcible—And made me feel as if I was a mere haphazard tiro in the art. It is however a more difficult thing than he allows to see clearly the sense of a passage. For any in the world may be varied by changing the emphasis. Evening, another agreeable conversation with my father. We discussed the political character of the close of the last Century. Pitt, Fox, Burke, Sheridan, Chatham, and the authorship of Junius.[2]

[1] Thomas Sheridan, *Lectures on the Art of Reading*, London, 1775.
[2] JQA had just received a letter from Dr. Waterhouse on the subject of the identity of Junius in which he had urged the claims of Lord Chatham and of Horne Tooke (JQA, Diary, 21 June).

TUESDAY. 22D.

As the weather was clear, and my father had business in town, we concluded to go in my Gig. My morning was spent as usual in a thousand little things—Making up bills and paying them. Received a short and snappish Note from Col. Tyler, inclosing the evidence of my brother's subscription, which I answered by sending him the Money.[1] Wrote to Spear my doubtful Tenant.[2] Mr. Woods called upon me about his Mother's affair, and talked it over. I told him I must go by the face of her Note, and if he had any statement to make, it must be submitted to the Judge of Probate. Mr. J. Q. Adams called about the Printing and I gave him his answer. Mr. Curtis spent a part of the morning at my room, but they could do none of the business they had contemplated.[3] I paid a short visit to Mr. Brooks and so the whole is explained.[4]

We returned to Quincy, and spent part of the afternoon in the Catalogue. But my father was dull and out of spirits. He had been talking Politics with Alex H. Everett. An effect is directly perceived. Evening Judge Adams and his Wife here. My Wife was quite unwell. My Mother and Mary sat down to Supper, but we had a stupid time.

[1] Enclosing payment, CFA wrote "it required only evidence of the fact, to produce payment of such an engagement" (to Col. J. S. Tyler, LbC, Adams Papers).

[2] The letter to John I. Spear is missing.

[3] The Treasurer of Harvard College had in the meantime changed his mind (JQA, Diary, 22 June).

[4] That is, CFA's and ABA's new plan to alternate between Quincy and Medford for the summer.

WEDNESDAY. 23D.

Morning clear and cool. Rode to town and passed all the morning as usual in a variety of pursuits. Having written my Journal and been to my House to dress, I walked down to see the progress of Mr. Hollis in covering my father's houses. Found the three completed, but neither of the sheds even commenced, nor were they working which I noted down, for I have a kind of notion they make me pay for it all. At my return to the Office, I sat down and read my father's further Chapters upon Turkey, in the Annual Register. His mind is a singular, certainly a powerful one, and though I am often tempted to doubt the correctness of his conclusions, yet I cannot help being struck with the power of his reasoning. Called in to see Mr. Brooks for a moment and found with him his son Edward and Mr. Everett. Talked a minute and then started for Quincy.

After dinner we went on with the Catalogue pretty rapidly, so that before evening we had finished one whole side of compact books. I read a little of Smollett's History of the last Years of George 2d in order to understand more clearly Horace Walpole's Memoirs which I propose to read.[1] But I always found Smollett very dull as a Historian. He hardly deserves the rank above a mere Annalist. Conversation in the Evening with my father upon Jeremy Bentham and Neal's Story about Platonic Trinitarianism.[2] He did not recollect it. After Supper, a discussion of the South Carolina Doctrines, and the nature of State and governmental Sovereignty.

[1] The reign of George II is encompassed in vols. 3–8 of the edition of Tobias Smollett, *The History of England from the Revolution to the Death of George the Second* ..., 8 vols., Basle, 1793–1794, now in MQA. The memoirs of Horace Walpole, 4th Earl of Orford, to which CFA refers were published as *Memoirs of the Last Ten Years of the* *Reign of King George II*, 2 vols., London, 1822.

[2] Probably in the memoir of Bentham written by John Neal (1793–1876) to accompany an edition of Bentham's *Principles of Legislation* published at Boston in 1830. See the *DAB* entry on Neal.

THURSDAY. 24TH.

Morning fine. Rode to town as usual. In reading the Newspaper I was very much struck with an Article in favour of the City's assuming the expense of Railroads.[1] Feeling myself as in some manner directly interested in this question, I felt very much disposed to answer it and accordingly began an Article for the purpose, but was obliged to leave it to go about Commissions for my Mother. These took me much time and were badly executed too. Mr. Merrill[2] called to pay me the sum due from J. T. Winthrop, to my brother George's Estate, which I had very little expectation of getting.[3] So far so good, but my Tenant Spear does not pay me. I had desired to finish my Article this morning but could not succeed. To Quincy to dinner. Afternoon employed in the Catalogue with my father in which we made no great progress, as it took much time to arrange the books. I had a little conversation with my father and mother upon the affairs of his property, and with the latter about the former. His condition worries me considerably, and I tried to induce my Mother to excite his almost blunted purpose, of writing upon my Grandfather. Louisa C. Smith and Abby S. Adams dined and spent the day here. My mother was unwell.

[1] In the letter signed "Honest Industry" (i.e. W. Foster), the use of tax money in the construction of a granite market (the Quincy Market) and a wharf is cited as a precedent for the construction at public expense of a projected railroad to the westward (*Boston Patriot*, 24 June, p. 2, col. 3).

[2] Probably James C. Merrill, counselor, of 39 Court Street (*Boston Directory*, 1830–1831).

[3] Apparently part of the balance owed on the loan made by GWA to the City Guards, of which Gen. Winthrop was commander (see entries for 3, 13 Oct. 1829; 10 April 1830, above; 10 Nov., below).

FRIDAY 25TH.

Morning fine. The Summer Weather seems to have set in at last. Went to town as usual and was occupied at the Office in making out the Accounts of the Quarter in order to see what the balance would be, as I contemplated taking advantage of the money, in a profitable opening which presented itself to me. The balance of the time was passed in reading the rest of my father's part of the annual Register, and finishing what I had written against "Honest Industry." Col. J. B. Davis happening to call in to ask if he should find my father at home if he went to Quincy, I told him of my Article which he consented to admit into his paper.

On Change I commissioned Degrand to buy me four Shares of Atlas

Insurance Stock, which he had spoken to me about, and in order to meet it decided upon selling out American Bank at the advance which it will probably bring. The rises and falls of Stocks are things not easily explicable to me. I do not see why now that Stock should be mounting which has been the source of so little profit for a long time back.

To Quincy to dine. Afternoon pursuing the Catalogue though languidly. It is a slow business and in this part of it not over interesting. It was terminated much sooner than usual by my accepting the determination of the ladies to ride. We went down to the Mount Wollaston Farm which looked pretty and wild enough. Had I wealth, I should like no better spot to beautify.[1] The Evening was passed in conversation with the family, in which my Mother took a very lively part.

[1] CFA's diary entries during the summer of 1830 reflect a delight in Mount Wollaston renewed with each visit. The attraction to it felt by four generations of Adamses, beginning with JA, found final expression when CFA's son JQA2 in 1877–1878 built his home upon it (Abigail Adams Homans, *Education by Uncles,* Boston, 1966, p. 5–10, illustra- tion facing p. 86). Located on the shore of Quincy Bay, the tract, origi- nally the property of AA's maternal fore- bears the Quincys, came into the pos- session of the Adams family after the death of Norton Quincy in 1801. On Mount Wollaston, see JA, *Diary and Autobiography,* 1:x, 141, 340, illustra- tion facing p. 256.

Quincy—Medford
SATURDAY 26TH.

Morning fine. My Wife and I left Quincy this morning for some days intending to make a stay for a short period at Medford, according to invitation. First to town, and I to the Office as usual. Inquired about my investment but found I had lost my chance. Still resolved to sell out of the American Bank if the Stock should go up. Finished a fair Copy of My Article about Railways, to send to the Patriot. Finished the whole of my fathers portion of the Annual Register with the Chapter on Greece. And consumed the remainder of my morning in going to make a bargain about my Mother's bathing tub, which I did not succeed in after all.

Went with my Wife to Medford and found upon our arrival Gor- ham Brooks and his Wife there, who came to dine and pass the after- noon. They are not favourites of mine. She has not character enough, he too much. Began upon Winthrop's Journal,[1] being resolved that if I must stay here, my time should not be altogether wasted. Evening, Conversation with Mr. Frothingham about Cromwell—Our views of his character.

[1] That part of John Winthrop's "Journal" known at the time was published in 1790 at Hartford. With the discovery in 1816 of a third section of the MS in the Prince Library, the Massachusetts Historical Society began at once to plan for a reissue of the earlier printed volume, corrected and annotated, and for the printing of the previously unpublished part in a second volume. With some help from the legislature and under the editorship of James Savage, the first volume was published at Boston in 1825, the second in 1826, both under the title *The History of New England from 1630 to 1649* (MHS, *Procs.*, 1st ser., I [1791–1835]:254, 374, 376). It was this edition that CFA was reading; see the next entry. His copy of the work is in MQA.

SUNDAY. 27TH.

Morning fine and warm. These two have been the first days in which the weather could be supposed to have shown us Summer. We attended divine service this morning, and heard Dr. Pierce [1] of Brookline preach in a manner not the most interesting to me. He dined with Mr. Brooks and as the Carriage was full, I walked home. The exercise not being usual to me at midday affected me a good deal—The heat being also considerable. It is a fair mile and a quarter in the Sun. I felt so fatigued that after dinner I fell asleep and declined attending Church. Dr. Pierce probably may not have relished it but I confess I return the compliment to his Sermons.

Mr. Frothingham preached at West Cambridge and dined at home which necessitated four walks like mine, and fatigued him pretty thoroughly. Read more of Winthrop in the afternoon. Mr. Savage does not please me. He writes some silly and other impudent Notes, and his book is altogether unworthy the labour he put upon it. The air was cooled by a thunder shower. Evening quietly spent—Every body being fatigued, soon went to bed.

[1] Long a minister at Brookline, John Pierce (1773–1849), Harvard 1793 (S.T.D. 1822), was a friend of JA. Pierce recorded in his MS diary (now in MHi) numerous meetings with JA at Quincy from 1796 onward, and also a detailed account of JA's funeral. A memoir of Pierce is in MHS, *Colls.*, 4th ser., I (1852):277–295; see also *NEQ*, 28:216–236 (June 1955), where accounts of his visits to JA are printed.

MONDAY. 28TH.

Morning very warm. I tried this morning Mr. Brooks' shower bath before breakfast and found myself exceedingly refreshed by it.[1] The feeling of the morning air though chilly is very delicious. There is a freshness about it, and the Country looks so verdant and still that it cheers the spirits to the task of the day. Rode to town and went to the Office. Mr. Spear my doubtful Tenant sent me two thirds of his Rent as did also Mrs. Wells. I believe in order to ensure punctuality it is highly necessary to keep persons in mind of their obligations. I was thus enabled to make a further deposit this month, and found that it had been the largest since my assuming the Agency. But this will avail little. My father seems equally satisfied if an Agent is minus a thousand dollars or if he scrapes faithfully every source. He came to town today much exhausted, and apparently depressed. I do not relish this in the least. He is in many respects an altered man. Returned to Medford to dine, but was caught in a very violent thunder shower which wet me very considerably.

Mr. Brooks and Mr. Frothingham did not dine at home, having gone to Charlestown to hear Mr. Everett deliver an Oration upon the Anniversary of it's being two hundred years since the first settlement.[2] I should like to have gone if I had not so violent a crowd to deal with. As it was I felt content in being able to sit and read Winthrop, though rather a dry study. The weather was showery. Evening, Mr. Stetson and Mr. Frothingham came home, afterwards Mr. Brooks. We got into a warm and animated conversation, or rather argument upon the subject of the Colonization scheme.[3] I confess I am rather inclined to think well of it as the only cool and apparently reasonable scheme which has been presented. But Mr. Brooks and Mr. Frothingham were against me.

[1] Peter C. Brooks had several years before constructed a "small house under the bank of the Canal" in which a shower bath was rigged. He delighted in the baths, prolonging them as late into the autumn as he could. CFA found the baths among the pleasant aspects of successive stays at Mystic Grove. See Brooks, Farm Journal, 24 Sept. 1826; below, vol. 4, entry for 22 Aug. 1832.

[2] The ceremonies had begun at Town Hall from where a procession moved up Main Street to Charlestown's First Church. There at 4 P.M. to an audience that crowded the hall "to excess," Edward Everett delivered an address "eminently able and eloquent" (*Boston Patriot*, 28 June, p. 2, col. 5; 30 June, p. 2, col. 2). The address is printed in Edward Ev-

erett, *Orations and Speeches on Various Occasions*, Boston, 1850, 1:215–245.

[3] The American Colonization Society addressed an appeal to the "Clergy and Congregations of all denominations of Christians throughout the United States" that was designed to be read in pulpits in support of "the establishment of colonies of the free people of colour on the African coast." The advancement of the colony of Liberia, it was held, would "relieve our country of a class injurious to the public welfare, ... elevate its character and confer upon it the most precious social and political blessings, ... suppress the slave trade, ... [and create] in Africa a Christian Republic" (*Boston Patriot*, 24 June, p. 2, col. 2).

TUESDAY 29TH.

Morning to town. At the Office nearly all day, busy in preparing my Quarterly Accounts, bringing them down to the present period and drawing out a Copy to present.[1] This has been the best Quarter since

I have had any thing to do with the Agency. Yet my father has the impression that his property in Boston is paying him nothing. So that aware as I am of the difficulty I have had to arrange it to the best advantage, I find that the expectations are always higher.

My reply to Mr. Foster's Article upon Railways appeared in this morning's paper, just after an article of his on the Constitutionality of it.[2] I did not relish it's appearance as I never do my own writing. Mr. Curtis called for a minute to see me, to speak of the Boylston affairs. After going to order a bathing tub for my Mother, I started for Medford.

The afternoon was again showery though with little thunder. I made great progress in Winthrop's Journal. Mr. Savage is a Tory, and a maker of very indifferent Notes. Strange that the Puritans should have fallen into such hands. Strange that a descendant should become so infected with the spirit of European dominion. Evening, Mssrs. Angiers came in on a visit of an hour.[3] Told us of a Robbery of the Branch Bank.

[1] CFA to JQA, 30 June (LbC, Adams Papers). The quarterly statement of the Agency showed a balance of $906.21 after payment of all repairs undertaken on the property. This amount did not include quarterly payments of $565 due to be met on 1 July nor any of the receivables due on the same day. CFA urged that the surplus that would be deposited to JQA's account be invested promptly. He reported as information that the income before expenses received by the Agency, 1 July 1829–30 June 1830, was $5,619.12.

[2] The second letter of "Honest Industry" urged the constitutionality of a grant by the city toward the construction of a railroad. CFA's letter, signed "A Calm Observer," followed this letter but was an answer to the earlier letter published on 24 June. Opposing the city's "dabbling in railways," CFA argued that government operation was inefficient and uneconomical, that railroad building was an artificial stimulant to the Boston economy, that "where capital is, there it will *naturally* seek advantageous investments." Summarizing, he wrote: "My choice is the slow jog of common sense, by which, though I lose in quickness of motion and perhaps opportunities for display, I am sure to get an equivalent—i.e. my journey's end without risk of my neck" (*Boston Patriot*, 29 June, p. 1–2).

[3] John and Luther Angier of Medford, masters of an academy for boys which several of ABA's brothers had attended (vol. 2:405; Brooks, Waste Book, 1821). On John Angier, who later married Abigail Smith Adams, see vol. 2:206 and Adams Genealogy.

WEDNESDAY. 30TH.

Morning fine, but it seems now hardly possible to go through a day without some rain. I went to town as usual, and passed my morning in making out my Accounts against the different Tenants and preparing my receipts as usual. This occupied much time. I have had little leisure to read any thing this season. My time seems short, and what with interruptions and small necessary jobs, I get on but indifferently in any studies I choose to lay down to myself. My intention was to have read Hutchinson and Minot, but I have not been able as yet to touch them. Returned to Medford to dine. Afternoon taken up with Company. Mr. Frothingham's relations, his Mother and sisters came to see him and the place. And they took tea.

Mr. Fuller the receiving Teller of the Branch Bank has gone off with forty thousand dollars—A Circumstance that produced considerable excitement here.[1] I saw him there so often that I had formed a kind of idea of his honesty which it seems circumstances prove very absurd. Every body *now* cries out how extravagant he was. The Bank would have thanked them perhaps if they had done it sooner. Evening at home. Winthrop.

[1] On the evening of 28 June, John Fuller, second teller in the Boston branch of the U.S. Bank, settled his accounts and handed over to the cashier his locked trunk, supposed to contain his balance of cash. The trunk was placed in the vault until morning. On the 29th Fuller did not appear; the trunk was opened and found empty. Reward was offered and a wide search begun. A week later he surrendered himself, returning all but $600 of the $40,000 taken. (*Boston Patriot,* 30 June, p. 2, col. 2; 10 July, p. 2, col. 3.)

THURSDAY. JULY IST.

Morning to town. Mr. Frothingham accompanied me. We agree very well on all subjects excepting political ones. He is much of a Tory. Astonishing how far these opinions and principles have crept into the instructed Classes of New England. How much the days of old are forgotten. Yet what can this Nation depend upon the moment it leaves those stays which have carried them hitherto through all trials.

I sent out my Quarterly Accounts, and received money from two of the Tenants in Court Street. Mr. Alexander H. Everett called to leave a package for my father. He talked a little while and looked at the Office opposite which he wished to have to hire. I hope he will take it, and for that purpose made the price moderate. Mr. Degrand came to offer me some Atlas Shares at 3 per Cent. Dividend which is 4 per cent off. I declined them but offered to take some Fire and Marine Shares if he could get them as high as two and a half. This is a bad speculation unless some change takes place in the affairs of the Company, which I think will happen, besides there being a considerable amount of Danish claims. These two things will probably run the Stock up when I can sell if I incline. In the mean time I sell out of the American Bank.

Returned to Medford and read Winthrop. Mr. Jonathan Brooks and Chardon Hall[1] made a short visit in the Evening.

[1] Peter Chardon Hall (b. 1809), youngest son of the Nathaniel Halls (Brooks, *Medford*, p. 548).

FRIDAY 2D.

Morning clear and warm. I arose very early to enjoy the freshness of the morning air. After breakfast, rode down with my Wife to Mr. E. Everett's at Charlestown where I left her, to pass the morning, and proceeded to town. My morning was taken up in usual little things. My hurry of business for the three last days prevented my writing my Journal for that time so that I had to make it all up at once today.

I forgot to mention that my Article drew me into Controversy, for Mr. Foster answered me and I took notice of his answer immediately. Whether he knows who it is I cannot say, but from certain allusions I conclude that he does. My reply was hurried and imperfect but a great point is to put it in quickly.[1]

I read today Mr. Alex H. Everett's article in the new Number of the North American Review upon British Opinions of American Literature written in his very best style.[2] This consumed the morning and I returned to Medford taking up my Wife on the way. Afternoon reading the second Volume of Winthrop, confirmed in my dislike of Savage. The Misses Osgood and Miss Ward[3] paid a visit to the House this evening, but I was so fatigued as to care very little about entering into Conversation. The Evening was brilliant and delicious.

[1] Foster in his reply charged that the arguments of "A Calm Observer" neglected the public benefit that would accrue and were addressed only to the question of whether the construction of a railroad would be advantageous to the wealthy (*Boston Patriot,* 1 July, p. 2, col. 3). CFA's answer asserted that the private and public interest are the same, "but a large body is always acting more blindly, and is therefore liable to be led wrong when a private man can clearly see his way." Further, "I do not mean to be understood as opposing railways.

If they are good, my belief is that capitalists will take hold of them, and that *their's* are the proper hands to undertake them" (same, 3 July, p. 2, col. 4).

[2] *North Amer. Rev.,* 31:26–66 (July 1830). A. H. Everett's observations on "An Article in the 99th Number of the *Edinburgh Review*."

[3] Perhaps Mary Gray Ward, daughter of Thomas W. and Lydia (Gray) Ward (*Medford Vital Records,* Boston, 1907, p. 160). See also entry for 26 July, below.

Quincy

SATURDAY 3RD.

Morning cloudy and warm. I took my last Shower bath. I have enjoyed them every day this week very much, and regret on their account leaving Medford, as I do on many others. They have there a quiet way of enjoying things which is extremely gratifying to a person after he gets accustomed to the ways of the family. But I felt obliged to leave for Quincy as I propose to make most of my visit as soon as possible.

At the Office. Mr. Conant my Tenant came in from Weston to make a final settlement of Accounts for last Year. He brought in all his demands and after setting them off paid me the balance. So far, so good. My Uncle, T. B. Adams came in and applied for his Quarterly Payment which I made to him. I then sat down to read my second Article in the Patriot, and afterwards, some of the North American Review, but was interrupted by Edmund Quincy who came and consumed the remainder of the time.

Went to Quincy to dine. Found my Mother better, but the family very much disordered by the conduct of a black fellow who came with them from Washington, whose looks I never liked. My father's servants have far too great licence. Nobody commands them but John and he is far too indulgent.[1] Went on with the Catalogue though rather slowly. Evening cool and damp. I felt restless and discontented.

[1] JQA dismissed William Taylor, paying him his wages "in full two months to the 18th," and sending John Kirke "to set him down at Boston." JQA's observation was that "it is scarcely possible to keep within any rule of order a family consisting partly of white and partly of coloured Servants." The next day John Kirke returned with a white boy, John Phillips, as a replacement. (JQA, Diary, 3, 4 July.) The generalizations of both CFA and JQA upon the incident are made less tenable by an occurrence a year later. At that time the same William Taylor proved to be the thief who entered and robbed in the night, JA2's house in Washington (JQA, Diary, 5, 6 July 1831).

SUNDAY. 4TH.

This is the great Anniversary of the Nation, and as it comes on Sunday, it would cheat people of their regular celebration if they had not the idea of making a succeeding day answer the purpose. My Mother as well as my Wife attended divine service this morning—An effort quite unusual to the former. Mr. Whitney gave us an occasional Address flat enough. Afternoon, my Wife and I went, and I was very sleepy. Nothing of any consequence happened, in the evening, I walked with my Father down to see Josiah Quincy and his Wife.[1] We found Miss Anna Q. there also.[2] A little affectation, and a great deal of family palaver with the latter lady, the former not much less, with a greater allowance of sentiment. We returned to sup at home.

[1] Sentence thus punctuated in MS.
[2] Presumably, Anna Cabot Lowell Quincy (b. 1812), youngest daughter of President Josiah Quincy, later Mrs.

Robert C. Waterston; see Adams Genealogy. Selections from her journals kept
during 1833 and 1834 are in *The*
Articulate Sisters, edited by M. A. DeW.
Howe, Cambridge, 1946, p. 193–244.

MONDAY. 5TH.

The morning threatened to be warm but a pleasant East Wind
came in time to cool us. I declined going to town, and passed my day
in reading Walpole's Memoires of the last ten Years of George the 2d.
with a volume of Smollett to illustrate. It is interesting, yet the very
miserable accommodations which I have for reading injure the interest
of my occupations very much. Continued my Work of Catalogue and
what with morning and afternoon did tolerably well. But my Father
was fatigued and indolent, and we were interrupted more than once.
Robert Buchanan, son of my Aunt, Mrs. Frye, came to Quincy to pass
a few days with us. He has just left West Point, and comes here to
pass a short time for the purpose of seeing the Country. He has altered
infinitely since I saw him last, and on the whole improved very materially.[1]

This was the day for celebration and noisy enough at the house at
Quincy, there being a celebration just above at the Railway.[2] We
drank John's birth day in a glass of pretty indifferent Champagne.
I was sleepy and stupid. Evening, a visit from Mr. Beale our Neighbour. Brilliant night.

[1]Robert Christie Buchanan (1811–
1878) was the son of LCA's sister, Mrs.
Nathaniel Frye Jr., by her first husband,
Andrew Buchanan. Robert Buchanan
had graduated from West Point a few
weeks before and was to have a distinguished military career. See vol. 1:4,
2:21; *DAB*; Adams Genealogy.

[2]Independence Day was celebrated at
Quincy beginning at 10 o'clock with a
procession to the Second Congregational
Meeting House in Milton, near the
Quincy and Milton ("Granite") Railway, where services were held at 12
noon. Following the services, there was
a dinner attended by two or three hundred persons in a tent erected in the
rear of the Railway Hotel (*Boston
Patriot*, 3 July, p. 2, col. 5; 8 July, p.
2, col. 1; 14 July, p. 2, col. 2). On the
Railway, see below, entry for 23 Aug.;
its proximity to the Old House is evident
on the "map of Boston and the adjacent towns" reproduced in the present
volume.

TUESDAY. 6TH.

Morning clear and very warm. I rode to town with the other Horse
in my Gig who has been sick. He is a very fine horse and brought me
into the City in amazing little while. At the Office. Owing to my absence from the City for two days I had a good deal of Journal to make
up, and with my interruptions, allowed me little time for reading.
Mr. Champney came in to present his Account in set off of Rent.

I balanced it and he promised to pay me directly. Mr. Gay gave me his money. Champney asked me also to make a Writ for him against him. It is now so long since I have made one that I felt as if it was quite a new business. I then went to the House for Abby S. Adams' receipt to make to her my regular payment. Found my man Benjamin Salter inclined to go away and he accordingly gave me notice that he should quit me upon my return.[1] Mr. Curtis called to ask me to draw a Deed, another little business Job. R. G. Wait, an appraiser of New's Estate came with a schedule of his desperate debts. He told me they intended making a return next week. Mr. Spear called to pay the balance of his Rent. Expressed himself well satisfied with the House. I called upon Stone and received the amount from the sale of G.W.A's Uniform and afterwards my own Dividend at the Atlas Office, which investment has so far turned out very well.

All this left me no more time, and I went out of town in a Shower, to meet the Directors of the Neponset Bridge Corporation at their Annual dinner at Squantum. They invite a number and make quite a party. The situation is very pleasant, though a great way to go round to reach it.[2] Mr. J[oseph] Head and his two sons Joseph and George, Mr. Miller, T. Greenleaf, Beale, J. Quincy Jr., Gourgas, J. H. Foster and his son Wm. E., Mr. T. B. Wales, my father, Uncle and myself constituted the party. We dined upon Fish and had on the whole a tolerably pleasant time. Returned and passed the Evening quietly. Edmund Quincy called with a young man from Halifax, by name of Sewall.[3] The ladies were out. I was very tired.

[1] CFA's manservant, Benjamin Salter, returned to CFA's employment after a few months (see below, entry for 23 Sept.).

[2] The dinner was probably held at the Old Squantum House located on the point and overlooking Quincy Bay. The area is included on the map referred to in the notes to the preceding entry.

[3] JQA identifies him as the grandson of JA's youthful friend, the loyalist Jonathan Sewall, and as of Montreal (Diary, 6 July).

WEDNESDAY. 7TH.

Morning warm. Rode to town as usual. At the Office regulating my Accounts both as Agent and in my private capacity. Wrote my Journal and drew the Deed for Mr. Curtis as requested, though he did not call for it. Drew the Dividend for the Neponset Bridge and received the rent of the House in Hancock Street from Miss Oliver, so that I was enabled to make a very good deposit. But all this and a call upon Mr. Brooks kept me much longer than I had any idea of so that I did not get to Quincy until half past two. Afternoon occupied in the

Catalogue which progresses gradually. But there is so little energy in the process that I am heartily tired and sick of it.

This day was one of my dispirited, discouraged days. I felt a disgust with the mode of life which I am pursuing, and with the manner in which my fathers family is conducted. The Servants being extravagant and unruly, my father dispirited, my Mother sick, my brother's Wife querulous, and all on the whole uncomfortable. I did little or nothing. Evening, Supper, and a short Conversation with my father upon Warren Hastings, but without much interest, as I was fatigued.

THURSDAY. 8TH.

The morning was cloudy, which became afterwards rain. Robert Buchanan went into town with me, and I left him at the end of Purchase Street for the purpose of starting in the Steam Boat to the Fort where he wished to go.[1] At the Office myself, in my usual avocations, which were not quite so much of a business kind today. Read a portion of Hutchinson's History of Massachusetts over again. Conversed with Thomas Welsh upon New's Affairs and made final arrangements respecting my brother George's Assets, by sending all the rest of the saleable things to be disposed of at Auction. Thus passed the morning. And after going to my House to obtain Elizabeth Adams' receipt, I went out of town with Robert to dine.

My father seemed unwell, and we made slow work with our Catalogue particularly as John arrived in the midst of our commencement and distracted us a little. I felt differently towards him this year from what I ever did before, which arises from many circumstances too numerous to mention but more particularly from the very uncomfortable condition in which the family is put by his Wife.[2] My own were not false anticipations. Judge T. B. Adams was here in the Evening. Retired early.

[1] Probably Fort Independence, at the entrance to Boston's inner harbor; a military garrison was maintained there.

[2] Mrs. JA2 was a semi-invalid, being in the last months of pregnancy. The space which she required along with that needed for her little girl and the child's nurse resulted in some inconvenience to JQA and LCA.

FRIDAY. 9TH.

Morning cold and cloudy. I rode to town with my Wife who came in for a Bath. At the Office as usual where I read another silly communication from W. Foster in the Patriot.[1] The time for decision is now rapidly drawing to us, and I today reflected upon the materials for a closing Article in this Controversy. My ideas would not come freely so I felt obliged to give up the point, for the day.

Mr. Degrand called to offer me some Atlas Stock at 2 per cent which I declined, not caring much about placing any more there. Mr. Curtis also called for the Deed I had drawn which I gave him. Mr. Holt a paper hanger called with a trifling bill for Work at the Tenement rented by Mrs. Welles. I would not pay it intending to do some more work there. Called to see Mr. Brooks who told me a comical story of Mr. J. Porter's going to Europe. It seems his Wife does not know her own Mind.[2]

Returned with my Wife to Quincy to dine, after which I was engaged with my father in making out his Catalogue, which occupied much time. We were interrupted by a visit from Mrs. Cruft and Pickman with their Mother Mrs. Smith, Mrs. Otis and her daughter Mary.[3] An old set on their annual visit. I then walked up to Judge Adams' to see Miss Elizabeth, to pay her quarterly interest but she as well as all the rest of the family were absent. The remainder of the evening with the family.

[1] *Boston Patriot*, 9 July, p. 2, col. 2.
[2] Probably Jonathan Porter, whose wife, Catherine, was the daughter of Samuel Gray of Medford by his first wife and was a ward of Peter C. Brooks after the death of her father (Brooks, *Waste Book*; *Medford Vital Records*, Boston, 1907, p. 113, 277).
[3] On Mrs. Edward Cruft, Mrs. Benjamin Pickman Jr., and Mrs. Samuel A. Otis; on their mother, Mrs. William Smith; and on Mary Ann Otis, see vol. 1:269, 270, 334, and Adams Genealogy.

SATURDAY 10TH.

Morning to town as usual. Passed my morning in writing and reading the North American Review. Interrupted once or twice, by persons calling, and by going down to see about the Dividend of the West Boston Bridge. Found that it had made one and considered it as on the whole good property. Called to see Mr. Brooks but he was not in town. On the whole did not progress much in the actual execution of business. Returned to Quincy to dine and spent the afternoon as usual in continuing the Catalogue of the Library. We finished the large room, and have now all the remainder in the room above and the Office to do. This will take more time than I have to give to it. My mother was not very well. She does not seem to recover as fast as I could have hoped.

SUNDAY 11TH.

Morning fine. Attended Divine Service all day and heard Mr.

Whitney preach a couple of Sermons upon the spirit which is now so prevalent, of Universalism.[1] He is himself as much inclined that way as was advisable, but he draws a distinction, by which he admits the probability of future though not eternal punishment, against the doctrines of probable salvation in any event. A more dangerous doctrine than this can scarcely be conceived yet the tendency is always towards it. Nothing is more dangerous than liberality as it is affectedly called, for vice slides in under so specious a mask that good men find they are left in the lurch before they are at all aware of it. Mr. Whitney is a good man but one of the weak ones who does not see where his doctrines will be likely to leave him. Already he is alarmed by the distant sound, but he is likely to feel what he has been so long bringing about much more harshly before he dies. Another sect is trying to gain a footing and will probably succeed.[2] The singing at this Church is horrible though called by the performers so fine as to inflict upon us a great deal of it.

In the evening I walked up to my Aunt Adams' to make another attempt to see Miss Elizabeth, which I barely succeeded in doing. She is always out, and her Mother is so silly as to try to excuse it to me as if I cared. They sent for her tonight, so that I finished that Quarterly business, much to my satisfaction. Returned home to a quiet supper.

[1] Although the history of Universalism began in Boston in 1785, its significant development as a church dates from 1817 when the Second Society was established and from 1819 when the *Universalist Magazine* was founded. By 1824 there were in New England and New York a dozen Universalist publications, and by 1830 there were four societies in Boston. (See A. A. Miner, "The Century of Universalism," in Winsor, *Memorial History of Boston*, 3:483–508).

[2] Universalist sermons currently were being preached in Quincy to a growing auditory, and a society was about to be formed. See Pattee, *Old Braintree and Quincy*, p. 259–260, and below, vol. 4, entry for 26 June 1831, note.

MONDAY. 12TH.

The weather was cold and disagreeable. The wind from the Eastward brought a driving sea mist, which wet me pretty thoroughly before I reached town, so that I thought it advisable to go home and change my dress. My particular object in coming was to attend the town meeting for the settlement of the question as to the amount to be borrowed to make a Railway. I went and saw for the first time in my life a primary assembly of the people in Boston. It was not agreeable, particularly as it was very evident the sentiment of the mob was clear and strong. The speaking was none of it good, though some of it was violent enough. I felt somewhat excited although there was in fact nothing material to occasion it. But I confess I regretted that the public feeling should run so strongly in favour of a measure which I hold to be ruinous.[1]

The whole morning was taken up however so that I had only a minute to go and see Mr. Brooks after which I went out of town. The afternoon was passed in taking the list of the remaining books in the Entry and lower floor, leaving now only what are in the Upper Story. Finished Walpole's 1st. Volume in the evening. An interesting account of a very uninteresting period.

[1] The meeting held at 10 A.M. in Faneuil Hall was for the purpose of hearing and debating the report of a committee recommending application to the legislature for authority for the city to take stock in a railroad from Boston to the north or west. Without taking action, the meeting was adjourned to 10 A.M. on 2 Aug. (*Boston Patriot*, 13 July, p. 2, cols. 1–4).

TUESDAY. 13TH.

The day was so rainy and disagreeable that I concluded not to go to town at all. My time was very much taken up in commencing upon an Alphabetical arrangement of the books. This is slow and difficult as I look at each Title and in a great many cases examine the account of the Author very fully. In this manner the acquisition of general knowledge of a description a good deal wanted will go on with the mechanical part of the Work. I accomplished this day, the letter A. which as I thought was doing pretty well. The afternoon was taken up in the prosecution of the same plan which carried me through a part of B. My mother being now unwell, deprives me of the chance of going through with the remainder of the books.

The rain continued without any cessation and confined us to the House. Conversation with John and Robert Buchanan. It is surprising to me how little John has cultivated elegant tastes. His steps ever since he has been at Washington, may be called retrograde, which is somewhat of a pity. Evening reading an Article in the Quarterly Review upon the Peerage of England.[1] A good article though breathing a spirit of a character questionable to say the least, in this Country.

[1] A review of four French works on nobility; of Debrett's *Peerage* . . . , 18th edn., 2 vols., 1829; and of Nicholas Harris Nicolas, *A Synopsis of the Peerage of England*, 2 vols., 1825; in *Quarterly Review*, 42:281–333 (March 1830).

WEDNESDAY. 14TH.

The morning was clear and as the Clouds that remained from yesterday were passing away, they gave to the Atmosphere a damp, sultry heat which is very unpleasant having the true character of a dog day. The roads were also in a shocking condition as we rode over them to town, Robert Buchanan being with me. As he called upon my time considerably, I was forced to pass over my own business. The Appraisers returned me the Account of New's Estate, about which measures must be taken as soon as possible. A client came but his application was a mere nibble. Rufus Davenport called with his Free Debt Rules, and I got rid of him as soon as possible.[1] Collected the balance of Rent due on the commencement of this Quarter and made the Deposit in the Bank.

The remainder of the day was taken up in showing to Robert Buchanan, the Athenæum Gallery and Library, in which last operation I saw more myself than I had ever done before. This made us late so that we got back to Quincy much after the usual hour. I was fatigued, so that we did not prosecute the Catalogue very zealously in the afternoon, though I did a little in the arrangement. Evening at home. Conversation with John after dinner.

[1] Rufus Davenport's address was 65 Congress Street; he has not been further identified (*Boston Directory*, 1830–1831).

THURSDAY. 15TH.

The morning was bright and clear. I arose early this morning in order to fulfil my agreement with Robert Buchanan and my brother, which was to go down on a fishing excursion to Cohasset rocks.[1] We started early in the little Carriage, and enjoyed our ride. The place I had never before seen. It is naked, and rocky, exposed to the action of the sea and the wind, much like Nahant, though not quite so much insulated. There is a beach here very similar to that and much longer. Having reached there, we went down to fish and very soon caught enough to make a considerable quantity. The sport for the first two hours was very good. It afterwards became less so until the latter hours of the day when it was nothing but nibbling.

The day was agreeable, but it is so long since I have had any kind of exposure to the Sun, that when we returned to the Hotel to dine, I found that I had got my face very thoroughly scorched, so much so as to be not a little painful. We found at the House,[2] my Uncle, the Judge, and Mr. Gourgas, his future son in law, and we joined parties at dinner. The Hotel can scarcely be called first rate, so that it needed a tolerable appetite to get along. With this we were all gifted to a considerable degree. We returned home about sunset. On the whole my time for parties of this kind is a little gone by. The suffering is a severe counterbalance to the amusement. I was so fatigued as to wish Edmund Quincy away, when he called to pay a visit.

¹ On "Cohasset rocks," a favorite fishing area seven or eight miles to the east of Quincy in Massachusetts Bay, and on the long association of the Adams family with the area, see JA, *Diary and Autobiography*, 4:7.
² That is, at the hotel.

FRIDAY. 16TH.

The morning was very warm, and I was feeling not a little, the influence of yesterday's sun, when I started with my Wife to go into town. Our household is very troublesome, as my manservant has concluded to go away, and we do not know what to do with our Cook. There was a consultation which resulted in nothing. I went to the Office where I was engaged in making up my Journal for some days back, as my occupations had prevented regularity. Several little things were also to be attended to which took up the hours so that I did little else. The weather was also of a nature to incapacitate one from much labour. We returned to Quincy to dine and I rarely recollect feeling the heat more than in that ride. The Thermometer ranged considerably over ninety degrees. My Wife was made quite sick by it all the afternoon, and my father made little progress with me in the Catalogue. After tea, my brother John and I started for the bath, which was quite delicious. Mr. Miller and Mr. Beale called in the Evening to pay a visit—After which we had much conversation.

SATURDAY. 17TH.

The day appeared as warm as any of the preceding, being entitled to the rank of our hottest weather. I rode into town and passed the morning at my Office and the house. I went to the latter in order to give final directions about shutting up the House. This proceeding is not by any means an agreeable one to me. I had hoped to have got rid of remaining in the Country but it seems that I must now stay longer than I had ever anticipated.

Occupied in drawing up the estimates of New's debts in order to present it to the Judge on Monday, and in my Journal. The day made me feel languid and illdisposed to action. Returned to Quincy to dine in the heat of the day. The ride was warm and uncomfortable. My Wife was extremely sick all day and the heat of the weather increased her suffering.

The house at Quincy is but poorly qualified either to be cool in Summer or warm in Winter. I sat and continued the Catalogue in my

Mother's room which by some chance was the very hottest in the House. We made some progress notwithstanding, and will soon finish as I hope. The work has now become a little tedious to me. My father is indifferent although he keeps up on the whole better than I expected. Evening, the family went to ride, and little was done of any kind.

SUNDAY. 18TH.

The heat had not relaxed in it's intensity this morning. I have rarely felt the Sun more powerful than it was today upon our going to the Creek to bathe after breakfast. The water was nevertheless very refreshing. We returned but I did not get dressed in time for Church. I was not very sorry for it. Read the History of Horace Walpole and a part of the Quarterly Review, which were on the whole quite amusing. My Wife was better today but still not recovered from yesterday. The family seemed all of them a little upset by the weather.

Miss L. C. Smith dined with us and in the afternoon, I attended divine service and heard Mr. Capen of South Boston who was very prosy and very disagreeable.[1] I felt sleepy and could not resist the influence. The Evening felt cooler to me, and I read a part of the Quarterly Review with much satisfaction. The other members of it [2] went to ride with the exception of my Mother and Wife.

[1] Lemuel Capen was the minister in the Hawes Place Church, South Boston (*Mass. Register*, 1830).
[2] Thus in MS.

MONDAY. 19TH.

The day was warm but an Easterly wind arose about the middle of the day to make it much more tolerable than any of the preceding ones have been. I rode into town as usual and was occupied, first in making up my list of demands against New's Estate, finishing the appraisement, returning the Inventory and making application for the sale of his real Estate. This took a large portion of time, but as the period within which I was limited expires next week, it is matter of much satisfaction that the whole affair is arranged.

I then went up to the house to give my Cook her directions as to going out of town. It was still very warm to walk so that all this exertion fatigued me. Warm weather is agreeable enough when a person has nothing to do but to sit at home, when much walking is necessary, it might as well be dispensed with. Returned to Quincy to dine. My father was so exhausted by the heat of last night that he could not prosecute the Catalogue, so that I was compelled to go on with the alphabetical arrangement, and this moved very slowly. Evening, a little more of the Quarterly Review and Supper. How time flies.

TUESDAY. 20TH.

The weather does not seem to moderate materially, but the East wind which rises in the day prevents one from feeling quite so much it's violence. I had not quite so much to do in the town today and therefore enjoyed my stay in town much more. Yet I do not know that in fact I spent my time a particle more usefully than usual.

Some few things to be obtained of different persons for my father, and my own hair to be cut, took up much of the morning, the balance passed in reading the Oration of Mr. Everett at Charlestown.[1] This is good. He has taken the right hold of the matter though in a tone a little too meek and lowly for my taste. The State of Massachusetts will exist firmly only while she sticks to the principles and feelings planted by the Puritans, and one of the worst of her signs at the present day is that their posterity is so ready to undervalue them.

I returned to Quincy as usual and occupied myself in the Alphabetical arrangement as my father was too warm and fatigued to do much. He overexerts himself and then complains.[2] The Evening was cool. I read Walpole when I was not conversing. Judge Adams' two daughters and Miss Mary Foster paid a visit.

[1] Edward Everett's address at the commemoration of Charlestown's settlement was published as a pamphlet only the day before (*Boston Patriot*, 19 July, p. 3, col. 3).

[2] JQA noted in the monthly summary of his *day* that his "worst symptom is a growing and unresisted repugnance to labour" (JQA, Diary, 31 July). His diary entries during most of the summer are given over largely to summarizing the passages from Cicero that he read each day.

WEDNESDAY. 21ST.

Morning exceedingly warm. I rode to town without being at all aware of the severe nature of the heat, or it is more than probable that I should have remained at home. At the Office occupied as usual, but as I felt extremely indisposed to make exertion I took the day very quietly to read Hutchinson in which I made considerable and good progress. The History interests me more and more, and satisfies me that my impressions formerly taken are correct. It is strange how the impressions concerning it are perverted.

Little or nothing took place of any consequence and owing to the warmth of the weather I was not much disposed to remain very long in town. Returned slowly. The heat was greater today than it has yet been. The Afternoon passed as usual, my father quite unable to do any thing, and I pursuing the arrangement of my Catalogue as rapidly as possible. But this is not very much when one melts visibly. The evening with the family. On the whole, pretty idle.

THURSDAY. 22D.

Another excessively hot day, so much so that I felt unable to advise my Wife to keep her engagement to go to Medford. The Sun seemed to strike a concentrated heat as I stood a little while in the Garden so that I recommended an entire absence of both of us from Boston. But Mr. Beale and Mr. Miller had invited the family to go to Squantum today with an abundance of ladies and gentlemen who were going from Quincy. I felt as if I ought to go or submit to be called fastidious in a great degree, so that after abundance of doubt, I decided in favour of going. My father, brother, John and I went in the Carriage. The ride was pleasant, having the air. We reached there to find a large collection of persons too numerous to name particularly. After a bath with the gentlemen and a sail with the ladies, we trifled away the rest of the time to a fish dinner. This was good though not the best. The afternoon went while I was watching the bowling alley. On the whole, as I was cool and did not feel very much ennuyé, my visit this day to Squantum turned out an agreeable disappointment. We reached home at six to warm weather again. But although the night was a dead calm, I did not suffer at all, on the contrary my evening was cool, and night's sleep sound.

Medford

FRIDAY 23D.

The weather changed during the night and this morning we found it quite cool with an Easterly Wind. This put us in mind of fulfilling our engagement. So that after breakfast Abby started with me to go to town. I drove to P. C. Brooks Jr. where she got out, and then went myself to the Office. Stopped to see Mr. Stephen Brown and inquire if he had any Atlas Insurance Stock for sale.[1] He thought he had ten shares but the man concluded to keep them, and I was disappointed of the Investment I had hoped to make for my father.

My time was much cut up. I was in State Street for some time and there met Mr. J. H. Foster who asked me to go and see the Shark caught lately, who was supposed to have destroyed the man from

Lynn.[2] Rather a terrific animal as I should think to meet single handed. His teeth are arranged with a singular economy, for prey. The inner row lie flat in the mouth unless when necessary for use, when they strike as firmly as the external row, and both are sharp as the teeth of a saw.

I read a little of Horace Walpole today also. It then became time for me to start for Medford, so that calling for Abby at Miss Julia Gorham's, I rode with her out of town. We found Mrs. Frothingham as usual, with Miss Phillips one of the large number from Andover. An innumerable quantity the *count* of whom it is difficult to keep.[3] I did little or nothing after dinner though I attempted to read the first part of Le Batteux, Principes de la Construction Oratoire.[4] Edward B. Hall, and afterwards Mr. Stetson called and passed the larger part of the Evening here in conversation, so that I had only a very short period of time to apply to *Winthrop* whom I have resumed.

[1] Stephen Brown was a broker and auctioneer whose office was at the Exchange (*Boston Directory*, 1830–1831).

[2] When Joseph Blaney of Swampscott, while fishing in a dory off Scituate, was attacked and killed by a shark, the event created a local sensation. Ten days later a ten-foot-long female shark, presumed to be the same, was taken by Blaney's son-in-law in the vicinity of the attack and put on exhibition in Boston (*Boston Patriot*, 16 July, p. 2, col. 2; 24 July, p. 2, col. 2).

[3] Of the thirteen children of John and Lydia (Gorham) Phillips, nine of the daughters were unmarried in 1830 (Henry Bond, *Genealogies ... of Watertown*, Boston, 1860, p. 886).

[4] In the edition of *Principes de la littérature* by Abbé Charles Batteux, published at Göttingen and Leyden in 5 vols., 1764 (a copy of which is in MQA), "Traité de la construction oratoire des mots" is the last of the three works contained in the fifth volume.

SATURDAY 24TH.

The morning was cloudy and from the exhaustion of last week I probably slept much more soundly than usual, for it was breakfast time before I arose. My wife had not a very good night, she being affected by some of the prescriptions given to her by the physician Dr. Holbrook.[1] After breakfast rode to town accompanied by Mr. Frothingham. The road extremely dusty.

At the Office, occupied in writing my Journal and arranging my accounts. Read a little of Horace Walpole's Memoires but my time slipped away so rapidly I did not accomplish much. My friend Richardson called in to see me for the first time for a considerable period. I was obliged to stop the conversation, in order to attend a sale of Stocks at Merchant's Hall where I wished to buy.[2] Insurance Stock went so high, I declined making any purchase, and now I feel it doubtful whether I shall be able to make any investment at all. Mr.

Degrand came in afterwards to ask me to get a power to sign for the State Bank Stock, as he was projecting a movement there. I told him I would see about it. Mr. Curtis came in to tell me that my father's picture had arrived and was ready for transportation. I called in at Doggett's to see it, and was disappointed in the effect of Sully's finishing.[3] Thence to Medford. Found P. C. Brooks and Lt. Griswold of the Army there to dine. The day turned out very warm, and I was so sleepy that my progress in Le Batteux was not very rapid, at least so far as being thorough was concerned. Evening passed in conversation.

When absent from Medford I think I like it, because I try to, but when I go back there, things are constantly presenting themselves to me in a very disagreeable way. The true secret is that there are no leading points of agreement in opinion and feeling between Mr. Brooks and myself.

[1] The Adamses' family doctor, Amos Holbrook (1754–1842) lived in Milton (Alden, *Medical Profession in Norfolk County*, p. 17; Edward P. Hamilton, *A History of Milton*, Milton, Mass., 1957, p. 253).

[2] The sale, advertised by Stephen Brown, was at noon in Merchants' Hall at the corner of Water and Congress streets. Insurance company stocks listed for sale brought advances of from six to fifteen and a quarter above par (*Boston Patriot*, 24 July, p. 3, col. 5; 26 July, p. 2, col. 4).

[3] See entry for 28 Jan., above.

SUNDAY. 25TH.

The Morning was as warm as any during the Summer, but it cooled off with rain and a thunder shower before night. We all attended divine service in the morning and heard Mr. C. T. Thayer deliver a discourse in quite a smooth, flowing manner. He imitates Mr. Everett and not badly. Indeed if his matter bore him out, I know no young man in the Pulpit who would succeed better. He dined with us and seemed pleasant enough though I have a prejudice against him from a resemblance to his brother. To think that he only a year before me in College has found a settlement in life, while I am as yet on the mere threshold.[1] Yet we are all advancing with rapid steps into the midst of active and bustling existence. There is no time to be lost by any one if he is wise enough to think.

As it rained, we did not go, (Abby and I) in the afternoon. She read French to me after which I read Le Batteux. Not much to be got from him. After all my notion is the true one. Oratory can hardly be acquired by learning the mere theory.

[1] Christopher Toppan Thayer, Harvard 1824, was the minister of the Congregational church in Beverly (vol. 2:175 and *Mass. Register*, 1831). The brother referred to here and at vol. 2:240 is probably John Holbrook Thayer, Harvard 1826.

MONDAY. 26TH.

The morning was cloudy and damp with a slight drizzling rain. I rode into Boston very uncomfortably, and passed my morning at the office. Much surprised to hear of the death of Judge Parker. He has been for many years a distinguished character in the history of this State, has played a part both as jurist and politician, and dies now with more name and reputation than would have been given him in 1812. I never admired his principles but am willing to admit his merit as the only good Judge upon our bench upon all questions not political, and as an excellent private character.[1] Peace be to his manes.[2] This generation are rapidly passing off, after having played a very respectable part. Their successors do not seem to equal them.

Heard also of a shocking accident which happened to the son of Mr. T. W. Ward at Medford; he was thrown from a horse and killed instantly. We had not heard any thing of it at Mr. Brooks' though the thing took place on Saturday.[3]

I read Walpole and wrote so that my time passed rapidly. Left town in a shower of rain and without Mr. Frothingham whom I had agreed to bring out, which troubled me much as I feared I had started too soon. He had walked in the morning. Mr. Brooks brought John Gorham. After dinner I read Winthrop and Batteux. The former has become very tiresome. And I have no resources at Medford. Here is the true superiority of Quincy to me which more than compensates for all the things of this world. Evening quiet at home.

[1] Judge Isaac Parker, Harvard 1786, was chief justice of the Supreme Judicial Court from 1814 to his death (see vol. 1:467). Following an apoplectic attack on the 25th, he died just after returning to Boston from Salem, where he had delivered a charge to the grand jury summoned to consider indictments in the murder of Capt. Joseph White (JQA, Diary, 27 July; *Boston Patriot*, 26 July, p. 3, col. 1; 27 July, p. 2, col. 2). Although antifederalist feeling ran high against Parker before he became chief justice, particularly in the several years that followed his presiding over the trial in 1807 of a prominent federalist, T. O. Selfridge, for the murder of Charles Austin (of which Selfridge was acquitted), Judge Parker's fairness and ability on the bench soon won general acclaim (*DAB*).

[2] That is, soul or spirit.

[3] William Ward, ten years of age, was the son of Thomas W. Ward, of Boston and Medford, and his wife Lydia, a daughter of Samuel Gray by his first wife (*Boston Patriot*, 26 July, p. 3, col. 2; *Medford Vital Records*, p. 317, 454; Brooks, Waste Book).

TUESDAY. 27TH.

The morning was very damp and wet. I had felt a slight twinge in the bowels upon getting up, so that I concluded not to go to town today. Instead, I remained at home and read Batteux upon Oratory. His instruction is excellent though most of it is taken from the old and standard sources which have been so often used as to become common-place. Yet good writing and speaking are not to be met with every day. The reason is that the theory though ever so excellent is nothing gained towards perfection unless the practice is carried on simultaneously. And the true art is missed in three attempts out of four. My own experience trifling as it is, tells me what a different thing it is to read in the Closet, and to speak before a thousand.

The weather was dull and evidently affected the family in spite of themselves. The afternoon passed in reading Winthrop. I cannot help sometimes reflecting how much better I should be doing if I was at home, but every thing in this world cannot be as we wish. We were all confined to the House, excepting to ride. And the day was stupid.

WEDNESDAY. 28TH.

Morning damp and stormy. This weather seems disposed to hold out a prodigious length of time. I rode to town with John Gorham who while he has been at Medford has had little to interest him in Country amusements. At the Office. Received a letter from my father with a power of Attorney to sign for the State Bank.[1] Apparently John came to town yesterday so that I missed him completely. Mr. Degrand called with his State Bank paper and I signed it for my father and myself. It is for a Meeting to make the building more profitable. No prospect however of investing.

I spent a large portion of the morning in drawing up my last paper upon the Railway subject. The town meeting comes on Monday and I feel desirous of one more attempt beforehand. The rest of the time passed in reading Walpole. Returned to Medford and spent the Afternoon in reading Batteux very lazily so as hardly to reach the marrow.

The Evening was distinguished by a discussion with Mr. Frothing-ham which was too warm to be pleasant. His views and feelings are rather stiff on one side and mine are equally stiff on the other. Our principles political and moral are totally at variance and when any subject happens to come up not of an ordinary character it sets us against each other. He happened to indulge tonight in a sarcastic sneer according to his custom upon the character of our ancient puritans which I with my feelings could not stand. So we had a sharp bout of it. After which I read Winthrops Journal and became more and more convinced of the correctness of my ground. But such arguments are useless, perhaps worse.

[1] Letter missing.

THURSDAY. 29TH.

The morning was damp and rainy, so much so that Mr. Brooks decided upon not going to town. As I had remained here once this week, and was anxious to go to town, I fixed upon disregarding the rain altogether. My ride was of course dark and I reached my office only to sit down quietly and read Walpole after finishing my Article for the Patriot, which I believe will close for the present at least, my writing in the Newspapers. It is at best an unprofitable business, and this a peculiarly unprofitable subject.

I was much interested in Walpole. On the whole he has made a favourable impression upon me. I like his warmth, his politics and his nature. Qualities which though they hurt him as a historian, yet increase my personal feeling for him. He writes English too, remarkably well. It is a style exceedingly flowing and easy yet very difficult to imitate well.

I rode out in the Rain though it did not wet me, and passed the afternoon in reading Batteux, whose remarks upon the manner of Oratory are exceedingly good. I also brought out a number of the Edinburgh in which I dipped.

Evening, finished Winthrop's Journal. Mr. Savage closes by saying that he died too early to hear of the *distressing* news of his old master's, (Charles') execution. A sympathy which I doubt if Winthrop himself had so feelingly entertained, particularly as his connexions in England were all engaged against the King, and he considers in one of his letters the account of his temporary success as *sad news*. All which Mr. S. does not condescend to consider.

FRIDAY. 30TH.

The morning opened with continued rain. This is the fifth day that we have not seen the Sun. A fact neither useful nor agreeable to us apparently. Mr. Brooks and Mr. Frothingham decided to go to town, so that I thought I would not. For some days back I have not felt very well from some cause or other which it is beyond me to divine and it did not seem to me altogether prudent to hazard the damp without a coat. Mr. Frothingham having today a use for his and I not possessing here any of my own.

I finished the Volume of Batteux upon Oratorical style, and the remarks upon Historical and Epistolary Style which are very good. The translation of the Oration for Archias though good in its way only explains the more clearly the deficiency of the French language and the fullness of the Latin.[1] Cicero was a master, and I must sit down when I get home and read his works as I have all along intended. They are all worth study.

But my reading now has come to an end here at Medford, so that for the remainder of the day I was obliged to recur to the Edinburgh Review most of which I read. This number has nothing in it very remarkable. A criticism upon a wretched poem which never had any merit though a good deal of popularity.[2] The evening was taken up in reading Mr. Stewart's answer to Mr. Channing's election Sermon.[3] He is an orthodox writer upon a subject not over interesting, but he handles his pen powerfully enough to take with one.[4]

[1] Charles Batteux, *Oraison de Cicéron pour le poëte Archias* (Latin and French), Paris, 1763.

[2] Apparently, the reference is to the anti-American *Vision of Judgment* by Robert Southey which is discussed at some length and unfavorably in the course of a review of Southey's new poem, *Sir Thomas More; or Colloquies on the Progress and Prospects of Society* (*Edinburgh Review*, 50:528–565 [Jan. 1830]).

[3] A week before there had been pub-lished *A Letter to William E. Channing, D.D. on the Subject of Religious Liberty* by Moses Stuart (*Boston Patriot*, 24 July, p. 3, col. 1). Stuart was a professor in the Andover Theological Seminary, and the pamphlet was part of the continuing attack emanating from the Seminary against the Unitarian wing of Boston Congregationalism of which Channing was a leader (Winsor, *Memorial History of Boston*, 3:474).

[4] Thus apparently in MS; the meaning may be "to take one with him."

SATURDAY. 31ST.

The day was not perfectly pleasant though clear—An East Wind coming with a peculiar chill over me, as I did not feel perfectly well. To sick people that wind is very dreadful, to those in firm health it matters exceeding little. Abby went with me this morning for the purpose of taking a bath.

I found that my Article was in the Patriot,[1] after which I read Walpole and wrote my Journal. Business is now multiplying upon me, and that not of an agreeable kind. My investment proceeds but slowly and I fear will not be effected at all. I went down to see a Mr. Watson on India Wharf who asked me five per cent advance upon some Fire and Marine Insurance Shares. A price I was totally unwilling to give. Saw Brown and Degrand, but they neither of them had any thing.

Returned to Medford early. In the afternoon Edward Brooks and his wife paid a visit and drank tea. Mr. Brooks was out to see his brother in law, Mr. Hall who has been sick. Evening quiet.

[1] In CFA's third letter on railroads, signed "A Calm Observer," he quotes at some length from a recent article in an English periodical on the complexity of running a railroad and the great expense attached to it; he deplores both the fail-

ure of many citizens who are opposed to a railway subsidy to attend the town meeting and the behavior of the proponents who did attend; and while acknowledging a probable present majority against his position, he prophesies a day when they will be in sackcloth and ashes (*Boston Patriot*, 31 July, p. 2, col. 4).

SUNDAY. AUGUST 1ST.

Morning cloudy but more mild. The season is not by any means settled. We all attended Divine Service morning and afternoon and heard Mr. Stetson preach upon the fashion of sudden religious conversions. Sensible but wearisome. The whole day passed with no peculiarity to mark it. No stranger visited, and I read but little. This is not a life best calculated to advance me in the path I feel so ambitious to pursue yet what can be done? I am not my own master, and circumstances will always obtain a control over the best formed resolutions. The evening went. I finished the Quarterly and nearly all of the Edinburgh Review for the last Quarter. Good but not remarkable, excepting the leading Article in the former upon the Peerage.

MONDAY. AUGUST 2D.

Morning cloudy but it cleared away and became pleasant in a short time. I rode to town as usual and found time enough to write my Diary, finish Walpole, and several little jobs, before the hour appointed for the Meeting of the Citizens to decide upon the Railway. This I attended and heard all the arguments if so they should be called both for and against the measure. The people were not overmuch disposed to hear those in opposition to the scheme and so I came off disgusted with the result.[1] A Town Meeting is no place to hear argument or attempt discussion. And when a people are taken with such schemes as these, they will often be led, by very inconsiderable persons. So it is now. Such men as Henry Williams, Henry H. Fuller, and David L. Child to direct the deliberations of the City of Boston[!][2] The idea is ludicrous when disjoined from the serious consequences which may it is feared ensue. The morning was nearly consumed however and after reading a little of Hutchinson, I returned to Medford. In the afternoon, Mr. Frothingham and I were left quite alone as the remainder of the family went to see their brothers and sisters at Watertown. So we had a solitary cup of tea and I a short stroll along the Canal. The night was beautiful.

[1] The meeting at Faneuil Hall with Mayor Otis presiding began at 10 A.M. and continued until 1 o'clock. It was marked by considerable hissing and unwillingness to hear certain speakers out. August 9th was fixed upon as the time for a municipal election or referendum on the resolution to contribute up to one

million dollars toward the building of a railway (*Boston Patriot*, 3 Aug., p. 2, col. 1).

² Child had evidently returned to the management of *The Massachusetts Journal*; Fuller was an attorney whose office was at 6 State Street (vol. 2:355; Bos-

ton *Directory*, 1830–1831); Henry Williams, otherwise not identified, may be the "Mr. Williams" who in company with Fuller had called upon CFA a little more than a year before (vol. 2:383).

TUESDAY. 3D.

Morning to town. Weather cloudy and it rained a little. I was very busy during the day, first in going to the House to get the Certificates of State Bank Stock. I felt a little melancholy upon going there. It is not to be denied that I should relish being there for my individual self above any other place. I dressed myself and returned to the Office from whence I went to meet Mr. Degrand and then effected the transfer of all my Father's Interest in the State Bank. I then deposited the money, and found my father in town and at my Office ready to finish. He then placed three thousand dollars at the disposal of T. B. Adams Jr. and finished the whole business.[1] He then gave me several bills to pay which carried me all the way to the Boylston Market, on my return dropped in to the sale of Stocks which went enormously high so I gave up the notion of buying. My Uncle, the Judge called in and Mr. Curtis to see my father, who went out at one and thus consumed my day.

Returned to Medford and after dinner, Mr. and Mrs. Edward, and Mr. and Mrs. Gorham Brooks with Miss Silsbee came over to spend the afternoon and take tea. The last young lady has had much fame, but a less pleasing young woman to me has seldom been seen in my experience.[2] I think Ellen[3] is a fine woman, and though there is much in her lot which might try many, she seems to bear it all with great patience. I see nothing in Gorham Brooks, which tells well for his character. My feelings may be prejudiced but they do not commonly deceive me. Quiet Evening.

[1] On the sale of JQA's shares in the State Bank and on the use of part of the proceeds to pay Thomas B. Adams Jr., on his twenty-first birthday, his de-

vise from JA, see 22 May, above.

[2] Georgiana Silsbee is identified at vol. 2:160.

[3] That is, Mrs. Gorham Brooks.

WEDNESDAY. 4TH.

Morning fine. Rode to town as usual and went to the Office. After remaining there some time to write up my Journal which has of late suffered a little from irregularity, I went to the Athenæum and changed my Walpole for the first volume of Dr. Parr's Works which contains his memoirs by a certain Dr. Johnson,[1] the legitimate *Writer* against the intruder Mr. Field whom I have already read. From this place I went down to my father's Estate in Tremont Street and put up a Notification that my Tenement was to let by way of jogging Hollis' Memory.[2] I propose to make a Revolution in all that business and that as soon as may be. My houses suffer and my father's income suffers, this is too much at once. Returned home and read a little of Hutchinson before my return to Medford.

Mr. and Mrs. Everett dined with us and we had quite a pleasant afternoon. Mr. E. was more communicative and I more easy than at any time in my recollection. The evening was beautiful and we enjoyed it, but I felt so fatigued that I was glad to go to bed early. I again felt the uneasy symptoms I complained of several days since.

[1] *The Works of Samuel Parr ... with Memoirs of his Life and Writings, and a Selection from his Correspondence by John Johnstone*, 8 vols., London, 1828.
[2] On 16 July CFA had written Daniel Hollis (LbC, Adams Papers) demanding payment of all claims due the Agency by 1 Aug. or his removal. Further notification is recorded in the entry for 21 Aug., below; his final departure was on 30 August.

THURSDAY. 5TH.

As Mr. Frothingham did not go to town today I concluded not to go in my own conveyance but to take a seat with Mr. Brooks. Accordingly we went down at his usual jog which is a little of the slowest. So that it was much after nine before I reached my Office.

Having done all my usual duties at the Office I thought I would go down to see how the pictures by Salmon would sell. They are all of them very pretty and went so very reasonably that I felt very much tempted to purchase. But I held in exceedingly well until the close, when one came up which I could not resist and immediately repented of the act. But it was too late.[1]

This was enough for a morning's work, so I left for the Office where I sat only a short time before the hour arrived to go out with Mr. Brooks which I did. The Afternoon went off quietly at home reading Johnson's Life of Parr which appears to me quite poor. Evening, reading French with my Wife. Mr. S. Swett and his daughter paid a short visit,[2] otherwise not interrupted.

[1] Robert Salmon, Scottish- or English-born painter of marine subjects, took up residence in Boston in 1828 and soon acquired a considerable local reputation (Groce and Wallace, *Dict. Amer. Artists*). A large collection of his paintings, including views of Boston harbor, its shipping and the nearby islands, along with views of Algiers, of the bombardment of that city, and of the fleets preparing for action there, had been on exhibition in recent months at Wash-

ington Hall, Market Hall, and the Athenæum Gallery. Seventy-five of the unsold
oil paintings were put up for auction at
the Julien Auction Room, corner of
Milk and Congress streets, at 11 o'clock

(*Boston Patriot*, 19 June, p. 2, col. 2;
Boston Daily Advertiser, 5 Aug., p. 3,
col. 5).
   [2] On Samuel Swett, a Boston merchant, see vol. 1:313.

FRIDAY. 6TH.

Morning pleasant. I have resumed my practice of taking the Shower
bath before breakfast which I found during my last stay so refreshing.
After breakfast Mr. Frothingham accompanied me to town, though I
put up my Gig in Charlestown as it was my design to dine at Mr.
Everett's, and we walked from there.[1] My first object was to go and see
Mr. Greene a broker in this place who advertises some Boylston Insurance Stock.[2] As I find none of the Atlas and it is becoming harder to
make investments, I thought I would try for some of this, but he asked
more than I could make up my mind to give without consulting some
person who has a knowledge of the Stock. I tried to see Mr. James H.
Foster but could not succeed. The rest of my time was taken up in
reading Hutchinson until the proper moment to go back to Charlestown.

Abby and Mr. Brooks were the only persons at Mr. Everett's. We
dined there, but I did not enjoy myself much. I cannot like Mr. Everett
and I was made to feel of so little consequence that I more than once
wished myself away. Perhaps this was vanity, and I ought to task
myself for it. But I can hardly do so, for it is no desire of mine to
intrude myself, if I am asked I expect to be made to feel pleasantly.
All this *may* be paying me for a day last Autumn. I was aware of my
fault then, but I could not correct it. I can hardly believe such unworthy retaliation could be resorted to.

After dinner, we went out to see the gardens of Mr. Breed and Mr.
Tufts on Breed's Hill, the gentlemen were not in, but we passed over
them. They are good, but laid out in wretched taste. Crammed together all kinds of things so as to produce nothing but a jumble of
good fruit.[3] We passed from there to the Dry Dock which is construct-
ing at the Navy Yard, a splendid work very creditable to the Nation.[4]
This made a call necessary upon Captn. Morris who was not at home.[5]

To finish our labours, we crossed to the State Prison and examined
throughout it's economy.[6] They have adopted there the principle of
the Sing Sing and Auburn prisons in New York. Labour without any
communication among the Prisoners. Their cells are small and separate, built entirely of Stone. They are kept at hard labour during the
day and inclosed at night. On the whole a tolerably good scheme but it
seemed to me that there is hardly sufficient discrimination in the dis-

grace attached to crimes. A man convicted for larceny of twenty dollars having for the period of his confinement precisely the same disgrace and suffering with one who has committed burglary or murder in the second degree. The length of time is the only distinction. Now the association of criminals for such very different offences for any period, produces an injurious impression both in their own minds and in those who see them—As we always attach our ideas more to the present than the future.[7] We returned to tea at Mr. Everett's. I was on the whole, very much satisfied with that visit. It is well to see human nature in all it's stages, and in none do questions of more importance to the whole Community present themselves than in this. We attended the religious exercises there and were edified by the Chaplain who does not deserve his place.[8] I rode home with my Wife thoroughly fatigued and glad to get home.

[1] The walk from Charlestown across the Charles River Bridge or the new Warren Bridge to the North End of Boston was a short one, less than half a mile (Winsor, *Memorial History of Boston*, 3:554–555).

[2] Simon E. Greene's brokerage office was in the lobby of the State Bank, 53 State Street (*Boston Directory*, 1830–1831).

[3] Breed's Hill rose to a modest height between the Navy Yard and the higher Bunker Hill. The estates of Ebenezer Breed and Nathan Tufts were two of the eight into which Breed's Hill was divided. The Tufts mansion was "placed far back from the street at the top of terraces covered by grass shaded by a few trees, and commanding a fine view towards the water." Later, the Tufts house was used as a boarding school, and the estate was called "Rydal Mount" (James F. Hunnewell, *A Century of Town Life . . . Charlestown, Massachusetts, 1785–1887*, Boston, 1888, p. 91).

[4] Construction on the granite dry dock was begun in 1827 under the superintendence and to the engineering plans of Loammi Baldwin (1780–1838). The dock was completed in 1834 at a cost in excess of $677,000 (Winsor, *Memorial History of Boston*, 3:354–356; a plan of the Navy Yard issued in 1828 is reproduced at 3:350).

[5] The Commandant's house in the Navy Yard, located almost at the foot of Breed's Hill and opposite to the Tufts estate, was "two stories high, of brick, square, with two bold swells towards a garden and the Yard and harbor." (Hunnewell, *A Century of Town Life* . . . , p. 91). On Commodore Charles Morris, see entry for 14 Aug., below.

[6] The State Prison, situated along the banks of the Charles in a bay, was built in 1804–1805 entirely of hewn stone. The complex is described fully in James F. Hunnewell, *Bibliography of Charlestown, Mass.*, Boston, 1880, p. 41; an engraving of the facade of the main building is reproduced in Hunnewell, *A Century of Town Life* . . . , facing p. 84.

[7] CFA's penological views are considerably in advance of those generally encountered during this period in the United States.

[8] Rev. Jared Curtis served as chaplain at the State Prison at an annual salary of $500 (*Mass. Register*, 1830, p. 164).

SATURDAY 7TH.

Morning cloudy, but it cleared up afterwards and became warm. Rode to town. My horse gave me a great strain as he took to running after being so unlucky as to trip. An affair attended with no little danger and fatigue. On the whole this horse of my father's is not troubled with many good qualities. At the Office where I wrote my Journal and read Hutchinson. Went upon Change and heard the news of the King's death from England.[1] A circumstance which may produce important results in Europe.

Being tired of hunting after investments I concluded to purchase some of the Boylston Insurance Stock after consulting Mr. J. H. Foster. I was compelled to give eight and a quarter advance but even at that rate I think it cheaper than nearly all other stock. So I bought fifteen shares for my father and three for myself.[2]

John came in from Quincy with my father and spent an hour at my Office. At the usual time, he went out with me to Medford. My father and Robert Buchanan went to Medford through Charlestown. Mr. and Mrs. Everett came also, and with the family constituted the Company to dinner. It was tolerably pleasant and in the afternoon we went over the grounds. They left us at six o'clock to return. John and Robert are both going next week. The latter looks quite sick. Evening warm and quiet. I felt extremely fatigued.

[1] The death of George IV occurred on 26 June.
[2] The $1,623.75 from the Agency account used to purchase the fifteen shares for JQA was largely the uninvested balance from the sale of State Bank shares remaining after paying Thomas B. Adams Jr. his legacy.

SUNDAY. 8TH.

Morning sultry. I did rejoice at the recurrence of this day, as somehow or other I was excessively tired from the labour of last week. This rambling life is a little too disagreeable, yet my Wife is not pleased in being alone, particularly when all the rest of the family are out of town.

Attended divine service and heard Mr. E. B. Hall in the morning and Mr. Stetson in the afternoon. The former succeeded very well. His manner is good, his delivery uncommonly proper in the Pulpit. He manifested today the evident superiority this gives to a man in other respects not remarkable. The latter gentleman exhibited precisely the reverse of the proposition.

The day was very warm. In the afternoon I read some of Dr. Parr's Life and felt more interest in it, though on the whole I am yet disappointed. It is not well arranged. Heard my wife's lesson of French which also took up time. We had a thunder shower in the evening. Mr. Jonathan Brooks and Dr. Swan paid a visit in the evening, and the former amused us as usual with his Yankee shrewdness.

MONDAY. 9TH.

Morning pleasant. Rode to town as usual. Prepared at my Office a Petition to compound with a debtor of New's Estate, and presented it to the Judge who made the decree. I then went to Faneuil Hall to vote against the projected Railway measure. The mass seemed to be going the other way, but I went nevertheless and performed my duty as conscientiously as becomes a good citizen.[1]

Some time passed reading Hutchinson and I had a visit from an old man, name unknown, who requested to know something about a right to land to make a road through Weston Farm. It seems that it is likely to be much benefitted by it and will yet involve considerable expense. Now the object of my father is to be run in debt by it as little as possible, for as to profit the idea is absurd. I gave him little or no decided encouragement, and he promised to call again before County Court. Dr. Davis called to inquire for Mr. Everett. Returned to Medford and in the afternoon and evening read Parr, which became much more amusing.

[1] On the vote to approve an appropriation not to exceed one million dollars, there were 1,966 yeas, 532 nays (*Boston Patriot*, 10 Aug., p. 2, col. 1).

TUESDAY. 10TH.

Morning cool and cloudy, but it cleared away subsequently. Rode to town as usual and went to the Office to my occupations. Felt restless however and therefore went to my house to see how things stood there. To all appearance they were perfectly safe. Returned and met Mr. Greene with whom I went to the Boylston Insurance Office and received the transfer of the Shares for which I paid and so that matter is settled.[1] Whether for good or for ill now remains to be seen. I have tried an experiment, and there are many reasons why I should wish it might turn out successfully.

Called to see if Hollis was moving but there did not seem any prospect of it. Provoking. Returned to the Office and read Hutchinson for the rest of the morning. Thence out of town. Found at Medford, P. C. Brooks Jr. and his Wife who dined and passed the afternoon. From some cause or other, my spirits were a little depressed. Yet I could scarcely tell the reason. Perhaps it is because this wandering kind of life has become fatiguing and reminds me that my life is wasting, without profit to myself or to others.

I read the remainder of the Memoirs of Dr. Parr this evening. It is an amusing work from the variety of characters introduced as well as the peculiarity of the subject, but I cannot think the mind of the writer was equal to the materials he possessed, he has not arranged clearly, or discussed thoroughly. He has compressed badly and not enlarged where his subject required. On the whole he has not done so well as Field.

[1] The office of the Boylston Fire and Marine Insurance Co. was at 475 Washington Street (*Boston Directory*, 1830–1831).

WEDNESDAY. 11TH.

The morning was cool, but as Mr. Brooks went to town alone I thought I would accompany him and not go in my own conveyance. He conversed much with me upon the Mount Wollaston Estate, and spoke of it as a valuable property to the family. I have thought so myself, but it cannot be made very available unless some member of the family itself undertakes to improve it. I have inclined to undertaking it myself, but my idea is rather speculation than practical. A house must be built, and with my limited means the idea is absurd. Yet it would be worth trying. To be sure I am no Farmer, and to be one, should begin quickly with the probability of great losses to get any experience. The undertaking is out of my line and on the whole I think it lucky, for my present way of life is proper enough, and has the advantage of certainty.

Morning passed at the Athenæum where I wasted my time in superficial and desultory examination of books, getting from them nothing. Read Hutchinson a little and returned with Mr. Brooks. The afternoon was lazily passed. I lounged in the grove and went to sleep there, then took up the remaining Articles of the North American Review for July, but did not get through a sleepy discussion of Stewart.[1] Miss Osgood, Mr. N. Hall and his sister Mary passed a short time here.

[1] A. H. Everett's review of Dugald Stewart, *The Philosophy of the Active and Moral Powers of Man*, in *North Amer. Rev.*, 31:213–267.

THURSDAY. 12TH.

Morning warm and pleasant, but my Wife was so unwell this morning with the disease incident to the season, that I abandoned the idea which I had taken up of returning on this day to Quincy. Rode to town accompanied by Mr. Frothingham. My time passed at the Office much as usual. I accomplished a good deal of Hutchinson, and then went down to the Boylston Insurance Office to try for the Certificates which however were not ready. I then went and looked at the Tenements in Common Street. Found Hollis not yet gone out, and Mrs. Wells still in. This woman notified me she must go, which is a matter of grievance. So it is sometimes. Those who are desired to go, stay and those whom we like to keep, leave us.

Returned to Medford. After dinner, Miss Glover and Miss Frothingham friends of Mrs. F., paid a visit.[1] We undertook a walk to the place in the Pond or lake called the Partings,[2] it was quite pleasant and took up a considerable time. On our return we found here Dr. and Mrs. Stevenson who took tea. On the whole, the time was very agreeably passed. They went away late, and the rest of the evening was passed lazily in skimming over Fontenelle's Pluralité des Mondes.[3]

[1] Miss Glover and Miss Frothingham are not otherwise identified.

[2] Opposite the six-mile line on the canal, still within the bounds of the Brooks estate but nearly a mile north of the house, the Mystic Pond narrowed and was crossed by a shoal called "the Partings." The location is evident on the plan of Medford reproduced in the present volume. The shoal, sometimes used as a road, divided the pond into nearly equal parts. At a later date a stone dam was built upon it, excluding the tidal water from the upper pond (Brooks, *Medford*, p. 17).

[3] An edition published at Paris in 1811 is in MQA.

Medford–Quincy

FRIDAY. 13TH.

Morning quite cool, so that it required a little courage to go into the bath. I have upon this visit found great advantage from this practice in the morning, and had I a convenient house for it, would always insist upon such an appendage. My Wife was so sick this morning that I was in doubt whether to leave or not, but after consideration of the difficulties on all sides I concluded that the wiser course would be to go. Accordingly, after breakfast, we started from Medford where I have enjoyed myself very well upon this visit, and reached town early.

My principal occupation was to go and see the Tenements in Common Street, two of which will now shortly be empty. They are in much better condition than I had anticipated, but after all real Estate is a great plague. It is always getting worn out, and requiring repairs. Returned and read a little of Hutchinson. Went early to Quincy, and found all the family much as I left them. John and Robert *not* gone. After dinner we resumed our Catalogue and progressed with it considerably. But the length of time which has elapsed has produced some confusion in my mind. My Mother seemed better. Evening quietly at home with the family. Conversed with my father about Junius and he read to us a part of the Rolliad.[1]

[1] "The Rolliad" came to be the title of a series of political satires directed against the Tory government of William Pitt. Written from 1784 to 1790, the satires originally took the form of critical reviews of an epic poem "The Rolliad," nonexistent but allegedly celebrating the exploits of Duke Rollo, a legend-

ary ancestor of John Rolle, M.P., one of Pitt's supporters. An edition of *The Rolliad* published at London in 1795, apparently not a complete collection of the several parts previously published, was JQA's and is in MQA.

SATURDAY. 14TH.

Morning pleasant. Rode to town as usual. My time very much taken up, first by going to the Athenæum, then to the Justice Court to attend to Champney's case, and then to see about a case Mrs. Wells has submitted to me. She is so poor that my advice is all a matter of charity. It seems she has been sued for a bill which she thinks has been paid, though she has no voucher of the fact. I thought the case a hard one, but did not make out enough to authorize me to recommend her appeal to Law. So I concluded I would go and see the Creditor. He told a different story, and seemed to insist upon it so earnestly that I did not know what to believe, and we came to no conclusion. Mrs. Wells has behaved so properly to me that I cannot think she has been to blame. The fault if any there is, lies between her son and the Creditor. My time was thus engrossed almost entirely, and I returned to Quincy a little late.

After dinner I went on with my Catalogue pretty rapidly, as my father was in a humour for it. Captn. Morris and his Wife paid a visit this afternoon.[1] Abby was quite sick all day so as not to be able to join the family. Her suffering is generally very great. In the evening, I sat with her some time, and not to disturb her, retired myself very early.

[1] Commodore Charles Morris, characterized as the "ablest sea officer of his day" by Farragut, was the commandant of the Charlestown Navy Yard from 1827 to 1832; see Winsor, *Memorial History of Boston*, 3:341, 353, and *DAB*.

SUNDAY. 15TH.

Morning mild and pleasant. I attended at Meeting during the whole of the day and heard Mr. B. Whitney of Hingham preach. A man who seems to keep no course with the current of the times. A true Country Parson, without any hopes or wishes out of the line of his station. He dined with us and I was struck with the limited character of his observations. He is one of the old school of Clergy, and serves to show pretty clearly that on the whole there has been some advance in Theological education.

It rained in the afternoon, but Mr. and Mrs. Russel of Boston[1] with Col. Quincy paid a visit notwithstanding. I continued my Alphabetical Catalogue during every minute of disposable time. Abby was much better today, so I sat up until eleven.

[1] That is, Joseph Russell (vol. 2:272 and JQA, Diary, 15 Aug.).

MONDAY. 16TH.

I rode to town this morning more rapidly than usual as my horse was changed for a much more clever one. At the Office, writing and reading when who should call in but my old acquaintance and Classmate Aylwin whom I had not seen for very many years.[1] He was altered but not so much that on a second examination I did not succeed in recognizing him. We talked a little while pleasantly, he has altered somewhat and become more manly, but we had little of a pleasant nature to recollect in his course and exit at Cambridge, and since there has been nothing to give us a common subject.

I had an engagement in the Probate Court, where I got my permission to sell New's real Estate. But much time was taken up in waiting. I was then occupied in filling up the Bond and arranging the rest of New's papers so that all my period for stay in Boston was thus consumed. The afternoon passed in a continuation of the Catalogue, my father after finishing my Mother's room, gave out when he went to the Office so that I pursued the Alphabetical Catalogue with steadiness. In the evening we went to pay a visit to Mr. Edward Miller which I owed him ever since my last visit here. Mrs. Miller was unwell and not visible, but we saw him for an hour. I sat two hours after, at work upon the Catalogue.

[1] Thomas Cushing Aylwin (d. 1871) entered Harvard with the class of 1825, but breaches in regulations led to his withdrawal after less than a full year; see Records of the College Faculty, 26 April 1822 (MH-Ar). In later years Aylwin became a judge in Montreal. He continued to maintain his association with the class; see entries in John Langdon Sibley, Private Journal (MS, MHi, deposited in MH-Ar).

TUESDAY. 17TH.

Morning to town as usual. Weather cloudy and warm. I thought I would take this opportunity to go and make a purchase of wine for my father, and at the same time get the Certificate for the Boylston Insurance Stock. Mr. Baldwin the President of it appears to be a very sensible man and manages on principles which I believe to be very secure.[1] Stock of this kind is always hazardous, therefore the wise course is to make it as little so as possible. I talked with him some time very pleasantly, and then went on my course. At Messrs. J. D. and

M. Williams, I purchased for my father one quarter Cask of Sherry and for myself half the quantity of Port Wine. They both seemed to me of excellent kinds, but the price to be paid for them was very considerable. I did not return to my Office until quite late and had only time for a very few minutes reading of Hutchinson. Returned to Quincy to dine and passed the Afternoon as usual making my Catalogue very busily indeed. But the labour of this work is no trifle. I felt very much fatigued.

¹ Aaron Baldwin was the president of the Boylston Fire and Marine Insurance Co. and of the Washington Bank (*Boston Directory*, 1830–1831).

WEDNESDAY. 18TH.

This is my Birthday Anniversary. And it has been usual with me to take the occasion to reflect upon the past and the future. A very important change has taken place in my prospects since the last year. I am now married, with many added pleasures as well as cares. Time passes with me swiftly, yet I feel dissatisfied with the progress which I make in keeping up with it. My ambition is extensive but not of an extravagant kind. It is rather a desire of distinction from reputation than from place. My hopes of popularity have always been so limited as to check any feeling which might arise in that direction, and to lead me to indulge rather in those over which I may be able to have some personal control. My own labour and personal character, on the whole I believe I can say that during the past year I have not gone backward in these respects though I have not done far enough towards advancing.

Rode to town as usual. Morning occupied, first in walking to the House for some little things, then at the Office where I finished Hutchinson's first Volume, the last Chapters of which are interesting as they give a very good account of the condition of the Colony in it's early times. Returned to Quincy, and spent the Afternoon in continuing the Catalogue. But I did not resume it in the evening as I got hold of the trial for the murder of Mr. White at Salem which is now producing such an excitement, and could not leave it quickly.¹

¹ The trial of Frank Knapp as principal in the murder of Capt. Joseph White began in Salem on 3 Aug. and was concluded on 13 Aug. in a mistrial. Pamphlet publications reporting the trial appeared at once. Much the fullest account was contained in a pamphlet entitled *Trial of George Crowninshield, J. J. Knapp, Jun. and John Francis Knapp, for the Murder of Capt. Joseph White . . ., Reported by John W. Whitman, Esq.*, Boston, 1830. This pamphlet actually contained the first trial of Frank Knapp and no other; it was published before the other trials began, as is made clear by a concluding note explaining the publishers' change of intention. Other pamphlets included *Re-*

port on the Evidence and Points of Law, Arising on the Trial of John Francis Knapp ..., Salem, 1830; Trial of John Francis Knapp ..., Boston, 1830; The Trial in the Case of the Commonwealth, versus John Francis Knapp ..., [Salem?, 1830]. The second trial of Knapp was begun on 14 Aug. and detailed accounts began to appear in the newspapers (Boston Patriot, 17 Aug., p. 1, col. 5). The trial was concluded on 20 Aug. with the conviction of Knapp.

THURSDAY. 19TH.

The Morning was extremely beautiful, and as my father was desirous of going to town to a Meeting of the Overseers of Harvard University, He, and John, Robert and I went together in the Barouche. The ride was extremely pleasant and we reached town in very good season. I went to the Office as usual, and read a little of Hutchinson. But my hours were interrupted by my brother and others. Besides, I walked down to Long Wharf to see about a case of Port Wine which had come for my father from Washington, and thence to several other places to get some little Articles on Commission. We waited much beyond my usual hour for my father and got to Quincy only before four o'clock.[1] The afternoon and part of the evening I spent in my Catalogue which progresses gradually. I am nearly through one half of it. But that not the most difficult half. Evening, conversation with the family quite amusing.

[1] The meeting of Overseers was convened at 12:30 and adjourned before 2 o'clock; it was held in the Council chamber of the State House with the lieutenant governor presiding (JQA, Diary, 19 Aug.).

FRIDAY. 20TH.

Morning delightful. Our weather now is extremely agreeable, being neither too warm nor too cold. Rode into town with Abby, and left her at the Bathing house,[1] from whence I went as usual to the Office. After finishing several little Commissions which as usual take up a large part of my time, I read Hutchinson's Account of the Witch excitement at Salem which on the whole appeared to me fair enough, although I do not exactly see through his statement of fraud. It is true much deception was used, but the great evidence of voluntary confession in some cases of the crime, goes far to prove disordered imaginations.

Rode out to dine, and in the afternoon went on with my Catalogue with only a single interruption in a visit from Mrs. Tufts, her daughter[2] and Miss L. C. Smith. The work is great, and I am apprehensive my time will not hold out very well to complete it. Worked also in the Evening.

[1] A "Bathing Establishment" was located near the Charlestown bridges but "below the bridges ... [to] possess all the advantages of having the water perfectly pure and clean." Both warm and cold baths were offered, the cold bath "built in such a manner as to be free and secure from any danger." The patronage of ladies was particularly sought, "a female attendant [being] in constant readiness to wait on" them (*Boston Patriot*, 29 May, p. 3, col. 3).

This was but one of several bathhouses erected in Boston beginning as early as 1805. A wood block of Braman's Baths, said to have been the largest of these, is reproduced in the present volume. See above, p. xv.

[2] That is, Mrs. Cotton Tufts Jr. of Weymouth (1763–1849, Mercy Brooks, first cousin of Peter C. Brooks, married to AA's cousin) and her daughter, Mercy Tufts, on both of whom see Adams Genealogy.

SATURDAY. 21ST.

Morning very clear and pleasant. Robert Buchanan went with me to town as he wished to see a few things of note before he went away. After performing several little jobs as usual, I accompanied him to the State House to see Chantry's Statue of Washington and the view from the top. It is ten or eleven years since I was in that spot before, and during the period how Boston has changed. Wealth has literally been poured upon it's Streets until the sources from which it came have felt the drain. Houses and public buildings are now crowded upon places which formerly were dreary heaps of barren mud.[1] We left that place and I then notified Hollis again to quit. He is a dog in the Manger. Will not work himself nor let others work for him.

At twelve o'clock we left town in the Steam Boat for Nahant.[2] Found on board Edmund Quincy and Mr. G. Meredith whom I knew formerly[3] and was glad to see them. We arrived barely in time for dinner and to get seats, the house being very much crowded. The Company was excellent, and our entertainment good. Arnold Welles and Charles C. [*i.e.* R.] Lowell, both young Members of the Bar came in and took wine with us.[4] Afterward Mr. Richd. C. Derby[5] who gave us Champagne and a Song, so that on the whole I do not think I ever enjoyed a convivial party so much. After rising from table we had barely time to go and look at the place a little before the hour came for returning.[6] And this was quite late enough. Our passage up was cold. We reached town at about a quarter after seven and proceeded immediately to Quincy, where we arrived barely in time to save them from considerable alarm, and I will add not a moment too soon for my fatigue.

[1] The prospect from the dome of the State House, especially to the north and east did indeed present striking changes from that visible a decade earlier. Extensive new building on reclaimed land had taken place or was in process in the area known as the Mill Pond and along the waterfront from the old Town Dock at Dock Square to the Long Wharf at the foot of State Street. Moreover, close

by the State House itself there had been much construction on the new streets and building sites available in the wake of the leveling of the summit of Beacon Hill. This earth moving project which began in 1810 and ended only in 1824 provided the fill for the Mill Pond's fifty acres of marsh and flats. The full development of the new area was not complete by 1830 but much building was already evident, stimulated perhaps by the opening in 1828 of the new Warren Bridge to Charlestown which had its Boston terminus at the center of the Mill Pond triangle. Southeastward from the Mill Pond the second large tract of made land had been created by 1826. There, over what had formerly been wharves, six new streets were laid out, and between Faneuil Hall and the new water's edge the three large and handsome granite structures that com-

prised the Quincy Market development were in use. (Whitehill, *Boston: A Topographical History*, p. 78–84, 96–98.)

[2] During the summer months the steamers *Ousatonic* and *Rush Light* plied between Boston and Nahant five times daily. Departure was from Tileston's Wharf, Purchase Street near Summer Street, and the fare was 25 cents (*Boston Patriot*, 24 June, p. 2, col. 6).

[3] On George Augustus Meredith, Harvard 1827, see vol. 2:277.

[4] Welles was also of Meredith's class. On Charles Russell Lowell, Harvard 1826, see vol. 1:265.

[5] Derby lived in Boston at 27 Chesnut Street (*Boston Directory*, 1830–1831).

[6] An engraving of Nahant and its hotel is reproduced in the present volume; see above, p. x–xi.

SUNDAY. 22D.

The morning was cloudy and damp as if it had been raining during the night. I walked into the Orchard with my Father and in discussing the subject of Trees I thought he seemed eager to close with my proposal of making a Nursery at Mount Wollaston. I think I will interest myself in this. But there are so many discouragements operating upon me in this regard that I do not know what to think of it.

We afterwards attended divine service and heard Mr. Whitney preach one Sermon upon controverted doctrinal texts and another upon the subject of a general judgment. In the evening, Abby and my father went down to pay a short visit to Mrs. Quincy. Saw her infant which is always brought in upon such occasions. A Thunder Storm in the Night.

MONDAY 23RD.

Morning cloudy. Rode to town as usual. At the Office where I performed my usual duties. Offered my bond for approval by the Judge of Probate but found it had no Seals and therefore would not answer, so that I was to carry it out to Quincy again. From thence I went down to see Mr. New's Estates which I propose to sell. Found them both tolerably good houses and situated well to rent. Indeed it seemed to me there was no reason why they should not sell for a great deal more than the Mortgage. However all these things are matter of chance.

Returned to the Office and after a short visit to Mr. Brooks went out to Quincy.

The afternoon was spent in strolling with my father to the Ledges at the Railway.[1] My purpose was to inquire of the conductors there the price of good stone, in case I should decide upon having the Store in Court Street done. He whom I saw referred me to Mr. Caleb Pratt in Boston.[2] My father's object was to examine his woodland for a spot fit to cut for consumption. We went to the top of the Tower and were pleased with the fine view which we had from there.[3] This Railway has been a great work, and the undertakers of it have certainly been entitled to considerable credit in carrying it on. It has moreover reduced the price of Stone very much, and thus brought it into much more extensive use, besides increasing the value of the Quarries.

We returned in time for the Ladies to take a ride, and I worked a little upon my Catalogue which I am now working off entire. Called with Robert Buchanan upon our Neighbour George Beale who seemed in no very good humour, which I attributed to his failure at Squantum.

[1] The Ledges was the local name for the stone escarpment in Quincy which Gridley Bryant purchased in 1825 with funds supplied by Dr. John C. Warren as a quarry for the granite to be used for the Bunker Hill monument. Faced with the problem of transporting the blocks the four miles from the Quarry to water-carriage on the Neponset River, Bryant conceived the idea of a railroad, obtained a charter from the legislature, and began construction. The first train of cars, horse-drawn, passing over the whole length of tracks of the Granite Railway in Quincy on 7 Oct. 1826, was the effective beginning of railroad enterprise in the United States (C. F. Adams Jr., "The Canal and Railroad Enterprise of Boston," in Winsor, *Memorial History of Boston*, 4:116–121). The route taken by the railway is marked on the "map of Boston and the adjacent towns" in the present volume. On the railway's cars, see above, p. xiv.

[2] Caleb Pratt, agent in Boston for the Railway Quarry (subsequently the Bunker-Hill Quarry), was a housewright on Sea Street (*Boston Directory*, 1830–1831, and entry for 31 Aug., below).

[3] Fifty-eight steps led to the top of the tower. The structure was built by Col. Thomas Handasyd Perkins, into whose hands the whole stock of the railway and quarry fell (JQA, Diary, 23 Aug., and Winsor, *Memorial History of Boston*, 4:118).

TUESDAY. 24TH.

Morning fair. Rode to town accompanied by my Wife. Left her at the Bath and went myself to the Office. Occupied in writing my Journal as usual, and afterwards in reading Hutchinson. My morning time escapes me almost without my being aware of it. It is very clearly the science of wasting life. And I am rapidly becoming tired of it. I do nothing which can be of any credit to myself. Conversed with Mr. Welsh a short time and then left town with Abby for dinner. The afternoon was taken up in continuation of my Library Catalogue which I am endeavouring to push to a completion, as my period for closing my country residence draws nigh. In the evening we were quietly at home.

WEDNESDAY. 25TH.

The morning was raw and blustering. As I had agreed to accompany Robert Buchanan to Cambridge today, we accordingly started early, and I drove him through Brookline and Brighton in order to show him some of the most cultivated spots in our vicinity. It was not a favourable day, but they looked well nevertheless. But it was rather a singular circumstance that after an absence from this Quarter of so short a period, I should yet feel so much at a loss for the road. Things have very much changed. One could hardly believe it who had been present all the time for with them improvements grow so gradually as to be nearly imperceptible.[1]

We reached Cambridge after the exercises for Commencement had been begun, and paid a short visit at Mr. Meredith's room before we went to the Church.[2] The exercises were much as usual. Some were tiresome, others I could not hear. The whole thing is a tax upon the patience of all excepting such as have relations present. I knew not a soul of the Speakers excepting T. Davis for the Master's Oration which as far as I could hear it was good.[3] We were delighted to close, and go to the dinner which though made for Graduates, I made to serve for Robert Buchanan also. The usual scramble for a bad dinner took place and the usual psalm, after which we left as rapidly as possible.[4] From this we went and paid a short visit at Mr. Quincy's, where we saw the ladies and a considerable number of dignitaries.[5] But on the whole, I never recollect to have seen a poorer, meaner, more unsatisfactory Commencement.[6] The glory of former days so far as it consisted of bustle, show and glare has departed, perhaps in truth there is no very great loss by the change. The weather threatened and we hurried off, but owing to the fatigue of our Horse did not reach home till a stormy night had set in.

[1] Revolutionary shifts in the flow of traffic to the western suburbs occurred in the wake of the construction in 1821 of Western Avenue (Beacon Street as extended), a toll road a mile and a half long built over the Mill Dam that stretched across the Back Bay from Charles Street to Sewell's Point (close to present Kenmore Square). There juncture was made with the Brighton Road which followed the course of the Charles River through Brookline, thence into Brighton to North Harvard Street, which, in turn, took one to the "Great Bridge" over the Charles and on to the present Boylston Street in Cambridge (Whitehill, *Boston: A Topographical History*, p. 92–94, 100–101). The developments can be seen on Bowen's "map of Boston and the adjacent towns"

in C. H. Snow, *A Geography of Boston
...* , Boston, 1830, and reproduced in
the present volume.

² Commencement exercises were held
in the fourth meetinghouse of the First
Church of Cambridge from 1756 until
it was replaced in 1833. The church
stood on a site southwest of the present
Lehman Hall in Harvard Square (Hamilton V. Bail, *Views of Harvard ...* ,
Cambridge, 1949, p. 41).

³ Thomas Kemper Davis' oration in
English had the title "Every Man a
Debtor to his Profession." The press reported that it was "well received ... , a
sound and sensible composition ... , elo-

quently spoken" (*Boston Patriot*, 25, 26
Aug., p. 2, col. 1).

⁴ At the commencement dinner in
University Hall, the Seventy-eighth
Psalm was traditionally sung (Morison,
Three Centuries of Harvard, p. 247).

⁵ For Maria Sophia Quincy's account
of the 1829 commencement reception
held from 5:30 to 7:30 in Wadsworth
House, see M. A. DeW. Howe, ed., *The
Articulate Sisters*, Cambridge, 1946, p.
182–183.

⁶ The Commencement of 1830 was
the first since 1798 at which no honor-
ary degrees were awarded (*Harvard
Quinquennial Cat.*).

THURSDAY. 26TH.

The morning opened very dark with a high wind, which in the
course of the day increased to a violent gale with floods of rain. I
decided upon remaining at home, very wisely as it turned out. My
time was taken up at home in continuing the Catalogue with which
I made very considerable progress. But the uniformity of the course
of proceeding prevents any particular notice of it. I find I do not get
as much information from it as I anticipated, excepting as to the titles
of books and names of authors, which is all superficial. In the afternoon my father asked me to begin upon the German books which I
did and we finished about one half of them. I know so little about
them as to make it very dull work. The house was flooded with rain
and leaked in so many parts as to satisfy me it must soon be repaired
or a new house built. It was cold and stormy and I wished myself at
home.

FRIDAY 27TH.

The Weather looked so exceedingly doubtful that I did not feel
very secure to move and in hesitating I lost the proper time. So I
occupied myself all the morning in continuing my Catalogue which
I now feel hurried to complete. My progress was quite considerable.
The afternoon was taken up in finishing the German Books which
completes the Catalogue as first taken, the only remaining work being
now to finish it in the other way and copy the whole. Enough in all
conscience.

The weather changed and became so fine that I asked my father to
ride down with me and look at the Mount Wollaston Farm. We accordingly went down and I never saw the place look more beautifully.

The natural advantages of the place are very great, and tempt me very much to commit foolish imprudences. I am sensible of an absurdity in my desire to go there, but the property is destined to hang in the family and upon me if any body, and I should like at least to think of improving it.

Our object ostensibly was to select a site for a young Orchard, but as it is commonly with my father we did nothing but talk and look round. It is a little singular how thoroughly speculative he is in his views, and how vain it is to hope for practical results which in any other case one might expect. Returned home and passed the evening as usual.

SATURDAY. 28TH.

The morning was clear and became very warm. I rode to town and passed a great deal of my morning in bringing up arrears in my Diary which had occurred for a considerable time previous. This irregularity from town puts every thing out of order. I also went down with Mr. Brooks to see Mrs. Sidney Brooks who has just come to town. She looks tolerably but not very well. Our visit was short and I returned to my Office to study the business of New's Estate. Made a draught of an advertisement of the Sale and then returned to Quincy. Pursued my Catalogue in the afternoon.

Robert Buchanan this day left us. During his stay we have been much enlivened though some things in him I did not altogether like. He had become so much pleased as to depart with great regret.

My Mother was not so well today. In the Evening, my Uncle the Judge called and Abby accompanied me to visit Mrs. Danl. Greenleaf at the foot of the Hill.[1] She was not at home but we spent half an hour looking at the place which is pretty. Bright Moonlight.

[1] Daniel Greenleaf and his wife Elizabeth were cousins; they had no children. He owned the wharf on Quincy Bay from which JQA customarily swam during the summer months. See entry for 25 Oct. 1829, above, and Greenleaf, *Greenleaf Family*, p. 210.

SUNDAY. 29TH.

Morning clear and pleasant. My Mother is again down with the Erisypelas and confined to her room.

We attended divine service and heard Mr. Hedge preach both morning and afternoon. His morning discourse was upon the existence of right and wrong and the limit to which the confusion between them is justifiable. The afternoon's was the same with that which I heard him deliver at Medford some time since upon eagerness for unnatural excitement, and was exceedingly well. He is one of the few among my Class for whose character and attainments I have some respect. Rarely has it fallen to man's lot to be associated with so ordinary a mass. I could not help being struck with it on Commencement day.[1] The larger part of the afternoon was occupied in continuing my Catalogue with as much rapidity as I could. But it drags nevertheless. Evening a short visit from Mr. and Mrs. Danl. Greenleaf.

[1] That is, at the Commencement just past.

MONDAY. 30TH.

Morning cloudy and threatening rain. I went to town nevertheless and was busy all the morning. I let the House which Mr. Hollis has at last vacated, directly—a circumstance which proves to me how much this Estate has been suffering from the preceding practice.[1] I hope to mend it altogether. Sidney Brooks called to make a short visit. He looks well and seems to be pretty well. I gave in my Bond as Administrator of New's Estate, which was accepted and then drew the Advertisement for the sale of his Equities which will wind up the business.[2] There is nothing else to receive or to sell.

Returned to Quincy to dinner and worked all the Afternoon at my Catalogue. But it did not show much progress. Saw my Mother in the Evening who appeared to be much better. Conversed with her a little about Thos. Hellen, who is it seems better than I thought he was. Continued my Catalogue after the family withdrew though it is awkward working.

[1] Tenement No. 2 at 101 Tremont Street was rented at $10.70 a month as of 1 Sept. to Henry Beals (M/CFA/3, p. 36).

[2] The advertisement announced an administrator's sale at public auction on the premises at noon on 6 Oct. of Robert New's equity in two parcels of land, one on Cambridge Street containing a wooden dwelling house and store, the second on Lynde Street (*Boston Daily Advertiser*, 31 Aug., p. 3, col. 6).

TUESDAY 31ST.

Morning pleasant. Abby accompanied me to town to see her Sister Mrs. Sidney Brooks who is now there. I left her at Mrs. Dehon's and went to the Office. Several persons called to see me, one concerning the empty house in Common Street, one as to the punctuality of Miss Longhurst as a Tenant, one upon Mr. New's Affairs, and my Carpenter, Mr. J. Y. Champney. Mr. Pratt is an Agent for the Railway Quarry and came about my Job of Stone Work. I explained to him what I wanted done and he left me promising to bring a plan and estimates. Called to see Mr. Brooks who was disappointed not to find us ready to go to Medford. My time in this manner vanished rapidly enough. Returned to Quincy and passed the afternoon in working upon my Catalogue. Mr. Beale came in and passed an hour of the Evening. My time seems like nothing, it goes so fast.

WEDNESDAY. SEPTEMBER 1ST.

Morning cool but pleasant. Rode to town as usual and passed my Morning in my common occupations. Went to look at the House which might have suffered by the rain although it did not. Felt grievously as if I wanted to be in it. Purchased of Mr. Brown ten shares of the Boylston Market Stock for T. B. Adams, and found a little time today to read Hutchinson. My morning flew and I returned to Quincy to work upon my Catalogue with new vigour, but it goes on rather slowly, and I am now apprehensive will not be finished in time for my return.

Purchased my Winter's Stock of Coal today at eleven dollars per Chaldron which appeared to me to be very moderate. The expense for Winter Fuel is always grievous. Evening a walk and visit to Mrs. T. B. Adams, where Abby had taken tea. We returned so that I pursued my Catalogue another hour.

THURSDAY. SEPT. 2D.

After arriving in town, I spent all my Morning in overlooking the taking in my Coal at my House—Not being willing to trust it to be done without my supervision. I like my purchase exceedingly, the Coal itself being fine and the price as low as any of this kind ever sold for. As it took up much time, I thought I would make some alterations in my Library so as to be more convenient upon my return. It is such fatiguing work that I have never yet done it properly.

Returned to Quincy a little late. In the afternoon pursued my Catalogue and made a finish of the mass of the books in the study, but all those upstairs remain to be done. Had a short Conversation with my Mother about the health of my Wife and sat working as usual until eleven o'clock.

FRIDAY. 3D.

This is the Anniversary of my marriage, one year has passed since that time and I can look back upon it with general satisfaction. If happiness is the end of man's existence I believe I have had as much of it as falls to the lot of man. My disposition is scarcely a complaining one, but rather thankful to the divine giver for the goods I have without grasping for more. The future remains with him.

Rode to town this morning, and spent the morning in a variety of little broken occupations. Paid for the Shares of the Boylston Market, and for my Coal, made several purchases for my Mother, and spent a short time looking for Peaches without success—At least I could find no good ones. Mr. Brooks called with his usual Quarterly Note and I arranged my affairs. My pecuniary matters for the past year have been prosperous, and this is something gained.

Returned to dine and found my Uncle the Judge and his Lady, Miss Smith and Miss Abby Adams who made a party to dine. We had a good and pleasant dinner. Afternoon pursuing the Catalogue, which as the time grows nearer I grow more and more doubtful of the accomplishment.

SATURDAY 4TH.

My Catalogue wanted so much of being finished that I concluded to remain at home today and work upon it. Accordingly I was very busy and accomplished a great deal. The Office and the Room upstairs remained to be done and the power to go on with them as I had done with the preceding did not exist which made me hurry faster than I otherwise should have done. Perhaps I did not finish quite so perfectly, and neglected much more the profit I had anticipated and which has made to me much the most amusing part of the Work.

My tastes are decidedly literary and if I had only the Room to exercise them which my father's Library gives me, or even my own. But at present I do neither.[1] I am tossing about in an ocean of nothing, and corrupting proper tastes in desultory reading—Gathering what men call a smattering of reading without the solidity proper to support it.

After a laborious day I went to pass part of the evening at our neighbour Mr. Danl. Greenleaf's, whose lady had asked my Wife to tea. She is a kindhearted woman very much disposed to be gratified with every thing, and I have felt desirous of treating her with corresponding civility. We there heard of some important news of a new Revolution in France which had overturned the Monarchy. But nobody seemed to put any confidence in the Report as it came. In the evening we returned in time for me to work somewhat longer.

[1] Thus in MS; the thought in obviously elliptical.

SUNDAY. 5TH.

The morning was clear and pleasant. My mother, wife and I attended divine Service and heard Dr. Richmond preach very sensible Sermons, but he is unfortunate in having a manner which is a little of the dullest.[1] I find it next to impossible to listen to him. The elder portion of the Clergy are more deficient than the younger, and yet they are all very indifferent. They show little or none of that fascination in manner which makes words, things.

My father obtained a Newspaper giving an Account of the Revolution as it is confirmed by the News from France.[2] This forms one of the most remarkable events of the present period. It astonishes and at the same time raises an involuntary enthusiasm. A people struggling for rights which fairly belong to them, always excite sympathy at the outset. It is only necessary that they should keep within those rights, to secure perfect approbation—hic labor, hoc opus est. We must wait and see.

I worked all day upon my Catalogue, progressing so rapidly that I hope now to finish very perfectly before I leave Quincy. Mr. Miller and Judge Adams were here in the Evening and Mr. Degrand from Boston who also spent the night.

[1] Edward Richmond, Congregational minister of Dorchester (JQA, Diary, 5 Sept.; *Mass. Register*, 1830). He is referred to in vol. 2:166, 386, but is there erroneously presumed to be Abel Richmond of Halifax.

[2] On the day before, the *Boston Patriot* (4 Sept., p. 2, col. 1) had carried a bare and unconfirmed "telegraphic" report, apparently signaled from shore to ship, that the monarchy had been overthrown on 28–29 July.

MONDAY. 6TH.

As our things were so numerous as not to be easily manageable in one day's transportation and I needed one day more to complete the Catalogue, I thought it would be advisable to stay until tomorrow. Accordingly we so decided, and Mr. Degrand thus got the chance of the Ride to town. I went to the Office and was busy about my Affairs. Received today two different payments from Debtors to the Estate of Mr. New, being the first money received from that property. I am now proceeding pretty rapidly to wind up the Affairs of that man. Next week I must apply for a Commission of Insolvency. Paid several demands for last Week. In the afternoon after dinner at home, I proceeded with the Catalogue in the Office and finished all that portion of it, and in the evening I completed the few remaining stragglers which I could find. This has been no trifling labour.

JOHN ADAMS 2D GEORGE WASHINGTON ADAMS (1823)

10–11. THE BROTHERS OF CHARLES FRANCIS ADAMS, BY CHARLES BIRD KING

See page xv

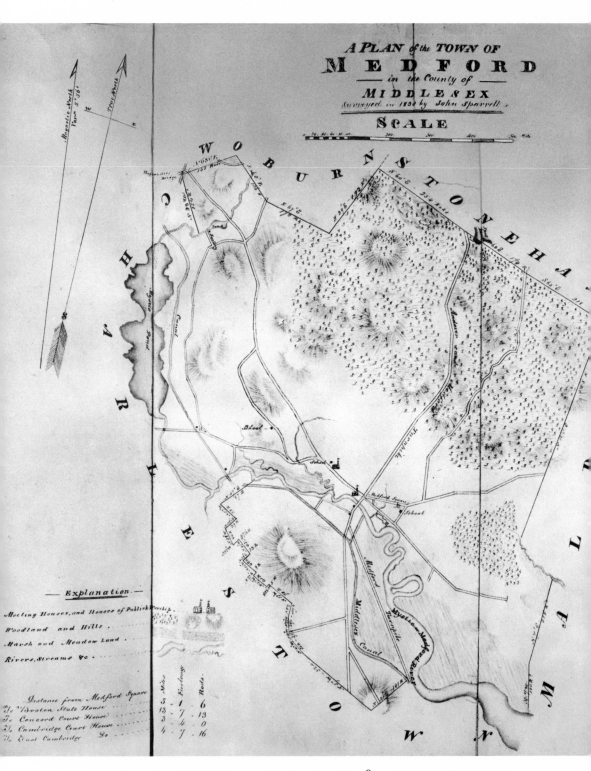

12. PLAN OF THE TOWN OF MEDFORD IN 1830, BY JOHN SPARRELL

See page xviii

13. RUINS OF THE STONE AQUEDUCT WHICH BORE THE MIDDLESEX CANAL OVER THE MYSTIC RIVER IN MEDFORD

See page xix

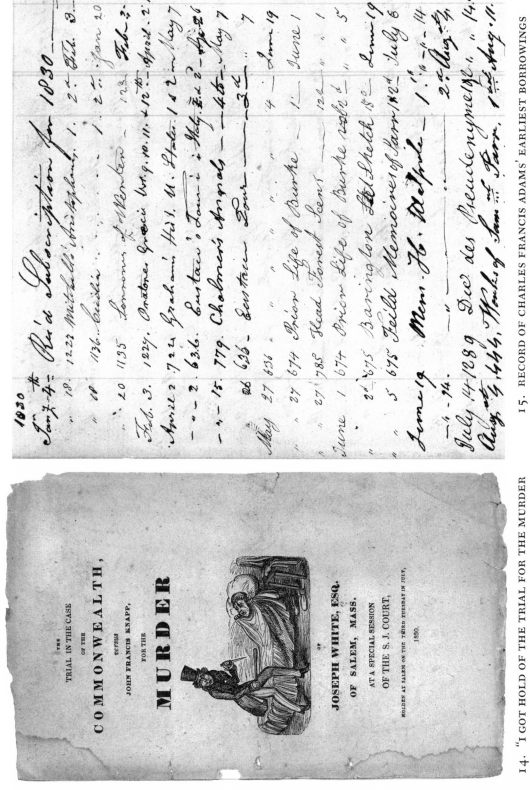

14. "I GOT HOLD OF THE TRIAL FOR THE MURDER OF MR. WHITE AT SALEM . . . AND COULD NOT LEAVE IT QUICKLY"

15. RECORD OF CHARLES FRANCIS ADAMS' EARLIEST BORROWINGS FROM THE BOSTON ATHENAEUM

TUESDAY. 7TH.

The morning opened dark and cloudy. So much so that I felt myself obliged to advise Abby to remain here a little while longer. Feeling as if I was bound to keep an Appointment which I had made with Daniel Adams the Pumpmaker[1] I went in but he disappointed me and did not come. It poured with prodigious violence during the last part of the time. I in fact accomplished very little during my stay. Some few small Commissions for Abby and my Mother, were finished, and I hastened after giving directions for transferring some things to Quincy by the baggage Waggon to make [my] way back as well as I could. Luckily for me the rain held up while I was going.

My father attended the Meeting of the Proprietors of Neponset Bridge and dined with them at Squantum. I was glad to be at home. My afternoon was passed without occupation, as I carried my Catalogue to town. I read for my amusement a part of Sevigniana or a collection of beauties from the Letters of Madame de Sévigné.[2] They are amusing and perhaps make the pleasantest way of reading that lady's voluminous Correspondence. But this occupation does not quite satisfy me. Something more serious ought to be my study.

Evening a conversation with my Mother in which I explained to her my views in the course which I had thought proper to adopt and gave my opinion of the disadvantages attending John's proposed course, perhaps more freely than was necessary.

[1] Daniel Adams, pump- and block-maker, had a "stone store" on India Wharf (*Boston Directory*, 1830–1831).
[2] JQA's copy of the edition published at Paris in 1768 of *Sévigniana, ou recueil de pensées ingenieuses ... tirées des lettres de Madame la marquise de Sévigné*, is in MQA.

WEDNESDAY 8TH.

The rain poured all day and precluded the possibility of our moving an inch. So that I made the best of it and commenced reading Rollin's Maniere d'etudier les Belles Lettres.[1] The critic in the French Dictionnaire Historique thinks it superficial and confused,[2] yet so far as I have gone it strikes me there is great merit and clearness. His method is perhaps not perfect, but in a work like this which is to give mere advice perhaps the best way to give it is the pleasantest or most agreeable manner. Not a regular course which must be studied but an easy one with occasional variety to keep up the attention. I pursued it nearly all day with little or no cessation as I had not any means to vary it properly. Took up however a book upon Gardening which I examined with a view to some improvement in the cultivation of the garden here in future, and to the cultivation of an Orchard at Mount Wollaston, a project entertained by my father and myself. Evening, Conversation with my Mother and having no work retired early.

[1] *De manière d'enseigner et d'étudier les belles lettres* by Charles Rollin, rector of the University of Paris, along with other works by him, had been among the favorite books of JA. See JA, *Earliest Diary*, p. 52; *Adams Family Correspondence*, 1:142–143; 2:40–41. His copy of an edition in English is now among his books in MB. At MQA there are two copies, one owned by JQA and published at Leyden in 1759 in 4 vols., the other also in 4 vols., Paris, 1741.

[2] *Dictionnaire historique et bibliographique portatif.* The edition at MQA was published at Paris in 1777 in 3 vols. and has JQA's bookplate.

Quincy—Medford

THURSDAY. 9TH.

It seemed as if Rain was the order of the day for we found no cessation of it, and were content with continuing our Quarters here this morning. I pursued the study or rather the reading of Rollin, all the morning and went through a Treatise upon the Instruction of Girls which was not quite so interesting to me as any of the rest of the Work. I then continued with Instruction in the French, and Greek Languages. His system seems to be good and I think on my return to my House I will adopt it. I have pretty nearly made up my mind to pursue eagerly Classical Studies, being satisfied fully that they are the only firm foundation for a Gentleman and Scholar.

My time hitherto, though I am far from admitting that it has been mispent, yet for want of a directing care has not been of the greatest possible service. My father gave advice but the misfortune of it was that in this case as in many others it was speculative. In itself excellent but not preserving that most necessary quality of being gradually given at moments when the use was immediately evident. Yet I will candidly admit that, that advice has been of infinite service to me even to do what I have done.

I worked an hour in the Garden and made an experiment with a Strawberry bed, cutting off the small shoots from the Bed made in the Spring and planting them anew. Called in to see the Judge, my Uncle who wanted the regular allowance for his Son John Quincy, which I gave him by drawing a Check for the Amount. After dinner, the weather looking decently, or at least not positively rainy, we decided upon going off to pay our visit to Medford. Our ride was not an unpleasant one and we arrived before six o'clock. We found the family much as usual with the exception of an addition in Miss Gorham who was there on a visit.

FRIDAY. 10TH.

Morning still cloudy and threatening. Mr. Frothingham accompanied me to town and I went to the Office as usual. Received a Note from Quincy by Joseph Adams stating the fact of Mary's having been delivered last night of a daughter.[1] This is well so far as safety and health go, but it is rather to be regretted on other accounts. It has now become doubtful whether I shall be blessed with any Children. I feel very far from sanguine about it, and it therefore is rather to be wished that some of John's Progeny should be male—If not, what becomes of the family which we love to cherish. Perhaps this is a part of fate. I know not but with a very good end, for it would be better that it should cease than degenerate to become a proverb.

I had all sorts of interruptions and did very little. Half an hour spent in Accounts, as much in Commissions, with a visit from my friend Mr. T. Davis and one from my Carpenter Mr. Champney consumed the time. The former chatted an hour pleasantly as usual, the latter gave me notice that his Mother intended leaving me. Another of the Tenements empty, and my arrangements for Work discomposed. Returned to Medford to dinner. Afternoon passed in reading Rollin, partly in seeing Visitors. Mr. Alfred Brooks, son of Jonathan, and his brother S. R. B., heretofore a merchant in Manchester but unfortunate in business who has returned to see his friends.[2] Others with them. In the evening I read and reviewed the first book of Rollin upon the study of Languages.

[1] JA2's second daughter, Georgeanna Frances. Joseph Harrod Adams, who brought the news of her birth, was the thirteen-year-old son of TBA. On both, see Adams Genealogy.

[2] Samuel Reeves Brooks (1793-1870)

had been nine years in England (Brooks, Farm Journal, 10, 19 Sept., 5 Dec.). Alfred (1801-1875) was the youngest of the three sons of Jonathan Brooks (Brooks, *Medford*, p. 529).

SATURDAY. 11TH.

Morning pleasant. Mr. Frothingham rode to town with me to remain over Sunday. I went to my Office after having collected the Dividend due at the New England Marine Insurance Office. A small affair of three per Cent in one year, which does not pay me for the risk of investing. My time was afterwards entirely engrossed by various people who came with or without purpose. Mr. Conant the Tenant from Weston came with his bill for Work, and I discussed with him the probability of a time for the sale of Wood. He gives very encouraging Accounts of the amount which remains. After him came Richardson who spent half an hour, during which time John Kirke came from Quincy with some Commissions. He also brought Books which I had expressed a wish to have. A Note from my Father and one from John required answering,[1] and some Commissions executed. These were hardly well through when Edmund Quincy came to talk about the Office opposite which he has some idea of engaging. In this manner I had barely time to write my Journal before returning to Medford. Mr. Brooks did not dine at home so that I was the only gentleman there. Read Rollin in the afternoon, but somehow or other with less gusto than at Quincy. Evening, Conversation.

[1] The original of JQA's letter to CFA is missing, but a facsimile is printed in James Grant Wilson, *The Presidents of the United States*, N.Y., 1894, facing p. 124. The note, principally on matters of business, concluded, "You know we have a new comer who was almost in time to bid you good by—but we do not miss you the less for that—nor your partner whose place it irks me to see vacant at breakfast. But we take Patience, and hope still to see you both often." JA2's letter to CFA and CFA's answers to both letters are missing.

SUNDAY. 12TH.

I have resumed the practice of taking Shower baths since coming to Medford although the temperature of the air has altered prodigiously since my last visit. The water is now very cool, but it has a bracing effect which is agreeable, and beneficial.

My Wife was not very well and did not go to Meeting. The rest of the family attended and heard Mr. C. Brooks of Hingham preach.[1] His Sermons were upon the character of the Saviour, and upon Christian Conversion. The former by far the best and the shortest. He considered the leading points of the character of Christ, to be benevolence, piety and humility and required them in all who professed to follow the Gospel, as necessary ingredients to form members of the true Church without regarding distinctions of Sect. The latter was long, more slovenly in arrangement of thought and repetition, but nevertheless conveyed many good passages very fairly. On the whole I was better pleased with him than ever before. Mr. Brooks who considers things often through a darkened medium was not suited.

I passed some time reading Rollin but in a loose way—The power of application being nothing. Mr. Frothingham brought out with him more French News of the same complexion with what had preceded. And we talked so much that I read little.

[1] Rev. Charles Brooks (1795–1872) was the oldest of the sons of Jonathan Brooks; subsequent to his Hingham ministry he wrote the *History of Medford* (Brooks, *Medford*, p. 448–449, 529).

MONDAY. 13TH.

Morning cloudy but with a cold East Wind, which was extremely disagreeable. I took the Bath however being quite determined to persevere as long as it would be tolerable. After breakfast I went to Boston accompanied by Mr. Frothingham. At the Office, writing my Journal up which has for two months past had a tendency to run constantly behindhand, owing to the irregularity of my presence in the City. I then thought it would be as well to prepare a list of debts of the Estate of Robert New in order to set about a Commission of Insolvency. All which was done. A Commission applied for and granted.

I then thought it would be advisable to go down and see the condition of the Tenements in Tremont Street which are empty. Found two of them deserted and the new occupant of the other dissatisfied so that I do not see but what I shall have them all three upon me at once, and this affects my spirits. More care and responsibility. Returned to my Office and from there went off again to Medford. Afternoon reading Rollin upon Rhetoric. A subject in itself so full of good matter cannot fail to be interesting, but this Author affords little matter which I have not seen before. The fact is that after a certain point all is repetition. Quiet evening. Gorham Brooks paid a short visit here.

TUESDAY. 14TH.

Morning cloudy and cold, with a drizzle from the Eastward. Went to town as usual. My first business was to go to my House to look at it's condition and being there I made several alterations in my Library to meet the new acquisition of Buffon—My father having sent one of his Copies for my use.[1] I feel always a great deal of pleasure in being in my study. It seems to be a literary atmosphere, in which I can indulge my favourite pursuits. But I could not stay at present. One fortnight will I hope see me back there.

One or two applications for the Tenements, a little of Hutchinson, and Accounts consumed the greater portion of the morning. Returned to Medford and found Mr. and Mrs. Everett with their children there to dine. Our dinner was pleasant as usual. My afternoon passed without any material occurrence excepting the doing nothing. A business of all others the most easy and least profitable.

Evening, Rollin upon the Eloquence of the Pulpit. He quotes much from the Fathers but on the whole his account is dry. The criticism of the Dictionnaire Historique appears in this case to be correct. His doctrine is superficial leaving no impression upon the mind. A mere series of passages from distinguished authors will hardly suffice, to get an understanding of style. They are various and confuse rather than teach.

[1] The *Histoire naturelle* of George Louis Leclerc, Comte de Buffon, published at Paris in 1800 in 74 volumes is in MQA and bears JQA's bookplate.

WEDNESDAY. 15TH.

Morning extremely fine, one of the first which we have had, for I rarely recollect a Season in which the Weather has been so cold. The Fruit has not had time to ripen and the foliage bears marks of it's influence. Rode to town accompanied by Mr. Frothingham and went to the Office, from thence to my house where I sent[1] and arranged the copy of Buffon, already spoken of. Felt as if I wished the time for my going there was come, but patience must be my guide.

Returned and read a portion of Hutchinson. Was detained in the Street for half an hour by an applicant who wanted one of the Tenements, but bored me upon every subject. He is a thoroughgoing democrat of the first water, and however much I may like the party, this specimen is not the most attractive portion of it. Glad to get away. Returned to Medford.

Afternoon broken by the arrival of Edward Brooks and his Wife who took tea here as well as Messrs. C. C. Emerson and J. Lyman.[2] Mr. Brooks was not at home, having gone to attend the funeral of Mr. Bridge in Charlestown.[3] Evening quiet. I finished the second Volume of Rollin.

[1] Thus in MS.

[2] Charles Chauncy Emerson (1808–1836), Harvard 1828, the son of Rev. William Emerson, was a lawyer (*Records of the First Church in Boston*, Col. Soc. Mass., *Pubns.*, 40 [1961]:467). J. Lyman may have been Joseph Lyman, Harvard 1830.

[3] Samuel J. Bridge of 16 Summer Street, Boston, died in New York City on 6 Sept. (*Boston Directory*, 1830–1831; *Columbian Centinel*, 11 Sept., p. 2, col. 4).

THURSDAY. 16TH.

Morning fine but cool. I rode to town as usual and was occupied at my Office. Went to the Athenæum for a few moments, with the view of looking at the Courier which nominated my father for Congress but there was no Copy there. I took the opportunity to obtain some books to assist me in my Catalogue, and returned. Found what I was looking for at the Reading Room in State Street.[1]

I worked a little upon my Catalogue but found myself stopped for the want of several things only to be obtained at my Study. I then read a little of Hutchinson, and the time came to return to Medford. My Wife was quite unwell all day and confined to her bed. I read Rollin although I do not feel so much interested in the historical portion of the work. It is matter a little too simple for me, it brings me back to rudiments so often worked over as to have become disgusting.

Mr. Theodore Lyman came to pay Mr. Brooks a short visit. I saw him only for a moment. He is rather a favourite with Mr. B. but I confess I see nothing in his character attractive or pleasant. And my mind is not given to bend in devotion to wealth, without any other quality.[2] I had a very quiet evening.

[1] The Reading Room was located in the Old State House at the head of State Street (*Boston Directory*, 1830–1831, p. 34). The issue of the *Boston Courier* for which CFA was searching was that of 6 September. In it (p. 1, col. 4) there appeared a paragraph, unsigned but apparently the work of J. T. Buckingham, the paper's editor and proprietor, as follows: "We would not wish to be considered meddlesome, but we take the liberty of suggesting to the National Republicans of Norfolk, that they would do well to elect Mr. ADAMS, the ex-president, as their next representative. There are many considerations which might make such an election desirable to them as a party, and, unless we mistake entirely Mr. Adams's disposition, there are as many which might render an election agreeable to him."

At first JQA dismissed the suggestion. "As the Editor of the Paper has been uniformly hostile to me, I supposed this nomination was made with the same Spirit, and did not imagine it was seriously thought of by any one" (JQA, Diary, 17 Sept.). However, he was soon visited by a number of persons including A. H. Everett, John Brazer Davis, and Joseph Richardson, the incumbent who refused to be a candidate for re-election, all presumably bent on urging JQA to run (JQA, Diary, 17, 18 Sept.).

[2] Theodore Lyman Jr., wealthy merchant, federalist, and lately a supporter of Andrew Jackson, was a fellow director with Mr. Brooks of the Massachusetts Society for Agriculture. His extensive estate was in Waltham. See vol. 2:103, 323, 326; also entry for 27 Jan., above.

FRIDAY. 17TH.

As this was the day destined for the Celebration of the Anniversary of the settlement of Boston, and about to produce a tremendous consequent fuss I thought it would be expedient for me to have nothing whatever to do with it.[1] I have a great horror of Crowds, and if I make up my mind to attend public days always have cause to repent it. So I remained at Medford and spent my day in reading Rollin.

The weather was exceedingly cold for so early in the Season and I found it absolutely uncomfortable without a fire. Indeed I felt altogether so chilly that I was obliged to take a quick walk to get warm. This was in the direction of West Cambridge Pond which is a spot always attractive in my eyes.[2] Susceptible of being improved into infinite beauty. The day except in the cold was exceedingly fine and gave animation to the spirits. These bracing days make strong frames stronger, and weak ones weaker. They are enemies to disease either in preventing or accelerating them. Nobody came through the day and we were very quiet.

[1] The celebration of the 200th anniversary of the settlement of Boston began with a grand procession from the State House down Beacon Street, across the Common to Tremont Street, ending at the Old South Church. There the oration was delivered by President Josiah Quincy. The day ended with an evening party at Lt. Gov. Winthrop's house (*Boston Patriot*, 16 Sept., p. 1, cols. 3–5). On JQA's participation in the observances of the day, see his Diary, 17 Sept., and Bemis, *JQA*, 2:205–206.

[2] CFA's allusion is probably to Spy Pond in West Cambridge, which was a comfortable walk from Mystic Grove.

SATURDAY. 18TH.

Morning fine but rather cold—There being quite a sharp frost. I took a bath but found the water cold and the air colder so that I nearly made up my mind to stop at least for the present. Mr. Frothingham not being at Medford, I decided to ride down with Mr. Brooks. On the road he opened the conversation about his prospects for the Winter. I gave him an invitation for the Winter, which he seemed disposed to decline, and under the circumstances in which I am situated, I did not urge it.[1]

At the Office. Occupied all the morning in work of different sorts, time flew imperceptibly. Worked a little upon my Catalogue. Called as a return visit upon Mr. Krehmer[2] and attended for a few moments an Auction.[3] Besides this a little of Hutchinson. I go on slowly. Returned to Medford with Mr. Brooks. Gorham and his Wife were there to dine. They are civil to me, but I cannot forget the former's conduct when I was differently situated. Consumed the whole afternoon in this manner. Evening passed quietly, finishing the Historical portion of Rollin's book.

[1] Mr. Brooks remained at Medford through the winter of 1830, moving to Boston in Nov. 1831 (Brooks, Waste Book).

[2] Probably George Krehmer, a childhood acquaintance in St. Petersburg, who was second secretary of the Russian legation in Washington; see vol. 2:289.

[3] Furniture, household goods, wines, hams, cigars, &c., were scheduled for auction at the Julien Auction Rooms (*Boston Patriot*, 17 Sept., p. 3, col. 5).

SUNDAY. 19TH.

Morning clear but so cool that I declined taking the Bath. I attended divine service at Mr. Stetson's Meeting house all day and heard him deliver two Sermons upon the verse in the first Chapter of Genesis affirming that God created man after his own image. They were good although they did not satisfy me upon the nature of the passage.

My day was otherwise much wasted. I heard my Wife read French to me and afterwards went down to see Mr. Jonathan Brooks and his English Son Samuel who drank tea. The children inherit the loquacity of their father and the English branch having additional sources of information and observation is just in so much spoiled by the further ease it gives to his propensity. A little of Rollin afterwards.

MONDAY. 20TH.

Morning to town with Mr. Brooks. Weather fine but cool. At the Office nearly all the morning engaged in my common occupations. Read a little of Hutchinson and made a settlement of some of the demands upon New's Estate. Mr. Beals, my Tenant of Mr. Hollis' house called to discuss the question of moving or reducing rent. I had heard a bad character of him and made no effort to compromise.

An Irish Woman came for advice, sent as she said by Mr. Consul Manners.[1] Why this gentleman should think proper to send the woman to me I cannot comprehend. She had no cause of complaint that I could discover against her lawyer Mr. A. Moore, with whose concerns I had no inclination to interfere. So I directed her to wait and see the end of her affair. She is a poor Irish woman whose case is a hard one as she has no friends and is unlucky enough to have a dishonest lawyer.

Returned to Medford with Mr. B. and found Mr. Frothingham there after an absence of several days. I wasted my Afternoon, excepting in a walk with Mr. Brooks to a part of Woburn to look at a great Elm Tree which is there. It is a noble sight. We measured it at two feet from the ground and found it twenty feet three inches in girth, which is with us prodigious.[2] Returned to tea and passed the Evening at Mrs. Hall's, tolerably dull.

[1] The British consul in Boston was George Manners; his office was at 3 Barristers Hall (*Boston Directory*, 1830–1831).

[2] The elm tree was perfectly sound at 136 years; it was on the land of Abel Richardson near the Blackhorse Tavern. Richardson, 94, and his wife, 92, were alive, looked after by a maiden daughter. The tree's only rival in the area was the elm on Boston Common which, 30 inches from the ground, measured 21 feet, 8 inches in circumference in 1825 (Brooks, Farm Journal, 20 Sept.). However, see the following entry for another measurement.

TUESDAY. 21ST.

Morning tolerably pleasant although there was a pretty thick fog came up from the Eastward in the course of it. I went in accompanied by Mr. Frothingham to Boston, and spent a considerable portion of time in overlooking things at my house, where the servants from Quincy came this morning. Gave directions about several things which I desired done before the Winter to make us a little warmer than we have been. Last Winter was the first trial of a new house and was therefore in many respects uncomfortable. I hope we may do better this.

Went down to the great tree on Boston Common to measure its circumference and compare it with that visited yesterday. I found it nineteen feet three inches, being one foot less. But it is much handsomer in shape.

Sidney Brooks called and settled all the Affair respecting the finding and removing poor George's body, and he returned me the balance of the sum appropriated for the purpose in his hands. Returned to Medford with Mr. Frothingham. Sidney Brooks and his Wife came to spend a few days. Afternoon Mr. and Mrs. C. Brooks of Boston with her friends from Portland came to visit the place.[1] The whole time was wasted, and the evening in talking about nothing.

[1] Charles Brooks was the son of Cotton Brooks of Portland and a first cousin of ABA. Charles and his brother, William G. Brooks, were partners in Brooks & Co., hardware, at 6 Dock Square. The Charles Brooks residence was at 9 Suffolk Place. (CFA, Diary, 18 May 1834; *Boston Directory*, 1830–1831.)

WEDNESDAY. 22D.

Morning cloudy and cold, threatening a storm. Rode to town as usual, and passed a large part of my morning at the House in pursuing the Catalogue of my father's books in Boston at my House.[1] I was also overlooking several changes which are going on at my House. I propose to mend the condition of things there a little. My study was so charming, I felt very much indisposed to leave it, but was obliged to.

Stopped at the new City Hall to a sale of the Stock and found that it was all as high as ever. Returned to my office late and found little or nothing to do. My time is now so much cut up that I cannot feel disposed to undertake large designs for want of it, and small ones use it up badly. Returned to Medford. Mr. and Mrs. Everett dined with us and it was tolerably pleasant. They went home early.

As the portion of time devoted to my stay here was rapidly vanishing I took an opportunity to ask Mr. Brooks to accompany me to see the Apple Trees for my Father's Garden which I wished to purchase from the Nursery of a man by the name of Warren. After examining them and ascertaining their origin and goodness, I concluded a bargain for eighty of them at twenty five cents a piece. This is to be a fair experiment as we can make to get an Orchard.[2] Returned to tea, and wasted the Evening in yawning and conversation.

[1] All of the books which had belonged to GWA became the property of JQA either by pledge or as a part of GWA's estate. CFA retained possession of the books, keeping them apparently both in his office and at his home.

[2] A similar account of the expedition and of the purchase of the "budded Baldwin apple trees" appears in Brooks, Farm Journal, entry for 23 September.

THURSDAY. 23RD.

Morning cloudy but rather warm. Mr. Frothingham accompanied me to Boston which was pleasant enough. He is a man of agreeable conversation and mild disposition, without any assumption. At the Office and from thence to the House where I passed an hour occupied upon the Catalogue. My old manservant Benjamin made his appearance today and applied to be taken back again. I was glad to see him, and to talk with him. He had repented of his bargain and therefore I thought might prove more satisfied of the advantages of my situation from his experience of that of others. I engaged him. Returning to the Office I read Hutchinson until dinner time.

Mr. Everett had invited all the Medford party to dine with him and so I went over at two o'clock. Mr. Alex. H. Everett was the only additional person. The dinner was very well but I did not like it. In the afternoon Mr. E's child was christened by Mr. Walker, before these members of the family and Mrs. Hale—the name was Edward Brooks. That such a man as Mr. Everett should manifest so much fawning sycophancy is enough to disgust me with my species. I believe this is the third Child with that name.[1] Returned to Medford accompanied by Mr. Frothingham. Mr. Stetson and Miss Eliz. Brooks paid a short visit.[2]

[1] Each of the three children of Peter C. Brooks who had sons who were alive in 1830 named a son for Edward Brooks, father of Peter C. Brooks: Edward Brooks (1822–1865), Edward Brooks Frothingham (b. 1825), Edward Brooks Everett (b. 1830) (Brooks, *Medford*, p. 452, 531; *Records of the First Church in Boston*, Col. Soc. Mass., *Pubns.*, 40 [1961]:451).

[2] Elizabeth Brooks (b. 1797) was a daughter of Jonathan and Elizabeth (Albree) Brooks (Brooks, *Medford*, p. 529).

FRIDAY. 24TH.

Morning remarkably fine, the air being warm and soft. I went to town accompanied by Mr. Frothingham. At the Office part of my time and the rest at my House to which I walked up twice. My picture came home today and I was confirmed in my opinion of it's merit.[1]

My Wife was in town, bringing in Mrs. Sidney Brooks who has finished her visit, which has been pleasant to us all.

My spirits were a little affected. Looking over the announcement of the new Number of the North American I found my Article *not* included. This is a little mortifying, and the proper course to take upon it is not absolutely clear. I shall wait until my return to town. Mr. Everett may think this fair to a young man struggling into life, but it may turn out unpleasantly. My prospects are respectable, and though it is in the power of others to check them, I trust, are not to be destroyed by any body but myself in this world.

I returned to Medford to dinner, and spent the afternoon in strolling over the Farm with Mr. Brooks. He showed me a body of Mud he was digging out of his Swamp with which he made Manure for his Land, and he went over the place to show me his quantity of Apple Fruit. It is very great. I hope to put the experience I gain here to some profit if I ever should be called to exercise any thing requiring some. Evening Rollin. I was quite fatigued.

¹ See entry for 5 Aug., above.

SATURDAY. 25TH.

Morning very thick with mist from the Eastward, and so damp that I felt pleased with my Coat, in riding into town. At the Office and from thence to my House where I passed a larger portion of time than usual. General Wool paid me a visit in return for mine, which detained me.¹ Then to the Office. Received a Note from my Father requesting our Company to the Christening of Mary's child, tomorrow.² A little too late for us easily to go. Read a little of Hutchinson and found it time to return to Medford. The day had cleared up and become fine.

Mr. Stetson was the only person to partake of the usual Salt fish dinner. He is a tolerably pleasant man though there is something I do not quite like about him. We sat until quite late. A practice I do not admire though no way occurs to me of easily killing the time remaining for my stay in the Country.

Sat with my Wife. Found her discouraged about her health and feeling poorly. I pity and sympathize with her. Married life has brought to her as many thorns as it has pleasures. This is the only cause of trouble in my mind. Evening quietly at home. Finished Rollin's book the latter part of which has been rather irksome.

¹ On Col. John Ellis Wool, inspector-general of the army, see vol. 2:110 and *DAB*.
² JQA to CFA, 24 Sept. (PHi, Dreer Coll.).

SUNDAY. 26TH.

The morning was exceedingly rainy and disagreeable so that the whole family remained at home. Having finished Rollin I hardly knew what to do with myself and wasted the time somewhat in doing little or nothing. Had a good deal of conversation with my Wife who is very much out of spirits respecting her health. She is weak and feels the effect of any kind of exertion. I tried to encourage her as well as I could although I myself think her complaint lasts most uncommonly.

In the Afternoon it cleared away and I attended Meeting. Heard Mr. Stetson preach a Sermon which might have been very good for all I knew to the contrary but I could not sufficiently fix my attention. In the evening, Amused myself with several Articles in the American Quarterly Review some of which are very good. That upon Napoleon though a warm and perhaps partial defence, is a very brilliant Article.[1] That upon Sunday Mails is more full of sense and sound judgment than the one on the same subject in the North American.[2]

[1] "Napoleon and Bourrienne," in *American Quarterly Review*, 8:32–71 (Sept. 1830).
[2] A review of *Report of the Committee of the House of Representatives of U.S. on Post-offices and Post Roads* ..., [on] *Transportation of the Mails and Distribution of Letters on Sunday*, same, p. 175–197.

Boston

MONDAY. 27TH.

Not during the whole Summer has there been a more beautiful morning than this was. The Sun rose clear and with that mellow and autumn light which spreads such a soft tinge upon every thing it touches. Arose and after breakfast made all my preparations for removal home. Three months have now been passed in this rambling way and I am heartily tired of it. To me it has proved worth nothing, except in blunting good resolutions and discouraging creditable undertakings. To my Wife it has not proved as beneficial as I anticipated. We reached our house early and I was busy during the morning in giving all the necessary directions incident upon setting a house going again.[1]

Then to the Office where I had a visit from Mr. Krehmer. A pleasant young man enough, but one of the Roué tribe for whom I feel exceeding little fondness. But he extracted from me an offer to go with him to Quincy for which I felt very sorry. Read a little of Hutchinson. Very dry. Returned home once more and dined. After which, I went to my study and began the Winter Campaign with Cicero which I propose to read through in course.[2] I began with the

Books de Inventione, and propose in the course of this study to make myself as much as possible master of the Latin language. It is one thing to read Latin, another to understand it's force. Evening, began a course with my Wife of French, by reading Mad. de Stael's Corinne,[3] and read to her an Article in the North American Review upon Moore's Life of Byron.[4] After which Logic. The first study day.

[1] Despite CFA's intent to restrict his and ABA's visits to Quincy and Medford during the summer to brief and intermittent ones, parental pressures and ABA's loneliness in a Boston from which other members of the family had removed (entry for 8 Aug., above) forced him to alter his decision. On 17 July the house on Hancock Avenue was closed for the summer and the servants were added to the staff at Quincy. Aside from one stay in Quincy during late August and early September extended some ten days beyond the usual, the periods spent at Quincy and at Medford were roughly equal. To prepare to reopen the Boston house Bridget McDonough, cook, and Elizabeth Caldwell, "nurserymaid," re-

turned to Hancock Avenue a few days earlier (JQA, Diary, 21 Sept.).

[2] Although there are numerous editions of Cicero's works in Latin at MQA, CFA makes it clear (entry for 29 Sept., below) that he was using the edition of the *Opera* published at Oxford in 1783 in 10 vols. The copy at MQA has JQA's bookplate and contains marginal notes in CFA's hand, mostly relating to typographical inaccuracies.

[3] This is a rereading. See vol. 1:437.

[4] A review, unsigned (by W. B. O. Peabody), of Thomas Moore's *Letters and Journals of Lord Byron, with Notices of his Life*, in *North Amer. Rev.*, 31:167–199 (July 1830).

TUESDAY. 28TH.

Morning fine. Arose early and devoted an hour to pursuing the Catalogue of my books at my House. Thence to the Office where I had several people inquiring about the Estate of Mr. New which is to be sold next week. Took a long walk myself to the Wharf of Mr. S. Child to obtain some Wood for the Winter.[1] The price of this Article has also fallen probably in consequence of the cheapness of Coal, so that my fuel will not cost me quite so much as it did last year. I hope to manage a little more discreetly it's use also.

Returned to the Office and then paid a visit to Mr. Krehmer, so that the morning was very much cut up. What was left at my disposal was devoted to Hutchinson which I do not read quite as attentively as I ought. After dinner, I sent for a conveyance and went with Mr. Krehmer to Quincy. We found the family all quite well excepting Louisa[2] who has a cold and sore throat.

No opportunity for Conversation of any kind excepting a few words with my Mother about the project of electing my father to Congress from Plymouth district which I regret exceedingly.[3] My father is a singular man. He wants the profound wisdom which gives knowledge it's highest lustre, he is not proof against the temporary seductions of popular distinction to resist which is the most solid evidence of greatness. Yet if he is not in character like Washington, he is a very extraordinary man for the times we live in. Returned by Moonlight, and Mr. E. Quincy paid us a short visit afterwards.

[1] The wood wharf of Stephen Child Jr. was on Front Street (*Boston Directory*, 1830–1831).

[2] That is, Mary Louisa Adams, aged two, the older of JA2's daughters.

[3] In the interim since the idea was first advanced (above, entry for 16 Sept.) JQA received calls from a number of supporters who sought his assurance that if the National Republicans of the district nominated him, he would accept the nomination. These visitors included Joseph Richardson, the incumbent not standing for reelection; John Bailey, the representative in Congress from Norfolk; John Brazer Davis; Deacon Daniel Spear; and Thomas Greenleaf. The two newspapers printed in the district, the *Old Colony Memorial* and the *Hingham Gazette*, came out in support of the nomination. (JQA, Diary, 18, 22, 25, 28 Sept.) However, LCA, either on her own initiative or after hearing CFA's objections, took a resolute stand against JQA's candidacy: "There are some very silly plans going on here and God only knows in what they will end, but I fear not at all to my taste" (LCA to JA2, 1 Oct., Adams Papers, and below, entry for 27 Oct. and note).

WEDNESDAY. 29TH.

Morning fine. My present time of rising is with the Sun, and on the whole I think this is the season in which I most enjoy my health. The weather is clear, cool and bracing. I work an hour after breakfast upon my Catalogue, then to the Office, where I employ myself as fully as I can in reading and writing with Accounts. This day I finished Hutchinson's second Volume most of which I have not read as well as I ought to have done. It is a valuable work, but exceedingly dry and difficult to pursue—The great simplicity of the style making it too even to prevent baldness. After dinner continued my attack upon Cicero. I find the large Oxford edition not quite so correct as I had anticipated. The Treatise de Inventione has much difficulty in it from the technical words of the Science which it is difficult clearly to transfer from one science to the other. I am also labouring upon the Port Royal Latin Grammar.[1] Read Corinne for an hour with Abby and finished the Article in the North American upon Moore's Life of Byron. It has many good points about it but has not *vis* enough. Passed two hours afterwards upon Hedge's and the Oxford Elements of Logic, which need more and more examination.

[1] *A New Method of Learning with Facility the Latin Tongue*, translated by T. Nugent from the French of "the Messieurs de Port-Royal." JQA's copy of the London edition, 2 vols., 1816, is in MQA.

THURSDAY. 30TH.

Morning fine but pretty cool reminding us of the approach of Winter. Went to the Office as usual, where I was occupied in making up the Accounts for the Quarter, and in drawing up the several distinct Accounts. My Uncle the Judge called in order to obtain his allowance for the Quarter a day in advance. He also brought a letter from my brother John to me in which he advertises the departure of some flour and hams from Georgetown, for me. A present for which I feel much obliged to him.[1]

A considerable part of my Morning passed in examining some grates and Stoves for two of my rooms which have not fire places. I also attended a sale of some but could not suit myself, though they went very low. The Judge dined with me, a civility I was glad to show him, as he had never dined with me or had any thing of the kind since I have been married. Nothing of any consequence occurred and I went to my Cicero only to turn back and review what I had already read. This is the only way, for one reading of an Author will give very little idea of his meaning, particularly if that Author is in a foreign language. Read Corinne an hour with Abby and afterwards read a part of Mason's Memoir of Gray the Poet, which is new to me.[2] Afterwards, two hours of Logic.

[1] The letter is missing. In return CFA wrote JA2 that he was sending him a box of fish and a half barrel of cranberries; in the same letter, though uncertain whether the intent in naming the new baby Georgeanna (for GWA) Frances was "applicable" to him, CFA assumed the compliment and thanked his brother for it (CFA to JA2, 2 Oct.).

[2] In the edition at MQA owned by JQA of *The Works of Thomas Gray*, 2 vols., London, 1807, the memoirs by William Mason appear in conjunction with Gray's letters in both volumes.

FRIDAY. OCTOBER 1ST.

This is the finest season of the year with us. The weather is clear though cold in the mornings and evenings, and the air has an elasticity very strengthening to the frame. I went to the Office and was busy for the greater part of the morning in making up my several Accounts for myself, my father and the Estate of R. New. This and an expedition to obtain a Stove which I completed consumed much time.

The balance was spent upon the new Number of the North American Review in which my Article does *not* appear and upon the Appendix to Hutchinson containing the Sketch of Plymouth History. I feel a little hurt with Mr. Everett for not inserting it according to promise, but my hands have *now* little power to resent even if I had the disposition so to do.

Returned home and after dinner passed my time as usual in reading Cicero. This book about Invention in its Rhetorical Sense has much merit as a Work though difficult in these times perfectly to comprehend. It has given me already new ideas upon the extent to which the disposition of materials may be mechanically ordered. And I hope it will not fail in the advantage it can confer if properly used to a practical [end].[1] Continued Corinne with Abby and Mason's Memoir of Gray. A book more agreeable than I had anticipated. Two hours passed afterwards upon Horne Tooke's Diversions of Purley.[2]

[1] Word editorially supplied.
[2] JQA's copy of John Horne Tooke, *The Diversions of Purley*, 2 vols., Phila., 1807, is in MQA.

[*Quincy*]

SATURDAY. 2D.

Morning delightful. Went to the Office. Occupied a considerable time in making out my Accounts, and in preparing a statement of New's affairs which is to be used at the sale on Wednesday, to finish this I was compelled to go down to the Office of the Assessors to obtain the schedule of Taxes chargeable to the Estates. And I did not complete the business before my father came in, after which he kept me at work in various little errands all the morning. So that I found exceeding little time to myself.

Returned home and found my Mother at my House, the first time she has come to town since she came to this part of the Country. I was of course glad to see her and she dined with us while my father went to Isaac P. Davis'. The afternoon was wasted as I did not feel as if I ought to leave her and pursue my occupations. We waited until after tea, and then concluded to go out with them and spend the Sunday at Quincy. The evening was very fine, the Moon beautiful and we arrived safe and sound in due time, at the old Mansion.

SUNDAY. 3D.

Morning clear but cold with a blustering wind which reminded us strongly of the approach of Winter. I copied a letter for my father,[1] and held some subsequent conversation with him upon the project of electing him to Congress. He does not disappoint me as I wish he had done. His is not the highest kind of greatness. And much as he may try to conceal his feeling under the cloak of patriotic inclination; My eye is a little too deep to be blinded by the outside. I regret the decision on his account. I regret it upon my own. To neither of us can it prove beneficial to be always struggling before the public without rest or intermission.

Went to Meeting and heard Mr. Whitney preach a couple of Sermons during the day which were dry and dull as usual. He is a persevering speaker of nothings. After service in the Afternoon, my father and I went to ride in the gig, round to the Mount Wollaston Estate. He went out in search of Acorns, and left me shivering in the Gig. I felt less partiality for the place this time. It is cold and bleak, and what are my ideas but vanity and vexation of spirit. I have no motive to hope for perpetuating the property.

Felt glad to return home, and after tea walked to the Judge's, my Uncle's. Saw him and the young ladies, but Mrs. Adams had gone to Haverhill. Passed an hour in conversation, and then did my regular Quarterly business, after which I returned to read two Articles in the Quarterly Review before retiring.

[1] Probably a letter from JQA to William Plumer Jr. at Epping, N.H., dated 30 Sept., which is in CFA's hand in JQA's letterbook (Adams Papers). The letter relates in some detail JQA's controversy with the New England Federalists (see above, entry for 31 Oct. 1829, note 4).

Boston

MONDAY 4TH.

The morning fine and clear again. After breakfast we made ready to return to Boston. My father did not seem in very good humour, probably from the course which I felt it my duty to take about the election. This matter is not an agreeable one to him nor is it so to me, but I feel as if he ought not to take any course without having the whole ground laid out before him. The precedent is important to the whole nation.[1]

Returned to town, and from thence directly to the Office. After arranging and looking over my papers here, I went down to the Meeting of the Stockholders of the State Bank, for the annual election of Directors. The excitement was very considerable as there was a design to overturn the President. Mr. Degrand figured away upon that occasion a little too much for the success of his cause. Our people are never over fond of foreigners and the moneyed men are wary of Brokers. The mass of the property of the Bank went in favour of the old system, while the young men and small Proprietors advocated a change; among the latter I may be classed. The excitement was notwithstanding very considerable.

I returned to the Office and passed the rest of the morning in reading, writing and Accounts. Mr. Frothingham dined with us. And I read Cicero afterwards, although I cannot make much of the Books de Inventione. They are a mere skeleton of a very intricate and subdivided system. Evening, Corinne, Mason's Life of Gray, and the Diversions of Purley.

[1] JQA makes no reference to the conversation with CFA, only to a miserable night caused by a return of his lumbago (Diary, 4 Oct.). His decision to accept a nomination if offered with a strong show of support had apparently been made. Despite efforts made by the Jacksonians to block the nomination, JQA was nominated by the Republican convention at Halifax on 12 Oct., as well as by the National Republican convention the next day (see JQA, Diary, 13, 14 Oct.; *Boston Patriot*, 16 Oct., p. 2, cols. 1–2). On 15 Oct. JQA responded to notice of the nomination: "If my fellow-citizens of the District should think proper to call for such services as it may be in my power to render them by representing them in the twenty-second Congress, I am not aware of any sound principle which would justify me in withholding them. To the manifestations of confidence on the part of those portions of the people, who, at two several meetings, have seen fit to present my name for the suffrages of the District, I am duly and deeply sensible" (*Boston Daily Advertiser*, 25 Oct., p. 2, col. 3). For a fuller account of the movement to make JQA a candidate and of the arguments advanced against his giving his consent, see Bemis, *JQA*, 2:206–211, in which account CFA's comments here and in the preceding entry are quoted and CFA's opposition presented in an unfavorable light. LCA's more intense and more sustained opposition is not mentioned by Bemis; on that see below, entry for 27 Oct. and note.

TUESDAY. 5TH.

Morning delightful, the air being a little warmer than it had been. I occupied my time as usual after breakfast until my Office hour, when I went down first to the American and Boston Banks, where I drew my Dividends of Profit and of Capital.[1] My Investments in both these Institutions have been partially returned to me but this time I got the start and have not only invested the surplus but am actually receiving at the same moment profits upon the same money in both situations. At the Office, preparing the Papers for New's sale, and arranging my father's accounts. The proceeds of his Estate come in slowly this Quarter. Returned home and passed a part of my afternoon in reading Cicero, just enough of which I understand to make me desire to keep more in my head.

Abby had been asked to go and take tea at Mr. Everett's, and accordingly I called for her at Mrs. Dehon's where she went to pay a parting visit to Fanny who goes tomorrow. We walked to Charlestown and found there Mr. and Mrs. Hale, Mr. and Mrs. A. H. Everett, Genl. Van Rensselaer and his son—The two latter just arrived from New York.[2] Evening tolerably pleasant and quiet return.

[1] CFA held three shares in the American Bank and six shares in the Boston Bank (vol. 2:286, 288, 339).

[2] Stephen Van Rensselaer (1764–1839), long a supporter of JQA and member of Congress from New York during his administration, had not stood for reelection in 1828. His son Henry Bell Van Rensselaer (1810–1864), in 1830 a cadet at West Point, was later a member of Congress and subsequently brigadier-general in the union army during the Civil War. (*Biog. Dir. Cong.*)

WEDNESDAY. 6TH.

Morning pleasant as usual. Went down to the Office and prepared my statement and other papers for the sale of New's Estate. Wrote my Journal and read a little of Minot's continuation to Hutchinson which I do not much fancy.[1] It is written with an ambitious and yet a diffuse style approaching to weakness. Busy also with my Accounts which progress slowly.

At twelve o'clock I went down and attended the sale of New's property. The Cambridge Street Equity of Redemption sold for three hundred and seventy five dollars. That in Lynde Street for one hundred and five.[2] The attendance was respectable and the building[3] pretty smart. I am inclined to think both sales were fair for each side, and certainly imagine neither was a great bargain. I have so little fondness for real Estate, that I should feel no ambition to assume either of these purchases.

Called upon Genl. Van Rensselaer and his Son. It was grand Muster day and every thing in confusion.[4] Spent the Afternoon in reading Cicero as usual and the evening in my usual way, with my Wife, first reading Corinne, then Mason, and afterwards Tooke.

[1] George Richards Minot, *Continuation of the History of the Province of Massachusetts Bay, from the year 1748 ... to 1765*, 2 vols., Boston, 1798–1803. In the second volume of the set at MQA, CFA has copied in his hand from JA's copy (now in MB) the marginal notes which JA had written. Each of the notes that is JA's is so indicated. In a note about the marginalia and about Minot's narrative of pre-Revolutionary events, CFA observed that JA's "account of the same scenes may be found in his letters to W. Tudor published as an appendix to the edition of *Novanglus*

... of 1819." On the publication of the letters, see below, entry for 24 Dec. and note; on *Novanglus and Massachusettensis*, see JA, *Diary and Autobiography*, 2:161.

[2] See above, entry for 30 Aug., note.

[3] Thus in MS, doubtless for "bidding."

[4] At noon three regiments, seven independent companies, a battalion of artillery, a corps of cavalry, and the Sea Fencibles passed in review before Gen. Capen on the Common. A sham fight followed in the afternoon (*Boston Patriot*, 7 Oct., p. 2, col. 2).

THURSDAY. 7TH.

Morning cool. Arose quite early and started immediately after breakfast for Weston according to an engagement made yesterday. The weather was cool and I enjoyed my ride far more than I did on a similar occasion last year. Called at his house for my friend Richardson and found much pleasure from his Company. We reached Weston before ten and proceeded to look at the Farm which does not amount to much, and after meeting with Col. Jones the Auctioneer, we went into the Woods and looked at the tract we propose to part with. When

I once get into this, I know very little where I am, so that I am compelled to trust very much to the representations of the Tenants on the place and Jones himself. Picked up a large quantity of White Oak Acorns for my Father, they are fresh and to all appearance of very good quality. We finished soon and I was enabled to start so as to be able to reach home by my regular dinner time. Afternoon passed in my usual avocations, Cicero, the first book, de Inventione, I finished, and began again. One examination of a book in a foreign language answers very little purpose. Evening at home. French as usual. Mason and Horne Tooke.

FRIDAY. 8TH.

Morning clear but rather cooler than it had been and so much so that I felt very much the want of a Fire. Having made up my Mind about the course proper to be taken with the Editor of the North American Review I wrote him a Note requesting the return of my Manuscript to which he replied by sending it to me with a Note stating that he should like to see me to give me some hints before revising it.[1] I felt exceedingly dispirited by this result of my labours. To have been kept in suspense so long, to have had the matter of it praised among connections with whom it is my ambition to stand well and then to be discouraged from pursuing the path I saw clear before me, were all a little severe upon me.

My time was very much taken up in attending to people of different sorts on various errands—Some in settlement of their demands, others upon other subjects. Not a moment was left for myself. According to agreement, we dined at P. Chardon Brooks'. I saw his Wife who is laid up for a considerable period with an accident by which her knee was affected. After dinner, returned home and pursued my review of Cicero's first Book which this time seems easy, but I follow it only by snatches, and the impression it makes wears out of my memory. Evening Corinne, a little of the Poet Gray and a visit from Edmund Quincy. But my spirits have not been so low since I was married.

[1] Both CFA's letter and A. H. Everett's reply are missing.

SATURDAY. 9TH.

Morning cloudy and it soon after began to rain, which lasted through the day. At the Office after a walk to the south end of the town to collect the Dividends due upon the personal property there and to look at the three Tenements which are now all empty. Found them in better condition than I anticipated, but felt a little anxiety about them, as they ought not to stand empty. Returned and was busy with various persons calling until my father came in, for whom I immediately went out on business.

Returning, found at my Office, Mr. Alex. H. Everett and his brother in law Mr. Peabody.[1] They called to examine the office opposite to me which he has been fiddling about so long. The real secret however, I suspect to be that he wanted to see about the effect produced upon me by that affair of my Article. He alluded to it, and I was very frank with him. After transacting business, my father returned with me to my House, where I found my Mother tolerably well and come in to dine and spend the Night.

The P[resident] and I dined with Mr. Everett at Charlestown. Company consisted of Genl. Van Rensselaer, Judge Johnson, Mr. Schroeder of Baltimore, Commodore Morris, Mr. Hale, Mr. Alex. H. Everett, Palfrey, Peabody, Batchelder and Son, and a Son of Mr. Johnson at Cambridge.[2] The dinner was a little dull. The persons in the Company being ill assorted. I sat between Peabody and Batchelder Jr. and extracted from the former more than I expected. I forgot to mention Mr. B. Gorham, the pleasantest of all. Returned in the rain and passed the Evening in conversation.

[1] Oliver William Bourne Peabody (1799–1848), Harvard 1816, brother of Lucretia Orne (Peabody) Everett. After A. H. Everett purchased the *North American Review* Peabody moved to Boston to assist in editing it (*DAB*).

[2] Josiah Stoddard Johnston (1784–1833), U.S. Senator from Louisiana, had earlier been a district judge in his state (JQA, Diary, 9 Oct.; *Biog. Dir. Cong.*). His son may have been Thomas Jones Johnston, originally a member of the Harvard class of 1821, who received his degree out of course in 1833 (Corporation Records, 5:254, 335, MH-Ar).

SUNDAY. IOTH.

Morning cloudy but became pleasant. My father and Mother left us this morning after breakfast, and I felt a sensation of loneliness at my home after they had gone which is somewhat new to me, and not very agreeable, neither does it forebode any good. My hopes have been sanguine for a year past, that if my domestic happiness was to be disappointed by the failure of children, I might at least have a substitute in the ardor for literary distinction, but my mind is easily discouraged and my avocations so divide me as to be fast destroying any hope I had to appropriate my time to any useful purpose.

Attended divine Service all day and heard Mr. Frothingham in the morning and Mr. Ripley in the Afternoon. Neither Sermon had any interest to me. My Wife remained at home all day excepting when she went to see Mrs. P. C. Brooks. I was occupied upon the Catalogue, which is drawing to a Close.

In the evening, Chardon came in to tell us his brother Gorham's child was dead.[1] Such a thing as this reconciles one to not having any, for I do pity with all my heart the person affected by a sudden blow of desolation. I have no ills in comparison with such as this.

[1] A daughter, born earlier in 1830 (Brooks, Farm Journal, 4 June and 11 Oct.).

MONDAY. 11TH.

Morning extremely mild and pleasant. Went to the Office as usual and occupied myself in writing my Journal and arranging my Accounts for my Father. Walked to the South end for the purpose of making the transfer to Thomas B. Adams Jr. of the Shares in the Boylston Market and seven Shares in the Boylston Insurance Company by which Investments two thirds of his property is disposed of.[1] Took the opportunity of looking at the Tenements which are all empty and felt as if there was a necessity of taking some immediate and vigorous measures. Collected the balance of my father's dividends and paid myself the Compensation due to me. Thus went the morning.

Afternoon spent in reading over Cicero's first book which I found easy and perfectly comprehensible. The advice is excellent. I would that I could keep it in my mind constantly. But I feel discouraged about myself. My efforts result in nothing and my studies are mere vanity. What is the use of labour without profit.

Evening read Corinne and Mason's Life of Gray, after which I took up the North American Review and read the Article upon the Tariff and Internal Improvement doctrine as at present treated by South Carolina. It is a Masterly Essay, by Edward Everett, and calculated to produce considerable effect. I particularly admired the close of it which is in his happiest manner.[2] I have also undertaken to read the British Essay Writers, which I never yet could succeed in doing.[3]

[1] Upon being notified on his 21st birthday that $3,000 had been deposited to his credit, Lt. Adams asked first for JQA's advice on its investment and subsequently that the money be invested for him. JQA delegated the matter to CFA, who purchased ten shares of the Boylston Market for $1,315. With the purchase of seven shares of Boylston Insurance Co., $936 remained in CFA's hands for investment. See above, entries for 3 Aug., 1 Sept.; JQA to Thomas B. Adams Jr., 28 Aug., 1 Sept.; JQA to CFA, 20 Oct. (all LbC's, Adams Papers).

[2] "Speeches made in the Senate of the United States on occasion of the Resolution offered by Mr. Foot, on the Subject of the Public Lands, during the First Session of the Twenty-First Congress," *North Amer. Rev.*, 31:462–546 (Oct. 1830).

[3] The daily reading in the British

essayists here begun was pursued until
23 Nov. 1832. During that time CFA
read the *Tatler, Spectator, Guardian,*

Rambler, Adventurer, World, and *Idler.*
On the edition CFA was reading, see
below, entry for 22 Jan. 1831.

[*Medford*]

TUESDAY. 12TH.

Morning delicious. I finished this morning the work of making the
Catalogue and now it only remains to take it off, in a fair Copy. Went
to the office where I found hardly a moment of leisure. My interruptions were so numerous that I could not find time to finish my
Journal. Mr. Hurlbert called and we discussed the matter of [doing][1]
his Store over. I felt frightened about the amount requisite to finish
it as I had projected and therefore we agreed to let him make his own
improvements upon a Lease of five years from next April.[2] Richardson
came in and talked over matters a little while. I then went to the
South end and gave directions about repairing the Tenements, besides
calling to get Thomas Adams' Certificate of Insurance Stock. Returned
to my Office where I finished the Deed of New's Equity in Lynde
Street and gave it to Mr. Minot[3] who paid over the sum necessary to
settle it, which finishes that part of the business. I had agreed to go to
Medford today so that we started as soon as I could get away. Mr.
Frothingham and ourselves dined there. Afternoon was passed away
by a visit of a Mr. and Mrs. Clapp and the lady's sister Miss Payne.
He is a wreck, a mere living atom, and miserable specimen of decayed
existence. They left early and we passed the evening in conversation.
N.B. This gentleman died but a few days after this was written.[4]

[1] Word editorially supplied.
[2] See above, entry for 11 March, note.
[3] Perhaps William Minot, counselor,
39 Court Street (*Boston Directory,*
1830–1831).
[4] On 25 Oct. the *Boston Patriot* (p.

3, col. 1) carried a notice of the death
of Elisha Clapp, aged 54, after a sickness of twelve years. He resided at 18
Winthrop Place (*Boston Directory,*
1830–1831).

Boston

WEDNESDAY. 13TH.

Morning cloudy and soon broke into a regular, steady rain. We
reached home however in good time and I went to the Office as usual.
Occupied all the morning by different persons coming to make appli-
cation for Houses. Judging from them I should think applications for
Dwellings were rising again, and in fact I am informed that real
Estate is improving.

Wrote my Journal and found half an hour to go to the Athenæum
to consult the Books there upon some points in which I was doubtful,

in making up my Catalogue. Returned to my House in a violent rain. Found there Chardon Brooks who dined with us—He being quite solitary at home owing to his Wife's accident which confines her to her bed. My afternoon was passed in reading Cicero in which I progressed considerably though I find it totally impossible to keep in my mind all the subdivided instructions which are given.

My wife was not over well but she read an hour in Corinne and I continued the sketch of Gray's character which presents him in a light very different from what I had expected. I afterwards began Symmons' Life of Milton,[1] and continued my undertaking with two papers of the Tatler. There was quite a smart thunder shower this evening.

[1] Charles Symmons' "Life of Milton" is in the last volume of *The Prose Works of John Milton*, 7 vols., London, 1806. JQA's bookplate is in the set at MQA.

THURSDAY. 14TH.

Morning at the Office as usual. My wife was not well and confined to her room. Mr. Grosvenor the purchaser of New's Estate in Cambridge Street called to say that he found the Title defective and accordingly I examined it and agreed with him. This resulted in a most troublesome and unexpected manner—For I must either get a release from the heirs or sell it over again for whatever it will bring. And this last measure will produce nothing but loss. On the whole I think it is a matter of regret that I assumed this trust, for it will pay me little or nothing in comparison with the trouble attending it. I also read Mr. Quincy's Address on the occasion of the Centennial Affair, and was quite pleased with it. The spirit of it is vastly different from that of almost every thing of the kind I have seen. It has more of the serious manliness of purpose becoming an Orator upon such an Occasion than the miserable seeking after effect commonly prompted by the personal interests of the Speaker.[1]

Upon returning home I found my Mother there who had come from Quincy to spend a few days, during Abby's indisposition. In the afternoon I read Cicero and passed an hour longer of the evening, in reading the Life of Milton. After which, two papers of the Tatler.

[1] Josiah Quincy, *An Address to the Citizens of Boston, on the 17th of September, 1830, the Close of the Second Century from the First Settlement of the City*, Boston, 1830.

FRIDAY 15TH.

Morning cloudy with occasional rain. The weather altogether being more like May than October. Went to the Office where I had much conversation with Mr. T. Welsh about this business of New's, and concluded that our best course would be to look up the heirs and see if they would do any thing to release us from our dilemma. I then had a good deal of Conversation with him about political affairs, in which we concluded that the nomination of Mr. Appleton was a tolerably poor concern, and not likely to go down among the Citizens.[1] I have half a mind to try my pen against it, and went so far as to draw up an Article for the purpose.

Returned home. Found there Miss Abby Adams and after dinner Horatio Brooks arrived from Gibraltar by the way of New York.[2] I read Cicero, finishing the first book de Inventione and beginning the second, the first passages of it are very pretty, and much more easy than the preceding book. Since we have returned from the Country, I have had more Company at my House than during all last Winter, and seem to promise to continue. However I like to have my Mother who keeps Abby company. Mr. Quincy came in and spent an hour of the evening, he was very pleasant. I sat up until quite late drawing up a little sketch of my proposed Article. Read my Numbers of the Tatler.

[1] Nathan Appleton, wealthy banker and textile manufacturer, had been nominated as a candidate for representative in Congress by the National Republicans of Suffolk at a meeting on 12 Oct. at the Exchange Coffee House (*Boston Daily Advertiser*, 13 Oct., p. 2, col. 1). On him, see vol. 2:267.

[2] Horatio Brooks (1809–1843), ABA's unmarried brother, had been at Gibraltar in the counting house of Hill & Blodget since June 1827, except for the period from Nov. 1828 to March 1829 when he left to escape a yellow fever epidemic. See Brooks, Waste Book and Farm Journal; Adams Genealogy.

SATURDAY. 16TH.

Morning at the Office. Occupied in writing my Journal, reading Minot and reflecting upon the business of the Election. Several little affairs took up some time, particularly some Commissions for my father which I was requested to execute, and attending a sale of Stocks for the purpose of attempting an investment for Thomas Adams. Things went however so high that I found the thing impossible. It is not a little surprising to me to see how high stocks run even now, and it shows an abundance of money existing unemployed.

Returned home and spent the afternoon as usual in reading Cicero a considerable portion of whose second book de Inventione I accomplished. It is more interesting than the other was. But I cannot help thinking that the reduction of all Oratory to method so clearly reduces somewhat it's power. Cicero was certainly a master of his art, he shows it by the ease with which he handles all it's parts, and by the regularity of the arrangement of his mind. He makes nearly mechanical what forms to others the hardest mental exertion.

After tea, I attended the Private Debating Society for the first time this Season. The meeting was small, and they discussed the question of the Rail Road. I took part in the Debate as usual and did not do quite as well as I ought to have done. Returned rather late.

SUNDAY. 17TH.

The day was very beautiful, being fine Autumn weather. I attended Divine Service both morning and afternoon and heard Mr. Frothingham deliver a Sermon in the Morning and Mr. Greenwood in the Afternoon. Neither of them remained on my mind at all. Indeed I felt rather indisposed from a dull headach during the day, probably arising from indigestion. It is the first I have had for a long time, and it indisposes me from performing any active exertion.

I did a little in the way of the Catalogue which I have commenced putting into it's final shape. Had some Conversation with Mr. Chadwick upon the approaching election to Congress and was surprised to find how many people designed voting for Mr. Lee.[1] This I consider as equivalent to an abandonment of all our principles and it has pained me not a little. It is much to be regretted that Mr. Gorham withdrew from this contest. I did very little but attempt to draw up an Article directly at variance with that of Friday, and in support of the County nomination. This I continued in the evening, after drawing up which I read a couple of papers in the Tatler.[2]

On the whole I was glad to retire for the pain in my head indisposed me much. A person who feels pain often gets accustomed to bear it well, but one who like me has known very little of it of late becomes impatient at the least sign of it.

[1] Henry Lee was the nominee of the Free Trade Party for representative to Congress to succeed Benjamin Gorham, who had declined reelection (*Boston Patriot*, 16 Oct., p. 2, col. 1).

[2] The absence of any statement by CFA that he sent off for publication the political article he had written may suggest that the article he wrote and sent to the *Courier* on the 18th was only a further revision of his earlier efforts to express his views on the Appleton-Lee contest. However, from his words in the entry for the 18th one might conclude that the article in the *Courier* was a different one. It should perhaps be noted that a communication signed "Medium" which appeared in the *Boston Daily Advertiser* on 19 Oct. (p. 2, col. 1) took essentially the position CFA had here reached.

MONDAY. 18TH.

The day opened cloudy and soon settled into a regular rain. My

Mother however finished her visit which has been a pleasant one to me, and returned to Quincy. I went to the Office and was surprised to find upon reaching there that the whole of the lower Staircase of the building in Court Street was removed by the Tenant of the Store, in order to substitute a new one more narrow and interfering less with his premises. The Communication with my office was by a ladder and once up, it was rather a difficult matter to get down. I mounted and spent my time in writing a political Article to send to Mr. Buckingham the Editor of the Courier. This is a singular choice on my part but it arises from the fact that he is the friend of the principles I peculiarly support.[1]

Returned home, where it appeared lonely after having had a house full. I read Cicero as usual and examined his method of dividing all questions which narrow the space of thought very much to the points in question in a case. This methodizing of thought is a great thing for a speaker. Evening, reading Symmons life of Milton and hammering out a new idea for another Number. But I feel exceedingly discouraged. My spirits have not got over the effect of Mr. Everett's course.

[1] The *Courier* and Joseph T. Buckingham, its editor, were spokesmen for the policies of Henry Clay. The likely reason for the suggestion by the *Courier* that JQA be elected to Congress was to remove him from contention for the Presidency in 1832 (Bemis, *JQA*, 2:206). The article sent by CFA may be the one signed "A," attacking Lee's position on the tariff and supporting Appleton (*Boston Courier*, 21 Oct., p. 2, cols. 1–2).

TUESDAY. 19TH.

The day was cloudy and dull. I went to the Office and passed my time in sorting the papers which have been accummulating upon me for a long time past. I used to think that in the disposition of my things I had a good deal of method but subsequently I have had great cause to change my opinion. Nothing seems in it's place, and it is a constant work to put them in order.

Mr. Degrand called and after conversation I concluded a bargain with him for Thomas B. Adams Jr. to buy with the balance of his money, some Fire and Marine Stock.[1] But the rate was very high. On the whole however, my Morning was wasted very much. These Carpenters in the Entry disarrange every thing. I am ashamed of my way of spending time, and discouraged at my ill success. Returned home.

Horatio Brooks dined with us. I am sorry to say he seems to like my House too well. Afternoon reading Cicero, but the matter was a little more difficult. The many shades of questions can hardly bear to be so nicely subdivided as they are by him. They will not remain in the memory, and are subject to be altered by circumstances. Evening Corinne and Mason's Life of Gray. After which Symmons' Life of Milton and the Tatler. The former is a little ultraliberal in his politics, to an extent that sometimes shocks me. Yet generally I agree with him.

[1] See above, entry for 11 Oct. and note.

WEDNESDAY. 20TH.

Morning beautiful and mild. I went to the Office as usual, and passed my time a little better than I have been in the practice of doing heretofore—As I was able to read and complete the first Volume of Minot's Continuation. A work I hold in very little estimation from its apparent labour in doing nothing. A history should have *substance* not be like a shadow always eluding the grasp. To be sure he has also the least interesting period of our history to deal with.

I was unavoidably occupied in trifles some part of the day, but this I never expect to get over. It seems the tax usual upon a man with an Office of his own. Returned home and passed the Afternoon in reading Cicero as usual. Completed a considerable portion but was stuck at one or two passages. This is always the case upon a first examination. Horatio Brooks returned and spent the evening so that our regular avocations having been interrupted I thought I would take the opportunity to finish Symmons. He is too abusive. I think he has the right side but does not manage it adroitly. His book is however on the whole interesting. Afterwards, two numbers of the Tatler.

THURSDAY. 21ST.

Morning clear again after the showery weather which came on last Evening. I went to the Office as usual, but passed a large portion of my morning at an Auction Room. The sale of the library of Edward J. Lowell took place today.[1] I could not help moralizing when I thought of the difference which had taken place between the views this young man had held out to himself and the actual state of things. It is melancholy to think that all our hopes and wishes, our ambition, our useful exertions hang upon so frail a tenure as human life. Lowell was a young man of great promise, few in this Community stood as high as he. He is now a fit subject to point a moral and adorn a tale.[2] I bought little or nothing as his books sold high.

Completed the purchase and transfer of the Fire and Marine Stock and settled several demands against my father and myself. After dinner, finished the second book de Inventione and resumed the same to review. My aim is to master the subject in all its forms.

Evening, went to Faneuil Hall to see and take part in a primary Meeting of the People.[3] It was large and respectable. Mr. J. B. Davis, A. H. Everett, Austin,[4] Gorham and Sullivan addressed the Meeting, and generally with more power than I had expected. On the whole, it was a favourable specimen of a Caucus, better than any I had seen.[5] Mr. Webster was received with great acclamation. He adjourned the Meeting, and I returned home to find my Wife suffering severely from one of her remedies.

[1] The library of a "professional gentleman deceased" consisting of about 400 volumes on the civil and common law and 600 other books was auctioned beginning at 9:30 A.M. at Cunningham's Auction Rooms, corner of Milk and Federal streets (*Boston Daily Advertiser*, 21 Oct., p. 3, col. 4).

[2] Edward Jackson Lowell (1805–1830), Harvard 1822, regarded in Boston as one of the most cultivated and promising young men of his generation, died at the home of his brother in Waltham during the preceding month (*Boston Patriot*, 11 Sept., p. 2, col. 5; 16 Sept., p. 2, col. 3; Ferris Greenslet, *The Lowells and their Seven Worlds*, Bos-

ton, 1946, p. 191–196).

[3] The National Republican caucus held at 6:30 P.M. announced its sponsors as "Friends of American Industry, Liberal National Policy, Internal Improvement, the Rail Roads, and the preservation of the Public Faith toward the Indian Tribes" (*Boston Daily Advertiser*, 21 Oct., p. 2, col. 3; 22 Oct., p. 2, col. 2).

[4] James T. Austin, Commonwealth attorney (*Boston Directory*, 1830–1831).

[5] The speeches of A. H. Everett, Jeremiah Evarts, and William Sullivan were printed in the *Advertiser*, 25 Oct., p. 1, cols. 3–6; 27 Oct., p. 2, cols. 4–6.

FRIDAY. 22D.

Morning clear and pleasant. At the Office as usual. Occupied in my Occupations of account and in settling some outstanding demands, until eleven o'clock, when I took up one of my books purchased at the sale yesterday. It is a work upon diplomatic style by one Meisel and so far as I have read contains some very good precepts indeed.[1] I was pleased with the simplicity of his advice and its aptness. A man in writing about a thing should always exemplify his advice as much as possible by his practice.

Returned home and passed the Afternoon in reading over the second book of Cicero de Inventione. I do not think more of it on a reperusal. It is on the whole a dry production. Useful to such as myself who are examining the subject with attention but totally without interest to people in general. It wants clearness, its allusions are intricate, its advice too multiplied. The mind cannot embrace at once so rapid a variety of points.

In the evening I attended a Ward Meeting of the friends of Mr.

Appleton to organize the system of voting, and returned home to read a little of Mr. Todd's Account of Milton,[2] which I do not like so well as that of Dr. Symmons. Two numbers of the Tatler.

[1] In the copy at MQA of *Cours de style diplomatique* by H. Meisel, 2 vols., Paris, 1826, is a notation in CFA's hand: "Bought at the sale of Mr. E. J. Lowell's Library. October 21st 1830, $2.00."

[2] Two copies of Henry John Todd's "Some Account of the Life and Writings of John Milton" are in MQA, both owned by JQA. One was published independently (London, 1809), the other is vol. 1 of Milton's *Poetical Works* in 7 vols., published in the same place and year.

Medford
SATURDAY. 23RD.

Morning clear and cool. Went to the Office and was busy all the morning at it, reading Mr. Meisel on a proper diplomatic style. He illustrates as he goes by examples from public papers of various kinds. Most of them are a little of the driest. It has been for some time past a matter of bitter reflection to me that I mispend my morning's time, and I am reflecting upon the proper method to cure it. Two acquisitions may be made either of which would be valuable—That of the German Language, or some knowledge of the Civil Law. I am now balancing between them as to which to take and waiting to get the necessary assistance from Quincy.

At half past one according to agreement I went out of town with Mr. Brooks to stay at Medford for a day or two. Found there Gorham B. and his Wife who is very dull owing to the loss of her child. I sincerely pity her. Living as she does so lonely in the Country makes it infinitely worse. P. C. Brooks Jr. was also there. Gorham is a kind of individual of a character so unpleasant to me that I never feel at ease in his presence. Sensible that he was averse to my introduction to the family and never treated me with common civility while I was single, I feel no desire to make those advances for acquaintance which I should be willing to do in most cases.[1] Evening quiet. Took up a new Number of the Edinburgh Review and was much interested by an Article on Mr. Jefferson's Works.[2]

[1] On Gorham Brooks and the earlier unpleasantness, see above, entry for 12 June and notes there.

[2] An essay-review of Thomas Jefferson Randolph's edition (*Edinburgh Review*, 51:496–526 [July 1830]).

SUNDAY. 24TH.

Morning clear but showing the advances of Winter upon us. The Country looks bleak and cheerless, and I feel no disposition to seek it.

Attended Divine Service all day and heard a certain Mr. Abbot[1] a young man preach two uninteresting and commonplace Sermons. This matter of preaching is rather a poor business in most cases— Particularly when young men undertake it. Yet young men must practise to become good. I continued my Number in the Edinburgh Review which I found uncommonly interesting. The Life of Bentley, the Roman History of Niebuhr and the Political Article are all good.[2] The spirit of the second I liked more particularly as it discourages the strong spirit of the age to doubt. My own ideas have always turned against the doctrine that makes every thing in the world unstable. Afternoon, a visit from Mr. Willm. G. Brooks and his brother from Maine.[3] They stayed an hour, after which I read Walter Scott's Dramatic Pieces, lately published. They have no great merit. Some pretty poetry, great ease, but no higher qualities and a total deficiency of Plot except that poorest of all which takes its rise from supernatural incidents—A quality which is visible in all the works of Scott and shows an inherent weakness in his mind.

[1] John S. C. Abbot, Congregational minister at Worcester (*Mass. Register,* 1831).
[2] In the July 1830 issue (vol. 51) of the *Edinburgh* were reviews of James Henry Monk's *Life of Richard Bentley* (p. 321–357) and of the translation of B. G. Niebuhr's *History of Rome* (p. 358–396); also an essay "The Country without a Government; or, Plain Questions upon the Unhappy State of the Present Administration" (p. 564–582).
[3] Sons of Cotton Brown Brooks of Portland.

Boston

MONDAY. 25TH.

Morning clear and pleasant but cold. After breakfast we returned to town with Mr. Brooks in the Carriage. I went to the Office after a visit from Miss Longhurst my quondam Tenant who told me a long story about her misfortunes occasioned by the conduct of a Custom House Officer. To be sure it was bad, but she explained enough of her course in the Spring to satisfy me that it was diamond cut diamond. I had for once an uninterrupted morning at the Office and read Mr. Meisel with some diligence. I begin to feel a little more settled there and as if I could pursue some regular occupation without having my time broken up. A man by name Hayden called and took one of the Houses in Tremont Street.[1] Two left.

After dinner I was busy in reading Cicero's second book de Inventione in which I made good progress and much more understandingly than before. There is a great deal in the connection which never is broken with impunity in reading Latin. Evening, my Wife read a good portion of Corinne and I a few Letters of Gray after which I accomplished a considerable part of Todd's Sketch of Milton's Life. I believe the events and the character of this Man's Life are now pretty well impressed upon my Memory. I afterwards read the usual quantity of the Tatler. But I find it very difficult to see the great merit of this species of Essay Writing.

¹ D. Hayden (M/CFA/3).

TUESDAY. 26TH.

Morning quite cold. After breakfast and the half hour to which I have now become limited in my Catalogue, I walked out first going down to see the Tenements in Tremont Street which are now nearly done. One of them is now occupied. The others I hope will soon go from my hands. At the Office, where I was busy in sorting and burning my brother's papers. This occupation I take up occasionally only to turn off from it in disgust. There is an insuperable melancholy comes over me when I reflect upon poor George's fate. When I think of the golden Spring, and then gradually draw my eyes to the cold and fruitless Summer.

I read a little of Mr. Meisel in which he talks of Treaties, Cartels, Conventions and the other formal acts of Diplomacy. This is not what I want. Returned home to find P. C. Brooks to dine with us. He was pleasant, and has softened a good deal of the roughness he used to have. Afternoon, finished the Review of the books de Inventione, from which I have benefitted so much that I believe I shall not go over it again, at least just now. Perhaps after I have read de Oratore I shall be able to understand it still better. Evening Corinne and Gray. After which I finished Todd's Sketch of Milton and began Johnson's. Was much struck with it's malignity.¹ Two numbers of the Tatler.

¹ Samuel Johnson's "Milton," one of the most captiously critical of his *Lives of the English Poets*, is in the 9th volume (p. 84–182) of the 12-volume edition of Johnson's *Works*, London, 1792, now in MQA. In an inserted note in CFA's hand issue is taken with one of Johnson's linguistic criticisms (p. 110).

WEDNESDAY. 27TH.

Morning thick, but it cleared away mild and pleasant. Went to the Office as usual and busied myself much of the morning in sorting and destroying Papers both of my late brother and Robert New. It is a poor business looking over such past affairs. It shows so strongly the vanity, the nothingness of Life.

My father sent me a Note ¹ and a Trunk to be forwarded, by which

I am in a degree informed that my Mother has resolved to pass the Winter here and that my brother's Wife goes on to Washington today without her. This is singular but not to me over agreeable. I had thought it probable, and yet when it comes out, so many objections present themselves as to make me dread it. The suitable time for this move has gone by.[2]

I read Meisel and finished the first Volume. At dinner with us today, Miss Julia Gorham and Horatio Brooks. I was dull. Began this afternoon upon Cicero de Oratore. The difference in the style is apparent. The former was the dry hard style of a beginner, this is the experienced pen of a practised writer. He flows with ease, and with dignity, having learned the art of amplification. Yet I was longer understanding the first ten Sections of this than the other. Evening, Corinne with my Wife and then Mason's Gray to her. After which, Johnson's Life of Milton and Critique. The latter is good though a little prejudiced. Two numbers of the Tatler.

[1] JQA to CFA, 27 Oct. (Adams Papers).

[2] The resolute opposition to JQA's re-entry into politics that LCA had expressed before JQA consented to be a candidate (see above, entry for 28 Sept., note) continued unabated after the fact. LCA having persisted in her determination announced to JQA a week earlier "not to go to Washington this winter" (JQA, Diary, 20 Oct.), JQA resigned himself to the decision and began to look to arrangements for making Quincy their year-round residence. In a letter to JA2 (27 Oct., Adams Papers), JQA asked that "all the boxes and cases of my effects, ... my manuscript Letter Books and Diaries, and my flannel and woollen Cloathing" be sent to Boston. Further, he instructed JA2 to advertise for sale JQA's "two houses in F Street with the land and buildings belonging to them" for $20,000. The possibility that under the changed circumstances JA2 might not wish to remain in Washington did not escape notice: "Whether you will deem it advisable to remain at Washington for the sake of the business of the Mills, is for your consideration." Beyond the attention given to the immediate consequences of the decision, he allowed himself only the observation: "The separation of the families is very painful to me, but I cannot help it."

Two days later, though plans for the winter in Quincy were reaffirmed, some doubts that announced decisions were immutable seem reflected in a letter modifying the earlier instructions: "You may for the present postpone shipping the boxes and cases, ... but send me my Letter Books, Diaries, and Cloathing" (JQA to JA2, 29 Oct., Adams Papers). However, if LCA was in fact weakening she gave no expression to it in a letter she wrote to JA2 the next day (Adams Papers):

"Do not condemn me for the choice I have made. It sprang from the conviction that I could not go on smoothly with my family holding the opinions which I do concerning the politics of the day without being looked upon as a treacherous spy by my husband and my children. I never was discreet and my feelings now run away with my judgment ere reason has time to act and my nervous system is too much shaken by long suffering to admit of my again plunging into the very focus of political machination. Do not imagine for one moment that I condemn your fathers choice. Family is and must ever be a secondary consideration to a zealous Patriot and in a world where alas I have found that the very best choice brings its evil it is ridiculous to complain of those casual disappointments which may and which will probably produce the most fortunate results."

LCA's stance seemed no less firm to CFA, now deeply troubled by the effect his own expressed opposition to his father's course may have had on his mother. In this mood he wrote somewhat disingenuously seeking his brother's support in the effort to convince their mother that she should change her mind on the question of residence:

"You may perhaps think that I have advised to this course, but I can say very certainly that I am not sensible of any such thing. The probability is that my father's accepting the nomination to Congress is unpleasant. Why it should be, I do not know.

"Under these circumstances I shall feel it my duty to recommend her to change her mind. A Quincy residence in her present condition is and always was an impossible thing. It is possible she might accept an invitation from me, which I shall give her if nothing better can be done, but my idea is she had better join you at W. soon. To this effect and as the case is a delicate one, I submit it to you whether it would not be advisable for you to write a mild letter, approving *indirectly* our Father's course, and *wishing* perhaps requesting her company this Winter. But do not *join* these things, or make it appear that one is in for the sake of the other. I am thus earnest about this matter, because I feel as if it was a case that demands some attention." (CFA to JA2, 4 Nov., Adams Papers.)

JA2, in his appeal to his mother (letter missing), seems to have followed CFA's advice, but LCA was unwilling to admit that she had been moved:

"My health is the plea upon which you have put the most stress in your Letter and it is the very reason why I chose my residence here. The Climate will never prove half so deleterious to me as a house which will become the focus of intrigue and in which all those feelings of deep mortification and agony already so painfully endured will be aroused anew in a heart already half broken by its former sufferings. I look around me in vain for anything like benefit that has resulted to any one as a reparation for this suffering or as a motion for future action! Where is it to be found? Is it in the grave of my lost child? Is it in the very necessity which induces you to claim this sacrifice? Is it in the advantages resulting to any of our connections of either side? Or is it to the grasping ambition which is an insatiable passion swallowing and consuming all in its ever devouring maw" (LCA to JA2, 14 Nov., Adams Papers).

Nevertheless JA2's letter (which JQA judged "kind and affectionate in its intentions" but "should have been rather more so in its form" [to JA2, 13 Nov., Adams Papers]), together with CFA's efforts perhaps (see entry for 7 Nov., below), elicited a grudging consent: "Your Letter my Son ... has answered your intention that is that I again sacrifice myself to my family convenience." However, LCA chose to base that acquiescence solely "upon the pecuniary principle.... I have no right to encumber the family with expences" (LCA to JA2, 14 Nov., Adams Papers). The im-we shall proceed to Washington" early passe ended, JQA was prepared to "hope in December (JQA to JA2, 13 Nov., Adams Papers). The decision taken, however, did not immediately effect a change in LCA's depressed state. Not until the month's end was more than temporary improvement to be seen (see entries for 20, 21 Nov., 1 Dec., below). She was able to begin her journey to Washington on 3 Dec.; JQA followed on the 8th.

THURSDAY. 28TH.

Morning foggy and thick, but it cleared away and became a mild and beautiful day. I went to the Office and passed my time in reading Monsieur Meisel. This book is after all a mere compilation of examples in the various kinds of Diplomatic Writing. I also did a little in the way of writing. Being dissatisfied with the old Exordium of my Article upon Graham, I wrote a new one. But my Father keeps the thing itself without any mercy. I feel discouraged about all this, but still it is worthwhile to try a little longer.

Afternoon, Cicero de Oratore in which I made some progress. The discussion turning upon the qualities necessary to an Orator Cicero gives it as his opinion that an Orator should be acquainted with all the Sciences. But I do not think his argument applies more to Orators than People of every Class. Knowledge is valuable in all it's shapes. It is power and can only apply more to Orators than other Classes when we define Oratory to be Speech. The style of the Book is fascinating.

I forgot to mention in its place that Mr. Brooks and Horatio dined with us. Evening, Corinne, and finished Mason's Life of Gray. On the whole an amusing work. Yet only two Poems have immortalized his name. The rest are not of much interest. I read part of the first Book of Paradise Lost[1] and Two numbers of the Tatler.

[1] Two editions of Milton's *Poetical Works*, both JQA's, are in MQA (2 vols., London, 1731; 7 vols., London, 1809). *Paradise Lost* and his other poems are also in vols. 10–12 of Johnson's *Works of the English Poets.*

FRIDAY. 29TH.

Morning bright and exhibiting all the beauty of Winter commencing. With us this Autumnal Season is the finest in the year. It braces and enlivens. At the Office as usual where I consumed an hour in looking over New's Papers and destroying them by hundreds. I then read a little of Mr. Meisel upon the diplomacy of Europe, and spent an hour in Accounts. But on the whole my Morning cannot be said to have been profitably used.

Returned home and occupied myself in the Afternoon though with some interruptions upon Cicero de Oratore. I was surprised to find that I could ever have passed over this book so utterly unconscious of it's worth. The recommendations it contains, the advice it gives, and the example it sets, have all been lost upon me until now. And every day now puts me in mind how much time has passed, that the season for *action* has come and I am barely opening the preparation. These thoughts and feelings discourage me, they throw a damp over my power of exertion which is I am afraid ominous of the result to take place. But I will persevere in my present course if for nothing else, at least for the pleasure the knowledge gives me.

Evening, Corinne with my Wife. After which Edward Brooks came in and sat an hour very pleasantly indeed. I finished afterwards the first book of Paradise Lost, and read two Numbers of the Tatler.

SATURDAY. 30TH.

Morning clear, beautiful weather. I went to the Office after walking up to see what was to be done at the Tenements in Tremont Street which I am overlooking. The repairs there must necessarily be considerable, as they have been suffered under Hollis' management to go to rack and ruin. This is a new leaf turned in the Agency which will as I suspect be the best that has been so turned for fifteen years. Indeed it always seemed to me wonderful that property should have depreciated so fast as my father's here in Boston has done. I hope that in a little while, I shall bring it up again, but it must take time. The estate in Court Street has been brought up considerably. That of the Tenements will soon be done. That in Hancock Street must be left to next Summer, and the other two will be continued on as well as they can be, until a final disposition can be made of that property.

Engaged at the Office much as usual. Received a Note from Alex. H. Everett requesting the return of my Article. I sent to Quincy for it.[1] Occupied after dinner upon Cicero de Oratore and finished the first book with which I have been exceedingly pleased.

Evening, went to Faneuil Hall, for the purpose of hearing Mr. Webster make his famous Speech. The Crowd was prodigious. I despaired almost of being able to hear him, and in effect was obliged to stand all the time. His Speech had commenced when I got there and lasted until after nine when I left.[2] It was powerful and convincing if any thing was necessary. But I cannot help thinking that he has been one of the converted. For let them all say what they will, the *principles* they opposed in 1820 were as good then as they are now whatever might have been the question of expediency. The principle has existed ever since 1789 though in 1820 it was not agreeable here.[3] Went to P. C. Brooks' for my Wife where after waiting a little while to eat a supper we returned home.

[1] The letters from A. H. Everett to CFA and from CFA to JQA are both missing.

[2] At the adjourned meeting of citizens friendly to the election of Nathan Appleton to Congress, Webster rose at 6:30 and addressed the gathering "for about three hours, at the expiration of which time, before he had finished his speech, Col. Perkins moved an adjourn-

ment to Quincy Hall at 6 o'clock on the following evening." An extended summary of Webster's speech was printed along with a promise of the future publication of the speech itself (*Boston Daily Advertiser*, 1 Nov., p. 2, col. 1).

[3] The supporters of Lee had republished a passage from a speech by Webster delivered at a time when he, reflecting the then prevailing New Eng-

land view, had opposed the adoption of a tariff for the protection of domestic manufactures. Webster, now a protectionist, devoted a major part of his speech of 30 Oct. to a justification of his changed position. He affirmed that the earlier opposition to protection was to its inexpediency at the time rather than to the principle; moreover, that he had never questioned that the right of Congress to protect manufactures was firmly embedded in the commerce clause of the Constitution (same).

SUNDAY. 31ST.

Morning cloudy but the day was clear, mild and beautiful. I attended with Abby in the morning at Mr. Frothingham's Church and heard Dr. Lowell preach a very pretty Sermon upon the fall of the year illustrating the life of man. It is true, the subject is trite, but in the pulpit who expects to hear new things. The search after novelty is there most dangerous, for it drives preachers to violent paradoxes, and artificial trains of sentiment, which injure rather than benefit the true tone of Christian morality. His language was appropriate, his figures animated, his end clear and apt. I know little more required in a Preacher.

Attended in the afternoon alone and heard Mr. Frothingham upon the History of Joseph. It struck me as a Sermon I had heard before with a new piece upon the late sudden death of Mr. Huskisson in England.[1] A true moral lesson to be sure.

I felt a head ach today and my general system so much out of order as to make me a little dull. I have experienced some internal palpitation which has troubled if[2] it has not distressed me. I therefore did little or nothing but write a little of my Catalogue. Read over the first book of Paradise Lost and two Numbers of the Tatler.

[1] The death of William Huskisson (1770–1830), British statesman, president of the Board of Trade and member of Parliament for Liverpool, excited more than ordinary interest in the United States. He was fatally injured on 15 Sept. at the celebration of the opening of the Liverpool and Manchester railway. As he went to greet the Duke of Wellington, a political rival, Huskisson fell on the tracks on which the steam carriage *Rocket* was approaching and was run over (*Boston Daily Advertiser*, 29 Oct., p. 2, col. 3; 2 Nov., p. 1, cols. 1–4; *DNB*).

[2] MS reads "it."

MONDAY. NOVEMBER 1ST.

It rained this morning but the weather was very mild and pleasant. I went to the Office and regulated my Accounts for last Month, bringing up my Bank balances. Mr. Ayer my Carpenter called upon me to see about my instructions respecting the Tenements. I told him to repair as well as he could, but not do more than was absolutely necessary. This was the day for the election of a member of Congress in this District and throughout the State. I went and gave my solitary suffrage for Mr. Appleton.[1] Not that I admire the Candidate but in a choice between two lines of policy and principle there can be no hesitation. Mr. Tenney called and paid me a Quarter's rent about which he is always punctual. My Tenants are on the whole very excellent.

My father sent me my Article with a Letter speaking well of it. I sat about to correct it and alter exceptionable passages for Mr. Everett.[2] On the whole if he will take it, I can do nothing better. I was about it all the Afternoon.

Dr. Stevenson called at my request and I conversed with him about my Wife's state of health. She suffers so much that something must be done for her. He talked very openly with me. But he evidently appeared puzzled. Evening, Corinne, and writing with two Numbers of the Tatler. I was today under the operation of Medicine.

[1] Election returns began to appear in newspapers on the 4th, but it was not until 8 Nov. that the winners in each of the thirteen districts were listed. Appleton was the winner in the Suffolk district.

JQA's election in the Plymouth district was one of the first announced as certain (*Boston Daily Advertiser*, 4 Nov., p. 2, col. 1). When the count was complete, he had received 1,817 votes out of 2,565 cast (JQA, Diary, 6 Nov.). After an evening spent in reflecting on the event and its significance, JQA concluded "My Election as President of the United States was not half so gratifying to my inmost Soul. No election or appointment conferred upon me ever gave me so much pleasure. I say this to record my Sentiments, but no Stranger intermeddleth with my Joys, and the dearest of my friends have no sympathy with my Sensations" (same, 7 Nov.).

[2] In his letter accompanying CFA's MS, JQA wrote: "It is not only well written, but well composed. The opinions and Sentiments contained in it, differ in some respects from mine, but ... a young man ... should think for himself." He advised that sarcastic reflections upon "4th of July Orations" be eliminated and that some comment be added upon those sections of Grahame's book which treat of Pennsylvania, Maryland, and New York (31 Oct., Adams Papers).

TUESDAY. 2D.

Morning clear and mild. After writing a little while I went to the Office as usual and was busy in writing and correcting my Article. But my father's Servant man Kirke came in from Quincy with a request that I should execute some Commissions, and the performance of them took up some time. I also called to see Mr. Everett and talk with him about my Article. He said he should like to have it and I concluded on the whole to send it to him. We talked of politics and of speaking after which I paid a short visit to his brother Mr. Peabody and Mrs. Everett.[1] This over, I thought it a favourable season to drop a Card for Mr. Blake, and one also for my old acquaintance Mrs.

Tarbell,[2] which is all the visiting I propose for the present. Returned home and passed the afternoon in writing over my Article with which I am again becoming disgusted. The ideas seem trite and the language diffuse. But I am resolved to try at all events, and see what practice may do.

Evening, Corinne with my Wife. Mr. and Mrs. Frothingham came in to tell us of an accident which had happened to Horatio Brooks at Fresh Pond. The particulars were not stated but from what could be gathered, it was ascertained that he had broken his Leg. This is an accident extremely unfortunate at this particular season. It is one of those troubles that will happen to disturb and confound all one's equanimity.[3] John Gorham also called in for half an hour.

[1] In the *North American Review* office.

[2] George Blake, who was replaced as United States district attorney for Massachusetts at the beginning of the Jackson administration, lived at 34 Summer Street quite close by the Thomas Tarbell residence on Avon Place (vol. 1:317; *Boston Directory*, 1828–1829, 1830–1831).

[3] Horatio Brooks' injury, a broken thigh, resulted from a fall from a building. He was confined at Fresh Pond until 8 Jan. 1831. When the screw was removed on 21 Dec. he was unable to bend his knee. He was still unable to walk without crutches when he returned home, but whether the condition was permanent is not known (Brooks, Waste Book, 31 Dec. 1830; Farm Journal, 29 Dec. 1830, 8 Jan. 1831).

WEDNESDAY. 3RD.

This was the day fixed for the sale of the Wood at Weston. But it looked so cloudy and dark in the morning that I hesitated much about going. At last I concluded that it would be advisable to go if only to stop the sale in time, if bad attendance or weather should cause any necessity for such course. Stopped for Richardson who was ready to go, and arrived there by ten. The sale had commenced, but the Company was large and responsible so that I felt no necessity to do any thing but look on. It was managed with a great deal more expedition than last year. And on the whole was as favourable to my father. The usual ceremony of dinner was performed at which I had an appetite for the rough fare greater than I do on common occasions for the best of food. I stopped the sale at about half past three o'clock when we returned to the House,[1] having done enough for one day. The necessary appendage of Tea followed which in the neatness of it's arrangement pleased me exceedingly. But we delayed too long, for I barely got to Richardson's House to save him from the rain, which came on with greater violence every minute, and I had for the rest of the time a dark and wet time of it. When I reached home, I was pretty well in the

Water. Having changed my Clothes, I felt heated and fatigued, and unable to do any thing. So I retired early.

¹ That is, to the farmhouse on the Weston property; see entry for 18 Sept. 1829, above.

THURSDAY. 4TH.

Morning clear after the Storm, though I felt heated and with a slight cold which did not do much to make me comfortable. Went to the Office where I spent some time in writing my Journal and looking over the sales of wood at Weston last year, from which I find that the one held yesterday will probably be considerably more productive than I had supposed. But as yet I have no evidence to judge certainly by.

My time passed in correcting and writing over passages of my Article. Returned home and after dinner, occupied myself in writing over what I had attempted to mature. The defence of the Puritans I have altered considerably, and put a little more care in it as it is the part of the whole which may be most questioned. I hope it will look like a good chain of reasoning at least if many people should hesitate about its soundness.

I was interrupted by the arrival of my father from Quincy who came in to be present at the marriage of Wm. Lee to Mrs. McLean.¹ He took occasion to speak to me of my Mother who is suffering from loneliness ever since the departure of her family from Quincy. He is fearful, she may be sick which would not do. I am desirous of doing what I can to prevent it, and therefore asked my Wife to write out an Invitation to come and stay here for a few days.² I hope she will do this, as she seems unwilling to have us go there. My father went at eight and I read Corinne with my Wife until nine. After which I was writing all the evening.

¹ At six o'clock at 44 Beacon Street, the home of Mrs. Ann Amory (widow of John) McLean, Mrs. McLean and William Lee, a widower, were married. Both had been friends of JQA "in the heyday of youth before either of them was first married." The bride, aged 57, was the youngest of the numerous Amory clan whom JQA called "social companions of my youth"; the groom, closer to JQA's age, was a friend from their days in the foreign service. The occa-sion gave to JQA the opportunity to see once again many of his contemporaries with whom he had been out of touch (vol. 1:50; JQA, Diary, 4 Nov.; *NEHGR*, 10:65 [Jan. 1856]). The passage from JQA's journal entry relating to the wedding is printed in *A Yankee Jeffersonian*, Cambridge, 1958, p. 233–234, being a selection from William Lee's diary and letters edited by Mary Lee Mann.

² Letter missing.

FRIDAY. 5TH.

Morning clear and cold. Went to see the Tenements which are

undergoing pretty thorough repair. The middle one strange to say does not let though the cheapest. Perhaps the difference is great but I confess I do not see it. Thence to the Office where my time was passed in writing, correcting my Article and reading Monsieur Meisel who is not very entertaining. On the whole I begin to feel as if I ought to hurry upon my reading of Law or German. My anxiety about my Mother is now very considerable and was increased rather by her not sending us any answer nor coming today.

The afternoon passed in my writing in continuation and with the aid of a small part of the evening finishing my Copy of the Article. I have now read, studied, and copied it so much that I feel in perfect disgust with it. But my pains ought not to go without some result now. So I am glad I have finished it. It shall with the blessing of Heaven, be sent on Monday to take it's chance.

I read French with my Wife, and tried to read a little Poetry, but a message from Chardon Brooks' wife about Horatio drove me to Edward Brooks to ascertain the true state of the case. Found as usual the thing was clear exaggeration. Read two numbers of the Tatler.

SATURDAY. 6TH.

Morning at the Office. Occupied myself in writing, making up Accounts, and reading Mons. Meisel. Took a short walk and by accident met Mr. Degrand with whom I had some conversation. He recommended to me some shares in the Suffolk Insurance Company, and I from a feeling of impatience at the difficulty of investment took them at the great advance of fifteen percent.[1] I felt the imprudence of the Step but not until it was too late to retract. It is imprudent not only as to the price paid, but as to my means to pay it, for it anticipates all my means for six months. But the advantage of this course on the other hand is that it prevents waste, it saves me from wild speculation, and it is a chance of Investment in the older Companies which will occur more rarely hereafter as the probability increases either of the payment of any of our claims on Europe, or of the prospect of a general war.[2] So that even the excess I may pay over the real value of the Shares, is not equal to the advantage I derive from investing well in small sums—Always a difficult operation. The management of money is a difficult and yet a fascinating business. It requires a coolness of head which belongs to few, and a closeness of calculation that sees beforehand as well as behind. This is not my strong forte, for I am frequently sensible of the danger in which I should be placed if I was tried, and by such a hazardous step as this, I am made sensible that sometimes one may be too hasty.

After dinner I went to the Athenæum to consult Winthrop's Journal upon a particular point in relation to my review. And afterwards spent the evening until seven o'clock reading the English Newspapers, after which I attended the Meeting of the Debating Society. It was the largest assemblage I have ever seen and was upon the question of expediency of the Dissolution of the Society. The question was well discussed and decided in the negative. I returned home and read two numbers of the Tatler.

[1] CFA purchased ten shares in Suffolk Insurance Co. for $38.33 a share (M/CFA/9).

[2] The July revolution in France was followed by unrest and demonstrations in Portugal, Spain, Italy, the Low Countries, &c., which seemed to augur the overthrow of regimes which in turn could well lead to intervention by the great powers. In this situation the threat of a general war was much discussed; see, for example, *Boston Daily Advertiser*, 9 Oct., p. 2, cols. 2–4.

SUNDAY. 7TH.

Morning dark and cloudy, so much so that I doubted the expediency of starting for Quincy, but considering on the whole that it was of some consequence I concluded to go, while my Wife went with her brother, P. C. Brooks Jr. to see Horatio at Fresh Pond.

I arrived at the House just as the bell was ringing for morning service, and I found my Mother rather better than I anticipated in health though evidently a little touched. I tried to discuss the matter of her determination with as much management as I could, and I went over all the ground that I could think of to do it, but my discourse did not produce a decided effect. Perhaps it may hereafter. I also talked with my father about his determination to go to Congress, and generally upon matters of a political character. This state of things is curious, but I sincerely hope that it will not last. I discussed matters as long as I was able and left them at five to return home.

Found my Wife had reached home before me, we spent the evening quietly, having a visit from Mr. Edmund Quincy to enliven the evening.

MONDAY. 8TH.

Weather dark and gloomy. I went to the Office as usual and occupied myself first in writing and making up my Accounts, afterwards in beginning upon the German Grammar, which I had brought from

Quincy yesterday, for the purpose of executing the scheme already alluded to here. I read that part of Mr. Meidinger relating to the substantives and on the whole derived a degree of benefit from the hours.[1] This ought not to be a language entirely new as once it was very well understood by me.[2] Indeed occasionally an idea seems to come back upon me like an old acquaintance.

But the state of my health is now becoming a matter of considerable alarm to me. My difficulty seems to be some obstruction about the heart, and makes itself felt by some kind of palpitation. The proper remedy for it, is air and exercise, which I propose in future to adopt. I began today by walking an hour, from one to two o'clock.

Miss Julia Gorham dined with us. I returned to Cicero de Oratore, and began a review of the first book, having been so long away as to lose the chain. Accomplished twenty sections. Evening, Corinne with my Wife, and some portions of Hazlitts Extracts from the English Poets.[3] After which I accomplished part of the second book of Paradise Lost. My purpose in reading this Poem over slowly at this time is to make myself master of the feeling which predominates in it, to understand perfectly the tone by which such a conception could have been sustained. Yet I find the Commentaries rather bald reading. Parallel passages from preceding Poets may be curious as exemplifying the manner in which different minds turn the same subjects, but to suppose that Milton had in his mind all these distinct passages strikes me as absurd. Two numbers of the Tatler.

[1] JQA's copy of J. V. Meidinger, *Nouvelle grammaire allemande-pratique, ou méthode facile et amusante pour apprendre l'allemand*, Liege, 1797, is in MQA.
[2] After the arrival of the Adams family in St. Petersburg, CFA, then two years old, was put in the care of a German nurse or governess and, as a result, soon acquired some skill in the German language. See Duberman, *CFA*, p. 8.
[3] William Hazlitt, comp., *Select British Poets*, London, 1824.

TUESDAY. 9TH.

The day was cloudy with rain. I went to the Office and busied myself all the morning in learning my share of the German Grammar. I found upon a review of the substantives a very considerable difficulty in ascertaining the distinctions drawn between the declensions. This is not over clearly explained in my Grammar. I therefore took up another, that of Gottsched,[1] to see if this would answer better. But I could not accomplish enough to judge, as I was forced to attend to advertising Mr. New's Estate in Cambridge Street which is again to be sold. This accomplished, I started upon my usual walk for health, tedious but necessary. "There is no enjoying life without thee" so says Ben Jonson I believe, and whether he does or not, so says the truth.

After dinner occupied with Cicero de Oratore, and reviewed about twenty five sections with much pleasure. Eloquence is a fascinating study, if Lord Bacon's Maxim be true that Knowledge is Power, the only way to understand it is by the implication of the proper means to convey it. Knowledge lying locked up in a man's head is as inert and useless a mass as so much gold in its primitive bed. It is *circulation* that gives both power. They differ in one thing alone, that the first has influence increasing in proportion to the attention bestowed to the shape in which it is circulated, the other seldom rises above a certain fixed value, attached to the native metal in its roughest state. But a truce with speculation. Evening passed in reading Corinne with my Wife, and a visit from Mr. Degrand who has again much against my will, showed his face at my House.[2] I finished the second book of Milton's Paradise Lost, reading with attention the famous Allegory of Sin and Death, and closed with two numbers of the Tatler.

[1] J. C. Gottsched, *Le maître allemand ou nouvelle grammaire* . . . , Paris, 1763.
[2] See above, entry for 29 Nov. 1829.

WEDNESDAY. 10TH.

Morning still cloudy and dark. I have not progressed much since my review took me away from it, in the Catalogue of my father's Library. But now that I have my time this ought to become a very serious consideration. For the last two mornings, Conversation with my Wife has taken up the time I generally devote to it, but my time is precious, and I am reminded of the necessity of labour.

At the Office where I devoted myself to the study of Gottsched's Grammar and liked the arrangement of it much better than Meidinger's. For he begins with a most necessary thing to understand, the Article, while the other hardly seems to treat it by itself at all. Mr. Stone, the Treasurer of the City Guards, called upon me to pay the balance of the demand of my late brother's Estate upon that Company. I was delighted to close the whole of that business and allow all his troubles and his pleasures to rest in peace. This demand I was particularly glad to collect, as it shows that his confidence was not always misplaced.[1]

I took my usual walk. After dinner, resumed and finished the first book of Cicero de Oratore in review. The argument is upon the necessity of all other Science to constitute the Orator. A question which involves no question when rightly considered, for it is solved by what may be made the definition of an Orator. The wider sense in which Crassus is made to understand it, is perhaps the pleasantest to minds generally, though that of Antony is likely to be the most accurate. Evening, Corinne and a little poetry in a desultory way, after which I read the first half of the third Book of Paradise Lost and two dry numbers of the Tatler.

¹ The unpaid balance on the loan made to the City Guards by GWA amounted to $71.20 (M/CFA/3).

THURSDAY. 11TH.

This day presented no pleasanter prospect to us than either of the preceding—The wind still holding to the Eastward, our Stormy point. I went to the Office after resuming a little work upon my Catalogue. Continued assiduously my perusal of Gottsched and Meidinger, and gleaned occasionally a profitable idea, but their Grammars are both too cumbrous for a student of elementary principles who ought not to have his mind crowded with so many ideas as to expel each other from a durable position. I read over the adjectives, numerals and pronouns without fixing a great deal that was material, but still reviving some old recollections.

I took my usual walk, and had a better appetite than usual for dinner. Miss M[ary] A[nn] Phillips dined with us and passed the whole day with my Wife. I had a very long afternoon in consequence, but as I fell into my old superficial way of accomplishing twenty five sections, I concluded to read it over thoroughly and did not finish. The second book is not so difficult as parts of the first, and yet to me perhaps not quite so entertaining. But I speak only from a partial examination. Abby sat with me tonight only for an hour, after which I finished and reviewed the third book of Paradise lost, and read two numbers of no great interest in the Tatler.

FRIDAY. 12TH.

The dark and dismal weather still continues without improvement. My spirits are not at this moment, I thank Heaven, particularly liable to depression or this would try them. At the Office, where after occupying myself with my Journal and Accounts, instead of continuing my German, I sat down to consider the subject proposed for discussion at the Debating Society tomorrow evening. As I gave it last Saturday, to be my opinion that a man should go prepared to take a part in the discussions of the evening, I feel in a degree bound to support my doctrine by my example. I laid out very good ground for my line, if I should conclude to take part in the discussion. My father's Servant, John Kirke came from Quincy with a Note,[1] and some Commissions to be executed. My Mother appeared in much better spirits than she had been.[2]

Tried to take my Walk but the weather was so bad, that I was somewhat disappointed about it. This is bad for to me now, regularity of exercise is of some consequence. After dinner, I read Cicero and accomplished pretty thoroughly what heretofore I had done slightly. The book is very interesting, there is a flow in the style so gentle and natural, the words seem to be placed with such peculiar fitness where they are to stand, that it holds forth a wonderful example for us pigmies to imitate.[3] Evening, Corinne with my Wife when we finished the first Volume. After which I read to her from Byron several of his smaller and sweeter pieces. I also read for the first time, the Critique in the Edinburgh Review of the Hours of Idleness,[4] which produced his famous Satire of the English Bards and Scotch Reviewers. It is rather harsh, and shows the danger in which Critics often are of undue severity. The Lion may be roused and use his teeth to some purpose. I afterwards went over two thirds of the fourth book of Paradise Lost, and read two Numbers of the Tatler.

[1] Missing.
[2] LCA apparently spent at least part of the day in Boston with ABA and CFA (LCA to JA2, 11 Nov., Adams Papers).
[3] In the literary debates during the 17th and 18th centuries on the superior-ity of the ancients or the moderns, mod-ern man was sometimes referred to as a dwarf or a pigmy on a giant's shoulders.
[4] *Edinburgh Review*, 11:285–289 (Jan. 1808).

SATURDAY. 13TH.

Nothing but rain. I went to the Office and was busy in digesting matter for the discussion at the Debating Society this evening. I wrote out the whole and arranged it in my mind in a fit manner for delivery. This cost me some labour but I hope it will benefit me inasmuch as I shall be better able to rely upon my strength on any occasion that may come up suddenly. Having a little head ach, I was driven to my usual walk to remove it notwithstanding the badness of the weather. Return-ing home, found my Wife quite unwell, and I therefore sat in her room and read Cicero as well as I could, during the Afternoon. But my progress was not perfectly satisfactory. I am so sensible of the influence of situation in reading, that when I am out of my study nothing seems to go well. I did not much more than half understand what I did read, and read only half the usual quantity.

In the evening I went through the rain to hear the Debate, found about twelve present and had a pretty sensible course of reasoning, for it is not debate, there is not warmth enough. On my return, finished the fourth book of Paradise Lost and reviewed a portion of it, and read two Numbers of the Tatler.

SUNDAY. 14TH.

Astonishing how the weather holds on stormy. It was as bad today as it has been at any time. My Wife was confined to her bed all day. I attended divine service morning and Afternoon. Heard Mr. Brazer of Salem.[1] He is a clear, finished Writer with a good though conceited delivery. I was pleased with his Sermons. One thing struck me as singular which was, that there was a paragraph almost precisely the same with one I had written in my Review, but which on correcting, I had struck out as too commonplace. Perhaps this is the greatest evidence of my correctness, yet it did not sound flat in his mouth. This may be true and still the same thing would not stand cool reading. Took a long walk also. My exercise has already gone far to correct my difficulty of which I complained.

In the afternoon I sat with my Wife and read partly aloud and partly to myself Drake's Essays upon the composition of the Tatler, Spectator and the other periodical literature of that day.[2] A book that is extremely necessary at this day to the reading and right understanding of those works. I received today much information which will carry me much more easily through my undertaking of these Essayists. I afterwards finished reviewing the fourth book of Paradise lost and read half of the fifth book, besides my usual number of Tatlers. I also omitted to record a little work upon my Catalogue.

[1] John Brazer, Harvard 1813 (*Mass. Register*, 1830).
[2] Nathan Drake, *Essays, Biographical, Critical, and Historical, Illustrative of the Tatler, Spectator, and Guardian*, &c., 3 vols., London, 1805.

MONDAY. 15TH.

The day was not an improvement upon any of the preceding. I went to the Office as usual and occupied myself in making up my Accounts as well as writing my Journal after which I sat down again to my German. My progress here is not very rapid and for a few days past has been very much confused by other occupations. I succeeded however in making a slight impression upon the verbs. Took my walk as usual between one and two o'clock.

In the afternoon I read a large portion of Cicero's second book de

Oratore, coming to the Account of wit which I did not taste. The application of language in this manner requires a most thorough knowledge of the conversational idiom of a Country, and the peculiar acceptation of words in Society. However good it may have been, and Cicero would scarcely have commended it if it had not been thought so, we can see nothing which merits being so strongly sustained.

Evening, Corinne with my Wife, after which Edward Brooks came in and spent the evening. Which was all very pleasantly done. I finished the fifth book of Paradise Lost, and reviewed two thirds of it. Two numbers of the Tatler.

TUESDAY. 16TH.

The wind changed and the weather which had been hazy became at last pretty clear. The Sun showed himself to us again and animated the scene which has so long been dark. I went to the Office as usual and after the usual duties, had just set myself down to study my German when my Father came in from Quincy. He sat at my Office all the morning and my occupations were entirely prevented by Mr. Curtis and Mr. Degrand who came in one after the other and consumed all the period. I was sorry to hear that my Mother was not well, but at the same time was glad to find that she had decided to go to Washington. This was produced by a letter from John which I had sent for, but which I fear was not precisely in the tone that I admire.[1] My father dined with me and consumed so much of the afternoon that I did not think it worthwhile to go upon Cicero this afternoon and spent it upon my Catalogue which I should wish could progress a great deal more than it does.

My day was on the whole a poorly spent one, and my mind always assumes a load of care when I think of my Parents. Their situation is a painful one, and it is always a hard thing for a Child to feel a doubt about the sound Judgment of either. But I see no way to avoid it. For I always find them in some species of embarrassment, and I do not often agree with their plans.

Evening, I read a little of Corinne with my Wife and a part of Crabbe's Tales which I never opened before.[2] They are not very astonishing. Part of the sixth Book of Paradise Lost with the review of the fifth and the Tatler.

[1] The letter from JA2 to LCA is missing; however, on its contents and character see above, entry for 27 Oct., note.
[2] In CFA's copy at MQA of the *Works of the Rev. George Crabbe*, London, 1823, the *Tales* are in vols. 5–8.

WEDNESDAY. 17TH.

The morning was fair and uncommonly mild. Our season here has been altogether of a soft nature so far, particularly when I come to compare it with the two preceding years. I went to the Office as usual and passed my morning in rather a desultory way, having only a little while to devote to German. I made a little progress in the verbs notwithstanding. The difficulties which meet one at the outset of languages rather deter one from pursuing them, but I trust a little in my usual perseverance. Took my walk at one o'clock.

After dinner I sat down again to Cicero but I read over his sections about Wit so superficially that it disgusted me and I turned over to the beginning of the second book again to review thoroughly. And this time I very much got the Sense of the Author, so far as I progressed. The great method of understanding foreign Authors, is as Wyttenbach[1] advises by constant reviewing. Thus the sense and force that may escape at one time will be caught at another. Evening, reading Corinne with my Wife. After which, I finished the sixth book of Paradise Lost and reviewed it. Read a little of Mr. Drake, and two Numbers of the Tatler.

[1] Probably Daniel Albert Wyttenbach (1746–1820), celebrated classical scholar.

THURSDAY. 18TH.

This was at last a clear day, and it was mild and beautiful indeed. Hitherto we have experienced hardly any frost to touch the ground which is very uncommon. I went to the Office and was occupied all the morning in arranging my room and clearing it from a mass of very superfluous papers which have accumulated. I find this the principal plague at my Office. The habit acquired by my brother George of amassing all his pieces of waste paper has deluged me with them ever since I have had any thing to do with them. My own inclinations also tend that way a little so that my task is made harder.

I went into State Street to see Mr. Quincy and give him the Papers relative to the Execution of my Grandfather's Will,[1] which he looked over and returned to me. Thus vanished the morning. I took my usual walk. I continued my review of the second book de Oratore, which I found much easier than before and became reconciled in the course of it to Wells and Lilly's Edition, notwithstanding the lettering and printing.[2]

Evening a portion of Corinne with my Wife and after it a little of Wordsworth's Poetry to diversify.[3] He is too simple for my taste, next to what the common people would call natural. I then read the seventh book of Paradise Lost containing the History of the Creation. After which I finished by a little of Mr. Drake and two Numbers of the Tatler.

[1] JQA and Josiah Quincy (1772–1864), coexecutors of the estate of JA, filed with the clerk of court their report No. 6 for the period 1 Jan. – 16 Nov. 1830 (Adams Papers, Microfilms, Reel No. 181).

[2] Wells & Lilly, Boston booksellers and publishers, brought out in 1815 in 20 vols. an edition of *M. Tullii Ciceronis opera omnia ex recensione novissima Io. Augusti Ernesti.* It is probable that CFA's comment on "the lettering and printing" was intended as no more than a contrast between this 12mo edition and the 4to Oxford edition he had used earlier; see entries for 27 Sept., note; 29 Sept., above.

[3] CFA may very well have read from one of the numerous anthologies of English poetry; however, there is in MQA an edition of Wordsworth's *Poetical Works*, 4 vols., Boston, 1824, which had been GWA's and became CFA's.

FRIDAY. 19TH.

Morning pleasant. Went to the Office as usual and occupied my time upon the German Grammar, upon which I made some progress. I think I have now got far enough properly to begin to read but I am stopped by not possessing any elementary work. This will drive me to reviewing my Grammar again and perhaps this exercise will not hurt me in the end. The verbs are tolerably easy, much the larger proportion of them being regular.

I wrote a letter to my father,[1] called to see Mr. Brooks, and went to read an article which appeared this morning in the Gazette against my Father. It was abusive enough, and after reflection the only source to which I could attribute it was Jonathan Russel, whose grief time has done nothing to alleviate.[2] I considered whether any notice should be taken of it, but reflected on the whole that it would not be advisable. Took my Walk.

After dinner, I read Cicero de Oratore, and completed the review of what I had read until the Wit which I was able to comprehend as little as ever. I must seek a Translation. In the Evening Corinne as usual. I then read over the seventh book of Paradise Lost, and part of the eighth. Finished by a little of Mr. Drake and two Numbers of the Tatler.

[1] Letter missing.

[2] Jonathan Russell's reputation had been severely damaged by JQA's pamphlet of 1822 relating to the negotiations preceding the Treaty of Ghent; see vol. 2:296–297. The "article" against JQA was presumably the letter with a Woburn dateline printed in the *Boston Commercial Gazette*, 18 Nov., p. 2, col. 4, in which the detraction of JQA is subsidiary to an attack upon Nathan Appleton.

Quincy

SATURDAY. 20TH.

The day was pleasant, although it afterwards became cloudy. I went to the Office as usual, where I was busily occupied in my common avocations of Accounts and writing, after which I began my German, but was interrupted by Mr. Conant from Weston, bringing me the first fruits of the Sale of Wood on the third. The amount was but small, and not as I hope any presage of what it is likely to be.

Presently, John Kirke my fathers Servant came in to let me know he was sent for us and accordingly I was obliged to prepare myself to go. We started at a little after one o'clock and reached Quincy before three. I found my Mother dull and cold in her manner of receiving us, and my father as kind as he commonly is. I am satisfied from what I hear that the proper course should have been to have started long ago, but as it is, this is better than remaining the Winter.[1]

I sat in conversation with my father all the afternoon, and we looked over the Garden, considering what should be done for the future. After which we discussed all his arrangements. In the evening I discussed the Comic Annual[2] and read passages aloud, to the amusement of the family but on the whole, it is a most indifferent production. The humour is of the gross kind and forced beyond the usual bounds, even of such things. We were tolerably comfortable although I felt quite strangely in my new Quarters at first.[3]

[1] That is, the return to Washington should have taken place early in November, but the plan to leave early in December was to be preferred to LCA's and JQA's remaining at Quincy through the cold months. JQA's election did not require his residence in Washington during the winter of 1830 since his term in the 22d Congress did not begin until 4 March, and the 1st session did not convene until 5 Dec. 1831.

[2] *The Comic Annual*, a production of Thomas Hood, London, vol. 1 (1830).

[3] Probably in the room which had been occupied by Mrs. JA2 during her long stay at the Old House.

SUNDAY. 21ST.

The morning was clear but cold. I passed the day very quietly, heard Mr. Whitney preach morning and afternoon, two Sermons very much in his usual style. He is very uninteresting and I think has almost brought his Parish to a crisis. The result of the present state of things is rather to be feared.

I conversed with my father during the day upon a variety of subjects relating to his situation here in Quincy. We do not often think alike upon matters of common life. He is a little more easy than I am disposed to be, under impositions of various kinds, and trusts as I believe we all do, a little too much to his own preconceived notions of right. But I am speaking perhaps more boldly than I ought.

My Mother was kept up in pretty tolerable spirits during the day, by the presence of my Wife. She is in low spirits from a state of depression resulting from her health, and from a general apathy to the ordinary run of the world, which is as unfortunate a thing as can befall a woman. I can give no account of any very profitable occupation during the day. Evening, Miscellaneous Conversation.

Boston
MONDAY. 22D.

The day opened in darkness and clouds. After breakfast it commenced raining and held on so pretty violently until night. We returned to Boston in the Carriage notwithstanding. I had several little things to do which consumed a portion of my Morning so that I did not reach the Office until late. When the time did come, I found a Note from Isaac H. Adams stating that his father had been thrown out of a Chaise and considerably hurt, therefore requesting I would see him and let the Carriage take him to Quincy. I went directly to Mr. Jas. H. Foster's where he was, and found him pretty comfortable, and able to go at 12 o'clock. It is very astonishing that his Neck was not broken.[1]

Returned to the Office and was busy there in my Accounts, as on this day I was to pay the Taxes upon my Father's Estate in Boston.[2] Mr. Curtis called to have the Certificates of certain shares belonging to the Estate of Mr. Boylston transferred to Mr. Greenleaf, and Mr. J. A. Welsh called also to be paid his Share of the proceeds of the Appraisement of Mr. New's Estate. I then went home to dress for the purpose of dining with Mr. A. H. Everett according to invitation. The party consisted of none but the family of Mr. Brooks and Mr. Everett, excepting that Mr. Brooks was himself prevented from coming by the rain. The dinner was dull, and gave me no satisfaction as I was not pleased with my part of it. I left to take tea with Mrs. Frothingham and ride home with my Wife. Milton's eighth book and the Tatler.

[1] The accident occurred on Hanover Street at Concert Hall when, on turning the corner, TBA's hired horse and chaise, "one of your new fashioned high seated wasp shaped gimcracks," struck the wheel of a wagon with such force that both shafts of the chaise were broken off, the chaise overturned and "shivered to atoms." One of the wheels passed over TBA's body in the thigh and hip area but no bones were broken. (JQA, Diary, 22 Nov.; JQA to JA2, 30 Nov., Adams Papers.)

[2] Taxes for the year amounted to $112 (M/CFA/3).

The morning was clear and only cool. I went to the Office as usual after a little progress upon my Catalogue. My time was taken up in making up my Accounts, and writing, so that as usual I could devote very little to my German. Mr. Welsh and I settled Accounts today, which finishes the last outstanding balance upon this Estate of my father's.[1] The more I see of all that is to be done upon these Estates, the more I am satisfied that what has heretofore been done has not been managed correctly. There is rarely any occasion with Tenants, for Arrears, if they can pay when they are asked, they will.[2] If not, they ought to make arrangements which should satisfy you or move. In my walk, I passed the Estate in Tremont Street and went in to see what was doing. I found that infinitely more had been done than I anticipated and I tremble at the accounts which are in prospect.

Took my usual walk and in the afternoon, read Cicero as usual. I got through his account of Wit, which is difficult enough and hardly pays one for the reading. Great assistance is to be experienced from the Copy by Olivet which contains the Commentaries.[3] As Abby had gone out of town, I spent an hour and a half at the Athenæum. Finished the evening with the first half of the ninth book of Paradise Lost and two Numbers of the Tatler.

[1] The long-standing indebtedness of Thomas Welsh Jr. for rental of an office in the 23 Court Street Building had been reduced in various ways (above, entries for 20 March, 1, 9 April), but apparently the elimination of any balance in the account had not earlier been achieved (M/CFA/3).

[2] Sentence thus punctuated in MS.

[3] CFA's copy of the *Opera* of Cicero, edited by d'Olivet and Ernest and published at London in 1820 in 12 vols. is in MQA; the commentary by Olivet constitutes the final volume.

Morning cloudy with occasional rain. I went to the Office as usual and occupied myself in a variety of ways. First in my Accounts which have latterly created some trouble, then in my Journal, and afterwards in my German which does not progress at all. I want some book to begin and translate, and I feel at this moment unwilling to afford one, my means being much shortened by the investment made some time since. Called for a few minutes to see Mr. Brooks and told him that I should not send for the Trees if it rained tomorrow, otherwise, I had made all the arrangements.[1] Mr. Hayden called to pay me his rent for one of the Tenements. He did not give a very favourable account of the other Tenant's ability to pay, so that these are not likely to be so soon off my hands. But he wants the front house, himself. I could not take my usual walk this morning.

Afternoon, read and finished Cicero's Second Book de Oratore, the latter part of which becomes interesting again. The doctrine of Artificial Memory is there very distinctly laid down and seems to have been used much more fully than it is in our day. Evening, Corinne with my Wife, after which I turned over the pages of Dodsley's Collection [2] without finding much of interest. Finished the Ninth Book of Paradise Lost, and reviewed the first half, and read two Numbers of the Tatler.

[1] On the Baldwin apple trees purchased in Medford for JQA's orchard at Mount Wollaston, see above, entry for 22 September.

[2] Robert Dodsley's *Collection of Poems by Several Hands* or his *Select Collection of Old Plays* is probably meant. There are editions of both in MQA.

THURSDAY. 25TH.

Our weather today was violently stormy notwithstanding the long continuation of the bad season. The rain set in at eleven o'clock and it continued all day. I had no expectation therefore of seeing my father's man, Kirke, though it was the appointed day for the Trees. He came however, and I sent him accordingly. He must have had a terrific day of it. I went to the Office and was busy in my Accounts, after which I spent a considerable and uninterrupted period upon my German. I tried to translate some passages that came in my way and felt quite encouraged by my success. I think my former knowledge must assist me insensibly, for on looking attentively upon words, I can trace their meaning often very easily.

Returned home and although my Study was exceedingly uncomfortable from the quantity of smoke that was in it, I succeeded in making a great deal of progress in the third book de Oratore, which is a model for beautiful style, being a practical example of a sound theory. Part of the Evening, Corinne, the other part, writing my Catalogue which the short days delay still more. Afterwards, I was occupied in reading part of the tenth Book of Paradise Lost, besides finishing the review of the Ninth. And two Numbers of the Tatler.

FRIDAY 26TH.

The air had a much colder feeling this morning, and more suitable to the advanced period of the Season. But it was still cloudy and drizzle. I went to the Office, where I read my German as usual, only interrupted by several applicants for my small House and by Mr.

Curtis who called expecting to meet here Mr. D. Greenleaf to finish the business of the Neponset Bridge Shares. But the latter did not come.[1] I then went to the Athenæum to obtain one or two books instead of my old ones which I have already kept too long. Met Edward Brooks there and we conversed some time upon indifferent matters taking up the time until two o'clock.

After dinner, I was occupied upon Cicero de Oratore for some time, but my study again smoked so much I had my attention very much broken. I completed however the second portion of the third Book—Though relapsing a little into my superficial mode of reading. This will cause a review, which will I hope be now pretty thorough. I think this book is worth most attentive study by any one who wishes to learn the principles of Oratory. I read besides the usual quantity of Corinne with my Wife, a little of Lady Morgan's Book of the Boudoir, a Work I have heard much derided.[2] Afterwards Finished the Tenth Book of Paradise Lost and reviewed a part of it, besides reading my Two Numbers of the Tatler.

[1] JQA had been deputed by the executors of the will of Ward Nicholas Boylston to effect the sale of the estate's six shares of Neponset Bridge stock to Daniel Greenleaf for $505 a share, a price he had earlier offered and had had rejected. Greenleaf had agreed to renew the offer; the time for settlement had been fixed. The sale was concluded on the day following. See JQA, Diary, 16, 19, 27 November.

[2] Lady Sydney Morgan, *Book of the Boudoir*, 2 vols., London, 1829.

[Medford]

SATURDAY. 27TH.

Morning clear and much colder than heretofore. I went to the Office as usual and received a visit from Mr. D. Greenleaf about the Shares of the Neponset Bridge Corporation. Read my German and made up my Accounts as usual. But owing to the fact that Mr. Brooks had sent for us to go to Medford, my time was too much broken to allow of any very material improvement of it. It is grievous to me to see how my mornings go in spite of all my best resolutions but so it is and, the more I try, the more impossible it seems to help it.

We started to go out of town at one o'clock in Mr. Brooks' Carriage with Mrs. Everett. The roads were not over good, and when we arrived at Medford, every thing seemed pretty desolate. This is the first time we have been up there since Mrs. Everett was established,[1] and the change does not seem very agreeable besides the different appearance which the House has when Winter approaches. I walked down in the Afternoon to see old Mr. Warren and get a receipt from him for the Trees purchased which he very readily gave. He is an old man of

Eighty two and writes with much clearness yet. Such is vigorous old age.

Evening, I read Mr. Everett's Lecture upon the Working Men's Party[2] and an article on the same subject in the Christian Examiner.[3] I liked them both, particularly as there is now a current rising in this Country upon that subject which needs checking. It deserves very attentive consideration from every honest Citizen.

[1] The Edward Everett family had moved to Mystic Grove on 3 Nov. (Brooks, Farm Journal). Edward Everett had left for Washington on 22 Nov., his wife and children remaining at Medford for the winter (Charlotte Everett to Edward Everett, 26 Nov., Everett Papers, MHi).

[2] Edward Everett's *Lecture on the Workingmen's Party*, delivered at the Charlestown Lyceum on 6 Oct., had been recently published in Boston as a pamphlet. It is included in Everett's *Orations and Speeches*, 4 vols., Boston, 1850, at 1:283–306.

[3] An unsigned essay-review by James T. Austin of Joseph T. Buckingham's *Address Delivered before the Massachusetts Charitable Mechanic Association ... Oct. 7, 1830*, Boston, 1830, in the *Christian Examiner and General Review*, vol. 9 (new ser., vol. 4), p. 250–268 (Nov. 1830).

SUNDAY. 28TH.

The day was a very fine one. I attended Divine Service all day, and heard Mr. Stetson preach a very able and useful Sermon upon the practice of Slander and Gossip which is so prevalent among us. I like that kind of address, for it is probable that not a single person sat in that Meeting house to whom his words did not in some degree apply. This is the true purpose of the divine Ministry as established on earth, and not the writing a mere collection of beautifully arranged sentences of morals.[1] This does not derogate from beauty of style or speaking because only that style of speaking can be worthy of the name of most beautiful, which most perfectly executes the purposes for which the whole Institution is designed. The afternoon's Sermon was more doctrinal and less valuable.

I amused myself during the rest of the day, dipping a little into Michel Montaigne, with whom I was more amused than ever before. He has much thought delivered in a rambling kind of way. Evening, Messrs. Jonathan Brooks and his son Saml., came up and passed the whole evening, tolerably pleasantly.

[1] Both the sermon on slander and gossip and CFA's strongly approving reaction to the choice of subject may have had a topical significance at this time beyond the general suitability of the lesson: "Boston has been in a state of consternation owing to a little scandalous peccadillo which has occurred and crushed all the interest of the European News and almost of internal politics. It is as high in its grade as the Knap murder and conducted with all the deliberation which rendered that incident so awful. The Lovelace began with bad

books at the age of 12 and completed the Seduction at 14 and it has come out on the eve of the marriage of the lassy aged 22 because she would not agree to infringe the rights of matrimony. It is a New Bedford affair. The Mother gone distracted" (LCA to Mrs. JA2, 26 Nov., Adams Papers).

Boston

MONDAY. 29TH.

The morning was cloudy and cold. It cleared away however in the course of the day. We returned to town with Mr. Brooks and had a pretty cold time. I got to the Office very late indeed so that I could do little or nothing, except write my Journal. Mr. A. H. Everett called to see me and gave a final answer about taking his Office. He agreed to begin upon the 1st of the month.[1] This is well, and now I have only the small house unrented out of all my father's property here. I hope this will not remain long upon my hands. Should it not, I should feel extremely gratified to have every inch of his Estate profitable at the same time. I walked down to see the repairs at the Wooden Tenements, and was glad to find that they were nearly finished. This has been a long and an expensive job.

After dinner I finished Cicero de Oratore, but the last has been read most superficially, so that I began the whole again for a final and thorough review. For this I am the better prepared as I have both the Notes of the edition d'Olivet, and a translation by Guthrie.[2] I accomplished the first seven sections fully. Evening, Corinne, and Lady Morgan, interrupted however by Edmund Quincy who passed two hours here. Finished the tenth Book of Paradise Lost in review, began the eleventh and read two Numbers of the Tatler.

[1] See above, entry for 9 October. The tenancy of a room in the 23 Court Street building as an editorial office for the *North American Review* continued until Dec. 1833 at an annual rent of $80 (M/CFA/3).

[2] William Guthrie's translation was published at London in 1742.

TUESDAY. 30TH.

Much to my surprise, I found the day as stormy as that on Thursday. The rain set in from the Eastward and continued with a high wind all day. I went to the Office as usual and was busy during my time in my German which I pursued with some success. At the same time I got my room prepared for Mr. Everett's reception. I am still so little satisfied with my morning's occupation that I am thinking of altering my arrangements, and resuming some review. My old undertaking of Williston recurs to my mind with a strong inclination. I will think about it.

Returned home and sat in the cold all the afternoon for fear of being overpowered with smoke, and though I suffered in feeling I gained in progress, for I accomplished Thirty Sections or one half of the first book de Oratore, which is by far the most amusing as I think.

Evening, the usual quantity of Corinne and then some of Lady Morgan. She is a vain, silly woman, and yet not unamusing—Though she fatigues from monotony. Afterwards, I read the remainder of Paradise Lost Book Eleventh and reviewed a part of it. After which, finished with two Numbers of the Tatler.[1] It continued raining in the Night.

[1] When CFA began his reading of the *Tatler* (above, entry for 11 Oct.), he also undertook to make a brief daily comment, sometimes no more than a word, on the subject or tone of each number or on his reaction to it. He entered these comments in what had been one of GWA's commonplace books, continuing the practice until this day on which he read Nos. 88 and 89, though on 24 Nov. he had recorded, "I am almost tired of my plan." (Adams Papers, Microfilms, Reel No. 294.)

DECEMBER 1830.

[*Quincy*]

WEDNESDAY. 1ST.

Morning cloudy but the weather became gradually mild and clear. I went down to the Market to see what Thanksgiving was to be seen. The display was not so great as I have seen but I made out to obtain provisions for a considerable period. Then to the Office but my occupations at the Office were almost prevented by a visit from Mr. Curtis who came by appointment to see my Father. He waited until twelve, when my father came. I thus barely had time enough to write my Journal, and arrange my Accounts for the month and close of my Quarter.

Returned home and dressed myself to go out to dine with Dr. G. Parkman. The Company consisted of my Father, Chief Justice Shaw, Messrs. Palfrey and Parkman, Clergymen, Messrs. Coolidge J. and T. B., R. G. Shaw, D. Parkman and P. O. Thacher. The dinner was very good and we got through exceedingly well, so as to start for Quincy shortly after five o'clock.

The weather has been so bad that the roads were very unpleasant, but we reached Quincy by seven o'clock. Found my Mother this time in remarkably good spirits. Strange it is, but the passage of ten days in which her mind has been occupied has produced a wonderful effect upon her feelings. We passed the evening very cosily in talking and on the whole amused ourselves very well until time to retire.

373

THURSDAY. 2ND.

This was the regular day allotted by the State Authorities according to custom, to the purpose of offering thanks for the manifold blessing received by us from the divine source.[1] It came today in unclouded beauty. I arose and was soon put into the service by my father to copy some Papers which he wished to arrange in the settlement of my Grandfather's Estate before he went away. It became time to attend at the Meeting House, where we heard Mr. Whitney preach an uncommonly brisk Sermon for him, and the regular howled Anthem upon this occasion. On our return, we had the usual bountiful dinner. I cannot help feeling how valuable a practice this is in a Community. It seems to be a kind of outpouring of the heart for a Season of Bounty.

After having made a larger dinner than I ought to have done I went with my Father to see his Orchard which he has set out on Mount Wollaston. I was very much delighted with it and cannot but hope that it will turn out well. We stopped at the Judge's on our return and paid a short visit after which we came home, took Tea and finished the Evening at the usual Thanksgiving Quincy Party at Mr. T. Greenleaf's, which was stupid enough.

[1] The observance of a Thursday during the fall of the year as a day of thanksgiving for the harvest became general in New England after 1730 when Connecticut shifted from Wednesday. While November was the more usual month for Thanksgiving, there were numerous instances of an October or a December observance. Moreover, the years both before and after the Revolution when the several colonies or states achieved a uniformity of date for the observance were quite exceptional. Early efforts to establish a national day of thanksgiving in the fall of the year foundered upon the church-state and federalist-antifederalist conflict. After national observances during the year 1777–1784 and in 1789, there were no further actions on the matter by the national government until 1863, from which year dates the annual observance of the last Thursday in November as a national Thanksgiving Day. See W. De-Loss Love, *The Fast and Thanksgiving Days of New England*, Boston, 1895, p. 364, 402–404, 408–409, 464–514.

Boston

FRIDAY. 3RD.

The day was warm but threatened with many Clouds. I spent more than an hour after breakfast, copying papers for my father. After executing these, I got ready to go to town. Madame my Mother this day took leave of Quincy on her return to Washington. She has proved to me over again that her residence there is not an agreeable one to her. I suppose she would be glad not to try it again. What a misfortune has this taste been to my Father. When I think upon it I feel grieved at the result, but it is not remediable.

We did not reach town until twelve o'clock when I went directly down to my Office. Of course I had exceeding little time to do any thing. I executed my work of every day and returned home. My Mother dined with us and started although with a lowering sky upon her Journey. She goes as far as Watertown tonight. I was glad that she went as it relieves us here from the responsibility which would have rested upon us had she been at Quincy alone. But I felt melancholy upon losing her. For she has been very kind to us.

I read Cicero as usual, though from the multitude of Notes I did not progress very fast. Evening, Corinne, and Lady Morgan for a short time, but as my Wife was very much wearied from a sleepless night, she retired early and I read Mr. Drake's Sketch of Addison, after which I reviewed the rest of the Eleventh Book of Paradise Lost, and read the Twelfth Book. Finished two Numbers of the Tatler.

SATURDAY. 4TH.

Morning opened very fine, for which I was very glad as I hoped it would afford a fine opportunity for my Mother to get on in her Journey. I went to the Office as usual. My time was very much taken up in little occupations so that I had no chance to do any thing very considerable in my German. I went to see the Exhibition of Butter to obtain the Premium, and made no effort to buy any as I thought it went too high. I then went with Abby to pay a visit to Mrs. Lee the new Wife of Wm. Lee of Washington. She did not please me much by her address. Returned to my Office and thus the whole morning passed.

Afternoon, busied in Cicero de Oratore, the first book of which I finished—To me much the most interesting and apt to our present modes of thinking. I think I have now mastered it pretty thoroughly.

Evening attended a Meeting of the Debating Society, the Question proposed for discussion was the probable influence of the French revolution. It was very tamely debated. I had prepared myself for a previous Meeting which I was unable to attend, and thought I would not lose the opportunity for trying my Powers this year. I found they had improved.

SUNDAY. 5TH.

Another fine day which I hope my Mother will be induced to improve, and thus take her out of the reach of our bad weather hereafter. According to my calculations she will reach Stafford Springs tonight.[1]

I attended divine service all day, while my Wife went with her brother Chardon to Watertown and Medford. Heard Mr. Frothingham in the morning and Mr. Motte in the afternoon, but neither of them were interesting enough to excite my attention. The latter is infinitely stupid. His manner is absurd, his matter, bad taste. I do not know a poorer Preacher in Boston.

I pursued my occupations very quietly in my study all day. Read a portion of Mr. Drake's sketch of Addison. Mr. Drake is a pleasant second hand Writer. His own thoughts are worth little, his compilations are in good taste and well selected to illustrate his subject. Proceeded with my Catalogue, and read a little of Enfield's History of Philosophy[2] in order to obtain a clearer idea of the Grecian Schools before passing to Cicero's Philosophical Works. My Wife was so fatigued with her ride that she retired early. E. Quincy called upon a short visit. I read the larger part of Addison's Critique upon Paradise Lost having finished my Review of the Twelfth Book last night. Two Numbers of the Tatler.

[1] The journey had been slowed by the extremely bad condition of the roads; LCA reached Waltham on the 3d, Worcester on the 4th, and Sturbridge on the 5th, reporting her arrival in each place by letter (Adams Papers).

[2] In MQA is JQA's copy of William Enfield, *The History of Philosophy*, 2 vols., London, 1819.

MONDAY. 6TH.

The morning was dark and cloudy and it commenced raining, changed afterwards to Snow and assumed the regular appearance of one of our North Easters. I regret that two days more were not allowed to my Mother to get beyond the reach of it all. But I hope she has gained so much on it as to make her Journey easy compared with what it might have been.

I went to the Office as usual and after arranging all my balances, paying off the sum chargeable upon me from my Fathers property, which makes my Investment complete, I sat down and progressed somewhat in my German. But the book I brought from Quincy is altogether too hard to begin with.

Returned home and the storm was so high I was afraid of having a fire in my Study. I sat in the basement room and accomplished twenty three Sections of the Second book de Oratore. They had been read pretty thoroughly before. But now comes the series of Jokes which is somewhat more difficult. I hope to accomplish this better than before. Evening, the usual portion of Corinne and Lady Morgan's nonsense. After which I completed Addison's Critique upon Paradise

Lost with Johnson's remarks upon the versification. This study has not been without benefit to me. It has served to give me a better idea of the nature of this great Poem. Two Numbers of the Tatler.

TUESDAY. 7TH.

I find I have got into a regular practice of beginning my daily Journal with an Account of the Weather. Perhaps this is not without it's use, though in the long run, it may have a tone of Monotony.[1] The weather was fine and clear with sharp cold.

I went to the Office as usual and spent my time in my usual occupations, making some little progress in German. My father's Trunk came in the course of the morning which warned me that he was coming in to take his departure. Received Letters from my Mother this morning, notifying us of her reaching Sturbridge before the Storm. This is not quite so far as I had expected but still it is a good way on.

Returned home, and after having seated myself quietly to proceed with my studies my Father arrived, cold and comfortless from Dedham.[2] The rest of the afternoon passed in arranging papers for my father, receiving directions from him upon the various little things he commissioned me with, and copying a series of the Papers which it was necessary to insert relating to the execution of my Grandfather's will. This is I hope the final charge likely to come upon my father's property.

Evening, Conversation with my father. I engaged him very pleasantly and could not help wishing that he could stay to give me the benefit of his conversation a little longer. But the Stages were so arranged, he was to start tomorrow morning. Col. J. B. Davis hearing that my father was here, called and spent an hour or two.

[1] In recording the weather as a part of each diary entry CFA was but following the practice of his father and of his grandfather, whose very first efforts at journal-keeping were primarily observations on the weather; see JA, *Earliest Diary*, p. 33–34.

[2] The date of JQA's departure had been fixed by the necessity that the executors of JA's will appear in the Probate Court at Dedham on 7 Dec. to submit their accounts for the Court's approval and to prepare for the second distribution of proceeds of the estate to the devisees on 1 Jan. (JQA, Diary, 7 Dec.; JA, Will, Inventory, and Estate Papers, p. 109–111, Adams Papers, Microfilms, Reel No. 181).

WEDNESDAY. 8TH.

Morning mild and clear but it clouded up before midday. I awoke with a most excruciating head ach and had been up only a few minutes before it was followed by nausea and vomiting. I have not felt so sick for a long time. My father started for Washington at about nine,[1] and I felt melancholy at having him go. For this transfer from one place to another, is getting to be a serious thing at his time of life. But so it must be.

I went to the Office as usual and was very busy in several occupations of money concerns that troubled me, being left by my father to be immediately done. The sale of New's Estate also took place today and I attended it and had it sold to Mr. Grosvenor the highest bidder again for $305.00.[2] This over, I found myself so unwell I thought it advisable to go home and barely reached it in time. I was so unwell I found myself able to do little or nothing but lie down and be as quiet as possible. I read a little of Mr. Drake and was not so well pleased as I went on seeing how evidently he is a Bookmaker.[3] Finished with two numbers of the Tatler and retired early.

[1] Because of the severe storm and of the reports of bad traveling conditions in LCA's letters, JQA modified his plans and took the stage for Hartford, planning to join LCA there (JQA, Diary, 7 Dec.).

[2] See entry for 14 Oct., above.

[3] In the disparaging sense of making a trade of the compilation of books or, as the current phrase has it, of non-books; see entry for 5 Dec., above.

THURSDAY. 9TH.

Morning clouds and rain. But the latter stopped soon. My head did not feel perfectly clear yet, and I was apprehensive I should be laid up. But by a long walk I got gradually better by evening. My time was taken up at the Office by a variety of little occupations. Mr. S. Brown called to be paid for his Sale.[1] Mr. Peabody my opposite Neighbour[2] to learn how to make a Coal Fire, and Messrs. Blake and Chapman at twelve o'clock on a Committee of the Debating Society business. They staid for an hour or so, after which I found it was time for my long walk. The Streets were not over favourable, but what is all that to health.

Afternoon, engaged in the second book de Oratore in which I made great progress, completing beyond the Fiftieth Section. It is all good so far, and continues so until we reach the specimen of poor Jokes. Evening, reading Corinne with my Wife and finished Lady Morgan's book, which will not tempt me to get the second volume. I cannot endure such nothingness. The remainder of the evening was devoted to pursuing the Catalogue, which I propose now to do constantly until I see some end to it. For it now drags. Read two numbers of the Tatler. It had been my intention to try a little criticism upon these, but such is the vanity of our hopes and resolutions. I take shelter in generalities.

FRIDAY. 10TH.

Morning clear and very windy. I went to the Office as usual and was busy in my common way without any definite result. I dispatched however all business immediately necessary by writing a letter to Miss L. C. Smith, notifying her of the arrangement of the Legacy,[1] and I called upon Mr. Quincy where I obtained the Letters to the other heirs which I sealed and forwarded. Mr. Grosvenor called upon me to finish the Deed of the Estate of R. New to him which I did, and the drawing up of this and it's execution consumed a tolerable portion of time. Mr. A. H. Everett called for a moment to ask about the paper he wished to see but he only received my father's answer.[2] My time was in this manner so much consumed that I had no opportunity for my walk, and my afternoon passed as usual in reading Cicero. I accomplished the portion which relates to Wit and was glad to find from my translation that more professed scholars understood it as little as I. It is a perishable material. Evening read with Abby, my portion of Corinne as usual, and having no book to read, I recurred to Shakspeare and read aloud the first Act of Hamlet. Continued my Catalogue and read two numbers of the Tatler.

[1] Letter missing.

[2] JQA had agreed to write a biographical notice of William Tudor for the *North American Review*, but in the press of other obligations before his departure was forced to postpone its completion (JQA, Diary, 6 Dec.). Subsequently, at the request of Tudor's mother who wanted separate publication in a volume of Tudor's writings, JQA informed Everett that the article would not be available for the *Review* (same, 5, 6 March 1831). JQA later revised his view on Mrs. Tudor's motives (same, 2 Dec. 1831).

SATURDAY. 11TH.

Morning clear and pleasant. I went to the Office as usual and was occupied first in reading a letter from my Mother, giving an Account of her perils as far as Hartford. She has had a pretty bad time of it since the snow fell. My father however had arrived safe.[1] I occupied part of my morning reading the President's Message which has just arrived. It is a strange mixture of singular doctrines not before heard in the Executive Chair of this Union.[2] Part of my morning passed in preparing a draught of my opening of the debate for the Committee of the Society that meets this evening. And a part I felt obliged to occupy in walking. My health ought not to be trifled with, for that is the foundation upon which every man should build.

Afternoon, finished the second book of Cicero de Oratore, and was pleased with all the latter part of it in which he describes the various duties of an Orator, clearly and in brief. A peculiarity of this book is, that in it he makes his Speaker contradict every thing he said in the other. In the evening, I went out to the Debating Society as usual, where we had a pretty good sized Company. The old discussion was continued and finished. I said only a very few words. Wrote a little of my Catalogue, and read two numbers of the Tatler.

¹ LCA had arrived at Hartford after a difficult trip in the evening of the 8th; JQA, after an even more rigorous journey, had joined her in the early afternoon of the 9th. Giving up plans to proceed by land, they took passage on the 10th on the steamboat *Victory* from Hartford to Saybrook and onward to New York on the 11th (LCA to CFA, 9 Dec., Adams Papers; JQA, Diary, 8–11 Dec.).

² The President's message, delivered to the two Houses on 7 Dec., appeared in the *Boston Daily Advertiser*, 11 Dec., p. 2–3.

SUNDAY. 12TH.

Morning bright but quite cold. The weather appears now to have become tolerably settled, and not more severe than one expects at this season. I attended divine service during the day and heard in the morning a discourse from Mr. Palfrey upon the subject of Truth. I do not know, whether I am right but this gentleman does not suit my taste much. He is not very agreeable as a Preacher, and there is a kind of Vinegar Acid in the tone, manner and character of the man, that repels his idea if I may so express it. Took a short walk after service before returning home. My Wife was not well enough to go out today.

As I have been pleased with Chapman's general conduct so far as I have seen any thing of it latterly, and as I have never in any manner taken notice of it, I thought I would ask him to come and dine with me, today. He accordingly came and was very pleasant. His amiable disposition and creditable conduct on the whole have produced rather a favourable impression upon my mind.¹ He went to Meeting with me in the Afternoon and we heard Mr. Frothingham, in a finished Sermon upon Social Worship. On the whole the day was pleasantly passed. I read in the Afternoon some of Enfield's History of Philosophy, and in the Evening conversed with my Wife. Continued upon the Catalogue and read two Numbers of the Tatler.

¹ Following the death of GWA and his own marriage, CFA, in keeping with the reformation he notes in his own be-behavior, had kept aloof socially from most of his old classmates and college friends, particularly those who had shared in his escapades and who re-mained unmarried. Jonathan Chapman

was later mayor of Boston (1840–1842); he also became a contributor to the *North Amer. Rev.* and the *Christian Examiner*. See Winsor, *Memorial History* *of Boston*, 3:247; John Langdon Sibley, Private Journal, p. 171–172 (MS, MHi, deposited in MH-Ar).

MONDAY. 13TH.

Morning clear and quite cold. I went down first to see the Irish Woman, Tenant of my Father's Tenement, and warn her to go out as she pays no rent.[1] This is an unpleasant business but it cannot be helped. I was wrong in letting her come in. Then to the Office where I did my usual duties and went round to pay a visit or two which I saw to be due. One to Mr. Brooks and another to Mr. Davis in his new office.[2] I also went to give in my vote for the City Officers though I could not swallow Mr. Otis. The Working men tried to raise an opposition but it was faint and heartless. Their handbill however made up in violence for their weakness. Mr. Conant called on my return, from Weston with some money on Account and he asked for some repairs which I was obliged to grant. Returned home, and spent the afternoon in reading the third book de Oratore in which I made good progress. The advice given in it, as to the language, and style to be used, applies as well now as it did when it was written. It is writing for all ages and nations. Evening, Corinne with Abby, after which her brother Edward came in and passed the evening, very pleasantly. I had an hour for my Catalogue, and then two numbers of the Tatler.

[1] Mrs. Elizabeth Arey had occupied tenement No. 1 at 101 Tremont Street since 1 Nov. (M/CFA/3).

[2] Thomas Kemper Davis, having been admitted to the bar, had moved into an office at 33 Court Street (*Boston Directory*, 1831–1832).

TUESDAY. 14TH.

Morning cold and cloudy. I went down on my usual walk to see my Irish Tenant, and thence went to the Office. Arranged my usual business and then went down to obtain the Dividend upon the New England Insurance Office Stock which was quite handsome and puts my father's Affairs here quite above Water.[1] This speculation was among the fortunate things of his life. It has saved his affairs here from embarassment several times. And now carries him through what is I hope the last of his undertakings for the Estate of my Grandfather.[2]

I read the short Account of the American Revolution and was pleased with every part of it but the Note in which bad doctrine is taught. In order to ascertain how far it was supported by its Authorities, I went down and read at the Athenæum certain papers written by Mr. Burke at the period when a secession from Parliament was meditated. I did not find what I wanted.[3]

Afternoon, reading Cicero and accomplished another portion of the third book de Oratore, which I had read before superficially. It is very good, and relates to propriety of language. Evening, Corinne and a little of Baroness Minutoli's Recollections of Egypt,[4] after which, more of my Catalogue, and two Numbers of the Tatler.

[1] The dividend received on 108 shares was $864 (M/CFA/3).

[2] In addition to the regular payments due quarterly under the terms of JA's will, portions of the legacies to John Peter de Windt (1786?–1870), Alexander Bryan Johnson (1786–1867), Louisa Catherine Smith, and T. B. Adams Jr. remained unpaid to a total of $485.63 and payable 1 Jan. 1831 (CFA to JQA, 16 Dec., LbC, Adams Papers; Adams Genealogy).

[3] [W. Shepherd], *History of the American Revolution,* London, 1830; a publication in the *Library of Useful Knowledge* issued by the Society for the Diffusion of Useful Knowledge, London. CFA sought corroboration for the statement therein that "when Lord Chatham was taken ill in the House of Lords, he was about to propose his plan for conciliation with America, and ... that this was generally understood to be a kind of *federal union* under the *British Crown*" (CFA to JQA, 16 Dec., LbC, Adams Papers).

[4] Baroness W. A. L. M. von Minutoli, *Recollections of Egypt,* London, 1827.

WEDNESDAY. 15TH.

Morning cloudy and warm with heavy rains, which came on at intervals more like the Summer than this season. I went to the Office, where after talking a little with Mr. Peabody, I sat down to my usual occupations. I read over carefully the pamphlet upon the subject of the Revolution and noted the passages upon which I desired information. Nothing of further moment occurred.

I returned home as usual and in the afternoon resumed and finished Cicero de Oratore. I have on the whole benefitted from this tolerably thorough perusal of this work. And although few ideas in it were new to me as they form the basis of all subsequent doctrines of eloquence, yet I have been a gainer by the study of a clear style, and the perception of beauties which never struck me before. Cicero was perhaps the greatest Master of the Theory of Oratory that ever existed, though perhaps in the practice he may have been equalled by Demosthenes. He understood the influence upon the passions so that when he speaks, we do not feel as if we were listening to a visionary. I should think that this very book was worthy of being always held as a Text book, although the influence of such a man as Edward T. Channing has rejected it at Cambridge.[1]

Evening, Corinne and after it, a visit from Mr. Edmund Quincy, so that I had little or no opportunity to continue my Catalogue, though I read two Numbers of the Tatler.

[1] On Edward Tyrrel Channing, Boylston professor of rhetoric and oratory at Harvard since 1819, for whom JQA and CFA entertained no high regard, and on his approach to the study of oratory, which, according to CFA, gave no emphasis to the classical orators, see vol. 1:176–229 *passim*.

THURSDAY. 16TH.

Morning clear and cold. I walked down to the Tenements to get out my annoyance of an Irish Woman. She has moved herself but one of her Tenants is still in the House and worries me. Thence to the Office where with a few interruptions I was busy nearly all the morning in writing a letter to my Father.[1] I received one from him at New York giving an Account of his progress tolerably amusing.[2] Mr. Jackson, Painter called upon me with his bills which I paid, finding them much larger than I anticipated.[3] This business of Houses requires a very skilful hand. I also had half an hour's conversation with Mr. Peabody.

Afternoon, engaged in copying my letter, and in looking over the Papers of Massachusettensis and Novanglus[4] to discover the point which I think represented in the Society's Pamphlet. I found abundance of matter in it, such as I wanted. Evening, Miss Julia Gorham came to see my Wife and I went out to be present at the Meeting of the Commissioners of Insolvency. Nothing was however done there. Returned and wasted the time excepting a little for my Catalogue and the Tatler.

[1] LbC, Adams Papers. For this letter, see above, entry for 14 Dec., notes, and below, entry for 28 Dec., note.

[2] JQA to CFA, 11–12 Dec., Adams Papers.

[3] Payment to E. Jackson amounted to $45 (M/CFA/3).

[4] On CFA's earlier reading of the "Novanglus" papers, written by JA in answer to Daniel Leonard's "Massachusettensis" papers, see vol. 2:233–240; on the papers themselves, see JA, *Diary and Autobiography*, 2:161; 3:313.

FRIDAY. 17TH.

Morning bright and clear. I went to the Office after having paid my usual visit to the Tenements to see how they are going on. Found the Irish Tenant had moved but the person she left was still there. This is a piece of work. At the Office where after reading some political articles upon the President's message I sat down to arrange what I proposed to say tomorrow at the Meeting of the Debating Society upon the Working Men's Party. I did not make very rapid progress and felt obliged to go to the Athenæum for the purpose of consulting the works upon America in the question that occurs to my mind.

As P. Chardon Brooks had invited Abby and me to dine at his house today, we accordingly went. It is the first time that I have dined there for I do not know how long. We found them pleasant as usual and I returned home in time to accomplish a considerable portion of Cicero's book called Brutus or de claris Oratoribus [1] which seems to be a mere account of such as have enjoyed reputation in the Republics of Athens and Rome. Evening at home. We read a little of Corinne and some of the Baroness Minutoli's Book, after which I made good progress in my Catalogue and read my usual numbers in the Tatler.

[1] In most editions of Cicero's *Opera* this work appeared immediately following the *De Oratore*.

SATURDAY 18TH.

Morning at the Office as usual. Received a letter from my Mother at Philadelphia but in the Account reached no farther than New York. She is well and has passed all the bad portion of the Journey pretty comfortably.[1] My time was passed in arranging what I had to say upon the Working Men's party, after going to Market which I tried this morning. I recollect that long before I was married, I used to laugh at this peculiar duty of Wedded Life in Boston, but on experience I think it is by no means unpleasant. My time is not however very well accounted for. I waste it nearly as badly as ever.

On my return home I designed taking a walk but was stopped by purchasing some Wood, a business I have been contemplating for some time past. This prevented my having a walk of any length. Afternoon, read Cicero de claris Oratoribus which is not over and above interesting. A dry detail of men who never were very distinguished as Orators and now forgotten is but uninteresting reading.

I took an hour to prepare myself for my evening duty, but I felt disinclined to it as I was forced to the wrong side. I went, but did not succeed as well as usual not only from the want of support but from my disbelief of the doctrines. I returned home and read two numbers of the Tatler.

[1] LCA to CFA, 12–15 Dec., Adams Papers; the tone and spirit of the letter indicate a restoration to health.

SUNDAY. 19TH.

The Weather was hazy and portended snow which however did not begin to fall until evening, at least in any quantity. I attended divine Service at the Church in Chauncy Place and heard Mr. Frothingham deliver two Sermons upon what he called the doctrine of Compensation, or the principle by which suffering or privation in one respect, is made up to us by enjoyment or possession in some other. This is in some lights a useful as well as a fascinating doctrine, but will bear application better to past than to future events. A man who shall rely upon happiness merely because he is suffering in misery will be likely to have that misery only increased by the bitterness of disappointment and will be led to forget that permanent dependance which he can justly place only upon the future of a beneficent Deity. This world is one of trial, in which the wicked often succeed, and the good are tried severely, so that compensation to either can only come from the final doom in another and a better world. But I don't design going so deep into this matter. I read a portion of Drake which I found trifling, and some of Hutchinson that convinces me the English Pamphlet is wrong, and some of Enfield's History of Philosophy upon the Greek Schools that was interesting, and some of Corinne, and Baroness Minutoli, after which my Catalogue, and the Tatler.

MONDAY. 20TH.

Morning cloudy and cold. Snow though not in large quantities had fallen during the night. I went to the Office and what with my Journal, my Accounts and the Newspapers I did not leave to myself a great deal of room for what I proposed doing which was to make my affidavit of the sale of the real Estate of Robert New. Being unwilling to have this hang on my mind any longer however, I worked away until I got it completed just ten minutes before the Court adjourned. It was no matter, I got it finished and filed today which puts an end to that business.

After dinner, with a single interruption of a few minutes by an applicant for one of the Tenements, I passed my time in reading Cicero's Brutus in which I made some progress. He gives here some Account of all the persons whom he introduces into his dialogue de Oratore, and this has been much the most interesting portion of it. Mr. Frothingham called but for an instant.

Evening, reading Corinne with my Wife the termination of which we are approaching. I afterwards closed the Recollections of Egypt, a woman's book, though not altogether without interest. Continued my Catalogue and read two numbers of the Tatler.

TUESDAY. 21ST.

Winter in Mr. Sparks almanack[1] is said to begin today, and certainly the weather looked not unlike it when we arose. The snow fell thick and heavily, but it did not last more than two or three hours.

At the Office as usual where I again spent a good deal of time in mere conversation to no useful purpose with my neighbour Mr. Peabody. I did afterwards find a useful hour in reading a book obtained from the Athenæum called acts relating to the Colonies.[2] This assumes the English Ground and it must be admitted reasons it well. Took a walk, in the usual direction of my Tenements, where I had a short and sharp conversation with the occupant of the first one. Then I returned home.

The Afternoon passed in a very rapid reading of a considerable portion of Brutus, with which I was better pleased. I think my acquaintance with the Latin Idiom is in some respects,[3] I am getting to that perfection of being able to take in the sense of a sentence often at a glance, which is the only way of enjoying a language. Evening, some more of Corinne, and having no regular book, I read to my Wife from a novel recommended to her as a good one, Pride and Prejudice.[4] It is not bad. Pursued my Catalogue and read two Numbers of the Tatler.

[1] Jared Sparks, comp., *American Almanac*, Boston, 1830 *et seq.*
[2] [Jonathan Lind], *Remarks on the Principal Acts of the Thirteenth Parliament of Great Britain ..., Vol. 1. Containing Remarks on the Acts Relating to the Colonies with a Plan of Reconciliation*, London, 1775.
[3] Thus in MS; a word is doubtless omitted.
[4] First published in 1813.

WEDNESDAY. 22D.

This was the coldest morning, we have yet experienced this year, and is no very pleasant presage of what we are about to suffer during this winter. I went to the Office this morning and held myself more to occupation than I have done heretofore. I finished the book called Acts relating to the Colonies, in which is condensed very ably all that can be given upon that side. I am not surprised that Englishmen should have held on so tenaciously as they did for to them it must have been convincing reasoning. My Uncle Judge Adams called for half an hour to see me and talk a little. Nothing else remarkable took place. I went to the Athenæum to get out one or two books and called to see Mr. Brooks but felt half frozen.

Afternoon, reading Brutus which I almost completed. The style of the latter part is interesting, more particularly as it gives us an insight into his method of pursuing the study of Oratory. It was highly laborious and moreover, it was in one particular[1] essentially different from any thing that is pursued in our day. We have no Masters of Rhetoric and Philosophy with whom to argue. Do we gain or lose by it? Evening, Corinne and a little of a new book called Nollekens and his times,[2] but Mr. Chapman came in and passed the Evening. Catalogue and Tatler.

[1] MS: "particularly."
[2] John Thomas Smith, *Nollekens and His Times*, 2 vols., London, 1828.

THURSDAY. 23D.

This morning was colder than yesterday and on the whole affords a bitter specimen of the severity of the Winter. I have rarely felt the action of the cold more even when the Thermometer was lower. At the Office as usual, where I read with attention the beginning of the papers of Novanglus, but I have given up the idea of writing upon the subject at present. It is too laborious in this cold weather. I wrote my Journal, and had one or two interruptions with demands to be paid. So my morning passed.

I had engaged with my Wife to dine with Mr. and Mrs. Frothingham so that I went down at the usual time. Nobody there but P. Chardon Brooks. I did not enjoy myself much, and returned only to get two hours of Cicero, but with it, I finished Brutus and began a review, which as usual strikes me much more pleasantly. The style seems then to fall into its place so much more easily. I hope to be able at the close to give a connected opinion about the book.

In the evening, Abby having returned, we sat down to read Corinne as usual, but Edward Brooks came in and passed nearly all of it with us in conversation. I did not sit up so long as usual this evening, as my fire went out but I still wrote in my Catalogue, and some of the Tatler.

FRIDAY. 24TH.

Much milder weather this morning. I went down to the Office as usual. Found there a letter from my Father, requesting information of some missing things, and giving an account of the rest of his Journey. He arrived on the 17th after a pretty fatiguing time of it.[1] My time was passed in reading my Grandfather's letters to Mr. Tudor about the circumstances of the American Revolution.[2] It is singular, but I have read these at least twice before and never have derived from them the kind of information I have now. Probably from the fact that I have obtained more information upon the subject generally.

Took a pretty long walk before dinner and concluded that as my father said he wanted information immediately,[3] I would go out to Quincy at once. So I started with my man Benjamin Sawtell,[4] and arrived there at a little after four. Found Mrs. Kirke had gone into Boston, so that after much delay and hesitation I was compelled to force the window of the second story to get into my father's study, where I found both the Letter book and the Bank book which he missed.[5] Having done this, I hastened to return and arrived at home shortly after seven o'clock in time to read Corinne with my Wife, to accomplish some of my Catalogue and to read a little of the Tatler.

[1] JQA to CFA, 18 Dec., Adams Papers.

[2] During 1817 and 1818 JA wrote a number of letters in which he rehearsed the events precedent to the Revolution as he recollected them. Many of these "Letters from the Hon. John Adams, to the Hon. Wm. Tudor, and Others, on the Events of the American Revolution" were published as an appendix (p. 229–312) to a collected edition of *Novanglus and Massachusettensis...*, Boston, 1819.

[3] JQA was fearful that his bankbook

and letterbook had been mislaid in one of the many trying episodes of the journey to Washington, or had been stolen. However, he admitted the possibility that they had been left behind in Quincy and therefore wished a search made (JQA to CFA, 18 Dec., Adams Papers).

[4] Earlier: "Salter." See entry for 6 July, above.

[5] A fuller account of this expedition is contained in CFA to JQA, 25 Dec., Adams Papers.

SATURDAY. 25TH.

Christmas day and a very stormy one. It did not prevent me from going to the Office as I considered that staying at home was impossible from the danger of smoke in my study in such a day. I was entirely uninterrupted and passed my time in examining the sayings of the seven wise Men found in Enfield's History of Philosophy and copying them with my own reflections attached to each.[1] They appear to me to embody much real wisdom. I also wrote to my Father a letter which engrossed all the rest of the time left to me.[2] The afternoon was also spent in copying the same, and in reading some few Pamphlets connected with the History of the Revolutionary Struggle. This took up all the Afternoon.

Evening passed partly in reading one of Jouy's publications[3] with my Wife in which however she did not take so much interest as I hoped. We were interrupted by Edward Brooks who again came in and talked very pleasantly during a part of the evening. He has latterly come here a great deal, and I am very glad to have him. For he talks pleasantly enough. I finished a volume of my Catalogue this evening, and read two Numbers of the Tatler.

[1] Certain of the apothegms of the so-called seven wise men of Greece were entered by CFA in a commonplace book originally used by GWA (now M/GWA/9 in Adams Papers). To each he added a paragraph of commentary or reflection; to the whole he gave the title "Elements of Knowledge." This was the same title

which GWA had given to the entries he had made in the commonplace book, and it is clear from CFA's note between GWA's entries and his own that he intended his to be a continuation of his brother's and something of a tribute to him:

"This volume is one of the remaining memorials of an unfortunate brother, and presents at its commencement one of the best specimens of his mind within my knowledge. *O! si sic omnia.* Had perseverance only been his to fill the sketch he was so fully able to lay out, perhaps he would still have been among us, our pride and support. But since it was not the will of Providence that it should be thus, all that remains to me is to benefit as much by his good purposes as I can, and supply the deficiencies which in him prevented their execution. I therefore adopt here all that has been inserted and shall con-

tinue the extracts, varying only my method of making them as I think may be most advisable. Boston, Decr. 25th 1830" (Adams Papers, Microfilms, Reel No. 295).

[2] CFA to JQA, 25 Dec., Adams Papers. For this letter, see below, entry for 29 Dec., note.

[3] Copies of a number of works by Victor Joseph Etienne deJouy are in MQA, particularly those which are descriptive of countries or cities and in which the central figure is a solitary or wanderer.

SUNDAY. 26TH.

This was a lovely day more like the softer air of the Spring Season than the weather common at this time of the year. My Wife went with me to Meeting in the morning, and I went alone in the Afternoon. The Sermons by Mr. Frothingham were in the morning upon the nativity of Christ as a moral lesson in it's Anniversary, in the afternoon, the close of the year. I thought neither of them in his best style. He labours too much. The finish of every sentence is the close of an idea, so that the next comes after it, without any absolute dependence upon that which has preceded it. My own notions of beauty are so different, they depend so much upon what I call flow in which the ideas seem almost to suggest themselves in a train of harmony, that I cannot listen long to Mr. F. without feeling fatigued.

At home I was occupied the remainder of the day and evening in reading Middleton's Life of Cicero over,[1] and I was surprised to find how little impression it had made upon me before. If this is to be always the result, I can think of no other fate but that of the daughters of Ixion. Am I right? for it is so long since I am forgetting mythology and have no means here of ascertaining.[2] My Wife read her usual portion of French this evening. I could not continue my Catalogue having no blank book but I read the Tatler.

[1] CFA had read Conyers Middleton's *Cicero* in Jan. 1828; see vol. 2:200–210 *passim.*

[2] Perhaps CFA is thinking rather of the story of Ixion himself who, despite divine favor and forgiveness, repeated and magnified his earlier transgressions, profiting less from experience than any other figure in mythology.

MONDAY. 27TH.

The day was one of heavy and constant rain and very dark. I went to the Office as usual and enjoyed a very quiet uninterrupted morning.

I passed my time in finishing my Accounts and settling their several balances for this Quarter, and in writing some more Notes upon the sayings of the Ancient Wise men. My plan was at first merely to transcribe them but afterwards extended itself to commenting upon each. Perhaps it is of no value, but it gives me room for reflection upon what I read. And this is the thing I want. I then sat down and read in the same style two or three of the Essays of Lord Bacon, one on Despatch, another upon Studies, which are wonderful concentrations of wisdom. This power of embodying thought, is the only thing truly valuable. The rest is secondary.

After dinner, I continued my review of Brutus which I had commenced two or three days since and progressed very considerably in it. Most of the early part however is hardly worth a review. Evening, with my Wife reading L'Hermite en Londres.[1] John Gorham, Miss Julia's brother came in soon after and spent the evening. I began the second part of my Catalogue and read the two Numbers of the Tatler.

[1] *L'hermite de Londres* ... is one of the works by deJouy in MQA; 3 vols., Paris, 1821–1822.

TUESDAY. 28TH.

Morning mild and pleasant. Went to the Office as usual, and received a letter from my father at considerable length, in which he answers a casual expression of mine which seems to have touched him considerably. The tone of his reply is painful as he seems to feel very unpleasantly. I regret that any thing I did could have induced such a feeling, more especially as I was very far from intending anything of the kind.[1] He has written me nothing of business matters which is another subject of regret as I had hoped to have acted upon good information and authority before the first of January.[2]

I was occupied as usual in prosecuting my affairs of business upon the coming Quarter, and in writing more Comment upon the Wise sayings. I then went down to the Athenæum and obtained some books for my study of Cicero. John Gorham dined with us today. Afternoon occupied in reading Brutus thirty Chapters of which I reviewed, it grows better towards it's close. On the whole it is interesting as a History of Oratory in the principal Ages of it's existence.

Evening, after accomplishing a considerable portion of L'Hermite en Londres, I read to my Wife for the rest of the evening from Evelina one of Miss Burney's Novels, and a very amusing one.[3] After which I continued my Work upon my Catalogue and read two Numbers of the Tatler.

[1] The letter from JQA (22 Dec., Adams Papers) is, in effect, an explanation and apologia of his concerns and activities during 1829 and 1830, and of those pursuits which he had had to postpone or abandon during that period; it is moreover a renewed defense of his decision to stand for election to Congress. The letter had been provoked by CFA's remark in his letter to his father of 16 Dec. (LbC, Adams Papers): "I always desire to obtain something from your knowledge which may be advantageous to me in my own occupations. I must confess that in the *whole* of my expectations for last Summer, I was somewhat disappointed. The preceding Season had raised them too high, the Washington Winter had turned your attention too exclusively to the present state of things, and it was not until about the period of your return there that I began to retrace what I saw the year before. This may be speaking very freely but I trust not disrespectfully."

JQA's interpretation of his remark continued to trouble CFA, who several times entered a disclaimer of broad intent. He wrote definitively on 9 Jan. 1831 (CFA to JQA, LbC, Adams Papers): "To constitute myself a Judge upon the suitable employment of your time never entered into my head and I hope never will."

[2] JQA's reply to CFA's questions on business matters was made in a separate letter on 25 Dec. (Adams Papers).

[3] First published in 1778.

WEDNESDAY. 29TH.

The day was a very pleasant one, and seems to be paying with the rest of our present week for the severity of the past. I went to the Office as usual and performed my usual work besides giving some attention to what is now my amusement, writing Commentaries upon the sayings of the wise men.

Two interruptions. Mr. Veazie is the Carpenter at Quincy who came in to see about the Posts about which Mr. Beale and I were talking. I discussed with him many points in relation to the old House, and concluded by asking him to provide estimates for the Stone, after which I would talk with him. This is a good opportunity to make a permanent improvement in respect to the externals of the old house and one which I should think it not undesirable to embrace.[1] Mr. Taylor called about my Uncle, the Judge's accident and asked me to interfere in his favour, which I declined wholly to do. I wonder what people will come for next. If the Judge will not pay, I suppose they think his friends must.

I also drew my few bills for professional Services which I may claim on the New Year. I wish they were more. Afternoon, finished Brutus and began the Orator which Middleton says was designed as a completion of the whole subject in connection. It seems to me by far the most finished piece of writing. The commencement of it is beautiful, but there is a little repetition. Evening, L'Hermite with my Wife, and Evelina aloud to her, after which, I went on with my Catalogue, and read two Numbers of the Tatler.

[1] The wooden posts supporting the fence on the side of the Old House had been renewed, but when work was begun on the front fence it was found that all new posts would be needed. It was the opinion of Mr. Beale and CFA that it was opportune to replace the gateposts with stone ones; that at least estimates should be secured (CFA to JQA, 25 Dec., Adams Papers). In his reply JQA approved replacement of the posts with ones constructed of hammered stone (JQA to CFA, 30 Dec., Adams Papers).

THURSDAY. 30TH.

Another very pleasant day. I went to the Office as usual and spent my time in preparing my Accounts for the Quarter, in writing my Journal and in continuing the Comments upon the Wise Men. All this took up much time.

The European news seems to give notice of an impending War,[1] the effect of which upon this Country remains to be seen. Probably it may be favourable for England though striving will hardly be able to keep perfectly clear.[2] I went in to see how Stocks were affected, and was surprised to notice the rise. They are enormously high.

I went to dine with Mr. and Mrs. Frothingham where Mr. Brooks also dined. It was very well, returned in the afternoon and found a Client, Mr. Champney in search of me. He wished to secure a debt of his, due by a Cabinet Maker for whom he had been building. His business occupied me for the afternoon and part of the evening. I made two Writs for him, read a little French with my Wife, and a little of Evelina, after which I went on with my Catalogue and read the Tatler.

[1] The latest dispatches from Europe indicated that affairs had assumed "a much more warlike aspect" and suggested that "a general war in Europe is at least probable." In England Wellington's ministry had fallen and there were disorders in London; on the Continent the separation of Belgium from the Netherlands had been effected with great destruction of property in Antwerp and a blockade of the Belgian ports by the Dutch, the death of the king of Naples had further unsettled matters in Italy, there had been further changes in the cabinet in France, Prussian troops were reported collecting along the Belgian border, and, most ominous of all, Russia was assembling a large army on her frontier and, it was rumored, had declared war against France, largely as a consequence of the overthrow of the monarchy and the accession of Louis-Philippe. Failures of banking houses in various cities accompanied the crisis. (*Boston Daily Advertiser*, 29 Dec., p. 2, cols. 1–2; 30 Dec., p. 2, cols. 1–5.)

[2] Thus in MS. By supplying commas following "favourable," "England," and "striving" a satisfactory reading is attained. The meaning would be as follows: Probably the effect of a war in Europe upon this country would be favorable, for England, though striving to keep perfectly clear of such a war, will hardly be able to do so.

FRIDAY. 31ST.

Morning dark and rainy. I went to the Office as usual, and was very much occupied in preparing my Accounts due at the close of this

Quarter and in drawing up my Letter in explanation of the Affairs of the whole year,[1] which engrossed all the time I had at my disposal, and more too, for I was taken up for two or three hours with an attempt to arrange the difference between my Clients and the person they had sued, but the whole conversation resulted in nothing, and I returned home some time after my dinner hour. The Afternoon was spent in the same manner copying what I had done in the morning. This work is on the whole rather tedious and somewhat exclusive, for it puts an entire stop to the regular train of study which is my delight.

Evening, we were just going on with our usual French studies when we were interrupted by Chapman my Classmate who came and passed a tolerably agreeable evening. I went on afterwards with my Catalogue and read two numbers of the Tatler. How different from the evening of last year. Yet to me how much more pleasant.

[1] CFA to JQA, 31 Dec., LbC, Adams Papers. For the most part the review was a comparison of the physical condition of JQA's Boston real estate holdings at the end of 1829 and of 1830, of the income received from them, and of the cost of repairs.

JANUARY. 1831

SATURDAY. 1ST.

Another year has come upon us, and has opened opportunity for reflection. The past is matter for consideration, the future for improvement. Though I have striven to do my best, yet I feel conscious of time misapplied and purposes unexecuted. I have laboured with some assiduity and I have not improved in proportion. When I look back upon the course of years however, I feel a reason to congratulate myself for the fortunate dispensations of Providence towards me, and to be reasonably gratified with my own situation. Fears which once tormented me have been dissipated, anxieties have been soothed, and on the other hand, desires have been gratified and hopes exalted.[1] When I consider in how many respects I am happy, my heart is full of gratitude, and I constantly warn myself as a lesson that this world is not permanent, to keep in mind not to be unduly elated, or to cease to exert myself to deserve as much as I can, the good gifts of a Deity. I have been faulty in many respects, I have indulged perhaps too much in the dreams which youth and success will excite, I have not laboured to deserve the claims which my vanity suggests to me to make, this is all matter to turn to profitable use in future and not unnecessarily to mourn over it now. One thing I may fairly pride myself upon, that I am not sensible of having done any thing for which to be ashamed. But enough of this.

I went to the Office after spending an hour trying to find for my Wife something for her to give to Mrs. Frothingham. She has made me a very pretty little gift of the kind, in an Inkstand for my Study. Her heart is full of affection. I was busy at the Office in making out my new Year's Accounts, and went to pay Miss Louisa C. Smith, her amount of Legacy left on the second Distribution of the Estate of My Grandfather. As my Wife and Mrs. Frothingham had gone out of town to dine I remained a little later at the Office and dined at Fenno's.[2]

This day my long written Article upon Grahame appeared, and I read it in the North American Review,[3] but so altered, I might say mutilated that it gave me no pleasure. On the whole, I have gained my point, but I do not know whether I shall not *now* be disappointed in the result. Perhaps instead of a forward it may be a backward step. Read a part of the Orator but it is difficult. Evening, attended the Debating Society and was put in the Chair. Returned late, but sat down to Catalogue as usual and read the Tatler.

[1] The first recorded allusion that CFA allowed himself to the fact that ABA was pregnant.

[2] William Fenno was the proprietor of a coffeehouse on Cornhill Square (*Boston Directory*, 1830–1831).

[3] *North Amer. Rev.*, 32:174–195

(Jan. 1831). The essay has recently been the subject of laudatory comments; see Michael Kraus, *The Writing of American History*, Norman, Okla., 1953, p. 99, 106; Duberman, *CFA*, p. 40–41. But see also entry for 23 Feb., below.

SUNDAY. 2D.

The day was pleasant although the weather was cool. I attended Meeting with my Wife in the morning and alone in the afternoon. Heard Mr. Frothingham preach a Sermon upon the opening of the year, and my Classmate Cunningham in the Afternoon on the same. I do not think the latter will be likely to take very much among the good people of Boston. I could not realise to myself that in that pulpit stood the man whom I had formerly known so well, and who was now trying to assume a tone which my preconceived notions of him made me feel to be unsuitable. His address is artificial, and his style far too figurative for the times.[1] I could not help reflecting what a severe hand had corrected my style, giving no Quarter to my Flowers, which were mere daisies along side of this man's lilies and Tulips. I afterwards read Middleton, in whom I made some progress. But not with much earnestness. My studies seem now a little aback. Evening, just as we were sitting down to read a little French, Edward Blake came in and spent an hour. He was quite pleasant. And after he left us, we had little inclination to resume. I went on however with my Catalogue and read the Tatler.

[1] CFA's earlier impressions of Francis Cunningham were not dissimilar to those he here expresses; see vol. 1:232–272 *passim*. What was worthy of remark was that those characteristics of style were now employed in the pulpit.

MONDAY. 3D.

Morning pleasant. I went to the Office, and was occupied nearly the whole of the morning in paying bills which were crowding in upon me. My father's considerably exceed the estimates I had formed and mine do not fall short. It is on the whole lucky that we are both decently provided. My Finances are rather intricate things as I manage them, but still I think I always see day through them. I had not any time to spare, as Mr. Boyd again called upon me in his case, which he was a little hasty in suing.

Returned home to dine and passed the afternoon in reading the Orator. I have been so much dissatisfied with my progress in it heretofore that I began over again to read it thoroughly and accomplished fifteen or sixteen sections in a proper manner. My studies must be more thoroughly attended to. Evening was passed in reading L'Hermite en Londres with my Wife, and also in continuing Evelina. But she was suffering so much that she seemed in no kind of spirits. I feel anxious about her present situation as it is a change from the past. After she retired, I continued my Catalogue lazily and read my regular Numbers of the Tatler.

TUESDAY. 4TH.

Morning doubtful but the present is an uncommonly mild time. I forgot yesterday to mention a Meeting of the Directors of the Middlesex Canal at Mr. W. Appleton's Office [1] upon the reduction of rates. The question was upon receiving the report of the Committee in favour of an agreement with the Concord and Boston Boating Company, by which they may be able to reduce their amount of freight. I assented to the proposal as an experiment but I am somewhat inclined to think that at this moment when the cry is out against Corporations, it is rather injudicious to both for one to throw a monopoly into the hands of the other. Nobody however expressed any such opinion. This ought to have been in yesterday's record.

I did very little but in the way of Accounts this morning. The Judge came up and I settled with him, and my Clients told me their business was settled, for which I am glad. I went to take a walk. My Wife is quite unwell and I feel for her. Afternoon reading the Orator which I still find great difficulty in understanding. My spirits are somehow or other very middling. Why, I cannot conceive for I have enough to be thankful for. But my progress is not what I want it to be. Evening, reading Evelina and French, after which I made considerable progress in my Catalogue and read the Tatler.

[1] The counting room of William Appleton, a director of the Middlesex Canal Company, was at 54 State Street (*Boston Directory*, 1831–1832).

WEDNESDAY. 5TH.

Morning very mild but inclining to rain, which came in torrents in the course of the afternoon. I went to the Office and received a letter from my Father very short, authorizing me to do what I liked about the Stone posts at Quincy.[1] Mr. Brown called to see me about some Shares of the Suffolk Insurance Office which I wanted and after conversation I agreed upon taking twelve for myself and three for T. B. Adams Jr. and thus getting rid of his balance. This is an attempt on my part, to make use of the floating balance of Money in my hands. I am sensible that there is hazard in it, and it may lead to much more and looser risks. This must be regulated by my Judgment.[2] Mr. Curtis called to pay me my Fees for Mr. Boylston's Estate and I obtained the Dividends upon different Stocks. The Tenants pay amazing slowly this Quarter.

Took a walk and returned home to dine at P. Chardon Brooks's. Found my Wife so unwell she could not go, so I went alone. Mr. Brooks was there and our dinner was agreeable enough. Returned home and read the Orator which is excessively hard and technical. It requires severe reviewing. Evening, read Evelina to my Wife and after she retired, prosecuted my Catalogue and read two Numbers of the Tatler.

[1] JQA to CFA, 30 Dec. 1830, Adams Papers.
[2] The shares were bought at $38.66 each. The funds for Thomas B. Adams Jr.'s investment were derived from the distribution made by the executors of the estate of JA. CFA's investment was made largely from funds on hand in the Robert New estate, a part of which represented CFA's compensation as executor (M/CFA/3; M/CFA/9). On the apparent impropriety, uncharacteristic of CFA, see further, the following entry.

THURSDAY. 6TH.

Morning very bright and clear, but somewhat colder than it has been. I went to the Office as usual and passed my time reading and occupied with my affairs which plague me not a little. I have left myself with rather too small a balance to do any thing, and I believe on the whole this shall be the last time I ever make such difficult experiments. If I did not feel every day the necessity of so extending my means as to meet the prospect of increased expenses, I should not expose myself to such straits, but I will not ask my father for any thing more, and I feel too much pride to think of being any farther assisted by my Wife's. It is true my progress must be slow, but if I see the means of helping myself I feel as if I ought to use them reasonably. I have inquired of my Father whether he would invest his money which he has declined doing so that it lies in my hands together with New's, without any call or use. Now I invest it to secure a Dividend in April and if by that time I cannot pay for the Stock out of my Income, to sell some other stock which may be likely to be less profitable.

I read a good deal of Enfield and reviewed the whole doctrine of Plato, which I am glad to know a little better. At one I returned home, as we were invited to go to Medford, and started with Mrs. Frothingham, my Wife and Chardon Brooks in the Carriage. Our ride was pleasant and we found there Mr. Gorham Brooks and his Wife with Mrs. Everett and Miss Phillips. The dinner was as usual, and we returned home after which I read Evelina to Abby, continued my Catalogue and read two numbers of the Tatler.

FRIDAY. 7TH.

Morning bright and clear. Mr. Ayer brought me this morning his Account which was not a little startling as it amounted to nearly double of my estimate.[1] I was a little shocked at this excess as by some strange chance the thing has happened in almost every other bill as well as this. At the Office where I was busy in reading and accounts as usual. I have been on the whole more troubled about Accounts this year than I ever was before. I accomplished however some portion of Enfield's History of the School of Aristotle.

Returned home and spent the remainder of the day in reading the Orator. Miss Julia Gorham dined here. The difficulty of the Orator is hardly paid by it's value for the whole doctrine of number is to us of little consequence. I finished it superficially and began a review.

Evening, about to read Evelina but was soon interrupted by Edmund Quincy who spent the Evening. After which I accomplished a little of my Catalogue and read the Tatler.

[1] CFA paid T. Ayer for his work on the rental property $177 (M/CFA/3).

SATURDAY. 8TH.

Morning clear. Mr. Ayer called after my leaving my House and followed me to the Office from whence I started with him to see the Houses in Tremont Street. I gave him such directions that I think they will soon be clear. Returned to the Office and was busy for much of the morning in settling the bills due by the Estate of Mr. New and drawing up an Account to present next Week. I also had the usual number of interruptions to pay bills, but none to receive money which a little shocks me.

In the afternoon I sat down and reviewed quite thoroughly the first half of the Orator, and found it improve[s] considerably upon acquaintance. After which I was engaged in writing a letter to my Father which did not satisfy my taste at all. This took all the time I had at my disposal, although my Wife had gone to her brother Chardon's to tea, until the usual time of Meeting for the Debating Society which I attended and heard an Argument upon Lawyer's Fees in which I take none but a practical Interest. So I took no part in the discussion, and went to Chardon's at nine o'clock, where I met Mr. Coit and young Mr. Oliver.[1] A pleasant Supper and return home at ten o'clock, when I continued my Catalogue and read the Tatler.

[1] Oliver was probably a cousin of Mrs. Chardon Brooks; see vol. 2:162.

SUNDAY 9TH.

Winter having kept off so long again comes down upon us with great force. The earth was covered with snow upon our rising in the morning, and it continued to fall the greater part of the day. I attended Divine Service this morning and heard a Mr. Malcolm, a Baptist Clergyman,[1] preach at Mr. Frothingham's. This rather surprised me, for such a degree of liberality is not usual, but upon hearing his Sermon against spiritual pride, or the pride of virtue, I was very much pleased. His manner strikes me as in many respects superior to any Clergyman's I have heard in Boston, and had it a little more impressiveness and grace would be calculated to strike very much generally. Any thing is better than tameness and his manner at times is decidedly eloquent.

It was so inclement, that I did not venture out in the afternoon, so that I employed my time in finishing and copying my letter to my Father,[2] which engrossed the whole time. This business takes up a good deal of valuable time and perhaps not so usefully as could be, for my letters do not improve.

Evening at home very quietly reading Evelina to my Wife, which I finished. This reading hardly pays one for the time. Continued my Catalogue afterwards which is now drawing to a close and read two Numbers of the Tatler.

¹ Howard Malcom, minister of the Federal Street Baptist Church, Boston (*Mass. Register*, 1831).
² CFA to JQA, 9 Jan., LbC, Adams Papers. For this letter, see above, entry for 28 Dec. 1830, note, and below, entry for 25 Jan., note.

MONDAY. 10TH.

This Snow makes every thing cheerless, and my walk to the Office very disagreeable. I went however and was busy in making up my Accounts at the Probate Office on Mr. News Estate. This took much time in waiting, and the business was not settled after all. But it is off my thoughts for the present. Mr. Champney called in to bargain about a House, but I could not come to any decision. On the whole my morning as usual is not to be accounted for and yet I feel as if I had done my best. But so it is, and I almost despair of any decided improvement.

Returned home and spent the afternoon in reading the Orator in which I now made great progress. Having cut the road, it is very easy now to smooth it. But the doctrine it contains is as useless now as it was before. Because we have lost the Art upon which it is based, and do not even know the pronunciation of the ancient Romans.

Evening at home quietly. Read French with my Wife and then read to her during the Evening from Camilla, another of Miss Burney's books.¹ Progressed with my Catalogue and read the Tatler.

¹ Published in 1796.

TUESDAY. 11TH.

The Snow was thick enough to make very good sleighing, and the Streets looked very lively. I went to the Office as usual, and passed my time in writing my Journal and reading Enfield's Philosophy, in which I made progress as far as the Cynic Philosophy. This is a very useful book and I am a little surprised I never took hold of it sooner. It has given me a better insight into the doctrines of the different Masters whose names we see perpetually in the Classics, than I ever possessed before. How much knowledge we ought to possess before even starting to read the older Authors, and yet we touch them first in boyhood when we do not even understand the Language, much less the multiplicity of allusions to mythology, philosophy, religion, habits and manners. No wonder there is so little taste for the Dead Languages.

My time was cut in halves by being obliged to go and see my Cousin Miss A. S. Adams who was in town, expecting to receive her Quarterly Interest. This however saved my going out of town as I had intended. After dinner I finished the Orator with which I have been on the whole edified. Though part of it is mysterious, yet it contains a vast deal of excellent matter to be practically exercised. The whole business of the choice of words, how vastly different from our Teachers. Yet who compares with Cicero in the most unerring test, success.

Evening. Began A Year in Spain, a new book by a young New York man.[1] Quite lively. Continued my Catalogue and read the Tatler.

[1] Alexander Slidell Mackenzie, *A Year in Spain*, Boston, 1829.

WEDNESDAY. 12TH.

Morning cloudy and mild, but it cleared off and became colder during the day. I went to the Office as usual, and with a few interruptions was engaged in arranging my Accounts which are very much in want of assistance, and in reading Enfield in which I made considerable progress. But this broken way of reading the Book makes it much less profitable and instructive than if I could have a continuity of time. My visitors were Mr. Forbes, Stable Keeper to be paid, a person about one of the Tenements and Mr. Sega about a subscription.

Returned home after taking a walk, and had Mr. Brooks to dine with us. After he went away, I pursued my study of Cicero by beginning the Topica, addressed to Trebatius, and owing to the great difficulty I had in understanding the great variety of allusions to their particular habits and laws, I thought ten Sections quite a Quantity of Work. Evening at home, reading French and continuing the very spirited book on Spain. After which, I continued my Catalogue which has arrived at W. and read two Numbers of the Tatler.

THURSDAY. 13TH.

The Season began again to show itself this morning in a severe degree of Cold. I went to the Office as usual, and from thence to an Auction Room where were to be sold two or three books that I wanted very much.[1] It is my rule to buy no books, yet how often I infringe upon it. Today however I really did not repent, for such a work as Middleton's Life of Cicero is to me almost necessary in my present pursuit and certainly beneficial.[2] To keep a work of that kind out of the Athenæum would be impossible so long as I must want it, and to buy a good Copy of it at Auction prices is rare. I also obtained Guthrie's translation of Cicero's Offices,[3] which is a valuable though not so very desirable an acquisition. Read Enfield at my Office and finished the History of the Ionic School which is a principal branch of Ancient Philosophy. But the Book must be often referred to, in order to fix the knowledge I acquire.

After dinner, reading the rest of the Topica, which is short, in this case a recommendation for it is both dry and difficult. Much of it the same with what is found in the books de Inventione and both taken from Aristotle. I began to review them also, for one reading does but clear the way. Evening, continued reading the book upon Spain, and much pleased with it. After which, I worked upon the Catalogue, until I brought it down to X which is cheering. Also read the usual numbers of the Tatler.

[1] The sale of "a collection of valuable books" began at 9:30 A.M. in Cunningham's Auction Room at Milk and Federal streets (*Boston Daily Advertiser*, 13 Jan., p. 3, col. 5).

[2] CFA's copy is in MQA; see vol. 2:200.

[3] The copy in MQA with CFA's bookplate is of the edition published at London in 1820.

FRIDAY. 14TH.

Morning cold again and clear. I went to the Office as usual and occupied myself with writing. Conversation with my opposite Neighbour Mr. Peabody, and reading Enfield in which I accomplished a portion of the book containing the Account of Pythagoras and his School. But day after day I find the insufficiency of my time. I received a letter from my Father[1] informing me of his paying Mr. Johnson[2] which puts me at ease about my funds here although the two Tenants, Spear and Oliver have failed to pay. This will not do at all. Miss Oliver owes now $250. Went to the Athenæum to pay my annual subscription and to try and find a book, but as I really could not see one that I felt as if I wanted, I only obtained a couple for my Wife and went home.

After dinner I continued and finished the review of the Topica, in which I was much helped by reading one of my father's Lectures upon the subject.[3] He seems fully to have studied and written from Antiquity, and I think his Book is much less valued than it should be.

In the Evening, we read French and I continued A Year in Spain to my Wife, after which I put a finishing hand to that Catalogue which has been so long in labour. This is truly delightful as it leaves room for an hour or two more of reading. I this evening accomplished a considerable portion of the North American Review, especially a heretical Article on the U.S. Bank by Mr. Bancroft.[4] After which, two Numbers of the Tatler.

[1] JQA to CFA, 7 Jan., Adams Papers. For this letter, see below, entry for 25 Jan., note.

[2] See above, entry for 14 Dec. 1830.

[3] In the *Lectures on Rhetoric and Oratory* by JQA, the "Topics" was the subject of lecture No. 9 (1:207–228).

[4] The article by George Bancroft on the "Bank of the United States" appeared in the *North Amer. Rev.*, 32:21–64 (Jan. 1831). The argument is directed against the conclusions stated in the report on the Bank written by George McDuffie of South Carolina as chairman of the Committee of Ways and Means of the House of Representatives, 13 April 1830. CFA discussed the article at some length and with reservations in his letter to JQA, 15 Jan., LbC, Adams Papers.

SATURDAY. 15TH.

It had been the intention for us to go to Medford and pass the Sunday, but we had not arisen more than an hour before a violent snow Storm set in from the North East and continued throughout the day. I went to the Office and was busy first in my usual affairs and afterwards in writing my weekly letter to my father.[1] This and Conversation with Mr. Peabody occupied me until time to return home.

The Storm was such as not to allow of a fire in my Study. I therefore pursued my occupation of copying my letter at home. After which I went on with Middleton's Life of Cicero. It does not meet my wants exactly as it contains only a sketch of his Actions and the History of the Period. This is interesting and valuable but not what I most need which is a Critique upon his Works.

In the evening French and the account of Spain to my Wife which is more and more pleasant as I go on. After which, for the first time, an uninterrupted space in which to read the North American Review, Article Hieroglyphics,[2] and the Tatler.

[1] CFA to JQA, 15 Jan., LbC, Adams Papers.

[2] The authorship of the article, which centered upon the contributions of Champollion, is attributed to Edward Everett; *North Amer. Rev.*, 32:95–127 (Jan. 1831).

SUNDAY. 16TH.

The Storm had abated very little when we arose this morning, and it continued during the day, piling its heaps around us. We have had no such storms for two years. I did not stir out of the House all day. My occupation was reading Middleton's Life of Cicero, and Drake's Account of the Authors of the British Essayists, which last in it's original shape I concluded. On the whole I have not experienced disadvantage from this reading. It has given me a view of the History of

Essay Writing in England which I had not before. The acquisition of new ideas is always of value. The same Author has continued the History since the age of Addison and Steele, which I propose also to examine.[1] I did not feel the pressure of time and accomplished a good deal.

Evening, reading to my Wife, from the Book upon Spain. This work of Mr. Slidell's[2] is really an acquisition in it's way, it does credit to our Country. I afterwards read the North American Review, Article, The American System,[3] which is a good Commentary upon Mr. Cambreleng's miserable misrepresentation of our affairs—A statesman who is for setting a foreign Country over his own by a series of perversions of fact. After this, I read my regular quantity of the Tatler.

[1] Nathan Drake, *Essays, Biographical, Critical, and Historical, Illustrative of the Rambler, Adventurer, and Idler,* 2 vols., London, 1809–1810.
[2] Thus in MS; the reference is to the book by Alexander Slidell Mackenzie.
[3] *North Amer. Rev.,* 32:127–174 (Jan. 1831); A. H. Everett was the author.

MONDAY. 17TH.

The Streets presented quite an extraordinary appearance this morning as the snow lay piled in heaps on every side. The People however turned out with great alacrity and began to clear out the paths for people riding, and walking. The horses had great difficulty to keep their course, as the snow was removed from the sidewalks only to be piled in their way.

Occupied at the Office with my Journal and with writing out a sketch of some papers on the present state of public affairs but the spirit does not yet come to me. Returned home after a walk to the Athenæum to get a book or two. Afternoon, reading the Oratoriæ Partitiones of Cicero which appears to be a mere summary of what has already been said, in the shape of a Dialogue between himself and his Son. It was therefore uninteresting although I succeeded in accomplishing one half of it. After what has preceded, it is not difficult.

Read French with my Wife and then continued the Year in Spain which gave us a clear sketch of a Spanish Bull Feast. My Ideas of Spain have obtained some clearness by this book. Afterwards, I began a book called Rhetorices Contractæ Libri 4 by Gerard Voss.[1] It is a mere abridgment of Cicero and Quinctilian, and after them is hardly worth the trouble of reading. Two Numbers of the Tatler.

[1] An edition published at Amsterdam in 1685 of Gerard J. Vossius' *Rhetorices contractæ, sive partitionum oratoriarum lib. V,* is in MQA.

Morning clear and pleasant. I went to the Office where after arranging my Accounts and crediting my Tenant Miss Oliver for the Money she has at last paid, I sat down to read Enfield whom I pursued with perseverance enough to finish the sketch of the Italic School, and the doctrines of Epicurus, which seem by no means so unreasonable as one would suppose from imagining those to be his which now bear his name. Pleasure is the chief good in life. Who denies it. But No syllogism should be formed upon this basis until the word Pleasure is defined. Epicurus explained it very correctly, his followers made it a Cloak for the indulgence of their Passions. And he has borne the public condemnation of Centuries for their Crimes. Such is the Justice of posterity.

Took a walk and returned home. The air was fine though cold. After dinner I continued and finished the Oratoriæ Partitiones of Cicero, and began a review of it. It wants interest but is a valuable Summary of the whole doctrine. I know not why I should read Vossius beside who only borrows the same substance, but I did continue him in the evening. And read Spain to my Wife. Afterwards the Tatler.

Morning clear and pleasant. Went to the Office as usual and was busy in writing my Journal, and drawing up my Accounts. Obtained the Dividend upon my fathers Stock in the Life Office which is steady and high. These two late receipts re-establish pro tempore my Father's Affairs. I am prepared to meet the larger demands upon him occasioned by his repairs at Quincy. I began the Second Volume of Enfield also, with the History of Philosophy among the Romans, and was rather surprised at the estimate which is formed of Cicero and of Cato. But it agrees with my natural feelings. Took a walk, where I was met by Edmund Quincy who is a terrific pedestrian.

After dinner, continued the review of the Partitiones Oratoriæ but I scarcely yet understand the full distinction which is drawn between the different portions of Oratory. First comes the general division, between the qualities of the Orator, those of the Oration, and what is called the question. These are each subdivided so as to produce confusion. I am not fully master of the ramifications. Read French and the book upon Spain to my Wife, who is yet scarcely able to listen, after which I continued the second book of Vossius upon the different affections. After which read two numbers of the Tatler.

THURSDAY. 20TH.

The Weather looked very much as if it was going to give us snow for the day, but instead, after a few flakes it cleared away and became cold. I went to the Office as usual, and was occupied in reading Enfield's Account of the Alexandrian Philosophy which is less interesting than the preceding portion of the work. For it presents a sad spectacle of the utter waste of human abilities. Took a walk with J. Chapman whom I happened to meet, and afterwards Mr. G. Lunt,[1] with both of whom I had a pleasant conversation.

I then went according to agreement to dine at Mrs. Frothingham's where were my Wife and Mr. Brooks, in order to be near and attend the funeral of poor Mrs. Sargent.[2] She is at last dead after a lingering illness. What a change since I was last in her House. Then I went to congratulate and sup with her immediately upon her Wedding.[3] Now it was to follow her to the last repository of mortal clay. But I remember still more strongly when she was a lively and blooming girl at Medford in the first Summer that I came here. She seemed to have every thing to enjoy in life. Fortune, friends, and health. What could one wish more. Happy in her marriage afterwards and with a blooming child, this was the period in which she was struck down from among us, to present another striking memento of the fleeting character of human happiness.

Returned home and passed the rest of the Afternoon in finishing the review of the Partitiones Oratoriæ and reading the short piece de Optimo Genere Oratorum. Evening French, and the book upon Spain after which a portion of Vossius and two numbers of the Tatler.

[1] George Lunt, Harvard 1824, is identified at vol. 1:128.

[2] Mrs. Ignatius Sargent (Charlotte Gray), ABA's first cousin; see vol. 2:155.

[3] The marriage was on 23 Dec. 1828, the supper party at the Sargent home was on 13 Feb. 1829; see vol. 2:326, 346.

FRIDAY. 21ST.

The coldest morning we have yet experienced. This may be considered as a truly bitter winter. I went to Market to obtain some things I especially needed and then returned to my Office to finish my Journal and read my usual portion of Enfield. But I am less interested in the result of the Philosophers of the particular time I am now about. The Account of Seneca is yet worthy of great attention.

I went down to the Athenæum for my Wife and then took a short walk but it was so cold there was no comfort in it. Returned home and passed my Afternoon in beginning upon the Orations of Cicero, a much pleasanter field. I took up the Oration for P. Quintius, which I found easy though upon an intimate question of private Law. I could not account for my understanding it so readily until I remembered I had read it when I first came to Boston though the name had escaped me.[1] It is a wonderful production as a first specimen of a young man's powers. It shows how strong he felt upon his past education.

Evening, French and the book upon Spain to my Wife who appeared quite unwell. After which more of Vossius and two numbers of the Tatler.

[1] See vol. 2:239–245 *passim*.

SATURDAY. 22D.

It had been the intention this morning to go to Medford, but our eyes were again saluted with snow which continued all day. I received a letter from my father requesting me to go to Quincy and get him those papers relating to Mr. Crawford.[1] This is a fine season truly for the purpose, but I suppose winds and weather must not prevent. At any rate I would not think of going until Monday. I sat down this morning after finishing my usual occupations, to write a little Article about our railroads which are again in agitation. This took up the whole time I had to spare.

In the afternoon, I read the remainder of the Oration for Quintius with which I was much struck. It is a powerful effort for a young man, but yet smells too much of the studies pursued. It does not reach that ars celare artem, which displays itself in other Orations, afterwards. As my father says in the Analysis he made of it, it is notwithstanding a study for a young speaker.

The Evening was so stormy I did not go out but sat at home and read to my Wife from the Book upon Spain, after which I read Vossius which I regret having taken up. It teaches me little more than I knew from Cicero. Afterwards, I began the last volume of the Tatler, and saw poor George's marks and comments before me. Among the latest Acts of his Life was reading the British Essayists.[2]

[1] William Harris Crawford (1772–1834) of Georgia was secretary of the treasury in President Monroe's cabinet while JQA was serving as secretary of state. In ill-health and bitter retirement after successive disappointments in his quest for the Presidency, he sought for several years after 1828 to foster a rift between President Jackson and Vice-President Calhoun by maintaining publicly that in the Cabinet meetings of July 1818 on the first Seminole War it was Calhoun who had proposed that Gen. Jackson be disciplined for having exceeded his authority in invading the Spanish province of Florida. In April 1830 Crawford's accusation was published in a letter and the controversy blazed. On 5 July he had written to JQA stating his recollections of those

meetings and asking for JQA's. JQA replied on 30 July, not speaking to the point of who proposed the censure of Gen. Jackson but affirming that he, JQA, had at that time opposed any censure and that he still adhered to that position. On 12 Jan. 1831 Calhoun wrote JQA (letter in Adams Papers), asking for a copy of JQA's letter to Crawford and requesting any further records or recollections that JQA had that bore upon the issue. On 14 Jan. JQA wrote to CFA (letter in Adams Papers) asking him to make copies of Crawford's letter and JQA's reply. Two copies of each letter in CFA's hand are in the Adams Papers. Subsequently, extracts from the correspondence and other documents relevant to the controversy were published in *Niles' Register*, 40:11–45 (5–19 March 1831). See also entry for 22 Feb., below; Bemis, *JQA*, 2:212–215; and JQA, Diary, 14 Jan. 1831, printed in JQA, *Memoirs*, 8:274–277.

[2] The *Tatler* is contained in vols. 1–4 of the edition of *The British Classics* published at London in 1813 in 24 volumes. The copy in MQA bears GWA's signature and the date 1823. At the opening of the first number, in CFA's hand, are the dates 10 Oct. 1830 and 12 Feb. 1855; following the last number of the *Tatler*, also in his hand, is the date 3 March 1831.

At the conclusion of the Preface to the final volume of the *Tatler* (vol. 4), in GWA's hand, is written: "The closing paragraph is admirable both in sentiment and style. And a very apt close of a moral and delightful book. The Tatler indeed abounds in the finest forms of English composition upon an immense variety of instructive and familiar topics." In the course of the volume there are marginalia in his hand, and GWA has written following the final paper the date, 18 Dec. 1828, and a comment which concludes: "I have this morning finished the Tatler.... Of its merits and value I shall speak elsewhere only saying here that this reperusal has strengthened the feeling with which I first closed it, that it is a useful instructive entertaining and agreeable book."

SUNDAY. 23D.

This was a severely cold morning. The winter has now set in with all vigour. We have snow as an alternation from intense cold. I attended divine service and heard Mr. Frothingham preach upon the subject of regeneration. I did not feel interested in the Sermon from the chill my feet had experienced from walking over the frozen ground. Heard of Abby's brother Edward having a daughter yesterday.[1] Returned home, and decided that it was not worthwhile to expose one's self to suffering for the mere possibility of hearing uncomfortably.

I read Middleton's Life of Cicero, in which my progress was considerable. This day is the only one in which I progress in that book and in Mr. Drake's. I also wrote to my Mother a long letter, to answer for the Winter.[2] Evening a visit from Mr. Tarbell, after which Vossius and the Tatler.

[1] Anne Gorham Brooks (d. 1848). Brooks, *Medford*, p. 531.
[2] CFA to LCA, 24 Jan., Adams Papers; an answer to LCA's letter to him of 5 Jan., Adams Papers.

MONDAY. 24TH.

This morning was colder than any we had yet experienced. I do not know how long this is going to last, but I think the sooner it is over the better. I wished to go to Quincy and actually ordered a Carriage for the purpose, but I was informed that the Snow was lying so deep that two horses could not get along and I felt too cold to venture out in an open Sleigh. So I gave up the idea.

My morning was passed partly in finishing my Article upon Railroads and partly at the Probate Office passing my second account upon the Estate of Mr. New, which I at last got through with. This is very good, for now the rest is plain. To be sure the Creditors have not received any satisfaction, but that is not my fault. I have not been paid for my trouble and am not likely to be. All I know about it is, that I have done my best.

In the afternoon, I began the Oration for Sext. Roscius of Ameria and read through the first half with ease, so that I found my previous study of them much more valuable than I had imagined. It is wonderfully able. The exposition of the whole conduct of the freedman of Sylla and the two relations of Roscius is in the very first style of an Orator. Evening, reading the book upon Spain after which, Vossius and the Tatler.

TUESDAY. 25TH.

The weather gave a very little, but it was still cold. I decided upon going to Quincy at all events, and ordered an open sleigh for the purpose. At the Office where I was entirely occupied in writing off a fair Copy of my Article which after all I did not entirely finish. This was owing to some interruptions for the Houses which are not occupied. I am an occasional writer for the Newspapers without much success, counting now upon some happy bit which may serve my turn rather than upon any credit their general reasoning may give me. Indeed, such is the effect of chance, that had I not read a chance passage in one of my father's letters to me, I should not have written again.[1]

Received a letter from my father which I did not fully read. I shall reserve it for future consideration.[2]

After dinner, my man Benjamin accompanied me in a single Sleigh to Quincy. I had a pretty bad time of it as the track was barely beaten out and passing was very difficult. I called at my Aunt Adams', at Mr. Brigham's about the Canal affairs,[3] and at the House, where I obtained the necessary papers and returned. Our ride was by Moonlight and more comfortable than I expected. Reached home early, and went to P. Chardon Brooks where the family were. Returned, read Vossius and the Tatler.

[1] In his letter of 7 Jan. (Adams Papers), JQA alluded to the negotiations which the executors of Ward Nicholas Boylston had in progress with the President and Fellows of Harvard College, represented by Nathaniel Bowditch, and which turned upon Bowditch's view of the limitations in the Corporation's powers. In the communication on railroads published in the *Boston Daily Advertiser*, 29 Jan., p. 2, cols. 2–3, which in all likelihood is the one CFA wrote, the central thesis is that the resolution passed at the public meeting in Faneuil Hall and submitted to the General Court on the support of railroad construction by a tax has no validity in that the acts of such a meeting are limited to the powers conferred, which do not include the right to levy a general tax, in the same way that private corporations are limited by their charters.

[2] JQA to CFA, 15–16 Jan., Adams Papers. The letter, a long one, dealt with a number of minor matters, but in large part it was a continuation of JQA's apologia for his concerns and activities during the two preceding years. The theme had been recurrent in the correspondence of father and son for a month, CFA several times insisting that his remark which had provoked JQA to justify himself had been interpreted by JQA in a way totally different from CFA's intent. CFA had hoped in his most recent disclaimer on 9 Jan. that the subject would be there concluded. For a fuller account, see above, entry for 28 Dec. 1830 and note.

[3] Because the meeting of the directors of the Quincy Canal was held in the evening, CFA did not attend and was not reelected as a director. It was voted to pay no interest on the Canal's notes (CFA to JQA, 5 Feb., Adams Papers).

WEDNESDAY. 26TH.

Morning clear but rather more moderate than it has been. I went to the Office as usual and was busy in despatching Jonathan Simple,[1] after which I wrote my Journal and then sat about copying my papers obtained yesterday. By some strange luck however, I was more than usual interrupted by persons upon various errands, so that I accomplished in fact only the letter of Mr. Crawford[2] which was very short. This certainly was not a very good morning's work.

Returned home to dine, and passed the afternoon in copying my father's reply,[3] and preparing two or three other short papers which it was necessary for me to finish to send off by the evening's Mail. No time was left me to make particular use of and so I used the fraction in reading a report of Col. Davis's upon Anatomy, which seemed a curious thing for the purpose it was designed to promote. He and I have different notions about the General Court.[4]

Evening, reading the Year in Spain which we have almost finished. It is a very good production for a young man and keeps up it's interest very well. Perhaps a little too much enthusiasm for the different classes of the Spanish Women, but that is very pardonable in a young man. I afterwards read Vossius, in his sketch of the different kinds of figurative language, and finished with two Numbers of the Tatler.

[1] Perhaps the nom de plume used by CFA in his communication to the *Boston Daily Advertiser*, but which when published was unsigned. More likely CFA

was using it as a generic name for anonymous letters to the press as an equivalent of "John Smith" or "John Doe."

² See entry for 22 Jan., above.

³ That is, to Crawford; same.

⁴ In the Mass. House of Representatives on 25 Jan. "on motion of Mr.

Davis of Boston, the bill more effectually
to protect the sepulchres of the dead, and
to legalize the study of anatomy in certain cases, was taken up for consideration" (*Boston Patriot*, 26 Jan., p. 2,
col. 1).

THURSDAY. 27TH.

Morning at the Office as usual but my time as unsatisfactorily accounted for as at any time. I wrote and read a little of Enfield walked
down into State Street to see if I could not find Mr. Curtis, to tell him
of the answer made by my father upon his proposition, relating to the
Affairs of Mr. Boylston.¹ Called in to see Mr. Brooks and read a little
of the Newspapers at the Reading Room and besides a walk, thus went
the day.

My Wife was quite unwell today and disturbed by some domestic
trouble—Our household having got into difficulty. She went to Medford with Mrs. Frothingham and I spent a long afternoon in finishing
the Oration for Roscius of Ameria, and began the review after reading
my father's letters upon it.²

How wonderful when I come to think of it, that in the midst of the
heat of his Presidential situation he could find time and inclination to
write such Letters. Is there another man like him at present in public
life. Perhaps Mr. E. Everett, in point of acquirement, but in moral
feeling not one.

A short evening in which we did nothing. I afterwards read Vossius
upon Figurative Language and finished with the usual Numbers of the
Tatler which have become dry.

¹ JQA's decision was to postpone the
application of the Boylston executors to
the Harvard Corporation upon which he
had had a conversation with Nathaniel
Bowditch (JQA to CFA, 7 Jan., Adams

Papers; also see above, entry for 25 Jan.,
note).

² JQA to CFA, 13, 17, 23 June 1828,
Adams Papers.

FRIDAY. 28TH.

Morning at the Office. The weather having very much moderated, is
no trifling source of satisfaction to me who am not fond of the excessive cold. I was busy this morning in my usual pursuits and read a
portion of Enfield. Two or three visitors interrupted me for very short
periods—Mr. Curtis about the application to the College, Mr. Quincy
with his Seal requested by me for my father¹—and I went out to see
Mr. Harding's Picture of Mr. Webster, in company with Mr. Peabody.

It is a great likeness and will I think do Mr. Harding much more credit than his picture of Judge Marshall. I saw also several other pictures at the same place of men whom I had formerly seen often enough. They were generally good likenesses but a little flattered I think. That is to say, the wrinkles are a little smoothed from the faces of Mr. Monroe and John Randolph. I was on the whole well pleased with the specimens I there saw of his painting excepting in the resemblance of my father which I abominate.[2]

Took a walk and returned home to dine, after which I finished the review of the Oration for Roscius, quite an able effort. The reading of these instead of giving me courage plunges me into despair. What can I do, that is not mawkish when I think of this. Evening a visit from Edmund Quincy. Finished Vossius and read the Tatler.

[1] Toward the end of 1830 JQA conceived the idea of having an heraldic design made for a copper plate that would contain, within its shield, elements from the seals of the Adams, Smith, Quincy, and Boylston families. It was his intent that the engraving should be "a memorial to my children of my father and mother" and that he would use impressions from it as his bookplate. He thereupon employed William J. Stone, Washington engraver, who had executed the 1823 facsimile of the Declaration of Independence, to design and execute the plate (JQA, Diary, 30 Dec. 1830; 14, 27 Jan., 1, 4 Feb. 1831). For Stone's use, JQA wrote to CFA for wax impressions of the Smith and Quincy seals, most recently in his letter of 15–16 Jan. (Adams Papers), in which he wrote, "I wait for the Quincy blazonry of Magna Charta." The plate was completed on 17 Feb. (JQA, Diary), and on 28 Feb. JQA sent to CFA an impression of it stamped on the upper portion of the first sheet of his letter paper. To this he subjoined an explication of each of the elements of the seal (JQA to CFA, 28 Feb., Adams Papers; printed along with a reproduction of the bookplate in *Catalogue of JQA's Books*, p. 142–144).

[2] The portraits by Chester Harding (1792–1866) were currently held in high esteem. Harding had made his residence in Boston since 1826 and at this time had his studio at 22 Beacon Street (*Boston Directory*, 1830–1831). Dur-

ing 1828 he had spent several months in Washington, where a large number of persons prominent in public life sat for him. At that time he did portraits of JQA, of Chief Justice John Marshall, and of Daniel Webster, among others (Margaret E. White, *A Sketch of Chester Harding, Artist*, Boston, 1890, p. 182–183, 194). However, it is probable that the portraits of Marshall and Webster to which CFA here refers were not those done in 1828. The Boston Athenæum in Jan. 1830 commissioned Harding to do a full-length portrait of Marshall standing, paid him $350 upon its completion, and exhibited it at its Gallery later in the year (Mabel M. Swan, *The Athenæum Gallery 1827–1873*, Boston, 1940, p. 118–120). The Webster portrait which CFA here reports seeing for the first time is probably the full-length one of Webster standing which Harding exhibited later in 1831 at the Athenæum Gallery, which was then purchased by several subscribers for $500 and presented to the Athenæum, and which was badly damaged in 1848 and repainted by Harding in 1851 (Swan, *The Athenæum Gallery*, p. 120). A smaller version of this portrait is now at the Massachusetts Historical Society and may be closer to the larger painting in its original state than the repainted one at the Athenæum. It is possible that CFA is referring to an altogether different portrait of Webster by Harding, for Webster was a favorite subject of his; nine portraits of Webster by him were listed in 1883 (MHS *Procs.*, 2d ser., 2 [1885–1886]:261–262), and others have since come to light. The Marshall portrait, still hanging at the Athenæum, is reproduced in Swan, *The Athenæum Gallery*, facing p. 118; the MHS's Webster is reproduced in Guy C. Lee, *History of North America*, Phila., 1903–1905, 13:259.

Harding painted at least two portraits of JQA, one in 1827, and another, partly from life and partly a copy of the first,

in 1828. CFA's earlier verdict was that though a likeness it was "not an agreeable one." See vol. 2:160, 177; also JQA, Diary, entry for 20 Feb. 1828. One of the two is probably the portrait now at the Redwood Library and Athenaeum, Newport, Rhode Island. It has been reproduced in Frederic A. Ogg, *Builders of the Republic* (*The Pageant of America*, vol. 8), New Haven, 1927, p. 240.

SATURDAY. 29TH.

Morning at the Office. My time as usual frittered away, for what with one thing and another, I did not sit down to write to my father which was designed to be the business of the morning until too late to finish the letter. Yet the only solid part of the morning to me was the portion occupied in that way.

I then went to the Athenæum to get a book or two which makes the usual alternation from my morning walks. Thence home where I passed my afternoon in reading over Guthrie's translations of the two Orations I have read. They are tolerable but not first rate. They show the laborious student but not the powerful genius—The reader of Cicero but not the spirit to grasp him. I was surprised to find how long it took me to read them in English, and could only account for it from the diffuse nature of the English Language when compared to the Latin. I believe now that I am very fully master of those two Orations and shall proceed to the rest with more confidence.

Evening attended for the first time for some weeks the Meeting of the Debating Society. The question the permanency of the Union. I did not intend to take part in it, but I did, and spoke without premeditation, with uncommon fluency. Home late. Read the Tatler.

SUNDAY. 30TH.

Morning chilly but fair weather. I went to Meeting all day, accompanied by my Wife in the morning. A certain Mr. Putnam preached,[1] in the morning a Sermon full of Common Places upon the mutability of human affairs. Quite a Common place, and totally useless Sermon. He is a young Man, my Junior in College, without much ballast. His discourse in the afternoon was upon the use of the world, and encouraged decidedly the disposition of men to attend to temporal matters. This I thought also indiscreet, the human mind is always prone enough to be engrossed with the love of the things of this world, and needs no authorized stimulus from the sacred desk. Let the fact be as it may, the actual operation of such language from a Preacher as this young man used, is to make all who are avid of gain still more so, with the further encouragement which their conscience quieted gives them. The love of Money is not perfectly in unison, with Charity or any of the expensive Virtues. A young Man may do Mischief when he treads upon doubtful ground.

I finished and copied a long letter to my Father, which engrossed the whole day, being the longest I ever wrote.[2] Evening finished the book upon Spain, and after my Wife retired, made progress in Middleton's Life of Cicero, also read the Tatler.

[1] George Putnam, Harvard 1826, was Congregational minister in Roxbury (*Mass. Register*, 1831).
[2] CFA to JQA, 29 Jan., Adams Papers. The letter is largely a part of the continuing dialogue of father and son on Cicero and rhetoric.

MONDAY. 31ST.

Morning mild and clear. Went to the Office as usual, and from thence to a Meeting of the Directors of the Middlesex Canal at Mr. W. Sullivan's Office. The question was upon the yearly Report of the Agent, and the Dividend. The Agent read his Report and the conclusion of it was that about six thousand four hundred dollars, remained in his hands, the Company being in debt something over seven thousand dollars to Mr. J. C. Jones.[1] The Majority of the Board were in favour of paying off this sum and releasing the Company from debt, thus making no Dividend. This is rather severe, but it cannot be helped. So much for the Middlesex Canal.

Returned home after taking a walk, having passed upon the whole a pretty useless morning. After dinner I read the Oration for Q. Roscius, the Comedian. It is a mere trunk like the Hercules Torso without head, hands or legs, but is still an able specimen of reasoning skilfully. His object was to prove that Roscius had made an arrangement for himself and not the Partnership. And his evidence is some of it curious. The first part is difficult owing to the peculiar law which it embraces.

Evening, I read Middleton's Life of Cicero which I finished. It does not say enough about his Works. Began the Port Royal Latin Grammar and read the Tatler.

[1] John Coffin Jones had been one of the incorporators of the Canal Company, was an early shareholder and director (Roberts, *The Middlesex Canal, 1793–1860*, p. 22 and *passim*). The current state of affairs in the Company is given in some detail in CFA's letter to JQA, 5 Feb. (Adams Papers).

FEBRUARY. 1831.

TUESDAY. 1ST.

The morning opened with another Snow Storm which bid fair to add considerably to the mass that was already upon the ground. It stopped however after heaping up about nine inches. I went to the Office as usual and occupied myself in writing and reading Enfield in whose work I made some progress owing to my quiet. But the History of Philosophy among the Jews and Saracens is of comparatively small interest to me. They had few very great men and my previous notions of them have not been heightened by reading this Account. Mr. Degrand called in for a moment to ask a question or two relative to the state of the Corporation Stock of the City of Washington. I gave him what information I had which was not much, nor very flattering.

Returned home and after dinner tried to sit upstairs but was driven out from the quantity of smoke. I reviewed however the Oration for the Comedian Roscius. Much of it is evidence exploded in our day from Courts of Law. Hearsay, Probability which are lean supports for eloquence. Yet the ingenuity of the argument is wonderful. The Oration is also remarkable for containing the account of the prices paid to Roscius for Acting, which are enormous, and prove to what a state of luxury the Romans had arrived. Evening wasted, excepting progress in the Latin Grammar and two Numbers of the Tatler.

WEDNESDAY. 2D.

Morning very mild, the snow melting pretty rapidly. I went to the Office as usual and was met in the first place by my punctual Tenant, in Court Street [1] with his Rent which was due yesterday. This is what I call good. I wish every body else was equally punctual. But Mr. Spear still hangs back. I sat down to read but did not accomplish much this morning. I will say however that I was agreeably disappointed this morning by the receipt of a letter from the publishers of the North American Review with a Check for $21, being in payment of my Article. This quite relieved me from feeling the effect of the failure in Dividend of the Middlesex Canal and came exactly at the right time. I ought to be thankful even for such little marks of fortune, and not repine when any thing looks badly.

Took a walk and went to the Athenæum. Streets very wet. Afternoon, occupied in reading the Oration against Cæcilius commonly called Divinatio being the first upon the business of the Prætor Verres. It is short and in some places rather difficult on account of the allusions to peculiar habits among the Romans. Evening. Read to my Wife and afterwards continued with the Port Royal Latin Grammar and the Tatler.

¹ That is, William Tenney (M/CFA/3).

THURSDAY. 3D.

Morning at the Office, weather quite mild. Went down directly to attend at the meeting of the Board of Directors of the Middlesex Canal, and afterwards that of the Proprietors. The old statement was read and accepted and the same board of Directors were elected for the ensuing year. On the whole a pretty indifferent way of passing one's morning. I went however to keep my place at the Board, which I thought it likely I might lose without. I care nothing about it, excepting that as representative of my father's Stock, I can see how his Interest stands and keep him informed of it. I returned home and found Mr. A. Spear the Tenant of Mount Wollaston, come to pay his Rent, and take up his Note. I was sorry for this not being anxious to receive the Money but as he wanted to pay it, I received about enough to counterbalance the loss of the Middlesex Canal Dividend.

Took a short walk and returned home where after dinner I read the Oration against Cæcilius over again. It displays power from the confidence of its tone, the method in which he depreciates his Antagonist, and yet the adroitness by which he avoids the invidious appearance of preferring himself. It is not remarkable for much else, not having any of the necessity for the kind of Oratory, he calls "grave" or sublime. Evening read some of Buffon—His introduction to the Natural History which is written well. After it the Latin Grammar and the Tatler.

FRIDAY. 4TH.

Morning at the Office. Nothing to interrupt me as a Southerly rain had set in which prevented much going out, and threatened to inundate the City. But it stopped in time to prevent much inconvenience. My time was wasted reading the Reports of the different sides of the Committee upon the question of repealing the 25th Section of the Judiciary Law.¹ I think neither of them have much merit. The question itself is a plain one and supports itself by it's own strength.

I received a letter from my Mother in very good spirits, which I was delighted to find.² Returned home and passed the afternoon in reading the first Oration against Verres, being the only one which Cicero

415

delivered. I did not have time enough to finish it though very short. The Law questions are puzzling. In the evening I looked over Buffon's Theorie de la Terre [3] but did not finish the paper upon it. After which I went on with the Port Royal Latin Grammar and read the usual numbers of the Tatler.

[1] The *Boston Daily Advertiser* on 3 Feb. reprinted the report of Warren Ransom Davis of South Carolina, chairman of the committee on the Judiciary, submitted to the House of Representatives on 22 Jan., in which the repeal of section 25 of the Judiciary Act of 1789 was recommended (p. 2, cols. 4–5, p. 1, cols. 1–3). The section objected to as unconstitutional provides for direct appeal from a state court to the Supreme Court of the United States. The assault upon it was a part of the states-rights effort to reduce the jurisdiction of the Federal judiciary.

[2] LCA to CFA, 29 Jan., Adams Papers.

[3] The "Théorie de la Terre" constitutes the first four volumes of Buffon's *Histoire naturelle* in the edition at MQA.

SATURDAY. 5TH.

A part of the morning was devoted to Marketing so that after writing my Journal and the usual duties at the Office I had not a great deal of time to devote to writing a letter to my father as I contemplated. I succeeded however in finishing more than one half of it. My letter writing comes much easier than it formerly did so that now my great difficulty is to compress enough. This is the trying part of style and the one which makes the happy medium between obscurity and weakness.

Returned home and passed the afternoon in reading and reviewing the first Oration against Verres. It has great points. Cicero was a great master of address. He knew how to touch the Audience he was talking to and to threaten, court, or despise exactly as it suited him. Is this an art or does it come from nature. Probably the latter heightened and improved by the former. Tact is not with some men, with others, it does more than great genius. He manages the Judges here with great dexterity.

In the evening I attended the Meeting of the Debating Society and heard a discussion upon the subject of Lyceums and their expediency which was very amusing though hardly instructive. The tone of argument there is rather low. We are not Men accustomed to argue unless we are made to. And the mind is always ready to fly off in a tangent upon the least opportunity. Quincy however who cultivates the ironical vein was quite happy this evening. Returned with the Wind piercing cold. I read a little of Buffon and the Tatler.

SUNDAY. 6TH.

Morning cold and clear. I went to Meeting all day, and heard in the morning a Sermon from Mr. Frothingham which my own personal suffering during the morning totally prevented me from listening to. In the Afternoon I heard Dr. Follen preach from a portion of the Sermon on the Mount. "Blessed are the pure in heart &ca." He did not handle it with the ability such a Sermon requires. He is a German and I cannot bear to see a German undertaking to talk to Americans in their own language. And when he takes the sublimest part of the New Testament to talk upon, he tries his abilities in a strong light. His Sermon in other respects, was very good. It would have done very well with a hundred other Texts or with none at all.

Returned home and finished my Letter to my father with the Copying.[1] Evening quiet. Read Buffon's Theory of the Earth which amused me, and also finished the first Volume of the Latin Grammar and two Numbers of the Tatler.

[1] CFA to JQA, 5 Feb., Adams Papers. For this letter, see above, entry for 31 Jan., note, and below, entry for 18 Feb., note.

MONDAY. 7TH.

Morning at the Office. Busy as usual in my avocations and had very little time to pursue my examination of the maxims of the wise men which I resumed after a lapse of some time. In truth during the intensely cold weather we have had, it is a severe thing to sit down and write at all. I have a good deal of that to do always in addition to which this comes hard. I find also that a good deal of my time is wasted in the reading of Newspapers. My morning evaporates in spite of myself.

After dinner I finished the first Oration against Verres, and began the second, all the early part of which is only a repetition of what he has already said. But he then enters into the heart of the subject. It is a pity that you are obliged to imagine this to have been delivered as the Delinquent fled the Contest, and made the whole series unnecessary.

In the Evening I attended the annual Meeting of the Proprietors of Boylston Market to see an Account of their expenditure and receipt. Upon the election of Directors, I was very much surprised to find myself put upon the list. It was not my wish to undertake this which is very certainly a more troublesome situation than that in the Middlesex Canal, but I did not feel at liberty to decline it. Upon the election of Clerk, I was again put in nomination and chosen, which I disliked exceedingly. Though of the two, I should have preferred having that alone to the other. Returned home at nine o'clock and read the Latin Grammar and the Tatler.

TUESDAY. 8TH.

Morning at the Office as usual. Occupied in my common avocations for the first hour. Mr. Plumer sent me down from New Hampshire my father's MS. upon the Letter of the Confederates, which I received today.[1] And as I had never read it, I sat down to do so but was interrupted by a request to meet Mr. Child at the Boylston Market which I immediately acceded to and went up there to see what came in my way as Clerk. He gave me up the Papers which I had deposited in their usual place excepting the Transfer book to be kept more conveniently at my Office. The arrangement of all the Accounts took me until one o'clock when I returned, and continued my Confederate Letter.

Afternoon pursued the same, and read a part of the second Oration against Verres which I admire exceedingly. It is a wonderful effort, displaying all the powers of which man is capable. It is by looking at such efforts as this that we wonder at the extent of his capacity. If there is any thing in this world which is calculated to display what man can do in perfection, it is probably to be found in the Orations of Cicero.

My Wife had gone to Medford and I was therefore able to extend my Evening. But I shall reserve my remarks upon my father's letter until I finish it. Evening, Latin Grammar and the Tatler.

[1] William Plumer Jr. had had for several months the MS of JQA's "Reply to the Appeal of the Massachusetts Federalists" and had been dilatory in responding to the request for its return; concerning the "Reply," see above, entry for 31 Oct. 1829.

WEDNESDAY. 9TH.

The Weather is now a pretty steady general cold, and for Winter is on the whole not bad, though I am longing for the return of the more moderate Season. I went to the Office and attended to my affairs as usual, reading the second Volume of Enfield. But I was again interrupted by an unwelcome Note from the Misses Haskins informing me that my Tenant Mr. Spear had quitted the House he occupied and left them as they were before. I went up directly and found the thing exactly as I feared, not at all to my gratification. Heard of the death of poor old Dr. Welsh, and took it a little to my conscience that I had neglected to go and see him. Poor old Man, his last days were passed in loneliness and poverty,[1] and I felt when thinking of him an indescribable kind of melancholy, which seemed hardly to be justified by the occasion. Mr. Vezey the Carpenter at Quincy, came in and I talked with him about the Stone Posts at Quincy which I agreed to have done provided it did not exceed a certain price. But the whole subject was postponed until the Spring. Thus passed the Morning.

Afternoon spent in reading Cicero's second against Verres in which I did not make much progress owing to its difficulty. Evening, French. Read to my Wife from the Tragedy of Douglas.[2] Not much pleased. It is a little singular I never read this before. After this, the Latin Grammar and the Tatler.

[1] In his last year Dr. Thomas Welsh lived apart from his children alone in a boardinghouse at 3 1/2 Sudbury Street (*Boston Directory*, 1829–1830; CFA to JQA, 13 Feb. 1831, LbC, Adams Papers). JQA, responding to CFA's information, wrote: "The decease of Dr. Welsh affects me on many accounts with a Sentiment of Melancholy. Four of the most trying years of my life [July 1790–June 1794], I had been an inmate of his house. All my children had resided in his family. In that middle station of Society, where it is said the greatest portion of human happiness is enjoyed, he had suffered many of its most distressing vicissitudes, and in his last days had been visited with the deepest afflictions" (JQA to CFA, 26 Feb., Adams Papers).

[2] First performed in Edinburgh, 1756, the work of Rev. John Home, *Douglas* was included in several anthologies of dramatic works. The play doubtless came to CFA's attention from the circumstance that it was chosen as the first of Master Burke's repertory of plays being presented at the Tremont Theatre (*Boston Daily Advertiser*, 31 Jan., p. 3, col. 5).

THURSDAY. 10TH.

Morning cold. At the Office as usual, where I spent my time in the occupations usual with me, after which I sat down and made considerable progress in Enfield. The Account of the philosophy of the Middle Ages is curious and wonderful for it manifests a strange stage of perversion of the human intellect. Afterwards I took a walk previous to going according to invitation to dine at Mrs. Frothingham's. I found Edward and Mr. Brooks were to be there with Abby and myself. The party was tolerably pleasant and I left it to attend the funeral of poor old Dr. Welsh. Had some conversation about him with Dr. Shattuck[1] and found it was as I had thought, that he was in a desolate situation and felt himself to be so. And that this operated upon his mind to shorten his career a little.

Returned home and instead of spending the remainder of the afternoon in reading Cicero, I thought I would devote it to the rest of my father's Paper. This is among the ablest of all his controversial efforts, and appears to me convincing. But it's present is not the best shape in which it could be put. The substance of it is singularly powerful, and when divested of the acrimony which runs through the tone, would be calculated to produce a great effect. It requires however repeated reading.[2] Evening Conversation with my Wife after which the Latin Grammar and the Tatler.

[1] Dr. George Cheyne Shattuck; see vol. 2:202.

[2] In his letter to his father on 13 Feb. (LbC, Adams Papers), CFA wrote similarly of JQA's "Reply to the Appeal of the Massachusetts Federalists," but at much greater length and included his reasons for not favoring publication of it until a later time and until its tone was modified.

FRIDAY. 11TH.

Morning as usual at the Office. But my time was passed in a singular way. The interruptions were so numerous, that they hardly left me the power even of doing nothing. I was desirous of conversing with Mr. Peabody but was unable owing to the very singular manner in which different persons kept coming. Mr. Jones the Auctioneer from Weston, an applicant or two for Houses, the old Tenant Mr. Spear all came in turn to talk and make their different requests or excuses. This took up the morning in a very desultory kind of way. I had time only for a short walk before returning home. I might say in further extenuation that I spent some time at Market.

Afternoon Engaged in reading the second Oration against Verres and with difficulty finished it. The last part of it is very hard to be understood from the entire allusion to the habits of the age. It is necessary to remember that they had customs which in themselves involve a knowledge of all the manners of the age. Since I began Cicero I have exceedingly enlarged this knowledge, but it is yet sadly deficient. And the acquisition of it implies an amount of time that I am afraid I should find it hard, unless I materially improve my present economy, to apply.[1] The Applicant for my House vacated by Mr. Spear called again in the Afternoon and having softened down in his demands, agreed to take it,[2] which will relieve me from any further trouble about it, I hope.

In the evening, I went to see the young Roscius who is making a great stir here. Master Burke in Shylock, and Looney McTwolter. A Wonderful boy certainly but not half so astonishing as he has been represented. Better in the latter than the former part.[3] Returned in good season, and read the Tatler.

[1] Commas editorially supplied.

[2] John Gulliver followed John I. Spear as the tenant of 103 Tremont Street (M/CFA/3).

[3] Master Burke, "the celebrated Irish Roscius," during the five weeks of his appearance in repertory in Boston regularly appeared in the leading role of the principal play on the bill, in the farcical afterpiece, and also conducted the orchestra between the two productions. The farce on this occasion was "The Review, or the Wags of Windsor," in which Burke played his acclaimed creation, Looney McTwolter (*Boston Daily Advertiser*, 11 Feb., p. 3, col. 5).

February 1831

SATURDAY 12TH.

Morning cold and clear. I went to the Office as usual and occupied myself with my Journal, Accounts and other duties, as well as with Enfield. But as there must always be something or other to distract my attention, so today it was taken off by the eclipse of the Sun which took place about noon.[1] I spent some time in observing this phenomenon. The Sun was not entirely darkened as the eclipse was not total, consequently the light was but partially affected. The cold however was considerable, and the temperature did not recover it throughout the day. The sight is a splendid one. It seems to bring so strongly before the mind the magnificence of the Solar System. The Planet Venus was visible, and a cloud which passed over the Sun presented a beautiful set of colours. Every body was looking and little was done. The appearance of the Streets was certainly curious. Men, Women and Boys all gazing at a spectacle the nature of which there were not many to comprehend.

I went to the Athenæum for a moment, and then returned home. Miss Julia Gorham dined with us. After dinner, I continued the Orations against Verres, beginning the one upon his Sicilian prætorship. My progress was tolerable. Evening went to the usual Meeting of the Debating Society. Few members present. I had a pleasant conversation, and returned early. Latin Grammar and Tatler.

[1] The solar eclipse occasioned considerable public interest in Boston; see *Boston Daily Advertiser*, 12 Feb., p. 2, col. 2; 14 Feb., p. 2, col. 1.

SUNDAY. 13TH.

The weather is steady and cold. No material variation in the Thermometer from about eight or ten, at sunrise, which is severe winter. I attended divine Service and heard Mr. Frothingham deliver a very clever Sermon upon the Eclipse of yesterday. The subject was a good one and he managed it well. Afternoon went alone and heard Mr. Gannett who is a shocking Proser. I like him less than ever since he has ceased to be regularly inflicted upon me,[1] yet he is not so bad as most people find him. He has good intention and earnest zeal, without tact or taste.

Returned home late but felt it my duty to sit down and write a Letter to my father at once, as I found by his of yesterday that his eyes are in bad condition.[2] This engrossed all my spare time. And I did not accomplish copying it either. This is a business which I feel as if I ought to do and yet as if I could hardly spare the time.[3] Evening,

French, and a little of Buffon upon the Earth which is interesting. Afterwards, Latin Grammar and Tatler.

[1] During the latter part of 1828 and the early months of 1829, CFA had attended services regularly at Dr. Channing's church in Federal Street, where Rev. Ezra Stiles Gannett, Channing's assistant, often preached; see vol. 2: 314–358 *passim*.

[2] JQA to CFA, 6 Feb.; CFA to JQA, 13 Feb., LbC; both in Adams Papers.

For CFA's letter see above, entry for 10 Feb., note, and below, entries for 17, 26 Feb., notes.

[3] The copy of CFA's long letter in his letter book is in ABA's hand. From soon after their marriage ABA served intermittently as copyist, but CFA generally made his own copies for many years.

MONDAY. 14TH.

Morning cool again. Went to the Office as usual and was occupied with my usual affairs a great part of the morning, so that I had little or no time to take up for reading. A visit from my new Tenant Mr. Gulliver took up a little, and I found him rather better humoured today. I also was busy in preparing the Papers for my application to be admitted as an Attorney to the Supreme Court.[1] A necessary step in the ascending series of a Lawyer's course. On the whole, Away went the morning as usual, and I was left to account for it as I might.

Afternoon busy with the second Oration of the Second Book against Verres in which I went on somewhat faster than heretofore. Though some passages were a little slighted. Evening quietly at home. Read to my Wife the remainder of Douglas, and two Acts of Sheridan's Comedy of the Rivals. After which I pursued the Latin Grammar and my regular Numbers of the Tatler.

[1] See below, vol. 4, entry for 2 March. To accompany the papers in support of his application, CFA wrote to Josiah Quincy Jr. under date of 14 Feb. asking him "to communicate to the Committee of the Bar my request to be considered as a Candidate for admission as an Attorney of the Supreme [Judicial] Court" (*The Influence and History of the Boston Athenæum from 1807 to 1907*, Boston, 1907, extra-illustrated copy in MBAt, facing p. 50).

TUESDAY. 15TH.

Morning at the Office as usual—After going to Market which made my time nearly eleven o'clock before I got there. Engaged in writing my Journal, with an occasional interruption from visitors. One upon the Affair with Robert New and the debt due to his Estate by one Byrd who asks time for payment. I told him to settle it with my Attorney. Then Mr. Conant from Weston with a little more money. And so wasted the morning.

At dinner, I received a summons from the parties in the case of Storer and Farmer which I had not heard of before. This is a shocking business to be made so public, but I do not now see how it can be avoided.[1] My poor brother's reputation must be mangled in a Court of Law, and that in a suit to which he had no kind of compulsion to belong. I did not get over it all the afternoon, but I still persevered in reading the Oration against Verres which I finished. It was to distract my attention.

Evening, at home, after in vain trying to get tickets for the Theatre.[2] I read to my Wife the rest of the Rivals. After which as usual the Latin Grammar and the Tatler.

[1] It had been almost a year since the litigation between Miles Farmer and Dr. David H. Storer in the court of Common Pleas, April term 1830, had been brought to CFA's notice, and at that time he had thought a settlement reached; see above, entry for 27 April 1830. However, the parties did not reach agreement and the case was continued to the July term when judgment for the plaintiff was entered by default.

Appeal was taken by the defendant to the November term of the Supreme Judicial Court, then carried over on technical grounds (*Farmer-Storer Trial*, p. 6–7). For an account of the issues, the public disclosure of which CFA found so painful, see vol. 2:403–404.

[2] *Richard III* and a farce, *The Irish Tutor*, were scheduled for performance (*Boston Daily Advertiser*, 15 Feb., p. 3, col. 5).

WEDNESDAY. 16TH.

The Winter which has been extremely severe on the whole, is now drawing to a close. This day we had a Southerly wind accompanied with rain by which the Snow began to disappear with considerable rapidity. I arose early and after going to my Office for a moment or two, obeyed the Summons to the Supreme Court. The Judge occupied some time in charging the Jury, and a Case was interposed by the Government so that the morning was entirely wasted. I was extremely shocked however to find Mr. J. C. Park engaged in the cause[1] and more so when I saw that he had summoned the Girl[2] as a Witness in the case. Dr. Tuckerman[3] who was also summoned exerted himself to effect a compromise to refer it to Arbitrators and the whole morning was spent in the negotiation. I went home still in doubt.

As it happened Mr. Brooks, and two of his Sons, Chardon and Horatio dined with us, and I was compelled to play the agreeable. This was perhaps quite fortunate as it kept me from thinking painfully. I returned to Court at half past three o'clock and the business appeared in so unpromising a state that I had braced myself up to an exhibition before a crowded Court of the whole melancholy Story, when by the exertion of Counsel, the case was finally referred to three Gentlemen, Messrs. Pickering, Curtis and Shaw.[4] This will at least make the affair more private and I thanked God with an overflowing heart that he had spared me this trial. Returned home, but I had been so excited during the day that I was not able to do any thing of consequence. Evening, French with my Wife. Read to her half of the Jealous Wife,[5] after which Latin Grammar and the Tatler.

[1] John C. Park, whose own marriage had been damaging to his reputation in Boston (see above, entry for 28 Nov. 1829), is not elsewhere mentioned as of counsel. Both the court docket and the *Farmer-Storer Trial* identify the attorneys as Samuel D. Parker for the plaintiff and Richard Fletcher for the defendant (SJC, November Term 1830, Docket No. New 104, 16 Feb. 1831, Suffolk County Court House; *Farmer-Storer Trial*).

[2] Eliza Dolph; see above, entry for 21 Sept. 1829, note.

[3] Joseph Tuckerman, D.D., was minister of the Congregational Chapel in Friend Street, to whose congregation Eliza Dolph had apparently belonged and perhaps Miles Farmer also. At some time after the birth of her child, Tuckerman had been able to place Eliza Dolph in domestic service. *Farmer-Storer Trial*, p. 12–14, 18, 22, 28; *Mass. Register*, 1831.

[4] John Pickering, Charles P. Curtis, and Robert G. Shaw, all of the Boston bar, were named as referees by agreement (SJC, November Term 1830, Docket No. New 104; *Farmer-Storer Trial*, p. 19).

[5] An English comedy by George Colman.

THURSDAY. 17TH.

Morning beautifully mild and warm even. This seems to give us a taste of a new Season. I went to the Office as usual and was occupied in writing, making up my Accounts and reading. I examined the transfer book of the Boylston Market Association and draughted an Alphabetical list of Stockholders, which was perhaps needless, but I like to arrange things regularly. I read a little of Enfield which did not interest me.

Upon my return home I found Miss Abby S. Adams, who had come in at last to spend a few days with my Wife. She looks ill, though not by half so badly as one would be led to suppose from her Account of it. She appears pleased with her engagement to Mr. Angier.[1] I hope it will prove fortunate with all my heart.

Evening and afternoon devoted by me to study. I continued the Orations against Verres beginning with that upon the Corn law, which I found easier than I had expected. I read also a little of Justinian's Institutes,[2] an Ode of Horace, the Grammar and the Tatler.

[1] When a few days earlier CFA wrote his father of the engagement of JQA's niece, Abigail Smith Adams, to John Angier, who conducted a large school for boys in Medford, CFA called him "a very respectable and worthy man," and to her brother he wrote, "we believe she has chosen well." His comments in later entries suggest that he modified this view on further acquaintance. See CFA to JQA, 13 Feb., LbC; CFA to Thomas B. Adams Jr., 20 Feb., LbC; CFA to JQA, 28 Feb., LbC; all in Adams Papers; also Adams Genealogy.

[2] At MQA are four editions of *Institutionum juris civilis expositio* including one with CFA's bookplate, Paris, 1757. At this time, however, CFA was reading a translation by George Harris, London, 1761, borrowed from the Athenæum.

FRIDAY 18TH.

Morning cold again and perhaps more trying to the feelings from the change we experienced yesterday. I went to the Office as usual and was occupied with my books and Papers, with a visit to Mr. Peabody and Enfield. The time flew much as usual. I received a letter from my father written in my Mother's handwriting from the first half page.[1] It was in tolerable spirits, and in a pretty good natured tone considering how I wrote to him. I believe I am pretty impudent.[2]

Mr. Horatio Brooks and Miss Abby Adams were with us at dinner, after which I sat up in my study as usual and read part of the Oration against Verres upon the supplies. Interrupted by Dr. Tuckerman upon that odious business. He came to see if he could not induce me to pay the sum but I would not do it. I told him precisely how I was situated, and gave him some information about the case which he had not had before. He left me saying that the matter of the reference was not settled yet as Mr. Pickering hesitated about accepting.

Evening we went together to the Theatre, Mr. Angier's attending Miss Adams. The performance was Romeo and Juliet with a silly afterpiece.[3] I was much more astonished at Master Burke's performance of Romeo than that of Shylock. It certainly was wonderful. The Theatre was full but very few acquaintances. Returned late, I read the Tatler.

[1] JQA to CFA, 11 Feb., Adams Papers. JQA's continuing trouble with his eyes did not permit him to write himself beyond the eight lines of verse on his affliction with which the letter begins.

[2] In his letter to his father on 5 Feb. (Adams Papers), CFA had written that there was an error in chronology in JQA's account of the composition of Cicero's "Topics." Perhaps more "impudent" in CFA's view, however, was the renewal of his effort to curb what he called JQA's tendency toward speculation in financial matters.

[3] The farce was *Barney Brallagan* (*Boston Daily Advertiser*, 18 Feb., p. 3, col. 5).

SATURDAY. 19TH.

Morning delightfully mild and pleasant. I went to the Office as usual and passed my time in writing my Journal and afterwards in reading a little of Enfield. But one or two interruptions. One from Judge Adams who came for the purpose of getting some Money for J. Q. Adams' Quarterly Allowance due tomorrow. I paid it. Mr. Peabody came in and talked very pleasantly also. I began writing a letter to my Father but could not progress much in it. Went down to the Fire and Marine Office to get Powers of Attorney for the repayment of Capital which is about to take place there. Thence to the Athenæum for books.

The Judge, my Uncle dined with us and was tolerably pleasant. After dinner I continued Verres and read twenty sections more in the Oration upon provisions. The Account given of the oppression exercised over the good People of Sicily is terrible enough. How thankful should we be who are able to consider what we have our own, without fearing rapine and extortion. But the detail is tedious.

Mr. Angier took tea with us in the Evening and I went to the Debating Society. A small Meeting. Question upon the present excitement in South Carolina.[1] Debate short and warm and the subject put over. After we adjourned as the Evening was delightfully mild, I took a long walk with several of the young men. Returned home and read the Tatler.

[1] There had been much public agitation in South Carolina for direct action unless legislation were passed in Congress to reduce or repeal import duties, particularly those on salt (*Boston Daily Advertiser*, 10 Feb., p. 2, col. 4).

SUNDAY. 20TH.

Morning quite cold. I finished the fourth volume of Drake's Essays and the literary life of Dr. Johnson before morning Service. I have not derived so much information from this as from the preceding part of the Work. Probably because the character and Works of Dr. J. are more familiar to me. The whole book is written with some affectation which I cannot bear, but otherwise decently enough.

Attended with my Wife and Miss Adams at Mr. Frothingham's in the morning. In the afternoon quite alone. Mr. Greenwood preached a dry Sermon upon the incomprehensible character of God and Mr. Frothingham an equally dry one upon some other subject. Returned home and was occupied the rest of the day in finishing and copying, to send away, my letter to my Father[1] and one to T. B. Adams Jr.[2] upon his affairs. This took me into the Evening, after which the Port Royal Greek Grammar[3] and the Tatler.

[1] 19 Feb., LbC, Adams Papers.
[2] 20 Feb., LbC, Adams Papers.
[3] *A New Method of learning with Facility the Greek Tongue,* translated by T. Nugent from the French of "the Messieurs de Port-Royal." JQA's copy of the edition published at London in 1817 is in MQA.

MONDAY. 21ST.

Morning almost as cold as ever. I went to the Office as usual and passed some time in examining the Newspapers which came to me in abundance. One, The Globe, from Washington, for what reason, I can not easily guess, for after looking it all over, I saw nothing excepting

Mr. Cambreleng's poor Speech.[1] The Intelligencer contained Mr. Calhoun's Preface which is a singular production.[2] I wasted the morning over these Papers and in getting rid of two or three interruptions.

Returned home and after dinner sat down to read the Oration against Verres which I accomplished. It has been rather superficially gone over but I design to review the whole Series after I have finished it. This one upon the grain is rather dry. Purchased a Landscape Annual with the Roman views for my Wife.[3] Took a walk.

Evening, I was at home alone with my Wife as Miss Adams went out to pay a visit to some of her friends. I rather wasted the time. Afterwards, I was busy in studying, the Port Royal Greek Grammar, and in continuing my regular reading of the Tatler.

[1] C. C. Cambreleng of New York spoke at length in the House of Representatives on 7 Feb. on the motion to strike from the Appropriations Bill for 1831 "so much as relates to an appropriation for the salary of the Minister to Russia" (*National Intelligencer*, 8 Feb., p. 3, col. 4).

[2] See the following entry.

[3] [Robert Jennings,] *The Landscape Annual*, London. Though a small section of vol. 1 for 1830 is devoted to Rome (p. 261–278, with 2 plates), the major treatment of Rome appears in vol. 2 for 1831, p. 130–220, with 10 engravings from drawings by S. Prout. The Adams copy has not been found.

TUESDAY. 22ND.

Morning mild and tolerably pleasant. I went to the Office as usual and was engaged in my avocations, writing and reading all the morning. Nothing of any particular importance occurred, and after sending out some accounts which are due to the Estate of my Father here, I sat down to reflect upon what I might be called to say at the Meeting of the Debating Society this week, as I had in some measure pledged myself to reply. I proceeded not far when I was reminded to take a walk. But this was half prevented by meeting with the publication of Mr. Calhoun's Pamphlet—Where I read several of the letters with some interest. It is however a poor concern on the whole.[1] A short walk and return home.

Afternoon, Began the next Oration against Verres and accomplished thirty Sections. It is easier and much more pleasant than the preceding though still nothing but an account of Robbery and Rapine. Such a Scoundrel never was seen on the face of the Earth. The Account must be exaggerated.

Evening quiet at home. Mr. Edmund Quincy came in and passed a couple of hours after which I continued with the Greek Grammar and the Tatler.

[1] In the preceding week Vice-President Calhoun had caused to be published a pamphlet containing *Correspondence between Gen. Andrew Jackson and John C. Calhoun* "on the subject of the course of the latter in the deliberations of the cabinet of Mr. Monroe, on the occurrences in the Seminole War." In addition to a prefatory letter to the People of the United States by Calhoun and supporting letters to and from a number of persons, including JQA, the pamphlet's core consisted of Calhoun's letter to President Jackson of 29 May 1830 in which he set forth his position. On the background of the controversy see entry for 22 Jan., above.

Upon the appearance of the pamphlet, newspaper publication of its contents, in whole or in part, followed at once. The *National Intelligencer* printed Calhoun's preface in the issue for 17 Feb., p. 3, cols. 3–4, and in its next issue printed all the correspondence, including JQA's letter to Calhoun of 14 Jan. (19 Feb., p. 1–4). The documents as published by Calhoun are in Calhoun, *Works*, ed. Crallé, 6:349–445.

WEDNESDAY 23RD.

Morning rainy and warm. The Snow began to go off in quantity and gave us some intimation of the decline of the Winter. I went to the Office and received from my brother the Pamphlet upon Mr. Calhoun's affair. Conversed also with Mr. Peabody upon an article in a Baptist paper criticising my Article in the Review. It is rather severe and in some particulars correct.[1] I read over some of the Correspondence again and on the whole passed my day pretty lazily for I am not sensible of having accomplished any thing.

Took a short walk though the weather was bad and returned home. Mr. Frothingham and Mr. Peabody dined with me upon venison. Tolerably pleasant. Mr. Angier, Abby's friend came in immediately afterward. I went to my study however at four o'clock and read twenty sections of the Oration de Signis. They were not difficult. This has more of the elegant fluency of Cicero's manner than any other of his upon this subject that I have yet read.

Evening at home. Miss Adams went out to spend the evening and I resumed the Jealous Wife to my Wife when interrupted by a visit from Mr. Degrand, who remained and talked Politics all the evening. No time afterward except to read the Tatler.

[1] In the issue of the *Christian Watchman* (the organ of the Baptist Missionary Society of Massachusetts) for 14 Jan., a communication signed "Secundus" (p. 2, col. 2), and in that of 18 Feb., another signed "Tertius" (p. 2, col. 5), took the author of the *North American Review* article on Grahame's *History* to task for the inaccuracy and unfairness of his comments on Roger Williams.

THURSDAY. 24TH.

Morning cold again. These alternations of weather are not so pleasant. The Winter still struggles for it's hold and sometimes gains a victory. I went to the Office as usual and occupied myself almost the whole morning in an examination of papers and authorities in relation to the business of Saturday Evening's Argument. I made a sketch of my remarks and tried to consider them over so as to avoid the trouble of a long Speech. This examination will not be useless to me. For the information it contains will do to lay up. How much information upon every subject a man must hunt after.

I took a long walk to J. D. Williams Store to try some Wine for table use and finally bought some. I find that it is too expensive to adhere to the plan I had fixed upon, to purchase first rate wine. So I bought some good middling quality. Returned home to a Capital dinner of venison. After which I finished the Oration de Signis and began that de Suppliciis, which the Commentator praises far above the rest.

Evening at home alone with my Wife. Finished the Jealous Wife and began the Critic.[1] Miss Adams was spending the day at a friend's. She returned at eight. I read some of the Greek Grammar and my usual Numbers of the Tatler.

[1] Sheridan's comedy.

FRIDAY 25TH.

Morning cold. Went to the Office as usual, and after performing my daily matters, I busied myself in perfecting my argument for tomorrow in case I should be called to make one. This is a good excuse if I should ever be obliged to deliver in public. I really am much inclined to the opinion that if ever I shall have to speak, my power of doing so will have been obtained by these efforts. For I well remember the time when I could not say three words.

Went to Mrs. Frothingham's to dine without company, P. C. Brooks Jr., Abby Adams, my Wife and I. At dinner much longer than usual and obliged to take a long walk afterwards for exercise so that I did not reach home for study until after five o'clock. As my Wife remained at Mr. Frothingham's I made it up in the evening and accomplished a large portion of the Oration de Suppliciis which is certainly a Masterpiece of Eloquence. Nothing seems to be left untried to produce one grand, burning whole. Returned for my Wife and took a little Supper. After reaching home, One of our Chamber bells rung in an unaccountable manner two or three times. We were all puzzled. I read the Tatler.

SATURDAY. 26TH.

Morning clear and pleasant. The Sun is gaining the Battle. I went to the Office as usual and received a letter from my Mother upon the matters relating to this Correspondence[1] but no Letter from my Father which makes me suspicious that mine has produced a disagreeable effect. For this I feel sorry, but I cannot disavow the sentiments it contains. It may not have been judicious just at this time to express them, but this is at least doubtful. For this may be the very time when truth will have most effect and lead him to make a deliberate revision. I hope this may be the consequence but in the mean time I have no letter.[2]

I was occupied in reconsidering my argument for this evening and amending it in some passages. Drew up my Accounts also for the month and found myself correct. Returned home and in the Afternoon, Completed the last Oration against Verres, de Suppliciis which is a splendid effort. On the whole, I doubt whether in the way of accusation any thing, can be done beyond this. Whether in arrangement, force of argument, and power of expression, it is equally admirable.

Evening. Mr. Angier at our House. I went to the Meeting of the Debating Society. Owing to the absence of the other side no regular argument was made, the discussion such as it was, had salt enough[3] in it. I took part in it, perhaps too much. We did not go home until ten o'clock after which I read the Tatler.

[1] That is, to the Calhoun-Jackson correspondence. LCA to CFA, 21 Feb., Adams Papers.

[2] See entry for 10 Feb., above, and the references there to CFA's letter of 13 February. CFA's fears that his father had been displeased by his comments on JQA's "Reply to the . . . Federalists" seem to have been groundless. JQA wrote: "Your observations are all kindly taken and shall be duly weighed." His failure to respond earlier seems to have resulted from his absorption in the Calhoun controversy (JQA to CFA, 26 Feb., Adams Papers).

[3] See above, entry for 19 Feb., note.

SUNDAY. 27TH.

Morning delightful. The Snow is now rapidly making it's disappearance and we hope soon to see again the face of the Earth. My Wife, Miss Adams and I attended Divine Service in the Morning and I went alone in the afternoon. Sermon by Mr. Frothingham. One upon the Season by Mr. Frothingham, part of which was very good, part not to my taste. Another upon substitution[1] which did not attract me.

Mr. Angier dined with us and I sat in my study, reading the Correspondence attentively which I have not done before. The whole betrays a tone and spirit in our public men which augurs ill to our Institutions. It is disgraceful to every body that meddles with it. I passed a portion of the Evening in writing upon the same subject to my Father, but I do not know that I shall send it. I did not feel perfectly well today and indeed for some days past I have experienced a disagreeable sense of fulness. After this, Greek Grammar and the Tatler.

[1] That is, upon the doctrine of substitutional or vicarious atonement. Protestant theology was divided on the extent to which the man who accepts the Redeemer is released from punishment by the sufferings of Jesus Christ for man. (In *OED*, the first recorded use of the word in its theological sense is in 1836; see also *Webster*, 2d edn., under "atonement.")

MONDAY. 28TH.

Morning clear and delightfully mild again. This weather is I hope the advance of an early Spring Season. I went to the Office as usual and passed my time in pretty useful employment for after the transaction of my regular business I sat down to Enfield and read a considerable portion of him. As the sketch comes down to more modern times, it again becomes interesting. Such names as Bacon, Leibnitz and Des Cartes excite curiosity. But after all how much vanity there is in all these studies. How little the human mind is capable of penetrating into the depths of science, and how abortive are all attempts to do so.

Took a walk with Mr. Peabody. After dinner I thought I would review Verres but upon trying, I felt as if it was quite unnecessary. I therefore took up the Oration for Fonteius. A mere fragment. My time was also taken up in conversation with my Wife upon matters relating to Abby S. Adams. This young lady having requested advice upon her affairs, sent my Wife to sound me, and upon the whole I was well satisfied with her arrangements.

Evening. I. H. Adams her brother was here so that I sat upstairs and wrote another letter to my Father.[1] Once critical about my letters and I am never satisfied. Greek Grammar and the Tatler. Horatio Brooks returned here from the Theatre to spend the Night.

[1] 28 Feb., LbC, Adams Papers.